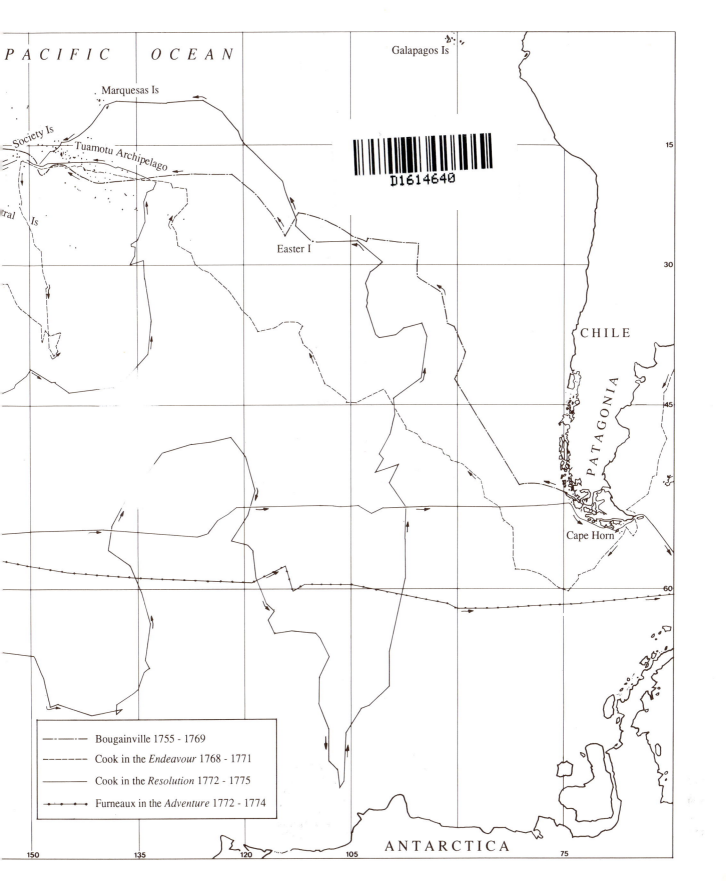

PACIFIC OCEAN

Galapagos Is

Marquesas Is

Society Is

Tuamotu Archipelago

ral Is

Easter I

D1614640

CHILE

PATAGONIA

Cape Horn

15

30

45

60

ANTARCTICA

Bougainville 1755 - 1769

Cook in the *Endeavour* 1768 - 1771

Cook in the *Resolution* 1772 - 1775

Furneaux in the *Adventure* 1772 - 1774

150   135   120   105   75

Observations Made

during a Voyage

round the World

Frontispiece. Portrait
medallion of Johann
Reinhold Forster by
Josiah Wedgewood,
designed by Joachim
Smith, white on blue
jasperware, 1775.
State Library of New
South Wales.

Observations Made during a Voyage round the World

JOHANN REINHOLD FORSTER

Edited by

Nicholas Thomas, Harriet Guest, and Michael Dettelbach

with a linguistics appendix by Karl H. Rensch

University of Hawai'i Press

Honolulu

© 1996 University of Hawai'i Press

Library of Congress Cataloging-in-Publication Data
Forster, Johann Reinhold, 1729–1798.
   Observations made during a voyage round the world / Johann
   Reinhold Forster ; edited by Nicholas Thomas, Harriet Guest, and
   Michael Dettelbach ; with a linguistics appendix by Karl H. Rensch.
      p. cm.
   Originally published: London : Printed for G. Robinson, 1778.
   Includes bibliographical references and index.
   ISBN 0–8248–1725–7 (alk. paper)
   1. Voyages around the world.
   2. Cook, James, 1728–1779.
   3. Oceania—Discovery and exploration.
   I. Thomas, Nicholas.
   II. Guest, Harriet.
   III. Dettelbach, Michael.
   IV. Title.
G420.C65F67   1996
910'.92—dc20
95–582
CIP

Publication of this book has been supported by grants from the National Endowment for the
Humanities, an independent federal agency, and the Australian Academy of the Humanities.

Endsheets: The Pacific Islands, Showing Tracks of the Voyages of Bougainville, Wallis, and Cook's
First and Second Voyages

University of Hawai'i Press books are printed on acid-free paper and meet the
guidelines for permanence and durability of the Council on Library Resources

Designed by Paula Newcomb

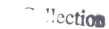

for Bernard Smith

Contents

APPENDIXES

Illustrations

Color Plates (follow page 320)

Maps

Preface

Johann Reinhold Forster's *Observations Made during a Voyage round the World*, first published in 1778, is the most significant and substantial analysis of exotic cultures that emerged as a result of the Cook voyages. Informed by eighteenth-century natural history, political theory, travel writing, and physical anthropology, it is a singularly rich source for European perceptions of, and reflections upon, such questions as the nature of scientific exploration, the progress of indigenous societies, the status of women, the meaning of national distinctness, and the role of climate in determining the character of varieties of plants, animals, and people.

Forster was typical of Enlightenment scholars in the sense that his interests and writings ranged widely across theoretical and applied inquiries and over subjects that subsequently became the provinces of distinct and segregated disciplines such as anthropology, botany, geography, and political theory. Because the book is so wide ranging, if primarily devoted to comparative ethnology, we have adopted what may be an unusual procedure, from an editorial viewpoint. Rather than introduce the text with a single introduction, we have prepared separate essays that discuss the book's author and composition, its approaches to natural history and comparative ethnology, and its analysis of women. Other topics, such as Forster's contributions to botany, might also have been addressed, but in our judgment these themes provide a way into the arguments of Forster's book that are of greatest contemporary interest yet liable to be misunderstood unless situated in the eighteenth-century debates.

Our most substantial debt is to Ria van de Zandt, who transferred the entirety of Forster's text to disk with meticulous attention to peculiarities of his capitalization, orthography, and punctuation. Martin Steer traced and checked Forster's classical quotations and citations, and Winifred Mumford drew the track chart and the maps of the Pacific and New Zealand. Victoria Luker assisted Nicholas Thomas in tracing Forster's references and provided some editorial comment on draft essays and annotations. Margaret Jolly, Jonathan Lamb, J. G. A. Pocock, Oskar Spate, and Bernard Smith all provided encouraging comment; and we are grateful to Niel Gunson, Lamont Lindstrom, Klaus Neumann, and Jeffrey Sissons for assistance with various bibliographic, ethnohistorical, and linguistic queries. Special mention must be made of Michael Hoare, to whom we are indebted for his foundational biographical and bibliographic work on Forster, and most particularly for his edition of Forster's *Resolution* journal, which we have turned to again and again, as will be plain from our annotations.

Nicholas Thomas' editorial and bibliographic work has been supported particularly by the Australian Research Council and by the National Library of Australia.

INTRODUCTION

Johann Reinhold Forster and His *Observations*

NICHOLAS THOMAS

Observations Made during a Voyage round the World was written on the basis of Forster's participation in Cook's second voyage of 1772–1775. The book is remarkable not only for its content, for its observations on what were then major questions of scientific and navigational debate, and for its reading of Tahitian and other Pacific societies in the terms of philosophical history, but also for its generic peculiarity. While the number of eighteenth-century travel books is very considerable, even those by scientific or philosophical travelers such as the French naturalists le Poivre and Adanson were narratives that interspersed remarks on landscapes, flora, fauna, and the inhabitants of places visited, through the account of a journey. Botanical or zoological findings were frequently published separately, usually in Latin volumes with illustrations and descriptions of specimens; but these systematizations were abstracted from the encounters constitutive of a voyage and did not include information on the human species. On the other hand, inquiries into natural history, the human species, social institutions, and morals were published by philosophers who often drew extensively on travel writers—as Montesquieu did, for example, on du Halde's account of China—but who had not traveled themselves and were not concerned to describe or analyze in detail circumstances in any particular part of the non-European world.

It would be misleading to suggest that there was a divide between the travel narrative and the systematic inquiry or treatise, since travel itself had undergone a good deal of systematization; but few works synthesized sustained reflections on fundamental questions—such as the progress of property, law, and social happiness—with the description of the manners and customs of particular peoples or the natural phenomena of an area. In the early eighteenth century, moreover, those travelers who described peoples in detail tended not to do so from a philosophical point of view (this is true for example of Chardin and Kolb, whose accounts of Persia and southern Africa respectively were widely read); those who were scientists, on the other hand, usually confined their attention to flora or the "brute organic." This is the complaint that Forster makes as he introduces his extended discussion of the human species in the South Sea islands, in the sixth chapter that constitutes two-thirds of this book. Although he was clearly defining a space for his own authority, and neglecting the few writers such as Lafitau who had in fact written theoretical inquiries into peoples with whom they had had extended personal contact, his claim that there was a gap between unphilosophical travel and philosophical speculation was a reasonable one, as his own book was indeed novel for its effort to synthesize "ethic philosophy" and travel.

Observations could be described as a geographically particularized philosophical essay, as a natural history that emphasized human physical and moral variety rather than plant and animal life, or as a travel book in which narrative was radically contracted to the skeletal journal at the beginning and displaced by an extensive reflective exposition of the kind that other writers presented piecemeal. However this generic hybridity is understood, it is important that it be seen not merely to emerge from Forster's desire or capacity to elaborate an undeveloped form, but significantly also from the politics of the voyage, or more particularly from a series of controversies about the publication of its results. On board the *Resolution*, Forster did not plan to write a book like this; events compelled him to do so. In this edition, our approach is not primarily biographical or psychological, but it is appropriate that a brief account be given of Forster's career and of the conditions under which the *Observations* was written.[1]

Johann Reinhold Forster was born near Danzig in 1729 and was educated in Berlin and at the University of Halle, where he completed theological studies in 1751. Briefly an apprentice pastor in Danzig, he moved to Nassenhuben in 1753 and began reading widely in natural history, languages, and ancient history. Dissatisfied, apparently, both with the limited character of his pastoral duties and their low remuneration, he undertook a survey of the new Volga colonies in Russia in 1765–1766. In this assignment, which included the investigation of natural resources, he was accompanied by his son George[2] (1754–1794), later a major figure of the German Enlightenment and an associate of Alexander von Humboldt; this collaboration of father and son prefigured a great deal of work together in field inquiries, and—less romantically but perhaps more consequentially—in writing and translating works of natural history, travel, and philosophy. Forster's report was critical of the planning and management of the colonies, and the pair left Russia without payment for England.

In London, Forster looked for employment and involved himself actively in the Royal Society, the Society of Antiquaries, and the Society of Arts; in due course he was admitted to each of these bodies (becoming a Fellow of the Royal Society in 1771) and published articles in their journals. He made the acquaintance of, and was supported by, a number of men with interests in natural history, antiquities, and travel, notably Thomas Pennant and Daines Barrington. Forster obtained a position teaching languages and natural history at the Warrington Academy, an important base of radical and dissenting thought, and worked intensively on a number of translations, particularly of works by pupils of Linnaeus, such as Pehr Osbeck and Joseph Gmelin, which are cited in the *Observations*; his own more substantial publications in this period included an *Introduction to Mineralogy* (1768).

Preparations were under way for Cook's second voyage from the latter part of 1771. It was assumed, until a late point, that the naturalist accompanying Cook would be Joseph Banks, whose participation in the first voyage in the *Endeavour* had occasioned great renown and some notoriety. Banks proposed to take a considerable entourage, including Solander and the painter Zoffany, and required alterations to the *Resolution* that were made but found to render the ship unseaworthy; dissatisfied with the less adequate quarters that remained, Banks withdrew himself and his party in May 1772. William Hodges was recruited in Zoffany's place, and Forster, with the recommendation of members of the council of the Royal Society, and Barrington's lobbying, was appointed as naturalist. It is of some importance that he went under virtually the terms that had been drawn up for Banks: the allowance of £4000, which far exceeded the £400 given each of the astronomers, William Wales and William Bayly, was or was understood to be behind some of the professional rivalries and animosities that were aired extensively in Forster's journal and in polemical, post-voyage publications (see Michael Dettelbach's essay). Forster was, it seems, first approached about joining the voyage on 26 May 1772; on 13 July the *Resolution*, accompanied by the *Adventure* under Tobias Furneaux, was at sea.

The principal purpose of the voyage was the investigation of the postulated great southern continent, long an object of geographical speculation, but of special interest in the late eighteenth century as a bountiful land of prospective settlement; its quest was a matter of imperial rivalry between Britain and France. To definitively confirm or disconfirm the existence of this land was Cook's purpose; the task was to be accomplished by summer cruises in far southern latitudes, which would be broken by periods of refreshment in the tropics. The first of the forays into the far south lasted more than four months, from late 1772 to early 1773; rest and provisions were then obtained at New Zealand; Tahiti, Tonga, and New Zealand were visited over the period up to October that year; further explorations were then made in the Antarctic; between March and August 1774, the *Resolution* visited and obtained refreshments at Easter Island, the Marquesas, Tahiti, and the western Pacific. In the latter region, particularly, much more was done than merely obtain supplies: though Quiros and Bougainville had visited parts of the northern New Hebrides (as Cook named the islands now known as Vanuatu), it was on this voyage that first contacts were made with the islanders in the southern part of the group, which was charted far more extensively than previously. Other inhabited lands "discovered," to use the notoriously Eurocentric term, included New Caledonia and the small Polynesian island of Niue, but in virtually all the island groups prior European cartographic and ethnographic knowledge was dramatically extended. New Zealand was visited a third time late in 1774, and further explorations were made in the far south, this time in the south Atlantic, early in 1775; the ships then returned to Britain via Cape Town in July of that year.[3]

Back in England, promotions, honors, and audiences with the king were bestowed; but for Johann Reinhold and George Forster all this was overshadowed by controversy that has been described in considerable detail by several writers[4] but must be briefly reviewed here. The key question was who would be the author of the official account of the voyage. The book, which would be well-illustrated with charts, plates from Hodges' paintings, and botanical and ethnographic engravings, was certain to be successful; fame aside, its author would do very well indeed financially. For this reason, among others, the Admiralty aimed to monopolize publication; voyage participants were required to surrender their logs and were not permitted to write unauthorized accounts.[5]

Forster's claim that he had been promised the opportunity of writing the history was regarded as fanciful by Cook's editor and biographer, J. C. Beaglehole, but seems to have had some basis, at least in a private understanding conveyed by Daines Barrington; Cook, dissatisfied with John Hawkesworth's account of the first voyage and himself anxious to obtain authorial renown and a share in the profits, resisted Forster's proposal. A series of negotiations and ruptures between September 1775 and June 1776 saw various proposals for co-authorship and divisions of reward mooted; but Sandwich, the first lord of the Admiralty, supported Cook, while Forster, backed by Daines Barrington, insisted that he should be permitted to write a voyage narrative rather than merely an appended volume of observations on natural history. Forster thus evidently perceived the narrative as the most attractive and prestigious form of publication, and conflict arose at one point because it emerged that, while he had conceded that Cook would write the principal voyage history and he the philosophical observations, he proposed, in any case, to present his remarks through a narrative. His concern may have derived in part from the fact that he had kept a full journal (now published in Michael Hoare's edition): making this into an account for publication would have entailed considerably less work than writing a fresh, differently organized, book—but clearly much more was at issue than saving labor. Forster had a deep familiarity with the philosophically informed travel narrative, a familiarity that derived as much from his translations as from his reading, and he no doubt hoped to emulate Linnaean travelers such as Kalm and Osbeck, while elevating their scientific sophistication through association with the singularly patriotic history of discovery from which the account of an official voyage could hardly be dissociated. Forster had made the 1772 translation of Bougainville's voyage (substantially George's work) a vehicle for this adoptive patriotism: editorial interventions had corrected certain Gallic distortions and emphasized the unequaled navigational accomplishments of the British. That nationalist rhetoric might have found a place in his publication from the second voyage, as conceived in the early stages of these negotiations, is suggested by the fact that Forster proposed for a time to introduce his volume of observations with a chronological history of exploration in the South Sea.[6]

Specimens of Forster's work went back and forth, and his written English was found wanting; substantial editing was proposed, which he found too substantial. He and Barrington fell out over the question of whether seawater could freeze; Forster's correct view that it could detracted from the possibility of a northwest passage, with which Barrington was preoccupied. Forster was left without a powerful supporter, and scope for agreement evaporated in mid-1776; Cook had for some time presumed that he would be writing on his own, and he completed his narrative before departing on the third voyage at the end of June 1776. George Forster's rival account appeared in print shortly before Cook's; though often acknowledged to be a far more engaging text than the official publication, it lacked the numerous plates of the latter and was relatively unsuccessful commercially. It was, however, attacked in a pamphlet by William Wales, who presumed it to be the work of Johann Reinhold, using George's name to bypass the Admiralty prohibition; George responded in his *Reply to Mr. Wales' Remarks* and pursued the whole controversy in his *Letter to the Right Honourable the Earl of Sandwich* in 1778, but the details of these debates need not be entered into here. Forster himself resolved to publish on his own; it is not clear exactly when he began concerted work on *Observations*, but it is likely to have been toward the end of 1776; the book was completed at the end of May 1778, and printed between June and August.

Despite the independence Forster gained by severing himself from the Admiralty, the scope of the book as published reflected the terms of an agreement—endorsed in April 1776 by Sandwich, Cook, the Admiralty secretary, and Forster—that had distinguished his contribution from Cook's. The latter's narrative was to be complemented by "Doctor Forster's Observations upon Natural History, and upon the Manners, Customs, Genius and Language of the several Islands, with his philosophical remarks in the course of the voyage, and a general introduction to his own work."[7] Forster, of course, may have suggested this wording, and it may be merely accidental that so far as the human species is concerned, it echoed a phrase in the Admiralty's instructions to Cook: "You are likewise to observe the Genius, Temper, Disposition, and Number of the Natives or Inhabitants, if there be any."[8] The point is not that this instruction, which was a secret document that Forster may not have seen, had any influence upon his concerns, but rather that *Observations* articulated with the agenda of the voyage's sponsors to an extent that is retrospectively obscured by the controversy and by Beaglehole's view that the book "would have been a curious mate for Cook's volumes."[9] Banks did not publish on the basis of his participation in the voyage of the *Endeavour,* but sections of remarks upon the South Sea islanders in his journal dealt, far more cursorily, with a similar range of topics that Forster considers in this book—population, color, size, food preparation, the status of women, and so on. What Banks did not venture to do and Forster did was make these observations merely the empirical materials for elaborate arguments concerning the progress of happiness, education, and civility. If what was at stake in not writing a narrative was a lapse into an "unconnected" sequence of remarks, Forster can be seen to have introduced thematic, moral, and developmental progressions, which supplied some coherence in place of a chronological order; this was the "compre-

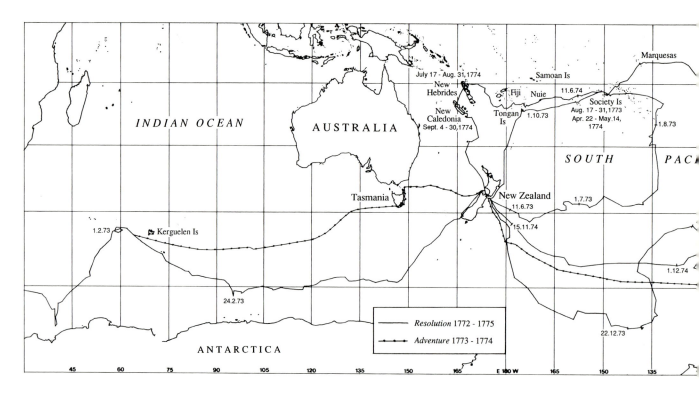

hensive and methodized view" referred to in the advertisment for the *Observations*, which we reproduce below. However, the combination of regionally peculiar and general histories and the ambivalence about progress, which echoes the writers of the Scottish Enlightenment, prejudiced the unity of the philosophical narrative in a number of ways.

Although the post-voyage polemics are almost nowhere directly referred to in the *Observations*, the text is marked by the context of the book's composition. As Michael Dettelbach shows, the project of natural history was deeply politicized. That Forster was preoccupied with power and its abuse does not indicate merely that his political concerns were those of the time; the issue was particularized in his own relationships and battles. His ambivalence about the effects of contact between the British and the peoples of the South Seas certainly refracted a negative view of the Admiralty: the common seamen were as corrupted as one would expect, given the despotic government to which they were subject. But these judgments are often implicit. Forster celebrated Cook's wisdom and achievement, as he did in other works published long after he could hope to gain much in or from Britain; he also wrote passages, such as the concluding section on the health of mariners, that retain the patriotic rhetoric of the extant draft on

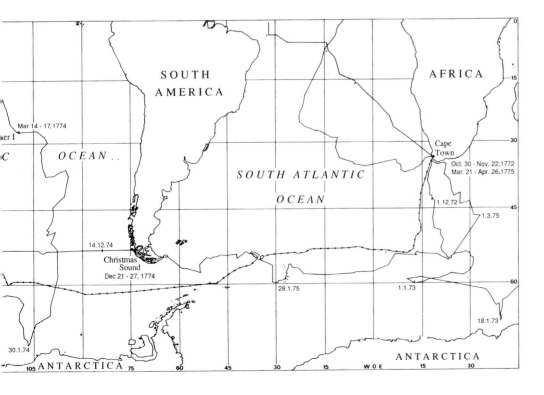

Track Chart of the *Resolution*, 1772–1775. Adapted from a map from Hoare, ed., *The* Resolution *Journal of Johann Reinhold Forster*, 1982.

the history of exploration in the south. The book, however, has a certain distance from the commemoration of a nation's discoveries that was so conspicuous in the official account and associated publications, such as Wales and Bayly's *Astronomical Observations*. Forster's section on the health of seamen, and the book as a whole, concludes by asserting the importance of sending men "versed in science" out on voyages: "it is not enough to send them out, but they ought likewise to be encouraged in their laborious task, liberally supported and generously enabled to make such enquiries as may prevent their fellow creatures in future times from becoming sacrifices to their own ignorance." Every reference of this kind in Forster's work is an affirmation of authority, a claim against the ways in which the tasks of the voyage had been ranked and privileged, a claim for his inquiries and a protest against those—common sailors and Admiralty Lords alike—who had thwarted or devalued them. That natural history as such, rather than Forster's work alone, suffered devaluation is attested to by Cook's decision to do without a naturalist on his third voyage, which was, over the months in which *Observations* was published, probing improbable northwest passages around Bering's Sea.

Facing mounting debts and no prospect of employment in England, the Forsters returned to Germany in 1780: George had traveled in advance of the family and had been able to raise support for his father, who was appointed in late 1779 to a professorship at the University of Halle, where he taught until shortly before his death in 1798.[10] He continued to publish extensively, and translated a considerable number of voyage narratives, including Rickman's account from Cook's third voyage, Dixon and Portlock's *Voyage*, several accounts from the 1788 settlement of New South Wales, and Bligh, Brissot, and La Pérouse. Among Forster's last translations into German was Fanny Burney's *Camilla*: though this was a very different kind of book, its themes of power, passion, and corruption were hardly wholly alien to him.

"On the Varieties of the Human Species": Forster's Comparative Ethnology

NICHOLAS THOMAS

In March 1772, as preparations were under way for Cook's second voyage, Lord Kames wrote to the surgeon James Lind, a member of Banks' proposed party on the circumnavigation, asking him to inquire into the relationships between human and animal varieties and different climates:

> There is no known plant or animal equally fitted for every climate. There are many various climates in our globe; and there are plants & animals fitted for every climate so as to flourish there and grow to perfection, and that degenerate in other climates. Whence the following question whether a plant or an animal that degenerates in a foreign climate may not in a long course of time be so habituated to that climate as at last to flourish there as well as in its original climate . . . so far as my experience goes or my reading, no length of time will ever make a plant or an animal do so well in a foreign climate or in a climate that once was foreign as in its original climate. . . . But here comes my subject. Are not men, like horses or wheat, apt to degenerate in foreign climes? In Charlestown [South Carolina] as observed they have not time to degenerate, for they die out in three generations. How is Batavia as to European inhabitants, are their numbers kept up by propagation or do they need continued supplies from Europe? In the course of your Voyage, you'll probably have many opportunities for enquiries of this kind. . . . This leads to a deep speculation viz what is the scheme of providence for peopling the earth with the human race. Abstracting from Revelation it is natural to conjecture, that as there are many different climates, there were formed originally different races of men fit for these different climates, in which only they flourish and degenerate in every other climate. Every experiment seems to correspond to this conjecture.[1]

Together with the rest of Banks' party, Lind withdrew from the expedition, and it is impossible to know what he would have made of this commission; but questions of this kind were of considerable importance for Johann Reinhold Forster, the natural historian who did join the voyage. Kames did not wait until the expedition returned to publish his *Sketches of the History of Man*, which opened with a rejection, along lines reminiscent of the letter I've just quoted, of the notion that humankind consisted of only one species. For Kames, the importance of this principle would seem to have been that the progress and dispositions of particular peoples could be explained partly on the basis of "original" differences between them, as well as on the basis of environment and, especially, economic and political organization: his interest was above all in the ways in which different forms of government were conducive to different degrees of progress, happiness, human vigor, and productivity; or rather, since the negative aspect of progress is extensively rehearsed, with the vice, degeneracy, and corruption he saw as accompanying and vitiating the higher stages of social advancement: "Good government will advance men to a high degree of civilization; but the very best government will not preserve them from corruption, after becoming rich by prosperity."[2]

Forster read *Sketches of the History of Man* as he was writing his *Observations* and referred to it at several points, but the book was only one of a number of texts he responded to, and it should not be unduly privileged as an influence upon his work; for one thing, Forster was definitely opposed to Kames' polygenetic doctrines. While Linnaeus and Buffon, among other natural historians, may appear more foundational for Forster's inquiry—a third of his book, after all, was concerned with physical geography and nonhuman life—Kames nevertheless provides a useful point of reference for an understanding of *Observations*. He, like other writers of the Scottish Enlightenment such as Millar and Ferguson, ranged across questions—such as taxation; the progress of property and commerce; and the effects of climate upon human customs, dispositions, and physiology—that would subsequently seem exclusively distributed among jurisprudential theory, economic policy, ethnology, and natural history. David Lieberman has detected in Kames' later work an "exasperating readiness to discourse upon virtually any subject at virtually uncontrollable length,"[3] and his remarks upon this range of topics in *Sketches of the History of Man* are, accordingly, never really subordinated to a unifying thesis. Forster's work, however, made more direct connections between political conditions, progress, and corruption and the problem that Kames alluded to in his letter to Lind: whether particular species or varieties were fitted exclusively to particular climates and what the effects of their transposition beyond those favored habitats might be.

When Kames wrote to Lind he could hardly have anticipated the extent to which a voyage aimed at confirming or disconfirming the existence of a great southern land would in fact produce a wealth of material for anthropological reflection: the range of contacts with Oceanic peoples was unprecedented. Most earlier voyages (such as those of Roggeveen, Wallis, and Bougainville) had stopped at Tahiti but then passed through other island groups or made only cursory visits in one or two other places such as Easter Island or northern Vanuatu. Participants in Cook's first voyage had indeed had more protracted encounters with several populations—Tahitians, Maori, and Australian Aborigines—though neither Joseph Banks nor Cook himself was especially interested in systematically discussing the differences and similarities among them. On the second voyage of 1772–1775, Easter Island, the Society Islands,[4] the Marquesas, Tonga, Niue, New Zealand, and the Tuamotu archipelago were visited; the inhabitants of these places were manifestly related, and the perceived distinctiveness of these Polynesians, as they were later categorized, was reinforced by contact with apparently unrelated peoples in neighboring regions, in the New Hebrides and New Caledonia in the western Pacific, and in Tierra del Fuego. Some islands were visited more than once or at length, others more briefly; fresh observations were complemented by the linguistic, ethnographic, and geographic knowledge accumulated from the first voyage.

In writing the *Observations*, Johann Reinhold Forster could draw upon a range of information concerning a region that was very different from the kind of geographical and ethnographic knowledge exhibited in most eighteenth-century works of travel or ethnology. Where these made any pretension to provide detailed accounts of indigenous peoples, they were generally restricted to whichever group the writer had lived with or observed closely, such as the Iroquois for Lafitau or the so-called Hottentots for Kolb. In so far as these texts were comparative, comparisons took the form of contrast with the civilized societies of Europe or (in the case of Lafitau) the points of similarity with the ancients. Forster, on the other hand, was both able and concerned to discuss the differences between Society Islanders, Easter Islanders, Tongans, Maori, and others; these peoples, as a number of voyage participants inferred correctly from linguistic cognates and similarities between customs and social forms, were all descended from an ancestral population that had dispersed itself across a huge triangle in the eastern Pacific (though the top point of that triangle, the Hawaiian group, remained unknown to Europeans until Cook's third voyage).

Forster's comparisons also differed from those pursued in more theoretical writing on the development of civil society. Although he regarded settled peoples as superior to nomads for much the same reasons as the Scottish writers did, and although their stadial differences between hunting, pastoral, and agricultural societies are implicit in his discussion, the larger evolution had to be in the background because most of the peoples encountered on the voyage were at the same stage in these terms: nearly all were sedentary horticulturalists. There was much, however, in physical appearance, sociality, and conduct toward Europeans that set the islanders of the New Hebrides and those of Tahiti apart, while less considerable but equally significant differences were apparent between more closely related groups, such as those of Tanna and Erromanga in the southern New Hebrides and those of Dusky Bay and Queen Charlotte's Sound in southern New Zealand. Forster, as natural historian and ethic philosopher, was prompted to characterize particular peoples in their specificity and to provide some sort of account of the differences among them. This essay explores the descriptive language he employed and the concepts he used to discriminate among and account for the varying degrees of "progress" he recognized among the "nations" of the South Sea.

Forster was a monogenist, but for him, as for Blumenbach and others, the affirmation of the unity of the human species was the premise for an exploration of its divisions into "races" or "varieties." As an order of classification the species was, of course, distinguished by the capacity to breed and produce fertile offspring, but varieties or subspecies were in other respects formally similar to species, in that they were assumed to be physically and temperamentally distinctive. In delineating varieties, the natural historian of course gave an account of their singularity, but was led also—given the environmentalism or qualified environmentalism that Buffon and Forster subscribed to—to account for this distinctiveness in terms of climatic situation and mode of life, among other factors. There was thus a tension between what can be seen as an essentializing project, which stipulated the natures of different races, and a comparative one, which emphasized their mutability: one moment of description privileged an "original" type, the other its "degenerated" derivations, which might approximate or merge into another variety.

At the beginning of the key section "On the Varieties of the Human Species, relative to Colour, Size, Form, Habit, and Natural Turn of Mind in the Natives of the South-Sea Isles," Forster foreshadowed the mode of typification he adopts, through a series of thumbnail sketches.

> The varieties of the human species are, as every one knows, very numerous. The small size, the tawny colour, the mistrustful temper, are as peculiar to the Esquimaux; as the noble and beautiful figure, and outline of the body, the fair complexion, and the treacherous turn of mind, to the inhabitant of Tcherkassia. The native of Senegal is characterized by a timorous disposition, by his jetty black skin, and crisped wooly hair. (153)

This descriptive language, which attributed peculiarities of size or hair, a particular color, and a characteristic disposition to a singular standard specimen, followed Buffon's style of characterizing animal species. Each section in the *Natural History* on a particular creature began by noting what was distinctive in teeth or bodily form and proceeded to the animal's supposed character and habit. "In his disposition, the ass is equally humble, patient, and tranquil, as the horse is proud, ardent, and impetuous"; "The badger is an indolent, diffident, solitary animal."[5] Though broadly similar, Buffon's descriptions of peoples were less structured and consistent; in emphasizing color or specifically physical characteristics in some cases and customs in others, they seem to reflect his sources rather than a clear method of his own.

National varieties in Europe had also long been written about in similarly essentialist terms, in genres such as grand tour writing and in encyclopedic grammars and atlases that included sections on the "genius" or habitual disposition of each nation. Though "the French," "the Spanish," and "the Irish" were mostly specified on the basis of temperament rather than physique, national characters were often seen as internalizations of the mode of life or education that amounted to "natures" or "second natures" and possessed almost the same stability as racial distinctness and character. As in the case of non-European populations, descriptions and analyses might alternate between moments at which national characters were stable types and those at which their modification or degeneration might be of particular interest. While the vocabularies of characterization varied considerably, according to the context and point of particular typifications, it is notable that the condition of a nation was often represented in terms of either torpor or vigor; social analysis frequently amounted to a specification of the factors that might rouse particular populations or on the other hand permit them to lapse into indolence and inactivity. This cluster of metaphors, together with the commonplace notion that high refinement, luxury, and opulence were conducive to effeminacy, enters conspicuously into Forster's account of the peoples of the South Sea.

Despite the essentialism that the passage on the Eskimo, the Tcherkassian, and the Senegalese suggests, Forster did not regard the characters of different human varieties or races as permanent or immutable. His discussion of the human species in the South Sea commences with an estimate of their numbers, an appropriate beginning since population was of foundational importance for his understanding of progress and degeneration. He argued that population growth was the cause and not an effect of civilization and particularly agriculture: because foraging could not support substantial numbers, people had to cultivate the ground, and therefore both exchange roots and seeds and respect and defend one another's plantations. These beginnings of law and cooperation not only led to distinctions of rank, power, and wealth; "Nay, they often produce a material difference in the colour, habits, and forms of the human species" (152). It was this question—of precisely how climatic, geographic, demographic, and civil factors produced "material" differences among the human varieties in the Pacific—that those of Cook's second voyage, who encountered related, distinct, and unrelated populations, were peculiarly equipped to address.

Forster began by contrasting two "great varieties" or "races" among the Oceanic peoples: "the one more fair, well limbed, athletic, of a fine size, and a kind benevolent temper; the other, blacker, the hair just beginning to become woolly and crisp, the body more slender and low, and their temper, if possible more brisk, though somewhat mistrustful" (153). The general coherence that each of these is accorded is, however, almost immediately prejudiced by the admission that each of these "races" is "again divided into several varieties, which form the gradations toward the other race"; yet despite there being almost a continuum between the two, Forster maintained that the first, if not the second, could be comprehended as "one tribe" possessing "a general character."

The "first" and "second" races postulated in the *Observations* corresponded closely with the Polynesian and Melanesian groups defined by Dumont d'Urville in the 1830s;[6] but if Forster's characterization and assessment of these peoples certainly anticipated those of nineteenth-century geographers and ethnologists in some respects, it is important that he not be read principally as a precursor. Though he certainly saw the peoples of the eastern Pacific as having progressed further than the "Melanesians" of the west, this evolutionism was informed by criteria distinct from those privileged later and was articulated with different arguments concerning the importance of climate, migration, and education, among other factors. In particular, while later writers tended to take nomadic populations as representatives of an originary and primeval condition, Forster noted their situations in temperate zones and saw them as degenerate branches of happier, tropical peoples.

The order in which the varieties are described is not so much evolutionary as aesthetic. While Buffon had begun anthropocentrically with domestic animals and those he considered most important (the horse, ass, ox, pig, dog, and so on), Forster commenced with the Tahitians and Society Islanders, which "contain the most beautiful variety of the first race," and moved to those "next in beauty" (the Marquesans), then through others to the peoples of "the second tribe," that is, the western islanders, discussing the peoples of New Caledonia, Tanna, and Malekula. The first "race" ranged in color from fair to tawny; the New Caledonians and Tannese were "swarthy," and the Malekulans "black." The Tierra del Fuegians were considered (as they in fact were) an unrelated population, but they stand at an extreme point on Forster's continuum, as an instance of an absolutely degraded type. This progression from most to least appealing entails shifts across a whole succession of criteria: bodily form, complexion, vigor, disposition toward Europeans, forms of adornment, and so forth. These matters are privileged in Forster's initial survey of the varieties; later sections of the text deal with particular issues such as the varying expressions of civility and the status of women and trace these through the range of peoples, usually in the same order from elevated Tahitians through the more debased groups.

Certain peoples are described initially as though they possessed the coherence and distinctiveness attributed to Senegalese, but Forster proceeds, in some cases, to acknowledge internal heterogeneity, which is then traced to climatic and behavioral factors. The population of Tahiti reproduces the "richness, luxury, and variety" that characterize the island's vegetation: neither is "confined to a single type or model" (154).[7]

> The common people are most exposed to air and sun; they do all kinds of dirty work; they exert their strength in agriculture, fishing, paddling, building of houses and canoes; and lastly, they are stinted in their food. From these causes, they degenerate as it were towards the second race, but always preserve some remains of their original type; which, in their chiefs or Arees, and the better sort of people, appears in its full lustre and perfection.

An "original type" subject to adaptation is thus postulated, and adaptation is directly recognizable in this case as a result of greater exposure to the elements and a harder mode of life; in the Marquesas, the men are less "fleshy" than the Tahitians, because of their greater activity: "as a very considerable part of them live on the slopes and the very summits of high hills . . . they must of course have a slender habit of body, from the frequent climbing of these high mountains, and from the keen air" (155). More generally, those eastern Pacific islanders such as the Marquesans, Tuamotuans, and Easter Islanders, who were "much exposed to air and sun" grew "thin and slender" and possessed bones that were "not strong, but solid and hard"; on the other hand, those in colder climates, or those such as the Tahitian chiefs, who avoided exposure to heat, acquired "a more soft, spungy, and succulent habit of body" (180).

In attributing variety to climatic determinations, Forster found it easier to explain degeneration than advancement. He inferred from the linguistic cognates, and quite correctly, that the Pacific islands had been settled from Asia and the Malay archipelago, and he saw migration from one tropical zone to another as producing some vague enhancement of the knowledge and character of a population; on the other hand, he theorized the loss of learning and the debasement of a people's character more powerfully and specifically, situating the process in movement from a tropical to a temperate or frigid zone. The Tierra del Fuegians provided one of his key examples: their peculiar misery was manifest not only in the flimsiness of their dwellings, in their harsh and broad features, and in their stupidity, but also in the fact that they expressed "hardly any desires or wishes to possess any thing which we offered" (193). An interest in novelties and a degree of acquisitiveness were thus two of the traits that enabled Forster to measure the advancement of the South Sea islanders over the occupants of this inhospitable place, and it was a measurement that produced certain ambiguities, as will be noted below.

While nineteenth-century evolutionism took populations such as the Tierra del Fuegians and the Tasmanians as living exemplars of primeval stone age ways of life, Forster saw the natural range of humanity as the tropics and argued that peoples closer to the poles had migrated into those colder climates and could generally be seen as debased variants of the populations from which they derived. The gradations could be detected not only in very broad contrasts between the inhabitants of mainland South America and those of Tierra del Fuego, but also at a local level, between the happier people of Success Bay, and the "little tribe" of apparent outcasts that Forster himself observed on the island, who seemed "occupied with nothing but their wants and wretchedness" (193). Degeneracy was marked not only by an evidently impoverished material culture, but also in physique: "The inhabitants of Tierra del Fuego, are all a chubbed race, probably because they are descended from a set of people of large limbs, living on the continent, but being stinted by cold, and wants of all kinds, are degenerated into a short and squat figure, which keeps always the original model, or type, in the size of the head; a circumstance almost generally observed in dwarfs" (180).

Forster may well have been influenced by Buffon's suggestion that the Laplanders were "a degenerated species,"[8] though Buffon rather crudely attributed the same nature and customs to the circumpolar peoples in general and put forward no elaborate argument to account for their condition. While obviously according the harshness of the climate a basic causative role, Forster saw its effect as mediated by knowledge and education, and he illustrated the contrast through juxtaposition of Tierra del Fuegians and the people of Greenland. That the latter were, in respect of their dwellings, their subsistence practices, and their clothes, clearly a more ingenious and happy people than the Tierra del Fuegians made it evident that life in frigid regions was not necessarily degraded; what was crucial was rather that a people that shifted from one climate to another tended to lose the accumulated knowledge of their ancestors, much of which might, in any case, be poorly suited to their new environment. Population was again a basic factor: although a transposed people might discover new ways of feeding and sheltering themselves, scope for invention was limited in small communities. This "smallness of their numbers," together with the resistance of savages to the ideas of others and the fact that the labor of inefficient foraging left little time for leisure and education, meant that the preconditions for improvement were lacking (207). While the people of the far south of New Zealand's South Island were per-

haps equally sparse and scattered as the Tierra del Fuegians, their happier condition arose from their relative proximity to people who sustained the larger
reserve of knowledge; the Tierra del Fuegians, on the other hand, were not only
nomads themselves, but the descendents of "a straggling tribe" and were therefore
at a greater remove from the intellectual resources conducive to improvement.

In New Zealand one of the key factors is the greater population: "their minds
have acquired a larger and more liberal circle of ideas" (208). Maori societies
struck Forster as violent and barbaric, but he perceived a dynamism in them that
suggested scope for progress toward a happier civility. Again, he does not construe
the harsh or brute attributes of the people as a direct result of climate, but rather
derives them from the mode of education: their social condition makes New
Zealanders "jealous of their liberty and independence," and they rouse themselves
into furious intrepidity in the face of perceived injuries and offenses; for Forster,
this warriorhood, courage, and fidelity toward kin and allies recalls the world of
fables and romances, but such attributes are prone to lapse into license through
lack of proper direction and government. He rejects the notion that their
extreme expression, cannibalism, is motivated by hunger, tracing it instead to
what education makes the passionate and ferocious second nature of the warriors:

> We find that their education is the chief cause of all these enormities. The men train
> up the boys in a kind of liberty, which at last degenerates into licentiousness: they
> suffer not the mothers to strike their petulant, unruly, and wicked sons, for fear of
> breaking that spirit of independency, which they seem to value above all things, and
> as the most necessary qualification for their societies; this naturally brings on an
> irascibility . . . they know not where to stop. (212–213)

Eating the corpses of the slain thus extends an unrestrained, frenzied aggres-
sion, and once the "bounds of humanity" are passed, the practice becomes habitual and is institutionalized "among the honours due to the conqueror" (213).

Forster notes that there is something paradoxical in ranking the Maori above
the Tierra del Fuegians, since though the former are definitely elevated above
the indifference and indolence of the latter, their vigor is marked as much by
inhumane practices as by anything that can be positively appreciated, such as
ingenuity in carving, canoe making, subsistence practices, oratory, and so on. At
a later point, Forster makes it clear that this combination of extremes is characteristic of the "step" that the Maori have reached, but he sees even its more negative manifestations as factors that may, in the course of time, be conducive to
improvement. Prolonged hostilities between two peoples must, he speculates,
lead each to realize that the depredations are destructive and that "a living man is
more useful than one that is dead or roasted" (214); warfare would thus eventu-

ally be pursued more cautiously, and conquerors would see the value of capturing and enslaving, rather than slaughtering, their enemies. Though conquest of this kind can clearly be oppressive, it is conducive to a larger and more united society and therefore also "prepares the way to a more humane and benevolent scene" (214). If Forster's concern to place cannibalism in its proper light appears contrived, the form of argument is pivotal because it dissociates the practice from a generic savagery and instead locates it in a particular form of rude society, martial barbarism, and in modes of education peculiar to that stage. Forster has no time for the argument that cannibalism is prompted by hunger, because it would preclude the connections he seeks to identify between it and particular forms of sociality; his interest, though ethnologically deeply nuanced by the range of societies observed, parallels that of Montesquieu and the many theorists he influenced, in the "consequences" of different kinds of government for laws, manners, principles of education, and so forth.

A tension might be detected here in Forster's exposition between two temporal models, or two fictions of historical contextualization. The first posits ancestral associations between peoples, migrations, and derivative or degenerate forms, and therefore situates the New Zealanders as an offshoot of the tropical South Sea islands population, the nomads of the Dusky Bay as debased further beneath the condition of the Maori in the north, and the Tierra del Fuegians, albeit an unrelated group, as the "last and most miserable of men" on the continuum, which extends beyond them into the uninhabited wastes of the Antarctic. The second form of argument is more abstracted from the actual histories about which Forster speculates; it renders the "degenerated" peoples at a point of extreme rudeness, from which unassisted improvement can either be projected (in New Zealand) or not (in Tierra del Fuego). In the second form of argument, the observed societies become imperfect or inchoate expressions of something more advanced, rather than historical outcomes of processes that later writers would describe as "devolution" in, or "adaptation" to, a harsher environment. The first strand of Forster's argument draws the societies observed into a particularizing, historical geography; the second assimilates them to a general narrative of political evolution. The effects of this combination are sometimes contradictory: New Zealand society is on the one hand the result of the transposition of something like Tahitian civility into the temperate zone; on the other, it is a precursor to Tahiti that enables Tahitian prehistory to be seen in the same way that primitive peoples generally made ancestral stages of European society visible. Hence cannibalism, which survived only as a historical memory of a barbaric epoch in the Society Islands, could be witnessed among the New Zealanders.

In the *Observations,* Tahitian society represents the highest form of civility encountered in the Pacific; in many respects, Forster finds the sense of common good and the happiness that he witnessed preferable to the condition of polished European societies. He does not, however, idealize Tahiti in the manner of Diderot, detecting in the island a kind of natural liberty or pre-social innocence; Tahitian civility is understood rather as a historically contingent political form, one that owes its happiness in part to adventitious climatic advantages, and one that is to some degree corrupted by its opulence.

Much follows from the relative density of population on a tropical isle: the inhabitants are compelled to practice cultivation and therefore to cooperate in tending gardens, in exchanging seeds and roots, in refraining from freely appropriating one another's produce, and in defending a tribe's plantations against invaders. This applies in some measure to all the tropical islands, but Tahiti's distinctly benevolent climate creates a general opulence, and thus scope for refinement in a variety of crafts and arts: Forster writes at length about the Society Islanders' accomplishments, not only in elementary matters of subsistence, dress, and ornament, but in such fields of knowledge as astronomy and geography, and he accords their religion a degree of reason and coherence. Although the elaboration of property and rank is fundamental to this cultural improvement, Tahitian society represents the apical point of human progress in the South Seas not because its polity is the most stratified but rather because a feudal stratification appears qualified by a simpler patriarchalism: a shift is postulated that amounts almost to a lapse from a politically evolved condition back to a less advanced form. The vocabulary of this positioning is ambiguous; again, something that might be assimilated to later evolutionary argument jostles with a more particular and historical account.

The especially appealing feature of the Tahitian polity, for Forster, is that the chiefs are committed to the common weal and are not dissociated from the people in general. The elaborate respect customs of Tongan society are compared unfavorably with Tahitian practices, and it is shown that Tonga—which also exhibits a more rigorous form of private property—retains the more strictly feudal form of government that Forster finds prevailed among all the islanders' Malay ancestors. This government is characterized by "oriental despotism and slavish subjection to chiefs and their LATOO, derogatory to that dignity and liberty, to which nature destined all her sons and daughters" (237). The contrast between the polities was reflected not only in a variety of observed customs, but also in the fact that Tongans were obliged to surrender goods obtained from Europeans to their chiefs, while ordinary Tahitians generally kept whatever they received; here, as at other points, Forster used responses toward Europeans, or the effect of their presence, as measures of the differing natures of particular indigenous societies. He suggested that two factors accounted for the marked despotism of the Friendly Islands: the population was greater, and they were situated "nearer to that country," meaning Asia, "from whence they came, and where abject humiliation for chiefs and princes are common" (237). The Tahitians, on the other hand, had "changed some of their manners, and laid aside part of that stiffness, formality and humiliating respect paid to their chiefs in proportion, as they removed from the country, which gave birth to their first ancestors" (229).

Forster's argument on this point is thus consistent with his notion of degeneration in the far south: as a nation is progressively removed from its original homeland, ancestral customs and knowledge are likely to be abandoned. This characterization of migration resonates with the debate that Kames alluded to in his letter to Lind—whether Europeans colonizing the tropics necessarily lost their moral and physical vigor; this was certainly thought to have taken place among the southern African Boers. If Forster did imagine a unitary process, the results were nevertheless different in the case of those who moved into temperate or frigid regions and those who moved within the tropics: the latter are understood not to suffer loss, but to either willfully lay aside certain practices or acquire "a new tincture of manners and customs" at each new land (228). Whether this is more a matter of subtraction or enhancement, the nation arrives at a "happy mean" or condition of political balance, whereby the king is shown only such decent and proper degree of respect that precludes tyranny or oppression. Forster was, of course, unaware of the highly stratified Hawaiian polities, which remained unknown to Europeans until Cook's third voyage; their greater remove from the original oriental despotism of the South Sea islanders' Asian ancestors would have prejudiced his hypothesis that hierarchical stiffness was gradually ameliorated through successive migrations but would not perhaps have altered the larger judgment, that the Society Islands were the only place where "civilization had made some progress, and where these advantages were not again over-balanced by defects in the constitution of government" (238).

Forster did, however, see Tahiti as possessing "defects" of another kind, and these introduce an ambiguity into the whole structure of his argument concerning the varying degrees of progress among the South Sea islanders. The peoples of the "second race," that is, those inhabiting the western Pacific, are manifestly inferior to those of the first, partly on the basis of familiar racial criteria such as color and alleged physical "deformity," but also because, like some less advanced groups among the "first race" and the Tierra del Fuegians, they do not welcome the Europeans or are uninterested in the novel goods that the Europeans have to offer.[9] This was apparent not just at the gross level of contrasts between one island or larger region and another, but at a more localized scale in New Zealand, between Dusky Bay and Queen Charlotte's Sound, at the southern and northern ends of the South Island: while the nomads of the far south accepted a few hatchets and trinkets, they were largely indifferent to them, and also far more restrained in their contact with the British, than the people farther north, who crowded around the ship and traded eagerly, to almost the same extent as the Tahitians and Tongans. While this differentiated response neatly mapped on to other criteria of relative advancement, such as evident political consolidation, density of population, and cultivation,[10] it was also associated with a form of license not evident in the far south: the people of Queen Charlotte's Sound were so anxious to obtain iron and other novelties from the ship's crew that they liberally and coercively prostituted their women to obtain them. Although Maori society had not advanced to a "commercial" stage, this was certainly a kind of traffic, and the brutality it required, and the venereal afflictions it produced, can be seen to literalize the corruption of the body politic by commerce and license, a kind of corruption that had long been postulated in the civic humanist political theories that shaped Forster's moral sense. The articulation between arguments elaborated in Europe and those appropriate to the islanders of the South Sea is marked by the fact that the British as well as the Maori are evidently corrupted by this commerce. This mutual corruption is most evident in George Forster's narrative, in which the Maori women are said to be repulsive: "It is astonishing," he wrote, "that persons should be found, who could gratify an animal appetite with such loathsome objects."[11] The persons who could be found were of course British sailors, and if it was astonishing that they should degrade themselves in this way, it is not astonishing that one Forster or the other should remark upon it, since they had been frustrated in quarrels with members of the crew on a number of occasions. George's charge that the seamen were degenerate, which was contested in particular in Wales' *Remarks*, resonated with his father's wider understanding of the effects of migration—not only because the seamen, like the Tierra del Fuegians, were isolated and remote from their point of cultural origin, but because the social order of the naval vessel was a tyrannical and despotic one; the effect of despotism upon the subjects of a regime was understood to be not only oppressive, but also debasing and stupifying.[12] Forster's ethnology was not a discourse exclusively of the "other" but one that encompassed a hierarchy of races in the unity of the species, that took Europeans of various classes and nations as well as "savages" and "barbarians" to be susceptible to the same processes, to common causes of improvement and degeneracy.

Forster pointed out that a happy feature of Tahitian society was its overall self-subsistence: except for certain ornaments and means of adornment, such as coconut oil, which was imported from the island of Bora Bora, most wants were satisfied without engagement in trade. If these are marginal exceptions, it emerges that they are consequential ones. Great value was attached to the red parrot feathers used in certain warriors' ornaments, and though some dyed cocks' feathers brought out from Britain were not esteemed, parrot feathers of the right kind obtained during the ship's visit to Tonga could be exchanged for almost anything:

The rage after these trifling commodities was so great, that Potatoa a chief, whose magnanimity and noble way of thinking, we never questioned before, wanted even to prostitute his own wife, for a parcel of these baubles. All kind of iron tools are likewise become great articles of commerce, since their connexions with Europeans. (232)

While Forster enunciates what was to become a familiar narrative of "fatal impact"—mourning the pollution of a happy society by new wants—the form of corruption alluded to here is not entirely exogenous, but derives rather from a licentiousness that was already habitual, and even institutionalized, in Tahitian society. Its direct association with the moral ambiguities of commercial society in Europe is marked by the word "bauble," which for Adam Smith and others referred to such articles of "frivolous utility" as ruined consumers laboring under the grand if necessary deception that identified wealth and happiness, that led them to labor indefinitely in pursuit of "vain and empty distinctions of greatness."[13] The baubles here are, to be sure, obtained through Europeans, but they are not themselves foreign to the precontact economy of the Society Islands, and they prefigure the islanders' interests in iron.

Potatou's attempt to prostitute his wife is not, therefore, an index of the Tahitians' widely cited promiscuity; this was a stereotype that both Forster and Cook endeavored to qualify. Rather, this attempt was interpreted in the *Observations* as a result of opulence, an opulence that might have been thought to differ conspicuously from the kinds of European luxury that were evoked in debate and was indeed understood to derive less from the mode of life than from the climate. Forster, however, stressed the similarities rather than the differences and appealed to general arguments that accounted for Tahitian licentiousness: "Opulence never fails to excite the appetite for sensual pleasure, and if no restraint is laid on its gratification, it grows stronger and stronger, so as at last to extinguish all the notions of propriety and decency" (254). The upshot, in the Tahitian case, was the Arioi society, an association of younger people, mainly of rank, who congregated occasionally in large groups for feasting, theatrical performances, and lascivious activities and who habitually practiced infanticide; their idleness, and the natural abundance and variety of food, led them also "to indulge themselves in the pleasures of the table beyond what is usual."

There is an ambivalence, rather than a mere inconsistency here, because Tahitian licentiousness is not an accidental excess or blemish, but a tendency founded in precisely the same conditions as the positive features of their manners and customs. Natural abundance, a relatively dense population, improvement in knowledge, and effective cultivation produce a degree of civilization marked by the breadth of native civil and political unions and the restrained government of an aristocracy: "the very moderate and mild servitude of their Toutous, the order and regulation in their domestic societies, the benevolent and paternal affection of their chiefs, their association for the security of property and liberty, their commerce, wealth, and enjoyments, give us the best idea of the more refined and exalted situation of the inhabitants of Taheitee," Forster writes, yet these factors are precisely also those that encourage a degree of luxury, an interest in novelties, and a desire to engage in traffic with the British. The contradictory value of this desire registers a larger contradiction in the whole process of improvement, which entails a willingness to learn from others but characterizes that willingness as curiosity, as a superficial and indiscriminate affection liable to be captivated by novelties, to be drawn into commerce and selfishness to the detriment of public virtue. Forster thus refrained from imagining Tahiti as a pristine space about to be corrupted; he instead saw the advancement of Tahiti as a process as double-edged as the progress of the polished European societies; if their very considerable elevation above the condition of ruder nations could not be doubted, they did, at the same time, possess faults almost in proportion, and such faults are present too in Tahiti, perhaps exacerbated by the levity characteristic of tropical nations, and perhaps about to be tragically magnified by the sudden introduction of European articles and demands.

Forster could be seen, in other words, to transpose to the Pacific not only the Scottish writers' general project of theorizing the history of civil society, but also the antinomy that more or less deeply qualified their endorsement of improvement and progress, which derived from the discourse of civic humanism: whether the argument was that wealth and opulence could only produce sensuality, vice, corruption, and effeminacy or that the particularization of labor subverted the ideals of active citizenship, it was manifestly the case that the social and moral character of civil advancement could only be qualified and uncertain; and, given the contingency that pervaded a history structured by migrations, expulsions, and chance findings of larger or smaller islands in meaner or happier climates; given that the novelties introduced through intercourse with Europeans could be as conducive to improvement as new varieties of plants or livestock, or as destructive as disease, this uncertainty was hardly much ameliorated by Forster's providentialism.

The foregoing has dealt mainly with the ways in which *Observations* describes and accounts for the differences between New Zealand and Tahiti. While Tierra del Fuego exemplifies to a more extreme degree the process of degeneration that Forster identifies in New Zealand, the argument is concerned basically with the difference between two related populations: both Maori and Tahitians belonged to Forster's "first race," that is, those later classed as Polynesians. The encounter in the western Pacific with a "second race" precluded any neat reduction of human variety to climatic determinations, since the peoples of Tanna, Malekula, and New Caledonia occupied the same latitudes as the Society Islanders; from our viewpoint, Forster's assessments of the latter frequently lapse into racist denigrations of bodies he found "ill-favoured" or "ugly and deformed"; it is telling that the classical parallels are made extensively and almost exclusively with the eastern islanders.[14] He suggests that certain differences between them are attributable to the mode of life: "The Taheitians, the fairest of all the islanders in the South Sea, go almost constantly dressed and covered. The inhabitants of Tanna, New Caledonia, and Mallicollo, on the contrary are always naked, and exposed to the air, and therefore infinitely blacker than the first" (176). But here the influence of climate figures as a consequence of prior difference, though it is also suggested that the evident inferiority of the western islanders proves that the two great tribes "from whom the two races of men in the South Seas descend, had unequally preserved by education and instruction, the systems of knowledge, which they had obtained from their more remote progenitors" (270); at some remote point, therefore, an equivalence is postulated, as if historical vicissitudes alone had intervened to leave one race at a less improved stage than another. What is shared and mutable is, however, for the most part in the background, as a clear racial difference is postulated and associated with stages in the life cycle or evolution of the species. At this point, again, an inversion in the temporality of Forster's analytical fiction can be detected: at one moment, both races represent the end points of a history in which their systems of ideas have either been preserved or lost; those that are "improved" rather than "degenerated" are seen to have maintained, rather than radically extended, an original reserve of knowledge and accomplishment. Against this paradigm, one race is rendered antecedent to another, through a developmental analogy that subsequently pervaded ethnological thought.

> If we compare the inhabitants of the more Western isles in the South Sea with the Taheitians, we find that the latter far surpass the former in every respect; which intimates that though the climate greatly influences the happiness of a nation, it is however not the only cause of its real felicity; that education contributes as much, if not more, towards the good state of a people; and that the removal from the tropics toward the colder extremes of the globe, together with the gradual loss of the principles of education greatly contribute to the degeneracy and debasement of a nation into a low and forlorn condition. Mankind is therefore to be considered in various situations, comparable with the various ages of man from infancy to manhood; with this difference only, that men in their collective capacity ripen but slowly from animality, through the states of savages and barbarians into a civilized society, which has again an infinite variety of situations and degrees of perfection. (342)

This passage was part of a recapitulation of the book's larger argument; the earlier section that defined humankind's "various situations" equated childhood with savagery and barbarism with adolescence in some detail. Like the adolescent, the barbarian had "the dawning of understanding and reason" but was prone to render the passions "subservient to reason" and degenerate into profligacy; education and improvement were therefore more crucial at this state than any other (200). But which Pacific islanders were in fact in this state? At no point did Forster explicitly equate different peoples with different "ages of man"; certain passages imply that he saw the "second" race as savages and the "first" as barbarians, but elsewhere he finds that the Society Islanders, Marquesans, and Tongans, by reason of the esteem in which women were held, "ought to be ranked one remove above barbarians" (260). If so, the "improvements" that Forster saw in any case as taking effect only gradually were perhaps not urgently necessary; and it was anticipated that vice could follow from commerce with Europeans as readily as any form of elevation.

In the diverse arguments of *Observations*, a number of major theories of nineteenth- and twentieth-century Pacific ethnology were prefigured, and it is easy to read the book largely retrospectively, for its anticipation of the Melanesia-Polynesia evolution or the notion that the Tahitian chiefs were descended from a race that had conquered the ancestors of the commoners. Forster's book may be seen as less satisfying than some of the subsequent writing, since it entertains several of these larger narratives without projecting a single one forcefully and unequivocally; or it may be seen as more adequate for its ambivalence in the face of human diversity and the hesitancy of its engagement in ethnological hierarchization. It would be foolish to imagine that readers do not either find the text commendable, for the liberality and relativism that characterize it in contrast to the harsher and more explicit racism of nineteenth-century anthropology, or sinister, to the extent that the division of the two "races," the remarks on the Tierra del Fuegians, and the analogy with the "ages" of man prefigure evolutionary discriminations that licensed mere conquest in some places and genocide in others. If it is in many ways unavoidable, and even appropriate, that the Cook voyages are seen as an early chapter in the colonization of the Pacific; if the voyage journals, and *Observations*, are therefore taken as texts that inaugurated the labor of colonial discourse in the region, it remains important that this historiography not merely invert that which celebrated Cook's navigational accomplishments as the prehistory of white settlement and nation building in Australia and New Zealand. The fault of both narratives is the extent to which eighteenth-century languages of description and adjudication would be impoverished; the meanings that Forster and his contemporaries attached to the status of women, to commerce, to education, and to geographic location depended on arguments that were proceeding at the time and that underwent substantial reorientation soon afterward. Whatever judgments may be made about *Observations*, one of its virtues must be that it exhibits the complex range of arguments and considerations that entered into the perception of Pacific peoples; no simple "representation of the other," this is a sustained and elaborate, yet divided and tentative, meditation on a voyage round the world.

Looking at Women: Forster's Observations in the South Pacific

HARRIET GUEST

Reflecting on the significance of navigation to the cultures of northern Europe, Johann Forster commented in 1784 that

> voyages made for the gratification of curiosity and for the extension of commerce, seem to have greatly contributed to the promotion of knowledge, and to the introduction of milder manners and customs into society. For it is highly cultivated nations only, that explore distant countries and nations for the sake of commerce, in like manner as seeking them for the gratification of curiosity, pre-supposes a still higher degree of cultivation and refinement.[1]

James Cook's second voyage to the South Pacific was represented as undertaken, above all, for the gratification of curiosity. The French ambassador reported that, in the space of a brief meeting, Lord Sandwich, the First Lord of the Admiralty, assured him more than twenty times over that curiosity was the only motive for the expensive and hazardous circumnavigation. Curiosity was one of the characteristics that those allocated to the lowest rungs of the ladder of cultivation were thought to lack, whereas, in contrast, its impartial or indiscriminate avidity was seen as a hallmark of high civilization. Sandwich's protestations of the political innocence of British expansion in the South Pacific imply that curiosity and civilization are so intimately intertwined that their relationship lends a kind of legitimating disinterestedness to what might seem to be the most blatantly acquisitive moves of European powers in their competition for extensive commercial empires in other continents and distant seas.[2]

Curiosity seems central to Forster's project in the South Pacific—and materially so, for the disputed value and status of natural and artificial curiosities was continually at issue in his transactions with the islanders and with the officers, gentlemen, and crew of Cook's ships. The journals of Forster and the other Europeans narrate numerous anecdotes of the natural philosopher's vexed and anxious attempts to distinguish the exchanges that stocked his cabinets from those of his companions. His commerce in philosophical curiosities was embarrassed by its proximity to trade in provisions, to sexual commerce, to appropriations by islanders and voyagers that were seen to involve no legitimating direct exchange and so were identified as theft, and to the energetic trade between Europeans and islanders in objects that seemed to have no curiosity or use value.[3] Forster's acquisitions, like the ambitious ventures of the British Admiralty, claim a curious status that seems ambivalently both to confirm their disinterestedness, their distance from the competitive fray, and to imply their energetic immersion in that fray of commercial and personal interests.

Curiosity, as motive and object, inspiration and end, indicates the quality of Forster's research that, he suggests, marks the difference between his *Observations* and the work of other writers of general histories of mankind. Forster pointed out that the "general fault" of other philosophers of the age was "to study mankind only in their cabinets; or, at best, to observe no other than highly civilized nations, who have over-run all parts of the world by the help of navigation, and from commercial views; and are more or less degenerate and tainted with vices" (143–144). Other writers' methods of study, as well as what they observed, seemed to Forster to fall short of his own "investigation of truth" (10). He suggested that they lacked empirical knowledge of the object of study removed from the context of their own civilized systems of value; they lacked knowledge of mankind refined from those contingencies that confuse the curious object with the trappings of commercial and libidinal desire, and that obscure those "facts [that] are the basis of the whole structure" (9) of his *Observations*. The point, I think, is not simply that Forster imagines himself as having encountered mankind in some exotic state beyond the social and present, in the natural space stripped of adventitious accretions that Rousseau explores in his *Discourse on the Origin of Inequality* (1755), for example. For Forster represents the cultures he observes in terms of their relative differences from those of Europe, rather than their absolute exotic otherness.[4] His comments suggest that his exotic experience has removed him from the civilized context that might have colored and obscured his gaze, but that in other writers the motivating capacity for mature and independent curiosity is weakened and tainted because their philosophical systems are "formed in the closet or at least in the bosom of a nation highly civilized, and therefore . . . degenerated" (9).

The ship's astronomer, William Wales, then, struck at the heart of Forster's conception of himself and his philosophical endeavor in publishing the claim that "there can be no good reason given why the seamen should not be as fond of curiosities as himself." Wales asserted that Forster's acquisitive enthusiasm had encouraged the seamen to trade in curiosities, for which they knew he would pay well, and that the libidinal appetites of the Forsters, like those of most of the voyagers, had involved them in sexual commerce with the islanders. What seems to me most revealing about Wales' attack is his insistent harping on the frailty of the distinctions between kinds of investigation and modes of exchange on which Forster's *Observations* were based. Wales' aspersions muddy Forster's claim to a curiosity that "presupposes a still higher degree of cultivation and refinement" than "commercial views" imply, for they indicate that Forster's avidity can be yoked and even identified with those wants and desires from which he was most anxious to free his civilized and enlightened philosophy. Forster's acquisitive hunger, Wales asserted, had competed with the officially sanctioned trade in provisions for the ship, had been no different from what the philosopher represented as the idle curiosity and profiteering of the seamen, and had even hindered the progress of scientific experiment. The philosopher's attempts to distinguish his own civilized inquiry had in Wales' view falsely "involved the whole ship's company, officers and men, in one universal censure of *ignorance, brutality, cruelty, wantonness,* and *barbarity.*"[5]

Forster's work as a natural philosopher in the South Pacific was conducted in a context in which curiosity, with its ambivalent implications of personal avidity and professional purity, seems constantly shadowed by the speculative form of commerce. As Forster's reflections on the art of navigation imply, curiosity depends for its advancement on commerce, but enlightened and professional or philosophical curiosity—curiosity freed from the implications of sexual and material desire that continually threaten to taint its propriety—is nevertheless defined by a hostility or distance from commercial views, a difference that appropriates to its perceptions a "higher degree of cultivation and refinement." This ambivalent relation between commerce and curiosity, which might be argued to characterize British cultural self-conceptions in the decades after 1760, provides the context in which, I think, we can best understand Forster's observations on the women of the South Pacific, and in particular of Tahiti. I will begin my discussion by looking briefly at some of the representations of the island women in Forster's private journals, which offer a very different account of them to that given in the text of the *Observations*. The contrast between these representations and those of the published text, I think, points up some of the implications of the complex relation between commerce and curiosity for the treatment of gender and sexuality in Forster's views on the islanders of the South Pacific.

The Women in *Otahaitee*, especially those of the better sort, are all inclined to grow fat, & some old ones are very unwieldy: this makes that even the youngest have a very relaxed habit of body, their flesh is flabby, & if you add to this the tawny, sallow, yellow complexion, they can by no means be so much praised for their handsomeness: & what makes these Women most insupportable to me, is their character of most accomplished Jilts: they know from experience that all the Europeans that have hitherto touched at their Isle, are fond of women; & therefore they avail themselves of this foible & coquet with every Man they see, & all this only to obtain some trifling presents of beads, nails, red & Silk handkerchiefs, etc. etc. & on the other hand they are very small in person, seldom is a woman of a moderate stature to be seen among these Isles, & they look when compared with the Men, as a race of dwarfs.[6]

Forster's comments, in his journals, on the women of the Society Islands, frequently express a striking degree of physical and moral distaste, or even revulsion, for what he seems to perceive as a debased femininity, grotesque in its exoticism. In this passage, the contrast between the "tawny, sallow, yellow complexion" of Tahitian women and the red and white of the British fair—"the roses on their cheeks & the lily bosom"—seems to leave the philosopher himself unsure of the implications of his forceful denial of the attractions of the islanders. The women of the Friendly Islands, he argues, are more pleasing than those of Tahiti, but neither can stand up to comparison with British women:

If I may mention in this depraved age the innocence & chastity of our Brittish maids, their improved minds & all the other accomplishments they so commonly are masters of, & all the virtues, which so early are instilled into their minds; not the least remembrance is left of all the charms of these copper beauties; all Ideas of them must be effaced from the mind of each of their warmest Admirers & force from them due hommage to Virtue, Elegance & beauty so superlatively united in Britannia's fair Daughters.[7]

British women are accorded the attributes of virtue, elegance, and beauty that are appropriate to a highly polished civilization, but hesitation may be suggested in the violence of language required to describe how their image supplants that of the islanders, and by the initial uncertainty of "If I may mention." Britannia's fair daughters, he seems to acknowledge, may either not possess or not earn admiration for the qualities that his contrast seems to demand of them.

Despite the protestations of the journal, the force of the opposition Forster attempts to construct between British and Tahitian femininity does not seem to turn on the issue of chastity and innocence, nor primarily, perhaps, on the racial otherness that this account stigmatizes with such repetitive insistence. Forster comments earlier, during his visit to Raiatea, that

the Character of these Islanders seems to be the same with the rest of them; they are friendly with us in appearance, in order to get something which they value *viz*, beads

& nails, & Iron tools, either by fair means or by theft. Their women coquet in the most impudent manner, & shew uncommon fondness for Foreigners, but are all Jilts & coax the Foreigners out of any thing they can get: & will not comply to sleep with them, unless they be common prostitutes, or the bribe very great & tempting.[8]

What distresses Forster most about these transactions seems not to be the sexual promiscuity he later attributes to the islanders, but their capacity to play fast and loose with the rules of (sexual) commerce. He deprecates the lack of chastity that their coquetry suggests, but the observation that they are not unchaste enough to fulfill the bargain seems even more deplorable. They participate in what he represents as an immoral black economy: the officially unsanctioned purchase or theft of curiosities and sex that disrupts and endangers the trade in provisions necessary to the ship. But it may be more significant for his account that their commerce complicates and confuses the status of his own professional desires for intimate knowledge of the islanders' manners and customs, and for possession of their natural and cultural curiosities. Forster's journals repeatedly represent the island women as figures central to those forms of trade that are most disturbing or distressing to the European officers and gentlemen (though perhaps not to the crew, who are frequently represented as culpable agents in these transactions). The island women are engaged in what Forster sees as prostitution, theft, and fraudulent coquetry, and the repeated incidents in which their often reluctant bodies are offered for sale by the island men damage Forster's respect for the cultures he observes, to the great distress of his liberal conscience.[9]

The recognition that encounters with Europeans have infected the people of New Zealand with venereal disease led Forster to reflect more generally on the effects of European commerce: "They have acquired nothing or next to nothing, by the Commerce & intercourse of our Ships crews, even the prizes of this libidinous intercourse with our young Sailors is so trifling *viz.* a Nail or a Shirt, that nothing is capable to compensate in the slightest manner the great injury done to their Society." Forster represents the "poor Natives of New Zeeland" as the victims of commercial exploitation. He suggests that the "brutal passion" of sexual desire, which "breaks through all social ties, extinguishes all principles of true honour, virtue & humanity," is, as it were, incidental to or symptomatic of the "principles of lust, avarice & ambition," which he implies animate commercial enterprise. Reflecting on the potential scourge that intercourse with Europeans has introduced, he argues:

Had the Man, who first infected the Female on this Isle, immediately after fulfilling his brutal lust, stabbed the object of his temporary passion, he would certainly deserve to be detested & abhorred as a most consummate villain: but if we consider

the fatal consequences, which must now attend his connexion with that woman, &
the general devastation his communicated evil must cause, I cannot help thinking,
that howsoever detestable the murder of such a poor wretch must be, it would be a
real benefit to the whole community & preserve a harmless brave & numerous
Nation from all the horrors of being poisoned from their very infancy, of fetching
infection in the embraces of love, & of instilling the same venom in the tender
embryo that is to be the result of love & the object of paternal piety & tenderness.[10]

The disease that is for Forster the sign of the evils of European exploitation here
becomes monstrously inflated, becomes not a representation or a symptom but
the source of the horrors that threaten this "harmless brave & numerous Nation."
All the evils he anticipates from commercial intercourse become embodied in the
figure of the first infected woman, an Eve whom he assumes to be one of "the
most abandonned of their Sex."[11] Her sacrificial murder, he implies, might even
have redeemed relations within the New Zealand family, which he more usually
represents as characterized by a lamentable and barbarous lack of feeling, especially marked in the treatment of women.

In his journals, then, Forster represents the women of the South Pacific as
both the agents and victims of commercial exploitation or malpractice. They provide a figure for the corruptions and vices that the Forsters believed intercourse
with Europeans had introduced to the societies of the Pacific. It is in the context
of that figuration that the text of the journals manifests a degree of violent revulsion and antipathy apparently at odds with Forster's self-image as a humane phi-
lanthropist. In the *Observations*, however, that image of Pacific women is less
marked, though it is not entirely absent. In his account of the people of the
Friendly Islands, the Society Islands, and in particular of Tahiti, Forster stresses
the active contribution of women to the relatively advanced state of civilization
that he identifies. He gives an unusually positive inflection to a commonplace of
the late eighteenth century in his assertion that "the rank assigned to WOMEN in
domestic society, among the various nations, has so great an influence upon their
civilization and morality" (258). In his argument the condition of women is not
merely the *index* to the degree of civilization achieved in any society, as it was for
most social and political theorists. The rank of women exerts influence on the
degree of civilization that nations achieve.

The rank that women have attained on Tahiti is assessed by Forster in terms that
involve a significant and remarkable departure from those of most discussions of
the role of women in these decades. Tahiti, "the Society, the Friendly Isles, and
the Marquesas," have to be recognized to have progressed "one remove above barbarians" because the island women exert civilizing influence and have gained "a

ABOUT THE EDITORS

NICHOLAS THOMAS is professor and Senior Research Fellow in anthropology at the Australian National University. Among his books are *Entangled Objects: Exchange, Material Culture and Colonialism in the Pacific* and *Colonialism's Culture: Anthropology, Travel and Government*.

HARRIET GUEST is lecturer in the Department of English and Related Literature, University of York. She has published numerous articles on eighteenth-century topics and is the author of *A Form of Sound Words: The Religious Poetry of Christopher Smart*, which was named Book of the Year (1989–1990) by the MLA conference on Christianity and Literature.

MICHAEL DETTELBACH is assistant professor of history at Smith College. His dissertation, "Alexander von Humboldt's Terrestrial Physics," provoked wide interest, and he has contributed chapters on Humboldtian science to two books currently in press: *Cultures of Natural History*, edited by N. Jardine, J. Secord, and E. C. Sparry, and *Visions of Empire: Voyages, Botany, and Representations of Nature*, edited by David Miller.

KARL H. RENSCH is a Reader in Linguistics at the Australian National University, Canberra. He has done extensive fieldwork in Wallis and Futuna, the Tuamotus, the Austral and Gambier Islands, and is currently working on communication problems in Polynesia at contact time. Among his publications are *Tikionario Mangareva-Farani*, *Fish Names of Western Polynesia*, and *The Language of Wallis Island*.

HAWAI Production Notes

Composition and paging were done in
FrameMaker software on an AGFA AccuSet
Postscript Imagesetter by the design
and production staff of University of
Hawai'i Press.

The text typeface is Goudy Old Style
and the display typeface is Trump.

Offset presswork and binding were done by
The Maple-Vail Book Manufacturing Group.
Text paper is Glatfelter Premier Matte, basis 60.

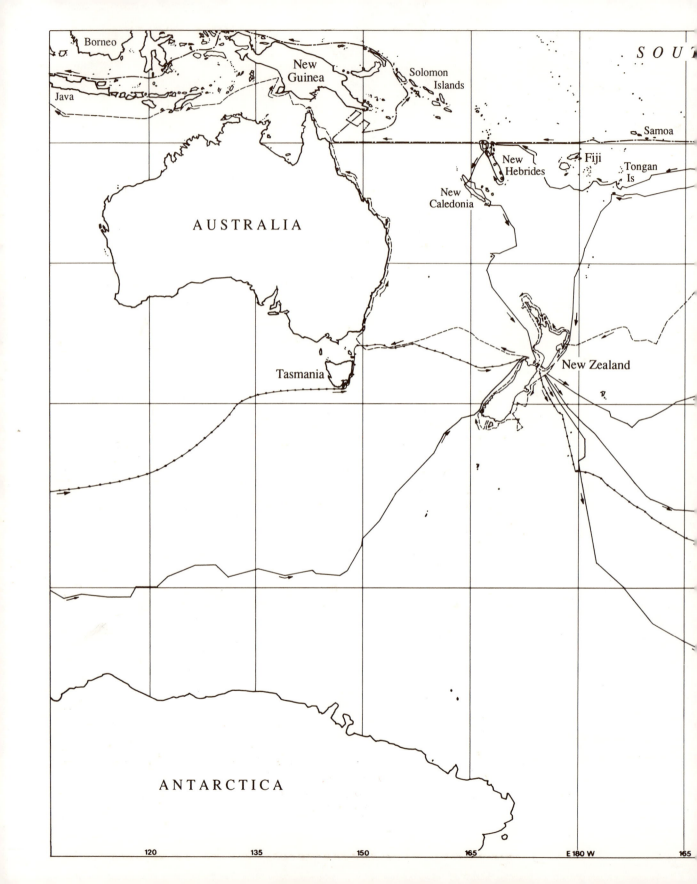

greater equality": their condition indicates but also somehow produces the characteristics of civilization. Forster comments on their rank that "if, from no other
reason, from this alone" the progressive state of these societies could be recognized. He explains that "the more the women are esteemed in a nation, and enjoy
an equality of rights with the men, the more it appears that the original harshness
of manners is softened, the more the people are capable of tender feelings, mutual
attachment, and social virtues, which naturally lead them towards the blessings of
civilization" (260). The text gives an unusual emphasis to the activity of women
as the agents of social change, stating unequivocally that "the female sex has
. . . softened the manners of their countrymen" (261). This emphasis on women's
agency may produce or account for his surprising insistence on the notion of
"equality of rights". The language of rights implies a political dimension to the
process of social change that women effect. That implication is also apparent
in Forster's observation that the charms of the island women have secured them
"a just and moderate influence in domestic *and even public affairs*" (260; my
emphasis).

    I can perhaps best indicate the striking qualities of Forster's argument here by
briefly contrasting his views with those John Millar advances in the lengthy discussion of the condition of women offered in his *The Origin of the Distinction of
Ranks* (1771). Like most theorists of the period, Millar represents the progress of
commercial civilization in Europe as double-edged—the signs of improvement
are for him inevitably also the symptoms of corruption and decline—and this
conjunction of improvement and decline is clearly apparent in the implications
of that progress for women. In advanced and affluent civilizations, women have a
greater, more visible importance in polite society. But these "improvements, in
the state and accomplishments of the women" work paradoxically to diminish
their importance, because they remove those restraints and obstacles that Millar
sees as necessary to the cultivation of romantic passion, and make women exclusively or only "subservient to the purposes of animal passion." The social promi-
nence of women in opulent civilizations, Millar concludes, is incompatible both
with their own interests and "with the general interest of society." Millar's argument represents the condition of women—and indeed of civilization—as more
unambiguously admirable and desirable in the stage of progress that immediately
preceeds the achievement of opulence. In that stage, the interests of women are
confined to "the members of their own family," and they are instructed only in
what "is thought conducive to the ornament of private life" or the "practice of all
the domestic virtues."[12] Like most British theorists of the period, Millar suggests
that the interests of women and of society are best served when women are
restricted to the arena of private life, and for his argument, privacy means a familial domesticity that is secluded from social as well as public visibility.

In *The Origin of the Distinction of Ranks*, the condition of women acts as an index or figure for the condition of civilization. Wherever commercial prosperity is perceived to be overstepping the thin line that divides it from "luxury and refinement", and so preserves its moral character, women embody and excite the vices of unbridled desire—passions that resemble Forster's "principles of lust, avarice & ambition."[13] The degenerate condition of women indicates the perversion of those passions that, in their moralized and contained form, had been the motors of commercial progress. This use of women as figures for the uneasy moral implications of commercial success is comparable with the function ascribed to them in Forster's journals. In the *Observations*, however, where the rank of women is explicitly linked with the achievement of civilization, the public role of women works physically and morally to lead or seduce men into desiring "the blessings of civilization" (260).

In part, of course, the importance that Forster attaches to the position of women in Tahitian society has to do with their domestic and familial roles and with what he perceives as the practice of virtuous monogamy. He argues that monogamy is prevalent on Tahiti because marital partners can be changed at will,[14] and he claims that "the beginning of their civil society is founded on paternal authority, and is of the patriarchal kind. The husband and wife of his bosom, whom love unites by the silken ties of matrimony, form the first society" (223). In that "first society," women discipline their children. They exercise a maternal authority perceived to be denied them in, for example, New Zealand, where the behavior of children was taken to show a barbarous lack of control. The bonds of feeling within the Tahitian family manifest that civilizing softness that it is the function of women to promote. The hearts of the Society Islanders, Forster writes, "are capable . . . of the most tender connexions, of which, in our mixed and degenerating societies, we have very few instances; perhaps none at all, where such a disinterested, generous love, or such an enthusiasm of passion forms the basis of the tender connexion" (222).

Forster's argument does not suggest, however, that the domestic family unit is the only or the most important arena for the exercise of feminine influence. In accounting for the tendency of peoples to degenerate from their civilized origins as a result of migration, he suggests that the family unit is in a sense antagonistic to the development of society. Groups of migrants "are deprived of the charms and choice of society, which is confined to the few individuals of a family" (197). Confined to their families, they become "strangers to social feelings, and still more so to social virtues" (198), and are incapable either of preserving and transmitting the knowledge they once had, or of inventing improvements. In North America, for example, Forster argues that the predominance of the family over potentially more extensive social groupings is the "true cause of the debasement and degeneracy" (207) that is perceived to characterize the savage state of the people. The fact that he sees the Tahitian family as the "first society" rather than as a "few individuals" is evidence of the softening powers of women, but the strength of bonds of feeling within the family does not necessarily lead to improvement or manifest the civilizing powers of women. Improvement may rather be the effect of the softer attachments and social feelings women have produced *between* families. For the authority women exercise within the Tahitian family is not limited to that arena. Despite his perception of Tahitian society as a sort of mixture of the feudal and patriarchal models, he describes what approximates to a matriarchal organization in the public and private life of the Society Islands: "The married women have . . . a great respect shewn to them, and their influence is great in all public and private affairs; and as soon as the heir of a family is born, the father in a certain manner loses his importance" (254). The influence of women within the family is represented as continuous with a much more extensive and public authority, and it is perhaps as a result of that continuity that the family is seen as the first society.

The civilizing influence of women in the Society Islands, as well as their role in public affairs, may be connected more directly in Forster's argument with the qualities he believes women acquire as a result of their oppression in nations that have not yet become civilized—qualities that "may perhaps prepare" barbarous men "for the first dawnings of civilization" (259). Forster, like most theorists of the period, asserts that among peoples categorized as savage and barbarous, women are treated as drudges and beasts of burden, and regarded as the property of their husbands. But Forster departs from the familiar theoretical model in his argument that

> this very oppression, and the more delicate frame of [the women's] bodies, together with the finer and more irritable texture of their nerves, have contributed more towards the improvement and perfection of their intellectual faculties, than of those of the males. The various objects surrounding them make quicker and more vivid impressions on the sense of the females, because their nerves are finer and more irritable; this makes them more inclined to imitation, and more quick in observing the properties and relations of things; their memory is more faithful in retaining them; and their faculties thereby become more capable of comparing them, and of abstracting general ideas from their perceptions. (259)

As a result of these qualities, he suggests, women are capable of producing "new improvements" and of controlling their passions into "cooler reflexion" (259). The absence of the first of these capacities is one of the principal characteristics of savagery, and the lack of the second is critical in distinguishing barbarism from civilization. Women here seem to be not the indices of the degree of civilization achieved by their nations, but the forerunners of that progress, apparently acting in advance of and out of step with the men. And the women seem to achieve this position, in Forster's argument, because their oppression has cultivated in them cognitive abilities that British theorists throughout the eighteenth century saw as the prerogative of educated or propertied men. These women are able to compare their perceptions and abstract general ideas from them. Forster's account of the qualities the oppression of women has produced suggests that if the women of Tahiti do "enjoy an equality of rights with the men" (260) it may be because they enjoy at least an equality of intellectual ability.

Forster's observations on the women of the Society Islands seem a surprising departure from the terms in which the position of women was understood in contemporary theories of commercial society, and from the representation of women in his own unpublished journals. The contrast with the first is sufficiently marked, indeed, to draw attention to the possibility that Forster perceives in the society of the islanders a kind of inverted image of European civilizations—an ideal projection marked by the absence of commercial prosperity with its attendant corruptions. In his introductory remarks on Tahiti, he writes that there "the inhabitants are hitherto fortunate enough to have none of the artificial wants, which luxury, avarice, and ambition have introduced among Europeans" (146). He argues specifically that marriage and reproduction are unproblematic, and a matter of "pleasing expectation" to Tahitians, and contrasts their happiness with "the many wants of our civilized state, the labours we must undergo in supplying these wants . . . and the many difficulties preceding and attendant on our marriages" (146–147). The connection between the "many wants" promoted in a commercial culture and the desires necessary to marriage and reproduction was most fully theorized in the 1770s by John Millar and by Henry Home, Lord Kames, in his *Sketches of the History of Man* (1774). But those theorists argued that sexual desire only became more than a transient brute appetite because of the leisure that civilized prosperity afforded, and that its refinement into romantic passion and companionate affection depended upon the "many difficulties" produced by inequalities of wealth, divergent occupational interests, and competition in commercial society. In the most advanced states of commercial prosperity, some of the obstacles to social intercourse between the sexes are removed, as affluence softens ambition into complacency, and women gain greater public or social visibility. In these conditions, sexual desire is freed from the vestiges of moral constraint or romantic chivalry, and degenerates into luxurious excess.

Forster's argument seems to resemble those of Millar and Kames in the close connection it assumes between the wants promoted by commercial culture and the "difficulties of marriage" that creates.[15] Later he seems to allude to the same theory in his account of the Tahitian Arioi, of whom he comments: "Opulence never fails to excite the appetite for sensual pleasure, and if no restraint is laid on its gratification, it grows stronger and stronger, so as at last to extinguish all the notions of propriety and decency" (254). The Arioi are explicitly compared to "our grandees" (257) and are represented as enjoying the immoral excesses of opulence in terms most usually appropriated to the later stages of commercial development.[16] But though Forster uses this account of the effects of commercial progress to represent the virtues of Tahitian society as those of an early or precommercial state, he also maintains that it is possible for most of the Tahitians to enjoy the pleasures of love in the absence of the difficulties created by the complexities evident in the advanced societies of Europe. He praises, as I have mentioned, the "disinterested, generous love" and "enthusiasm of passion" that characterize the domestic manners of the Tahitians, and he does not suggest that their pleasures are diminished because "love, and all its concomitant, and most mysterious endearments, enjoyments, and consequences" have never "been stamped in these happy isles with a notion of turpitude" (244).[17] Though he does acknowledge depravity and licentiousness in the behavior of those Tahitians he perceives as belonging to either the highest or the lowest classes, that acknowledgment does not seem to infect the ideal he attributes to the majority of the islanders.[18] He suggests that the island women charm and seduce the men into civilization, but the "softness" they instill seems to lack the implications of luxury and corruption that make the term ambivalent in the context of European notions of progress.

In their ability to gratify, with apparently unproblematic ease, their sexual and material desires, the Tahitians seem to have their cake and eat it. But they are not represented as enjoying this satisfaction simply by virtue of living in a precommercial state; when Forster mentions commerce between the islands of the South Pacific, he represents it as one of the signs of their civilized progress. In the *Observations*, internal commerce in the South Pacific seems to be free of vice, and seems not to have corrupted the islanders' sexual and material desires with artificial wants and complications. This is apparently a result of the fact that there is in these societies no advanced division of labor: occupations are uniform, and men and women experience no wants and desires they cannot readily supply. Forster writes that the

pampered epicure in Europe hardly knows the multifarious ingredients of his disguised ragouts, and his palled appetite remains indifferent to the almost infinite variety carried to his table from every quarter of the globe; nor has he the satisfaction to know how or where these things are produced, or manufactured, while the more happy inhabitant of Taheitee plants his own breadfruit tree, and plucks the fruit for his own use; . . . there is not a single article of his food, which owes not its existence to his or his fathers industry or care. (345)[19]

It is because Tahitian society lacks the complexities and inequalities of advanced commercial civilizations that "these people enjoy a happiness which is more attainable by every individual" (346) than it is in Europe.

It is this degree of social equality that Forster suggests is most immediately threatened by contact with Europeans. Early in his account of Tahitian society he writes that

> the facility of procuring the necessaries of life, and even those articles which are here reckoned to be luxuries; together with the humane and benevolent temper of these nations have hitherto happily prevented the oppression of the Toutous; and if the morals of these people are not influenced and corrupted by the commerce and intercourse with European profligates, and by the introduction of new luxuries, which can be procured only by hard labour and drudgery, the happiness of the lowest class of people, will, probably be of long continuance. (230)

Commerce with Europeans threatens Tahitian society with the "introduction of new luxuries," artificial wants that require the exploitation of social inequality in an oppressive division of labor for their satisfaction. This argument clarifies the sense in which the representation of the island women in Forster's journals functions as an index or figure for the moral corruption that he attributed to intercourse with Europeans. They were there perceived in the terms made available by the discourse of the division of labor, which usually recognized no respectable occupational category for women. Women, as The Sex, could usually only be recognized as appropriate subjects of this discourse if they marketed their sexual labor in prostitution. If they failed to fulfill the requirements of that job description, then they appeared doubly immoral, for their chastity became the sign of their failure to accept the terms the discourse made available to them. And the immorality of the island women is of course further accentuated by their exoticism, by the racial otherness on which Forster's account insists. For their exoticism should have preserved them apart from the division of labor in the first place.

Forster's account of the condition of women in the *Observations*, on the other hand, seems to some extent to represent it as an index to what is most utopian and enviable about society in Tahiti. Tahitian women can be understood as doubly excluded, by virtue both of their gender and their exoticism, from the inequalities attendant on the division of labor. They may be out of step with their society, and even morally superior to it, in ways that are comparable to the position of the British women described in the journals, of whom virtues seem to be demanded that are inappropriate to "this depraved age." For late eighteenth-century writers who attempted to describe the history of social organization in terms of the division of labor, women embody qualities that are seen to be excluded from and somehow prior to the corruptions of commercial modernity—qualities that Forster may represent as produced by their oppression in the states of savagery and barbarism he saw as antecedent to civilization.[20] The equality they enjoy might in these terms be understood as having an indexical relation to the condition of their society insofar as it is perceived as a society prior to division, and in a state where happiness is attainable by each individual.

The *Observations* does not represent Tahiti only as a utopia excluded from the implications of the division of labor, however, nor does it represent women simply in terms of their moral superiority and happy equality. I have argued that Forster attributes an unusual public and political role to the island women, which seems connected with their possession of intellectual capacities more usually seen as exclusively masculine, as a result of which they become agents of progressive civilization. That role, I think, might best be understood in the context of the late-eighteenth-century argument that knowledge itself was divided by the division of labor, an argument repeatedly articulated in the text in passages which confirm the superiority of European civilization despite the degeneration attendant on commercial prosperity. Forster asserts, for example, that "all inquisitive individuals, and the more polished nations of Europe have free access" to the "joint-stock of knowledge of all mankind." He rehearses the familiar argument that

> this immense store of knowledge can at present no longer be viewed and examined by one person: it is too vast to be comprehended by one individual, be he ever so great a genius. It is enough in the present condition of highly civilized European societies, to perpetuate the bulk, by dividing it into various branches, open for the exercise and investigation of a multitude, and their various circumstances and choice. Thus we have contrived not only to preserve each small branch in that perfection in which it is found, but likewise to make new improvements, and to add to it new discoveries. (268)

In the terms of this argument, progress is entirely dependent on division and specialization. It is the division of knowledge that produces those notions of professional status that Forster was so keen to defend in his dealings with his fellow voyagers as well as with the islanders. In the representation of the condition of the women of the Society Islands, the text seems to project a kind of doubled utopian ideal: the ideal of an equality figured as possible only prior to the division of labor and of a public influence, founded in intellectual capacity, that is figured in the notion of the division of knowledge as the sign of the progress of civilization. This doubled ideal might be understood as the mirror image of Forster's own aspirations to a scientific curiosity that is at once disinterested or comprehensive and a professional specialism, a curiosity that participates in the division of knowledge, but transcends the division of labor.

It may be as a result of the sense in which the condition of the island women recapitulates Forster's own dilemma that his account of them is so marked by hesitations and inconsistencies. His account of their public role seems particularly elusive and evasive. After the passage I have quoted on their equality of rights and their capacity to lead men toward civilization, for example, he adds that they

> are possessed of a delicate organization, a sprightly turn of mind, a lively, fanciful imagination, a wonderful quickness of parts and sensibility, a sweetness of temper, and a desire to please; all of which, when connected with primitive simplicity of manners, when accompanied with a charming frankness, a beautifully proportioned shape, an irresistible smile, and eyes full of sweetness and sparkling with fire, contribute to captivate the hearts of their men, and to secure them a just and moderate influence in domestic and even public affairs. (260)[21]

The elaborate eroticization of the women of Tahiti serves to gloss over the problematic conjunction of their "primitive simplicity of manners" and their civilizing powers. It suggests that the island women do literally "seduce" the men by virtue of their sexualized art of pleasing into civilizing softness, into forms of desire that harmonize their social differences. This seductive role more closely resembles that attributed to them in commercial societies that have not yet—in the terms of Millar and Kames—become immoral. It works to blur the representation in the text of the women's equal rights and public role by returning them to their more familiar private and domestic status. It also serves to conceal the sense in which the condition of the island women reflects Forster's own claim to a specialized knowledge free of occupational bias. As I have mentioned, Forster represented the distinctive quality of his *Observations* as produced by his own distance and alienation from "the bosom of a nation highly civilized, and therefore . . . degenerated" (9). That distance is marked by the analogy between his position and that of the island women, but their eroticization is the sign of the utopian and perhaps impossible status of that position for the European philosopher.

"A Kind of Linnaean Being":
Forster and Eighteenth-Century Natural History

Fifteen weeks from their last land at the Cape of Good Hope, surrounded at the end of the southern summer with ice islands towering above the topmasts, Johann Reinhold Forster, naturalist aboard HMS *Resolution,* found himself sharing a cabin with three ill sheep, "who, raised on a stage as high as my bed, shit & pissed on one side, whilst 5 Goats did the same on the other," and vented his despair:

> I must confess, if twice 4000 pounds were offered to me to go again on such a Voyage, & go through all the Scenes I was obliged to pass now: I would willingly give Up this great inducement & which is so powerful with very many, & exchange it as willingly with the necessity of writing & working very hard for the Support of myself and my Family: & after all, I had, when I left England a fair prospect of getting a place at the British Museum, my friends having interested themselves very much in my favour, & obtained the promiss of His Grace the Archbishop & of the Speaker of the House of Commons; this place & a little industry would have kept me from want and necessity. Had it not been, for the pleasing hopes of making great discoveries in Natural History in this Expedition, I would never had so great an inclination of going on it. But instead of meeting with any object worthy of our attention, after having circumnavigated very near half the globe, we saw nothing, but water, Ice, & sky.[1]

The rigors of the situation had, at least momentarily, reduced expeditionary natural history to an unwise risk, a poor speculation on his and his family's future happiness. At other difficult moments, though, Forster might transcend hopes of directly realizing profits from his speculations in natural history and locate his reward in the world-historical mission of the British nation:

> I will toil & strive as much as lies in my power, & oppose to all these Inconveniences & hardships a mind superior to all these things: my Conscience reproaches me with nothing; I have done as much as I could in those circumstances; the rest I leave to providence & the generosity of my Friends & patrons. The great Impartiality & Jus-

Johann Reinhold Forster and George Forster, Father and Son, aquatint by Daniel Beyel after a painting by John Francis Rigaud, c. 1781. 332 × 253 mm. Rex Nan Kivell Collection, National Library of Australia.

tice of the English Nation is so well known & so well attested by eternal Monuments, that she no doubt will reward one way or other, Her brave Sons, who navigated these inhospitable Seas, & went through the hardest duty with Spirit & vigour, & brought an Expedition to a happy Issue, which no Nation will in future times undertake. Britannia's glorious sons will stand unrivalled in this arduous task: the Track of the Resolution will remain forever an eternal & only monument of the power & greatness of the Nation, of the wisdom & attention of the Men, who are at the head of the Affairs & of the Conduct, bravery, & perseverance of the people who went on this perilous & difficult Expedition.[2]

Somewhere between this spiritual transcendence, this dissolution of the natural historian in the "eternal Monument" to the nation that was the *Resolution* voyage, and the disillusionment of the credulous speculator, tempted by "great inducements" and "pleasing hopes" to risk more immediate "promises" and engage himself for three years as a natural historian on an Admiralty ship, lay the vocation of the eighteenth-century natural historian. Between such outbursts in his journal, Forster, his son George, and their assistant Anders Sparrman proceeded with the business of collecting, preserving, and describing the rocks, plants, and animals they encountered, impelled both by prospects of fame and patronage and by their sense of the historical mission of the human spirit, conducted by nations. My object here is to show how, in Forster's career as a natural historian, collecting and classifying nature in the eighteenth century engaged the ideas of "nation" and the progress of civilization.

The various levels on which this engagement occurred were linked by the notion of "oeconomy." I have used this term, with its archaic spelling and manifold meanings, to describe the object of the natural historian for two reasons. First, the archaic form stresses that economics and natural history emerged as sciences *together*, only after the latter half of the seventeenth century. Until the late eighteenth century, the term "economy" had primarily theological and moral meanings, indicating a wisely, even divinely calculated arrangement of parts for achieving almost any end; it only rarely referred to money and wealth and to "the nation."[3] In Forster's lifetime, "the economy," like "the nation," had not yet become an identifiable object; "oeconomist" is meant only to gesture toward that event and the political economists of a generation after Forster. Second, as we shall see, "oeconomy" figures heavily in the discourse of natural history itself, to describe everything from the arrangement of a flea's internal organs, to the maternal instinct of hens and the social instincts of bees, to the defecation and decay of animals, all "oeconomies of nature" that tend to preserve and perpetuate the chain of being. Natural history was the discursive bridge by which nature's economies became metaphorical and the nation's economy literal; as an "oeconomist," Forster was on the cusp of modernity.

Theodicy and "Oeconomy": Linnaean Natural History

In the middle of the seventeenth century, the hoary genre of "natural history," which could trace a more or less continuous lineage back to Pliny, endured a remarkable metamorphosis. Renaissance natural histories had been concerned to link natural bodies to celestial and terrestrial powers through narrations of their habits, forms, and life histories. A particular stone, insect, or flower entered the natural history compendium as the bearer of singular virtues, material emblems of immaterial forces that might be expressed as the ability to cure a disease or to excite a strong passion in the beholder. The sensual representation of a natural body, for instance, in a still life, could be as efficacious as the object itself. By 1700 these links had been severed, and natural history was divorced from the activity of chronicling and emblematics and accorded an abstract, "scientific" method. Form became the key to placing a natural body in a more or less abstract taxonomic scheme and no longer referred directly to its particular virtues.[4]

At the same time, the equally ancient analysis of the prince and his dominion suffered a similarly dramatic shift in focus, from maintaining the power and glory of the court to producing the prosperity of the "common weal." The new discourse has been variously comprehended under the terms "mercantilism" or "cameralism." Currency and specie formed the chief object of the new discourse. The prohibition on the export of gold and silver (which, along with the concern for maintaining a positive balance of trade and preventing the outflow of specie, is usually used to characterize mercantilism) was only a secondary policy effect of the internal activities of nation building out of princely domains, centered on the encouragement of the internal circulation of a national currency.[5] The transformation of both natural history and political analysis were considerably more complex than I could indicate here, both temporally and spatially. The important point is that they coincided, each supporting the other, that state building participated in the constitution of natural history and that natural history participated in the constitution of the nation as a natural unit of analysis and action. The natural historian was, at least in Northern Europe, often the Protestant pastor, the representative of the state church on the territory's frontiers. The same trading companies that managed and monopolized colonial enterprises and maritime trade under royal charters sponsored the natural historians who in the East and West Indies and the Cape of Good Hope procured specimens and engravings for the royal cabinets and gardens or for those of the chief stockholders.

In fact, the new natural history developed its most definitive and militant form in a state with few colonial possessions but eager to define and mobilize its nationhood, Sweden, in the hands of a Lutheran pastor's son, Carl Linné (Carolus Linnaeus, 1707–1778). Linnaeus described the system of nature for a Sweden that understood itself as a nation endowed with certain wealth and resources that had to be exploited and defended on behalf of the common weal.[6] Linnaeus intimately connected the enterprise of methodical classification and description of the natural world with a personal, heterodox theology and mercantilist ideals of national integrity in Northern Europe. These three aspects converged in the notion of the "oeconomy of nature": a picture of the self-regulating, self-justifying world, in which the moral universe of human action is dissolved in the larger universe of natural arrangements. The Linnaean natural historian was the interpreter and discoverer of these arrangements, not least in the very act of classification: every inscription in the Linnaean sexual system added another instructive little sexual "oeconomy" to nature's exotic and erotic workings, the multifarious, nefarious arrangements by which nature contrived to maintain itself—a man with two wives there, here a woman with six husbands, sleeping in separate beds, and so on. The natural historian thought of himself as *nature's* husband, her oeconomist, and thereby also the nation's oeconomist, responsible for defending the nation's autonomy, free from the evil of dependence upon a foreign power.[7]

As a professor (1741), then rector at the University of Uppsala, Linnaeus trained an army of "apostles." The evangelical metaphor (Linnaeus' own) is apt. By drilling students in the practices of naming and classification that he codified between 1735 and 1766 in successive versions of his *Systema naturae* and *Fundamenta botanica* and sending them on expeditions *within* Sweden, Linnaeus trained a regiment skilled in making forays into unknown territory, capable of quickly orienting themselves, recruiting native populations as both informants and spokespersons, and returning with "useful knowledge," that is, with collections of objects and manuscripts that, by maintaining sufficient material and formal integrity over the long, wet distances, could serve as the basis for "matters of fact" back home and for the next trip out. Between 1746 and 1792, sixteen of Linnaeus' doctoral students participated in long-distance discovery voyages. The "Linnaean method" was truly definitive only after about 1790, but in the 1750s it already had a strong, well-organized, international corps of practitioners and patrons.[8]

Linnaeus believed his students bound to serve Sweden and their *praeses*, and vast collections did reach Linnaeus' cabinet and garden in Uppsala, which soon comprised a central dissemination point for exotic seeds and information. But ambitious students, attracted by the rigors of Linnaean method, saw natural history as a career. "Ungrateful Solander," as Linnaeus called Daniel Solander (1733–1782), who sailed as Joseph Banks' assistant on Captain Cook's first circumnavigation (1769–1771) and was one of only three apostles to return to Europe with his specimens, was a "mercenary" for keeping his collections and drawings in Britain. Linnaeus eventually looked to Forster as Solander's replacement and his consolation.[9]

Forster as Linnaean

> Although I am not a pupil of Linnaeus, however I know his method and reckon myself to be a kind of Linnaean being.[10]

The sense of office and vocation that informed Linnaean natural history in the mercantile economies of Europe animated Johann Reinhold Forster. Trained for the cloth at Halle, the seat of German mercantilism, he would exchange the discipline of the church for that of Linnaean economy.[11] His preparation for the Reformed pastorate, to be sent out into the Marches or rural East Prussia to minister to the populations of peasant farmers and local merchants, would have required preparation in husbandry as part of managing the spiritual lives of his congregation.[12] Stationed in a small parish outside the merchant town of Danzig during 1753–1765, he sought the patronage of local landowners, who displayed their own interest in agricultural improvement by forming societies and brotherhoods of Linnaean naturalists.[13] Forster ministered conscientiously enough to win the attentions of his superiors in Danzig. In 1765, Forster's pastoral talents attracted the attention of the Russian resident in Danzig, who sought a minister to the Reformed congregation of German colonists on the Volga, near Archangelsk, who might impose some general order there. The Russians, Forster wrote his friend the philologist J. D. Michaelis at Göttingen, "seemed very impressed with my knowledge of natural history, theoretical and practical husbandry, and many European languages." He told Michaelis he hoped to found a flourishing settlement on the barren steppes.[14]

The Russian commission began Forster's career as a natural historian seeking state patronage. Forster's activities in the Volga wilderness ended, however, with his angry departure from St. Petersburg without payment, and this indicates the ambiguous character of the office of the Linnaean naturalist, somewhere between land speculator, political philosopher-governor, and intelligence gatherer. Catherine II authorized the establishment of colonies on the Volga steppes in 1764 to raise tax revenue and secure her southernmost borders against Cossack encroachment. By 1766 the rosy prospects painted by Russian agents were inducing 30,000 Germans to embark for the new settlements, 18,000 from Lübeck alone, despite reports of inadequate building and farming materials, poor roads, corrupt officials, and few provisions.[15] According to Forster, the czaress' colonial office had commissioned him to rebut these rumors and to recommend improvements if needed; but when he returned to St. Petersburg scandalized at the treatment of his countrymen, armed with a list of grievances and drafts of a new plan for the colonies, he was ignored and denied compensation.[16] Forster found sympathy with the French ambassador in St. Petersburg, who told his counterpart in London that "the jealousy which characterizes the Russian nation" had prevented the just appreciation of Forster's talents and reported in cipher to his superior in Paris that Forster was "quick and clever" and would certainly be of use to the French. Meanwhile, the British envoy, George Macartney, disapproved of French efforts to cultivate "malcontents" in St. Petersburg and suspected that to sabotage Russian expansion the French themselves were spreading the very rumors Forster was supposed to quash. Macartney gave a different version of Forster's activities to his superiors, reporting (in cipher) that Forster had arrived in St. Petersburg with his own colonial scheme:

> [Forster] laid a Plan before the Government here, for engaging a considerable Number of his Countrymen to settle in those desert but fertile Plains which lay on the Banks of the Volga, between Casan and Astracan; for this Purpose he made a Journey to those Regions, in order to pitch upon a proper Spot for the Foundation of his Colony, and with indefatigable Pains and Industry, during a very short Residence, not only made himself Master of every Thing relative to the Soil, Advantages, Resources and possible Improvement of that Country; but drew the most accurate Plans and Charts of it, that ever were made.

Clearly, Macartney, too, thought Forster's talents could be quite useful, but also dangerous: Forster was "a Fellow of quick parts . . . and of a very ambitious and enterprising Turn, which has often engaged him in extraordinary Projects," and he had the Home Office put Forster under surveillance when the latter disembarked from the packet *Liebste* in London in autumn 1766. The official Russian account fleshes out Macartney's: the Russians claimed that Forster had actually been engaged not by the colonial office but by one of its patented "entrepreneurs" (a Baron de Beauregard) in an independent speculation to found a colony and that he had actively fomented discontent among the settlers.[17] The conflict of perspectives is telling, betraying the close association between Protestant ministry, natural history, financial speculation, and territorial expansion. If we are to believe Peter Simon Pallas, the next German naturalist in Russian employ, Forster proposed "to make Plantations of Oak and other useful Timber in these plains, where not so much as a shrub comes up, & which is as fit for that purpose, as the desarts of Syria or Arabia."[18]

Forster in England

When Daniel Solander had reached England in March 1759, he had immediately applied to Linnaeus for a certificate attesting to his "progress in those parts of natural history that lay the grounds for economics."[19] Arriving in London seven years later, Forster did not have the advantage of such testimonials, and he began advertising his "oeconomic" skills, sending papers on Polish methods of carp farming and beekeeping to the Royal Society in search of potential patrons.[20] He exhibited the collection of marine flora and fauna he assembled during the passage across the North Sea around the British Museum and through a growing network of contacts marketed his natural history of the Russian steppes and a detailed map of the Volga to potential patrons in the Royal Society.[21] When he secured a position teaching modern languages and natural history at the Dissenters' Academy in Warrington, Lancashire, in 1767, he confidently proposed to publish an entire "system of Natural History" with the financial backing of the school's rector, the Reverend John Seddon.[22]

In his lectures on natural history, Forster showed his young pupils Nature's ingenious "oeconomies," the keys to which had been provided by "Dr. Charles Linnaeus, the greatest man whom the Learned World ever had in this Respect."[23] The sublime structure of mountains, which as "the Laboratories of Nature" manufactured minerals and purified metals "from First Principles" and gathered water from the clouds (19); the global distribution of grasses, that most useful of foods (21); the "marvellous structure" of zoophytes, which "shews that there is no Jump, but a wise & intended Gradation in Nature, to fill up all the immense scale of possible Beings" (25); the remarkable maternal instincts of hens, "laid deep in the Nature of Parents for preventing the destruction of its Species" (28)—all these smaller examples of the "Oeconomy of Nature" pointed to the overarching "oeconomy" that defined the object of natural history:

These considerations bring us at last to this, that it is the strongest demonstration of this eternal Goodness of God, when Men behold the whole Creation surrounding them, as each part of it maybe useful to Mankind, in supplying its most urgent Wants, in generously providing them with the Comforts & Ornaments of Life; & certainly every Moment presents us with new Instances of it. (29)

Natural history impressed upon its students their duties as "Beings, loaded in every part of their Lives with an infinite variety of Benefactions."

And even this Enjoying of the Creation gives us the strongest Reasons of studying Nature. . . . Would a Lord not cut a poor figure, who should not know, what was the extent of his possessions, & is it also not for the Lords of the Creation impardonable Negligence, to be ignorant of the Extent of their Dominions, of the Beings subject to them, and of the Use of the Things they are in possession of; and what proper Use can a Man make of a thing, whose Qualities he is not acquainted with? (30)

The chief aim of natural history was thus to manage this larger divine "oeconomy," to direct the "lordship" of Man over Nature. Forster took his examples from triumphs of mercantilist policy: for instance, Linnaeus' recent discovery that the coveted cinnamon tree, long believed to be exclusive to the Dutch Indies, was a kind of laurel had prompted the London Society for the Encouragement of Arts, Manufactures, and Commerce to offer premiums for those planters in the British West Indies who could plant the most cinnamon trees, freeing England from a pernicious dependence in "the Spirit of Liberty [and] Patriotism" (33–34). Every class of person benefited from the study of natural history— the architect "raising lasting monuments of the Grandeur and Power of Nations" and the laborer building "his mean Cottage," the physician applying the *materia medica* and the patient guarding against quacks, the stranded traveler, the soldier. Knowledge of natural history would teach the merchant

> where he can get a certain Commodity, the cheapest, nearest & best of all; this would teach him the Nature & Property of each Branch of Trade & how it must be preserved & kept; it would teach him the Goodness & Qualities of the different Merchandises, & prevent him from being imposed by avaricious & fraudulent dealers. In a word, a Merchant with the knowledge of Nature is a true Merchant & a respectable Man in human society; without it, he is but a Man who gains Money by buying & selling. (35–36)

In short, natural history transformed base, selfish, and corrupt commerce into a noble and patriotic activity and elevated the short-sighted, uncoordinated work of individuals into the activities of a nation.

Natural history not only supported every rank and every station in society, so that each could fulfill its role fully and credibly, but also brought the marks and distinctions, the expression and self-representation of social order, to perfection:

> These different Cloths & Stuffs intended for Garments are yet beautified by the Application of various productions taken from the Animal, Vegetable & Mineral Kingdom in the Vats of the Dyer & the House of the Callico & Linen-Printer, so that each Age, each Business, and each Station of Life, from the Throne to the Footman may have its Choice & its Distinction. (44)

Combined with the ingenuity of human industry, the variety of natural products displayed and organized by natural history made rank and station part of a natural display. The greater the variety of goods supplied by nature and commerce, the clearer and finer the distinctions between different stations and the less the chance of confusion, disorder, and miscegenation. The social plenum was as much an "Argument for the immense Wisdom of that Being, which was capable to give to each [creature] as much perfection as their allotted station in the universal immense Plan would allow" (25) as the finely graded plenum of nature; while the latter was displayed by natural history, the former was preserved and perfected by it. In a closing image, certain to attract his pupils, Forster made the desire attached to a woman's body a function not of its native "charms" but of those marks of rank and beauty with which nature, through commerce, could adorn it.

> And certainly behold yonder fair Daughter of the Creation, her conquering Look brings to her Feet a Crowd of Adorers: is all this owing only to her superior Charms? I believe not! for wrap her up in rags, she may have the same sweet & victorious Countenance, she never will be the Admiration of the Nobleman, of the Squire, of the Clerk, perhaps not even that of some honest gardian of Horses: but wrap this same Person in the finest Dutch Linnen, in the best chosen Silks, let Nature bring her Toilette to this fine Lady, some Vermillion to colour her cheeks, some precious Stones to rival the brightness of her Eyes, some fine filaments of Flax artfully tied into Brabant Laces, to conceal slyly some of her natural Beauties . . . let the Flowers lent her their Balm, distilled into essences to spread her odoriferous Smell wherever she moves. All Rangs [ranks] of Life will come & sacrifice at the Altar of this Divinity, Hommage of Desire. (41–42)

Here was a goddess in which the natural and social order could be worshiped at once, as an object of "desire," and her priest was the natural historian.

Such a vision of social order fitted Forster well for the patronage of those elements of British society identified with the empire. When he lost his position at Warrington in 1769, his association with the naturalist Thomas Pennant cemented Forster's Linnaean vocation in the British colonial context, a vocation made all the more pressing by Forster's dire financial situation. The two planned a nine-volume series of translations of "Journeys of the Linnaean School," of which Forster's own Russian travels were to make two. Eventually, three "Voyages of Pupils of Dr. Linnaeus" were dedicated by the pair "to the English Nation": Pehr Kalm's to North America (1770–1771), Pehr Loeffling's to Spain and South America (1771), and Pehr Osbeck's to China (1771), the last dedicated to Pennant. Forster's sixteen-year-old son, George, translated, Reinhold updated the natural history, and Pennant provided the credit with the publishers and the financial backing to sustain the Forster family.[24]

Forster was just as industriously promoting his own talents in natural history, publishing catalogues of British insects, North American and Chinese fauna and flora (as appendices to the Kalm and Osbeck), and several papers to the Royal Society describing birds, fishes, and mammals recently arrived from the Hudson's Bay Colony. He also published essays exposing *Short Directions for Lovers and Promoters of Natural History. In what manner Specimens of all kinds may be collected, preserved, and transported to distant Countries* (appended to the Kalm translation) and *An easy method of assaying and classifying mineral substances, containing plain and easy Instructions for any person to examine the Products of his own Land, or such as are obvious in Excursions or Travel in Foreign Countries* (1772).[25]

The return of Joseph Banks and Daniel Solander from Cook's first circumnavigation in July 1771 made the pair the toast of London. News of a second voyage to the South Seas convinced Forster he had to be on that boat. Here was a unique chance to prove his natural historical talents in the service of the British empire. Along with dozens of others—gentleman-amateurs, medics, scholars, and several professional natural historians—who saw their fortunes in the opportunity, Forster advertised his ambition to the pair. He dedicated the catalogue of North American plants to Solander and a 1771 catalogue of insects to Banks and quickly translated and critically annotated the accounts of two French expeditions, Bossu's travels in Louisiana (1771) and Bougainville's circumnavigation (1772), displaying his familiarity with the latest researches of Britain's chief colonial competitors.[26] The reviewer of his Bougainville in the *Critical Review* wished that "a gentleman, whose improvements in natural history we have, on several occasions, perused with so much satisfaction, should be induced to accompany his two congenial philosophers [Banks and Solander] on the intended navigation around the globe" as a member of a philosophical "triumvirate."[27]

The events that in May and June 1772 put Forster and his son on the *Resolution* in place of Banks and Solander need not be rehearsed here. Let it suffice to point out that the German's berth was already the product of an Admiralty decision to value the *Resolution*'s speed and seaworthiness more than the philosophical skill and authority that Banks and his entourage and equipment might have brought to the voyage.[28] The tensions, if not their scope, were not lost on Forster. "I shall do for Natural History whatever lies in my power; my efforts will be great, as I have great Antagonists & the Expectations of my Patrons and Friends are likewise great," Forster vowed to Pennant, imbued with a sense of holy mission.[29] On the way to meet the *Resolution* at Plymouth, Forster, the royally appointed economist and "philosophical observer" to the king, surveyed the Cornish tin mines, evaluated Devonshire agriculture, and projected forests of oak replacing the sheep on treeless Bagshot Common, as he had on the Volga steppes.[30] The stage was set in Forster's own mind for the trials of the Linnaean naturalist against foes natural and human.

Expedition as Experiment: The Trials of a Natural Historian

June ye 25th [1773]. We dined this day upon beef, which our crew called *Experimental-beef*: To understand this, I only will observe, that every thing which our Sailors found not to be quite in the common way of a man of war, they call *Experimental*. The beer made of the Essence of beer, or Malt they called *Experimental beer,* the very Water distilled from Sea Water by *Mr. Irwin's* method was *Experimental Water, Mr. Wales,* the Astronomer, *Mr. Hodges,* the painter, Myself and my Son were comprehended under the name of *Experimental Gentlemen.*[31]

Aboard HMS *Resolution,* natural history was one set of practices among many, all aimed at making the ship an effective long-distance instrument in colonial speculation and control, like seawater distillation, antiscorbutics, and ship's painters. It was developed by long trial and negotiation to produce a particular form of stable, consensual knowledge. Both the natural historian and his patron had an interest in that stability and consensus. A natural historical fact would do the Admiralty no good if it found only tenuous purchase among other natural historians, if it could not be made the basis of future actions and help stabilize the unknown territory. On the other hand, a fact that lacked the social and material sponsorship afforded by patrons like the Admiralty, including the prospect of being "useful" on future voyages or even in projected colonies, was considerably weakened in the far-flung and competitive networks of natural history, where others might revise a classification or blatantly plagiarize and appropriate one's "discoveries." Natural historical facts, like the people and ships that carried them, were fragile things.

Even when practiced close to "civilized" Europe, in Lapland or Siberia or the Scottish Highlands, preserving, drawing, describing, and naming, like all practices, were subject to challenge or reinforcement: they became experimental. Every ascription and observation was a potential revolution. But proximity to gardens and books and other natural historians generally meant that novelty was quickly domesticated by means of communication (of letters, specimens, drawings) and negotiation. Beyond the reach of such channels, on long-distance voyages of discovery, the experimental character of natural history could become uncomfortably permanent. It was a constant struggle against creeping mold, flooding waters, hungry sailors, inquisitive islanders, exhaustion, to maintain sufficiently stable facts.[32] One could not even be sure of the identities of the islands one was surveying, when the charts gave different accounts of their positions, histories, and names.[33] Far from books, museums, dry rooms and paper, patrons, and societies, immersed in a physical universe of unparalleled bleakness and a social universe—the *Resolution*—where civilian categories of authority and social station did not hold, every aspect of natural historical practice was under test, and might be challenged or reinforced on each iteration.

This was as true of chronometry, astronomy, and navigation as of natural history, although their longer history of incorporation in the regime of a man-of-war reduced the uncertainty produced by months without being able to correct time-keepers, match eclipse observations, or consult the latest occultation tables. The Admiralty had charged William Wales, the *Resolution*'s astronomer, with three experimental chronometers by John Arnold and another experimental time-keeper by Larcum Kendall, a copy of one that in 1765 had won its maker £10,000 of a Bureau of Longitude prize. Keeping time was the key to more exact long-distance navigation and orientation, and Wales was under immense pressure to make these experiments "succeed." The voyage itself was the community of these experimental practices and people—an uneasy community, because exactly what was under test in these experiments could never be limited or fixed ahead and could grow to include the ship's social order (already confused by the ambiguous status of our foreign "experimental gentleman") as well as the natural order. They were all "experimental gentlemen" in more ways than they would have admitted.[34]

All the way to the Cape of Good Hope, then, Forster surveyed their landfalls with the same confident "philosopher's" eye that had evaluated the Cornish tin mines before departing. In his journal he restructured the political economies of Madeira and Funchal. At the Cape, Forster could still receive mail and, more important, send crates of natural history news to Pennant, the Royal Society, and Linnaeus. He sent Pennant news of many trophies: numerous new bird species, several new plants, and an entirely new genus of mammal, a "great Mole." He subcontracted with Linnaean collectors based in the colony and expected "to find great collections ready for me [on the return trip] & I will carry every Spoil from the Cape."[35] From there on, though, whatever they collected or observed would have to be preserved with them, at least in words and picture, around the world.

Soon enough, prospects of returning to England as another Banks dimmed. Forster made himself ill with the thought that Cook was sailing past land brimming with new plants, that three days were spent on a barren rock to determine its longitude, that months were spent crisscrossing the high latitudes of the South Pacific in search of a continent that did not exist, and that meanwhile, in Banks' London townhouse museum, Solander was describing and drawing new plants and animals from the very lands he was bypassing, while Banks bankrolled sumptuous engravings of them.

How did Forster and his collections survive these daily trials, these ubiquitous threats of moral and material chaos? Affirming in his arguments with the officers and in his journal that he was an accepted, reliable member of the ranks of Natural History, tilling a cooperative field, sons of a common discipline, enabled him to preserve his identity before and after the voyage. Forster's self-consciousness as a natural historian, affirmed under challenge over and over again in his journal, both enabled him to bear the encroaching chaos and secured him the enmity of those who felt their own self-consciousnesses thereby infringed upon. Obstacles like the impossible damp, which made his living quarters seem a moldy "house of the dead"; contradictions from the officers or even Cook; or any other contrary things were ascribed to forces of evil, selfishness, meanness, brutishness, and prejudice against the public-minded natural historian. Forster showed himself only too ready to dispute the competence and character of others or arrogate authority not necessarily his in order to account for natural historical uncertainty to himself and his prospective public. He developed a natural-historical self-righteousness. Characteristic is a journal outburst from 4 July 1774, off the island of Vatoa in Fiji, where Forster balked at Cook's apparent willingness to indulge the turtle-hunting fancies of his crew while dismissing Forster's requests to go ashore for collecting:

> Whosoever knows, what it is to meet with such treatment, may easily conceive how mortifying it must be for a man of Spirit, & zealous to promote his favourite Science, & eager to fulfill the expectations of the public, & the trust reposed in him by his Employers; to see an Isle full of plants as it were in reach, & not enjoy the pleasure, which he thought to taste by enlarging the limits of Science: but such patriotic notions & sensations were strangers from all times, to people who have nothing in view, but the aggrandisement of their rank & fortune, without any tincture of Science or a heart capable of friendship & of true social virtue.[36]

Of course, Forster the aspiring natural historian is always thinking of returning home with discoveries and accomplishments in natural history such as would make his own fortune among the ranks of natural historians. But as this is "science" and a public good, it offers a foil to the selfish and antisocial characters that motivate those who oppose him. This sense of being part of a larger discipline addressing "nature in its greatest extent" (Observations, preface) that goes beyond self-interest or even the commercial interests of Great Britain—what we might call professional consciousness—guarantees his "credibility" and "good faith" in both himself and his prospective audience. Threats to this consciousness were quickly ascribed to meanness and baseness. In his entry for 9 September 1774 he lamented: "I [his 4,000 pounds] am the object of their Envy & they hinder me in the pursuit of Natural History, where they can, from base and mean, dirty principles, beneath any man of Sense.... But it cannot be otherwise expected from the people who have not sense enough to think reasonably & beyond the Sphere of their mean grovelling passions."[37] Those who would be contrary are worse than the barely social savages he describes in the Observations. "We are indefatigable, but cannot prosper if every step is taken by envious persons to cross & hinder me."

By the time the *Resolution* reached the Cape for the second time, in March 1775, Forster had recovered sufficiently to prepare a triumphal naturalist's homecoming, sending off letters and specimens to Pennant, Barrington, and Linnaeus and spending lavishly at the Cape for plants and animal skins, along with several live springbok for the royal menagerie.[38] Still aboard the *Resolution,* the Forsters frantically readied their collections, drawings, and manuscripts for immediate delivery to the publishers once back in England. Anxieties about securing credit for their discoveries plagued them. Not only did Forster still think Banks and Solander ready to publish at any moment; he was anxious to establish his place in the voyage, his philosophical authority. By September 1774, according to Hoare, Forster stood completely alienated from most of the crew and officers. Indeed, rumors of the Prussian's inflated and pretentious bearing on board quickly spread, reaching England well before landing and Göttingen by July.[39] Meanwhile, plenty of others aboard ship were ready to bespeak the natural history of the South Pacific. Midshipmen had made ornithological drawings, which the captain's clerk showed to Solander; the surgeon's mate, William Anderson, had made collections of shells and plants; and plenty of sailors had kept their own journals, which, though surrendered to Cook on the Admiralty's demand upon reaching the Cape, could challenge and discredit Forster at the Admiralty.[40]

The Admiralty was not ready to admit Forster's claim to philosophical authority, however. The break apparently came over the amount of credit Forster was willing to give to the reports of a southern continent, with which Barrington, Dalrymple, and others had promoted this voyage to the Admiralty and Parliament. Forster had concluded by 1774 that a land in the southern polar ocean sufficiently large to interest Britain—"a small island at such a distance from Great Britian can be of no use & consequently of no consequence to this Great Nation"—was a geographical impossibility, and he rebelled at Cook's insistence on further reconnaissance.[41] In remarks on the formation of ice, submitted to the Admiralty in a preliminary draft of his narrative, Forster concluded that seawater could freeze and that the large ice sheets taken as evidence of land proved no such thing: the enthusiasm of Barrington and Dalrymple had made the Admiralty incautious. An alarmed Barrington challenged Forster, employing Charles Blagden and Jesse Ramsden, both fellows of the Royal Society, to conduct experiments showing that ice meant land. Forster could not tolerate Barrington's philosophical pretensions and had young George publish a polemical pamphlet against the "tyranny" of his patron:

> If the patron maintain that salt-water cannot freeze, and his friend ventures to trust his own eyes and believe the contrary; or if the great man dreams of a Southern continent, and his client has the audacity to divulge that he has sailed over the spot

where it should have been;—woe to the poor *quondam* friend; not the sea but his patron's heart will be instantly turned to ice, and from thence forward to find one single sentiment of philanthropy or even common justice in the frozen mass, will be as utterly impossible as to meet with lands where it has pleased heaven to place an ocean.[42]

In the end, the Admiralty did not need Forster's natural history as much as Forster needed the patronage and protection of the Admiralty. Without the genteel status of a Banks to enable the two worlds of credit to exist independently, the uneasy accommodation between the British Navy and the impecunious Linnaean naturalist fell apart. Taking up a large subscription, mostly among the Oxford divines interested in his philological work, Forster published the *Observations Made during a Voyage round the World* in 1778 as a demonstration of the true philosophical compass of the natural historian.

Forster's Observations

> The British Legislature did not send out and liberally support my father as a naturalist, who was merely to bring home a collection of butterflies and dried plants. . . . So far from prescribing rules for his conduct, they conceived that the man whom they had chosen, prompted by his natural love of science, would endeavour to derive the greatest possible advantage to learning from his voyage. He was only therefore directed to exercise all his talents, and to extend his observations to every remarkable object. From him they expected a philosophical history of the voyage, free from prejudice and vulgar error, where human nature should be represented without any adherence to fallacious systems, and upon the principles of general philanthropy; in short, an account written upon a plan which the learned world had not hitherto seen executed.[43]

The *Observations Made during a Voyage round the World*, the elder Forster's chief "philosophical" reflection on his three years on the *Resolution*, does not at first appear concerned primarily with natural history. Forster and his son planned to display the natural historical yield of the voyage in separate, expensively illustrated folio volumes devoted to the Linnaean classification of the plants, birds, mammals, and fish they collected or recorded; but although the two worked furiously to complete publishable manuscripts as the *Resolution* approached Portsmouth in 1775—anxious as they were to establish priority over Banks and Solander and those seamen who had been making their own collections and to profit from the sensation of Cook's return—only the *Characteres generum plantarum* (London, 1776), the Linnaean diagnoses of their plants, minimally illustrated, emerged, and then to poor and even scandalized reviews that claimed he had stolen from Solander. The *Observations* contains only brief, geographical summaries of the natural bodies encountered in the South Seas, identifying by their Linnaean labels the minerals, stones and earths, plants and animals populating each land. How then did the book advertise the competence of the natural historian?

The final chapter on maintaining a materially and morally happy ship's company over long distances away from civilization, preventing the physical and moral decay inevitably attendant upon such separation, was a clear selling point, and its position at the very end of the long volume is fitting for a book so preoccupied with the degeneration of nature and humankind in the absence of countervailing forces. Forster highlighted this chapter in presenting copies of the book to the Swedish king, the president of the Swedish Medical College, and the secretary of the Royal Swedish Academy of Sciences, citing its importance for any colonial enterprise.[44]

But the whole work advertised the "philosophical" natural historian's insight into the economies of nature, the forces that shaped the globe, its productions and its human inhabitants, and how they might be best disposed to fulfill the moral advancement of the human species. Forster spent much of the first four chapters steadily undermining Buffon's dismissal of vulcanism as a major earth-building force, documenting the prevalence of volcanoes and their importance in the formation of dry land in the South Seas. The global distribution patterns of land, water, heat, and organic bodies is a prominent concern. The formation of soil, a spiraling cycle of growth and decay and defecation—"so that by this grass, and the excrements of seals, penguins, and shags, the soil of the country gradually becomes more and more elevated" (43)—of putrification and the accumulation of "the precious treasure of fertile mould," exemplifies the dirty-but-divine Linnaean economy: "All this seeming scene of destruction and confusion is one of the oeconomical actions of nature, thus hoarding up a precious quantity of the richest mould, for a future generation of men, who, one day or other, will live upon the rich products of this treasured soil" (43). The earth, Forster says, quoting the beginning of Pliny's discourse on geography, "always serves the needs of mortals. Which of her productions are forced, what does she expend without purpose! What delights of smell and texture, taste, touch, and color! With what good faith she repays with interest whatever is entrusted to her! What she nourishes for our sake!" (44).[45] Nature, for Forster as for Linnaeus, was the soul of economy. Always in the background was the prospect of a beautiful, cultivated nature, built by the genius of mankind out of the imperfect materials supplied by the raw forces of vulcanism, sedimentation, and soil formation:

> Where man the lord of the creation on this globe, has never attempted any change on it, there nature *seems* only to thrive; for in reality it languishes, and is deformed by being left to itself. Impenetrable woods cover the surface of these regions; its trees are no doubt here and there large and fine, but many are decayed, and still more lying on the ground rotting; here is a tree without its rind, another without a top; all the ground below is over-run with briars, and weeds, and climbers, which hinder you from setting a foot forward: all that seems to vegetate and thrive is suffocated, and buried under mosses, lichens and mushrooms. The water stagnates every where, and causes immense swamps, which are unfit to serve either the inhabitants of the land, or those of the water; being over-run with gigantic but coarse plants, affording very little food to the more useful parts of the animated creation. (99)

By itself, though tending toward development and life out of the "appearance of barrenness, the horrors of desolation and silence of death" (41), nature represented only waste and disorder. Untended, it was "deformed" and uneconomical. But "how beautiful, how improved, how useful does nature become by the industry of man! and what happy changes are produced, by the moderate care of rational beings!" Nature could become a "beautiful" garden, nothing unused, everything serving its function in the divinely designed "economy."

Forster's most sustained and systematic defense of his authority as "philosophical observer," however, might be located in the treatise on "ethic philosophy" that comprises two-thirds of the *Observations*. Recruiting native customs, languages, arts, and culture and normalizing translations with vocabularies and behaviors with anthropologies were as necessary in stabilizing these new worlds as describing a plant according to Linnaean rules or naming an island "New Caledonia." Without the native names for the islands in the Marquesas recorded on older charts, only myriad Spanish, French, and English names and roughly matching descriptions, no one on the *Resolution* could be sure exactly what they were passing: "Had all the former Navigators taken the prudent Step to inquire the Natives, for the Names of the Islands they saw," Forster choked back the frustration, "we might be able to ascertain with certainty, what are new discoveries & what are not. We take always the trouble to ascertain the true Name, & then all the future Navigators can enquire for the Name of what they see, & then they will easily make out, whether it is new or not."[46]

Hence Forster's ire when the natives themselves threatened this allegedly mutual philanthropic understanding. To make any use of native informants, Forster had to create a familiar moral world of credit and honor on these strange islands; when "robbery" or "deceit" appeared to rupture that world, Forster could become terribly vindictive, insisting that the natives "knew" they had done wrong and would welcome punishment. Recall for instance the scene that developed around the identification of a "nutmeg tree" on Tanna.[47] Forster, desperately

A KIND OF LINNAEAN BEING

wanting to know what tree a magnificent flower he has been given comes from and what its name is (the perfect tree to discover and name for an important patron), became infuriated when he began to think the islander he had been questioning was lying to him. Forster spat at his informant and vowed to punish him for his "evil." (Forster, driven by "paternal love," actually shot an islander who he believed was attempting to steal George's gun in order to shoot him; we find out that at least part of what was going through Forster's mind was a previous incident in which Cook refused to discipline the natives after the theft of clothes and a microscope from Sparrman.) When Cook's officers prevented Forster from disciplining the native, and Cook himself scolded Forster for endangering relations with the islanders, Forster was beside himself with indignation. His honor and authority as a naturalist, who *needs* to identify that tree, had been offended by both the "cunning" of the islander and the officiousness of the officers. Understanding and sympathy stopped at the tools and transactions of the naturalist.

Consider Forster's last words in the *Observations*, then, less as a plea for humane treatment of native peoples and more as a promotional advertisement for the natural historian:

> Mankind ought to be considered as the members of one great family; therefore let us not despise any of them, though they be our inferiors in regard to many improvements and points of civilization; none of them is so despicable that he should not, in some one point or other, know more than the wisest man of the most polished nation. This knowledge may be easily obtained from them by friendliness, kindness, and gentleness; and if so bought is cheaply obtained. (376)

The native peoples, in whatever degree of civilization, are authorities whom Forster makes it impossible not to listen to; they cannot be shot or alienated without losing valuable and important, perhaps lifesaving, and certainly cost-saving knowledge; they are ignored at the outsider's peril. The "philanthropy" cultivated by "men versed in science" thus made them indispensable to voyages of discovery. Indeed, the source of much of the naturalist's authority was his ability to convincingly recruit the natives, to interpret their words and behaviors, and to communicate with subjects others might abandon as closed to communication.[48] This was a crucial resource for one's credibility back home and is one reason William Wales focused his attacks on Forster's linguistic competence, not only in the Polynesian tongues, but in English. The ability to attach the right names to the right things, which Forster claims depends upon understanding the natives, was essential both to the Admiralty's strategic aims and the naturalist's philosophical ambitions.

Such "philanthropic" understanding as Forster urged upon his patrons was important for more than its utility to the colonial enterprise. It made the "other" into a potential source of communication and information rather than an incomprehensible, unpredictable, and ultimately inhuman presence. It established the ground of intercourse between the English and the islanders. Forster's harshest judgments were in fact reserved for those peoples like the miserable Fuegians, who did not even show an interest in communicating and exhibited utter indifference to his attempts: this he diagnosed as a complete inability to abstract from their material wretchedness. Commerce started with the "commerce of ideas" (which was, in Forster's anthropology, one of the first beneficial effects of increasing population density). The original "cheap" purchase of natural history by the natural historian from native informants laid the basis for the substitution of conquest by commerce.

Forster's failure to accommodate with the British Admiralty was not the product of any fundamental incompatibility between the aims and methods of natural history and those of territorial expansion and colonial speculation, within or outside the country's boundaries. Indeed, as Forster's attempts to secure patronage and fame as a natural historian suggest, the two enterprises sustained one another through the originally theological idea of "nature's oeconomy," to issue eventually in the delineation of the nation's "political economy" in the discourse of Scottish civics. The commission from the Russian Colonial Office to inspect the Volga settlements, which first took him from his Danzig pastorate in 1765, revealed a discipline that combined the church with land speculation, administration, and intelligence. Lecturing to young Dissenters in the Midlands, Forster developed a natural history that clearly revealed divine order in the natural world and guaranteed it in the social world, by showing the nation where and how to satisfy its wants, create a closed commerce, and permit all "stations of life" to fulfill and perfect their given functions. All this was brought into sharp relief by the chaos of the long circumnavigation in the Admiralty man-of-war, which issued in the *Observations*. With its comprehensive expositions of natural and human history, physical geography, and anthropology in one global description, the *Observations* marks a high point in the development of the eighteenth-century natural historian's self-consciousness as "oeconomist."

Textual Note

This text follows that of the only English edition of 1778, printed by G. Robinson, which presents few technical complications. There are no significant variations among copies we have consulted, though the list of subscribers is sometimes bound in at the beginning rather than the end, and some early copies lack the Comparative Table of languages. Tupaia's map is usually found around page 424, rather than at page 513, as indicated in a direction to the binder and as is clearly appropriate. A few obvious printer's errors and the errata listed at the back of the 1778 edition, have been corrected here; otherwise this edition closely follows the spelling and punctuation of the original. Michael Hoare (*Tactless Philosopher,* 344–345) has listed translations and later editions in other languages.

Forster's footnotes have been printed as such, with asterisks and devices similar to those he employed; those of the editors are marked by superscript numbers and appear as endnotes. We have standardized the 1778 printer's uses of roman and italic fonts in notes to make Forster's references clearer; otherwise these have not been modernized or standardized. Details of the works cited appear in the second part of the bibliography at the end of the book. Wherever possible we have listed the editions used by Forster, though some of the works he refers to, and especially the travel narratives, were extensively reprinted and anthologized in the eighteenth century. In a number of cases it is not clear from the truncated references he provides which of several possible editions, abridgments, or extracts are drawn upon. For important works which readers of the *Observations* may wish to consult, we have sometimes added references to reprints or recent scholarly editions where available.

No full manuscript of the *Observations* has been located, but a few short draft sections are preserved in Forster's papers in the Staatsbibliothek der Stiftung Preussischer Kulturbesitz, Berlin (MS. germ. oct. 79). (For a full list of the Forster papers in this repository, see, again, Hoare's *Tactless Philosopher.*) Two of these ("On the Human Species in the Isles of the South Sea. On its Numbers and Population" and "On the Diseases Incident to Europeans in these Climates, & on the

Preservation of their Health in Long Voyages") are closely related to the text as published. Two others ("Geography of the South Sea" and "Essay on the South Sea Islands") are more preliminary and do not correspond with particular sections of the published text. These drafts, though not printed in full here, are discussed and quoted in endnotes to the relevant sections.

LONDON, FEBRUARY 16, 1778.

In APRIL *next will be Published,*

OBSERVATIONS

DURING A

VOYAGE ROUND THE WORLD,

ON

1. THE EARTH, AND ITS STRATA:
2. WATER, AND THE OCEAN:
3. THE ATMOSPHERE:
4. CHANGES OF THE GLOBE:
5. ORGANIC BODIES: *And,*
6. THE HUMAN SPECIES.

BY JOHN REINOLD FORSTER, LL.D. F.R.S.

This Work will be comprehended in a handsome Volume, large Quarto, on a good Paper, with an entire new Type; Two Thirds of the Whole being already printed off. The Subscription will be *Fifteen Shillings* in Boards; but on the Day of Publication the Price will be considerably raised.

N.B. Those who subscribe, or collect Subscriptions, for *six* Copies, have the *seventh* gratis.

Subscriptions are received at DR. FORSTER's, No. 16, Percy-street, Rathbone-Place; Mr. GEORGE ROBINSON's, Bookseller, Pater-noster Row; at Mr. B. WHITE's, Fleet-street; Mr. P. ELMSLEY's, in the Strand; Mr. J. ROBSON's, Bond-street; and the principal Booksellers in Town and Country, from this Time to the End of *March.*

The object pursued in this work, is an investigation of NATURE, in its greatest extent; the earth, the sea, the air, the organic and animated creation, and more particularly mankind itself, so far as all these came within the reach of examination, in the course of a voyage round the world.

IT has been owing to several untoward circumstances, that voyagers have seldom been able to divide their attention equally between so many different objects, to view them with critical discernment, in an unprejudiced manner, and to collect and arrange their observations, with a competent knowledge of every branch of Natural History, and Philosophy. By sending out a person, who had made these his particular study, and by directing him to employ all his time, during the voyage, in making enquiries to this purpose, there was some probability of a benefit accruing to science, and of a considerable addition being made to the stock of human knowledge. The author of this work, who was so sent out, in the Resolution, with Captain Cook, on his late voyage towards the South-Pole, and round the world, now means to lay before the public the result of his researches. It is his aim to give, in a comprehensive and methodized view, all the information which has been obtained in these late voyages, relatively to his science, and to deduce from thence such remarks as may be of general use, and particularly acceptable to the friends of humanity. He has therefore made MAN his principal object, and contemplated him with the greatest attention, under various points of view. The history of our own species, is in reality our most important and most attractive study; the pictures of manners and characters, ever varied and ever new, teem with useful instruction, at the same time that they lead the mind to the most pleasing reflexions. The author has endeavoured to look upon *mankind* in general, as one large family, and described the various tribes of the South-Sea with this retrospect, which must make them more interesting, by adverting to their different degrees of civilization. The characters of nations in a *high* state of civilization, are sufficiently known from the writings of philosophers, who have spent their lives among them. But we are by no means equally well acquainted with the inferior stages of human nature, from that of the most wretched savage, removed but in the first degree from absolute animality, to that of the more polished inhabitant of the tropical islands. These have been seldom visited, and still more rarely contemplated with a philosophical eye; therefore, what the author may have collected among them, will, it is hoped, have the charms of novelty, as well as importance; and tend to shew, by what accidents and misfortunes men may, for want of mutual support, degenerate to savages; and by what steps they may gradually emerge from the darkness of barbarism, and uniting in social compacts, behold the dawn of civilization.

It may not be improper to add, that these Observations were originally intended to be printed at the end of Captain Cook's Journal of his Voyage, as a second part of the work, published under the auspices of the Admiralty-Board, but that circumstances, hereafter to be mentioned, prevented this plan from taking place. It still, however, remains in the power of every reader to put it in execution, by purchasing this publication, which, from the similarity of the subject, is equally calculated to serve as a Companion to Captain Cook's, or to George Forster's Account of the Voyage, not interfering, with the contents of either of these works.[1]

OBSERVATIONS MADE DURING A
VOYAGE ROUND THE WORLD

[ACCORDINGLY FOR MY OWN PART I ADOPT THE PURSUIT OF PHILOSOPHY IN ITS ENTIRETY BOTH (SO FAR AS I AM ABLE) AS A GUIDING PRINCIPLE OF LIFE AND AS AN INTELLECTUAL PLEASURE, NOR DO I THINK THAT A GREATER OR BETTER GIFT HAS BEEN BESTOWED BY THE GODS UPON MANKIND]

Translation (*above*) of quotation by Cicero (*opposite*), which appears on the title page of Forster's *Observations*, 1778.

OBSERVATIONS

MADE DURING A

VOYAGE ROUND THE WORLD,

ON

PHYSICAL GEOGRAPHY,

NATURAL HISTORY,

AND

ETHIC PHILOSOPHY.

ESPECIALLY ON

1. The EARTH and its STRATA,
2. WATER and the OCEAN,
3. The ATMOSPHERE,
4. The CHANGES of the GLOBE,
5. ORGANIC BODIES, and
6. The HUMAN SPECIES.

By JOHN REINOLD FORSTER, LLD. F. R. S. and S. A.

AND A MEMBER OF SEVERAL LEARNED ACADEMIES IN EUROPE.

TOTUM IGITUR ILLUD PHILOSOPHIÆ STUDIUM, MIHI QUIDEM IPSE SUMO, & AD VITÆ
CONSUETUDINEM & CONSTANTIAM QUANTUM POSSUM & AD DELECTATIONEM ANIMI: NEC ULLUM
ARBITROR AUT MAJUS AUT MELIUS A DIIS DATUM MUNUS HOMINI.

M. Tullius Cicero. Acad. Quæst. lib. i.

***

LONDON:

Printed for G. ROBINSON, in PATER-NOSTER-ROW.

M DCC LXXVIII.

TO

THE PRESIDENT,

COUNCIL,

AND FELLOWS OF THE

ROYAL SOCIETY

OF LONDON,

INSTITUTED FOR PROMOTING

NATURAL KNOWLEDGE,

THE FOLLOWING SHEETS,

AS THE

RESULT OF ENQUIRIES

MADE IN THE COURSE OF A

VOYAGE ROUND THE WORLD,

BY A FELLOW OF THE SOCIETY,

WHO WAS APPOINTED NATURALIST ON THAT

VOYAGE,

AT THE RECOMMENDATION OF

SEVERAL MEMBERS OF THEIR COUNCIL IN 1772,

ARE WITH PROFOUND RESPECT

AND GRATITUDE

INSCRIBED

BY THEIR MOST HUMBLE

AND MOST OBEDIENT SERVANT

JOHN REINOLD FORSTER.

Contents of the Observations

CHAPTER VI

Preface

The present performance has undergone so many changes in its form since my return from my voyage, that the public will excuse my delay in publishing it, and some of my friends, will I flatter myself, be able to judge, what considerable improvements it has received both from their friendly strictures, and my own meditation and reading. The subject I have treated is so varied, that I have been obliged to have recourse in many points to the Sages of every age: and I have either been instructed by them, or led by their hints to some new observations, or obliged to dissent from their opinions. In regard to the Physical Geography of our Globe I am much indebted to the Count de Buffon, and to the ingenious Chevalier Torbern Bergman; in regard to the Philosophical History of the Human Species, I have been often delighted with the ideas of that excellent Philosopher of Basle Mr. Isaac Iselin.[1] And the works of Dr. Blumenbach and Dr. John Hunter (the author of a Dissertation, *de hominum varietatibus*) have furnished me with some anatomical facts.[2] Besides these works I have consulted many others, and transferred into these observations several ideas which though analogous to mine, were however new to me, and some of my own I was much pleased to find had been already adopted by the most ingenious men of the age. My object was nature in its greatest extent; the Earth, the Sea, the Air, the Organic and Animated Creation, and more particularly that class of Beings to which we ourselves belong. The History of Mankind has often been attempted; many writers have described the manners and characters of individuals, but few have traced the history of men in general, considered as one large body. What is extant on that head in the French and English languages, contains either slight sketches and fragments, or systems formed in the closet or at least in the bosom of a nation highly civilized, and therefore in many respects degenerated from its original simplicity. None of these authors ever had the opportunity of contemplating mankind in this state, and its various stages from that of the most wretched savages, removed but in the first degree from absolute animality, to the more polished and civilized inhabitants of the Friendly and Society Isles. Facts are the basis of the whole structure, a few fair inferences enabled me to finish the whole. My aim has been instruction, and the investigation of truth, as far as lies in my power. I cannot expect to have satisfied every body. To receive the approbation of the good and learned will be my ambition. If proofs be brought that my opinions are not admissible, and if these arguments be communicated without rancour, I am open to conviction, and shall think myself much indebted to the man, who will be kind enough to convince me of my mistake in a friendly manner: if on the contrary, scurrility and abuse serve instead of arguments, the public will not, I hope, have a worse opinion of me for thinking such treatment beneath any resentment and unworthy of reply.

London, May the 30th, 1778

A Journal of the Voyage round the World in the Resolution[1]

JULY[2]

13.   His Majesty's sloops Resolution and Adventure sailed from Plymouth.
20.   Made the coast of Gallicia in Spain, between the Capes Prior and Ortiguera.
22.   Saw the light-house of Corunna.
23.   Passed three Spanish men of war, one of which insulted the British flag.
28.   Saw Porto-Santo and Madeira. — Anchored in the road of Funchal.

AUGUST

1.   In the evening, sailed from Madeira.
4.   Saw the Island of Palma, one of the Canaries.
5.   Saw the Isle of Ferro, another of the Canaries.
11.   Passed Bonavista, one of the Cape Verd Islands.
12.   Saw Mayo and San Jago, two of the Cape Verd Islands. — In the afternoon anchored in Porto-Praya, on the latter.
14.   Sailed from San Jago.

SEPTEMBER

9.   Crossed the equinoctial line.

OCTOBER

29.   Made the Cape of Good Hope.
30.   Anchored in Table Bay.

NOVEMBER

22.   Sailed from the Cape of Good Hope for the South.

DECEMBER

10.   Saw ice floating in the ocean the first time, being in 51° ± S. lat. and 21° ± E. long. from Greenwich.
14.   Saw great fields of ice, nearly in 55° S. and between 22° and 24° E.

JANUARY

2.   Our latitude about 59° S. and long. 9° 30′ E. We turn back to the Eastward.

17. Crossed the antarctic circle the first time, and advanced to 67° 10′ S. in 39° 40′ E.

FEBRUARY

2. In search of M. de Kerguelen's Land, we reach 48° 36′ S. and 60° ± E.

8. Lost company of the Adventure, for the first time, in a fog.

24. Saw field ice in about 62° S. and 95° E.

MARCH

25. Saw the coast of New Zealand, to the south of West Cape.

26. Anchored in Dusky Bay.

27. Removed into a cove called Pickersgill Harbour.

APRIL

29. Sailed out of that cove.

MAY

11. Cleared the North entrance of Dusky Bay.

17. Saw several water spouts in Cook's Strait.

18. Anchored in Queen Charlotte's Sound, where we rejoined the Adventure.

JUNE

7. Sailed from Queen Charlotte's Sound.

JULY

9. In lat. 43° ± S. and long. 146° ± W.

AUGUST

11. Discovered a new low island, which we called Resolution, in 17° 24′ S. and 141° 39′ W. — In the evening discovered another, which received the name of Doubtful Island, in 17° 20′ S. and 142° 38′ W.

12. Discovered a low island, which we named Furneaux Island, in 17° 5′ S. and 143° 16′ W.

13. Discovered a fourth, which we named Adventure Island, in 17° 4′ S. and 144° 30′ W. — Passed Chain Island in the afternoon.

15. Saw Maâtea, which captain Wallis calls Osnabruck Island, in 17° 48′ S. and 148° 10′ W. — In the evening saw Taheitee.

16. The Resolution struck on the coast of Taheitee, but was got off again.

17. Both ships anchored in Aitepèha harbour, in the lesser peninsula of Taheitee, named Tiarraboo.

24. Sailed from Aitepèha harbour.

25. Anchored in Matavaï Bay, on the greater peninsula of Taheitee, named Tobreonoo. Its North point, called Point Venus, is situated in 17° 29′ 15″ S. and 149° 35′ W.

SEPTEMBER

1. Sailed from Taheitee.

2.   Saw Huahine, one of the Society Islands.

3.   Saw Raietea, Tahà, and Borabora, three of the Society Islands; and anchored in Wharrè-harbour, on Huahine, in 16° 44′ S. and 151° 7′ W.

7.   Sailed from Huahine.

8.   Anchored in Hamaneno harbour, on Raietea, situated in 16° 45′ S. and 151° 34½′ W.

14.   Two boats were sent to the Isle of Tahà.

17.   We sailed from Raietea. — Passed by Borabora, in 16° 27′ S. and 151° 50′ W. also passed to the Southward of Mowrùa, in 16° 25′ S. and 152° 8′ W.

23.   Discovered a low island, which we named Hervey's Island in 19° 18′ S. and 158° 54′ W.

OCTOBER

2.   In the evening saw Eäoowhe, which Tasman calls Middleburg Island, which is about four leagues long; its middle lying in 21° 22′ S. and 174° 42′ W.

3.   Anchored in the road off its N.W. end.

4.   Sailed, and in the evening came to an anchor in Van Diemen's road, at the N.W. end of Tonga-Tabboo, the Amsterdam Island of Tasman, which is nearly twenty leagues in circuit, its middle being in 21° 11′ S. and 175° W.

7.   Sailed from Tonga-Tabboo.

8. } Saw Pylstaert Island in 22° 26′ S. 175° 59′ W.
10.

21.   Made the coast of New-Zeeland near Portland Island.

29.   Lost company of the Adventure a second time, and never rejoined her afterwards.

NOVEMBER

2.   Anchored in a bay under Cape Tra-Whittee on the North side of Cook's Strait.

3.   Anchored in Queen Charlotte's Sound the second time.

25.   Sailed from New Zeeland.

DECEMBER

6.   In the evening crossed the point of the Antipodes of London.

12.   Saw the first ice this season in 62° ± S. and between 172° and 173° W.

15.   Saw field-ice in 66° S. and 158° W.

20.   Crossed the antarctic circle, advancing a second time into the frigid zone in 147° 30′ W.

25.   Left the frigid zone in 135° W. after sailing upwards of 12° of longitude within it.

JANUARY

11.   Reached the latitude of 47° 51′ S. and longitude 122° 30′ ± W.

26. Crossed the antarctic circle again, and entered the frigid zone the third time in 109° 40′ W.

30. We were stopped by immense ice-fields in 71° 10′ 30″ S. and 107° ± W. that being the furthest point towards the South Pole which has hitherto been made.

FEBRUARY

22. ⎧ Went in quest of the supposed continent of Juan Fernandez, without
TO ⎨
25. ⎩ finding it, between 36° and 38° S. and between 94° and 101° W.

MARCH

11. Saw Easter Island, or Waihù, situated in 27° 5′ 30″ S. and in 109° 46′ 45″ W.

14. Anchored at its S. W. end.

16. Sailed from Easter Island.

APRIL

6. Discovered Hood's Island, a rock hitherto unknown, belonging to the cluster of islands called the Marquesas.

7. Saw Heevaroa, (la Dominica) Onateyo, (St. Pedro) and Waitahù, (St. Christina) three of the Marquesas. — In the evening anchored at Waitahù in Madre-de-Dios harbour, otherwise called Resolution-Bay, situated in 9° 55′ 30″ S. and 139° 8′ 40″ W.

10. Sailed from the Marquesas.
    Saw Mr. Byron's King George's Islands. — Landed on the Easternmost, called Teoukea, situated in 14° 28′ S. and 144° 56′ W. — Fell in with four low islands, which were named Palliser's Islands, their middle being in 15° 36′ S. and 146° 30′ W.

21. Saw the island Taheitee the second time. — Anchored at Matavaï Bay.

MAY

14. Sailed from Taheitee.

15. In the afternoon we anchored at Huahine, in Wharrè-harbour.

23. Sailed from Huahine towards Raietea.

24. Anchored in Hamaneno harbour.

JUNE

4. Sailed from the Society Islands.

6. Passed by Howe's Island, or Mopeehàh, in 16° 46′ S. and 154° 8′ W.

16. Passed a low island, unknown before, in 18° 4′ S. and 163° 10′ W. and called it Palmerstone's Island.

20. Saw an island in 19° 1′ S. and 109° 37′ W.

21. Landed upon it, and left it, calling it Savage Island.

25. Saw some of the islands belonging to the Archipelago of Namocka.

26.   Anchored on the lee-side of Namocka, (Rotterdam Island of Tas-man), which is about 5 leagues in circuit, situated in 20° 17′ S. and 174° 32′ W.

29.   Set sail from Namocka, and passed by the Friendly Islands adjacent.

30.   Passed through the strait between two high islands of small size, one called O-Ghào, and the other Tofoòa. The latter has a volcano, and lies in 19° 45′ S. and 174° 48′ W.

July

2.   Saw an island, and stood towards it.

3.   Passed by it, finding no anchorage, and called it Turtle Island. It lies in 19° 48′ S. and 178° 2′ W.

16.   Saw the islands of Whitsuntide and Aurora, discovered by Capt. Quiros, and visited by M. de Bougainville.

18.   Passed between M. de Bougainville's Pic de l'Averdi (or Pic de l'Etoile) and Aurora Island. The latter is about 12 leagues long, and 4 or 5 miles broad. Its middle lies nearly in 15° 06′ S. and 168° 24′ E. Came in sight of the Isle of Lepers, so called by M. de Bougainville.

20.   Passed between the Isle of Lepers and Aurora, towards Whitsuntide Island. The Isle of Lepers is found to be about 20 leagues in circuit, its middle lying in 15° 20′ S. and 168° 03′ E. Whitsuntide Island is about 12 leagues long, and about 6 miles broad, in the broadest part; the middle in 15° 45′ S. and 168° 28′ E.

21.   Saw an island to the South of Whitsuntide Island, which (as we after-wards learnt) the natives call Ambrrym. Its extent E. and W. or there-abouts is 7 leagues, and its circuit near 20. Its middle lies in 16° 15′ S. and 168° 20′ E.

    Soon after discovered another island to the West, of considerable extent, named Mallicollo, two others to the S.E. named Pa-oom and Apee, and another to the South, which was called Three-Hills Isle. In the afternoon anchored in Port Sandwich, on the isle of Mallicollo.

23.   Sailed from Mallicollo, in the morning. This island lies about N.N.W. and S.S.E. 20 leagues long, and about 55 in circuit. Its North point is in 15° 50′ S. and 167° 23′ E. and Port Sandwich near the S.E. end, is in 16° 28′ S. and 167° 56′ E.

    Left the Isle of Pa-oom to the N.E. of us in the afternoon; we remained dubious whether it does not consist of two islands, of which the Eastern-most is a high peak, situated in 16° 25′ S. and 168° 30′ E. The whole cir-cumference of the island does not exceed 5 leagues. The island of Apee, a little to the Southward of it, is about 7 leagues long, and its middle is in 16° 42′ S. and 168° 36′ E.

1774

24. In the morning ran close up to the Three-Hills Island, which is not above two leagues long, and lies in 17° 04' S. and 168° 32' E.

    In the afternoon examined some small isles off the S.E. end of Apee, which were called Shepherd's Isles.

25. Passed by a small island, which we called Two-Hills Island, to the South of Three-Hills, and saw a rock near it, which received the name of the Monument. In the evening we were becalmed near a large island, which we had discovered the day before.

26. Passed the new island in the afternoon, and called it Sandwich Island. Its middle is in 17° 45' S. and 168° 30' E. It lies nearly S.E. and N.W. and may measure 25 leagues in circuit. Two small islands, one to the East, the other to the North of it, were called Montagu and Hinchingbrook.

27. At day-break we discovered another new island to the S.S.E.

28. Discovered another still more to the S.E. and a great way further off.

AUGUST

1. Ran along the Western shore of the island discovered on the 27th of July, where we saw a harbour.

3. Anchored on the North side of this island, of which the middle lies in 18° 48' S. and 169° 20' E. Its circumference appears to be above 30 leagues.

4. Sailed from this island, which (as we afterwards learnt) the natives call Irromanga, and advanced towards the more Southerly one.

5. Anchored in a port on the new island, which has a volcano. The natives call their island Tanna; it lies in 19° 30' S. and 169° 38' E. Its circuit appears to be about 24 leagues.

20. Sailed from Tanna. A small low island, named Immer, lies a few leagues to the North of it; a high island, called Irronàn, lies about 12 leagues to the Eastward of it; and another, called Anattom, to the South-Eastward. This last is situated in 20° 3' S. and 170° 5' E. We stood to the North Westward, along the lee-side of the cluster of isles we had hitherto discovered, which were named the New Hebrides.

24. Having coasted the W. shore of Mallicollo, we sailed round its North point, through a passage already discovered by M. de Bougainville, and formed by another great island to the Northward, near which we saw several small isles, along the S. and E. coasts.

25. We entered a vast bay about 8 leagues deep, on the North end of the great island. It appeared to Captain Cook to be the same which Capt. Quiros has dedicated to St. Philip and St. James. Its West point, which we called Cape Cumberland, lies in 14° 38' S. and 166° 52' E. and the East point, named Cape Quiros, in 14° 55' S. and 167° 14' E.

27.   Sailed out of the bay of St. Philip and St. James, on Quiros's Tierra del Espiritù Santo.

31.   Left the Tierra del Espiritù Santo, after coasting its Western shore, down to Bougainville's Passage. The S.W. point of the land, or Cape Lisburne, lies in 15° 35′ S. and 167° E.

SEPTEMBER

4.   Discovered a very extensive tract of land, to which we gave the name of New Caledonia.

5.   Came to an anchor in a harbour on the North shore. A small island in the harbour, which we called Observatory Island, lies in 20° 15′ S. and 164° 40′ E.

13.   Sailed out of the harbour to the North Westward along the shore. The point we first fell in with or Cape Collnet, lies in 20° 30′ S. and 165° 02′ E. An island to the Westward, which the natives call Balabéa, about 12 miles in circuit, lies in 20° 06′ S. and 164° 18′ E.

16.   The Northernmost land, which looked like broken islands, lies nearly in 19° 37′ S. and 163° 40′ E. We sailed to the South Eastward again along the coast.

24.   Saw the Easternmost extremity of New Caledonia, which we called Queen Charlotte's Foreland, in 22° 15′ S. and 167° 15′ E. In the evening discovered another island, which we called the Isle of Pines. It is 15 or 18 leagues in circuit, and lies in 22° 40′ S. and 167° 40′ E.

29.   Came to an anchor under a small isle, which Capt. Cook called Botany Island, in 22° 28′ S. and 167° 16′ E. The Southernmost point of New Caledonia, which we called the Prince of Wales's Foreland lies in 22° 30′ S. and 166° 58′ E.

OCTOBER

1.   Cleared the reefs of New Caledonia at day break, and sailed to the Southward.

10.   Discovered a small island, on which we landed in the afternoon, and which we left in the evening. It was named Norfolk Island, and lies in 29° 2½′ S. and 168° 16′ E.

16.   In the evening saw the Coast of New Zeeland, near Mount Egmont.

18.   Anchored in Ship Cove, Queen Charlotte's Sound, the third time. This harbour is situated in 41° 6′ S. 174° 25′ 30″ E.

NOVEMBER

10.   Sailed from Queen Charlotte's Sound.

DECEMBER

18.   Made the coast of Tierra del Fuego near Cape Deseado, soon after midnight.

20.   Anchored in a spacious Sound, which we called Christmas Sound.

28.   Set sail from Christmas Sound. The West point of its entrance called York Minster, lies in 55° 30′ S. and 70° 28′ W.

29.   Passed Cape Horn in the morning, and found it situated in 55° 58′ S. and 67° 46′ W.

31.   Anchored under some small islands on the North side of Staten Land, after passing Strait le Maire. We called these isles New Year's Islands, situated in 54° 46′ S. 64° 30′ W.

JANUARY

3.   At day break sailed to the Southward.

14.   Saw land in the morning at a vast distance.

16.   Passed between two little islands at the N.W. end of this land. The passage was not above a league across. The Southermost was named Bird Island, the Northernmost, or Willis's Island, lies in 54° S. and 38° 25′ W.

17.   Landed in a bay, which we called Possession Bay, in 54° 15′ S. and 37° 15′ W.

19.   Reached the S. E. end of the new land, which was called the Isle of Georgia. A small island at the S. end lies in 54° 52′ S. and 35° 50′ W. and was called Cooper's Island. Some rocks to the South Eastward about 15 leagues off were called Clerke's rocks, and lie in 55° S. and 34° 50′ W.

23.   Very near being lost upon Clerke's rocks.

28.   Having crossed 60° S. we were stopped by field-ice.

31.   At seven o'clock saw very high land close to use, through the fog.

FEBRUARY

2.   Saw the Northernmost parts of this land, which was named Sandwich Land. Its Southernmost extreme, or Southern Thule, lies in 59° 30′ S. and 27° 30′ W. The point which we first fell in with, or Freezeland Peak, in 58° 55′ S. and 27° W. A sinuosity of the coast between Thule and Freezeland's Peak was called Forster's Bay. An island called Saunder's Island, in 57° 48′ S. and 26° 35′ W. and two other islands, called Candlemas Islands, in 57° 10′ S. and 27° 6′ W.

18.   Passed over the place, where M. des Loziers Bouvet, supposed to have seen land, which he called Cape Circumcision.

23.   Passed over the spot, where we had seen field-ice in December, 1772.

MARCH

18.   Made the coast of Africa, near Mossel-Bay.

22.   Anchored in Table-Bay, at the Cape of Good Hope.

APRIL

27.   Sailed from the Cape.

15. Saw the island of St. Helena, and anchored about midnight in James's Bay.
21. Set sail in company with the Dutton Indiaman.
28. Saw Ascension Island, and anchored in Cross Bay.
31. In the afternoon we sailed from Ascension.

JUNE

9. We saw and passed the isle of Fernando Noronha.

JULY

13. Saw the Azores, or Western Islands.
14. Anchored in Fayal Road.
19. At day-break set sail from Fayal.
20. Left the Azores.
29. Passed the Lizard; saw the Start, and Eddistone.
30. Anchored at Spithead.

OBSERVATIONS MADE DURING A VOYAGE ROUND THE WORLD

CHAPTER I

Remarks on the Earth and Lands; their Inequalities, Strata, and constituent Parts

INTER CRIMINA INGRATI ANIMI ET HOC DUXERIM, QUOD NATURAM EJUS (TERRAE) IGNORAMUS.
  Plin. *Hist. Nat.* lib. 2. c. 64[1]

SECTION I
Large Lands

The globe of the earth contains, as far as we know, three large masses of land. In the Eastern hemisphere we find first that mass, which is commonly called the *Old World*, and which comprehends three large parts, bearing the appellation of Continents, and distinguished by the names of *Europe, Asia,* and *Africa.* The next in size, and in the order of time, when it was made known to European nations, is situated in the Western hemisphere, and called *America.* The third large mass of land lies in the South-East part of our hemisphere, and its Eastern limits have been but lately ascertained by that indefatigable and intelligent navigator, Capt. *Cook,* in the year 1770. Its Western and Northern limits were first discovered in 1616 and the following years, by the Dutch navigators, when a noble spirit of discovery still animated the governors of their Indian settlements. Since that time it has been visited, and severally seen, by Dutch and English navigators, and the whole was called in 1644 *New-Holland,* from its first discoverers. Perhaps many will dissent from me, and refuse to call it a *Continent,* though it be little, if at all, inferior to Europe, to which no one has hitherto hesitated to give that name. It must be allowed, that New-Holland is at present the most backward of all the lands called Continents, in point of population, and utility to Europe; but this objection is of little weight, since it may perhaps, in future ages, become as populous as any of the other continents, and equally useful; as I believe it to be very likely to supply the wants of European colonies.

We know this land but imperfectly, and all our navigators seem to complain that it is deficient in fresh water and large rivers; but, had they properly and carefully examined its circuit, especially its South-Western shores, their enquiries would perhaps have been rewarded with success; for it is highly probable, that a land of so great extent contains high mountains in its interior parts; and wherever those are, there must be rivers. These would invite European settlers; especially such as would be willing to withdraw themselves from the oppressions of growing despotism in Europe.[2] To such sons of liberty this continent would offer a new and happy asylum: by which means it might become the seat of sciences and arts; happy in its cultivation, the riches of its productions, and the number of its inhabitants.

The rest of the lands, not comprehended under those now enumerated, are only islands. In our voyage we touched at the Cape of Good Hope in Africa: we saw only the last fragments of America along the coast of Tierra del Fuego, and besides these, our own continent from which we came, and to which we again returned. We have therefore nothing to say in particular relative to large lands, if we except a single remark, which we collected from the accounts of our friends on board the Adventure, who saw part of New-Holland in 1773. The Southernmost extremity of this continent has a great familiarity to all the Southern points and extremities of continents, and therefore appears black, rocky, and of considerable elevation*; though farther to the North, the country is even, and without any remarkably high hills, at least near the shores.

I pretend not to defend any particular hypothesis relative to the theory of the earth; but, if we cast our eyes on the two hemispheres of our globe, such as they are known since our last voyage, they seem to offer some curious particulars to our view.

All the remarkable Southern points of lands on our globe, have a great and striking similarity in regard to their conformation, and the situation of islands in their vicinity. They are all high and rocky; each seems to be the extremity of a range of high mountains running northward. All have to the eastward one or more large islands. Nay, if we continue the comparison, all continents have a great sinuosity on the west-side towards the north. So many coinciding circumstances seem, not to be merely accidental, but rather to proceed from one and the same general cause. I do not pretend to point out this first cause, but cannot help suspecting, that a violent flood coming from the south-west has produced this

* The Cape of Good Hope presents a high, bleak, and rocky point. Cape Comorin in India, and Cape Froward in America, are both of the same nature.

striking identity of conformation in these lands, though I can neither point out the time when this great revolution happened, nor assign any reason for its operating in this manner. It suffices to have mentioned the fact, and hinted at the next cause, without any ostentation.

America has the Andes running from the South to the North, and ending in Cape Froward, nay, extending even beyond the streight to Cape Horn. The sinuosity on its West-side is evident about the tropic of Capricorn, and to the East of its South-point are Tierra del Fuego, Staten Land, and the Falkland Islands.

Africa, on its West coast, has a great sinuosity to the North of the Line. The high rocks of its Southern extremity at the Cape of Good Hope are continued by a long range of high mountains running in the direction of North East from the Cape. Madagascar, and several small islands, are to the East or North-East of its Southern extremity.

Asia terminates at Cape Comorin in a high, rocky point, formed by the extremity of a chain of the mountains of Gatte: beyond *Cambaya,* towards the river *Sind,* there is a sinuosity similar to those already mentioned; and on the East-side of Cape Comorin is the island of Ceylon.

New-Holland has a high rocky point on its Southern extremity, which, according to the accounts of Tasman and our last navigators, seems to be continued in a series of mountains extending a good way up to the North. Whosoever casts a glance on Africa and New-Holland, must, upon the whole, be struck with the similarity of their general outlines; the sinuosity to the West being very remarkable in both: and Eastward of New-Holland are the two large islands, which form New-Zeeland.

SECTION II

Islands

All the islands which we saw during our voyage are either situated within the tropicks, or in the temperate zones. The Tropical Islands may be again divided into high and low.

The high Tropical Islands are either surrounded by reefs, and have flats near the sea-shore, or they are without reefs. Of the first kind are O-Taheitee with all the Society Isles and Maatea, the higher Friendly Isles Tongatabu, Eaoowe, Namocka, Turtle Island and new Caledonia.

Amongst the highest Tropical Isles without a reef, we reckon the Marquesas and all the new Hebrides, together with Savage Island; and Tofooa and Oghao among the Friendly Isles.

The Low Isles of which we have any knowledge, are Chain-Island and four other isles, which were perhaps seen by Mr. De Bougainville; also Tethuroa, Teoukea with four more called Palliser's Isle, Tupai, Mopeeha or Howe's Isles; Palmerstone's Isles, with Immer, one of the new Hebrides, and the Archipelago of the Low Friendly Islands.

These isles are so different from each other in their nature, that we cannot help at first sight observing the striking and material difference. The Low Isles are commonly narrow, low ledges of coral rocks, including in the middle a kind of lagoon and having here and there little sandy spots somewhat elevated above high-water mark, whereon coco nuts and a few other plants will thrive: the rest of the ledge of rocks is so low, that the sea frequently flows over it at high and sometimes at low water. Several of the larger isles of this kind are regularly inhabited; some are only resorted to, now and then by the inhabitants of the neighbouring high isles, for the purposes of fishing, fowling and turtling; and some others are absolutely uninhabited, though they are furnished with coco nut-trees and are often resorted to in great flocks by man of war birds, boobies, gulls, terns and some petrels.

The high islands of both kinds appear at a distance, like large hills in the midst of the ocean, and some of them are greatly elevated, so that their summits are seldom free from clouds. Those, which are surrounded by a reef and by a fertile plain, along the sea-shores, have commonly a more gentle slope; whereas the others are suddenly steep. It must be allowed, however, that the hills in some of the new Hebrides *viz.* Ambrrym, Sandwich Isle, Tanna and others have likewise in several places an easy ascent.

The islands seen by us in the South Sea in the temperate Southern zone, are Easter Island, Norfolk Island, and new Zeeland, and these are all high, and have no reef surrounding them. Norfolk Island is however situated upon a bank extending more than ten or twelve miles round it. New Zeeland as far as we had an opportunity of examining it, consists of very high hills, of which some in the very interior parts have summits almost always involved in clouds, or when free, shewing their snowy heads at more than twenty or thirty leagues distance. The lower hills of the same islands are almost every where covered with woods and forests, and none but the higher summits appear to be barren.

Tierra del Fuego as far as we could discover, appears to be a cluster of isles intersected by various deep sounds and channels. The land consists of craggy, bleak and steep rocks, whose summits are covered with eternal snow, especially in those interior parts which are less exposed to the mild and humid air of the sea. Its Easternmost side about the streights le Maire, has an easy slope, and is in some parts wooded. Staten Land has the same appearance as the barren part of Tierra del Fuego: nor was the snow wanting in the beginning of January or the very height of summer.

Southern Georgia is an isle of about eighty leagues in extent, consisting of high hills, none of which were free from snow in the middle of January, except a few rocks towards the sea: and the bottoms of all its harbours we found filled with ice.

The last land we saw in these cold, dismal regions we called *Sandwich Land,* and the Southernmost part of it, *Southern Thule*. All this land or cluster of isles, is full of ice and entirely covered with snow.

> . . . *Pigris ubi nulla campis*
> *Arbor aestiva recreatur aura:*
> *Quod latus mundi, nebulae, malusque*
> *Jupiter urget.*
> Hor. lib. i. od. XXII[1]

SECTION III

Strata

No soil appears on SOUTHERN GEORGIA, except in a few crevices of the rocks; all the rest is a ponderous slate which contains some irony particles, lies in horizontal strata or nearly so, and is here and there perpendicularly intersected by veins of quartz.

The rocks of *Tierra del Fuego* near the sea, are of the same nature and have on the higher parts, coarse granite rocks. (*Saxum*)

The Southern isle of NEW ZEELAND which we visited in two different places, is on its surface covered with a stratum of fine black light mould, formed of putrified mosses, deciduous leaves, and rotten trees (*humus daedalea & ruralis*, Linnaei.) This stratum is in some places about ten or twelve inches thick, but in general not so deep; under it we found an argillaceous substance nearly related to the class of talcous stones, which is turned into a kind of earth, by being exposed to the action of the sun, air, rain and frost, and is of various thickness: still deeper the same is indurated into stone, running in oblique strata dipping generally to the South: their hardness varies considerably, for some of the most indurated and compact will strike fire with steel. Their colour is generally a pale yellow, sometimes with a greenish hue. These strata are intersected perpendicularly or nearly so, by veins of white quartz (*quarzum lacteum* Linn.) and sometimes contain a green kind of stone of a lamellated structure, and nearly related to the talcous stones. On shingly beaches I have, though seldom, found a few black smooth stones of the flinty order, and some large detached pieces of a solid, ponderous, speckled grey or blackish green lava, employed by the natives to form their emittees, or weapons for close engagement. A few pumice-stones (*pumex vulcani* Linn.) were likewise collected on the shingly beaches of this isle: but whether they were thrown up by a volcano in the neighbourhood, or carried there from remote parts by the sea, I cannot determine. Among the fossil productions of this country, we must likewise reckon a green stone, which sometimes is opaque, and sometimes quite transparent, manufactured by the natives into hatchets, chissels, and ornaments, and seems to be of the nephritic kind (*talcum nephriticum* Linn.)

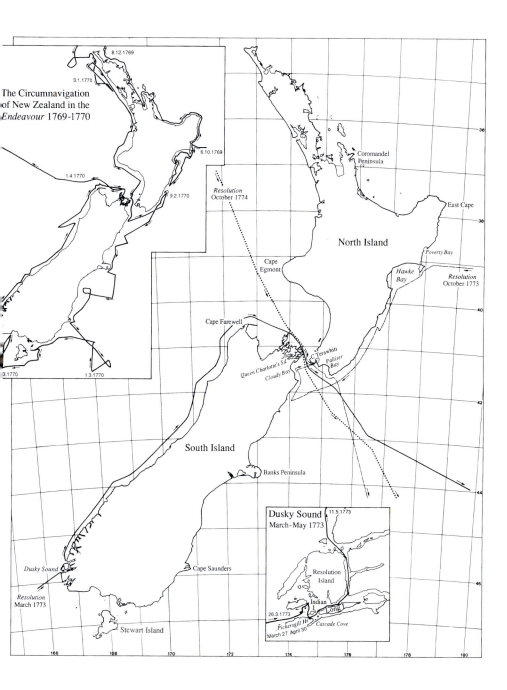

The Circumnavigation
of New Zealand in the
Endeavour 1769-1770

8.12.1769

3.1.1770

6.10.1769

1.4.1770

9.2.1770

Resolution
October 1774

3.1.1770

1.3.1770

Coromandel
Peninsula

East Cape

North Island

Poverty Bay

Cape
Egmont

Hawke
Bay

Resolution
October 1773

Cape Farewell

C. Terawhiti
Palliser
Bay

Queen Charlotte's Sd

Cloudy Bay

South Island

Banks Peninsula

Dusky Sound
March-May 1773

11.5.1773

Resolution
Island

Dusky Sound

Indian

Long

Cape Saunders

26.3.1773

Resolution
March 1773

Pickersgill Hr
March 27   April 30

Cascade Cove

Stewart Island

166   168   170   172   174   176   178   180

36

38

40

42

44

46

New Zealand

This stone is commonly brought by the natives from the interior parts of Queen Charlotte's Sound to the South West, in which direction they pointed. We asked for its native place, and they called it *Poënamoo*, from whence probably the abovementioned part of the country obtained the denomination of Tavai Poënamoo: but next to *Motoo-aroo*, on the little islet, where the natives formerly had one of their hippa's or strong holds, this stone is found in perpendicular or somewhat oblique veins, of about two inches thickness, in the above-mentioned strata of talcous greyish stone. The nephritic is seldom solid or in large pieces, for the greatest fragments we saw, never exceeded twelve or fifteen inches in breadth, and about two inches in thickness. On the shores we commonly met with a blueish grey, argillaceous slate of a lamellated structure, easily crumbling to pieces, when exposed to the weather: sometimes this slate is more solid, ponderous, and of a darker colour, probably on account of some metallic irony particles, which I suppose it to contain. The fragments of this slate scattered on the beach our seamen call *shingle*. We found in NORFOLK ISLAND almost the same strata as in New Zeeland, and also red and yellow fragments of a spungy lava: this island likewise contains the same plants and birds.

EASTER ISLAND has strongly the appearance of a land that has lately undergone a great alteration by fire. All its rocks look black, burnt and cavernous, resembling slags or dross. The soil is a reddish brown, dusty mould, as if it had been burnt, and might with justice be deemed a kind of *Puzzolana*,* spread with innumerable fragments of *tarras stone*, some rocks which I saw were of a brown or reddish ochreous volcanic tufa,† (*tophus tubalcaini* Linn.) full of caverns, and some ferrugineous particles. Of this substance the gigantic statues of Easter Island are formed, and therefore they cannot be of very remote antiquity, as the stone is of an extremely perishable nature. On the South side of the isle, the whole cliff towards the sea for more than a quarter of a mile consists of solid ponderous rock of a honeycombed slag or lava, which may be expected to yield some portions of iron. Besides these, we saw several black glassy stones, which to mineralogists are known by the name of black agate (*pumex vitreus* Linn.) found in Iceland,‡ near the Vesuvio in Italy,* the Mongibello in Sicily, and on the Isle of Ascension;✦ in short in all the neighbourhoods of volcanos. We observed likewise a stony, light, spungy kind of lava, of a whitish grey colour.

THE MARQUESAS have a rocky shore, consisting of indurated clay; a ponder-

---

* See Ferber's *travels through Italy*, translated by Mr. Raspe, p. 130.
† See Ferber's *travels*, p. 128.
‡ Ferber's *travels*, p. 158. Mr. Raspe's note.
* Ferber's *travels*, p. 157.
✦ Cronsted's *mineralogy*, sect. 295. p. 269.

ous, solid slate, of a blueish grey colour, containing some iron particles; and lastly a stony lava, which is either grey, spungy with lamellated, vitreous, pentagonal or hexagonal sherl, of a brownish and in some of a greenish, or of a blackish colour, with brownish and sometimes white starlike or radiated sherl. The surface of the soil is a clay mixed with mould, which the natives manure with shells. Under this mould is an earthy argillaceous substance, mixed with tarras and puzzolana. As we staid but a few days here, we had not much time to examine the higher parts of the isle.

O-Taheitee and all the Society Isles are no doubt of the same nature. Their shores are coral rock extending from the reef encircling these isles to the very high-water mark. There begins the sand, formed in some places from small shells, and rubbed pieces of coral rock; but in others the shores are covered by a blackish kind of sand, consisting of the former sort mixed with black, sometimes shining and glittering particles of coarse daze or glist (*Mica*) and here and there some particles of refractory iron ores called in England Shim (*ferrum micaceum*, Linn.) and Kall (*molybdaenum spuma lupi*, Linn.) The plains from the shores to the foot of the hills, are covered with a very fine thick stratum of black mould, mixed with the above-mentioned kind of sand, and when the natives cultivate some spots for raising the inebriating pepper plant (*piper methysticum*) or the cloth plant (*morus papyrifera*) they often use shells as a kind of manure. The first and lower range of hills are commonly formed of a red ochreous earth (*ochra martis* Linn.) sometimes so intensely red, that the natives use it to paint their canoes and cloth: and in this earth I found here and there pieces, as I believe of the osteocella (*tophus osteocolla* Linn.) The higher hills consist of a hard, compact, and stiff clayey substance, which in the strata that are out of the reach of sun, air and rain, are hardened into a stone. There are at the top of the valleys, along the banks of the rivers, large masses of coarse granite stones (*saxum*) of various mixtures, and at a place of the same nature, near a cascade formed by the river *Matavai*, there are pillars of a grey, solid basaltes, (*nitrum basaltinum* Linn.) and here and there I saw fragments of black solid basaltes or paragone, which the natives commonly employ to make their paste beaters, hatchets, chissels and cutting tools. At *O-Aite-peha* the natives brought me on board a kind of pyrites having the exact form of a stalactite, or of a substance that had been melted and congealed while running down. The existence of sulphureous pyrites confirms the account I was favoured with by the learned and ingenious Dr. Casimiro Gomez Ortega, F.R.S. the King of Spain's Botanist, and Intendant of the botanical garden at Madrid, intimating that the Spanish men of war, which had been at O-Taheitee, brought from thence a large mass of the finest crystalline transparent native sulphur, now placed in the royal cabinet of natural history at Madrid. At the top of the numerous valleys, which intersect these isles, are large, rocky masses, black and cavernous, full of various white and other specks of sherl, in a word, real lava. There is likewise a grey, stalactitic, porous lava to be met with, which contains black sherls, and lastly we found an argillaceous, lamellated iron stone of a dull reddish brown colour.

The FRIENDLY ISLANDS have, in my opinion, the same soil as the Society Isles; with this difference only, that they are not so high or so rocky as the latter. When we came to A-*Namocka* in the year 1774, we saw on the isle of Tofoòa a smoke in the morning, which appeared fiery at night. When we passed between it and O-Ghào, we observed great clouds of smoke rising from the middle of the isle, attended with a smell similar to that produced by burnt turf; some particles filled the atmosphere, and fell down on the ship, and coming in contact with the eye, occasioned an acute pain. On the North side of the isle we saw a large place with the evident appearance of being lately burnt by fire. On the shores of A-Namocka, pumice-stones were frequently thrown up by the sea. The natives of all these isles used likewise pieces of black, solid basaltes for hatchets and tools, as in the Society Isles. Among the fishing implements of these islanders, we found conic pieces of calcareous stone; but we could not determine whether they were made of spar, or of coral-rock: though I am inclined to believe these cones to be a kind of sparry substance.

The soil of the NEW-HEBRIDES seems to be very much of the same kind with that in the above islands.

At MALLICOLLO, it appeared to consist rather of a yellowish clay, mixed with common sand. The rocks along the sea-shore, are formed of corals and madrepores; and higher up of an indurated clay. The isle of AMBRRYM has certainly one, if not two, volcanos; and we found pumice-stones on the opposite shores of Mallicollo. IRROMANGA we saw only at a distance, and it seemed to be much of the same nature with the former isles. TANNA has on its shores coral rocks and madrepores: the beaches are covered with a blackish sand, consisting of minute pieces of sherl and pumice-stone, which are formed by the ashes constantly thrown up by a volcano, and scattered over the whole surface of the island. (*Pumex cinerarius*, Linn.) The surface of the whole isle consists therefore of this pumice-sand mixed with a black mould formed by the putrified vegetables. The pumice-sand is very abundant; for there is at certain times, several leagues distant from the volcano, not a leaf of any tree or plant, nor any grass, which is not entirely covered with ashes, which I examined, and found to be this very pumice-sand: however, this forms a most admirable ashy, fertile soil, in which all vegetables thrive with the greatest luxuriance. We found a few single detached rock-stones; being a mixture of quartz and black daze or mica; nay, one of these pieces was a coarse dissolved granite, covered with black button-ore, which is a sort of iron-ore.

The chief strata of the isle, as far as I could form a judgment of them, from the various cliffs surrounding the harbour, are of a clay mixed with aluminous earth, interspersed with lumps of pure chalk. The strata of the clay are about six inches more or less, deviating very little from the horizontal line. In a few places I found a soft, blackish sand-stone, composed of the ashes spread by the volcano, and some parts of clay. Here and there I observed a substance commonly called *rotten-stone*, which is a brown clayey tripoli; and, between the rotten-stone and the above-mentioned sand-stone, is a stratum containing both mixed together. High on the sides of the hills towards the volcano, I found a whitish, argillaceous substance, through which aqueous and sulphureous steams, from the very neighbourhood of the volcano, were continually rising, and made the place intensely hot: its taste is styptic, and I believe aluminous*. Some native sulphur was to be seen in this earth, together with several green specks or marks of copper. Under these solfataras (which, at each eruption from the volcano, emitted greater quantities of hot steams), are several hot wells, close to the high-water mark, which, however, seem not to be in the least sulphureous. I found likewise, in the vicinity of the hot steaming places or solfataras, a red ochre, or vitriolic earth, similar to the *colcothar vitrioli*, used by the natives for painting their faces. Everywhere in the isle we met with pumice-stones of purple, black, and white colour, and of different specific gravity. On the South-side of the isle is a cliff, in which I found several pieces of lava, some of which were black and solid, others porous and filled with greenish and white sherl crystals; others were grey and porous, containing yellow and black sherl. Besides these, we found a reddish lava or tarras, very light and similar to a pumice-stone. On the shores were calcareous *tophi* to be met with, containing several *nidi* of *pholades*.

---

* All the neighbourhood of the solfataras in Tanna contains volcanic productions. The stones near it are lavas; the sand consists of volcanic ashes, and the soil is clay mixed with this sand. It is therefore beyond any doubt, that the clayey white substance, found in the very spiraculum, is nothing but a new modification of the volcanic productions. The first who ever had this idea, that clays are produced by an operation of the vitriolic acid vitrescent or vitrified substances, is the ingenious Mr. *Beaumé*, who founded it on a series of experiments. But the very first, who applied this idea to the great operations of nature in the solfataras, is Mr. *Ferber*, the most intelligent, and most accurate mineralogical writer of this age, which may be seen more at large in his xith letter, dated February 17, 1772, published in his *Travels through Italy*, translated by Mr. *Raspe*. Sir William Hamilton, that indefatigable observer of volcanos, had already examined the solfatara in 1771; but he seems, at that time, not to have had the least intimation of this remarkable process; since, in his letter to Dr. Maty, dated March 5, 1771, he calls the operation going forward at the solfatara a *calcination*: and he mentions to *have seen half of a large piece of lava perfectly* CALCINED, *while the other half, out of the reach of the vapours, has been untouched; and in four pieces, the centre seems to be already converted into* TRUE MARBLE. These whitish clays *might, even by their appearance*, says Mr. Ferber, p. 165, *be mistaken for lime-stone*; no wonder, therefore, that they should suggest the idea of CALCINATION and of TRUE MARBLE.

The neighbouring isle of ANATTOM, I suppose to contain likewise volcanic productions, as well as Tanna, because the natives of the latter had hatchets of black, solid basaltes or paragone, and said they came from *Anattom*, to distinguish them from hatchets made of a white shell, and which came from the isle of *Immer:*[1] the first kind they called *Pahà-bìttas*, and the latter *Pahà-bùshan*. To our iron hatchets they gave the first name.

NEW-CALEDONIA, and its adjacent isles, are surrounded by a reef of coral rocks and madrepores. The shores consist of shell-sand and particles of quartz. The soil is, in the plains, a black mould mixed with the above sand, and when watered and cultivated, very fertile. The sides of the hills, which I visited, are composed of a yellow ochreous clay, richly spangled with small particles of cat-silver, or a whitish kind of daze. (*Mica argentea.* Linn.) The higher parts of the hills consist of a stone, called by the German miners *gestell-stein*, composed of quartz and great lumps of the above cat-silver (*Saxum quarzo & mica argentea compositum.*) The cat-silver is sometimes of an intensely red or orange colour, by means of an iron-ochre. To the West of our anchoring-place, near the shore, are large, extremely hard masses of a blackish-green horn-stone, (*talcum corneum.* Linn.) full of small pieces of garnets, of the size of a pin's head. (*Saxum corneum, granatis mixtum.*) In several places, fragments of white and very transparent quartz, sometimes tinged red in the cracks, are found scattered: these stones the natives contrive to break in such a manner, that a sharp edge is produced, and use them to cut their hair. The natives carry stones for their slings in small bags. These stones are of an oblong roundish figure, and pointed at both ends, consisting of a kind of soap-rock or smectites. Besides these, we met with some coarse, fibrous, greenish asbestos.

If I except the coral rocks and madrepores, which form the shores of a great many of these isles, I cannot say, that I met with a single petrefaction of any denomination, in all the isles we visited in the course of our expedition.

From the above account it appears, I think, evidently, that all the tropical high isles of the South-Sea have been subject to the action of volcanos. This is strongly confirmed by the actual ignivomous[2] mountains, which we observed at Tofoòa, Ambrrym, and Tanna.

Pyritical and sulphureous substances, together with a few iron-stones and some vestiges of copper, are no doubt found in several of them: but the mountains of New-Caledonia are the most likely to contain the richest metallic veins; and the same opinion, I suspect, may be formed of the mountains in New Zeeland. For the metallic substances, in all the other volcanic isles are probably destroyed and scorified by the violence of the subterraneous fire: those in New-Caledonia and New-Zeeland seem to be as yet undisturbed, as the species of fossils prevailing in these two isles are substances, which mineralogists have hitherto looked upon as primogenial, in which all the metallic veins* on our globe are constantly found. We can offer nothing besides this general, but probable, conjecture; as our short stay, and the multiplicity of other business, prevented us from enquiring more minutely into the nature of the fossil productions of these isles.

* I speak of veins only, and not of flatt-work or floors, which contain likewise sometimes metallic ores, but have an origin different from that of the primogenial mountains.

SECTION IV

Mountains

If we examine the isles, visited by us in the different seas, which we navigated, it will appear, that they all ought to be considered as a range of submarine mountains: for, if the bottom of the sea is to be looked upon as land, these isles certainly are elevations or rising grounds; and therefore, as they are so near one another, and lying in the same direction, they can be nothing but chains of mountains. I will at present, therefore, only give an idea of the various ranges of these submarine elevations, which fall under the above description.

When we were at the Cape of Good Hope, in November, 1772, we were informed, that the French had discovered some land in the Southern Indian ocean, about the meridian of Mauritius, and the latitude of 48° South. After having gone beyond the antarctic circle, we hauled up towards the above situation, and found no land; but, from all concurring circumstances, it was highly probably, that we had been at no great distance from it. At our return to the Cape in March, 1775, we found there Capt. Crozet, who had made a voyage on discovery with the unfortunate Capt. Marion,[1] and had found several small isles and a large one, all lying in a direction from West to East, or nearly so: these isles, and those seen by Mr. de Kerguelen, are expressed in a chart published under the patronage of the Duc de Croy, by Robert de Vaugondy.[2] Though we had not the good luck to fall in with them, we have, however, no reasons to disbelieve their existence; and probably their situation will be ascertained by that able and indefatigable navigator, Capt. Cook, in the expedition in which he at present is employed. These isles seem to be a series or chain of submarine mountains, running nearly from West to East. The lands, visited by us and others, in the Southern parts of the Atlantic ocean, are Sandwich Land, South-Georgia, Falkland Islands, and Staten Land, together with the broken lands belonging to Tierra del Fuego, and these form another chain of submarine mountains, lying almost in the same direction with the former. The low isles to the East of O-Taheitee, with the Society Isles, the Friendly Isles, the New-Hebrides, and New-Caledonia, together with the intermediate isles of Scilly, Howe, Palliser, Palmerstone, Savage, and Turtle-Island, as well as the isles of Hope and Cocos, Capt. Carteret's Queen Charlotte-Isles, and several more, as far as New-Hibernia, New-Britain, and New-Guinea, are one great chain of submarine mountains; extending through an immense space, or three-fourths of the whole South-Sea.

Norfolk-Island, and New-Zeeland, seem to belong to a range of mountains branching out from the great chain, and running from North to South. If we consider this direction of isles or submarine mountains, it should seem they were designed to give greater solidity and strength to the compages of our globe.

The next circumstance relative to the mountains is their HEIGHT. The highest of all the mountains, which we saw in the course of this voyage, is, in my opinion, Mount Egmont, on the Northern isle of New-Zeeland, whose summit was covered with snow a great way down, and almost constantly capt with clouds; though at intervals we saw its top very distinctly.

In France, in about 46° of North latitude, the line of eternal snow is found at the height of about 3280 or 3400 yards above the level of the sea. On the Pico de Teyde, on the isle of Teneriffe, in about 28° of North latitude, the snow is to be met with at the height of 4472 yards. Mount Egment is very nearly in 39° of South latitude: but, as we constantly found, that in Southern latitudes the cold is much more intense than in the corresponding degrees of the Northern hemi-

William Hodges, *In Dusky Bay, New Zealand*, wash and watercolor, 1773. 382 × 543 mm. State Library of New South Wales.

sphere, I will suppose the climate of Mount Egmont equal to that of France, and therefore the line of snow to be at the height of 3280 yards; and, as the snow seemed to occupy one third of its height, the mountain will be 4920 yards high, or 14,760 feet, which is somewhat less than Dr. Heberden[3] found the Pico of the isle of Teneriffe* to be. The summits of the other mountains, in the interior parts of New-Zeeland, both in Queen Charlotte's Sound and in Dusky Bay we found constantly covered a good way down with eternal snow.

We observed these snow capt heads all the way along, when we sailed from Dusky Bay to Queen Charlotte's Sound in May, in the year 1773, and we took notice of the same circumstance in the same year in October, on the other side of the Southern isle, when contrary storms brought us a good way along its South East shore, almost as far as Banks's Island. This I believe, sufficiently proves, that these mountains form, as it were, one continued chain, running throughout the whole Southern Isle, and that they are little inferior in height to twelve or fourteen thousand feet. This long series of mountains, running in the same direction, gives room for a probable conjecture, that the metallic veins, which in all likelihood are to be met within the mountains of New Zeeland, are of a very rich and valuable nature.

The hills of *Tierra del Fuego, Staten Land, South Georgia,* and *Sandwich Land* are constantly covered with snow; however, in the two first only the summits of the hills had snow, but in the latter the snow and ice reached in most places to the very edge of the sea, in the midst of their summer; which certainly proves the extreme rigour of the climate, as the line of eternal snow comes down so low. What is still more remarkable, this happened in isles surrounded by the moist and therefore mild sea air, which undoubtedly weakens the intenseness of the frost, and commonly mitigates the rigour of the climate.

The mountain in the middle of the great peninsula of O-Taheitee or of Tobreonoo, is as far as I can form any idea, the highest of all the mountains in the Tropical Isles: it is in some places of an easy and gentle slope, and intersected by numerous and very deep valleys, converging towards the middle of the isle, where

---

* The Chevalier DE BORDA has in August, 1776, measured the height of the Peak of Teneriffe, and found it to be 1931 French toises = 12,340 English feet, and very near the same quantity he obtained by trigonometrical measurement. Dr. Heberden's operations gave 15,396 English feet as the height of the Peak of Teneriffe. *Phil. Trans.* vol. xlvii. p. 356. The same Dr. Heberden remarks there that the *Sugar-loaf,* or *la Pericosa, is an eighth part of a league to the top,* and that it is *covered with snow the greatest part of the year.* Deducting, therefore, 1980 feet = to one eighth part of a league, from 15,396 feet, the total for the height of the Peak according to Dr. Heberden, there remain 13,416 feet = 4472 yards, to the line of snow. Or, if these 1980 feet be deducted from 12,340, or the height according to the Chev. BORDA, there remain 10,360 feet = 3453 yards, as the line of snow in about 28° and some odd minutes North latitude.

its summits are to be met with. The highest point of this hill is at a very just estimate, about seven miles from Point Venus. According to Captain Cook's map, it
seems to be nine miles distant from thence; but as I have been twice up to this
hill, I rather think the distance in the map to be too great; and the more so, as the
valley, wherein Matavai-river runs, scarcely extends at its very extremity to more
than six miles, and this valley is almost at the same distance from the sea, with
the highest part of the hill. Mr. Wales our Astronomer took from his observatory
on Point Venus the height of the hill, by the astronomical quadrants, and found it
to be exactly 15° above the level of the sea; for the observatory is but a few feet
above that level. If we allow these premises to be right, it will follow from a trigonometrical calculation, that this hill is 9565 feet high.*

The little Peninsula of O-Taheitee or Téarraboo, has likewise hills towards
its centre, but their summits are so steep, so craggy and so like spires in some
instances, that the sight of these convinces the beholder, that they have undergone a great convulsion from violent causes, and especially subterraneous fire.
The hills in all the other Tropical Isles are very moderate, and at least one third
less than those of Tobreonoo. Though they be high enough to attract the clouds,
and often to have their summits involved in them, they are however far removed
from the line of eternal snow, which in Peru under the line, was found to be at
5,340 yard above the ocean. These observations on the difference of the line of
eternal snow, give us an opportunity of communicating some hints or conjectures
on the causes of this difference. *First* it appears that the beams of the sun falling
more vertical on the earth, cause a greater degree of heat, and in proportion as
they fall in a more oblique direction, they produce less warmth: *secondly* the
nearer to the general level of the earth, the more is the atmosphere heated, probably the beams being there reflected from the unequal surface of the earth, and
crossing one another in various directions cause greater warmth; and moreover
the atmosphere being denser and more filled with vapours near the common level
of the earth, when once warmed to a certain degree, preserves the heat for a
longer time.† The contrary must take place in a situation more remote from the
common level of the earth, where the atmosphere is thinner and less capable of
retaining the warmth. These two principles will contribute to explain the phenomenon. Under the tropicks, the atmosphere and surface of the earth is more
heated than towards the poles, because the sun operates at the first place more

---

* If the effect of refraction be taken into the account, then the height will be 9530 feet; If nine
miles distant, then the hill is 12,250 feet high.
† Inferiora quoque tepent, primum terrarum halitu, qui multum secum calidi affert, deinde quia radii
solis replicantur & quousque redire potuerunt, replicato calore benignius fovent. Seneca *Nat.
Quaest.* l. 2. c. X.[4]

MOUNTAINS

vertically, and at the other more obliquely, and therefore less effectually: the hills being under the line in a more heated atmosphere, the line of eternal snow, is there naturally more removed from the common level of the earth, than towards the poles, where the air is neither so intensely nor so constantly heated, which consequently brings the line of eternal snow much lower.

The atmosphere being a fluid environing our globe, must consequently be subject to all the laws of nature to which the whole globe is subject. As the power of gravity near the equinoctial line is known to be less than towards the poles, the atmosphere naturally must be less attracted between the tropicks than beyond them; and consequently being besides more heated and therefore more rarefied, it must extend to a greater height between the tropicks; and probably this may contribute, with the before mentioned causes, towards removing there the line of eternal snow to a greater distance from the common level of the earth.

The probable causes, of the Southern hemisphere being colder in corresponding degrees of latitude, than the Northern hemisphere, shall be explained in the section, wherein we speak of the formation of ice.

SECTION V

Formation of Soil

The TROPICAL ISLES have all the appearance of a long existence and fertility. But the Southernmost parts of NEW-ZEELAND, TIERRA DEL FUEGO, STATEN-LAND, SOUTHERN-GEORGIA and SANDWICH-LAND are still unimproved, and in that rude state in which they sprung up from the first chaos; with this distinction, that the farther you proceed towards the line and the climates capable of being assisted by the benevolent influence of the sun, the greater advances you discover towards improvement and fertility.[1]

All the various particles of mineral bodies whatsoever are dead, and only the organic bodies of vegetables and animals are capable of life. Wherever we meet the first only, there nature has all the appearance of barrenness, the horrors of desolation and silence of death. But the least addition of vegetation enlivens the scene, and even the slow motions of unwieldy and torpid seals and grave pinguins on the shore, infuse life and chearfulness into the beholder. But when the surface of a land is clad with plants and diversified with birds and animals, then first we have an idea of the vivifying powers of nature and its great Lord. This previous observation therefore, will enable us to form a just idea of each of the above unimproved, rude lands. The barren bleak rocks of SANDWICH-LAND seem not to be covered by the least atom of mould, nor is there any vestige of vegetation to be seen: immense loads of eternal snow, bury these barren rocks, *as if doomed to be under the curse of nature, and continual fogs involve it in perpetual darkness.* *

SOUTHERN-GEORGIA has on its North West point a little isle which is covered with greens, and in Possession Bay we saw two rocks, where nature has just begun her great work, in producing organic vegetable bodies, and in forming a thin coat of soil, on the tops of barren cliffs; and so sparing was she of these her presents, that no more than two plants would vegetate here, the one a grass (*Dactylis glomerata*) and the other a kind of burnet (*Sanguisorba.*)

---

* Pliny's words, *Hist. Nat.* l. 4. seem therefore to be best applicable to this miserible land: *pars mundi damnata a rerum natura & eterna mersa caligine.*[2]

FORMATION OF
SOIL

To Tierra del Fuego, the next land to the Westward, I will join *Staten-Land* on account of the great similarity they bear to each other, in the general face of the country. In the cavities and crevices of the huge piles of rocks forming these lands, where a little moisture is preserved by its situation, and where from the continued friction of the loose pieces of rocks, washed and hurried down the steep sides of the rocky masses, a few minute particles, form a kind of sand; there in the stagnant water gradually spring up, a few algaceous plants from seeds carried thither on the feet, plumage, and bills of birds: these plants form at the end of each season a few atoms of mould, which yearly increases: the birds, the sea, or the wind carries from a neighbouring isle, the seeds of some of the mossy plants to this little mould, and they vegetate in it during the proper season. Though these plants be not absolute mosses, they are however nearly related to them in their habit: we reckon among them the Ixia *pumila*; a new plant which we called Donatia, a small Melanthium, a minute Oxalis and Calendula, another little dioicous plant, called by us Phyllachne, together with the Mniarum*. These plants, or the greater part of them, have a peculiar growth, particularly adapted to these regions, and fit for forming soil and mould on barren rocks. In proportion as they grow up, they spread into various stems and branches, which lies as close together as possible: they spread new seeds, and at last a large spot is covered; the lowermost fibres, roots, stalks and leaves gradually decay and push forth on the top new verdant leaves: the decaying lower parts form a kind of peat or turf, which gradually changes into mould and soil. The close texture of these plants, hinders the moisture below from evaporating, and thus furnishes nutriment to the vegetation above, and clothes at last whole hills and isles with a constant verdure. Among these pumilous plants, some of a greater stature begin to thrive, without in the least prejudicing the growth of these creators of mould and soil. Among these plants we reckon a small Arbutus, a diminutive myrtle, a little dandelion, a small creeping Crassula, the common Pinguicula *alpina*, a yellow variety of the Viola *palustris*, the Statice *armeria*, or sea pink, a kind of burnet, the Ranunculus *lapponicus*, the Holcus *odoratus*, the common celery, with the Arabis *heterophylla*. Soon after we observed in places that are still covered with the above-mentioned mossy plant, a new rush (Juncus *triglumis*) a fine Amellus, a most beautiful scarlet Chelone, and lastly, even shrubby plants, *viz.* a scarlet flowered, shrubby plant of a new genus, which we called Embothrium *coccineum*; two new kinds of berberis, (Berberis *ilicifolia & mitior*;) an arbutus with cuspidated leaves (Arbutus

_____

* See Forster. *Nova Genera Plantarum*.

mucronata) and lastly the tree bearing the Winter's bark (DRIMYS *winteri*) which however in these rocky barren parts of Tierra del Fuego never exceeds the size of a tolerable shrub; whereas in Success Bay, on a gentle sloping ground, in a rich and deep soil it grows to the size of the largest timber. The falling leaves, the rotting mossy plants, and various other circumstances increase the mould and form a deeper soil, more and more capable of bearing larger plants. Thus they all enlarge the vegetable system and rescue new animated parts of the creation from their inactive, chaotic state.

I cannot pass over in silence the peculiar growth of one species of grass on New Year's Isle, near Staten Land, and which we likewise observed at South-Georgia: it is the well-known *Dactylis glomerata*, or one of its varieties. This grass is perennial, and bears the rigours of the coldest winters: it grows always in tufts or bunches, at some distance from each other. Every year the shoots form, as it were, a new head, and enlarge the growth of the bunch, till at last you see these bunches of the height of four or five feet, and at the top two or three times broader than at the bottom. The leaves and stalks of the grass are strong, and often three or four feet long. Under these tufts the ursine seals and pinguins take shelter; and, as they come so often dripping out of the sea, they make the lanes between the tufts extremely dirty and muddy, so that a man cannot walk, except on the tops of the tufts. In other places the shags (*Pelecanus carunculatus*) take possession of these tufts, and make their nests on them; so that by this grass, and the excrements of seals, pinguins, and shags, the soil of the country gradually becomes more and more elevated.

In the Southern parts of New Zeeland we find the formation of mould and soil much more forward, because its climate is milder, the summer longer, and vegetation more quick and strong: but, upon the whole, we observe the same analogy in its origin. All sorts of ferns and of small mossy plants, especially the MNIARUM, occupy large spots; which, by their continual spreading and yearly decay, increase the mould, and thus form a soil for the reception of numerous shrubs. Their foliage every year putrifies, and accumulates the precious treasure of fertile mould, in which at last the largest trees grow to an immense extent and bulk; till, decaying by old age, a violent, impetuous storm breaks them down; and they, in their fall, crush numberless bushes and shrubs, that pass together into a state of putrefaction, and afford space and nutriment for a whole generation of young trees, which must in their turn decay, to make room for others.[3] All this seeming scene of destruction and confusion is one of the oeconomical actions of nature, thus hoarding up a precious quantity of the richest mould, for a future generation of men, who, one day or other, will live upon the rich products of this treasured soil.

FORMATION OF
SOIL

Terra nos nascentes excipit, natos alit, semelque editos sustinet semper: novissime complexa gremio, jam a reliqua natura abdicatos, tum maxime ut mater operiens—Benigna, mitis, indulgens ususque mortalium semper ancilla, quae coacta generat, quae sponte fundit! quos odores, saporesque! quos succos! quos tactus! quos colores! quam bona fide creditum foenus reddit! quae nostri causa alit!
    PLIN. *Hist. Nat.* lib. 2. c. lxiii[4]

CHAPTER II

Remarks on Water and the Ocean

[AQUA.] HOC ELEMENTUM CAETERIS OMNIBUS IMPERAT.
  Plin. *Hist. Nat.* lib. 31. c. 5[1]

SECTION I

Springs

In the SOCIETY ISLES we found very copious springs, of the most limpid, cool, and fine water; one of them especially, in O-RAYETEA, might vie with Horace's *Fons Blandusiae*.[2] The natives had enlarged it to a fine reservoir, surrounded by large stones, in a rustic manner, blended with pleasing simplicity. Some groups of the finest trees and flowering shrubs, together with the impending venerable rocks from whence the water issued, involved it in a constant shade, and preserved a delicious coolness. The chrystalline stream, constantly running from the reservoir, the verdure of the trees and environs, invited the traveller, in these hot regions, to a refreshing ablution of his wearied limbs, from which he rose with new vigour to support the sultriness of the climate, and to go chearfully through the duties of life.

In TANNA we discovered on the side of the harbour towards the Volcano, several hot springs, called by the natives *Doogòos*. The water came out of the black stratum of sand-stone mentioned before, close to the edge of the sea; and at high-water the wells were sometimes covered by the sea.

We saw several of these hot springs near each other; and, as there were little cavities under them, we cleared them of the rubbish, and after the water had filled the cavities and overflowed for some time, I took my portable thermometer, with Fahrenheit's scale, made by Mr. Ramsden,[3] (which had been that day, in my cabin, at 78° and which, having been carried close to my body in a pocket,

I found at 80°,) and having placed it in the hot well, so that the whole bulb and tube were covered, the quicksilver rose soon to 191°, but after having been for five minutes in the well, it did not rise above that degree. I took the thermometer out, and cleared the well still better, and made the excavation of the stone below deeper, and then immersed it again during ten minutes, but found it all the time at 191°. This was done August the 17th, 1774, at 4^h 30′ P.M. at high-water. We returned the next morning about nine o'clock, when the water was low; and, upon immersing the thermometer as before, we observed the quicksilver to rise to 187° in the space of one minute and a half; at which degree it remained, though the thermometer continued several minutes longer in the water. I threw some small fish, and some muscles, into the hot water, and they were boiled in a few minutes. The water is clear and limpid, and has no peculiar taste, except that I thought it to have a very faint astringency. I put a piece of fine and bright silver into it, which having lain for more than an hour in it, came out untarnished. I put a small quantity of solution of salt of tartar in it, but it did not precipitate any thing, though I increased the quantity of the tartar. I had no other substances with me to try the water by other methods.

On the same cliff, but close to the sandy beach, at the bottom of the harbour, there are two other hot springs. We came on the same morning, Aug. the 18th, half an hour later, to these springs. I hollowed out the sand to gather some of the hot water, and immersed my thermometer just at the place where the water bubbles up, and in about two minutes time the quicksilver rose to 202°, and remained for several minutes in the water without rising higher. On the same cliff, on a brow about 60 or 80 fathoms higher, we found a place clear of trees, where in cool weather, especially after rain, we could discover from the ship, steams rising, which were still more distinctly observed when we came close to the place. We found ourselves, after a few minutes stay, in a profuse perspiration, occasioned by the hot steams, and the heat of the ground we stood on, which in some places was intolerable. When the volcano made an explosion, we always saw a new quantity of vapours and steams pierce these spiracula, which are apparently shut up, but seem to have a cavity underneath; for the whole mountain gave a hollow sound, when we were walking on the footpath leading to these solfataras; and I likewise traced a train of these spiracula, both above and below on the sides of this hill, as far as within a few yards of the hot wells. I saw the solfataras three times. The second time I took my thermometer with me, and having dug a hole about a foot deep, I hung the thermometer in it by the ribbon on its top, to a stick laid across the hole; and I saw it rise from 80° in a few seconds to 170°: having left the thermometer for four minutes in the hole, I found it still at 170°, and though I repeated this at one minute's interval, three times, the mercury was still at the same degree. When I took it out, it fell in a second's time to 160°, and gradually lower. In my cabin on board the ship, it stood at 78°; having been carried close to my body up the hill, by a long ascent, it rose to 87°; I hung it therefore in the open air, in the shade of a tree on the hill, about twenty yards from the smoking place, for about five minutes, and found it to stand at 80°, and to remain at the same height for a long while after. When I was digging the hole for the reception of the thermometer, the natives seemed uneasy, and were apprehensive the place would be on fire.[4] This happened on August the 12th at about ten o'clock in the morning.

I went up again on August the 14th in the forenoon, and repeated the experiment with this difference only, that we entirely buried the thermometer in the hole, by putting loose earth round it. It had stood that day in my cabin at 78°, on the hill at 80°; but after having been buried a minute, it rose to 210° and there it remained stationary for five minutes. As I could trace the spiracula of hot steams, blended with some sulphureous smell, all along the side of the hill, down to the hot wells; it is probable, that a stream of water, in a subterraneous chasm or crevice, coming too near one of the places, that are violently heated by the neighbouring volcano, is resolved into steams; and forced through the earth and stones; parts of it however seem again to gather somewhere in small streams, oozing out at the hot wells, close to the sea-side. I am even apt to believe, that this chasm or crevice is connected with the crater of the volcano: for on August the 11th, when the volcano was heard making great explosions, and seen throwing up very large masses of stones, ignited ashes, and immense clouds of thick smoke, we observed on the hill, that at each explosion, there came new quantities of steam through the spiracula.

At the bottom of the harbour near the beach, is a small pond containing some fresh and palatable water; it is tinged somewhat brownish and though perfectly good when fresh, it soon contracted in the casks a much greater degree of putrefaction and foetid smell, than had been observed of any other water during the whole voyage, which I believe proves that some foreign, perhaps inflammable particles are contained in this water. This pond was connected, within the bushes, with a range of stagnant, muddy waters, for more than a mile or two, along the plain opposite the harbour. These waters, are it seems gathered here during the rainy season; and as they have no visible drain, they collect in the lowest parts and stagnate, and as the whole surface of the soil of the isle is formed of volcanic ashes, containing all more or less saline or sulphureous particles, the water may dissolve them, and strike the brown colour by extracting the vegetable substances gradually falling into or coming into contact with it.

In the rest of the isles belonging to the NEW HEBRIDES, we frequently observed large streams of water forming cascades on the steep descents of hills, and thus precipitating themselves down and soon mixing with the briny fluid of the ocean.

The FRIENDLY ISLES seem to be destitute of springs: for though on some of them, as *Eaoowhe* and *Namocka*, there are small hills and rising grounds, they are however far from being so high as to attract the clouds or to cause from their perpetual mositure a continual flow of spring-water. The natives have ponds, some of which are large, wherein they collect the rain-water: but it is somewhat brackish from the vicinity of the sea. Besides these ponds of fresh water, there is in *Namocka* a large lagoon of salt water about three miles long, full of small isles, beautifully ornamented with clusters of trees, crowded with wild ducks, and surrounded by bushes of mangroves and hills forming a romantic landscape.

In HUAHEINE, one of the Society Isles, there are on its North point likewise two large salt water lagoons, with a very muddy bottom; as they are shallow, considerably within the land, surrounded by thick bushes and large trees, and therefore very little agitated by winds, they stink most immoderately, and must I suppose, spread noxious effluvia; and I must confess, I saw only a few habitations on its South side near the hills, and those were not quite contiguous to the lagoons.

In NORFOLK ISLAND we found a small spring, and I believe if we had searched the whole isle over, we should have found more.

EASTER ISLAND has no other water, but what is found in some reservoirs in forms of wells or ponds, collected I suppose from rain. It is stagnant, bad and somewhat brackish.

The MARQUESAS have abundance of the finest springs, forming many beautiful streams and cascades: for their cloud capt hills, are constantly moistened from the vapour of the clouds, and therefore yield plentiful supplies for the springs in this hot climate.

NEW-ZEELAND no doubt has abundance of springs and rivulets; and there is hardly an islet or rock, which is not blessed with a spring of fresh water. In *Dusky Bay* there are several rich springs; but all the water running and being drained through a rich, spungy, loose mould formed from putrefied vegetables, has acquired a deep brown colour; it is nevertheless free from foulness, has no peculiar taste and keeps at sea remarkably well.

TIERRA DEL FUEGO is richly provided with the finest springs and large ponds of fresh water, from the melted snow, on its high and barren rocks. In some places we observed large and high cascades, which greatly contribute to soften the harshness of its wild scenery.

In SOUTH-GEORGIA and SANDWICH-LAND, we met with no springs: but as there is ice enough in its vicinity and even as far as the parallel of 51° South latitude, in their spring season, and in the depth of summer and autumn higher up in

67° and 70°, a navigator cannot be at a loss for fresh water in high Southern lati-tudes.

If I except the water at Tanna in the hot wells, which perhaps may contain some saline particles on account of a faint astringency I tasted, we did not meet with any other medicated water whatsoever in the course of our expedition.

William Hodges, [*View
in Dusky Bay with a
Maori Canoe*], oil on
panel, 1776. 262 × 343
mm. National Maritime
Museum, London.

SECTION II

Rivulets

All the springs of the Society Isles, Marquesas, and New-Zeeland form rivulets; but none of them are so considerable as to deserve a particular notice. In Dusky Bay where all the inlets of the sea are very deep, we always found, that wherever the bottoms of bays or creeks have a stream of water coming down, the water gradually shoaled, so that at a good distance from the bottom of the bay, the boats ran a ground; which I think confirms the opinion, that these streams having by their impetuosity after a heavy rain or melting of snow from the sides of the steep hills, carried a great many earthy particles down to the very mouth of the rivulet, they deposit them there gradually: being, as I suppose, necessitated to this deposit by the resistance of the briny and therefore heavier fluid of the ocean, by the winds and tides meeting the stream, and other such causes.

We observed, in the several inlets and arms forming this spacious bay, some-times *cascades* rushing rapidly down, and falling from vast heights before they met with another rock. Some of these cascades with their neighbouring scenery, require the pencil and genius of a SALVATOR ROSA to do them justice: however the ingenious artist, who went with us on this expedition has great merit, in hav-ing executed some of these romantic landscapes in a masterly manner.

The upper parts of all the rivulets in the Society Isles, are not so useless or neglected, as might be imagined. Wherever the natives observe that the valley between the steep sides enlarges, there they form a wear, by piling large stones so high, that the water is raised on a level with or even higher than the plain; which they surround with a small bank, make it level and plant it with eddoes[1] or *arum esculentum*, a plant which likes to be under water and thus grows into large tuber-ous roots; they then admit the water into these plantations from above the wear and discharge it at the opposite end. The wears serve the natives at the same time for a bridge, they being extremely skilful in jumping from one large stone to another, and sometimes carrying at the same time a burthen on their backs.

SECTION III

Ocean

The last and most considerable body of water is the ocean. It highly deserves to be examined on many accounts, and though the remarks we have to make on it are but few and perhaps trivial, we will venture to communicate them, as they may serve to confirm some known positions.

The Depth of the Ocean

The Depth of the ocean is certainly one of the most remarkable circumstances. We now and then even out of sight of any land, tried to measure this depth; for instance in the year 1772 Sept. 5th. being near the line in 00° 52 North latitude, we could find no ground with 250 fathom. On February 8th. 1773, when we were in something more than 48° South latitude, a little to the East of the meridian of the isle of *Mauritius*, we had 210 fathom line out, but found no ground. On November the 22nd. 1774 being in the middle of the Pacific Ocean, we sounded with 150 fathom and found no ground.

It has been laid down as a maxim by the learned and ingenious Count DE BUFFON* "that the depth of the sea along the coasts is commonly so much greater as these coasts are more elevated, and again so much less as they are lower, and that the inequality of the bottom of the sea generally corresponds with the inequality of the surface of the soil of the coast;" and Dampier is quoted in confirmation of this assertion. Though the learned author certainly merits the applause of the world, it has however been the fate of his work to have the common stamp of all human productions; viz. to have some imperfections, and even to recount some false assertions upon the faith of other authors and travellers: the illustrious author, is so well-known for his love of truth, and for the variety of his erudition,

---

* *Historie naturelle* tom. 2d p. 199 & 200. Edit. in 12 mo.[1]

that he will no doubt find it just to give his work all that perfection, which it is capable of, by correcting whatsoever is not strictly conformable to truth and nature. I will therefore, on the strength of his supposition and the encouragement personally given me by himself,[2] remark that his observation will hold in regard to large lands; it is however equally true, that in regard to all the low isles in the South seas, and even in regard to the low reefs surrounding the Society Isles, this rule admits of many exceptions. In New Zeeland, Tierra del Fuego, New Caledonia and all the New Hebrides, I believe the rule to be true: for all these lands are high and have generally bold coasts; and the soundings are deep close into the shore without decreasing. I have however in some instances observed just the contrary; as off the South entrance of Dusky Bay we had about 45 fathoms water; but in the bay itself we had no ground with 80 fathom line. Off the South coast of Tierra del Fuego between Cape Noir and Christmas Bay, we had 45 and 50 fathom water, which increased to 60 or 70; but when we stood in for Christmas Bay we had no ground with 80 fathom of line, in the very entrance. When we were off the coast of South Georgia we had regular soundings, but in the entrance of Possession Bay we had no ground with 54 fathoms. According to the above rule of Mr. de Buffon, the low isles in the South-Seas should have gradual soundings; but we found the contrary to be true: for close to the reef forming these isles, the water is almost unfathomable. The same may be said of O-Taheitee and all the Society Isles, which are surrounded by a fertile plain extending from the hills to the sea, and then included in a reef, beyond which the sea immediately becomes excessively deep. Near Turtle-Island we saw an oblong reef, which was no where free from water, had a deep sea included, and on its outsides there was a great depth close to the reef. All these instances here enumerated, seem to be exceptions to Mr. de Buffon's rule.

The Colour of the Ocean

Wherever there is an extensive bank or shoal, there the COLOUR of the sea-water is changed; but even this is subject to many exceptions: sometimes we find places which are amazingly clear, and the ground, at the depth of several fathoms, may be seen as plainly as if it were within a few yards of the surface; sometimes the sea assumes a grey hue, and seems turbid, as if it had lost its limpidity. But often you are deceived by the situation of the sky and clouds. Dark, cloudy weather involves likewise the whole ocean in a grey hue. A serene and clear sky tinges the waves with the finest berylline or blueish-green colour. If a cloud appears, it gives to a spot of the sea a hue quite different from the rest; and, if not well attended to, often alarms the navigator with the fear of soundings, or even shoals.

A judicious eye, conducted by long experience, can alone distinguish properly in these cases. But, upon the whole, it cannot be too much recommended to navigators, especially in unexplored seas, to make use of the lead in every doubtful situation.*

Of the Saltness of the Ocean

It has been suspected, that the *saltness* of the ocean is not every where equal. Some assert the sea to be salter under the Line than towards the Poles[†]; that the great oceans are salter than the smaller seas, which are almost included by land, viz. the Baltic, the Mediterranean, the White Sea near Archangel, the Persian and the Arabic Gulphs, &c.; that its saltness increases with its large depth; and lastly, that the high sea, at a great distance from land, is salter than near it, and especially near places where large rivers fall into the sea. I had no opportunity to make the necessary experiments to ascertain or to refute these assertions, as I was obliged to set out upon this expedition almost at a moment's warning, and could not therefore provide any apparatus necessary for that purpose. The above remarks may, however, serve to future navigators, as a hint of what is still wanted to be observed, relative to the saltness of the ocean. I should therefore propose to them, to procure the apparatus described by Mr. *Wilke*, in the *Memoirs of the Swedish Academy*, vol. 33, n. 6 of the 1st quarter, which serves to bring the water of the ocean up from any given depth: they ought also to be provided with an accurate and nice hydrostatical balance, in order to ascertain the specific gravity of any water or liquid; or they may make use, for convenience sake, of a *haloscopium*, consisting of a hollow globe of ivory, into which a tube of about five or six inches must be inserted, on which the different specific weights of pure water, and its various mixtures with certain quantities of common salt, are marked in degrees; so that, by immersing this simple machine into sea-water, it would be easy to ascertain the degrees of its saltness. This machine would likewise serve to ascertain the comparative purity and weight of every water found in rivers, wells, &c. &c.

It has likewise formerly been believed, that, besides the common saltness, the water of the ocean contained particles, which communicated to it a kind of bitterness, that made it next to impossible to distil drinkable water from sea-water. The ingenious Dr. LIND,[3] of Haslar-hospital, near Portsmouth, has long ago shewn how little foundation there is in this prejudice, and likewise taught the

---

* See Mr. Dalrymple's *Memoir of a Chart of the Southern Ocean*, p. 7.
† Buffon's *Histoire Naturelle*, tom. 2. p. 79. edit. in 12 mo.

British nation, without any public reward or encouragement, an easy and approved method for obtaining, by distillation, potable water from sea-water.* When we made use of Dr. Irving's distilling machine, we likewise found, that the water thus distilled was not only entirely freed from its salt, but, besides this, we never could discover the least bitter particle in the drinkable water. But it must not by any means be concluded from hence, that there are no such bitter particles contained in the sea-water; for everyone knows too well, that, after the fresh water has been evaporated from sea-water, and salt has been thereby formed, there remains always a thick, gelatinous lie, which cannot be crystallized, and which is nothing but a mixture, containing marine acid and *magnesia alba*; and, besides these ingredients, the sea-brine always contains some Glauber's salt and some selenitic particles; so that it seems as if the whole were a mixture of fresh water, marine acid, vitriolic acid, fixed mineral alkali, magnesia, and lime. However, though several of these substances form a bitter salt by their mixture, they nevertheless will not hinder the sea-water from affording a clear, limpid, potable water by distillation, because the particles being all fixed, remain in the salt-brine, which is left in the copper; and the water being alone volatile, rises in steams, and is distilled. Or even if, by distillation, a few acid or saline particles should be volatilized, and mix with the distilled water, their proportion is certainly so small and insignificant, that no detriment can be derived from thence. On the usefulness and practicability of the method of distilling water, I can say nothing, as it is not my province, and as a report has been made to the Admiralty by persons, whose proper business it was.

The Warmth, or Temperature of the Ocean

To ascertain the degree of *warmth* of the sea-water, at a certain depth, several experiments were made by us. The thermometer made use of, is of Fahrenheit's construction, made by Mr. Ramsden, and furnished with an ivory scale: it was, on these occasions, always put into a cylindrical tin case, which had at each end a valve, admitting the water as long as the instrument was going down, and shutting while it was hawling up again. The annexed table will at once shew the result of the experiments.

From this table it appears, that under the Line, and near the Tropics, the water is cooler at a great depth than at its surface. In high latitudes, the air is colder sometimes, sometimes very near upon a par, and sometimes warmer than

---

* Lind's *Essay on Diseases incidental to Europeans in hot climates*. Appendix, p. 351.

DATE	LATITUDE	DEGREES OF FAHRENHEIT'S THERMOMETER			DEPTH IN FATHOMS	STAY OF THE THERMOMETER IN THE DEEP	TIME IN HAULING THE THERMOMETER UP
		IN THE AIR	ON THE SURFACE OF THE SEA-WAT.	AT A CERTAIN DEPTH IN THE SEA			
1772 September 5	00°52′N.	75½°	74°	66°	85 F.	30′	27½′
27	24°44′S.	72½°	70°	68°	80 F.	15′	7′
October 12	34°48′S.	60°	59°	58°	100 F.	20′	6′
December 15	55°00′S.	30½°	30°	34°	100 F.	17′	5½′
23	55°26′S.	33°	32°	34½°	100 F.	16′	6½′
1773 January 13	64°00′S.	37°	33½°	32°	100 F.	20′	7′

the sea-water at the depth of about 100 fathoms; according as the preceding changes of the temperature of the air, or the direction and violence of the wind happen to fall out. For it is to be observed, that these experiments were always made when we had a calm, or at least very little wind; because, in a gale of wind, we could not have been able to make them in a boat. Another probable cause of the difference in the temperature of the sea-water, in the same high latitude, undoubtedly must be sought in the ice; in a sea covered with high and extensive ice islands, the water should be colder than in a sea which is at a great distance from any ice.

The Phosphoreal Light of the Sea-Water

It is very well known, that the sea-water has sometimes a luminous appearance, or, to use a more philosophical word, a *phosphorical light*. Many have endeavoured to give us the real causes of this phaenomenon*; and, in consequence, some have brought us the drawing of a curious submarine insect, related to the shrimp kind, which had a peculiar luminous appearance, and asserted this to be the cause of the phosphoreal light of the sea†. Others again ascribe it to the great number of animals of the mollusca-tribe, swimming every where in the sea. The above-mentioned shrimps, as well as the mollusca, may contribute to make the sea appear luminous; but I would not venture to assert these to be the *only* causes of the phosphoreal light, after the observation of the various phaenomena I made in the course of this long voyage.

First, I found reason to doubt, whether all the luminous appearances in the sea are of the same nature; for one kind of these phaenomena never extend to a great distance from the ship; that part of the sea only appears luminous which is close to the ship, and the light is likewise communicated only to the top of the next waves, that break obliquely from it; and this happens commonly in a fresh gale.

Another kind of phosphoreal light I observed commonly in, or immediately succeeding a long calm, after hot weather; it spread more over, and even mixed with the body of the sea, than the former. When we took the sea-water in this condition into a tub, it there became dark as soon as it was free from motion: but, at each violent agitation of the water, it appeared luminous, where the motion was produced, and seemed to stick for a moment only to the finger or hand, which agitated the water, but disappeared as instantaneously.

The third kind of phosphoreal light is no doubt caused by mollusca‡, whose whole figure may be distinguished in the water by their own luminous appearance. I have observed, though rarely, the same effect to be occasioned by fish and shell-fish*; and there may be likewise some shrimps and other insects✦, that are

---

* The Father Bourzes, in the *Lettres Edifiantes,* tom. ix. Par. 1730, speaks of the phosphoreal light of the sea with judgment; and still more so, the late ingenious philosopher, Mr. Canton, *Phil. Trans.* vol. ix. p. 446, in his paper on the luminous appearance of the sea.

† See the *Gentleman's Magazine,* for 1771; and Basteri *Opusc.* subsec. Tom. I.P.I. p. 31. Tab. iv. *fig.*

‡ The genus of *Sepia* or cuttle-fish, and that of *Medusa* or blubber, shine in the water in the dark. See among others *Linné. Syst. Nat. ed.* xii. *p.* 1095. Also, Hawkesworth's Compilation of Voyages, vol. ii. p. 15.

* Dactyli (Pholades.) His natura in tenebris remoto lumine, alio fulgere claro. Plin. *Hist. Nat.* lib. 9. c. 87. (61.)[4]

✦ Some of the genus of *Scolopendra* or Centipes, shine during the darkness of the night, *viz.* the species called *electrica* and *phosphorea,* and perhaps some other species, or even genus. The last-named species fell on board of a ship several hundred miles from any land, and has, perhaps, wings like the water-beetle *(Dytiscus),* which, at certain times leaves the water, and takes a flight through the air, which may account for the above fact. See Linne. *Syst. Nat. ed.* xii. *p.* 1064.

phosphorescent, though I have never seen them. But the most singular and sur-prizing appearance of this nature, I observed in the night preceding Oct. 30, 1772, when we were off the Cape of Good Hope, at the distance of a few miles from the shore, and had a fresh gale. Scarcely had night spread its veil over the surface of the ocean, when it had the apperance of being all over on fire. Every wave that broke had a luminous margin or top; wherever the sides of the ship came in contact with the sea, there appeared a line of phosphoreal light. The eye discovered this luminous appearance every where on the ocean; nay, the very bosom of this immense element seemed to be pregnant with this shining appear-ance. We saw great bodies illuminated moving in the sea; some came along-side of the ship, and stood on along with her; others moved off from her with a veloc-ity almost equal to lightning. The shape of these illuminated bodies discovered them to be fishes. Some approached near one another, and when a small one came near a larger, it made all possible haste to fly from the danger. I had a bucket full of this luminous sea-water drawn up for examination. We found, that an infi-nite number of little round luminous bodies were moving in the water with amaz-ing quickness. After the water had been standing for a little while, the small sparkling objects seemed to decrease in quantity, but, by stirring the water again, we observed the whole to be again entirely luminous; and leaving the water undisturbed, we saw the little sparks moving very briskly in different directions. Though the bucket with the water was suspended, that it might be less affected by the motion of the ship, the sparkling objects still moved to and fro', so that this first convinced me, that these luminous atoms had a voluntary motion, quite independent of the agitation of the water or ship; but, at each agitation of the water by a stick or the hand, we plainly perceived the sparkling to increase. Sometimes, by stirring the water, one of these phosphoreal sparks would stick to the hand or finger. They were scarcely of the size of the smallest pin's head. The least magnifier of my microscope discovered these little atoms to be globular, gelatinous, transparent, and somewhat brownish. By putting one under the microscope, we observed first a kind of thin tube going into the substance of this little globule, from a round orifice on its surface. The inside was filled with four or five oblong intestine bags, connected with the tube just mentioned. The same appearances were observed by the greatest magnifier, and were only more distinct. I wanted to examine one in the water, and then bring it under the microscope, but I could not provide a live animalcule: they were all dead, on account of their tender structure, before I could separate them from the finger to which they were flicking. This attempt was accordingly frustrated. When we left the Cape of Good Hope, on November the 22d, we had that very night the same luminous appear-ance of the sea, and a very hard gale. Thus we have again a new cause of the phos-phoreal light. But, before we proceed with our remarks, let us only follow the idea arising from this phaenomenon. The immense ocean, filled with myriads of animalcules, which have life, loco-motion, and a power of shining in the dark, of laying that power aside at pleasure, and illuminating all bodies coming in contact with them; this is a wonder which fills the mind with greater astonishment and reverential awe, than it is in my power justly and properly to describe.

If I were now to say something on the different species of phosphoreal light, I could by no means give my assertion, that degree of certainty which philosophers would require. I will therefore confine myself to some probable hints concerning their real causes.

The first species of luminous appearance seems to be produced by a cause altogether different from the rest, and if I may venture to declare my opinion on the subject, I should think, that this light is owing to electricity. We know very well, that the motion of a ship through the water in a gale, is extremely swift, and the friction caused by this motion very great: for we find that the sea agitated by a gale of wind is remarkably warmer, than the air*. The bituminous substances, which cover the sides of ships, the nails sticking in the bottom, and the conducting power of water will equally serve to explain the possibility of such an electricity.

The second species of luminous appearance in sea water seems to be a real phosphoreal light. It is very well known, that many animal bodies putrify and are dissolved in the sea, and that almost every part of animal and many mineral bodies, and the air itself, contains the acid of phosphorus as an integrant part†. The addition of any inflammable principle to this acid, will produce the substance we call *phosphorus*. Every one who has seen salted fish drying, must know that many of them become phosphoreal. It is likewise a well established fact, that the ocean, itself after a long continued calm, becomes stinking and highly putrid‡, arising probably from the putrefaction of a great many animal substances, that die in the ocean, float in it, and in hot calm days frequently and suddenly putrefy. That fishes and mollusca contain oily and inflammable particles is equally well known. The acid of phosphorus disengaged by putrefaction from its original mixture in animal bodies, may easily combine with some of the just mentioned inflammables, and thus produce a phosphorus floating on the top of the ocean, and causing that luminous appearance, which we so much admire.

Lastly the third kind of phosphoreal light no doubt arises from live animals

---

* See *a voyage towards the North Pole*, by Capt. Phipps. *Appendix*. p. 147.

† See *Elemens de Mineralogie docimastique* par M. Sage, Paris 1777, 8vo. Preface p. xi. vol. II. p. 376, 377, 378.

‡ See Boyle. T. III. p. 222,[5] he relates that some navigators, in a calm which lasted thirteen days, found the sea becoming putrid.

OCEAN

floating in the sea and is owing to their peculiar structure or rather the nature of their integrant parts, which perhaps might be investigated, by analyzing chemically some of the mollusca, which have a luminous appearance.

On the Question concerning the Existence of a Southern Land[6]

A suspicion was long since entertained by the author of the Universal History, and by the learned and ingenious President DES BROSSES,* of a great Southern continent, founded on the argument, that in case there should be no more land in the Southern hemisphere, than what we knew before, it would be insufficient to counterpoise the weight of lands in the Northern. An ingenious author, whose disinterested zeal for the promotion of geography, navigation and discoveries is not less conspicuous, than his many virtues as a man, a citizen and a friend, has lately† endeavoured to set these arguments in a stronger light. Our present circumnavigation has, I believe, put it beyond doubt, that there is no land on this side of 60° in the Southern hemisphere, if we except the few inconsiderable fragments we found in the Southern atlantic ocean. If therefore we should even suppose, that the whole space from 60° and upwards, where we have not been, be intirely occupied by land, this would be still too inconsiderable to counterpoise the lands of the Northern hemisphere. I am therefore apt to suspect, that nature has provided against this defect, by placing perhaps at the bottom of the Southern ocean such bodies as by their specific weight will compensate the deficiency of lands; if this system of the wanted counterpoise be at all necessary. But there may perhaps be other methods to obviate this defect, of which our narrow knowledge and experience have not yet informed us.

---

* *Modern Universal History, Folio Edit.* vol, V. p. 2. note c. or 8vo edit. vol. XI. p. 275. *Voyages aux Terres Australes*, vol. I. p. 13.
† Dalrymple's *collection of voyages to the South-Sea*, vol. p.

SECTION IV

Ice and its Formation[1]

Nothing appeared more strange to the several navigators in high latitudes, than the first sight of the immense masses of ice which are found floating in the ocean; and I must confess, that though I had read a great many accounts on their nature, figure, formation and magnitude, I was however very much struck by their first appearance. The real grandeur of the sight by far surpassed any thing I could expect; for we saw sometimes islands of ice of one or two miles extent, and at the same time a hundred feet or upwards above water. We will suppose, that ice of parallel dimensions swimming in sea-water, only shews one part out of ten above water*; which is a moderate supposition, because according to Mairan† ice swimming in fresh water had one fourteenth part of the whole above its surface; nay, Dr. Irving‡ plunged a piece of the most solid ice in melted snow water and fourteen fifteenth parts sunk under its level. A piece therefore of only one mile in length, a quarter of a mile in breadth, and 100 feet above water contains 696,960,000 cubic feet of solid ice; but as the 100 feet, are only the contents of the ice above water, the same must be taken nine times more for the contents under water; and the whole will then amount to 6,969,600,000 cubic feet of solid ice, which must of course be a stupendous mass. But the enormous size of these icy masses is not the only object of our astonishment, for the great number of them is equally surprizing. In the year, 1773 on the 26th, of December, we counted 186 masses of ice all in sight from the mast head, whereof none was less than the hull of a ship. At other times we were every where surrounded by ice islands, or obliged to alter our course, because it was obstructed by an immense field of ice. On these occasions we saw first small pieces of loose, broken ice, full of holes and pores like a spunge, thus wafted by the continual agitation of the waves; behind

---

* Boyle *Philos. Trans.* No 62.[2]
† Mairan *sur la glace* p. 264.
‡ *A voyage towards the North Pole* by Capt. Phipps. *Appendix.* p. 147.

them appeared large flat and solid masses, of an immense extent. Between them we observed stupendous large and high ice islands, likewise solid but formed in the most strange manner into points, spires and broken rocks. All this scene of ice extended as far as the eye could reach. However, it is likewise remarkable, that in different years, seasons and places of the sea, we found the ice differently situated. In the year 1772, December the 10th, we saw the ice between 50° and 51° of Southern latitude. In 1773 on December the 12th, we found the first ice in 62° South latitude. In 1775, in January the 27th, we saw ice in about 60° South latitude. On February the 24th, we came to the same place, where about 26 months before, we had met with such an impenetrable body of ice, as had obliged us to run to the East; but where at this last time no vestige of it appeared no more than at the place, where BOUVET[3] had placed his Cape Circumcision, we having sailed over the whole tract, which he suspected to be land; nor could we be mistaken in its situation, as we had been on the same parallel for a considerable time: so that it is impossible to have missed the land, if any had existed, as we had frequent opportunities to ascertain our latitude.

Another circumstance worthy of notice is, that all ice floating in the sea yields fresh water when melted. However care must be taken never to collect such ice which is spungy and honeycombed from the agitation of the waves, as this kind of ice always contained considerable quantity of brine in the interstices and spungy cavities which does not entirely drain from it by suffering it to lie on the deck of the ship, and therefore is less fit for yielding good potable water. This kind of ice may well be distinguished from the more solid sorts both by its appearance and by its situation, as it commonly is the outermost at the approach of any large quantity of ice, and therefore more exposed to the agitation of the waves. To leeward of large ice masses, commonly loose pieces of ice are drifting of various sizes; those that are nearest the large mass, are commonly the most solid, and therefore the most proper for supplying the ship with water. Of this ice, such pieces are taken up as can be conveniently lifted into the boat; and then they are piled up on the quarter-deck, where the salt-water, adhering to its outside, soon drains away; and, as the contact of the deck and warmer atmosphere contributes to dissolve some part of the ice, the rest becomes quite fresh. With this ice the boiler is filled, that it may the more readily be dissolved. Other ice is broken into such pieces as will go through the bung-holes into the water-casks; and when there is not room for more, the interstices are filled up, with the water from the boiler, which soon melts the small pieces of ice in the cask.

When we came to leeward of extensive *portions* of small drifting ice, or such as the Greenlandmen call *packed,* i.e. on the edges of which, by the sea and pressure of the ice, small pieces are forced up, we always found the sea smooth; and this was the appearance, when we entered the loose ice on January the 17th,

1773, in 67° 15′ South latitude; but, on the weather-side of the ice, there was a great swell and high surf. Whenever we approached large tracts of solid ice, we observed, on the horizon, a white reflexion from the snow and ice, which the Greenlandmen call *the blink of the ice:* so that seeing this phaenomenon appear, we were sure to be within a few leagues of the ice; and it was at that time likewise, that we commonly noticed flights of white petrels of the size of pigeons, which we called snowy petrels, the common fore-runners of the ice.

It has been observed, that the large masses of ice floating in the ocean, cool the air considerably; so that, upon approaching them, the change may be sensibly felt.

On the 11th of December, 1772, on a clear mild day, before we reached a large mass of ice, of about half a mile in length, and a hundred feet high, the thermometer on deck, fixed on the capstan, was at 41°. When we were to leeward of

ICE

William Hodges, *The Resolution & Adventure 4 Jan 1773 Taking in Ice for Water. Lat 61S*, wash and watercolor, January 1773. 380 × 545 mm. State Library of New South Wales.

it, the thermometer sunk to 37½°; and when we had passed it, which was at about five o'clock in the afternoon, it had risen again to 41°. On December the 13th, 1772, in the morning early, the thermometer was at about 32°, and it had continued to snow all the night and morning. In the morning, between seven and eight o'clock, we approached a great many ice-islands, some of which were of vast extent. At eight o'clock the thermometer pointed at 31½°; it remained there when we were just to leeward of the largest of them; and, after we had passed it, the thermometer did not rise higher than 31½°. I believe the cold was not lessened, because the deck being wet from the snow, caused a great evaporation, which cooled the air: and we were likewise every where surrounded by large ice-masses, which had so much cooled the atmosphere all round, that it remained in the same temperature. Both these instances seem therefore to prove, that the ice-masses contribute considerably towards cooling the atmosphere.

The ice floats in an ocean, which in the summer of the Southern hemisphere was observed to be many degrees above the freezing point; it must therefore continually melt and decay; and, as the difference of the specific gravity of common air to fresh water is nearly as 0.001 or 0.000¼ to 1.000; supposing both of the same temperature; it is evident that fresh water must melt the ice, more than common air, as the particles of water in contact with the ice are so much heavier; and, for the same reason as sea-water is to fresh water as 1.030 to 1.000, sea-water must act still more upon the ice than fresh-water*. We had frequent opportunities of seeing the effect of the sea-water upon the ice, in dissolving and crumbling large masses to pieces, with a crash not inferior to the explosion of guns; and sometimes we were at so small a distance from them, that we were scarce out of the reach of the danger of being crushed by an ice-rock splitting in pieces, which were oversetting, each of them having gotten new centers of gravity. The water melted from the ice, and mixed with the ocean, must likewise cool the temperature of the sea-water in the latitudes between 50 and 60° South, where these particulars were chiefly observed by us.

It seems to be undeniable, that the ice we met with in the open ocean, in 50° and 67°, or even 71° South latitude, is formed still farther to the South. For it had its origin either near some land, or in the open ocean. In the first case it must evidently come from regions lying beyond the tracks of our ships, i.e. beyond 60°, 67°, and 71° South latitude, as we found no lands, where these enormous quanti-

* However large masses of ice require a long time and a warm climate entirely to dissolve them. Sometimes in 40° North latitude, ice-islands have been met with in the Atlantic: and I have been told by an officer, who spent several years at and about Newfoundland, that a very bulky ice-island was driven into the *Streights of Belleisle*, where it was grounded, and continued a whole summer, and was not entirely dissolved before the summer of the next year.

ties of ice could possibly have been generated. Or, in the second case, if the ice be formed far from any land, this climate must likewise be farther to the South than our tracks, as we never fell in with ice, which we would with certainty consider as stationary, but, on the contrary, found it commonly in motion. At least, the loose ice between 71° and 50° South latitude, must have come from the fast, solid ice beyond 71° or some higher latitude. Other navigators*, as well as ourselves, have met with ice in low Southern latitudes, i.e. 49°, 50°, 51°, and 52°, early in spring and summer; consequently it is evident, that it must have drifted to these low latitudes from beyond 60°, 67°, and 71° South latitude. In the Northern seas, it is a common and obvious phaenomenon, observed almost every year, that the ice moves towards warmer climates. These instances, therefore, seem to prove, that there is either a strong current, an attraction, or some other cause acting regularly, which carries these large masses of ice from each pole towards the equinoctial line.

I should here finish these remarks on the ice, if it were not necessary to say something concerning its formation. I know that Mr. de Buffon,[†] Lomonosof[‡] and Crantz[*] were of opinion that the ice found in the ocean, is formed near lands, only from the fresh water and ice carried down into the sea by the many rivers in Sibiria, Hudson's Bay, &c. and therefore when we fell in with such quantities of ice in December, 1772, I expected we should soon meet with the land, from whence these ice masses had been detached. But being disappointed in the discovery of this land, though we penetrated beyond the 67° twice, and once beyond 71° South latitude, and having besides some other doubts concerning the existence of the pretended Southern Continent, I thought it necessary to enquire, what reasons chiefly induced the above authors to form the opinion that the ice floating in the ocean, must be formed near land, or that an Austral land is absolutely requisite for that purpose[♦], and having looked for their arguments, I find they amount chiefly to this; "that the ice floating in the ocean is all fresh, that salt water does not freeze at all, or if it does, it contains briny particles; they infer from thence, that the ice in the ocean cannot be formed in the sea, far from any land; there must therefore exist Austral lands; because in order to form an idea of the origin of the great ice masses agreeably to what is observed in the

---

* Dalrymple's *Collection of Voyages, chiefly in the Southern Atlantic Ocean.* Capt. Halley's *Journal, p. 34, and* Capt. Bouvet's, *p. 4.*
[†] De Buffon *Histoire Naturelle,* edit. in 12mo. tom. I. p. 313, 319. and tom. 2. p. 91, 100.
[‡] Lomonosof *Memoire on the ice mountains of the Northern Sea,* in the *Swedish memoirs of the academy of Stockholm,* vol. XXV. Germ. edit.
[*] Crantz's *history of Greenland,* p. 18, 42.
[♦] Buffon *Hist. Naturelle,* tom. 1, p. 314. speaks of the Austral Lands as necessary for the formation of the ice, & tom. 2. p. 99.

Northern hemisphere, they find that the first (*point dáppui*) point for fixing the high ice islands is the land, and secondly that the great quantity of flat ice is brought down the rivers." I have impartially and carefully considered and examined these arguments, and compared every circumstance with what we saw in the high Southern latitudes, and with other known facts, and will here insert the result of all my enquiries on this subject.

First, *they observe the ice floating in the ocean to yield by melting, fresh water:* which I believe to be true; however hitherto it has by no means been generally allowed to be fresh, for Crantz* says expressly, that, "the flat pieces (forming what they call the *Ice-Fields*) are salt, because they were congealed from sea water." The ice taken up by us for watering the ship was of all kinds, and nevertheless we found it constantly fresh, which proves, either that the principle of analogy cannot be applied indiscriminately in both hemispheres, and that one thing may be true in the Northern hemisphere, which is quite otherwise in the Southern, from reasons not yet known or discovered by us: or we must think that Crantz and others are mistaken, who suppose the ice floating in the ocean to be salt.

The next remark is, *that salt water does not freeze at all, or if it does it contains briny particles.* Mr. *de Buffon*†, the most ingenious and the most elegant writer of Natural History, tells us, "that the sea between Nova Zemla and Spitzbergen under the 79° North latitude does not freeze, as it is there considerably broad, and that it is not to be apprehended to find this sea frozen not even under the pole itself, for indeed there is no example of having ever found a sea wholly frozen over, and at a considerable distance from the shores; that the only instance of a sea entirely frozen is that of the Black Sea, which is narrow and not very salt, and receiving a great many rivers coming from Northern regions, and bringing down ice; that this sea therefore sometimes freezes to such a degree, that its whole surface is congealed, to a considerable thickness; and, if the historians are to be credited, was frozen in the reign of Emperor Constantine Copronymus thirty ells thick, not including twenty ells of snow which was lying on the ice. This fact, continues M. *de Buffon,* seems to be exaggerated, but it is true however, that it freezes almost every winter, whilst the high seas which are 1000 leagues nearer, towards the pole do not freeze, which can have no other cause than the difference in saltness and the little quantity of ice carried out by rivers, if compared to the enormous quantity of ice which the rivers convey into the Black Sea." Mr. *de Buffon* is not mistaken when he mentions that the Black Sea frequently freezes. STRABO‡ informs us, that the people near the Bosporus Cimmerius pass this sea in

* Crantz's *Hist. of Greenland,* p. 31.
† Ibid vol. I. p. 318.
‡ Strabo. *Geogr.* Lib. vii. p. m. 212.[4]

carts from Panticapaeum to Phanagorea, and that Neoptolemus, a General of Mithridates Eupator, won a battle with his cavalry on the ice, on the very spot where he gained a naval victory in the summer. MARCELLINUS COMES* relates, that in the XIV Indiction, under the Consulship of Vincentius and Fravita, in the year 401 after Christ, the whole surface of the Pontus was covered with ice, and that the ice in spring was carried through the Propontis, during thirty days, like mountains. ZONARAS† mentions the sea between Constantinople and Scutari frozen to such a degree, in the reign of Constantine Copronymus, that even loaded carts passed over it. The Prince DEMETRIUS CANTEMIR‡ observes, that in the year 1620–21 there happened so intense a frost that the people walked over the ice from Constantinople to Iskodar. All these instances confirm Mr. *de Buffon*'s assertion; but as this great natural historian says, that the Black Sea is the only instance of a sea being entirely frozen*; I must beg leave to dissent from him, for it is equally well attested, that the Baltic is sometimes entirely frozen according to CASPAR SCHUTZ's account✦. In the year 1426, the winter was so severe that people travelled over the ice across the Baltic from Dantzick to Lubeck; and the sea was likewise passable from Denmark to Mecklenburgh, and in the year 1459, the whole Baltic was entirely frozen, so that persons travelled both on foot and on horseback, over ice from Denmark to the Venedick Hans-towns, called Lubeck, Wismar, Rostock and Stralsund, which had never happened before; people likewise travelled across the Baltic over ice from Reval in Estland to Denmark and to Sweden, and back again without the least danger♥. But according to SAEMUND

---

* Marcellinus Comes in Scaligeri edit. Euseb. p. 37.

† Zonaras in Constantino Copronymo and Nicephorus Patr. p. 43, 44, as well as Theophanes, p. 365, 366. mention, that in the winter 76⅔ almost during five months the Black Sea was covered from Zichia, (the country between the Kuban and Awchas) to Chazaria (the Crimea) and even to Bulguria with ice thirty ells thick.

‡ Demetr. *Cantemir hist. of the Othman Empire* in the *Modern Universal History*, vol. V. in fol. p. 347.

* In the year 860, the mediterranean was covered with ice, so that people travelled in carts and horses across the Ionian Sea to Venice. (*Hermannus Contractus ap. Pistor. Script.* t. II. p. 236.) And in 1234 the mediterranean was again thus frozen, that the Venetian merchants travelled over the ice with their merchandize to what place they chose, *Matth. Pariss.* p. 78.

✦ Caspar Schutz *Historia rerum Prussicarum*. Leipzig, fol. 1599, p. 114. and 281.

♥ In 1296 the Baltic was frozen from Gothland to Sweden. (*Incerti auctoris Annales Denor. in Westphalii monument. Cimbr.* t. I. p. 1392.)

In 1306, the Baltic was during fourteen weeks covered with ice, between all the Danish and Swedish islands. (*Ludwig reliquiae. MSStor.* t. IX. p. 170.)

In 1323, there was a road for foot passengers and horsemen over the ice on the Baltic during six weeks. (*id. ibid.*)

In 1349, people walked over the ice from Stralsund to Denmark. (*Lucerti auct. cit. ap. Ludwig.* t. IX. p. 171.)

FRODE* even the great German Ocean between Denmark and Norway was frozen in the year 1048, so that the Wolves frequently ran over the ice from one country to the other. The great Northern Ocean is likewise most certainly sometimes frozen to a great distance from any land, for MULLER[†] relates, that in the year 1715 a Cossack called MARKOFF with some other persons was sent by the Russian Government to explore the North Sea, but finding it next to impossible to make any progress during summer, on account of the vast quantities of ice commonly filling this ocean, he at last determined to try the experiment during winter; he therefore took several sledges drawn according to the custom of the country by dogs, which commonly go about 80 or 100 wersts per day, 105 of which make a degree. And on March the 15th, Old Style, with this caravan of nine persons, he left the shores of Sibiria at the mouth of the river Yana, under the $71°$ of North latitude, and proceeded for seven days, together Northward, so that he had reached at least the $77°$ or $78°$ North latitude, when he was stopped by the ice, which there began to appear in the shape of prodigious mountains. He climbed up to the top of some of these ice mountains, but seeing from thence no land, nor any thing except ice, as far as the eye could reach, and having besides no more food for this dogs left, he thought it very necessary to return, which he with great difficulty performed, on April the 3rd, as several of the dogs which had perished for want, were employed to support those that remained alive. These facts, I believe, will convince the unprejudiced reader, that there are other seas besides the Black Sea, which really do freeze in winter, and that the ice carried down the rivers, could not at least freeze the German Ocean between Norway and Denmark, because the rivers there are so small, and bear a very inconsiderable propor-

---

In 1408, the whole sea between Gothland and Oeland, and likewise between Rostock and Gezoer were frozen. id. ibid. 196.

In 1423, the ice bore riding from Prussia to Lubeck. (*Crantzii Vandal.* l. X. c. 40.) The whole sea was covered with ice from Mecklenburg to Denmark. (*Incert. auct. ap. Ludw.* t. IX. p. 125.)

In 1461, (says Nicol. Mareschallus in *annal. Herul. ap. Westphal.* t. I. p. 261.) Tanta erat hyems, ut concreto gelu oceano plaustris millia passuum supra CCC merces ad ultimam Thylen. (*Iceland*) & Orcades veherentur e *Germania* tota pene bruma.

In 1545, the sea between Rostock and Denmark, and likewise between Fionia and Sealand was thus frozen, that the people travelled over the ice on foot, and with sledges, to which horses and oxen were put. (*Anonym ap. Ludwig.* t. IX. p. 176.)

In 1294, the Cattegat or sea between Norway and Denmark was frozen, that from Oxslo in Norway, they could travel on it to Jutland. (Strelow *Chron. Juthiland*, p. 148.)

These historical notes were communicated to me, by Prof. Thunman at Hall in Saxony, and sent me by the Rev. Dr. Bushing, for which communications I return my best thanks.

* Saemund Frode apud Thormod. Torfaeum. Serie Dynast. regum Daniae. Hafniae 4to. 1705. p. 41.
[†] Muller's *Russische Samlungen*, vol. III. p. 41.

tion to the immense ocean, which according to experiments made by Mr. Wilke[*] is very salt, though near the land, in the Swedish harbour of Landscrona.

Now, if six or seven degrees of latitude, containing from 360 to 420 sea miles, are not to be reckoned a great distance from the land, I do not know in what manner to argue, because no distance whatsoever will be reckoned far from any land. Nay, if the Cossack Markoff, being mounted on one of the highest ice-mountains, may be allowed to see at least to the distance of 20 leagues, the extent alluded to above, must then be increased to 480 English sea-miles; which certainly is very considerable, and makes it more than probable, that the ocean is frozen in winter, in high Northern latitudes, even as far as the Pole. Besides, it invalidates the argument, which these gentlemen wish to infer from thence, *that the ocean does not freeze in high latitudes, especially where there is a considerably broad sea:* for we have shewn instances to the contrary.

But M. de Buffon speaks of ice carried down the rivers into the Northern ocean, and forming there these immense quantities of ice; "and in case, says he[†], we would suppose, against all probability, that at the Pole it could be so cold as to congeal the surface of the sea, it would remain equally incomprehensible, how these enormous floating ice-masses could be formed, if they had not land for a point to fix on, and from whence they are severed by the heat of the sun. The two ships, which the India Company sent in 1739, upon the discovery of the Austral lands, found ice in 47 or 48° South latitude, but at no great distance from land; which they discovered, without being able to approach it. This ice, therefore, must have come from the interior parts of the lands near the South Pole, and we must conjecture, that it follows the course of several large rivers, washing these unknown lands, in the same manner as the rivers Oby, the Yenisea, and the other great rivers which fall into the Northern sea, carry the ice-masses, which stop up the streights of Waigats for the greater part of the year, and render the Tartarean sea inaccessible upon this course." Before we can allow the analogy between the rivers Oby, Yenisea, and the rest which sail into the Northern ocean, and those coming from the interior parts of the Austral lands, let us compare the situation of both countries, supposing the Austral lands really to exist. The Oby, Yenisea, and the rest of the Sibirian rivers, falling down into the Northern ocean, have their sources in 48° and 50° North latitude, where the climate is mild and capable of producing corn of all kinds. All the rivers of this great continent increasing these great rivers, have likewise their sources in mild and temperate climates, and the main direction of their course is from South to North; and the coast of the Northern ocean, not reckoning its sinuosities, runs in general West and East. The

---

[*] *Memoirs of the Swedish Academy*, vol. 33. p. 66.
[†] Buffon *Hist. Nat.* tom. I. p. 313.

small rivers, which are formed in high latitudes, have, properly speaking, no sources, no springs, but carry off only the waters generated by the melting of snow in spring, and by the fall of rain in the short summer, and are for the greatest part dry in autumn. And the reason of this phaenomenon is obvious, after considering the constitution of the earth in those high Northern climates. At Yakutik, in about 62° North latitude, the soil is eternally frozen, even in the height of summer, at the depth of three feet from the surface. In the years 1685 and 1686, an attempt was made to dig a well; and a man, by great and indefatigable labour, continued during two summer-seasons, succeeded so far in this laborious task, that he at last reached the depth of 91 feet; but the whole earth at this depth was frozen, and he met with no water, which forced him to desist from so fruitless an attempt*. And it is easy to infer from hence, how impossible it is, that springs should be formed in the womb of an eternally frozen soil. But let us now compare with this, the situation of the pretended unknown Austral lands. The coast of this land must be to the South of our navigation, in 60°, 67°, and 71° South latitude; and its direction we will allow to be East and West; the course, therefore, of the rivers must be from South to North, i.e. from the interior parts of the land towards the ocean. When we came towards the 54° South latitude, we found a small isle of about 80 leagues in circumference; the thermometer continued at about 30°, 32°, and 34°, in its neighbourhood, in the midst of summer; though isles have in general a milder climate than continents, we found, however, all this country entirely covered with immense loads of snow, the bottoms of its bays were choaked up with solid masses of ice, of 60 or 80 feet above water, and we saw no vestiges either of rivers or of springs. If this be the case in 54° South latitude, how can we then expect any springs or rivers in 60° or 71° South latitude, or rather still higher up to the South, where the sources of these imaginary rivers of the pretended Austral land, must be removed? It is therefore impossible to say, that the rivers of the Austral land carried those ice-masses into the ocean, which we met with in such stupendous quantities.

There is one circumstance more, which surely most evidently proves, that there is no land in those latitudes, which are still capable of vegetation. In all the high Northern seas, there is constantly such a prodigious quantity of wood thrown on the shores of all the lands, *viz.* Nova Zemla, Spitzbergen, Greenland, Beering's-Island, &c. &c. that though none is growing there, the unfortunate individuals, that are obliged to spend a winter there, however, are sufficiently provided with this most necessary commodity. In all the Southern seas, there is no drifting wood to be met with. The French searched a great extent of the shores of the Falkland Islands, with great care, but found not above one or two pieces of

---

* Gmelin's *Voyage to Sibiria*, vol. 2. p. 520–523.

wood thrown up by the sea; nor did we see any on the island of South-Georgia: all which sufficiently evinces the truth of the above assertion.

The argument, therefore, is now reduced to this, "*That salt-water does not freeze at all, or, if it does, the ice contains briny particles.*" But we have already before produced numberless instances, that the sea does freeze; nay, CRANTZ* allows, *that the flat pieces of ice are salt, because they were congealed from sea-water.* We beg leave to add a few decisive facts relative to the freezing of the sea. BARENTZ[†] observes in the year 1596, September the 16th, the sea froze two fingers thick, and next night the ice was as thick again. This happened in the middle of September; what effect then must the intense frost of a night in January not produce? When Capt. JAMES[‡] wintered in Charleton's Isle, the sea froze in the middle of December 1631: it remains therefore only to examine, whether the ice formed in the sea must necessarily contain briny particles. And here I find myself in a very disagreeable dilemma, for during the intense frost of the winter, in 1776, two sets of experiments were made on the freezing of sea-water, and published*, contradicting one another almost in every material point. The one by Mr. Edward Nairne F.R.S. an ingenious and accurate observer; the other by Dr. Higgins, who reads Lectures on Chemistry and Natural Philosophy, and consequently must be supposed to be well acquainted with the subject.[5] I will therefore still venture to consider the question as undecided by these experiments, and content myself with making a few observations on them; but previously I beg leave to make this general remark, that those, who are well acquainted with Mechanics, Chemistry, Natural Philosophy and the various Arts which require a nice observation of minute circumstances, need not be informed, that an experiment or machine, succeeds often very well, when made upon a smaller scale, but will not answer if undertaken at large; and *vice versa* machines and experiments executed upon a small scale will not produce the effect, which they certainly have when made in a more enlarged manner. A few years ago an experiment made on the dying of scarlet, did not succeed when undertaken on a small scale, whereas it produced the desired effect when tried at a dyer's house with the large apparatus; and it evidently confirms the above assertion, which I think I have a right to apply to the freezing of salt-water. It is therefore probable, that the ice formed in the ocean at large, in a higher latitude, and in a more intense degree of cold, whereof we have no idea here, may become solid, and free from any briny particles, though a few

---

* Crantz. p. 31.

[†] *Recueil des Voyages qui ont servi à l'Establissement de la Compagnie des Indes Orientales.* vol. 1.

[‡] *Histoire des Voyages*, vol. LVII. edit. in 12mo. p. 421.

* Mr. NAIRNE's experiments are found in the *Philos. Trans.* vol. LXVI. p. 249. and Dr. Higgins's in a *second supplement to the Probability of reaching the North Pole.* p. 121, 142.

experiments made by Dr. Higgins, in his house, on the freezing of salt-water produced only a loose, spungy ice, filled with briny particles.

The ice formed of sea-water by Mr. Nairne, was very hard, 3½ inches long, and 2 inches in diameter; it follows from thence, that the washing the outside of this ice in fresh water, could not affect the inside of a hard piece of ice. This ice when melted, yielded fresh water, which was specifically lighter than water, which was a mixture of rain and snow water; and next in lightness to distilled water. Had the ice thus obtained, not been fresh, the residuum of the sea water, after this ice had been taken out, could not have been specifically heavier than sea-water, which however was the case in Mr. Nairne's experiment. It seems therefore, in my opinion, evident from hence, that salt-water does freeze, and has no other briny Particles, than what adhere to its outside. All this perfectly agrees with the curious fact related by Mr. ADANSON*, who had brought to France two bottles of sea-water, taken up in different parts of the ocean, in order to examine it and to compare its saltness, when more at leisure; but both the bottles containing the salt-water were burst by being frozen, and the water produced from melting the ice, proved perfectly fresh. This fact is so fairly stated, and so very natural, that I cannot conceive it is necessary to suppose†, without the least foundation for it, *that the bottles were changed, or that Mr. Adanson does not mention the circumstance by which the sea-water was thus altered upon its being dissolved:* for as he expressly observes the bottles to have been burst, it is obvious that the concentrated briny parts ran out and were entirely drained from the ice, which was formed of the fresh water only.

The ice formed by Dr. Higgins from sea-water, *consisted of thin laminae, adhering to each other weakly.* Dr. Higgins took out the frozen ice from the vessels, wherein he exposed the sea-water, and continued to do so till the remaining concentrated sea-water began to form crystals of sea salt. Both these experiments therefore by no means prove what the Dr. intended to infer from thence; for it was wrong to take out such ice, which only *consisted of thin laminae, adhering to each other weakly.* Had he waited with patience, he would have obtained a hard ice as well as Mr. Nairne, which, by a more perfect congelation, would have excluded the briny particles intercepted between the *thin laminae, adhering to each other weakly;* and would have connected the laminae, by others formed by fresh water. The Dr. found afterwards, it is true, thicker and somewhat more solid ice, in the vessel B: but the sea-water had already been so much concentrated by repeated congelations, that it is no wonder the ice formed in it, became at last

---

* Adanson *Histoire naturelle du Senegal.* Paris 1757, 4to. p. 190.
† *Second supplement, to the Probability of reaching the North Pole,* p. 119.

brackish: it should seem then, that no conclusive arguments can be drawn from these experiments.

There are two other objections against the formation of the ice in the great ocean; the *first* is taken from the immense bulk and size of the ice masses formed in the ocean, which is *the deepest mass of water we know of**. But the reader is referred to the table communicated above where it appears, that in the midst of summer, in the latitudes of 55°, 55° 26′, and 64° South, at 100 fathoms depth, the thermometer was at 34°, 34½° and 32°; and that in all instances, the difference between the temperature at top and at 100 fathoms depth, never exceeded 4 degrees, of Fahrenheit's thermometer, or that the temperature of the air did not differ five degrees from that of the ocean at 100 fathom deep. If we now add to this, that beyond the 71° South, the temperature of the air and ocean must be still colder, and that the rigours of an antarctic winter are certainly more than sufficient to cool the ocean to 28½°, which is requisite for congealing the aqueous particles in it; if we moreover consider, that these severe frosts are continued during six or eight months of the year, we may easily conceive that there is time enough to congeal large and extensive masses of ice. But it is likewise certain, that there is more than one way, by which those immense ice masses are formed. We suppose very justly, that the ocean does freeze, having produced so many instances of it; we allow likewise that the ice thus formed in a calm, perhaps does not exceed three or four yards in thickness†; a storm probably often breaks such an icefield, which Crantz allows to be 200 leagues one way, and eighty the other; the pressure of the broken fragments against one another, frequently sets one upon the other piece, and they freeze in that manner together; several such double pieces, thrown by another pressure upon one another, form at last large masses of miles extent, and of twenty, forty, sixty and more fathoms thickness, or of a great bulk and height. MARTENS‡ in his description of Spitzbergen, remarks that the pieces of ice cause so great a noise by their shock, that the navigator in those regions, can only, with difficulty hear the words of those that speak; and as the ice-pieces are thrown one upon another, ice-mountains are formed by it. And I observed very frequently, in the years 1772 and 1773, when we were amongst the ice, masses which had the most evident marks of such a formation, being composed of strata of some feet in thickness. This is in some measure confirmed by the state in which the Cosack Markoff found the ice at the distance of 420 miles from the Sibirian coasts. The high masses were not found formed, as is suspected in the *Second Supplement to the Probability of reaching the North Pole*,

---

* Dr. Higgins's experiments, in the *second supplement to the Probability*, &c. p. 141.

† Crantz, p. 31.

‡ Martens *Voyages au Nord*, tom. II. p. 62.

p. 143–145, near the land, under the high cliffs, but far out at sea; and when these ice-mountains were climbed by Markoff, nothing but ice, and no vestiges of land appeared as far as the eye could reach. The high climates near the Poles, are likewise subject to heavy falls of snow, of several yards in thickness, which grow more and more compact, and by thaws and rain, are formed into solid ice, which increase the stupendous size of the floating ice-mountains.

The *second* objection against the freezing of the ocean into such ice as is found floating in it, is taken from the *opacity* of ice formed in salt-water; because the largest masses are commonly transparent like crystal, with a fine blue tinct, caused by the reflection of the sea. This argument is very specious, and might be deemed unanswerable to those, who are not used to cold winters, and their effects; but whosoever has spent several winters in countries, which are subject to intense frosts, will find nothing extraordinary or difficult in this argument: for it is a well-known fact in cold countries, that the ice, which covers their lakes and rivers, is often opaque, especially when the frost sets in, accompanied by a fall of snow; for, in those instances, the ice looks, before it hardens, like a dough or paste, and when congealed it is opaque and white; however in spring, a rain and the thaw, followed by frosty nights, change the opacity and colour of the ice, and make it quite transparent and colourless like a crystal; but, in case the thaw continues, and it ceases entirely to freeze, the same transparent ice become soft and porous, and turns again entirely opaque*. This, I believe, may be applicable to the ice seen by us in the ocean. The field-ice was commonly opaque; some of the large masses, probably drenched by rain, and frozen again, were transparent and pellucid; but the small fragments of loose ice, formed by the decay of the large masses, and soaked by long continued rains, we found to be porous, soft, and opaque.

It is likewise urged as an argument against the formation of ice in the ocean, that it always requires land, in order to have a point upon which it may be fixed†. First, I observe, that in Mr. Nairne's experiments, the ice was generated on the surface, and was seen shooting crystals downwards; which evidently evinces, in my opinion, that ice is there formed or generated where the intensest cold is; as the air sooner cools the surface, than the depth of the ocean, the ice shoots naturally downwards, and cools the ocean more and more, by which it is prepared for further congelation. I suppose, however, that this happens always during calms, which are not uncommon in high latitudes, as we experienced in the late expedition. Nor does land seem absolutely necessary in order to fix the ice; for this may be done with as much ease and propriety to the large ice-mountains, which remain undissolved floating in the ocean in high latitudes: or it may, perhaps, not

---

* Martens *Recueil des Voyages au Nord*, tom.2. p. 62.
† Buffon, *Hist. Nat.* vol. I. p. 34.

be improper to suppose, that the whole Polar region, from 80° and upwards, in the Southern hemisphere, remains a solid ice for several years together, to which yearly a new circle of ice is added, and of which, however, part is broken off by the winds, and the return of the mild season. Wherever the ice floats in large masses, and sometimes in compact bodies formed of an infinite number of small pieces, there it is by no means difficult to freeze the whole into one piece, for, amongst the ice, the wind has not a power of raising high and great waves. This circumstance was not entirely unknown to the ancients; and it is probable they acquired this information from the natives of ancient Gaul, and from the Britons, and other Northern nations, who sometimes undertook long voyages. The North-ern ocean was called by the ancients the *frozen*, the *dead*, the *lazy*, and *immovable sea*: sometimes they gave it the name *mare cronium*, the concrete sea, and *mori-marusa*, the dead sea*. And, what is very remarkable, in all the Northern cold countries, the frost sometimes is so intense, that all the waters become suddenly coagulated into a kind of paste or dough, and thus at once congeal[†]. We may therefore, with great propriety, think, that the intense cold in the high Austral regions has the same effect, suddenly to congeal parts of the ocean, especially as, according to our last observations, and those of other travellers, the Antarctic cli-

---

* DIONYS. PERIEGETES. v. 32. 33. Ποντον μεν καλεουσι ΠΕΠΗΓΟΤΑ τε, ΚΡΟΝΙΟΝ τε
            Αλλοι δꝛ αυ και ΝΕΚΡΟΝ εφημισαν, εινεκꝛ αφαυρου
            Ηελιου
  ORPHEUS *Argonautic.* v. 1079. 1080. Εμπεσε δꝛ Ωκεανω, ΚΡΟΝΙΟΝ δε εκικλησκουσι
            Ποντον ΥΠΕΡΒΟΡΕΗΝ μεροπες, ΝΕΚΡΗΝ τε θαλασσαν.
  STRABO, lib. ii. p. m. 71. says, after Pytheas of Marseilles, that near Thule, to the North, the sea is neither land, nor sea, nor air, but a concrete of them all, like sea-lungs; which plainly proves, that the famous traveller of Marseilles had heard some account concerning the congelation of the sea, which, when compared with the other accounts, and the names given to this North sea by the ancients, are together a strong proof, that the whole account originated with the Gaelic and Celtic nations; for it is in their language, that we must look for the meaning of those names, which are found in Pliny, viz. *Morimarusa*, the *dead sea*; Mor in the Welch is the sea, and *marω*, *dead*; so that *mor-marω* signifies the *dead sea*; in the Irish, *muir-croinn* is the *coagulated, thick, concrete* sea; (see TOLAND's History of the Druids, in the *Collection of several Pieces*. London, 1726. 8vo. vol. I. p. 149.) So that the *Cronian* sea was not called from Cronus or Saturn, but from its congealed, coagulated state.
  TACITUS, *de Mor. Germ.* c. 45. Trans Suionas, aliud mare *pigrum*, ac prope *immotum*——quod extremus cadentis jam solis fulgor in ortus edurat, adeo clarus, ut sidera hebetet.
  PLINIUS. *Hist. Nat.* lib. iv. c. 13. Septentrionalis Oceanus; *Amalchium* eum Hecataeus adpellat, a Paropamiso amne, qua Scythiam alluit, quod nomen ejus gentis lingua significat *congelatum*. Philemon *Morimarusam* a Cimbris vocari, hoc est *mortuum mare*, usque ad Promontorium Rubeas: ultra deinde *Cronium*. Et cap. 16. A Thule unius diei navigatione *mare concretum*, a nonnullis *Cronium* adpellatur.[6]
† See Gmelin's *Voyage to Sibiria*.

mate is undoubtedly colder than the Northern hemisphere, in corresponding degrees of latitude.

The ingenious M. de Buffon* says, "The navigators pretend that the continent of the Austral lands is much colder than that of the Arctic Pole; but there is not the least appearance that this opinion is well founded, and probably it has been adopted by voyagers on no other account, than because they found ice in a latitude, where it is seldom or never to be met with in our Northern seas; but that may be produced by some peculiar causes." If we compare the meteorological observations made at Falkland's Islands, at about 51° South latitude, and communicated by ALEXANDER DALRYMPLE, Esq, in his *Collection of Voyages chiefly to the Southern Atlantic Ocean,* with such as are every where made in Europe, in corresponding degrees of latitude of the Northern hemisphere; if we consider, that in Tierra del Fuego, Staten Land, and South-Georgia, from 54° to 56° South latitude, and in Sandwich Land, in about 58° and 59° South latitude, the whole land is covered with eternal snow to the shores of the sea, in the months of December and January, corresponding to our June and July; every unprejudiced reader will find it necessary to allow the temperature of the Southern hemisphere, to be remarkably colder than that of the Northern; and no one will, I believe, for the future, venture to question this curious fact in the Natural History of our Globe.

But, as the inquisitive reader may require of me a solution of this curious and difficult phaenomenon, I will venture to deliver my opinion on the subject; and hope, that if it prove not entirely satisfactory, it may, however, contribute towards an explanation or many things, which perhaps were not before considered in this point of view. Having maturely considered every circumstance, I find that, with other causes founded on the apparent motion of the sun, the absence of land in the high latitudes of the Southern hemisphere, creates this material difference in the temperature of the air, between the corresponding degrees of latitude in the Arctic and the Antarctic hemispheres.

In the Arctic regions, from 60° to 66½ degrees and upwards, there is much land to be met with, *viz.* Iceland, Spitzbergen, the North of Norway and Sweden, all Lapland, all the Northern parts of European and Asiatic Russia: beyond its Eastern extremities in Kamtchatka, are those numerous isles lately discovered by the Russians; and the lands of North-America, about Hudson's and Baffin's Bay; and last of all, New and Old Greenland. Some of these lands are inhabited, and even cultivated, and bear various kinds of fruit and corn; and, during the short summers they enjoy, there is sometimes an intense heat, very little inferior to that between the Tropics. Let us now compare this with our experience in the Antar-

* Buffon's *Hist. Nat.* vol. I. p. 312.

tic hemisphere. We found no land wherever we sailed, about 60° and upwards to the South, except the two little spots in the Southern Atlantic ocean. The thermometer, in the height of summer, in these high latitudes, was never five degrees above the freezing point, and we saw it frequently pointing below it. We often had snow and sleet, and found our water in the skuttled watercask on deck, frozen during some nights. If all this happen in the midst of summer, what must the condition of these climates be during winter? The accounts of the Spanish*, Dutch†, French‡, and especially of our English* navigators, relative to the temperature of the Austral regions about Patagonia, Tierra del Fuego, Falkland's Islands, and the neighbouring seas, perfectly correspond with our experience. And in the Falkland's Islands, the thermometer, during a whole year, did not vary, at a medium, above 20°♦. It is therefore evident and beyond all doubt, that there is no large continent from 60° to 71° and upwards and that the inconsiderable fragments existing there, are much colder than the lands in any corresponding Northern degree.

The sea being a transparent body, the beams of a sun penetrate a great way into it, but at last at the depth of about 271 feet English measure the rays of light do not pass any farther, and a body of the above-mentioned height of sea-water, becomes perfectly opaque.♥ Wherever therefore no bottom is to be met with at the depth of 45 fathoms, the sea cannot reflect any beams of the sun, which are absorbed, and as it were swallowed up in the depth of the ocean: and as the reflection of the beams of the sun chiefly contributes to the warm temperature of the air, it hence becomes evident, that seas of great extent, which commonly exceed 45 fathoms in depth, have never so warm a temperature of the air, as the lands lying under the same parallel; and for the very same reason, islands of a moderate size, surrounded by a great ocean, are not so hot, as large continents situated under the same parallel. To these particulars may be added, the famous experiment of the burning mirror, whose focus, when directed on a quantity of water, produced no heat, whereas, in the same focus, any metal would instantaneously melt, vitrify and evaporate; nor can we omit the well known circumstance, that the sun moves eight days longer in the Northern, than in the Southern signs of the zodiac. This makes the winter eight days longer, and their summers eight days shorter; which all together must cool the Southern hemisphere, by a $22^{13}/_{16}$ or very near by a 23rd part more than the arctic regions.

---

* Amerigo Vespucci, 3d Voyage. Garcia Nodal. Sarmiento.[7]

† Roggewein, *Recueil des Voyages pour l'Establissement des Indes Orientales*, tom. 4.

‡ Bougainville, M. de Gennes, Frezier, Beauchesne Gouin, Bouvet.

* Drake, Cavendish, Sharp, Sir John Narborough, Wood, Woods Rogers, Halley, Anson, &c. &c.[8]

♦ Dalrymple's *Collection*, and *Philos. Trans.* vol. 66.

♥ Bouguer *Essai d'Optique sur la Gradation de la lumiere*.

ICE

Cuncta gelu, canaque aeternum grandine tecta
Atque aevi glaciem cohibent, riget ardua montis
Aetherii facies, surgentique obvia Phoebo,
Duratas nescit flammis mollire pruinas.
   Silius Italicus lib. iii. v. 480[9]

I might have been less prolix in regard to the observations on the ice, its formation and causes of the cold, had I not thought, that by collecting here as it were every material circumstance, relative to the ice in the Southern hemisphere, into one chapter, and examining what has been said on both sides of the question, some future navigators might be better enabled to judge, how far the observed facts correspond with the assigned causes. If they should find reasons to be of a contrary opinion, they will certainly be induced to publish the facts, upon which that opinion was founded; they will point out my mistakes, and shew the causes of my error; in short they will assert truth, by which science will be benefited and human knowledge enlarged. If on the contrary, the arguments alledged in behalf of my assertions are found incontrovertible, they probably will give my arguments new support and strength, and place beyond the reach of doubt, what I have endeavoured to hint at, as the only truth. In either case, I have endeavoured to do my part, I have represented facts as they really occured to me, and on that account I hope my prolixity will be less offensive.

I might here have subjoined many other particulars relative to the ocean; I might have given some account of its currents, and of the different constitution of its bottom, where we had any soundings; of the various tides; and of the dipping and variation of the magnetical needle; but I forbear to speak on these subjects, as they are partly the objects of the nautical observations, made by the officers of ships sent on this expedition, which have been presented to the Lords Commissioners of the Admiralty, and by their command are published in Captain Cook's nautical account;[10] and as the board of longitude, had likewise charged two astronomers, to make accurate observations on magnetism and the tides, it would therefore be very improper, to attempt a business so ably discharged by others; who with proper instruments for that purpose, more leisure, and with more command of assistance, had better opportunities of making more perfect observations on these subjects.

CHAPTER III

Remarks on the Atmosphere, and its Changes, Meteors, and Phaenomena

MUNDI PARS EST AER QUIDEM NECESSARIA.
  Seneca[1]

SECTION I

Aqueous Meteors

We proceed now to the consideration of a less dense element, and its various changes and phaenomena, and shall treat first, of the aqueous meteors; because more closely connected with the former section.

First, The climate within the tropics being very warm, and the nights rather long, the vapours raised in the day time by the heat of the sun, are condensed towards night, and fall frequently, as a *dew* on every part of the ship: and this we sometimes observed in the midst of the atlantic ocean, though at a great distance from any land. We had a few instances of a strong dew falling in the higher latitudes, of which I will only select one on January 8th, at 10 P.M. 1775; when we were sailing between 50° and 60° and far enough from land, we found the whole deck and all the rigging moistened by a copious dew. I am therefore inclined to believe, that a heavy fall of dew, cannot any longer be considered as a certain or infallible sign of the neighbourhood of lands.

Secondly, The Tropical isles having been visited by us at two different times, *viz.* once from August to October, in 1773, and again from March to September, 1774, we can hardly from thence form an idea of the changes and the returns of the seasons, as, each time, during our whole stay, the sun was in the Northern hemisphere: however, if we consider that we were at O-Taheitee at the latter end

of August, and again in April and the beginning of May, and that we found a very
material difference in the external appearance of vegetation, we may be allowed
to conclude, that this was owing to the difference of seasons; for, in countries
between the tropics, Nature seems to be more uniform and constant in the setting
in of winds and rains, than without the tropics. The difference was too striking
not to be noticed; and, if it were not caused by the natural return of the seasons, it
must have been produced by a very extraordinary deviation from the uniform
tenor of the changes produced within the tropics; which may be possible, but
hardly probable.

The hills in O-Taheitee were covered in August with dry and dead herbage,
a great part of it had been burnt by the natives, and gave the country a barren and
dreary look. The isle had very little bread-fruit, few or no apples, and the ban-
nanas were scarce: and if we except the eddoes, the greater part of vegetables were
but moderately plentiful, and hogs scarcely to be had at all. But when we arrived
eight months after, in April, the hills as far as their very summits, were clad with
the most agreeable verdure; the trees on the plains were bending under the
weight of bread-fruit; in the valleys the largest apple-trees were loaded with their
excellent fruit;[2] all the shores fringed by innumerable coco-nut trees, offered a
vast profusion of these useful nuts; nay the valleys between the higher hills, were
entirely covered with immense clusters of the horse-plantain, while each cottage
was surrounded with considerable plantain-walks of the better sort, richly providing a more delicious food: we obtained in a little time a great quantity of large and
well tasted hogs from the natives, and saw every where, more left. This so material difference was, in my opinion, caused by the natural change of seasons. When
we came there the last time, the sun had then just left the Southern hemisphere;
and it has been generally observed, that wherever the sun is vertical within the
tropics, there its powerful beams accelerate the rising of the vapours, and cause a
profusion of rain; which together with the vivifying influence of the sun, of
course refreshes and quickens vegetation, infuses new life in all the animated part
of nature, and produces plenty every where.

But this very idea leads me to another view of nature. O-Taheitee and all the
high islands, are in general more happy and more fertile, than the low islands,
and those of a moderate height. The high hills in the middle of the first, attract
by their situation, all the vapours and clouds that pass near them; there are but
few days, on which their summits are not involved in fogs and clouds; and though
it does not constantly rain there, yet such a regular supply of moisture is derived
from these hills, that their very tops are crowned with lofty trees, and their sides
fringed with shrubs and agreeable plants during the whole year; and all the surrounding valleys collect in their bosom the salutary humidity, which is not
absorbed by these plants, and which is generously screened by them against the

sun's power; so that in every one a gentle stream is collected from the smaller rills, which unite into one bed. This rivulet the natives stem here and there by wears, made of large stones, in order to water the plantations of eddoes; the frequent trees that are growing along the banks of the sweet purling stream, extend their shady branchs, give a coolness to the virgin-water, and thus bring refreshment, and the principles of life into the plains, where the rivulet begins to meander between the rich plantations of bread-fruit, apple and cloth trees, and bannana's, and spreads happiness and plenty. These rivers become the fountains and chief causes of the great variety of fruit, which grow every where; they enliven the picturesque scenery, and afford a cooling liquor for the inhabitants. Whereas the natives of the lower isles, have no other but coco-nut trees round their habitations, which thrive well in a sandy soil, and close to the sea-shore often within the reach of the spray; and the rain water preserved in deep filthy pits and ponds, full of green, slimy, aquatic plants, and stinking from its stagnation, is the only refreshing liquor they enjoy after they have been exposed on the reef (where they must resort for the fishery) to the parching sun and spray of the seas. Such is the difference in the dispensation of the salutary rains, caused by the different structure of the isles.

Though the high hills constantly attract the moisture of the clouds and cause many rains during the whole year, there is however a season, when the rains are more copious; and this was just passed, when we came the second time to O-Taheitee; for all the streams and rivulets were full of water, whereas before, they had hardly water enough to moisten the ground.

The very hills which are the cause of the fertility and happiness of these isles, produce likewise another phaenomenon, viz. as they attract the rising vapours, and passing clouds of the atmosphere: the temperature of the air is therefore frequently changed, and consequently sudden gusts of winds are produced by the change, with concomitant squalls of rain; this is an intimation to navigators of the vicinity of land, as we several times experienced. We had squalls and lightning on the 23d, of September 1773, when we discovered Hervey's Isle. The same happened after we had passed Mopeeha or Howe's Isle on June 7th, 1774; when we fell in with the Marquesas and O-Taheitee, we had some sudden gusts of wind with rain; when we came to Tofooa one of the Friendly Isles, when we came into the vicinity of Whitsuntide isle, and during a good while, that we were about the New-Hebrides; when we came to Norfolk-Isle, and near New-Zeeland, we experienced the same sudden gusts of wind with showers of rain; all which seems to have been likewise noticed by that intelligent observer, Mr. de Bougainville*.

Thirdly, That in the course of our voyage, we should especially to the South

---

* See his *voyage*, p. 278, and 284 of the English edition.

have FOGS is very natural, from the nature of the climate, and the analogy in the Northern hemisphere; nor would it deserve any further notice, was it not for a very curious, and as far as I know, quite new observation, first kindly communicated by that great and experienced navigator, Capt. Cook, and which I afterwards had frequent opportunities of seeing confirmed, by my own experience.

If after a hard gale, with a high sea and a swell, we met with a calm, and a fog fell in at the same time, we observed that the swell, instead of gradually abating, as should be the natural consequence of a calm, always increased; which seems to be caused by the pressure of the atmosphere, loaded with such a quantity of aqueous particles, as is always the case in a fog.

Fourthly, The repeated approach of our ship to the Antarctic circle, was often announced by the fall of SNOW, SLEET, and HAIL: but the first year in 1772, we had snow very early in the latitude of 51° on December 11th. In the course of the following years, we never had snow, except when we came into the neighbourhood of that circle. However, it must be observed, this happened during the height of summer: what weather then must not the winter-season afford? We were happy enough to meet with no land to the South; which might have seduced us to spend a cold season somewhere on it, and to experience the rigors of an Antarctic winter.

Fifthly, When we were going into Queen Charlotte's Sound, in the year 1773, May 17th, we found ourselves nearly abreast of Cape Stephens, between three and four o'clock in the afternoon; the wind abated gradually, and we had almost a calm. It had rained the day before, and blew hard all the night; and in the morning the weather had been mild, pleasant, and warm, the thermometer standing at 56½°. At a quarter after four o'clock, we observed to the South-West some thick clouds; and to all appearance it rained on the Southern parts of the Cape. Immediately we saw a whitish spot on the surface of the sea, from whence a string or column rose upwards, while another soon after came down from the clouds, and joined the former.[3] A little while after, we saw three more of these columns forming, the nearest of which was at the distance of about three miles; at its base, where it was considerably the largest, (its diameter appearing at that distance to be of 70 or 80 fathom in extent) the water of the sea was violently agitated, rose in vapours and steam, and, being illuminated by the sun, looked bright and yellowish, especially against the black clouds behind; but, before the sun shone out, it looked white. As these columns came nearer towards us down the streights, we had an opportunity of examining them more particularly. Their diameter above, towards the clouds, was larger than that in their middle, which latter seemd not to exceed *two or three feet.* The water was whirled upwards in a spiral: sometimes it seemed that there was a hollow space within the column, and that the water formed only a cylinder; for the body of the column had, towards its axis, a hue different from the rest, and much the appearance of a hollow glass tube. As these columns moved forwards on the surface of the sea, the clouds did not follow them equally fast; and this circumstance gave them an oblique position, and sometimes a curved shape. Their motions seemed not to be of equal velocity, nor apparently in the same direction; one seemed therefore to pass the others, and they were viewed across one another. In proportion as they came nearer to us, the sea appeared more and more agitated, by short, broken waves. We had then some wind, but by no means settled, for it blew in one quarter of an hour, almost from all points of the compass. The first of these four columns was the Southernmost, and lasted the longest; the Northernmost of them was the nearest to us, and moved apparently Southward, and likewise towards us; and, as the clouds, with which the upper parts of the columns were connected, did not follow with the same velocity, with which the lower parts moved on the surface of the water, they disappeared soon after; because the columns being drawn out, as it were, to too great a length, were necessarily broken.

Whilst we were still observing these four water-spouts, we remarked, not above half a mile from the ship, on its starboard quarter, a spot on the sea of about

ATMOSPHERE

"Waterspouts in Cook's Straits, in New Zealand," engraving after William Hodges, in William Wales and William Bayly, *The Original Astronomical Observations, made in the course of a Voyage towards the South Pole*, 1777, Plate 4. National Library of Australia.

50 or 60 fathoms in diameter, more agitated than the rest. The water moved quick towards the center, in short and broken waves, and there being resolved in steam, rose up in spirals towards the clouds; but we could not so well distinguish the pillar, while it rose in this water-spout, as in the others, because the steam raised from the sea, obstructed the sight. The noise it caused, was like that of a cascade rolling down a deep glen. As this spout moved along towards the ship, it came abreast of it, and was, when nearest, within two cables length. A few hail-stones fell during this time on deck. Soon after, another water-spout was discovered behind this last. A cloud of steam formed below, and moved upwards in a spiral, in a shape gradually decreasing towards the summit. Another cloud of a long slender form, tapering towards its lower extremity, seemed to descend towards the rising spout, and both ends united and became very cylindrical and erect; but in time moving to the South-East, it assumed an oblique and curved form; and at last, when it broke, we observed in its neighbourhood, a flash of lightning, but heard no explosion. The spout next to us had disappeared a short time before. It was then just five o'clock, and the thermometer was at 54°. We had several showers during the time of the appearance of the water-spouts, and had hauled up the courses, and clued up the top-sails.

After the hard gale, which had blown the same year, from the 22d of October, at noon, till we were off Cape Palliser on the 29th, the gale still continuing strong, and the sea turbulent, I was told by the officers of our ship, that in the morning-watch several water-spouts had been seen. At eight o'clock we had a slight shower of rain, and immediately after the wind changed, the thermometer being at 51½°.

From these facts, I beg leave to draw the following corollaries. *First,* Water-spouts seem to be formed by eddies of winds, which, in their conflict, cause a circular motion of the air, contributing towards the raising of the sea-water in steam; and the vacuum, caused by the rarefied air in the midst of the column, seems to attract the clouds, and to give them a conic shape, whose point stands downwards.

Secondly, From the flash of lightning, it should seem, that the clouds were then electric; and that therefore the coalition of the two tubes from the sea and the clouds, may be owing to electric attraction*.

Thirdly, Water-spouts are commonly formed near lands having projecting

---

* In the *Philos. Transactions*, vol. xlvii. n. 80. p. 478. it is said, that a water-spout in Lincolnshire ended in a fiery stream. The spout, which made so great a havock at Rome, June 14th, 1749, observed by Father Boscowich, was continually emitting flashes of lightning on all sides. The spout also described by DAMPIER, vol. iii. p. 182, came out of a black cloud, that yielded great store of rain, thunder, and lightning. See Dr. FRANKLIN's *Experiments and Observations on Electricity,* 5th edit. London. 4to. 1774. p. 229 and 280. Mr. Adanson likewise observed a water-spout preceded by a thunder-storm, and found the spout extremely hot, which may be chiefly owing to the inflamed air, conveyed in this spout by an Easterly wind from the inland parts of Africa. ADANSON's *Voyage to Senegal.*

promontories, within narrow seas, straits, and other places where the winds form currents and eddies, and coming in conflict with other winds, take a contrary direction from the position of some promontory or strait. Those water-spouts, which Thevenot has described, were observed in the Persian Gulph, between the isles of Guésomo, Laréca, and Ormus.[4] A friend of mine saw several in the inundated rice-fields along Canton river in China. Dr. Shaw observed some in the Mediterranean, near the Capes Carmel, Greego, and Laodicea.[5] Both our water-spouts were formed within, or near the entrance of Cook's Straits, between the two isles of New Zeeland, among many projecting head-lands, at the mouth of sounds and bays, extending several leagues up the country, and forming remarkable windings*.

Fourthly, Water-spouts are commonly observed in a calm, after hard gales, and sometimes after warm, mild weather, especially when the upper region of the air is remarkably cooler; for we had met with smart showers of rain the preceding day, and it blew hard all the night before: in the morning, the violence of the wind gradually abated, and it became mild. When the water-spouts were just forming, the thermometer was at 56½°, which had been at 51½° the day before. During the time that one of them approached us, some hail fell, which proves the upper region of the atmosphere to have been cooler than the lower, by 20 degrees at least; and, after the spouts had all disappeared, the thermometer was at 54°; consequently even the atmosphere below, had been remarkably cooled in three quarters of an hour.

Mr. de Buffon, vol. ii. p. 287. edit. in 12mo, finds it necessary, in order to account for all the phaenomena attending water-spouts, to suppose that there is always a place under the sea, where some subterraneous fire releases a great deal of air, which raises the sea, causes a bubbling and a smoke, and unites the clouds with the sea, by a spout. But we cannot help remarking, that the vapours appeared to all of us, as steam raised by violent winds, and by no means as smoke produced by fire. Nay, had the place been heated by a subterraneous fire, the thermometer would certainly have risen higher; but we observed it to fall, which clearly proved the air to have become cooler. I will only add, that the rarefaction of the air and electricity, are certainly more than sufficient for the explanation of the various phaenomena of this meteor.

Vocatur & columna, quum spissatus humor rigensque ipse se sustinet. Ex codem genere &
in longum veluti fistula nubes aquam trahit.
    Plinii *Hist. Nat.* lib. ii. c. 49[6]

---

* Whoever is desirous of meeting with more instances of water-spouts being formed near lands, or in the eddies between two winds, may have recourse to the *Philosophical Transactions*, and Dr. *Franklin's* above-mentioned ingenious book.

SECTION II

Aerial Phaenomena

First, Frezier observed under the tropic, at sun-setting, a GREEN CLOUD; and he describes it as a thing very singular.[1] Those who are acquainted with colours, and the various effects of their mixtures, know that green is naturally produced by mixing yellow and blue. The natural colour of the sky, and of a great many clouds, is blue: the setting sun commonly gilds all the sky and clouds near the horizon, with a lively gold-yellow or orange; it is, therefore, by no means extraordinary to see, at sun-setting, a greenish sky or cloud, and it may be observed frequently in Europe. But, as the rising and setting sun causes, between and about the tropics, the tincts of the sky and clouds to be infinitely brighter than any where else, it happens now and then, that all the appearances of the sky and clouds, are more striking and brilliant, and therefore more noticed. I had an opportunity to observe, in the year 1774, April 2d, in 9° 30′ South latitude, at sun-setting, a beautiful green cloud; some others at a greater distance were of an olive-colour, and even part of the sky was tinged with a lively, delicate green.

Secondly, The refraction of light through clouds and rains, causes a RAINBOW opposite to the sun; a phaenomenon which, however beautiful and striking, is so common, and the manner of its formation so well known, that it hardly requires here any particular notice: but I cannot pass by in silence, that whilst we were going, in 1773, from New Zeeland, the first time, to O-Taheitee, I had an opportunity of observing, from June 7th to July 12th, every morning constantly, a rainbow, or part of a rainbow, on the horizon. Though this remark is but trivial, it proves, however, that we had almost daily small showers of rain, and that we paid particular attention to every object which deserved observation.

The fainter light of the moon causes likewise rainbows, but they are less noticed on account of their faint and weak colours; I observed one with remarkably bright colours on June 29th, 1773, another on July 6th, the same year, and another on March 19th, 1775, when near the Cape of Good Hope. Aristotle is, I believe, the first who observed this phaenomenon.

Thirdly, When the air is charged with dense vapours, and often when they are frozen into snow or sleet, there appears a HALO about the sun or moon, which is by no means remarkable upon the whole; but it has been observed that Halos precede high winds, squalls and often rain and snow. Though I had frequent opportunities to see this observation confirmed, I did not however always minute it down in my journal; I find only the following memorandums. On February 25th, 1774, we saw a large Halo about the moon, and that very night came on squalls with rain, and the next morning we had the same weather, with loud thunder claps. On January 5th, A.M. 1775, a large Halo, occupying more than 44° of the heavens, was seen about the sun, dark in the middle, bright and whitish with some colours of the rainbow in the circle, and we had rain, and now and then squalls.

AERIAL

PHAENOMENA

SECTION III

Fiery Meteors

FIERY METEORS

First, our atmosphere is not only frequently charged with aqueous particles, which are productive of different appearances and various changes of the weather, but there are besides, so many heterogeneous particles dispersed through the whole mass of the circumambient air, that we are not yet apprized of the quantity and variety of them. Accurate observers discover from time to time some new ones, and make us acquainted with their effects, when variously combined. The electric matter has been found often to be one of the curious and powerful ingredients, that enter the mixture of the atmosphere. This matter causes in various instances different phaenomena. LIGHTNING and THUNDER are in all parts of the Globe caused by it. However we heard from the inhabitants of St. Helena, who were born there, and grown up to a good old age, that they never had observed a thunder storm on their happy isle. As the highest hills on it, and all the rocks surrounding it, are a kind of lava or vitrified slags of dross, which I suppose are, like all vitrescent bodies, electric *per se,* or non-conductors; the electricity of the atmosphere is perhaps not conducted by them, and causes therefore no explosion.

The isles in the South-Sea are, as far as we know, subject to lightning and thunder storms; for we experienced some at different places and seasons, in the several parts of our voyage over this ocean; and we were now and then obliged to fix the electric chain, to prevent fatal accidents. Once at O-Taheitee, the man who was sent up to the main top-gallant mast head, had scarcely fixed the chain, and another man was still clearing it of the main-chains and shrouds, when the latter received an electric shock, and the fire was seen running down the chain into the water, without doing any damage.

Secondly, on August the 17th, 1772, after we had left St. Jago, at eight o'Clock in the evening, we observed a fiery meteor, of an oblong shape, a bright but blueish light, and descending towards the North West, and then moving in an oblique direction towards the horizon: its duration was momentaneous. We had about that time, frequent showers of rain, attended with sudden and violent gusts of wind, both before and after its appearance.

88

On the 30th of September, 1774, at half an hour after seven o'clock in the evening, after we had left the South East point of Caledonia and Pine Island, all those that were on the deck observed to the North-ward, a luminous globe, of the size and brightness of the sun moving downwards with great velocity towards the horizon. Its light was pale, and it burst without any explosion whatsoever; for all the noise which could be heard, seemed to be a loud hissing, familiar to that caused by oakum when set on fire. After its bursting, several bright sparks flew as it were from it; the lowermost of which had the shape of a pear, and could be traced by a blueish light it left behind. We were then becalmed, but as, according to the observation of several intelligent persons, the appearance of a fiery globe, has been the forerunner of a fresh gale, I expected one; and it was really verified that very night by such a gale, with squalls and rain. Though I am far from asserting that this, and perhaps a few more instances are sufficient to make this rule general, I think however that if these phaenomena and the following weather, were by further observers more carefully noticed, experience might lead us to some more general and more certain conclusions.

Thirdly, the appearance of NORTHERN LIGHTS (*Aurora Borealis*) in the higher latitudes of our hemisphere, is at present a very common phaenomenon; and the inhabitants of Sweden, Norway, Ice-Land and Russia, have the sight of this meteor in the winter, almost every clear night; but I never heard or read of any one who had seen the SOUTHERN LIGHTS (*Aurora Australis*) before us;[1] and though we spent three different seasons in or near the antarctic circle, we however observed them the first time only in the year 1773, on seven different nights. We were at that time from 58° to 60° South latitude, and the thermometer at eight o'Clock in the morning, stood from 31° to 33° in the open air, on deck. Their appearance was much the same as that of the Northern Lights; they were observed shooting up to the zenith in columns or streams, of a pale light, from a dark segment as a base near the horizon, and often spread over the whole Southern hemisphere; sometimes these lights were so transparent, that stars could be observed through them, and at other times the stream seemed to be white and more dense or opaque, and would not transmit the light of the stars. We saw the meteors on February the 18th, 19th, 20th, 21st, 26th, and on March 15th, and 16th.

Winds

Some of the most remarkable and general changes of our atmosphere are produced by the winds. Their history is as yet very imperfect, and will still remain so, for want of a sufficient number of accurate and faithful observations; and because mankind is strongly inclined to reap the benefit of their own labours as soon as possible, without leaving it to posterity, to make the conclusion from premises, for which the present, a second, and perhaps a third age should collect the materials. As soon as we have a tolerable number of facts before us, we begin to build thereon a system, filling up from guesses, surmises and doubtful inaccurate experiments the rest of the structure, which is afterwards found so tottering, that it soon either falls down, or is by adversaries torn to pieces.

We shall therefore confine ourselves to the enumeration of facts, and leave the conclusions to others, or at most, offer them as, what they really are, conjectures.

I. Regular Winds

We found within and near the tropics the regular winds, as other navigators had done before us. In the year 1772, we left England in July, and at Cape Finisterre, met with a North East wind, which carried us within a few degrees of the line, where, towards the latter end of August, we had rain and a S.S.W. or S.W. wind, which forced us to sail S.E. or S.E. by E. On September 8th, when we were near the line, the wind came to the South, but in two days more it veered round to S.S.E. so that we could run S.W. As we approached the tropic, the wind came more round to the East to E. by N. and even N.E. and we stood S.E. about the end of Sept. having just passed the tropic. On the 11th, of October we could stand E. by S. or nearly so, and Eastward, on the 16th, the wind being N. and N. by W. On the 25th of October, we found the wind coming more Eastward, though now and then for a short time it blew from the West, so that we sailed briskly towards the Cape of Good Hope, and had the satisfaction to enter Table Bay, having had a fresh gale the preceding night. This view of the winds during our passage will shew at once the extent and the changes of the trade winds. Wherever one wind fell and another began, there we had faint breezes and calms, though of short duration.

In the year 1773, in our run from New-Zeeland to O-Taheitee, we had, on the 20th of July, a S.E. wind in about 36° South latitude, which we thought to be the trade wind, though we were soon undeceived, having many changes of winds after it; and we did not fall in with the true settled S.E. trade, till August the 7th, in about 19° South latitude; this wind blew sometimes fresher, sometimes fainter, especially when we came near the isles, and it carried us to O-Taheitee on August 16th.

After we left the Society Isles, we ran towards the Friendly Isles by help of the South East trade; though at the approach of a hard shower of rain and some lightning it shifted to various points; but we soon recovered the true trade wind, and perhaps the direction of the wind was likewise altered by the vicinity of some land; for though we saw no more than one low island in the whole run, we might pass several, at no great distance, without seeing them, either in the night, or on account of their low situation; for the next year we ran a little more North of this course and fell in with several isles; and this very South East wind brought us to Eaoowhe and Tonga-tabu.

The same trade wind with very little changes, carried us after leaving Tonga-tabu, out of the tropics and even to about 32° South latitude. In the year 1774, when we returned from the South to the isles, we met the South East trade wind in about 29° South latitude on the 6th of March; it continued constant while we sailed to Easter-Island and after we left it. On March 21st, at three o'clock P.M. in about 22° 45′ South latitude, the wind took us all on a sudden a-head, and we had soon after a smart shower of rain, but it was no sooner over than the trade wind returned, and blew fresh, and continued so, except in a few instances more, when we had some showers of rain. About the Marquesas we had rain and several gusts of wind.

After we left the Marquesas, we stood S.S.W. then S.W. and at last W½ S. and had the same S.E. trade setting us forward; now and then changing our course, on account of five low isles we fell in with, till at last we came a second time to O-Taheitee.

In our second run from the Society to the Friendly Isles, we had the same South-East trade wind, and now and then a foul West wind, when we came near land, or while a hard shower of rain was coming on, and sometimes we were becalmed. Having been a few days at A-Namocka, and passed between Oghao and Tofooa, we found a S.E. wind, which hindered us from going to Tonga-tabu as we originally intended; this breeze continued, with a few changes, till we fell in with the New Hebrides, where we had frequent squalls and rain, and sometimes calms. We had again Easterly winds in going to New Caledonia, and when near it were often becalmed, with now and then a squall and a hard shower of rain. After we left New Caledonia we had the wind South, but it veered gradually to W.S.W. and W. by S. and so on to the Westerly quarter, where it remained, and brought us to Queen Charlotte's Sound for the third time.

In the year 1775, when we left the Cape of Good Hope, we had a fresh South-East breeze, which now and then became somewhat more Easterly, and at last we were becalmed from May 10th to the night of the 13th, when the true South-East trade set in, and carried us to the islands of St. Helena, Ascension, Fernando de Noronha, and to the 4th degree North latitude, where we were becalmed. From the time we left St. Helena, we had now and then squalls and showers of rain, which were more common about the Line. The calm lasted from June 15th to the 19th, and was accompanied with hard showers of rain, and set in with thunder and lightning. After this, we met again a breeze at North, which during the night veered to N.N.E. and N.E.; but, as we advanced farther to the North, the wind became more settled.

Having passed the tropic of Cancer again, we found the wind became more Easterly, *viz.* E.N.E. and even sometimes E. by N. Half E.; till, in 27° or 28° North latitude, we again met with the variable winds.

From this circumstantial account, the following inferences may be drawn.

Firstly, The trade-winds extend sometimes beyond the tropics into the temperate zones, especially when the sun is in the same hemisphere; and the extent of the trade-winds within the tropics, seems to be proportionate to the sun's distance in the opposite hemisphere.

Secondly, The trade-winds in the South-Sea, are sometimes interrupted by calms and contrary Westerly winds; and in particular, rains and thunder-storms are not uncommon at these changes.

Thirdly, The trade-winds are likewise sometimes interrupted at the approach of land, especially if it be of considerable height.

Fourthly, At the intervals, where one wind leaves off and the other sets in, commonly calms, and not seldom rains, are to be met with.

It has hitherto been allowed, that, in the space within the tropics in large oceans, the regular winds reign, which come from the East; and the cause of this is thought to be the sun, which, being vertical, or nearly so, within the tropics at noon, rarefies the air, as his effect is then most powerful; but, as the sun is every moment advancing to the meridian of some other place on the globe, the rarefied part of the atmosphere of course moves from East to West. As soon as the cause of the rarefaction ceases by the removal of the sun, the columns of air in the neighbourhood of the rarefied place, rush in to cause an equilibrium. This current forms the trade-wind, and gives it continuance, within and near the tropics. The cause, however, is not so general, as that it may not be altered by some more powerful agent; such as the vicinity of land, or a cloud pregnant with vapours and electric matter.

Though the lands in the South-Seas be of no considerable extent, they have however, generally, the benefit of the sea and land-breezes; so that the reigning trade-wind only operates in the daytime on the windward-side of the isle, and afterwards follows the direction of the shores, and falls every where perpendicular, or nearly so, upon them; nay, on the lee-side of the isle, it becomes contrary to the trade, but extends only a few miles more or less out to sea, in proportion to the size of the land and other accidental causes. In the night-time, the same wind, as it were, returns and goes out to sea from the land, keeping within the common limits of these alternate breezes.

As the Easterly winds reign with a peculiar constancy within the tropics, it has been likewise observed, that, without them, the Westerly ones are the most general, but their constancy, both in strength and direction, must never be compared with that of the Eastern trade-winds.

When we came far to the South, and were either within or near the antarctic circle, we found again, that the East winds are the most constant, and prevail the longest.*

If therefore, there is any dependance on these observations, it is probable that these Easterly winds are, as it were, only a kind of an eddy-wind, formed by the more general Western winds in the temperate zone. So that we might, perhaps, consider the whole in this manner: within the tropics, the great rarefaction of the atmosphere caused by the heat of the vertical sun produces the Eastern trade winds: this constant motion of the *Aërial Fluid* to the East, causes towards the temperate zones a kind of eddy, so that the winds turn gradually South and North, and lastly West, which is the prevailing winds of both the temperate zones. But this streaming of the air to the East, is again in the cold frozen zones counterpoised by another kind of eddy wind from the East. We have already mentioned, that we wish that the facts we relate may be distinguished from our inferences, and guesses; the former are materials towards the history of the winds on our globe; the latter are private opinions, which, though they may be condemned, may nevertheless serve as hints, towards forming a more perfect system.

---

* See the *Recueil des Voyages qui ont servi à l'établissement & au Progres de la Compagnie des Indes Orientales*, vol. i. in the Third Voyage of Barentz.

See Dalrymple's *Collection of Voyages in the Southern Atlantic Ocean*, Capt. Halley's *Journal*, p. 52.

The same East wind has been observed by other Navigators within or near the Polar Isles. Barrington's *Probability of reaching the North Pole*, p. 104.

Summary Observations and Facts, by Mr. Valtravers p. 20. The common current from the East is strong and rapid in those seas.

II. Variable Winds

Though we have given a general view of the more prevailing winds in the temperate and frozen zones, we meant not by any means to say, that there are no other winds blowing in these zones; nay, we are so far from asserting this, that we will now give an instance to the contrary. When we crossed the Pacific Ocean, between 40° and 46° South latitude, in the year 1773, directing our course Eastward, we found in this run, contrary Eastern winds frequently to prevail; and what is more remarkable, when the winds again began to change, we observed four different times, between June 5th and July 5th, that they gradually went round the compass, but alway's against the sun.

About New Zeeland, we observed the winds to be for the most part Westerly, and they are often in the winter very furious.

In the seas between New Zeeland and Tierra del Fuego, in November and December, in the year 1774, we found a Western wind reigning from 42° to 54° South latitude.

The neighbourhood of Tierra del Fuego, has been observed by other navigators, as the most tempestuous; but we found this sea remarkably smooth, and the weather mild; and though we experienced a few squalls, they were however, by no means more violent than some we had met with before in other seas.

III. Storms

We met with very little tempestuous weather, upon the whole, during our three years expedition; and had not any remarkable storms, except twice.

When we left the Cape of Good Hope, on November the 23d, 1772, and were standing to the South, we had during three weeks, very hard gales and a high sea.

And the second time, when we were running along the East coast of New Zeeland, towards Queen Charlotte's Sound, in October 1773, we met a hard gale, which gradually increased into a tempest; we were obliged to hand all our sails, and to lye to under our bare poles. The sea was long; the gale blowing off shore, tossed our poor ship strangely to and from, in a tempestuous ocean. The storm roared in the rigging, and broke the waves against the sides and over the decks of the ship. In one moment, being on the top of a mountainous wave, we could overlook an immense tract of this turbulent element; and with awe and terror, we beheld on both sides, the abysses scooped out as it were by the enraged winds; another moment hurried us down between the hollow waves, and we were overwhelmed by a deluge of brine. The furious tempest raises the sea, it breaks on the very summit of the wave, which by the storm is dissolved into atoms of vapours, involving the surface of the ocean in clouds of smoke and fog. Such was our situation, with very little relaxation for several days, and happy did we think ourselves, after having been disappointed several times, when, in a moderate interval, we could take refuge in the desired port.

CHAPTER IV

Remarks on the Changes of our Globe

IN NOVA FERT ANIMUS MUTATAS DICERE FORMAS CORPORA.
   Ovid[1]

Having briefly treated of the nature of the land we met with in the course of our navigation, of the waters, and the constitution and changes of the atmosphere, we have still some few remarks to make on the changes our globe has undergone, both from causes which come on in the regular course of nature, and likewise from others which are accidental.

SECTION I

Regular Changes

The constant succession of summer and winter, of heat and cold, is in the temperate zones, in general more striking and remarkable than in the torrid zone: but I may, perhaps, with equal truth assert, that the tropical isles of the South Sea, enjoy more eminently than any others, an equal temperature and constant mild weather, by their happy situation in a great ocean, where constantly alternating sea and land breezes, mitigate the violence of a vertical sun.

New-Zeeland enjoys, according to the kind informations of Capt. Cook, more settled and more distinct seasons, changing the temperature of the air from warm to cold. This able navigator certainly could give the best account of it, having passed in the Endeavour, about six months, during their summer, along the coasts of New-Zeeland. We came afterwards, in March, to the same isle, and remained till June; and twice we were there in October, and in November; so that, by this means, a very good judgment might be formed of the seasons of this isle. In its Southern parts we found in March still mild weather, which continued partly in April; but in May, the tempestuous winds, constant rain, with sleet, hail, and snow, and very great storms of lightning and thunder, began to set in; the verdure every where faded, many trees shed their leaves, and the snowy summits of hills, attended by a piercing cold, convinced us, that the winter-season was begun.

In the month of June, in Queen Charlotte's Sound, we found the climate milder than in Dusky-Bay; which, however, changed considerably during our three weeks stay: but, when Capt. Cook was there in the Endeavour, in 1770, he found the finest warm, and even hot weather, in the summer-season, and every thing vegetating in the greatest luxuriance.

We, who had spent our winter in the tropical isles, and the spring in New-Zeeland, and felt the effects of a most uncomfortable summer in Tierra del Fuego and South Georgia, could not but think ourselves completely unhappy; and a single momentary recollection of the winters of those wretched climates, is even now sufficient to make us shudder at the very thought of it.

However, we find that these changes of the season in the tropical and temperate zones, cause considerable alterations; which produce likewise, a very considerable effect upon our globe, and is infinitely more conspicuous there, than in the more rigid climates. The constant succession of vegetation within the tropics, infuses every where life, and affords food to millions of animated beings, of the human and animal kind; the temperate zones have still vegetation enough to enliven the scene, and to feed many thousands; but the whole creation seems lifeless and torpid, in the frozen climates of Tierra del Fuego, and Staten Land; and the little life which is left to nature, is confined to a very short space of time; and even its greatest activity, in the motion of whales, seals and pinguins, the only numerous inhabitants of these regions, is absolute torpor, when compared with the agility of the animated beings of warmer and more happy regions.[2] In proportion as places lie nearer to the course of the sun; soil and mould, the great promoters of vegetation are increased; and in the same proportion all organic bodies animate the lifeless, chaotic part of the strata of our globe. But as I have already spoken of these changes, it may be sufficient here to hint at them only.

SECTION II

Accidental Changes

If we consider the changes our globe has undergone from accidental causes, we find the ARTIFICIAL CHANGES made on the surface of our globe by mankind, not to be the least considerable.

Where man the lord of the creation on this globe, has never attempted any change on it, there nature *seems* only the thrive; for in reality it languishes, and is deformed by being left to itself*. Impenetrable woods cover the surface of these regions; its trees are no doubt here and there large and fine, but many are decayed, and still more lying on the ground rotting; here is a tree without its rind, another without a top; all the ground below is over-run with briars, and weeds, and climbers, which hinder you from setting a foot forward: all that seems to vegetate and thrive is suffocated, and buried under mosses, lichens and mushrooms. The water stagnates every where, and causes immense swamps, which are unfit to serve either the inhabitants of the land, or those of the water; being over-run with gigantic but coarse plants, affording very little food to the more useful parts of the animated creation.[1]

As soon as the lord of the creation appears in these regions, he eradicates all those vegetables, which afford no nutriment to him, and to other useful animals. He opens a passage for himself and his assistants. He preserves those plants, and cultivates those vegetables, which afford food, and other useful productions. All that is broken, decaying, and rotting, he carefully clears away, preserving the air from putrefaction and noxious effluvia. He opens a channel for the dead, motionless, stagnating waters, which, being endued by motion, with new life and limpidity, become serviceable to a whole world of creatures, for whom its fluid was originally destined. The earth becomes dry; its rich soil is soon covered with a new verdure, forming a brilliant sod, enamelled with the most fragrant flowers. Every where animals feed in these new meadows, which are created by the industry of

---

* Mr. de Buffon, *premiere Vue de la Nature*, [i.e., vol. 12 of the *Histoire naturelle*] vol. xxiv. de l'Edit. en 12mo.

man, and supported by his ingenious contrivances. The violence of the vertical sun no sooner begins to fade this new paradise, than man spreads, for a short time, the refreshing and salutary waters of the purling, limpid stream over its surface, and restores life and vegetation. Here a bread-fruit spreads its shady branches, and on their extremities, offers an agreeable food to its planter. The apple-tree, covered with its golden fruit, seems to vie with the former, in the number and agreeable taste of its production. There the young shoots of a mulberry-tree grow up luxuriantly, whose bark is soon to become the garment of its cultivator, and screen him against the heat of the sun, and the cold of the nocturnal air. How beautiful, how improved, how useful does nature become by the industry of man! and what happy changes are produced, by the moderate care of rational beings![2]

Every one must perceive, though we forbore to name the countries which we have thus compared, that the former is the picture of the wildes of New-Zeeland, in the Southern isles; and who can fail to discover Taheitee, the happiest isle of the South-Seas, in the latter representation?

Among the ACCIDENTAL NATURAL CAUSES of the changes on our globe, the most remarkable ones are, the winds, the rains, the waters of rivers, the tides of the ocean, the currents therein, subterraneous fires, and earthquakes: but, as we did not stay long enough in the several isles of the South-Sea, to make accurate observations on these changes, we can say nothing on that subject.

But, as we had an opportunity of seeing three different volcanos in the year 1774, and were for several weeks, very near to one of them, I will here insert my remarks on that subject.

Two days after our arrival at Namocka, at day-break we were agreeably surprized by the sight of more then 13 low islands, none of which we had seen before; besides them, we discovered two high ones, the Westernmost of which, constantly emitted great quantities of smoke.[3] The natives call this isle To-foòa. Two days after, we passed with the ship between it and Oghào, another high isle, divided from the former by a narrow channel. To-foòa was covered up to its summit, with great quantities of clubwood (*casuarina equisetifolia*), and we saw many coco-nut trees, and some plantains. The natives assured us, there grew bread-fruit and yams on it, and that it had a run of fresh water. Its shores consisted of black rocks, that had the appearance of being burnt, and the greater part of them had the form of pillars, and were much honey-combed. The beaches were covered with a black sand; and we found, on the shores of the neighbouring isle of A-Namocka, many pumice-stones. The smoke rolled out of the summit of the hill in the middle of the isle. When we came to the leeward of it, it rained, and our people on deck complained that the drops falling on their eyes produced pain and uneasiness; they smelled likewise something like the burning of turf, or of some vegetables and fern; but I did not observe these two latter particulars, though I was likewise all the time on deck. With the rain, some ashes fell down, which seemed to be pieces of small pumice-stone. On the North-West side of the isle there was a large part of the hill, from whence the smoke issued, which appeared to be lately burnt, for it was all black, and the bushes were without foliage and verdure, and only here and there, in craggy places and crevices, a few greens appeared. As we found no anchorage near this isle, and squally weather was coming on, we had no opportunity to make farther observations on this volcano.

When we were in the midst of the NEW-HEBRIDES, having passed WHITSUN-TIDE ISLE, we saw a large fine island to the South of it, which had all the appearance of the greatest fertility and highest cultivation. We remarked on its summit, in two places, a smoke rising, of a much greyer hue, than that from ordinary fire, which we could likewise see rising here and there on the isle, where the natives dressed their victuals. Coming afterwards to MALLICOLLO, we learned from the natives, that this isle was called AMBRRYM, and that there was a fire coming out from hills.[4] We observed on the South-East side of the isle, which is gently sloping, and has a very beautiful appearance, white columns of smoke, rolling with great velocity and strength out of the summit of one of the inland hills, which, however, was not the highest hill on the isle. The North shores of Mallicollo were covered with pumice-stones of various sizes.

These obvious remarks on this volcano, were all that our very short stay at Mallicollo, and in its neighbourhood, would permit us to make.

The isle of TANNA was seen by us, after we left IRROMANGA.[5] The night preceding our arrival, we observed a very great fire on this isle, and we saw it every now and then blazing up with great violence. In the morning we were a few miles distant from the isle, and saw plainly a volcano on its South-East side, at the end of a low range of hills, not elevated more than 120 or 150 yards above the surface of the sea; beyond which there appeared another ridge, at least as high again. It seemed not above four miles distant from the sea, and looked like a truncated cone, quite barren, of a reddish grey, and had the appearance of being formed by ashes, pumice-stones, and lava. Every four or five minutes we perceived a strait column of smoke, of a reddish grey cast, rising with great velocity and violence; and soon after we heard a rumbling noise in the volcano like that of thunder. After the smoke, or rather mass of ignited ashes, had risen to a considerable height, the resistance of the air, and its own gravitation, brought it down: it varied from the columnar shape, and branched out into separate masses, assuming a surface and out-line, not unlike a large cauliflower*. Sometimes these ashes appeared

---

* Nubes (incertum procul intuentibus ex quo monte: Vesuvium fuisse postea cognitum est) oriebatur, cujus similitudinem & formam non alia magis arbor quam pinus expresserit. Nam longissimo velut trunco elata in altum, quibusdam ramis diffundebatur. Credo quia recenti spiritu evecta, deinde senescente eo destituta, aut etiam pondere suo victa, in latitudinem vanescebat; candida interdum, interdum sordida, prout terram cinerembe sustulerat. PLIN. *Epist. lib.* vi. *Ep.* xv.[6]

white, sometimes they had a dirty grey, and sometimes a very red cast which happened, as I suppose, when the hot ignited ashes were thrown up, or when the smoak and ashes were illuminated by the fire at the bottom of the crater.

After we came into the harbour, the volcano seemed to be about 6 or 8 miles distant, its explosions continued for several days, and lasted sometimes, together with the rumbling noise, for about half a minute: the whole deck was covered with ashes and minute cinders, which was very hurtful to the eyes. One morning after rain, the volcano, which had ceased its loud explosions, did again now and then blaze up. I observed this before 4 o'clock in the morning. The clouds of smoak which were emitted, had all the various hues from yellow, orange, red, and dark purple, dying away into a reddish grey, or into a darker hue. When night had spread its veil over all the objects, surrounding us, the stars were observed to shine through some lucid spots. As often as fresh clouds of smoak appeared, they were illuminated from the bottom of the crater. Each neighbouring object, when exposed to this light, was on its edges tinged yellow, orange, red, or purple. Some days after, the volcano was quiet, and no more noise was heard, and but few clouds of smoak appeared, which however, during night were illuminated.

Seven days after our first arrival, I made an attempt to go to the volcano, in hopes of examining this great object somewhat nearer; and went therefore on a path up the hill towards it. It had rained the night before, and we were not gone a mile up the sides of the hill from the watering-place, when we came to a spot clear of wood and of reeds, where we saw a smoak or steam rising from the ground: its smell was strongly sulphureous; and the earth was so intensely hot, that we could hardly stand on it. The soil about these spiracles looked whitish like clay: and in other places of its neighbourhood like red ochre. The fumes rising were real steams, and in all appearance not noxious to vegetation; for I observed several fig-trees loaded with fruit, within 2 or 3 yards of them. I traced these solfataras up the hill, in several other places, and as that day the volcano made a great many loud explosions, we could plainly see, that a new quantity of vapours rose from these spiracles after each explosion. I traced these spiracles another time likewise, down the hill, within a few yards of the sea, where at high water mark, several hot wells were found by us.

From the ship we observed, that the volcano threw up ignited stones of an immense size: for as we were about 6 or 8 miles off, the stones must be of a considerable bulk to be visible at such a distance. When we left the island, there appeared on the outside of the volcano among the ashes, a smoking ridge, which was not observed at first when we came into the harbour. And as I had before seen on a cliff near the sea, some pieces of lava, it is probable this smoking place, contained a stream of ignited slags, forming, when cold, the lava. All the environs of the volcano are covered with ashes, the sand on the sea shore consisted of them, and the soil on the hills was mixed with them: which I found to consist of small pieces of pumice-stone, of small portions of shining, irregularly shaped glasses, semitransparent slags of white, pellucid, irregular pieces like SHERL, or glass, of shining, fibrous, acerose particles like asbest; and lastly, of some black, opaque, irregular atoms. These ashes fell at the distance of 8 or 10 miles on one side or the other, according as the winds blew. From the preceding account I have reason to draw the following corollaries.

First, Volcanos are not always formed on the highest mountains, but are sometimes on a lower ridge, in the neighbourhood of still higher hills. I will not deny that there may be instances, where volcanos occupy the summits of great, high mountains, but I suppose they are found both in high and low hills.

Mr. de Buffon in his most ingenious work, on the Theory of the Earth, pretends that volcanos are never to be met with but in high mountains. This assertion seems not to correspond with our experience, for a hill of about 150 yards at highest, deserves scarcely to be called a high mountain, nor are those volcanos we saw at To-foòa and Ambrrym much higher.

Secondly, A great many volcanos, if not the greater part of them, are found on isles or on the continent, at no great distance from the sea. Such are Aetna, Stromboli, Lipari, and Vulcano, Fuogo, the Peak of Teneriffe, Volcano Island, in the Queen Charlotte Islands, the volcanos near New Guinea, and the Moluccas, the Manillas, in Japan, Iceland, and the new discovered islands between Kamtchatka, and North America: of the latter sort is Vesuvio, the volcanos in Kamtchatka and California: and the only ones that should seem to make an exception, are the volcanos in the Andes, in South America and Mexico; but even there, none is above 100 miles in a straight line, distant from the sea. Those which we found in To-foòa, Ambrrym, and Tanna, belong to the first class.

Thirdly, Volcanos are to be met with, only in countries containing a good many pyritical, sulphureous substances. The red ochre we found on the sides of the hills in Tanna, where the spiracles were seen by us, looked exactly like the remains of a pyrites containing sulphur and an iron earth, which had been ustulated and calcined in a strong fire. Those who have visited the neighbourhood of other volcanos, know very well that such red, ochreous strata are very common in their neighbourhood.

Fourthly, We found that after rain, the volcano in Tanna began to rage and blaze more violently than before; which seems to imply, that the moisture of the rain, insinuating itself into the interior parts of the volcano, through various crevices and chinks, and meeting these pyritical strata, caused a new fermentation, followed by new eruptions and violent explosions.

Fifthly, Volcanos, no doubt, cause great changes on the surface of our globe, by accumulating the ashes and pumice stones, which they continually emit, and

ACCIDENTAL
CHANGES

by the streams of lava, which often are thrown up by them and run a considerable distance, causing great ravages in cultivated regions: we certainly have reason to believe, that the whole hill where the volcano was at Tanna, had been considerably enlarged by the ashes, pumice stones, and lava. Nay, the soil of the whole island had been altered by the continued fall of ashes. I observed besides this, a cliff to the East of the volcano near the sea, at more than ten miles distance from it, which certainly contained vestiges of a great revolution. It consisted of a black sandy or gritty stratum, full of pumice stones, a great many red, ochreous stones, and pieces of lava.

SECTION III

On the Diminution of the Sea and Water

This subject has of late been treated in various manners by the learned world. Some have endeavoured to prove, that the sea gradually made a regular recession from the land, and they have corroborated this opinion, with every argument they could possibly devise. In Sweden it has been the favourite opinion of the most eminent philosophers. But as all opinions may be carried too far, so it has happened in this particular instance. One of the historians of that kingdom, Mr. DALIN, pretends that the ocean falls 45 Swedish inches = 37^{13}⁄$_{16}$ English inches in 100 years, and consequently 0.45 = 0.37 in one year: and by this means proves when Sweden first became HABITABLE, which he immediately considers as the time when it was actually INHABITED. There are others who have opposed this very opinion; so that it seems by no means, to be a point as yet decided; nor is it yet, as far as I am able to judge, a proper time to decide the question: we are first to collect a great many facts, and by no means to form systems from a few particulars, which perhaps may be proved to arise from other causes, than the recession of the sea; and if in one place, the sea uncovers some ground, we ought likewise as carefully and faithfully to record the places where the sea has made encroachments upon the land; which, if rightly compared, might shew, that what in one place is gained, is lost in another. Nor do these gentlemen consider, that, should the ocean decrease, nothing but the aqueous particles would naturally be diminished, and the saline, as fixed particles would remain, which of course must constantly increase the saltness of the ocean; and such fish and submarine animals as can now subsist in the ocean, would, in course of time, find themselves in an element by no means suited to their life and necessities: nay, as their organs for swimming are by no means adapted to so dense a fluid, they would lastly die, and the ocean would in a little time after, shoot into crystals of salt and become entirely solid. Rain, dew, and vapours would be formed, every century more and more sparingly, and at last no vegetation or animal life could be supported, and would end with the subversion of this our globe.

I met with one instance only, during our expedition, where I could fairly observe, that the ground had been raised. It is well known, and often remarked in the South Sea, that the animalcules forming the lithophytes, create in the sea curious structures: they are commonly narrow below, and have as it were only one stalk: the more they grow, the more they spread above, so that some of them are found above 15 feet high, expanding from a base of two or three feet, to 18 or 20 on the top, but as the animalcules inhabiting these lithophytes, cannot live out of water, they never extend their structure higher than to the waters edge, at low water mark.

When we came on the 3d of July, 1774, to Turtle Island, we saw on the reef several such lithophytes of the abovementioned heighth and size: they were perfectly above water, and on their spreading tops, some plants were already growing; which shews that they are above high water mark: and besides this, should they be now again covered by the sea, half of the isle, which is not very high, would certainly be drowned, with all its trees, and the habitations of the natives. It appears therefore evidently, either that the water had receded, or that these objects had been raised above water; but what might be the cause of either, I will not pretend to decide. It might be owing to the recession of the sea, and its gradual yearly diminution. But an earthquake, and a subterraneous fire, are most likely to have raised these lithophytes and parts of the neighbouring isle above water.

SECTION IV

The Theory of the Formation of Isles

Having thus offered a few remarks on the various changes of those parts of the globe, which we visited during our circumnavigation, I might here leave the subject, were it not in some measure necessary, to add a few observations, which may serve to establish a theory for the formation of the tropical isles in the South-Sea.

When we first came within the tropics in 1773, I applied particularly to study the constitution and nature of the tropical isles. When we visited them again in 1774, I added many more observations; and, after all, I found the nature of these isles to be just such as I represented them in the section, where I described the lands we had fallen in with.

We found low isles, connected by reefs of coral rocks; we met with islands more elevated, some without a reef, and other surrounded by a reef of lithophytes.[1]

All the low isles seem to me to be a production of the sea, or rather its inhabitants, the polype-like animals forming the lithophytes. These animalcules raise their habitation gradually from a small base, always spreading more and more, in proportion as the structure grows higher. The materials are a kind of lime mixed with some animal substance. I have seen these large structures in all stages, and of various extent. Near Turtle-Island, we found, at a few miles distance, and to leeward of it, a considerable large circular reef, over which the sea broke every where, and no part of it was above water; it included a large, deep lagoon. To the East and North-East of the Society-Isles, are a great many isles, which, in some parts, are above water; in others, the elevated parts are connected by reefs, some of which are dry at low-water, and others are constantly under water. The elevated parts, consist of a soil formed by a sand of shells and coral rocks, mixed with a light black mould, produced from putrefied vegetables, and the dung of sea-fowls; and are commonly covered by coco-nut trees and other shrubs, and a few antiscorbutic plants. The lower parts have only a few shrubs, and the above plants; others still lower, are washed by the sea at high-water. All these isles are connected, and include a lagoon in the middle, which is full of the finest fish; and sometimes there is an opening, admitting a boat or canoe in the reef, but I never saw or heard of an opening that would admit a ship.

The reef, or the first origin of these isles, is formed by the animalcules inhabiting the lithophytes. They raise their habitation within a little of the surface of the sea, which gradually throws shells, weeds, sand, small bits of corals, and other things on the tops of these coral rocks, and at last fairly raises them above water; where the above things continue to be accumulated by the sea, till by a bird, or by the sea, a few seeds of plants, that commonly grow on the sea-shore, are thrown up, and begin to vegetate; and by their annual decay and re-production from seeds, create a little mould, yearly accumulated by the mixture with sand, increasing the dry spot on every side; till another sea happens to carry a coco-nut hither, which preserves its vegetative power a long time in the sea, and therefore will soon begin to grow on this soil, especially as it thrives equally in all kinds of soil; and thus may all these low isles have become covered with the finest coco-nut trees.

The animalcules forming these reefs, want to shelter their habitation from the impetuosity of the winds, and the power and rage of the ocean; but as, within the tropics, the winds blow commonly from one quarter, they, by instinct, endeavour to stretch only a ledge, within which is a lagoon, which is certainly entirely screened against the power of both: this therefore might account for the method employed by the animalcules in building only narrow ledges of coral rocks; to secure in their middle a calm and sheltered place: and this seems to me to be the most probable cause of THE ORIGIN of all THE TROPICAL LOW ISLES over the whole South-Sea.

We come now to the HIGHER ones. I must confess, there is hardly one of them, which had not one way or other, strong marks and vestiges left, of its having undergone some violent alteration in its surface by fire, or, as I should rather say, by a volcano.

It is very well known, that many isles* have been raised out of the sea by the action of a subterraneous fire. The islands of SANTORINI, and the two KAMENIS†,

---

* Plin. *Hist. Nat.* lib. ii. c. 88, 89. lib. iv. c. 22. — Seneca *Nat. Quaest.* vi. c. 21, 26. & lib. ii. c. 26. — Strab. Almeloven. p. 94, 100. — Plutarch. *de Pythiae Oraculis*, ex edit, Xyland. Frst. 1620. p. 399. — Pausan. lib. viii. c. 33. — Justin. lib. xxx. c. 4. — Niceph. Patriarch. *Brev. Hist. Paris*, 1648. p. 37. ad ann. 727. ad eund. Theophal. *Chronogr.* refert. — Cedren. & Paul. Diacon. *Coronelli Isolario*, p. 243. edit. Venet. 1696. fol. — *Philos. Trans.* vol. xxvii. No. 332. — Dio. Cass. lib. lx. c. 29. — Aurel. *Victor.* in Claudio. — Amm. Marcell. edit. *Vales.* Paris, 1681. fol. lib. xvii. c. 7. — Pindar. Ol. Ode 2. — Diod. Sic. lib. v. c. 55. — Heraclid. *Pont. de Polit. Graec. ad calcem Cragii, de Rep. Laced.* — Philo Jud. *de Mundi incorrupt.* p. 959.
† *Nouveaux Memoires des Missions.* tom. i. — *Philos. Trans.* vol. xxvii. n. 332.

in the Greek Archipelago, and the isle formed in 1720, in the Western Isles*, are incontestible proofs of it. These seem to have been a kind of volcano coming out of the bottom of the sea. We visited isles that had still volcanos; others, that had only elevation, and marks of being formed in remote ages by a volcano; and lastly, we found isles, that had no remains of a volcano, but even strong and undoubted vestiges of having been violently changed, and partly overturned by an earth-quake, subteraneous fire, and a volcano. TOFOOA, AMBRRYM, TANNA, and PICO, are of the first class. MAATEA, O-TAHEITEE, HUAHEINE, O-RAIEDEA, O-TAHAW, BOLA-BOLA, MOURUA, WAITAHU, or St. Christina, and the rest of the MARQUE-SAS, with several of the NEW-HEBRIDES, and FAYAL, belong to the second; and I cannot help referring EASTER-ISLAND, ST. HELENA and ASCENSION to the last.

I will not from hence insist, that all the isles now enumerated, were origi-nally produced by earthquakes and volcanos, but I may venture to assert this of several, from their external appearance, and of others I am certain, that they existed above water, before they had a volcano, and were entirely changed, and partly subverted by subterraneous fire.

ASCENSION, in the Atlantic Ocean, an isle which we saw last, after all the others, furnished me with some very curious and pertinent remarks on the sub-ject. We anchored in Cross-Bay, and saw the highest hill of the isle at about five miles distance from the shore; it consists of a gritty lime-tophus, mixed with marle and sand. Some parts of this stone being decayed by length of time, form, together with a little mould, the surface, which is covered with purslane, and some grasses. The nature of this hill is, in every respect, different from the rest of the isle, especially about Cross-Bay. For, as soon as we had reached the elevated plain, situated between the bay and the hill, which is a-breast of the bay, we found it about two miles in diameter, covered with black, gritty slag-ashes, and in some places with a dusky yellow ochre. At sixty or eighty yards distance, the plain is all over incumbered with little hummocks, about ten or twenty feet high, formed of very rugged slags and porous cinders; in short, of lava. All this plain is inclosed by several hills, of a conic form, and of a reddish-brown or rusty-coloured cast, consisting entirely of small ashes, and gritty dissolved slags; some of which are black, and others of an ochreous nature, and of a yellow or red colour. On one side of the plain is an elevated ridge of rocks of the most craggy appearance, lying in very irregular masses, and terminating in the most curious manner, in points and sharp prominencies. Part of this ridge we could trace towards the sea, where the slags, if possible, assumed still more horrid shapes, intersected by deep gullies,

---

* Gassendi de Vita Epicuri. vol. ii. p. 1050. — Hist. de l'Acad. de Paris, de 1721. p. 26. & 1722. p. 12. — Philos. Trans. abridg. tom. v. sect. ii. p. 154. Comment. Bonon. tom. 1. p. 205.

forming a tremendous, inaccessible shore. The slags or lava ring like bells; and, if a piece of it be broken and thrown down the sides of these steep craggy masses, it produces a sharp clanging sound. At the very first sight of these objects, nothing is more obvious to every beholder, than that the high peak in the middle of the isle, is one of the primogenial lands, whereof, perhaps, the whole isle consisted before its present desolation. The elevated plain seems to have been the crater of the volcano; the conic hills were probably thrown up by the cinders and ashes. The ridge of slags is the stream of lava, and some of it ran probably towards the sea. The elevated hummocks in the plain, are the masses of slags and lava, such as they remained after the action of the volcano ceased. They have gradually decayed, and this, together with the foreign matters, washed down by violent rains from the hills of ashes and cinders, have contributed to fill the crater up, and make its surface level. It seems therefore to follow, that Ascension was originally a land or island; but, when the volcano was formed in its bosom, part of it was entirely changed and destroyed, and now shews nothing but nature in ruins:

> . . . nec restat in illa,
> Quod repetas; tantum cinis, & sine semine terra est.
>   Corn. Severus[2]

St. Helena has on its outside, especially where the ships lye at anchor, an appearance, if possible, more dreadful and dreary than Ascension; but the farther you advance, the less desolate the country appears; and the most interior parts are always covered with plants, trees, and verdure: however there are every where the most evident marks, of its having undergone a great and total change from a volcano and earthquake, which perhaps sunk the greatest part of it in the sea.

Easter-Island, or Waihu, is another island of the same nature. All its rocks are black, burnt, and honey-combed: some have perfectly the appearance of slags; nay, even the soil, which is but thinly spread over the burnt rocks, has the appearance of a dark yellow ochre. We found a great many black glassy stones, scattered among the great quantity wherewith the whole isle is covered, which are known to mineralogists by the name of Iceland-agate, and are always found near volcanos, or places exposed to their violence: thus, for instance, they abound in Italy and Sicily, and in Iceland near the volcanos, and likewise in Ascension. We found the whole isle very poor in vegetables; and, though I walked over a great part of it, I found no more than about twenty plants, including those that are cultivated, and no trees at all, which is very remarkable in an isle of this extent, under so fine a climate, and inhabited for a long time past: for, when Roggewein first discovered it in 1722, he even then found those stone pillars, which we likewise saw, and which seemed to us to have been erected many years ago.[3] The writers of Roggewein's voyage saw likewise woods on this isle; it should therefore seem, that since that time, some disaster had befallen this spot, and ruined the woods, and thrown down many of the huge stone pillars, for we found several on the ground. Perhaps this happened in 1746, when Lima and Callao suffered so much by an earthquake; nor is it uncommon for earthquakes to extend their power a great way. Capt. Davis, in the year 1687, being 450 leagues from the main of America, felt an earthquake very strongly, when at the same time its most violent effects were observed at Lima and Callao.

But I will, by no means, insist upon the circumstance, that the isle was full of woods and forests in Roggewein's time, upon the mere authority of these writers, as a corroborative proof of any changes, which I suppose this isle to have undergone; for one of these writers at least seems to contradict his own report, by telling us, that the man who came on board, had a canoe made of small pieces, none of which was above half a foot in length; which we found really true, and is very natural, because they have no wood: but unluckily, upon the whole, the history of the giants twelve feet high, deprived him entirely of the character of a faithful historian. And, besides this, we found the figures or stone pillars, all made of a porous tufa, which had undergone a violent operation by fire. These pillars were already existing in Roggewein's time; consequently the isle, its stones, and strata, had already undergone the violence of fire; so that it evidently appears, that whatever changes the island has undergone, must have been anterior to Roggewein's arrival there in 1722. However, it was obvious to every one, that the isle had been subject to the violence of a volcano, which had perhaps destroyed a part of it.

But the tropical isles in the South-Seas bear likewise the most undeniable marks of violent changes from fire and earthquakes; though their present cultivated state, the fine mould covering their surface, and the various vegetables on it, partly hide the vestiges of these revolutions, and require therefore the eye of a man used to these enquiries, and acquainted with nature in its various states. The excavated tops of the peaks of MAIATEA, BOLA-BOLA, and MOURUA, the spires and shattered rocks of the interior parts of TE-ARRABOO, or the little peninsula of O-TAHEITEE, together with the honey-combed black rocks and lava of TOBREO-NOO and the MARQUESAS, are such proofs of these revolutions, as nobody will dispute, who is well acquainted with the subject, and has formerly examined the neighbourhood of volcanos. Nay, all the New-Hebrides, the Marquesas, and Society-Isles, together with the Azores or Western-Isles in the Atlantic, have all more or less, the same marks of those great changes, which they have undergone in former ages. But if we remember, that earthquakes and subterraneous fires have in all ages raised isles from the depth of the ocean; if we read the accounts of the origin of THERASIA and HIERA, or SANTERINI and VOLCANELLO, of the two

KAMENIS, of an isle between Tercera and St. Michael; if we compare the strata and structure of these new isles, and of some in the Atlantic, and the South-Seas; if we recollect, that some of these isles have still volcanos, and that others are still subject to earthquakes; we cannot help suspecting, that these isles might probably have had the same origin, by being raised from the bottom of the ocean by a fire, or, as I may call it, a sub-marine volcano. The O-TAHEITEANS and inhabitants of the Society Isles seem to be very well acquainted with earthquakes. Their mythology acknowledges a God, called O-MAOOWE, whom they think to be the God and Creator of the sun, and who in his anger shakes the earth, and causes earthquakes; which they express by the phrase O-MAOOWE TOORORE TE WHEN-NOA, (i.e.) Maoowe shakes the earth; which certainly seems to me to prove, that they are not quite strangers to this tremendous phaenomenon.[4]

I must not assert that the foregoing observations, make it certain that these isles were raised by earthquakes and fire; but I think the opinion probable; nor do I imagine that all the high isles, were thus thrown up by fire and earthquakes, from the bottom of the sea. Many of them may have existed before, nay, they have perhaps constituted greater lands, and were only dismembered by the sinking of the intermediate parts: and as we have already once entered into the land of fables and mythology, I must beg leave to return again to it. The natives of the Society Isles, pretend their isles were produced when O-Maoowe dragged a great land from West to East through the ocean, which they still imagine to be situated to the Eastward of their islands: all that time they say, their isles were broken off as little fragments, and left in the midst of the ocean. This tradition seems to indicate, that the inhabitants themselves have some idea of a great revolution, which happened to their isles. The god of earthquakes, mentioned before, proves, that they some how refer the present condition of their isles, to a great earthquake as a general cause: and the great land they remember, and of which their isles are fragments, seems to imply, that they have not forgotten that their habitations formerly were parts of a great continent, destroyed by earthquakes, and a violent flood, which the dragging of the land through the sea seems to indicate.

CHAPTER V

Remarks on the Organic Bodies

OMNIS NATURA VULT ESSE CONSERVATRIX SUI, UT & IN GENERE CON-
SERVETUR SUO.
    M. Tullius Cicero *de Fin. Bon. & Mal.* l. 4[1]

The next article which demands our attention in the lands of the South Sea, is the history of the organic bodies, which partly form, and partly dwell on their immediate exterior surface. They constitute the vegetable and animal kingsdoms in the system of nature, the latter being distinguished from the first, by the powers of perception, or the senses, the peculiar attributes of animal being.

SECTION I

Vegetable Kingdom

The vegetation which cloaths our earth, VARIES considerably in every country we met with during our circum-navigation, even as the appearances of the lands themselves, are new and singular in almost every one of them. Between the tropics, we met with the Low Islands, consisting of mere coral rocks, scarce covered with sand. The Society Isles of vast height, surrounded by rich plains, and included in coral reefs: and many other clusters of mountainous islands, destitute both of reefs and plains. We have observed how much the least attractive of these tropical countries, surpasses the ruder scenery of New Zeeland: how much more discouraging than this, are the extremities of America; and lastly, how dreadful the southern coasts appear, which we discovered. In the same manner, the plants that inhabit these lands, will be found to differ in number, stature, beauty, and use.[2]

Low Isles

The Low Islands which are dispersed in the Pacific Ocean between the tropics, are of an inconsiderable size, and consequently produce few sorts of plants: however, the great abundance of coco-nut palms on them, gives them a pleasing aspect at a distance; some trees and shrubs that flourish on the shores, a few anti-scorbutic simples, and some plants which have the quality of intoxicating fish,[3] compose their whole Flora.

Society Isles

But nature and art have united their efforts in the Society Isles, to strike the beholder with the magnificence of prospects, and to awaken every idea of beauty, by the variety of harmonious forms and colours. They consist of plains, hills, and a high range of mountains, in each of which, vegetation is different. The plains which encircle these isles, give greater room for cultivation than mountainous exposures: in consequence of this, we see them and the remotest extremities of the vallies which run between the hills, covered with plantations; we find them inhabited by a numerous race, in a higher state of civilization than any of their neighbours;[4] we enter a country improved by art, and from the rough walks of

Sydney Parkinson, [A View in Tahiti with Taro, Yams and a Breadfruit Tree], wash, 1769. 241 × 375 mm. British Library.

uncultivated nature, pass into the lovely variety of a flourishing and well kept garden; the ground is no longer loaded with heaps of putrid branches and leaves, that give nourishment to briars, climbers, ferns, and the whole tribe of parasite plants; but a bed of grasses adorns the whole surface, and forms that luxuriant sod, which is always the effect of cultivation. The fruit trees rise at proper distances from each other, and the shade which their foliage throws, shelters the green turf below, which the rays of a tropical sun would otherwise soon scorch and destroy.[5] The dwellings of the natives have the same advantage, being generally situated in the midst of a group of trees, and frequently surrounded with various shrubs. The first range of hills that rise within the plains are entirely destitute of trees, by which means, the sun having full scope to operate, permits no grasses or other tender plants to grow there, so that the whole is covered with a very dry kind of fern, among which, two sorts of shrubs are dispersed that can equally support the utmost fury of a vertical sun.

As we advance higher, we find the sides of the hills beginning to be wooded, and at last arrive at the highest summits, which are wholly covered with forests of

VEGETABLE KINGDOM

"Chart of the island Otaheite," engraving by J. Cheevers after James Cook and Isaac Smith, from John Hawkesworth, *An account of the voyages undertaken . . . for making discoveries in the Southern Hemisphere,* London, 1773.

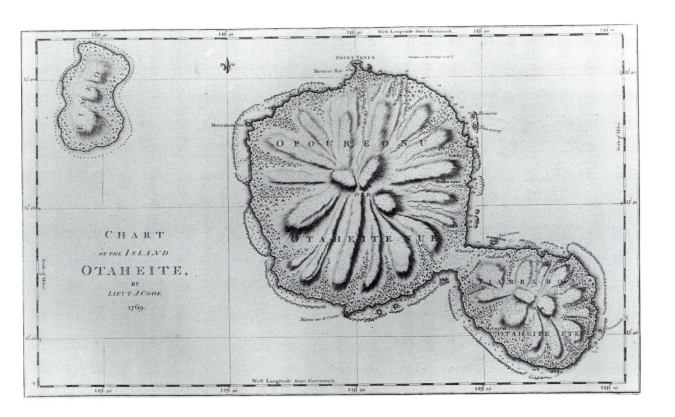

very tall trees. As these tops are frequently involved in clouds, the temperature of the air is very mild, and causes all kinds of vegetables to thrive with luxurance. Among the rest, mosses, ferns, epidendra, and the like, which particularly delight in moisture, cover the trunks and branches of the trees, and over-run the ground.

Marquesas

To the North Eastward of the Society Isles, lie those islands which Mendanna named the Marquesas de Mendoza. They might be aptly compared to the Society Isles, if these last were destitute of reefs and of plains. The Marquesas are also more wooded, though the variety of plants is not, by far, so great, owing to the room which the plantations take up in the woods themselves.

Friendly Isles

Next to the Society Isles for richness of productions, and beauty of appearance, we must place that group discovered by the Dutch navigator Taesman, and not unaptly to be distinguished by the name of Friendly Isles, from the peaceable, kind disposition of their inhabitants. They are raised so high above the level of the sea, that they can no longer rank with the Low Islands; and being destitute of mountains, they are equally distinct from the High Islands. They are extremely populous, their uniform surface therefore, gives the people an opportunity of carrying cultivation very far; and from one end to the other, they are intersected by paths and fences, which divide the plantations. At first one might be apt to think that this high cultivation, would give the botanist very scanty supplies of spontaneous plants; but it is the peculiar beauty of all these elegant isles to join the useful to the agreeable in nature, by which means a variety of different wild species thrive among those that are cultivated, in that pleasing disorder which is so much admired in the gardens of this kingdom.

New Hebrides

The more Western isles named the New Hebrides, appear with a very different vegetation. They are high and mountainous, without plains or reefs, though their hills have gentle slopes, and their valleys are extensive: they are fertile, and almost totally covered with forests, in which, the plantations of the natives, are so many insulated spots, especially as the number of inhabitants is but small

for the size of the isles. The spontaneous plants therefore, occupying the greatest space, the variety of species is also greater here, than in the more Easterly
islands.

New Caledonia

The arid soil of New Caledonia, totally distinct from all others in the South Sea,
produces nevertheless, a variety of plants, most of which form *genera* very distinct
from those before known. A reef of coral rocks surrounds the shores here at a considerable distance, in the same manner as at the Society Isles, and the only cultivated parts of the country, are likewise some narrow plains. But it seems, that
though the natives bestow great labour on them, yet they barely yield them a
scanty subsistance, which probably, is the cause of their very inconsiderable
number. From the unanimous testimony of several gentlemen, who made the
voyage in the Endeavour Bark, as well as this last in the Resolution, we have the
greatest reason to assert, that the productions of this large island, (the plains
excepted) entirely resemble those of the coasts of New Holland, which are not far
distant.[6]

New Zeeland

New Zeeland, which lies in the temperate zone, presents a very different aspect
from any of the tropical countries. Its northern isle though mountainous, like the
other, has however very extensive slopes, which the natives have known how to
turn to advantage by culture; but as we never landed on that part, we shall confine ourselves to the Southern isle, at each of whose extremities we touched. The
prospect here consists of several ranges of mountains, one higher than another,
the highest capt with snow: their sides are steep, their valleys narrow, and the
whole covered with immense forests. The only difference between the Northern
and Southern ends of the isle, consists in this, that the latter still degenerates into
ruder rocks; whilst the former in some places has level spots, clear of wood, and
covered with grasses, rushes, &c. The climate of this isle is so temperate, that all
sorts of European garden plants (which we had sown) vegetated very luxuriantly
in the midst of winter: the indigenous Flora is therefore very prolific, and the
variety of genera and new species considerable: but as the country has probably,
never since its first existence, undergone any changes from the hand of industry:
its forests are perfect labyrinths, which innumerable climbers, briars, and shrubberies, twining together, render almost wholly impenetrable, whilst they in great

VEGETABLE
KINGDOM

measure prevent every herbaceous plant from coming up: these last therefore, are only found on the beaches, along the edge of the valley, and are almost entirely composed of antiscorbutics and pot-herbs.

Tierra del Fuego

Still, as we advance to the South, the appearance of countries becomes more and more barren. Tierra del Fuego, at the South extremity of America, always labours under the rigors of cold, and all its Western coasts are barren, rocky mountains, whose tops are continually covered with snow. In a bay where we anchored to the North-West of Cape Horn, we found scarce any traces of vegetation, except on some low little isles, whose thin turf, which covered the rock, was quite marshy; and in the lowest bottoms of vallies, or the crevices of mountains, where some ill-shaped, wretched shrubberies were to be found, scarce ever growing to such a height, as to deserve the name of trees. All the higher parts of the mountains are black rocks, perfectly naked. In the small catalogue of plants, we however find the celery, which Providence has distributed so universally, as one of the best

"Christmas Sound, Tierra del Fuego," engraving by W. Watts after William Hodges, from Cook, *A Voyage towards the South Pole*, 1777, Plate 32.

remedies against the scurvy. The North-East side of Tierra del Fuego, slopes into a kind of plain, and looks more rich in vegetables; but we did not land upon it.

New Georgia

When we saw the barren side of Tierra del Fuego, we had scarce an idea of a more wretched country existing; but after standing sometime to the Eastward, we met with the isle of New-Georgia, which, though in the same latitude, appeared so much more dreadful, that before we came close up with it, it was suspected to be an island of ice. The shapes of its mountains are, perhaps, the most ragged and pointed on the globe; they are covered with loads of snow in the height of summer, almost to the water's edge; whilst here and there, the sun shining on points, which project into the sea, leaves them naked, and shews them craggy, black and disgustful. We landed in Possession-Bay, and found the whole Flora to consist of two species of plants, one a new plant* peculiar to the Southern hemisphere, the other a well-known grass; both which, by their starved appearance and low stature, denoted the wretchedness of the country.

However, as if nature meant to convince us of her power of producing something still more wretched, we found land about four degrees to the Southward of this, apparently higher than it, absolutely covered with ice and snow (some detached rocks excepted) and in all probability incapable of producing a single plant. Wrapt in almost continual fogs, we could only now and then have a sight of it, and that only of its lowest part, an immense volume of clouds constantly resting on the summits of the mountains, as though the sight of all its horrors would be too tremendous for mortal eyes to behold. The mind indeed, still shudders at the idea, and eagerly turns from so disgusting an object.

I. Number of Species

From what has been said, it appears, that the rigorous frost in the antarctic regions almost precludes the germination of plants; that the countries in the temperate zones, being chiefly uncultivated, produce a variety of plants, which only want the assistance of art to confine them within proper bounds; and lastly, that the tropical isles derive a luxuriance of vegetation from the advantage of climate and culture. But the number of vegetables is likewise commonly proportioned to the

---

* Ancistrum. Forster's *Nova Genera Plantarum*, p. 3, 4.

VEGETABLE
KINGDOM

extent of the country. Continents have therefore, at all times, been remarkable for their immense botanical treasures; and, among the rest, that of New-Holland, so lately examined by Messrs. BANKS and SOLANDER, rewarded their labors so plentifully, that one of its harbors obtained a name suitable to this circumstance, (Botany Bay). Islands only produce a greater or less number of species, as their circumference is more or less extensive. In this point of view, I think both New-Zeeland and the tropical isles rich in vegetable productions. It would be difficult to determine the number in the first with any degree of precision, from the little opportunities we had of examining its riches: our acquisitions of new species from thence amount to 120 and upwards; the known ones, recorded already in the works of Linnaeus, are only six, and consequently bear a trifling proportion to the new ones; but there is great reason to suppose that, including both the isles of New-Zeeland, a Flora of no less than 400 or 500 species, on a careful scrutiny, might be collected together; especially if the botanist should come at a more advanced season than the beginning of spring, or not so late as the beginning of winter; at which times we had the only opportunities of visiting this country.

In the tropical isles, the proportion of new and known species is very different. All our acquisitions of new ones from them amount to about 220 species; and the collection of the known or Linnaean, to 110, which gives the whole number 330; and shews, that one third were well known before. Cultivation contributes not a little towards this, because it probably contains such plants, as the first settlers of these isles brought with them from their original East-Indian seats, which of course are most likely to be known; and, with these cultivated ones, it is to be supposed there might come the seeds of many wild ones, also of East-Indian growth, and consequently known to the botanists. The new plants, therefore, can only be those which originally grew, peculiar to these countries, and such as have escaped the vigilance of the Europeans in India.

The number of individual species (330) which we found in the tropical isles, (old and new) is by no means to be considered as a perfect Flora, for which purpose, our opportunities of botanizing were greatly insufficient. On the contrary, I am rather inclined to think, that our number might almost be doubled on a more accurate search, which must be the work of years, not of a few days, as was the case with us. The greatest expectations are from the New-Hebrides, as they are large, uncultivated, but very fertile islands. The jealous disposition of their natives would not permit us to make many discoveries there; yet, from the outskirts of the country, we might form a judgment of the interior parts. As an instance, that we often have had indications of new plants, though we could never meet with the plants themselves, I shall only mention the wild nutmeg of the isle of Tanna, of which we obtained several fruits, without ever being able to find the tree. The first we met with was in the craw of a pigeon, which we had shot, (of that sort, which, according to Rumphius,[7] disseminates the true nutmegs in the East-India islands): it was still surrounded by a membrane of bright red, which was its mace; its color was the same as that of the true nutmeg, but its shape more oblong; its taste was strongly aromatic and pungent, but it had no smell. The natives afterwards brought us some of them. Quiros must have meant this wild nut, when he enumerates nutmegs among the products of his Tierra del Espiritù Santo.[8] This circumstance gives a strong proof (with many more of another nature) of the veracity of this famous navigator; and, as he likewise mentions silver, ebony, pepper, and cinnamon among the productions of Tierra del Espiritù Santo, and the isles in the neighbourhood, I am inclined to believe, that they are really to be met with there.

Another material obstacle to our compleating the Flora of the South-Seas, and which indeed is connected with the former, arises from the changes of seasons: for though, between the tropics, they be not strongly marked with the alternatives of heat and cold, yet, according to the approach or recess of the sun, vegetation is more or less active. This we experienced, by touching at some of the isles, two different times, after an interval of seven months. The first was in August (1773) or the height of the dry season; when we found every thing wearing a yellowish or exhausted colour; many trees had shed their leaves, and few plants were in flower. The second time, being in April (1774), soon after the rainy, or at the beginning of the dry season, we were surprized beyond measure by the lively hues which now appeared in those very objects, that had seemed as it were dead at our first visit: we found many plants which we have never seen before; observed many others in flower, and every thing covered with a thick foliage of a fresh and vivid green: and from this circumstance, and the longer time we spent at the Society Isles, our collections from thence are the most perfect. It is true, the difference of dry and rainy seasons is not so strongly marked as on continents, or in isles contiguous to them; especially as fruits of all kinds chiefly ripen during the wet months, which would be impossible, were the rains constant; and secondly, since even the dry months are not wholly exempted from showers: but the relative distinction holds notwithstanding, as the proportion of rain in one, is considerably greater than in another.

It is owing to the exceeding small size of the low isles, that their vegetable productions are so inconsiderable; though I must confess, we never landed on any one without meeting with something new. SAVAGE-ISLE, which is in fact no more than a low island, raised several feet above water, and clearly manifests its origin, by the bare coral rocks of which it consists, has some new plants, which, in the out-skirts of the isle, grew in the cavities of the coral without any the least soil. We might have made several acquisitions on this island, but the savage disposition of the natives forced us to abandon it.[9] As a contrast to the tropical isles, we ought to mention Easter-Island, which lies so little without the tropic, that is may well be classed with those isles which are actually included in it. This isle is either grossly misrepresented by the Dutch discoverers, or has since then been almost totally ruined.[10] Its wretched soil, loaded with innumerable stones, furnishes a Flora of only 20 species; among these, ten are cultivated; not one grows to a tree, and almost all are low, shrivelled and dry. In the opposite, or Westernmost part of the South-Sea, lies a small isle, which has obtained the name of Norfolk-Island: almost its whole vegetation corresponds with that of New-Zeeland, whose North end is not far distant from it; only some allowances must be made for the greater mildness of the climate, which gives every plant a greater luxuriance of growth. Peculiar to this isle, and to the Eastern end of Caledonia we found a species of coniferous tree, from the cones probably seeming to be a cypress: it grows here to a great size, and is very heavy but useful timber.

II. Stations

As the South-sea is bounded on one side by America, on the other by Asia, the plants, which grow in its isles, partly resemble those of the two continents; and the nearer they are either to the one or the other, the more the vegetation partakes of it. Thus the Easternmost isles contain a greater number of American, than of Indian plants; and again, as we advance farther to the West, the resemblance with India becomes more strongly discernible. There are, however, singular exceptions to this general rule: thus, for instance, we find the *gardenia* and *morus papyrifera*, both East-Indian plants, only in the Easterly groupes of the Friendly and Society Isles; the TACCA of Rumph, which is likewise an Indian species, is only found in the Society Isles.[11] On the other hand, some American species do not appear till we reach the Western Isles, called the Hebrides, which are however the farthest removed from that continent. Part of these exceptions are perhaps owing to the inhabitants, who, being of a more civilized nature in the Easterly isles, have brought several parts with them from India, for cultivation, which the others have neglected. The same circumstance also, accounts for the arrival of the spontaneous Indian species in these Easternmost isles; they being probably, as I have already observed, brought among the seeds of the cultivated sorts. In confirmation of which, it may be alledged, that the Indian species are commonly found on the plains in the Society Isles, and the spontaneous American species on the mountains.

A few plants are common to all the climates of the South Sea; among these is chiefly the celery, and a species of scurvy grass (Arabis) both which are generally found in the low islands between the tropics, on the beaches of New Zeeland,

and on the burnt islands of Tierra del Fuego. Several other species seem to have obviated the differences in the climate by a higher or lower situation: a plant, for instance, which occupies the highest summits of the mountains at O-Taheitèe, (or any of the Society Isles) and grows only as a shrub, in New Zeeland is found in the valley, and forms a tree of considerable height; nay the difference is sensible in different parts of New Zeeland itself: thus a fine shrubby tree at Dusky Bay or the Southern extremity, which there grows in the lowest part of the country, dwindles to a small inconsiderable shrub at Queen Charlotte's Sound, or the Northern end, where it is only seen on the highest mountains. A similarity of situation and climate sometimes produces a similarity of vegetation, and this is the reason why the cold mountains of Tierra del Fuego produce several plants, which in Europe are the inhabitants of Lapland, the Pyrenees, and the Alps.

III. Variety

The difference of soil and climate, causes more varieties in the tropical plants of the Southern isles, than in any other. Nothing is more common in the tropical isles, than two, three, four, or more varieties of the same plant, of which, the extremes sometimes, might have formed new species, if we had not known the intermediate ones, which connected them, and plainly shewed the gradation. In all these circumstances, I have always found that the parts most subject to variation, were the leaves, hairs, and number of flower stalks, (pedunculi) and that the shape and whole contents of the flower (partes fructificationis) were always the most constant. This however, like all other rules, is not without exceptions, and varieties arising from soil sometimes cause differences even there, but they are too slight to be noticed. A cold climate, or a high exposure shrinks a tree into a shrub, and vice versa. A sandy or rocky ground produces succulent leaves, and gives them to plants, which, in a rich soil have them thin and flaccid. A plant which is perfectly hairy in a dry soil, loses all its roughness, when it is found in a moister situation: and this frequently causes the difference between varieties of the same species in the Friendly Isles, and in the hills of the Society Isles: for the former, not being very high, are less moist than the hills of the latter, which are frequently covered with mists and clouds.

IV. Cultivation

That cultivation causes great varieties in plants, has been observed long since, and can no where be better seen than in the tropical South Sea isles, where the bread-fruit tree (*artocarpus communis*) alone, has four or five varieties; and the DRACAENATERMINALIS Linn. two; the TACCA, in its cultivated state, has quite a different appearance from the wild one, and the plantane, or *musa paradisiaca*, varies almost *in infinitum* like our apple. The vegetable kingdom furnishes the natives of the tropical lands in the South Sea, with the greatest part of their food, their clothing, their dwelling, furniture, and every convenience. In New Zeeland, the natives live chiefly on fish, and the spontaneous plants furnish them with vestments, so that they care not (especially in the Southern island) to have recourse to agriculture. The plant of which they make all their clothing, fishing lines, cords, &c. is a new genus, which we have called PHORMIUM, and properly belongs to the natural order of the *coronariae*, which it closely connects with the *ensatae* or flags. But in the tropical isles, where the climate softens what is savage in human nature, and as I may say naturally leads to the civilization of mankind, the people are fond of variety of food, of conveniencies at home, and of neatness and ornament in dress; hence it happens that they cultivate (one island with another) almost fifty different species, besides making use of several that are spontaneous. The little trouble which agriculture is attended with, and the great advantages which arise from it in the Society and Friendly Isles, are the reasons why the number of plants cultivated in those isles, so much exceeds those of the others. In the more Westerly isles of the New Hebrides, the country being very woody every where, it became a more difficult task to till the ground; for this reason, only some of the most necessary plants are selected there for cultivation, and we find the manners of the people, more unpolished, and savage. New Caledonia seems to be but a refractory soil, and therefore the few inhabitants on it, can barely procure a subsistence at the expence of much toil and labour.

V. Classes and Sexes

It is an observation of a very remote date, that cultivation often takes from plants the power of propagating by seed: this is clearly seen in most of the plantations of the isles, and more especially in the bread-fruit tree, where the seeds are shrivelled up, and lost as it were, in a great quantity of farinaceous pulp;* in the same manner it also happens in the plantane, which sometimes hardly preserves the

---

* Mr. *Sonnerat* found in the Philippines likewise the bread-fruit tree wild, and as this plant had there not undergone so many changes from cultivation, it bears ripe seeds, of a considerable size, which he has delineated and engraved.

rudiments of seeds.* The O-Taheitee apple, which contains a hard capsula, commonly has no seeds in the loculaments or divisions; the gardenia, hibiscus and rosa sinensis almost constantly bring flowers where the number of petals is multiplied, and neither of them have seed. But the cloth tree or morus papyrifera, is the most extraordinary of all, inasmuch as it never blossoms in these isles; the reason is obvious, for the natives never suffer it to grow till the time of flowering comes on, as the bark would then be unfit for their purpose. The great fertility and exuberance of the soil in some of the tropical isles, is perhaps one of the reasons why such a number of their plants belong to the Linnaean classes of monoecia, dioecia, and polygamia, and it is remarkable that plants which bontanists have observed to be hermaphrodites in America, here bear their male and female flowers on two distinct shrubs, and this may confirm the opinion, that most dioicous plants, are somewhere or other also found in the hermaphrodite state; which, if it were general, would entirely set aside that class: it has likewise often been thought that it would be an improvement to the sexual system, if the classes of monoecia and polygamia were expunged, and their genera placed according to the number of stamina; but, if we consider how many of them would fall to the share of such classes as are already numerous, it must be obvious, that this would only render the science more intricate. The number of five, according to the great Linnaeus's observation, is the most frequent in nature, (Phil. Bot. 60). Hence the class of pentandria is so crowded with genera; and hence also our acquisitions chiefly belong to it. It was with a kind of regret, that we saw so many plants accumulating to the increase of that class, which was already too extensive; as this circumstance seemed to hasten the overthrow of the sexual system, it contributed to make us extremely cautious in creating new genera. Those classes, which in Europe are the most copious, the *umbellated*, the *Syngenesia*, the *Papilionaceae*, the *Bicornes*, the *Siliquosae*, the *Personatae*, and the *Verticillatae*, have very few congeners in the tropical isles; the beautiful classes of *Ensatae*, *Coronariae*, *Sarmentaceae*, are equally rare. The *grasses* are not numerous, and are chiefly of the class of Polygamia. The *Piperitae*, *Scitamineae*, *Hesperideae*, *Luridae*, *Contortae*, *Columniserae*, and *Tricoccae*, chiefly compose the Flora of these isles. Among the *Orchideae*, a great variety of Epidendra inhabit the uncultivated parts. Most of them are new, and their flowers so very various, that they could be distinguished into several different genera, with the same ease that botanists have separated the *Convolvulus* and *Ipomaea*, or the *Nyctanthes* and *Jasminum*, only from slight differences in the formation of the flower. The species of Convolvuli are

---

* Mr. Banks, it is said, met with one kind of the musa wild in New Holland, which there bore and perfected its seeds.

very copious in the South-Sea isles, and so closely connected with each other, that it becomes very difficult to determine them. The genus of peppers (*piper*) has been placed among the diandria by Linnaeaus; though he has taken the greatest part of its species upon the authority of PLUMIER. We had opportunities of exam‑ ining many species of it, and always found the number of stamina irregular and indeterminate, and the shape and number of stigmata different in almost every species: it is therefore but just, that this genus should be restored to the class GYNANDRIA, where it properly belongs, and with which its fructification perfectly agrees. But, allowing, even that some species of pepper regularly have two stamina to each germen, this cannot be sufficient to remove them out of the class; since we see the *Arum seguinum, macrorhizon,* and *esculentum,* the *Dracontium,* and the *Pothos,* which have all either four, six, or seven stamina regularly round each germen, still continue in the class *Gynandria Polyandria.*

This is an abstract of the observations, which we were able to make on the classification of plants, and of the classes which are chiefly found in the isles of the South-Sea. I shall only add, concerning the descriptions or definitions of the known species in Linnaeus, that we have found them, in general, very exact in the American plants, but more inaccurate in those of the East-Indies; a circum‑ stance, which I can only attribute to the following cause: The American plants have had the good fortune to be examined and described in their native soil, by the most expert botanists of the present age; the late favourite disciple of Linnaeus, Peter Loefling; the great and consummate observer, Jacquin; Dr. P. Browne; Mr. Jussieu, &c.[12] On the contrary, the Indian plants are chiefly known from herbals, and the more inaccurate, unfaithful, and unscientific accounts of the botanists of the last age; for we can hardly expect much from the few opportunities, which the disciples of the great father of botany have had, of snatching up a few plants, as they have been chiefly confined to the voyage to China; during which they seldom go ashore, and much less make any stay in places, which are worthy the attention of the curious observer. And this circum‑ stance likewise shews, how much that immense part of our globe, India, with its isles, wants the labours of a new, accurate, and modern observer, accompanied by a faithful draughtsman, used to drawings of natural history, in order to make us better acquainted with the rich treasures of these extensive regions; and it raises a wish in each patriotic breast, that, as the British empire in India is so extensive, so much respected, and its subjects there so wealthy and powerful, that some of them would engage men capable of searching the treasures of nature, and exam‑ ining the several objects of sciences and arts in these climates.

Before I conclude this article, I shall only add a word or two on the received opinion, that sea-weeds are certain indications of land. I shall not need to men‑ tion the immense beds of weed, which are annually found in the midst of the

Atlantic ocean, to disprove this assertion, since I can have recourse to an ocean infinitely broader, namely, the South-Sea in the temperate zone, which is at least 1500 leagues broad from New-Zeeland to America, in which space, we are now well assured, there is no land, though we saw from time to time bunches of weeds in every part of it. Indeed, nothing is so probable, as that some weeds never take root, but grow floating on the water, as other aquatic plants do. But, supposing this were not the case, nothing is more easily to be conceived, than that the almost constant strong Westerly winds in that part, may detach these weeds, and carry them over all the ocean. If this last circumstance were well ascertained, it is most likely, that the weeds once torn up, begin from that time to decay, and a kind of random-guess of the vicinity of land, might be formed upon the bare inspection of the state of the weeds.

VEGETABLE
KINGDOM

SECTION II

Animal Kingdom

The countries of the South Sea, and the Southern coasts, contain a considerable variety of animals, though they are confined to a few classes only. We have seen by what degrees nature descended from the gay enamel[1] of the plains of the Society Isles, to the horrid barrenness of the Southern SANDWICH LAND. In the same manner the animal world, from being beautiful, rich, enchanting, between the tropics; falls into deformity, poverty, and disgustfulness in the Southern coasts. We cannot help being in raptures, when we tread the paths of O-Taheitean groves, which at each step strike us with the most simple, and at the same time the most beautiful prospects of rural life; presenting scenes of happiness and affluence to our eyes, among a people, which, from our narrow prejudices we are too readily accustomed to call savage. Herds of swine are seen on every side; by every hut dogs lie stretched out at their ease, and the cock with his seraglio, struts about, displaying his gay plumage, or perches on the fruit trees to rest. An unintermitted chorus of small birds warbles on the branches all the day long, and from time to time, the pigeons cooe is heard with the same pleasure as in our woods. On the sea shore, the natives are employed in dragging the net, and taking a variety of beautiful fish, whose dying colours change every moment: or they pick some shells from the reefs, which, though well known to the naturalist, yet have a right to the philosopher's attention, who admires the wonderful elegance of nature alike, in her most common as in her rarest productions. To enhance the satisfaction we feel, this happy country is free from all noxious and troublesome insects; no wasps, nor mosquitoes, infest the inhabitants, as in other tropical countries; no beasts of prey, nor poisonous reptiles ever disturb their tranquility.*

Let us remove from hence to the temperate zone: what a falling off from the

---

* The common flies are, indeed, at some seasons troublesome, on account of their immense numbers, but they cannot be called *noxious* insects: the only disagreeable animal in O-Taheitee is the common black rat, which is very numerous there, and often does mischief by its voracity.

soft scenes of domestic quiet, to the wilds of New-Zeeland! The rocky mountains, the forests, yea, human nature itself, all look savage and forbidding. The animal creation are already less happy than between the tropics, and hawks and owls, the tyrants of the wood, prey upon the weak and defenceless: still however the whole country rings with continual songs, of which the sweetness, emulates that of our first songsters. But as we advance to the South, and cross an immense ocean, in the midst of which we see some lonely birds, skimming the waves, and collecting an uncertain sustenance; we arrive at the South-end of America, and view a barren coast, inhabited by the last and most miserable of men, and but scantily clad with low and crooked shrubs: we find a number of vultures, eagles, and hawks, always hovering about, upon the watch for prey: and lastly, we observe that the greatest part of the other birds live gregarious in a few spots; whilst the rocks are occupied by a race of seals, which in comparison with the rest of animals, seem monstrous and misshapen.[2]

The classes of birds and fishes, are the only numerous ones in the countries which we have visited: those of quadrupeds and insects are confined to an exceeding small number of well known species. Those of cetacea, amphibia and vermes, are likewise not numerous, and the two first especially contain scarce anything new.

Quadrupeds

In the tropical isles they have but four species of quadrupeds, two of which are domestic; and the remaining ones are the vampyre and the common rat. This last inhabits the Marquesas, Society-Isles, Friendly-Isles, and the New-Hebrides; it is also found at New-Zeeland; but whether it may not have been transported thither by our ships is uncertain; at New-Caledonia, however, it has never been seen. Rats are in incredible numbers, at the Society-Isles, and especially at O-Taheitee, where they live upon the scraps of meals, which the natives leave in their huts, upon the flowers and pods of the erythrina corallodendron, upon plantanes and other fruits, and for want of these, on all sorts of excrements; nay, they are some-times so bold, as to be said to attach the toes of the inhabitants whilst they are asleep. They are much scarcer at the Marquesas and Friendly-Isles, and seldom seen at the New-Hebrides.

The vampyre (*vespertilio vampyrus)* which is the largest known species of bat, is only seen in the more Western isles. At the Friendly-Isles they live gregarious by several hundreds, and some of them are seen flying about the whole day: I found a large casuarina-tree, hung with at least 500 of them in various attitudes, some by the hind and others by the fore-feet. They live chiefly on fruits: they

skim the water with wonderful ease, and though we saw one swimming, I think
this single fact, gives me no right to pronounce them expert swimmers. It is
known that they frequent the water, in order to wash themselves from any filthiness or to get rid of vermin which might accidentally stick to them. Their smell
is somewhat offensive. When irritated they bite hard, but are for the rest quite
inoffensive. In Tanna there are, besides these larger bats, myriads of a minute species, which we saw and heard, but never could obtain for examination. At New-
Caledonia the natives use the hair of the great bats in ropes and in the tassels to
their clubs; and they interweave it among the threads of the grass (*cyperus squar-
rosus*), which is made use of for that purpose.

The two domestic quadrupeds are the hog and the dog.[3] The Society-Isles
alone are fortunate enough to possess them both: New-Zeeland and the low
islands must be content with dogs alone; the Marquesas, Friendly-Isles, and New-
Hebrides have only hogs; and Easter-Island and New-Caledonia are destitute of
both. The hogs are of that breed which we call the Chinese, having a short body,
short legs, belly hanging down almost to the ground, the ears erect, and very few
thin hairs on the body: their meat is the most juicy, and their fat the most agreeable and the least cloying I ever tasted, which can only be attributed to the excellent food they are used to; consisting chiefly of the bread-fruit or its sour paste,
yams, eddoes, &c. They are very numerous at the Society-Isles, where you hardly
pass a house that is without them, and frequently meet with some that keep a
great number. There is likewise abundance of them at the Marquesas and a considerable number at Amsterdam, one of the Friendly-Isles; but they are more rare
at the Western-isles of the New-Hebrides. The dogs of the South Sea isles are of a
singular race: they most resemble the common cur, but have a prodigious large
head, remarkably little eyes, prick-ears, long hair and a short bushy tail. They are
chiefly fed with fruit at the Society Isles; but in the low isles and New Zeeland,
where they are the only domestic animals, they live upon fish. They are exceedingly stupid, and seldom or never bark, only howl now and then; have the sense
of smelling in a very low degree, and are lazy beyond measure: they are kept by
the natives chiefly for the sake of their flesh, of which they are very fond, prefer-
ring it to pork; they also make use of their hair, in various ornaments, especially
to fringe their breast plates in the Society Isles, and to face or even line the whole
garment at New Zeeland.

Besides the dog, New-Zeeland boasts four other quadrupeds, one is the rat,
the other a small bat, resembling that described in Mr. Pennant's[4] Synopsis of
Quadrupeds, No. 283, under the name of New-York bat; the third is the sea-bear,
or ursine seal, Penn. Syn. Quad. No. 27 (*Phoca ursina.* Linn.) and the fourth, the
animal which Lord Anson calls a Sea-lion, (*Phoca leonina.* Linn. leonine seal,
P.S.Q. No. 272).[5] Some sailors on board the Resolution, affirmed they had seen a
little quadruped at Dusky Bay, in New-Zeeland, of the shape of a fox or jackal; but

as we never on our frequent excursions in the woods, met with any thing of this kind, nor have, on the most careful enquiry, found that any gentleman who had visited New-Zeeland in the Endeavour, had ever seen such an animal, we are of opinion, (especially considering the transient manner in which, and the time when this was seen, being in the dawn of the morning) that it must have been a mistake. As the Southern coasts which we saw, have both these seals, and another cogeneric animal, besides the seal with a mane, (*Phoca jubata*) all in greater number, and size, I shall now mention them together. It is an observation of the great naturalist M. de Buffon, that the large animals in the creation, are all to be considered as so many genera (espèces isolées) to which we can refer no other species; and to prove the truth of this, he mentions the instances of the elephant, rhinoceros, tapir, hippopotamus, and giraffe, which are really so many genera, to which only one species belongs: and adds likewise the cabiai, the beaver, and the lion.

We shall mention a circumstance making against his assertion: the species of seals in the antarctic hemisphere, are as large as most quadrupeds on the globe, except the elephant and rhinoceros. But two of them, which undoubtedly are distinct species, can hardly be defined, unless by the colour and mensural difference. One of these is the ursine seal, the other the jubated seal. This last is mentioned, and described by the great zoologist, the late M. Steller,[6] in his account of the animals of Beering's isles, near Kamtchatka: there is also a tolerably good account of this animal in Don Pernetty's voyage to the Malouines or Falkland Isles: they both call it the sea lion; a name given to it with the greatest justice, as its anteriors bear a great resemblance to the lion, which its shaggy mane and tawny colour helps to strengthen, while Lord Anson's sea lion with its wrinkled nose, has not the least similarity with it.

As there is not one animal entirely new, among the eight quadrupeds of the South Sea, it may seem to indicate that this class is already more compleat than is generally supposed; but what we have already observed in regard to plants, holds good equally in the animal kingdom: for never were small islands known to abound with a great variety of quadrupeds. It is from the interior parts of Africa, India, and perhaps too of New-Holland, that we must expect those supplies to the science, whenever the munificence of princes shall enable the naturalists, ever ready to undergo fatigue and hardships, for the sake of discovery, to search the hidden treasures of those vast continents.

Cetacea

The cetaceous animals which we saw in the South Sea, are the fin fish, (*Balaena physalis*, Linn.) the bottle nosed whale, the grampus, the porpesse, and the dolphin of the antients. The two last are seen all over the ocean from the line to the antarctic polar circle. We had no opportunity of examining any but a female of the dolphin, (*Delphinus Delphis*, Linn.) which we found perfectly to answer to the accurate descriptions of the various zoologists. It was struck with the harpoon, and we feasted on it with as much, or perhaps more appetite, than they did in the time of Dr. Caius. (*See* Mr. Pennant's *British Zoology*, vol. 3. p. 63. edit. in 4to.)

Birds

The birds of the South Sea, and of Tierra del Fuego, are numerous, and form a considerable variety of species; among which are two genera entirely new, and a third hitherto confounded with several others (the pinguin). They live secure in every bush, and on every tree, undisturbed for the greatest part by the inhabitants; they enliven the woods with their continual songs, and contribute much to the splender of nature by their varied plumage. It is a received notion that birds of many colours do not sing well, but not to mention the common goldfinch, which is perhaps, one of the most beautiful birds in nature, and has a very melodious note, we have numerous instances here to the contrary. The wild forests of New Zeeland, and the cultivated groves of O-Taheitee, resound alike with the harmony of the shining songsters. There is only one tame species of birds, properly speaking, in the tropical isles of the South Sea, *viz.* the common cock and hen; they are found numerous at Easter Island, where they are the only domestic animals: they are likewise in great plenty at the Society Isles, and Friendly Isles, at which last they are of a prodigious size: they are also not uncommon at the Marquesas, Hebrides, and New-Caledonia; but the low isles, and those of the temperate zone, are quite destitute of them. We can hardly reckon certain parroquets and pigeons among domestic birds; for though the natives of the Friendly and Society Isles, sometimes catch and tame them, yet they never have any breeds of them. The number of our new birds from New-Zeeland, is thirty-seven; that of the tropical isles, is forty-seven; the species from the ocean, the Southern extremities of America and the Southern lands, are upwards of twenty. The whole number thus amounts to 104; of which one half are aquatic: we have besides these, met with about thirty Linnaean species, of which above twenty are aquatic; and I am well persuaded that we have not been able to procure every species in the same manner, as we have not obtained a compleat Flora of every country we visited; the number of new birds therefore is astonishing, when compared to that of the known system, and must prove what great expectations are to be formed of those continents, which have not hitherto been much examined. The aquatic genera are, as we have already observed, very numerous, and among them we have the same remark to make which we have already made on the plants, namely that the most copious genera have still received the greatest additions. To the genus of *Anas* we have added nine new species, to that of the *Pelecanus* five, and to the *Procellariae* twelve. In the same manner among the land birds, we have seven new parrots, six pigeons, and eight fly-catchers.

Amphibia

The few amphibia which we met with in the South Sea, are confined to the tropical countries; they are, 1st. the caret turtle which gives the tortoise-shell proper for manufacture, (*testudo imbricata* Linn.) 2d, the green turtle, (*testudo midas*) which is fit for eating; 3d. the common lizard, (*lacerta agilis*, Linn.) 4th. the gecko, (*lacerta gecko*) 5th. the amphibious snake, (*coluber laticaudatus*, Linn.) and 6th. the *anguis platura*, Linn. among which, none is poisonous.

Fishes

The South Sea is rich in fish, and has a great variety of species; for though no branch of natural productions, was attended with more difficulties in the collection to us, not only from our very short stay in many places, but likewise because we were obliged almost wholly to depend upon the natives of the several countries, for this article, there being no expert fisher-men on board; yet the sea in various places yielded us the number of seventy-four species unknown heretofore; besides about forty which are described in the System of Nature of the celebrated Linnaeus. Among them we have only made one new genus, which till now has lain latent among the *chaetodontes*, but ought justly to be separated from them. The accurate observer, Prof. Forskal, whose premature death in Arabia, every lover of science must sincerely lament, had the same idea, though I knew nothing of it, as his book was not published till after my return to Europe; he calls the new genus *acanthurus*, and I gave it the name of *harpurus*.[7] The greatest part of the fish in the South Sea are very good eating, many of them are delicious, and would do honour to a Roman feast; only a few of the branchiostegous are noxious, of which we felt the fatal effects, as I shall mention in the sequel. M. de Buffon has observed, that nature seems to please herself in casting several beings very nearly in the same mould, as if certain conformations were more easy to her than others; he might have added, perhaps, with great propriety, because such conformations are most useful and necessary in the whole system of organic bodies. Hence we have found that certain classes of plants are remarkably copious, likewise, that the most extensive genera of birds, have still received a greater number of new species; and that in the fishes also, the rich genera of *gadus blennius, sparus* and *perca,* are most enlarged in the same manner; we may at the same time, I think, with the greatest probability suppose, that the unknown treasures in this last class are still immense; first, from the great additions which it has been in our power to make, though we laboured under the difficulties aforementioned: and secondly, from the more imperfect state of the definitions, which, according to the best method extant, must still depend upon the very precarious number of rays in the fins.

Insects

No countries in the world produce fewer species of insects than those of the South-Sea: it is surprizing how very few we met with, and those of the most common and well-known sorts. The only place where we saw them rather more abundant, was in New-Caledonia, and this I suspect is owing to its proximity to New-Holland; but our short stay there did not allow us to make the least acquisition in this branch. The most numerous sorts are undoubtedly the crustaceous; but, among them, we saw none that were not well marked in the Linnaean system. Here I must also remark, that there is a small species of scorpion in the tropical isles of the South-Sea, but more common to the Westernmost than the Society Isles, where I never saw one. The native, who was with us eight months, told us they were harmless; however, they were armed exactly as their cogeneric species. It is therefore reserved for future enquiry, to determine by what accidental circumstances the *virus* of the scorpion's sting becomes more or less deleterious; especially as the experiments made by Mr. de Maupertuis seem to intimate, that even the individuals of the same species are not all equally poisonous; and that one and the same individual is, at different times, more or less dangerous. *Academie des Sciences,* 17.[8]

Shells, and other Vermes

The shells of the South-Sea are far less various than might at first be expected; and the reefs of the tropical isles generally yielded the most common Linnaean shells, such as cowries, episcopal mitres, murices tritonis, the most common buccina, turbines, and neritae. A few species at New-Zeeland, are new, though the greatest part of them are minute. In regard to the mollusca, what little discoveries we made, are confined to the Atlantic ocean; and of the remaining *orders* we no where found any thing new.

I. Number

The whole number of species in the greater classes of animals, *viz.* quadrupeds, cetacea, amphibia, birds, and fish, which we saw in the South-Sea, according to the above enumeration, amounts to between 260 and 270, of which about one third are well known. Let us allow, that this number comprehends two thirds of the animals of those classes, actually residing in the South-Sea, though we have reason to think, that the fauna is much more extensive, we shall have upwards of 400; and supposing the classes of insects and vermes to give only 150 species, the whole fauna of the South-Sea isles will consist of at least 550 species, a prodigious number indeed, when compared with that of the Flora.

II. Station

Though many of the birds in New-Zeeland are remarkable for the gay colors of their plumage; yet we found, when we came to Norfolk-Island, (which, as I have observed in my account of the plants, contains exactly the same species) that the same birds appeared there arrayed in far more vivid and burning tints, which must prove, that the climate has a considerable influence on colours. There is also a species of king-fisher common to all the South-Sea isles, of which the tropical varieties are much brighter than that of New-Zeeland. The plumage of birds is likewise adapted to the climate in another respect; for those of warm countries have a moderate covering, whilst those of the cold parts of the world, and such especially, as are continually skimming over the sea, have an immense quantity of feathers, each of which is double; and the pinguins, which almost constantly live in the water, have their short, oblong feathers lying as close above each other as the scales of fishes, being at the same time furnished with a thick coat of fat, by which they are enabled to resist the cold: the case is the same with the seals, the geese, and all other Southern aquatic animals. The land birds, both within and without the tropics, build their nests in trees, except only the common quail, which lives in New-Zeeland, and has all the manners of the European one. Of the water-fowl, some make their nests on the ground, such as the grallae, which breed only in pairs; whilst several species of shags, (*pelecani*) live gregarious in trees, and others in crevices of rocks; and some petrels (*procellariae*) by thousands together, burrow in holes under-ground close by each other, where they educate their young, and to which they retire every night. The most prolific species in the South Sea, are the ducks, which hatch several eggs at one brood, and though the shags, penguins, and petrels, do not hatch more than one or two, or at most three eggs at a time, yet by being never disturbed, and always keeping together in great flocks, they are become the most frequent and numerous. The most palatable spe-

ANIMAL KINGDOM cies of fish are likewise the most prolific; but it must be observed, that there is no where such abundance of fish in the South-Sea, as at New-Zeeland, by which means they are become the principal nourishment of the natives, who have found that way of living to be attended with the least trouble, and consequently suited to that indolent disposition which they have in common with all barbarous nations.

III. Variety

It does not appear, that the individuals of the animal kingdom are so much subject to variety in the South-Seas, as those of the vegetable. Domestication, the great cause of degeneracy in so many of our animals, in the first place, is here confined to three species; the hog, dog, and cock: and secondly, it is in fact next to a state of nature in these isles: the hogs and the fowls run about at their ease the greatest part of the day; the last especially, which live entirely on what they pick up, without being regularly fed. The dog being here merely kept to be eaten, is not obliged to undergo the slavery, to which the varieties of that species are forced to submit in our polished countries; he lies at his ease all the day long, is fed at certain times, and nothing more is required of him: he is therefore not altered from his state of nature in the least; if probably inferior in all the sensitive faculties to any wild dog; (which may perhaps be owing to his food) and certainly, in no degree, partakes of the sagacity and quick perception of our refined variety. Among the wild birds, the varieties are very few: two species of pigeons, two of parrots, one of king-fishers, and one or two of fly-catchers, are the only I know of, that vary any thing in different isles; and it is much to be doubted, with regard to some of them, whether what we count varieties are not either distinct species, or only different sexes of one and the same; circumstances, which it is well known, require a long series of observations, not to be made on a cursory view. The varieties in other classes are still less considerable.

IV. Classification

The animals of the South-Seas, as we have already observed, are most of them new species. The known ones between the tropics, are chiefly such as are generally found all over the maritime parts of the torrid zone; those of the temperate zone being principally aquatic, are common to those latitudes in every sea; or consist of European species. Upon the whole, we found no more than two genera, which are distinct from those already known, and all the remaining species rank under old genera. But it is not possible to refer those to the two continents of Asia and America, as was done with the plants; because there are so very few genera, which are not common to both of them. We shall therefore, at present, confine our observations on the classes of animals, to the Southern aquatic birds, and the new genus of fish, which we established. The genus of petrels, which contains only six species according to Linnaeus's last system, has received an addition of twelve new species from the Southern seas. The largest of them is the bird, which the Spaniards call the *Quebrantahuessos,* or OSPREY-PETREL; the least is the common stormfinch, *(Procellaria pelagica)* which is seen alike in the North sea and in the South sea, and in almost every latitude. Mr. de Brisson, whom Mr. de Buffon justly censures for multiplying species, and subdividing genera, has divided the few known species into two genera, from some slight difference in the bill, which is not even worth remarking here. At the same time, M. Scopoli, with as little propriety, unites the diomedea or albatros, with the procellariae; and hath been led to this method of classing, by a real species of the last genus; which, upon what foundation I cannot imagine, he mistakes for the bird Linnaeus calls a DIOMEDEA.[9] There are but two circumstances which have occasioned the errors of the various naturalists; the one, that they attached themselves too much to the investigation of individual species, without every now and then stopping to take a view of the general chain of nature; and, to this we must ascribe the many mistakes in subdividing, or combining genera; the other, that, by continually fixing on the general view of the whole extent of nature, they forget to descend to the particulars of classification, which the imperfect state of the science requires. It is from keeping a just medium between these extremes, that the illustrious Linnaeus has acquired so great a fame in the literary world, and methodized all the productions of nature with such judgment, that future ages will ever own him as the father of the science. It is from falling into the first error, that some untravelled naturalists load their books with the enumeration of varieties, instead of species. On the other hand, the great zoologist, and most elegant writer of this and many other ages, M. de Buffon, wholly solicitous to view his subject in all its grandeur, makes light of exposing here and there a neglect. After-ages may bring the science nearer to perfection, by combining what is valuable on both sides. Great as the loss of Linnaeus must certainly be to science, it will not be so severely felt, whilst we have so enlightened botanists, as Mr. Banks and Dr. Solander, and such acute zoologists as M. de Buffon and Professor Pallas. The genus of pinguins Mr. Pennant set in its proper light, after it had lain lost, as it were, among the genera of DIOMEDEA and PHAETON, which are utter strangers to it. Mr. Pennant's Magellanic pinguin, the two misplaced Linnaean species, and our three new species, have increased it considerably. The bill, though various in regard to thickness, has, however, the same character in them all, except that some species have the lower mandible truncated; the nostrils are always linear apertures, which further proves their distinction from the diomedea. The feet are exactly of the same shape in them all. They have only the rudiments of wings, enlarged by a membrane into a fin, and covered with a kind of feathers, but so closely, that they seem like scales. It is this, besides the shape of bill and feet, which distinguishes the genus of auks or murrs (*alcae*) from them; for these last, though sometimes incapable of flying, are only so on account of the *shortness*, not the *deficiency* of quills. The body of the pinguins is entirely covered with oblong, thick, hard, and glossy plumes, which form a coat of mail, impenetrable to wet, because they are obliged to live almost continually in the sea. They are confined to the temperate and frigid zones, at least I know of none between the tropics. The genus of pelicans (*pelecanus*) might perhaps be separated into three genera with greater justice, than authors have used in many of their dilacerations. The true pelican (*onocrotalus*) is greatly different from all the rest of the species: the man of war (*p. aquilus*); the gannet (*p. bassanus*); and the several sorts of boobies (*p. sula, fiber & piscator,*) form another division; from which the cormorant and shag (*p. carbo & graculus*) and four new species, are again widely different. But the characters of the feet, and the naked skin in which the eyes are situated, being common to them all, they may still be continued in one common genus. The gannets and boobies, though they frequent particular places for breeding, are however, not gregarious as the sorts of shags: some of these last build in vast numbers on the same tree; others sit by thousands in the cavities of overhanging cliffs along the seashore, and again, another sort build their elevated nests on the ground, by whole myriads.

Among the fish we have only separated a genus from the *chaetodon*, which differs from it by having no scales on the fins, a spine on each side of the tail, and a different number of branchiostegous rays. Of this genus which has obtained the name of HARPURUS, there are seven species, viz. three new ones, (4, the *ch. nigricans,*) (5, *lineatus*) (6, *fasciatus* of Linnaeus) and 7, one described by Hasselquist, and erroneously quoted for the *ch. nigricans* by Linnaeus. We have augmented the Linnaean genus of SCIAENA, with eight new species, which have every one the same generic characters, so that this genus now stands more firmly among the rest, to which it is related. The genera of LABRUS and SPARUS merit the utmost attention of the naturalists, since every writer gives us different, and often contradictory characteristics of them, which may be seen by comparing the definitions of Linnaeus, (Syst. Nat. xii.) Gouan, (genera piscium) Brunniche, (icthyolog massiliens.) Pallas, (spicileg. zool.) and Forskal, (Faun. Aegypt. arab.) some of which are certainly found from the examination of a few species only.

I shall now briefly mention the USE which is made of the various animal productions in the South Sea isles.[10] The animal kingdom has at all times furnished

1.

2.

3.

4.

5.

Chapman, Del.

Published Feb.? 1.st 1777 by W.m Strahan in New Street Shoe Lane & Tho.s Cadell in the Strand London.

Record sculp.
N.º XVII

"Ornaments and
Weapons at the
Marquesas," engraving
by John Record after
Charles Chapman, from
Cook, *A Voyage towards
the South Pole*, 1777,
Plate 17.

mankind with a variety of necessaries, conveniencies, and luxuries; the first step towards the civilization of nations, is the adoption of such things as serve to make life more easy and comfortable; and the first consequence of a civilized state, is the introduction of such articles as captivate the various senses, and flatter the appetites. Hence in the South Sea we find the natives of the Society Isles in the highest state of civilization; they possess the comforts and even luxuries of life: the more Westerly nations lose the luxuries, and retain only the conveniences: the New-Zeelanders more savage, have even these in an inferior degree; and the wretched inhabitants of Tierra del Fuego, can hardly be said to have more than the bare necessaries of life, and therefore, of all our brethren, approach the nearest to brutes.[11] Almost every species of fish is eaten at the tropical isles, and generally looked upon by the inhabitants as a dainty, which they prefer to pork and dog's flesh. Their birds, on the contrary, are seldom taken for the sake of any thing else than the feathers, (excepting the domestic fowls and wild ducks) of which, they make a variety of ornaments, and upon which, as real luxuries, they set a very high value: nay, so far are they from eating all birds, that they have a kind of superstitious regard for herons and king-fishers, almost like that which is paid to the stork, the robin red-breast, the swallow, and other familiar harmless birds in England. The natives of the Society Isles, have their immense helmets and targets covered with the shining plumes of a pigeon, and edged round with a vast number of the long white tail feathers of the tropic-bird: but what they value as much as diamonds and pearls are esteemed in Europe, are the crimson feathers of certain parroquets, of which, they make tassels to ornament the warriors. We accidentally procured a quantity of these feathers at Amsterdam, one of the Friendly Isles, where they fastened them on pieces of their stuffs.[12] These being carried to *O-Taheitee*, and shared out in little pieces, procured us a great number of hogs; for a bit of two inches square, covered with feathers, would at any time, be eagerly purchased with a hog. The rest of the tropical islanders make a variety of ornaments of birds feathers, such as crested caps; at Easter Isle, and the Marquesas, fly-flaps, &c. The hair of the dog is employed in fringing their targets at O-Taheitee, and nothing is more common than vast bunches of human hair tied round the knees, ancles, &c. among the natives of the Marquesas. The Easter Islanders make an ornament hanging on the breast of the porposse's bone, the O-Taheiteans make saws and various utensils of bone, shark's teeth, &c. The tails of the sting ray (*raja pastinaca*) are universally employed to arm the spears of the natives; the Mallicolese point their arrows with bone; and the inhabitants of Tierra del Fuego have fish gigs armed with jagged bones. A variety of shells are also made use of in the tropical isles, some are eaten, some make necklaces, some bracelets and fish hooks, others weights to sink their fishing lines, and they wear some mishapen pearls in their ears. Not even the coral is without its use, for it is employed to smooth and polish the surface of their canoes. The New-Zeelanders living continually on fish, are glad when they can get a dog or bird to eat, which with them, always is reckoned a dainty. They employ the skins of dogs for their cloaths, but merely for convenience, namely, to keep them warm: their ornaments are however, a comb of the bone of some cetaceous animal, which is stuck in the hair; and feathers of gulls, parrots, &c. The first they wear on their head, the last on their battle axes; lastly, they have some ornaments which are taken from the mineral kingdom. Among the tropical isles, the natives dress all their meat over the fire, with as much cleanliness and nicety as we could do it ourselves, so that the delicate appearance of their victuals often tempted us to yield to their invitations, which their hospitable disposition never failed to express in the most engaging manner. At New-Zeeland too, the inhabitants though less hospitable, and more uncleanly, yet dress their fish with so much care, that a man with a good appetite would not refuse to eat with them. But the people of Tierra del Fuego are not only miserable in their appearance, being scarce covered with a bit of seal's skin, but they are likewise highly disgustful in the manner of taking their food, which consists of raw seals flesh, almost putrid, and of which the rank fat is to their taste the most delicious part: in other places where seals are more scarce, they derive their subsistence from the muscle-shells, which are common on the rocks. We found vast refreshment from the animals in the various countries we met with, and only in a few instances suffered by eating some species of fish. The one of these was a *Sparus,* of which three were caught at Mallicollo, the largest about fifteen inches long: about sixteen persons eat of these three fish, and found themselves affected with a prodigious numbness, which soon made them quite giddy, and incapable of standing; they had afterwards excruciating pains in all their bones, which did not go off till ten days afterwards, by the continual use of vomits, and sudorifics.[13] A hog that eat part of the entrails, swelled prodigiously, and died a few hours after: several dogs also which eat of the offal, lay for a fortnight in the greatest agonies, howling and foaming at the mouth, utterly incapable of standing on their legs. A little favourite parroquet, which eat a bit of the fish, likewise died in consequence of it. Sometime afterwards, I was told that a fish of the same species was caught at Tanna by some of the sailors, who salted it and eat it, without any ill effects; from whence it is to be supposed that this species is not poisonous in itself, but only from the food which it accidently meets with, in the same manner as many fish in the West Indies, otherwise very wholesome to eat, are said to become deleterious, by feeding on the manchineel apples. The other sort was a new species of TETRODON, whose ugly appearance alone might have prejudiced us against it, had we been any ways nice; but so much is the value of fresh provisions enhanced by being long at sea, that we were glad of even this opportunity of eating an ill-looking animal. Only three of us eat a very small bit of the liver, not above two or three morsels each at supper; before two o'clock the next morning, we were all up, complaining of the effects of the poison, which operated exactly as that of the sparus had done before: we immediately took vomits, and having evacuated all we had eaten, escaped with a giddiness, lasting only a few days, without any of the acute pain experienced in the other instance. Another hog then on board, unfortunately tasting the entrails, swelled as the other had done and died: sometime after, another TETRODON of the same species, was caught, and being opened, one of the dogs eat a small quantity of the entrails, and lived in the most dreadful agonies for a fortnight after, so that he was at length thrown over board as incurable. The sparus seems to have been mentioned by QUIROS, under the name of PARGOS, which he says at one time poisoned great part of his ship's company. The tetrodon again is related closely to the *Tetrodon ocellatus,* which in Japan is commonly made use of in cases of self-destruction, and the virus of which is enhanced by the *Ilicium anisatum,* an otherwise salutary plant. (*See* Kaempfer *Hist. Japon.*)

It remains now that I should say something on the animals, which are looked on as signs of the approach of land: and I ought here to add, that the sight of birds is not more to be depended on, than that of sea-weeds, unless we are well assured that the birds we see, are land birds, or never range to any distance from land; a circumstance not easily ascertained. Seals, pinguins, petrels, and albatrosses, are seen six or seven hundred leagues from land, in the very middle of the South Sea, so that they cannot be depended on. Between the tropics, men of war birds are seen a hundred leagues from land, and as the isles of the South Sea there, are much nearer together, they cannot be looked upon as signs of land. Boobies and shags do not wander so far; and the last, commonly not out of sight of land; but one knows not how far accident may sometimes carry them.

These are the few remarks on animals which occured to me, during the course of this expedition.

CHAPTER VI

Remarks on the Human Species in the South-Sea Isles

MIRANTUR ALIQUI ALTITUDINES MONTIUM, INGENTES FLUCTUS MARIS, ALTISSIMOS LAPSUS FLUMINUM, ET OCEANI AMBITUM, ET GYROS SIDERUM — ET RELINQUUNT SEIPSOS, NEC MIRANTUR.
Augustinus[1]

THE PROPER STUDY OF MANKIND IS MAN.
Pope[2]

Though we have many accounts of distant regions, it has been a general misfortune, that their authors were either too ignorant to collect any valuable and useful observations, or desirous of making a shew with a superficial knowledge, have given us their opinions, embellished with surmises, and trite reflections, borrowed from other writers. If they happened to be capable of collecting and communicating useful information, relative to the study of nature, they have usually confined themselves to the inanimate bodies of the creation; or have principally considered part of the brute organic; while Man,

> *"A creature form'd of earth . . .*
> *Exalted from so base original*
> *With heav'nly spoils, . . . "*
> Milton[3]

is entirely neglected and forgotten, amongst other less important pursuits.

It must likewise be acknowledged, that several learned and ingenious works on the human species, have appeared in the present age, written by philosophers, whose names alone should seem to be a sufficient recommendation. I have, however, early observed, that, being misled by the vague reports of unphilosophical travellers,[4] which they have sometimes wilfully changed and moulded, to suit their own opinions; their systems, though ever so ingenious, are seldom agreeable to nature. It appears indeed, to be the general fault of these writers, to study mankind only in their cabinets; or, at best, to observe no other than highly civilized nations, who have over-run all parts of the world by the help of navigation, and from commercial views; and are more or less degenerate and tainted with vices.[5]

As we met with many tribes in the course of our expedition, who had never seen any European or other polished nation, I thought it my duty to attend to this branch of the great study of nature, as much as my other occupations would permit. I collected facts, and now communicate them to the impartial and learned world, with a few inferences, as an imperfect essay.

SECTION I

On the Numbers of Inhabitants in the South-Sea-Isles, and their Population

Non temere & fortuito sati & creati sumus, & profecto est
quaedam vis, quae generi consulit humano.
  M. Tullius Cicero[1]

We shall begin with O-Taheitee, one of the largest, most populous, and best-cultivated islands of the Pacific Ocean.[2] The high hills of this happy country are without inhabitants; and, if we except some fertile well-watered vallies, containing a few cottages, in the midst of the mountains, the whole interior country is still unimproved, and such as it came out of the hands of nature. The flat grounds, surrounding the island towards the sea, contain chiefly the habitations of the natives; and nothing can be seen more beautiful, more cultivated, and more fertile, than these extensive plains. The whole ground is covered with coco-nut and bread-fruit trees, which yield the chief subsistence for its inhabitants: all is interspersed with plantations of bananas, young mulberry-trees for the manufacture of their cloth, and other useful plants; such as yams, eddoes, sugar-canes, and many others too tedious to enumerate. Under the shade of these agreeable groves, we every where beheld numerous houses, which we should have considered as mere sheds, were they not sufficient to screen the owners from rain, moisture, and the inclemencies of the air, which is always mild and temperate in these happy regions. All the houses are filled with people, and the largest habitations contain several families. Wherever we walked, we found the roads lined with natives, and not one of the houses was empty, though we had left the shores opposite the ship, crowded with people. All these circumstances indicate, that there is an extraordinary population in this queen of tropical isles; and we have every necessary argument to corroborate the assertion.

The mild and temperate climate, under the powerful, benevolent, and congenial influence of the sun, mitigated by alternate sea and land breezes, quickens the growth of the vegetable and animal creation; and therefore, in some measure also, benefits and improves the human frame, by this happy combination. Such is

POPULATION

145

the great abundance of the finest fruit growing, as it were, without cultivation, that none are distressed for food. The sea is another great resource for the inhabitants of this and all the Society Isles. They catch great numbers of fine and delicious fish; they collect numberless shells, cray-fish, sea-eggs, and several kinds of blubbers, along the reefs, both by day and night; and often go to the low islands a few leagues off, in quest of cavallas,[3] turtles, and water-fowl. There is not a house or cottage, about which you do not observe a dog, several cocks and hens, and frequently two or three pigs. All this not only affords a superfluity, but likewise a great variety of animal and vegetable food. The bark of the *morus papyrifera*, the bread-fruit tree, and some others, afford them materials for an easy, light, and warm kind of clothing; which they manufacture of various qualities, cut into various shapes, and dye with various colours. Food and raiment, the two great wants of the human species, are therefore easily supplied, and the inhabitants are hitherto fortunate enough to have none of the artificial wants, which luxury, avarice, and ambition have introduced among Europeans.[4]

The call of nature is heard at an early age in this genial climate: the inhabitants therefore soon begin to chuse an agreeable partner for life, happy in the pleasing expectation of seeing themselves represented, and as it were reproduced in a numerous offspring.

These circumstances, when compared with the many wants of our civilized

William Hodges, *The Otaheite Fleet and Appany Bay* [Pare], pen and wash, 1774. 370 × 545 mm. State Library of New South Wales.

"Otoo [Tu] King of Otaheite," engraving by J. Hall after William Hodges, from Cook, *A Voyage towards the South Pole*, 1777, Plate 38.

state, the labours we must undergo in supplying these wants, and especially those which are most indispensible in our climates, and the many difficulties preceding and attendant on our marriages, will be sufficient to prove, that in the natural course of things, population must be great in these happy regions. But this reasoning does not give a clear and precise idea of the subject. I will therefore attempt to enable the reader to make a near estimate of the real population of this and all the adjacent isles.

When we came the second time to O-Taheitee in April, 1774, we found the inhabitants busied in making preparations for a great naval expedition against Morea, a district in Eimeo. We saw a fleet of their war-canoes collected together, with a great number of small craft: we saw the natives preparing the war-canoes in several districts, and in some they were already launched; we found them exercising their rowers and warriors; and the armaments of two districts actually appeared in review before the great chief's house, at O-Parre. The district of Atahooroo is one of the greatest, and that of Tittahaw one of the smallest. The first had equipped 159 war-canoes, and about 70 small vessels intended for the chiefs, the sick and wounded, and probably to carry some provisions. The second district sent 44 war-canoes, and about 20 or 30 smaller ones. That part of O-Taheitee, which is called T-Obreonoo, or the great Western peninsula, contains 24 districts in all; the lesser Eastern peninsula, or Te-Arraboo, is divided into 19. Let us suppose, that each district of the first is capable of sending the medium between the largest and least number of war-canoes, as mentioned before, which would amount to 100: nay, to be more moderate, let us suppose each district can send no more than 50 war-canoes, and 25 small attending boats; and we shall find the war-canoes of T-Obreonoo to amount to 1200, and the small vessels to 600. We observed in the large war-canoes 50 persons, including warriors, paddlers, and steerers; and in the smaller about 30. (We found, indeed, some war-canoes, that required 144 paddlers, eight men to steer, one to command the paddlers, and about 30 warriors for the stage; but, as there are only one or two vessels of that size in each island, we can make no inference from thence.) To be very moderate in our computations, we will suppose no more than 20 men in each of these war-canoes; and, according to this last supposition, the men required to defend and navigate 1200 vessels, will amount to 24,000. Each of the small attending boats contained at a medium five men; consequently the crews of all the small canoes of the 24 districts, at the rate of 25 vessels from each district, form a number of 3000, which, added to the complement of the war-canoes, are 27,000 men. Let us further suppose each of these men to be married to a woman, and to have one child; and in this case, we shall have the number of 81,000 persons.[5] Every one will allow, that this is the very lowest computation that can be made, and that the number of living inhabitants of T-Obreonoo must be at least double the above number. For all the inhabitants are not warriors; nor are all employed in navigating the vessels; there remain besides, many old men at home; and it is certainly insufficient to allow a single child for every married couple; for marriage here is commonly blessed with a numerous offspring. I have seen more than one family, wherein there were six or eight children. HAPPAI, the father of O-Too, the present king of T-Obreonoo, had eight children, seven of whom were still alive, when we came to O-Taheitee. Many other families had from three to five children. But some will be ready enough to question this great population, and to doubt, whether such numbers can find food in proportion to support them all: it is but just to establish the fact on a firm basis. We have frequently spoken with warmth of the extraordinary fertility of these regions; we are likewise able to demonstrate the truth of what we have advanced. When we visited the Society-Isles, the natives often told us, that three large bread-fruit trees were sufficient to feed a full-grown person during the bread-fruit season, that is, during eight months. The largest bread-fruit trees, with their branches, occupy a space in diameter about forty feet; consequently every tree occupies 1600 square feet, or if round 1256⅔ feet. An English acre contains 43,560 square feet; it follows, that above 27 large bread-fruit trees in the first case, and 35 in the second, would stand on an acre; and these will feed ten persons for the space of eight months in the first case, and 12 persons in the second. During the remaining four months of the year, the natives live upon the roots of yams and eddoes, the banana, and the fruit of the horse-plantanes, of which they have immense plantations, in the vallies of the uninhabited mountainous part of the isle. They likewise make a kind of sour-paste of the bread-fruit by fermentation, which keeps for several months, and is both healthy and palatable to those who are once used to its acidulated taste. Now let us compare this to the greatest fertility in known countries. In France*, on a square league, containing about 4867 French acres (*arpents*), no more than 1390 persons can live by agriculture, and 2604 by vintage: in the first case, one person requires 3½ *arpents* to live upon, and in the latter nearly two *arpents* must be allotted for the subsistence of one individual. In O-Taheitee, and the Society-Isles, about ten or twelve persons live eight months on one English acre, which contains 43,560 square feet; whereas the arpent, containing 51,550 square feet English measure, feeds but one person six months in France. This calculation proves, that taking such parts, as are best cultivated in both countries, the population of O-Taheitee is to that of France, nearly as 17 to 1. Moreover, let us suppose, that on the whole isle of O-Taheitee, there are no more than 40 square English miles of land planted with bread-fruit trees, which supposition cer-

---

* *Discours sur les Vignes Dijon*, 1756, 12mo.

tainly does not err in excess. Each mile consists of 640 acres, and 40 miles must accordingly contain 25,600 acres. Ten or twelve men live eight months on one acre; consequently thirty or thirty-six men can subsist the same time on three acres, and twenty or twenty-four men find food during a whole year on three acres; consequently, on the whole extent of 25,600 acres, 170,660 persons, according to the first supposition, or 204,800 according to the second, can be supported yearly. But we have seen above, that only 44,125 individuals are supposed to exist on O-Taheitee, according to our first calculation, which is nearly less by 26,535 persons in the first instance, or 60,675 in the second, than the isle can support, upon the most moderate calculation. Having thus fairly stated the possibility of so great a population, we shall certainly not be thought unreasonable in our estimate.

Te-Arraboo has 19 or 20 districts, and is equally well cultivated and populous: for its natives not only withstood the whole power of the inhabitants of T-Obreonoo, but even beat their forces and ravaged their shores. It might therefore be deemed very little, if at all inferior, in power and in numbers: but we will reckon them to be only one half of the population of T-Obreonoo; and the number of its inhabitants will be 40,500.

Imeo is a little but well-cultivated isle, subject to the king of T-Obreonoo. According to the accounts of the Taheiteans, it opposed and beat off the whole force of Te-Arraboo; and the great armaments we observed going forward in T-Obreonoo, for the reduction of Iméo, prove that they have no mean idea of their strength; notwithstanding this, we shall allow them no more than one fourth of the population of

T-Obreonoo, *i.e.*	20,250,	which,
added to the inhabitants of Te-Arraboo	40,500,	and of
those of T-Obreonoo	81,000,	makes
the number of inhabitants of all O-Taheitee, and of Iméo, amount to	141,750.	

All these are subject to O-Too, king of T-Obreonoo; for though Te-Arraboo has a king of its own, yet that king is a vassal to O-Too.[6] We conclude therefore, that allowing 150,000 persons for the population of O-Taheitee and Iméo, the computation must be considered as very moderate.

The isles of Huahine, O-Raietea, O-Tahà, Bola-bola, Mourua, Tabu-a-Manoo, and Maâtèa, are certainly very populous; for we saw three of them, and found them all well-cultivated, and equally well-peopled; and, as the king of Bola-bola has subdued O-Raietea, and O-Tahà, it is highly probable, that his power, and consequently the population of Bora-bora and Mourua, must be nearly upon a par with that of the two conquered islands. If we allow 200,000 inhabitants for all these seven isles, the account will by no means be exaggerated.

The five Marquesas are likewise very populous, for the natives cultivate and inhabit all the slopes of their hills. Between them, and the Society-Isles, are a vast number of low isles full of inhabitants.[7] To the East and South-East of O-Taheitee are still more. We saw about five in the year 1773; and as many, if not more in 1774. In the Endeavour several more were discovered; and Capts. Wallis and Carteret found many also. We cannot think the allowance too great, when we suppose all these islands, and the Marquesas to contain 100,000 inhabitants.

Farther to the West is a cluster of isles, which we call the Friendly Isles. Tonga-Tabu the largest of them, is in every part highly cultivated; the barren sandy outskirts towards the sea, and the road leading through the isle alone excepted, all the rest seems to be private property, is fenced in, and inhabited by a numerous, industrious and friendly people. E-Aoowe is less in size, nor is it wholly cultivated, any more than A-Namocka: nevertheless there are great numbers of inhabitants in both. About A-Namocka is a collection of small isles, all full of people: and if we consult Taesman, we find the same archipelago continued under the name of Prince William's Isles. I suppose the inhabitants of all these isles amount to about 200,000.

Still more to the West is that cluster of large islands, to which we gave the name of the New Hebrides. These, though far from being so populous as the Society and Friendly Isles, yet being infinitely larger, contain a considerable number of inhabitants. We found a great croud of people on one of them, named Mallicollo, and if we may form a judgment from the cultivation in Ambrrym it must be equally, if not better inhabited; the isles of Aurora, of Lepers, and Whitsuntide, seem to be less populous; Tierra del Espiritu Santo is large, and perhaps in proportion to its size, has many inhabitants. The isles of Pa-oom, A-Pee, Three-hills, Shepherd, Mountague, Hinchinbrook, and Sandwich, are all inhabited, and the latter seemed to be very fertile and populous. Irromanga, and Tanna, from our own observations, and the isles of Irronan, Immer, and Anattom according to the informations we received at Tanna, are full of people: all these therefore, together may be supposed to contain at least 200,000 inhabitants.

If we suppose the number of souls in New-Caledonia and its adjacent isles to be 50,000, the allowance, it is apprehended, cannot be deemed very faulty; for though these parts be not so highly populous as some others; an extent of eighty leagues in length, will justify the guess we have made concerning its state of population.

The Southern isle of New-Zeeland has very few inhabitants; but the Northernmost, according to the accounts we had from Capt. Cook, and from what we saw in some few places, as we passed by, is much better peopled, nay, in some spots very populous; therefore allowing 100,000 souls to both isles, we rather think our estimate to fall short of the true population.

If we take the sum	150,000	O-Tahaitee and Iméo
of these numbers,	200,000	Society Isles
we find the whole of	100,000	Marquesas and Low Isles
the inhabitants of the	200,000	Friendly Isles
isles in the South Sea	200,000	New Hebrides
	50,000	New Caldonia
	100,000	New Zeeland
Amounting to	1,000,000	

The population in Tierra del Fuego is so thin, and they live in so small tribes, or rather families, that I can hardly believe they exceed in all, two thousand individuals, scattered over a surface of land, containing at least, as much as would form the half of Ireland.

This account of the population of the isles we visited, in the South Seas, I will now conclude with the two following remarks.

First, I do not pretend that my estimate of the numbers of the inhabitants is perfectly accurate; at best it is but a guess approaching as near to truth as the data which we had opportunities of collecting would permit; and if upon the whole there is any fault in it, it rather consists in having formed too small an estimate, or if any particular account should exceed the true number, it must be in New Caledonia.

Secondly, The population of countries encreases in the same proportion with civilization and cultivation.[8] Not that I believe civilization or cultivation to be the true causes of a greater population; but they are rather, in my opinion, its effects. As soon as the numbers increase in a confined place, viz. an island, to such a degree, that its inhabitants are obliged to cultivate some plants for their food, because the natural wild productions are no longer sufficient, they then devise methods for performing this task in an easy and proper manner; they find themselves obliged to obtain from others, the feeds and roots, to stipulate among themselves, not to destroy each others plantations; to defend them jointly against the violence of invaders, and to give each other mutual assistance. Such are the beginnings of arts and cultivation, such is the rise of civil societies; sooner or later they cause distinctions of rank, and the various degrees of power, influence, and wealth, which, more or less are observed among mankind. Nay, they often produce a material difference in the colour, habits, and forms of the human species, of which, we shall now treat more at large.

SECTION II

On the Varieties of the Human Species, relative to Colour, Size, Form, Habit, and Natural Turn of Mind in the Natives of the South-Sea Isles

Εστι δε τι και παρα τα κλιματα ωστε τα μεν φυσει
Εστιν επιχωρια τισι, τα δε θεσει, και ασκησει.
   Strabo lib. 2[1]

The varieties of the human species are, as every one knows, very numerous. The small size, the tawny colour, the mistrustful temper, are as peculiar to the Esquimaux; as the noble and beautiful figure, and outline of the body, the fair complexion, and the treacherous turn of mind, to the inhabitant of Tcherkassia. The native of Senegal is characterised by a timorous disposition, by his jetty black skin, and crisped wooly hair. A majestic size, red hair, a blue languishing eye, a remarkably fair complexion, and a warlike, intrepid, but open and generous temper distinguish the Teutonic tribes of the North of Europe, from the rest of mankind. But to enumerate all these varieties, requires too much time; and the subject has been so fully treated of by others, that it would be highly improper to repeat their observations. I will therefore confine myself to a sketch of the different varieties peculiar to every country we have visited, and then endeavour to enumerate their various and probable causes.

    We chiefly observed two great varieties of people in the South Seas; the one more fair, well limbed, athletic, of a fine size, and a kind benevolent temper; the other, blacker, the hair just beginning to become woolly and crisp, the body more slender and low, and their temper, if possible more brisk,[2] though somewhat mistrustful. The first race inhabits O-Taheitee, and the Society Isles, the Marquesas, the Friendly Isles, Easter-Island, and New-Zeeland. The second race peoples New-Caledonia, Tanna, and the New Hebrides, especially Mallicollo. The Pesserais, are not I think, to be ranked among the natives of the South Sea, as it is not to be doubted, that they originally came to Tierra del Fuego, from the American continent. Each of the above two races of men, is again divided into several varieties, which form the gradations towards the other race; so that we find some of the first race almost as black and slender as some of the second; and in this second race are some strong, athletic figures, which may almost vie with the first; however, as we have many good reasons for comprehending in one tribe all the islanders enumerated under the first race; we could not help giving to all a general character, from which, on account of the extent and compass, wherein these nations are dispersed, the outskirts or extremes must deviate.

I. *First.* O-TAHEITEE, and the adjacent Society-Isles, no doubt contain the most beautiful variety of the first race: but even here nature seems to follow that richness, luxuriance, and variety which we have observed in its vegetation; it is not confined to a single type or model. The common people are most exposed to air and sun; they do all kinds of dirty work; they exert their strength in agriculture, fishing, paddling, building of houses and canoes; and lastly, they are stinted in their food. From these causes, they degenerate as it were towards the second race, but always preserve some remains of their original type; which, in their chiefs or Arees,[3] and the better sort of people, appears in its full lustre and perfection. The colour of their skin is less tawny than that of a Spaniard, and not so coppery as that of an American; it is of a lighter tint than the fairest complexion of an inhabitant of the East-Indian islands; in a word, it is of a white, tinctured with a brownish yellow, however not so strongly mixed, but that on the cheek of the fairest of their women, you may easily distinguish a spreading blush. From this complexion we find all the intermediate hues down to a lively brown, bordering upon the swarthy complexion of the second race. Their hair is commonly black, strong, naturally falling in the most beautiful ringlets, and shining with the perfumed coco-nut-oil. I saw but few with yellowish-brown or sandy hair, and often no more than the extremities were yellowish, and the roots of a darker brown. A single man in O-Tahà had perfectly red hair, a fairer complexion than the rest, and was sprinkled all over with freckles. The features of the face are generally regular, soft, and beautiful; the nose something broad below; the chin is overspread and darkened by a fine beard. The women have an open, chearful countenance, a full, bright, and sparkling eye; the face more round than oval; the features arranged with uncommon symmetry, and heightened and improved by a smile, which beggars all description. The rest of the body, above the waist, is well proportioned, included in the most beautiful, soft outline, and sometimes extremely feminine. Many of the Arees and Manahounes[4] are of an athletic habit, but always blended with a degree of effeminacy. The feet are rather large, and what might be thought out of proportion. The common people are likewise in general well-built and proportioned, but more active, and with limbs and joints that are well knit. The women are in general finely, nay delicately shaped. The arms, hands, and fingers of some are so exquisitely delicate and beautiful, that they would do honour to a Venus of Medicis. Unfortunately the habit of walking barefooted, has destroyed that beautiful figure in their legs, which are commonly large and rather clumsy. Of the men, the Arees are in general of a tall stature. I saw several who exceeded six feet three inches, and one man was six feet four inches; nor are the common people always confined to a short size. The women are rather of low stature, and but few are of a size approaching that of men, though I saw a girl six feet high, and others very tall. The natives of these isles are generally of a lively, brisk temper, great lovers of mirth and laughter, and of an open, easy, benevolent character. Their natural levity hinders them from paying a long attention to any one thing. You might as well undertake to fix mercury, as to keep their mind steady on the same subject. The relaxation of their solids, under a powerful sun, causes a great indolence, and an unconquerable aversion to any laborious undertaking.[5] Those that are in power and affluence, generally indulge themselves in eating, and distend the frame of their body to its utmost stretch. They are absolutely inactive, refuse to take even their victuals, and permit themselves to be crammed. The great plenty of good and nourishing food, together with the fine climate, the beauty and unreserved behaviour of their females, invite them powerfully to the enjoyments and pleasures of love. They begin very early to abandon themselves to the most libidinous scenes. Their songs, their dances, and dramatic performances, breathe a spirit of luxury. They are, for the rest, hospitable: the lower sort like to pilfer from foreigners, being too powerfully tempted by the sight of new and curious things, which are very valuable to them. In their wars, they fight with great bravery and valour. In short, their character is as amiable as that of any nation, that ever came unimproved out of the hands of nature.

Secondly. The variety of men, next in beauty to those of the Society-Isles, are the inhabitants of the MARQUESAS. They are in general more tawny than the former being situated in the latitude of 9° 57′ South, nearer the line than the Society-Isles; and they are also more accustomed to go without any covering; their privities excepted: both which reasons are sufficient to account for the darker hue of their skin. However, there are some few more fair among them; and their women, who generally go covered, are almost as fair as those in the Society-Isles. Their men are generally stout-limbed, but none are so fleshy as those in the last-mentioned isles, owing, as I suppose, to their greater activity; for, as a very considerable part of them live on the slopes[6] and the very summits of high hills, where their habitations have much the appearance of the ayries of eagles, on the craggy summits of inaccessible rocks, they must of course have a slender habit of body, from the frequent climbing of these high mountains, and from the keen air, which they breathe in regions almost constantly involved in clouds. They have black beards and fine hair on their heads. Their females and younger people have beautiful, regular features, and oval faces; but the grown men lose their sprightli-

"The Chief at Sta. Christina" (in all likelihood, Honu, chief of Vaitahu, Tahuata), engraving by J. Hall after William Hodges, from Cook, *A Voyage towards the South Pole*, 1777, Plate 36.

REMARKS ON THE HUMAN SPECIES IN THE SOUTH-SEA ISLES

ness, by the general custom of puncturing closely, all their body and faces, in the most strange, but regular manner, in scrolls, circles, lines, and chequerwise; which of course destroys all the features, and the regularity of lineaments.[7] The bodies remain, however, fine and proportioned, all the limbs strong and muscular, with an agreeable outline. The young people are generally most beautiful, and would afford many a fine model for a Ganymede. The women have a soft, melting outline, the finest symmetry, and the most delicate extremities. Their size runs in general to the middle stature of men, and few or none, are what we could call little. They appeared to us courteous, civil, and hospitable; had a great deal of curiosity, and the same levity, which is the general character of tropical nations. But, as our stay among them was short, we cannot enter into any more particular detail of their character.

We made but half an hour's stay at TEOUKEA, one of the low isles between the Marquesas and O-Taheitee; and in this time we observed the natives to be of a very tawny colour, common to both sexes. They were a stout people, with well-proportioned limbs, and black hair; had on the breast, belly, and sometimes on the hands, some figures made by puncturing the body; and were of a middling size. They received us with kindness; gave us coco-nuts and dogs for nails; and, though very numerous and well-armed, did not attempt to insult us. I cannot, however, say what they might have done, had we made a longer stay, especially as their numbers increased every moment.

Thirdly. The inhabitants of the FRIENDLY ISLES are little inferior, if not equal in beauty to those of the Marquesas. Their complexion, no doubt, is of a darker hue, than that of the commonalty of the natives in the Society-Isles; though, in my opinion, it partakes of a lively brown, inclining so far towards the red or copper colour, as not to deserve the appellation of swarthy. However, many among them, especially the better sort of people, and the greater part of their women, approach near to the complexion of O-Taheitean fair ones. They are generally of a middling stature, or rather above it; and their features regular and manly. The men seldom let their beards grow to any length, generally cutting them with two sharp shells; their ears are perforated by two holes, through which they run a small stick horizontally across. The outlines of their bodies are not so beautifully feminine, as those of the chiefs in the Society-Isles; but they are compact, well-proportioned, and more muscular and expressive; as moderate industry has assigned each muscle its place and size, without distorting any part of their frame. The stature of their females nearly approaches that of the other sex; none are so fat and unwieldy, as many individuals in the Society-Isles. Their brown complexion becomes their regular features, their roundish faces, and fine, full, and lively eyes. Their countenance is overspread with an inexpressible smile; their shapes and outlines are elegant, and all their actions accompanied with ease and freedom. Among others we observed in the croud, at Tonga-Tabu, a young girl of about ten or twelve years, with the most regular features, an oval face, and the sweetest countenance; her eye was bright, lively, and all soul; her long, black hair hung negligently down, and was ornamented with bunches of odoriferous flowers; her actions were easy, brisk, and free. She had with her five apples, and threw every one of them up into the air, catching them again with amazing activity and skill. The character of these people is really amiable; their friendly behaviour to us, who were utter strangers to them, would have done honour to the most civilized nation. We were presented in every house with food, and the refreshing liquor contained in the coco-nuts, with a spirit of hospitality, which is truly patriarchal. All their actions bespoke a noble mind, and a wonderful, charming simplicity of manners. They have, however, all the little faults we observed in the O-Taheiteans, though not in the same degree. Their utensils, weapons, manufactures, agriculture, and music, bespeak their inventive genius and elegant taste.

Fourthly. Next to this nation, we come to a set of men, but few in number; for they do not exceed 900 in all, and much inferior in every respect to those already-mentioned; I mean the natives of EASTER-ISLAND. They are of a tawny complexion, rather darker than that of the Friendly-Isles: their men have hardly a bit of cloth round their reins to cover their privities, but the women have commonly more covering. They are of a middle size, between five and six feet, of a slender habit of body, having well-proportioned limbs, but not the most pleasing features. The women are not quite disagreeable, and rather small in proportion. The males are punctured almost all over the body, have black hair and thin beards. Their ears are perforated by a large aperture, and part of the outer rim of the ear is separated from the rest by being cut: in this monstrous hole, the natives frequently put a scroll made of a leaf of the sugar-cane. They are a friendly, harmless set of people, and some of them exercised hospitality in its utmost extent, and original purity; but they were also much addicted to thieving. The soil is strong and barren, and has extensive plantations of potatoes, sugar-canes, bananas, and eddoes; though wood and water are very scarce articles in this poor country. The vestiges of former plantations on the hills, together with many huge stone-pillars, erected near the burying-places, to the memory of their deceased chiefs and heroes; some of them 27 feet high, are the only remains of the former grandeur and population of this isle; while some toys, finely carved, were evident proofs of their ingenuity and taste.[8]

Fifthly. Far remote from this, and all the other isles in the South-Seas, inhabited by the first race of people, we find, near the South-West extremity of this spacious ocean, two large isles called NEW-ZEELAND, peopled by the same race of men. They are of a tawny complexion, still more darkened in their faces by the custom of puncturing, or rather carving into them, the most curious and regular volutes, which hinder, in some measure, the growth of a black and bushy beard. Their size is generally tall, their body strong, and formed for fatigue; their limbs proportioned and well-knit. The knees, however, are very much enlarged, from the constant custom of sitting on their hams in their canoes, and their legs turned inwards. The females are generally thin, a few only have tolerable features; the rest are ill-favoured, though their shape and limbs are not without proportion. Their knees are equally enlarged with those of the men; and they are harshly treated by their husbands, for whom they are obliged to do all the drudgery, as is common in all barbarous nations*.[9] They are hospitable, sincere, and generous friends; intrepid and bold warriors; implacable and cruel enemies, carrying their thirst of revenge even to such a degree of inhumanity, as to feast upon their unfortunate prisoners, the wretched victims to a ferocious and uncultured disposition. They are generally men of sound understanding, and have taste and genius; as proofs of which, may be mentioned, their curious carvings, and other manufactures.[11]

II. The varieties of men belonging to the second tribe or race of people in the South Seas, are all confined within the tropics to its most Western parts.

First, The extensive country of NEW-CALEDONIA though near the continent of New-Holland, is inhabited by a set of men, who are totally different from the slender diminutive natives of that country, and in many respects distinguished from all the natives belonging to the first tribe, living in the Eastern isles of the South Sea. Many of these New-Caledonians are very tall and stout, and the rest are not below the common size; but their women, who appear here again, under

---

* According to Strabo, lib. iii. p. 114, and Tacitus *de morib. German.* c. 15.[10] The ancient inhabitants of Spain, Liguria, Celtica, and Germany, had likewise the barbarous custom of leaving husbandry, and all laborious work to their women, whilst they themselves remained perfectly idle. There are likewise in the present age, many barbarous nations, who treat their women harshly, and leave all drudgery to them. Upon the river Orenoco, this custom prevails. Gumilla *in Orenoco illustrado.* The same is observed in California, by Father Venegas, *Hist. of California,* part i, sect. i. The men among the Eskimaux are extremely indolent, and the women are the greatest drudges upon the face of the earth. Lieut. Curtis, *Philos. Trans.* vol. lxiv. P. ii. p. 385. In Tcherkassia women cultivate the ground. Chardin. *Voy.* The Bulgarian women were found to work in the vineyards, by Father Boscowich, *Voyage de Constantinople.* p. 93 and 164. In Africa, nothing is more common, than that the most laborious part of all work is delegated to women; for this takes place among the Hottentots, according to Kolben's *Descr. of the Cape of Good Hope.* vol. i. p. 160. and La Caille's *Voyage au Cap. de B.E.* The women about Sierra Leon were seen hard at work by Keeling, *Voy.* The nation of the Giagas are described to be most unfeelingly cruel to their women. Lord Kaime's *Sketches of the Hist. of Man.* p. 187. Mr. *Falkner* observed of the women among the Puelches, Tehuelhets, and other Patagonian tribes, that their lives are but one continued scene of labour; for, besides nursing and bringing up their children, they are obliged to submit to every species of drudgery. Falkner's *Description of Patagonia.* p. 125.

"Man of Easter Island,"
engraving by F. Barto-
lozzi after William
Hodges, from Cook, A
*Voyage towards the South
Pole*, 1777, Plate 46.

William Hodges, *A Woman of New Zealand*, red chalk, 1773–1775. 544 × 372 mm. National Library of Australia.

the humiliating and disgracing predicament of drudges, are commonly small. They are all of a swarthy colour; their hair is crisped, but not very woolly;* their chins are surrounded with respectable beards, which they now and then tie up in a knot; their features are strong and masculine, the ear-laps are cut and enlarged in the same manner as in Easter Island. I saw one man, who had eighteen tortoise-shell ear-rings of one inch diameter, and three quarters of an inch breadth. Their limbs are strong and active, marked by fine outlines. Their females have generally coarse features, few having any thing agreeable or pleasing in their round face, with thick lips and wide mouths. Their teeth are fine, their eyes lively, the hair finely curled, the body in such as have not yet borne children, is well proportioned, with a flowing outline, and fine extremities. The generality are of a mild and good natured temper, ready to please their guests in every thing in which they can be serviceable: but the ungrateful soil affording them only a sparing subsistence, and that too, not to be procured without much labour, they could not supply us with any roots or vegetables; and we were obliged to provide them with the first dog and bitch, and the first boar and sow, which in time to come may perhaps supply them with a new and acceptable change of food.

Secondly, The inhabitants of TANNA, one of the New Hebrides, are almost of the same swarthy colour as the former; only a few had a clearer complexion, and in these the tips of their hair were of a yellowish brown: the hair and beards of the rest are all black and crisp, nay, in some woolly. The generality of them are tall, stout, and well made, none of them are corpulent or fat. The features of the greatest part are manly and bold, and but few are disagreeable. Their females are of the same complexion, have before child-bearing, generally a fine outline, but they are

---

* As some of my readers, not having seen a variety of nations, may think the distinction between crisped and woolly hair, either improper or insufficient, I must beg leave to observe that the woolly hair of negroes, is not only frizzled and crisped, but likewise that each hair is found to be extremely thin, and proceeding from a root or bulb, remarkably smaller than that observed in other human hair; on this account it is called woolly, and its remarkable thinness probably arises from a too copious perspiration, which carries off likewise many humours, otherwise secreted for the express nutriment and growth of the hair: where this perspiration is not so considerable, it can only crisp and blacken the hair, but not to such a degree as to render it woolly. Perhaps the cause of this difference lies in the greater mildness of the climate, or is founded on the way of living of such a people. For instance, though the natives of *Taheitee*, the *Society Isles*, *Marquesas*, and the *Friendly Isles*, dwell in the same latitude with the *New Hebrides*, yet they have never woolly hair, because they frequently rub their hair and head with coco-nut oil, which hinders the too copious perspiration; and I shall hereafter prove these fair people to be originally descended from a fairer and less swarthy or parched race, whose type or model is commonly preserved in their offspring. Upon the whole, a moderate heat accelerates the growth of human hair; this needs no proof, as it is well known that hair grows stronger in summer than in winter; every body is apprised of the common fact, that the marks of puberty appear sooner with people in hot climates, than with those who dwell in colder regions.[12]

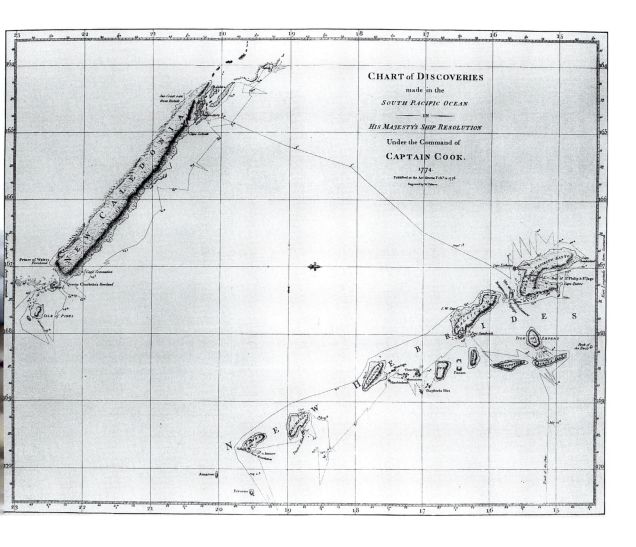

"Chart of Discoveries Made in the South Pacific Ocean," showing New Caledonia and the New Hebrides, from Cook's *A Voyage towards the South Pole*.

all ill-favoured, nay, some are very ugly: I saw but two, who had less harsh lineaments, and a smile upon their countenance. Both sexes have large holes in the lap of their ear, and wear several large rings of tortoise-shell in them; the *septum narium* is likewise perforated, and they wear a stick or whitish cylindrical stone in it. The hair of these people is dressed in the most curious and singular manner; for they take a small parcel of their hair, of the thickness of a pigeons quill and *queue* it up in the outer rind of a convolvulus, and thus they go on till they have finished the whole, which grows very copiously; by this means their heads bear some resemblance to a porcupine covered with prickly quills. Their whole body is naked; and the genitals only, are curiously wrapped up in leaves tied by a string, and then tucked up to a rope which they wear round their waists. On their breasts and arms are figures cut in, to which they apply some plant that raises a scar above the rest of the skin. They are a good natured, friendly set of men, exercising hospitality in a high degree. They seem to be valorous in encountering enemies, who are equal to them in arms; nay, before they perfectly knew how far our arms were superior to, and more destructive than theirs, a single man with a dart or sling, would often stand in a path, and hinder a party of eight or ten of us from going higher up into the country. They were mistrustful and jealous in the beginning; but after we had learnt a few words of their language, and convinced them that we did not intend to do them any harm, they let us freely pass and repass. I have gone accompanied by one or two persons only, several miles up the country. I hardly know an instance of their stealing any thing from us. They shewed at times, almost as much levity as the other nations of the South Seas; though in my opinion they were in general more grave; however they are lively, brisk, and ready to do any service that lies in their power or to give any information that is wanted, provided the enquirer can make himself understood.

Thirdly, The natives of MALLICOLLO are a small, nimble, slender, black and ill-favoured set of being; that of all men I ever saw, border the nearest upon the tribe of monkies.[13] Their skulls are of a very singular structure, being from the root of the nose more depressed backward, than in any of the other races of mankind, which we had formerly seen. Their women are ugly and deformed, and as I have before remarked in each of the varieties of men of the second race, they were here likewise obliged to act the part of pack-horses, in carrying provisions for their indolent husbands, and to do all the most laborious drudgery in the plantations. The hair is in the greater part of them woolly and frizzled. Their ears and noses perforated, for the insertion of large rings in the one, and of sticks or stones in the other. Their complexion is sooty, their features harsh, the cheek bone and face broad, and the whole countenance highly disagreeable. Their limbs are slender, though well shaped, and the belly constricted by a string to such a degree, as no European could bear without the greatest inconvenience. The genitals are wrapped in and tucked up, in the same manner as at Tanna and New Caledonia. One of their arms is ornamented by a bracelet fixed on it when young, and which therefore, can never after be removed in grown persons. I observed several among these people, who were very hairy all over the body, the back not excepted; and this circumstance I also observed in Tanna and New Caldonia. They are nimble, lively, and restless; some of them seem to be ill-natured and mischievous; but the generality, of a friendly and good disposition. They seem to love joy and merriment; music, songs, and dances. Though their poisoned arrows had no effect upon our dogs, I am however, not yet clear that they are entirely harmless; if so the natives would not have so anxiously withheld our hands, whenever we wanted to try the points of these infected arrows with our fingers: nor can I conceive for what reason they should take so much trouble in smearing and preserving the resinous substance on the boney points of these arrows: Quiros who saw the same nation, likewise suspected their arrows to be poisoned.[14] I am therefore apt to suspect them to be very cruel and implacable enemies. I cannot at the same time omit to do them justice, in observing that they were not destitute of principles of humanity and equity. We saw the greater and more rational part of them extremely cautious in giving us any reason for complaint, and to such a degree were they anxious to prevent hostilities being commenced by their people, that they seem to have been sensible of the unjustice of giving the first provocation, which might bring on a retaliation on our side; nay, they hindered several of their people from giving even the least umbrage to us.[15]

Medio vera terrae salubris utrimque mixtura, fertilis ad omnia tractus, magna & in colore temperies, ritus molles, sensus liquidus, ingenia faecunda, totiusque naturae capacia.
   Plinius *Hist. Nat.* lib. ii. c. 78[16]

Though the inhabitants of TIERRA DEL FUEGO belong to neither of the races of men in the South Sea, being most probably descended from some of the natives in South America, yet we cannot entirely pass them by in silence. But finding at the same time, that the greater part of voyagers and compilers, and likewise those authors who have made use of the various accounts of voyagers, frequently confound the different nations on the extremity of South America, I will previously endeavour to fix our ideas relative to the various tribes that are to be met with in these parts of the world.

   The people at the entrance of the Magellanic Strait were seen and measured by Captain WALLIS:* he found the stature of the greater part of them, to be from five feet ten inches to six feet high; several were six feet five inches and six feet

* Hawkesworth's *Compilation,* vol. i. p. 374.

VARIETIES OF MEN   six, and one of the tallest was six feet seven inches high. Mr. DE BOUGAINVILLE*
found none below five feet five or six inches French measure, and none above
five feet nine or ten inches: but the crew of the *Etoile* had seen several in a preceding voyage six feet high: these measurements when reduced to the English
standard, give five feet ten inches and six feet two inches, but the last amounts to
six feet 4.728 inches. Mr. DE LA GIRAUDAIS†, of the Pink Etoile, says, the least of
those he saw in 1766 was five feet seven inches French measure, which is above
five feet eleven inches English. Mr. DUCLOS GUYOT,‡ in the Eagle frigate, informs
us, that the shortest of the people seen by him in 1766, measured five feet seven
inches French measure = 5 feet 11.498 inches English: the rest were considerably
taller. PIGAFETTA,* in the ship Victoria, saw with Magalhaens[17] at Port St. Julian,
people, eight Spanish feet high, which are equal to seven feet four inches English.
KNIVET,✦ who went with Sir Thomas Cavendish, in 1592, into Port Desire, found
there, people, that were 16 hands high, which amounts to six feet, reckoning a
hand at 4½ inches. RICHARD HAWKINS♥ likewise speaks of tall people at Port St.
Julian, in 1593, so tall that they are often taken by voyagers for giants. There are
some Spaniards, who pretend that in the back of Chili, are a people of ten or
twelve feet high: but as this account is too vague, and has not authority which
may be depended upon, we will make no use of it. However, from the above mentioned numerous accounts, it appears, that on the continent of America, near
Cape Virgin Mary, there is a nation, whose individuals undoubtedly are most
remarkably stout and tall, none of them seem to be below five feet ten inches,
several are above six feet, one was measured six feet seven inches high; nay,
according to Pigafetta, some are said to be seven feet four inches; in the more
interior parts of South America, are tribes of a size still greater than those who
were measured by Captain Wallis; for Mr. FALKNER,★ who spent several years
among these nations, describes the great Cacique Cangapol, who resided at
Huichin upon the Black River, as being seven feet and some inches high, because
on tiptoe, he could not reach to the top of his head: and he adds, that he did not
recollect ever to have seen an Indian that was above an inch or two taller than
Cangapol; and the brother of this tall Cacique, was about six feet high: these

---

* Bougainville's *Voyage*, English translation, p. 142.
† Pernetty's *History of a Voyage to the Falkland Islands.* English translation, p. 288.
‡ Ibid. p. 273.
* Pigafetta, ap. Ramusio, vol. i. p. 353 fol.
✦ Knivet's *Voyage.*
♥ Hawkins's *Voyage to the South Seas.* London, 1622.
★ Falkner's *Description of Patagonia*, p. 26, 111, 112.

brethren belonged to the tribe of *Puelches*. These nations seldom resort to the sea, or the neighbourhood of the Straits of Magellan, and are therefore little known to such navigators as touch at those unfrequented places. It will perhaps appear to us a strange phaenomenon, that a whole nation should preserve that remarkable tall stature. But we are united in societies, where the constant intercourse with for-eigners, makes it next to impossible to preserve the purity of races without mix-ture; and pity it is, that the guiles of art and deceit are so great in one sex, and curiosity, levity, and lewdness, are so common in the other, in our enlightened and highly-civilized societies, that they contribute still more to make the preser-vation of races precarious. This depravation prevailed so far, that even OMAI became the object of concupiscence of some females of rank.[18] The Puelches, on the contrary, and the other Patagonian tribes, whatever be their names, live in a country, which is little frequented by nations different from their own; their neighbours, the Spaniards, in Chili and Rio de la Plata, having very little inter-course with them, and being happy to live undisturbed from the incursions and depredations of such dangerous enemies. They procure, with great facility, their livelihood by the chace, and from their own numerous herds, in a country rich in pastures, and of immense extent, bounded by the sea, and separated by high ridges of mountains from all other nations. These are the most effectual means of preventing the degeneracy and debasement of their noble and athletic race; and we may conclude from thence, that constant intermarriages in the same tall tribes, render the great size of body more fixed, and invariably settled; nor must it be omitted, that as growth depends on *food, climate,* and *exercise,* in these nations, all these circumstances concur to make them a strong, stout, and tall race of men. The chace provides them plentifully with food, which is both varied and salubri-ous. The climate is moderate, and they have cloth made of the best skins and furrs, to serve them in any season. Lastly, they are seldom at rest, they move and roam over all the immense parts of America, South of the river of Plate, to the very straits of Magellan; they hunt, ride, and learn the use of their arms, and therefore take the most salutary exercise, communicating to their body and its parts sufficient strength and consistence, without crippling their limbs by too early, too violent, or too long continued labour, or starving them into a puny figure, by too close application, drudgery, and the exhaustion of their animal and vital spirits. This argument is likewise confirmed by a curious instance in our Northern climate. The guards of the late king, Frederick William of Prussia, and likewise those of the present monarch, who all are of an uncommon size, have been stationed at *Potzdam,* for fifty years past. A great number of the present inhabitants of that place are of a very high stature, which is more especially strik-ing in the numerous gigantic figures of women. This certainly is owing to the

Omai, engraving by F. Bartolozzi after Nathaniel Dance, 1775. State Library of New South Wales.

connections and intermarriages of the tall men with the females of that town.*
Having therefore stated both the probability and reality of such a tall race of men
in Patagonia, from the best authenticated testimonies of respectable writers, and
from arguments founded in nature; I shall take leave of this subject with the obvious remark, that it is as unjust as it is illiberal to rail at those who are still of opinion, that such tall people are found on the extremity of South America.

    To the South of the straits of Magalhaens, on Tierra del Fuego, are a tribe of
people apparently much debased, or degenerated from those nations which live
on the continent. Their broad shoulders and chests, large heads, and the general
cast of their features, would prove them to be descended from the men living next
to them, though that faithful and intelligent writer, Mr. *Falkner* had not informed
us, that they belonged to the *Yacana-cunnees*.[†] But at the same time I shall likewise observe, that it appears from the accounts mentioned before, that the tall
race of men seen by Admiral Byron, Captain Wallis, Mr. Bougainville, Mr. de la
Giraudais, and Mr. Du Clos Guyot, were all provided with horses, of which all the
families of the *Yacana-cunnees* are destitute; for which very reason they derive
their name; *Yanaca-cunnee*, signifying *footmen*: and as those observed by Captain
Cook in his first voyage,[‡] and by several Dutch,[*] and French navigators,[♦] had no
horses, and commonly navigated bark canoes, the above assertion of Mr. Falkner
becomes more confirmed. Nevertheless it may be very possible, that the inhabitants of the more Western parts of Tierra del Fuego, may be descended from some
branches of the *Key-yus*, a tribe of the *Huilliches*, who belong to the nation of the
Moluches; and are rather of low stature, but broad and thick set.[♥] And really somewhat similar to them were the few people, whom we met with at Christmas Bay.
We found them to be a short, squat race, with large heads; their colour yellowish
brown; the features harsh, the face broad, the cheek-bones high and prominent,
the nose flat, the nostrils and mouth large, and the whole countenance without
meaning.[19] The hair is black and straight, hanging about the head in a shocking
manner, their beards thin, and cut short. All the upper part of the body is stout,
the shoulders and chest broad; the belly straight, but not prominent; and the
scrotum very long. The feet are by no means proportioned to the upper parts; for

---

* Though I have been myself at Potzdam, it is however so long ago, and at so early a period of life,
when people are not mindful enough, or capable of making observations, that I never took notice of
it; but I owe this information to a gentleman whose spirit of observation, and literary talents make
his authority indisputable.
[†] Falkner's *Description of Patagonia*, p. 91, 111.
[‡] Hawkesworth's *compilation*, vol. 2. p.
[*] *Recueil des Voyages pour l'Etablissement de la Comp. des Indes-Orientales*, v. 4
[♦] Bougainville's *Voyage*.
[♥] Falkner's *Descr. of Patagonia*, p. 112.

"Man in Christmas
Sound, Tierra del
Fuego," engraving by
J. Basire after William
Hodges, from Cook, *A
Voyage towards the South
Pole*, 1777, Plate 27.

the thighs are thin and lean, the legs bent, the knees large, and the toes turned inwards. They are absolutely naked, and have only a small piece of seal-skin hanging down and covering part of their back. Their women are much of the same features, colour, and form as the men, and have generally long hanging breasts, and besides the seal-skin on their backs, a small patch of the skin of a bird or seal to cover their privities. All have a countenance announcing nothing but their wretchedness. They seem to be good-natured, friendly and harmless; but remarkably stupid, being incapable of understanding any of our signs, which, however, were very intelligible to the nations of the South Sea. We could observe no other word distinctly, than that of *pesserai*,[20] which they frequently repeated, in a manner to make us believe they intended to signify that they are friends; and that they find a thing good. When they talked, I particularly remarked, that their language included the *r*, and an *l*, preceded by an English *th*, something like the *Ll* of the Welsh, and many other lisping sounds. They stunk immoderately of train-oil, so that we might smell them at a distance;[21] and in the finest days, they were shivering with cold. Human nature appears no where in so debased and wretched a condition, as with these miserable, forlorn, and stupid creatures.

SECTION III

On the Causes of the Difference in the Races of Men in the South Seas, their Origin and Migrations

INDE VENUS VARIA PRODUCIT SORTE FIGURAS:
MAJORUMQUE RESERT VOLTUS, VOCESQUE COMASQUE.
  Lucretius[1]

CAUSES OF
VARIETIES

Having stated the differences of colour, size, habit, form of body, and turn of mind, as observed in the various nations of the South Sea, it remains to assign the most probable and the most reasonable causes of these remarkable differences of the two races. This would be an easy task, by having recourse to holy writ only, and from thence laying it down as a fundamental position, that all mankind are descended from one couple; for it must then follow that all are of one species: and that all varieties are only accidental. But in this age of refinement and infidelity, some modern writers use every possible means to invalidate the authority of revealed religion, and though they employ the scripture, when they endeavour to support their own unphilosophic opinions, they never admit arguments taken from thence in others; and if we look around we find so general a tendency in all ranks of men towards saying and writing new and uncommon things, that the generality of literary productions teem with the most eccentric and monstrous opinions.

  . . . Velut aegri somnia, vanae
  Finguntur species.
    Horatius[2]

  Some therefore divide mankind according to its colours into various species; others, instead of being contented with bringing all men under one kindred, choose to extend the human species even to ouran-outangs, a kind of well known apes from the East-Indies.* This certainly enlarges the subject, and renders the discussion more intricate, and the arguments more varied and difficult.

---

* The author of the *Origin and Progress of Language*, v. i. p. 289, says: The ouran-outangs are proved to be of our species by marks of humanity, that I think, are incontestable; and likewise p. 175.[3]

I could easily appeal to common sense, and to reason as the great characteristic, exclusive privileges of mankind, which are not found in any of the quadrupeds, though some of them are misrepresented as being rational in an eminent degree; I could from the very helpless and defenceless state of children when they are first born, from the long duration of that state, from the want of instinct, of connate[4] faculty of defending themselves against external injuries, or of finding and choosing salubrious food, &c. &c. infer, that man was originally intended for a being living in society, who should be taken care of and educated by others, and who has therefore received the embryo of reason improvable by the various degrees of education. It might be proved from the organs and the gift of speech in men, who are alone capable of this language of reason, that they ought to be wholly distinguished from all animals; as every species of the brute creation is destitute of the variety, power, and extent of voice and articulation: and though endued with passions, and possessing the advantages of a mechanical sensation, are strangers to the exercise of reason, the formation of ideas, the language of the heart, and the refinement of moral sentiment.* I could have recourse to the Hallers, the Hunters, the Daubentons, the Le Cats, the Meckels, the Campers, and all the great anatomists of this and former ages, and with them prove from the structure of the brains and from the skulls, from the occipital hole, from the connexion, movement, structure and length of the cervical vertebrae, from the structure and shortness of the pelvis, the breadth of the ilia, the narrowness of the ischia, from the form and structure of the acetabulum, and the head of the femoral bones, from the structure and connexion of the musculus gluteus with those of the legs, from the whole compages and structure of the feet and their parts, from the number and structure of our hands, and many other wonders of our frame, that man is the only creature of the class which suckle their young ones, who is intended to walk erect:† for though, perhaps apes and monkies accidentally walk erect; it is not, however, natural to them, and they prefer crawling on all fours; and though even men in a wild state, have accustomed themselves to walk on all fours, it has been observed, that this habit caused a preternatural tumour of the hypochondria.‡ But I should be obliged to repeat and to transcribe the arguments, so ably set forth by the most learned men, which, though they are known by the studious, nevertheless remain as unknown to the pretenders of learning, as if they never had been published: for it is the fate of science to be only skimmed by the witty fashionable writers, but never to be thoroughly studied and meditated:

---

* Mr. Court de Gebelin, *Plan General du Monde Primitif*, p. 10.

† *Blumenbach* de generis humani varietate nativa. Gotting, 1776, 8vo. and W. Hunter, *de codem Argumento*. Edinburg. 1776, 8vo.

‡ Tulpius, *obs*. IV. 10.

I cannot therefore enter into any serious argumentation with the patrons and advocates of the long exploded opinion, that monkies are of the same species with mankind. I appeal rather to an argument taken from the better half of our species, the fair sex; we all assent to the description which Adam gives of his partner; a creature

> . . . *So lovely fair,*
> *That what seem'd fair in all the world, seem'd now*
> *Mean, or in her summ'd up, in her contain'd*
> *And in her looks; which from that time infus'd*
> *Sweetness into his heart, unfelt before,*
> *And into all things from her air inspir'd.*
> *The spirit of love, and amorous delight.*
> *Grace was in all her steps; heav'n in her eye,*
> *In every gesture dignity and love.*
>   Milton[5]

I cannot think that a man looking up to this inimitable masterpiece, could be tempted to compare it with an ugly, loathsome ouran-outang! If he still in good earnest be of this opinion, the whole heavenly sisterhood of Eve's fair daughters ought for ever to exclude him from their bright circles: and in case he then persists obstinate, may none but ouran-outangs vouchsafe and admit his embraces.

The next class of writers represent the inhabitants of Greenland, and those of Senegambia, as beings specifically[6] different from those of Europe or Tcherkassia:* and, indeed, if we are at once to make a sudden transition from the contemplation of the fairest beauty of Europe to that of a deformed negro; the difference is so great, and the contrast so strong, that we might be tempted to think them of a distinct species: but if we examine the insensible gradations, in the form, habit, size, colour, and some external differences, we shall find that they are by no means so widely remote from each other in the scale of beings, as to form separate species. Anatomically considered, they perfectly agree, in all the material great parts of their frame, and even in the particulars of their structure, and consequently they cannot constitute different species. For considering that if the most remote tribes of mankind cohabit together, they always procreate children similar to their parents and capable of procreating others, the difference cannot be so material; especially if we remark, that by continually repeated marriages of a

---

* Voltaire, *Philosophie de l'histoire & questions sur L'Encyclopedie,* tom iv. & tom vii.

Mulatto (who is the offspring of a black and white person) with white persons, the progeny after each marriage, becomes fairer and fairer, so that at last not the least difference is observable; or that if the Mulatto marries a black person, their offspring is blacker, and after a few inter-marriages the race is reduced to absolute negroes: after these remarks, I say it must become more and more evident to minds free from prejudice or rancour against religion, *that all mankind, though ever so much varied, are, however, but of one species.* If therefore this class of antagonists, should deny the scripture that veneration, in which it is held by Christians, they cannot, however, refuse it with any colour of justice, the authority of an old historical account; and as such we find it corroborates strongly the above result of philosophical enquiry, by telling us, *that all mankind are descended from one couple.*

If all mankind be of one species, and sprung from the same original stem, how then does it happen that the negroe of Senegal is so different from the inhabitant of the North of Europe? What occasions the inhabitants of O-Taheitee to be so much distinguished from the Mallicolese? We have hinted before, that these two varieties of men in the South-Seas, are descended from two distinct races.[7] This is not decisive, and only leads us further into the same discussions, and requires us to shew what causes have produced these two distinct races or varieties of men?

The question cannot be discussed unless we consider the subject under various heads. The differences are either observed in the organic part of man, or they respect his mental and moral faculties: of the last we shall treat at large in subsequent sections; at present we intend to confine ourselves to the corporeal varieties, consisting in, 1st, colour; 2d, size; 3d, form and habit; and 4th, peculiar defects or excesses, or modifications in certain parts of the human body.

First, The COLOUR of the human body depends no doubt upon these three great causes: 1st, exposure to the air; 2d, the influence of the sun; and 3d, some particular circumstances in the mode of living. From the best enquiries set on foot by anatomists, it appears, that all the difference of colour lies in the human *skin,* and especially in the outer-integument called the *cuticle,* which again is considered by them under the two denominations of *Epidermis* and *Malpighi's reticular membrane.* In white people, the *Epidermis* is a very thin, pellucid, indurated lamella, transmitting the colour of the *reticular membrane* immediately lying under it, which is a white or colourless, viscous or slimy substance: whatever colour the substance has which is immediately under the Epidermis, that colour appears and becomes visible to the eye. The blood suddenly mounting into the blood vessels of the face, tinges the same with a vermillion blush. The blood being coloured by the extravasated bile, causes the yellow colour of the *jaundice.* The yellow lymph deposited in the cutaneous vascula, imparts the yellow tint of those who in the West Indies are afflicted with the *yellow fever.* The tattowing of

the O-Taheiteans, and gunpowder accidentally forced into the skin, forms a black or blueish appearance. And in negroes, the late ingenious Mr. *Meckel** discovered the reticulum of Malpighi to be black; but the medullar substance of the brain, the pineal gland, and the spinal marrow, together with the *plexus nervi optici*, he found grey and blackish. Others[†] have found the blood of negroes to be deeper coloured than that of white people. The ancients[‡] knew that the spermatic liquor of negroes is of a dark hue, and this curious observation is confirmed by moderns.**
In a word, we find, that many of the fluids in negroes are tinged darker, and such of their solids as are of a tender and delicate texture, are likewise coloured blackish. *Meckel* suspects, that the blueish liquor which colours the medullary substance of the brain, and so easily evaporates in negroes, contributes towards the dark complexion of the mucous membrane of the cuticle, being secreted by the cutaneous nerves into the viscous reticular substance.

But let us now investigate the causes of this phaenomenon in negroes; we have already indicated the three most striking causes; the *exposure to the air*, is undoubtedly one of the most powerful: for do we not see this daily proved in our own climate; our ladies, and other people who are little exposed to the action of the air, have a fair complexion; whereas the common labourers are brown and tawny; nay our bodies furnish us with sufficient proofs; those parts which are constantly covered, are fair and delicate, but the hands being constantly exposed to the action of the air, acquire a darker hue. The negroes live in a climate which permits them to wear little or no covering at all; accordingly, we really find all the negroes naked, or very slightly covered, which undoubtedly must increase the black colour of their skin. The Taheiteans, the fairest of all the islanders in the South Sea, go almost constantly dressed and covered. The inhabitants of Tanna, New Caledonia, and Mallicollo, on the contrary are always naked, and exposed to the air, and therefore infinitely blacker than the first.

The *operation of the Sun* is undoubtedly another great cause of the dark hue in negroes; we find that nations in the same proportion, as they approach the equator, likewise become darker coloured; however, this observation is not quite universal, and ought to be modified under many circumstances. Inhabitants of islands are seldom so black as those of great continents; in Africa, between the tropics, the Easterly winds prevail the most; and as in Abyssinia these winds come over a large ocean, where they are mitigated and cooled in their passage, the inhabitants of that country are not so black as those about Senegal, which is situ-

---

* Meckel in the *Memoires de l'Academie de Berlin*, 1753.
† Towns in the *Philos. Trans.* on the blood of negroes.
‡ Herodorus *Thalia*, No. ci.[8]
** Le Cat *Traité sur la couleur de la peau*.

ated in the broadest part of Africa, and where the Easterly wind having passed over the burning sands of the immense continent, is become infinitely more fiery and parching than in any other part. A higher exposure above the surface of the sea, makes a great difference in the temperature of the air; the inhabitants of Quito in Peru, though living under the line, are by no means black or swarthy. The vicinity of the sea, and its refreshing and gently fanning breezes, contribute greatly to mitigate the power of a tropical sun. This cause cannot be applied to the difference of colour in the Taheiteans and the Mallicolese, as both nations enjoy the same advantage.

But the *peculiar modes of living* likewise, strongly co-operate with the above causes, in producing the many changes of colour in the human species. The Taheiteans are constantly cleanly, and practise frequent ablutions, encreasing by this simple elegance the fairness of their complexions, though they live within the tropics. The New Zeelanders living in the temperate zone from 34° to 47° South latitude, are more tawny, which may be in part ascribed to their uncleanliness, abhorrence of bathing, and sitting exposed to smoak and nastiness in their dirty cottages.

Secondly, The *size* of the natives of Taheitee, and all the isles peopled by the same race, certainly distinguishes them from the tribes in Mallicollo; however this difference is not so general in these nations, as to extend even to Tanna and New Caledonia, where we found many very tall and athletic persons. But the chiefs in the Society Isles, again distinguish themselves from the rest of the inhabitants, by their tall stature and corpulence. According to the doctrines of those who are skilled in philosophy, growth and size depend chiefly upon climate, food, and exercise.

The *climate* is either warm or cold. Heat adds to the action of the heart a stimulus, and accelerates its pulsation; and since in a warm climate, the solids are more relaxed, than in a cold one, the impulse of the blood in the arteries finds less resistance, and therefore more powerfully expands the whole frame of the body; because, every function of the parts and secretion of the liquids, is promoted with greater vigour. This we find conformable to experience, for in hot climates mankind grow more powerfully, and attains earlier maturity and puberty. On the other hand, cold assuages the stimulus, and constricts the fibres, which naturally throws the whole system into a torpor or languid state. The heart does not act powerfully enough to carry on the functions with that vigour which is required, not only to accelerate growth, but likewise to overcome the greater resistance caused by the rigid state of all the solid parts. We find in consequence of these principles, the poor inhabitants of Tierra del Fuego, a small race of people, though descended from tribes, who, on the continent of South America, in a milder climate, and more happy circumstances, are very tall and athletic.

CAUSES OF
VARIETIES

Food another great article, both as to *quantity* and *quality*, exerts its powerful influence upon size and growth. The great abundance and excellence of tropical fruits and roots, together with a variety and plenty of fish, and now and then a fowl, a hog, or a dog, contribute to the luxuries of the table of Arees and other people of rank, in the Society Isles; and as they are used to indulge very much in these luxuries, we find them remarkably tall, stout, and athletic. The Towtows have only the bare necessaries;[9] and we were informed that now and then there are years of scarcity, when the poorer sort of people are driven to great distress; but the Arees feel nothing of these inconveniences. The Towtows never, or at least very rarely partake of the feasts, where pork is devoured by the chiefs, but must rest contented with the more homely vegetable fare, and think themselves fortunate, if they catch some fish, or collect some wretched small shell fish, and even blubbers. In the Marquesas animal food is more scarce in proportion; nor are the islands upon the whole, overstocked with other eatables: for which reason we found, that though the natives were not small, very few however, if any, were so tall and so athletic as on the Society Isles, and above all, the difference between Arees and Towtows was not so striking. In the Friendly Isles, the abundance of vegetables is great, because private property has been the cause of a higher degree of cultivation; and animal food seems likewise to be plentiful: here however, the disparity in the size of Arees and Towtows is not so great as in the Society Isles.[10] In New Zeeland, the inhabitants are in general well provided with fish, and they are not without extensive plantations of roots in the Northern isle; nor do they seem famished or stinted, as the greater part are tall and strongly built. The isles of Tanna and New Caledonia have plenty of vegetable food, though little of the animal kind; nay, in New Caledonia, they had before our arrival, neither dogs nor hogs; but the extensive reefs surrounding their isle, afford them great plenty of fish: this circumstance no doubt, contributed to the formation of their strong and tall bodies. Lastly, the Mallicolese seem to have plantations of all kinds of fruit in great abundance, some hogs, fowls, and plenty of fish, but they are the only nation who seemed not to be benefited by this affluent and excellent food; nor could we assign the reasons of their diminished size. The inhabitants of the Western parts of Tierra del Fuego, have doubtless no other food than what the sea affords them, which is very precarious in so high a latitude, especially in stormy weather. Of vegetables, they have only a few berries; which seems to indicate, that from time to time they are distressed, and their wretched appearance does not contradict it; their diminutive size, and small thin legs and thighs rather prove that they are famished and stinted: nor can the half rotten pieces of raw seals-flesh and fat be very salubrious and nutritive; which we saw them devour with a voracity that did not indicate either the abundance or the excellence of their provisions.

Exercise in a moderate degree, is absolutely necessary to give the various part of the human frame, strength and due consistence. *Inactivity* hinders the secretion and circulation of the fluids, necessary for the increase of the body, and therefore causes in young people a weakly constitution, and flaccid limbs, without stability, consistence, or vigour. *Violent* labour is equally hurtful in regard to the increase of the body; for too long an exertion of muscular fibres in young men causes a rigidity, and entirely exhausts the vital powers. Let us only cast an eye on the wretched objects, who, from their infancy toil in confinement, and observe their distorted, disproportioned limbs, their ghastly faces, and their puny stinted size. On the contrary, the whole body acquires by a moderate and equal use of all our parts, a constitution which is gradually steeled against decay and diseases: an equal share of agility is imparted to all the limbs, which knits the joints to their due consistence and stability. The inhabitants of the South Sea isles, are by their lively temper in their early age prevented from being inactive. The happiness of their climate, the fertility of their soil, the luxuriance of vegetation, and the fewness of their wants, also make too great an exertion unnecessary: it is therefore *moderate exercise* which, among many other happy circumstances, contribute to form these tall and beautiful figures, which are so common among them.

Thirdly, Form and *habit*, are likewise subject to the same influence of climate,

William Hodges,
*Resolution Bay in the
Marquesas*, wash and
watercolor, 1774. 373 ×
550 mm. State Library
of New South Wales.

food, and exercise; this spares us the trouble of repeating the above mentioned
arguments: for it is evident that heat dries the limbs and whole frame of body in
the Mallicolese, the inhabitants of Easter-Island, the Marquesas, the Low Islands,
the Towtows and lower ranks of people in the Society and Friendly Isles, who all
go naked, and are much exposed to air and sun: hence, they become thin and
slender; for even their bones are not strong, but solid and hard. On the other
hand, cold climates give a more soft, spungy and succulent habit of body; which is
easily observable in the people of Tierra del Fuego, who are a thick, squat, bony
race of men. The New-Zeelanders are likewise in a milder climate, fleshy, boney,
and succulent, and the Arees and better sort of people, in the Society and
Friendly Isles, who carefully study, and endeavour to keep themselves cool, and
avoid as much as possible, an exposure to the heat of the sun, are succulent,
fleshy, and fat.

Fourthly, The *peculiar defects, or excesses, or modifications of certain parts of the
human body* have endemial[11] causes, dependent upon peculiar customs, which
sometimes are obvious, but at other times not easily investigated, especially when
the observer has not more time to study them, than we had. However, we will
point them out, and leave it to others to make further discoveries.

In Mallicollo, we observed that the greater part of the skulls of the inhabitants, had a very singular conformation; for the forehead from the beginning of the
nose, together with the rest of the head, was much depressed and inclining backward: which causes an appearance in the looks and countenances of the natives,
similar to those of monkies. Whether the inhabitants use some art to give the
heads of their children this figure, or whether it be owing to some other cause, or
to an original defect of the whole generation, which in the first couple from
whom this tribe descended, was modelled by chance or art into that form, and
afterwards became inherent and natural to their offspring, it is impossible to
determine. The inhabitants of Tierra del Fuego, are all a chubbed race, probably
because they are descended from a set of people of large limbs, living on the continent, but being stinted by cold, and wants of all kinds, are degenerated into a
short, and squat figure, which keeps always the original model, or type, in the size
of the head; a circumstance almost generally observed in dwarfs.

The feet are generally thin, and by no means proportioned to the rest of the
body, in the New-Zeelanders, and the people of Tierra del Fuego, and they likewise have large knees.[12] This may be easily accounted for from their general practice of fishing, which confines them for days together to their canoes, without
allowing them the usual exercise; and from their constant sitting upon their
hams, which stretches and expands the knees, and prevents the legs from being
furnished with the supplies necessary for the increase of those parts. The people
in the isles walk much, but likewise sit on their hams, and we find their knees

also, and their whole legs enlarged, from the great exertion of those parts, which are not compressed and restrained as ours, by shoes and other articles of dress.

The faces are in general strongly marked with large features, and somewhat broad, but prominent noses, in all the islanders of the South Seas; and this seems to be, in my opinion, the character of the nation, or tribe, from which they are descended. The more Western tropical isles have inhabitants with less prominent noses, larger mouths, and broader lips, which again must be referred to the original tribe from whence they are derived.

The laps of the ears are certainly cut and enlarged by constantly keeping a sugar-cane leaf scrolled up in this hole, in Easter-Island, New-Caledonia, and partly in Tanna. The inhabitants of Tonga-Tabu, and the Friendly-Isles, enlarge the laps of the ears likewise, but without making an incision, and have only two perforations in them, through which they thrust horizontally a small stick, of the thickness of a strong goose-quill. The greater part of the same nation want the two first joints of one, and sometimes both the little fingers, which they cut off as marks of their grief, for deceased parents or relations.

The inhabitants of O-Taheitee and the Society-Isles, are circumcised; but properly speaking, a part of the prepuce is not cut off, but a round smooth stick being thrust into it, it is slit through the upper part, with a bamboo, to which they have given a sharp edge; and then the parts are kept divided, that they may not cover the glans again.

The breasts of the women of O-Taheitee, the Society-Isles, Marquesas, and Friendly-Isles, are not so flaccid and pendulous as is commonly observed in negro-women, and as we likewise noticed them in all the Western islands, in New-Zeeland, and some of the females of the lower sort at the Society-Isles. This has been lately ascribed to the manner of suckling the children;* but I am of opinion that it cannot be solely owing to this; for the women of the Arees never have them so pendulous and long. I should rather ascribe it to the greater relaxation of the body in the women of the lower class, who are more exposed to the air and sun, than those of the Aree tribe. In the same manner the negroe-women, as well as those in the Western Isles of Mallicollo, Tanna, and New-Caledonia, are for the greater part more exposed to the air and sun, being constantly naked above the waist. The gentle constriction of the upper part of the body, by the finer sorts of cloth in which the O-Taheitean women of quality gracefully wrap themselves, contributes likewise to keep the breasts high, and to prevent their flaccidity and pendulous state. I saw some very old fat women in the Society-Isles, whose breasts were relaxed and enlarged, but by no means long and pendulous, which, however,

---

* Blumenbach *de Generis Humani Varietate Nativa*, p. 73.

was a very common circumstance in all the women of the Western-Isles, who had
borne and suckled children.

The chiefs in the Society-Isles value themselves on having long nails on all,
or on some of their fingers; it is an evident proof of their indolence, and that they
are not obliged to work, which would soon deprive them of this distinguishing
mark of their pre-eminence; they are, however, very careful in keeping these long
nails clean, and free from any impurity; the custom of tattowing the faces in
spirals and various scrolls, which prevails in New-Zeeland, and the various figures
with which the natives of the Marquesas puncture their faces, naturally destroys
the growth of hair, and to this we must ascribe it, that in both places, those who
are much punctured, have very little or no beards at all.

These are the most remarkable particulars which chiefly form the variety of
the two great tribes, observed by us in the South Sea isles; from whence may be
inferred the powerful influence of climate, food, and peculiar customs upon the
colour, size, habit, and form of body, and certain defects, excesses, or modifications of the parts; but it must be acknowledged at the same time, that the causes
here enumerated are not the only ones, and particularly that climate alone does
not produce such extraordinary effects; for we find that the Dutch, who have
been settled at the Cape of Good Hope, during an uninterrupted course of 120
years, have constantly remained fair and similar to Europeans in every respect;
notwithstanding, if we compare them with the Hottentots, the native inhabitants
of that part of the world, it appears, that exclusive of the way of living and food,
the climate alone cannot occasion this material and striking variety; nay, that
even these causes, when united, are not sufficient to produce this effect, as some
of the very remote Dutch farmers live almost in the same manner as their neighbours the Hottentots; they have wretched huts, instead of houses; lead a rambling
nomadic life, attend their herds and flocks all day long, and live upon milk, the
produce of the chace, and the flesh of their cattle; it is therefore evident, that if
climate can work any material alteration, it must require an immense period of
time to produce it; and as our lives are so short, our historical accounts so imperfect, in regard to the migrations of the human species, and our philosophical
observations on the subject, all of a very modern date, it cannot be expected we
can speak with precision on the subject.[13]

It must however be observed, that when the fair Northern nations are
removed into the hot tropical climates, they themselves and their progeny soon
change, and gradually become somewhat more analogous in colour, and other circumstances, to the former inhabitants, whose migration is of so old a date, that
no memorial of it is presented; still, however, they may be easily distinguished
from these aboriginal tribes: it is likewise true, that nations removed from the
vicinity of the line towards the poles, keep their native colour longer without

alteration than any other people coming from older climates, and going to live in hotter regions; but such incidents must always be compared under similar circumstances: for if two Europeans, equally fair, are removed to the same hot climate, and the one is well dressed and avoids, as much as possible, being exposed to the action of the air, and power of the sun; whilst the other finds himself obliged to work in the open air, and has hardly any rags to cover his skin; they will, of natural consequence, become widely different in colour; moreover, if this diversity in the mode of living be kept up for several generations, the character of both must of course become more strikingly different.[14] If we look upon the inhabitants of Denmark, we find them remarkably fair, and with blue eyes, and red hair. The Bohemians, Poles, Russians, and in general all the Slavonian nations, have a brownish complexion, dark eyes, and black or brown hair, though some of the latter undoubtedly live in higher latitudes than the former. The reason here certainly is not the climate, but the cause is to be found in their migrations; the Gothic nations are no doubt the most early inhabitants of the North, and therefore have had more time to become gradually fairer, than the greater part of their neighbouring European tribes; and they likewise have had less opportunities of marrying or becoming connected with such Southern nations, as had a brown complexion and black hair. The Slavonian nations or Sauromatae, are later descended from the Medes,* a nation formerly living in modern Persia; they were long settled to the North of the Caucasus and Black Sea, a country which is very hot in summer; and in the fifth century they were near the Danube, from whence they gradually spread to the countries, which they now occupy: this account rationally resolves the strange phaenomenon, viz. that they still keep the national character, of a Southern tribe. They migrated from the South in a later period than the Goths, and other Teutonic tribes; and have had more opportunities of mixing with Asiatic tribes of a brown complexion, than the Northern Danes and Goths. This instance, I believe, confirms the above assertion; and it likewise appears from thence, that the fairer nations being exposed to a more powerful sun in hot climates, soon acquire a browner complexion. However, when they have once attained to a certain standard character, they preserve it with very immaterial alterations; but I suppose that they make no considerable change in their food, in their mode of dressing and living, and that they do not promiscuously intermarry with negroes, mulattos, or other aboriginal or mixed tribes of hot climates, in which cases, there are just reasons to suspect that their character and complexion must gradually degenerate, and become more and more debased; but if negroes, and other swarthy tribes, be transplanted into temperate, or nearly

---

* Diod. Sicul. lib. 2do. & Plin. *Hist. Nat.* lib. vi. c. 7.[15]

cold climates, they do not immediately change, nor do they easily become fairer, but preserve their original complexion for a longer space of time. When they only intermarry in their own race, the change, if any, is imperceptible in their offspring for many generations. I will here only hint, at the probable causes of this phaenomenon; the transition, from being brown in complexion to fair, is, it seems, more difficult, than that from fair to brown; the *Epidermis* admits the beams of the sun and the action of the air, in colouring the *reticulum mucosum* brown; but when once it is coloured, nothing is sufficiently powerful to extract the brown colour; and this seems to be founded in daily experience; a man being perhaps only one day exposed to a powerful sun, shall become strongly tinted with brown; when, to remove this hue, perhaps six or eight months of close confinement, are not sufficient. It seems therefore more and more probable, that the first stamen of an embryo partakes, much of the colour, size, form and habit of the parents; and that two different tribes, having gradually undergone a different round of climates, food, and customs; and coming afterwards at different periods of time, and by different ways, into the same climate, but preserving a different mode of living, and being partly supported by different food, may nevertheless preserve an evident difference in their character, colour, size, form, and habit of body.

If we apply this induction to the two different tribes, whom we found in the South-Sea, it will appear to be highly probable, that they may be descended from two different races of men; and though living in the same climate, or nearly so, might, however, preserve a difference in character, colour, size, form and habit of body; and if I could now prove, by an historical argument, that they really are descended from two different races of men, nothing will be wanting to conviction. How far I shall succeed in this historical argument, will be easily seen from the following observation.

It has always been customary among the more critical and chaste historians, to reckon all such nations as speak the *same general language*, to be of the same tribe or race; unless there be a positive proof to the contrary, in a good, authentic, contemporary writer; or one who has made enquiries on the subject from old materials, now no longer existing. By the SAME GENERAL LANGUAGE, I understand all the various subordinate dialects of one language. No one for instance, acquainted with the subject, will deny, that the Dutch, Low-German, Danish, Swedish, Norwegian, Icelandic, and the English (in respect to such words as owe their origin to the Anglo-Saxon) are dialects subordinate to the *same original language*, together with the present High-German, and the remains of the Gothic in Ulfila's New Testament. But allowing this, yet we find that these dialects differ in many respects, each having peculiar words, for ideas which the nation acquired later, after parting from the original tribe; and other words, which they obtained by connexions with, or the conquest of, another nation: many words, however, though somewhat modified, always preserve enough of the original type, to satisfy the critical etymologist, that they belong to the *same general language*, as subordinate dialects. This short digression will therefore open a way to prove that the five races, which I enumerated as belonging to the first tribe, are really descended from the same original nation; for they all speak a language that has in the greatest part of their word, a great and striking affinity.

I took particular care in collecting the words of every peculiar nation we met with, that I might be enabled to form an idea of the whole, and how far all the languages are related to each other. I soon perceived, that in general, the five nations already enumerated, spoke a language differing only in a few words, and that for the greater part, the difference consisted in a few vowels or consonants, though the words still preserved a great affinity; nay, many were absolutely the same in all the dialects. I could therefore no longer doubt, that they were all descended from the same original stem, and that the differences in the language arose only from the difficulty of pronouncing consonants, which some sounded more easily, whilst others, either changed, or entirely omitted them. When a migrating race found in their new country, new birds, new fishes, and new plants, they must of course find new names for them, which could not exist in any other of the cogeneric dialects. The qualities of these new animals, the preparation of the new vegetables into food and garments, required other new names, and thus it happened, that their language gradually assumed a distinct appearance, though after all, it was the same with that of the original tribe, being modified only to suit the organs of the tribe, and the new objects of their country.

Having now determined, that these people use the *same general language* in various dialects, we have only to prove, that the other nations are of a different race, from that, to which the first varieties own their origin; and this is very easy to prove in the same manner by their languages, which are not only wholly different from the abovementioned general language, but are likewise distinct from each other: so that one might with as much propriety say, that they are descended from as many different nations, were it not improper to multiply them without necessity, and as they really have some similarity in their customs, colour, form, and habit of body.

If we are desirous of tracing the races of all these islanders back to any continent, or its neighbourhood, we must cast an eye on a map of the South Sea, where we find it bounded to the East by America, to the West by Asia, by the Indian Isles on its North side, and by New Holland to the South. At first sight, it might seem probable, that these tropical isles were originally settled from America, as the Easterly winds are the most prevalent in these seas, and as the small and wretched embarkations of the natives in the South Seas, can hardly be employed in plying to windward. But if we consider the argument more minutely, we find that America itself was not peopled many centuries before its discovery by the Spaniards. There were but two states or kingdoms on this immense continent, that had acquired any degree of population, and made considerable progress in civilization; and they likewise did not originate earlier, than about 300 or 400 years before the arrival of the Spaniards. The rest was occupied by a few straggling families, thinly dispersed over this vast tract of land, so that sometimes not more than 30 or 40 persons, lived in an extent of 100 leagues at very great distances from each other. Again, when the Spaniards discovered some of these islands in the South Sea, a few years only after the discovery of the continent of America, they found them as populous as we have seen them in our days: from whence it appears to be highly improbable, that these isles were peopled from America. If we moreover consult the Mexican, Peruvian, and Chilese vocabularies,* and those of other American languages,† we find not the most distant, or even accidental similarity between any of the American languages, and those of the South Sea Isles. The colour, features, form, habit of body, and customs of the Americans, and these islanders, are totally different; as every one conversant with the subject, will easily discover. Nay, the distances of 600, 700, 800, or even 1000 leagues between the continent of America and the Easternmost of these isles, together with the wretchedness and small size of their vessels, prove, in my opinion, incontestably, that these islanders never came from America.

We must therefore go to the Westward; let us begin with New Holland. All the former navigators, and especially Capt. Cook, in the Endeavour, found this immense continent very thinly inhabited. The diminutive size of its inhabitants, the peculiarity of their customs and habits, their total want of coco-nuts, cultivated plantanes, and hogs, together with the most miserable condition of their huts and boats, prove beyond all doubt, that the South Sea islanders, are not descended from the natives of New Holland. But, what is still more convincing, their language is totally different, as evidently appears from the examination of a vocabulary obligingly communicated to me by Capt. Cook. We have therefore nothing left but to go further to the North, where the South Sea isles are as it were connected with the East Indian isles. Many of these latter are inhabited by two different races of men. In several of the Moluccas is a race of men, who are blacker than the rest, with woolly hair, slender and tall, speaking a peculiar language, and inhabiting the interior hilly parts of the countries; in several isles

---

* In Reland's *Diss. Miscellan*, vol. iii.
† A Manuscript Vocabulary of the Brazilian language, obligingly communicated by his Excellency the Chevalier PINTO.

these people are called ALFOORIES.* The shores of these isles are peopled by
another nation, whose individuals are swarthy, of a more agreeable form, with
curled and long hair, and of a different language, which is chiefly a branch or dialect of the Malayan. In all the Philippines, the interior mountainous parts, are
inhabited by a black set of people, with frizzled hair, who are tall, lusty, and very
warlike, and speak a peculiar language different from that of their neighbours. But
the outskirts towards the sea are peopled with a race infinitely fairer, having long
hair, and speaking different languages: they are of various denominations, but the
Tagales, Pampangos, and *Bissayas*, are the most celebrated among them. The
former are the more antient inhabitants, and the latter are certainly related to the
various tribes of Malays, who had over-run all the East India islands before the
arrival of the Europeans in those seas. Their language is likewise in many
instances related to that of the Malays.† The isle of Formosa or Tai-ovan has likewise in its interior hilly parts, a set of brown, frizzly haired, broad faced inhabitants; but the shores, especially those to the North, are occupied by the Chinese,
who differ even in language from the former. The isles of New Guinea, New
Britain, and Nova Hibernia have certainly black complexioned inhabitants,
whose manners, customs, habit, form, and character, correspond very much with
the inhabitants of the South Sea islands belonging to the second race in Nova
Caledonia, Tanna, and Mallicollo; and these blacks in New-Guinea, are probably
related to those in the Moluccas and Philippines. The Ladrones, and the new discovered Caroline Islands, contain a set of people very much related to our first
race. Their size, colour, habit, manners, and customs, seem strongly to indicate
this affinity; and they are according to the account of some writers,‡ nearly
related in every respect to the *Tagales* in Luçon or Manilla, so that we may now
trace the line of migration by a continued line of isles, the greater part of which
are not above 100 leagues distant from each other.

We likewise find a very remarkable similarity between several words of the
fair tribe of islanders in the South Sea, and some of the Malays. But it would
be highly inconclusive from the similarity of a few words, to infer that these
islanders were descended from the Malays: for as the Malay contains words found
in the Persian, Malabar, Braminic, Cingalese, Javanese, and Malegass,* this

---

* Franc. Valentyn *Beschryving van Amboina*, ii deel. p. 71,–84. and Dan. Beeckman *Voyage to Borneo*, p. 43. who calls the Aboriginal people on Borneo *Byajos*.
† Hernando los Rios Coronel, *Relacion de las Islas Malucas*. Navarette *Trattados Historicos de la Monarchia de China*. Gemelli Carreri *il giro del mondo*. Fr. Diego Bergano, *Vocabulario de Pampango en Romance*, Manila, 1732, fol. P. Juan de Noceda y el P. Pedro de San Lucar *Vocabulario de la Lengua Tagala*, Manila 1754, fol.
‡ Pere Gobien *Historie des Isles Marianes*, Paris, 1700, 12mo.
* Reland's *Dissertationes Miscellaneae*, vol. iii.

English.		Society-Isles.	Friendly-Isles.	New-Zeeland.	Easter-Island.	Marquesas.	New-Caledonia.	Tan
The Numerals	1	A-Tāhāi	a-tāhāw	Tahāi	Ko-tāhāi	bo-tāhāi	pārū	Reitee
	2	A-Róoā	Lóoā	Róoā	Róoā	bo-hooā	pā-rùo	cārroo
	3	a-Tòroo	Tòloo	Tòroo	Tòroo	bo-tò-oo	pār-ghen	kāhār
	4	a-Hāā	T'fā	T'fā	Hāā	bo-hā	par-bai	kàfā
	5	a-Rèemā	Neema	Reema	Reema	bo-hèemā	pānim	karirrom
	6	a-Hòno	Vàno	Hònnoo	Hòno	bo-hā	pānim-ghèe	Me-riddee
	7	a-Hiddoo	Fidda	Widdoo	Hiddoo	bo-hiddoo	pānim-rùo	Me-càrroo
	8	a-Wàrroo	Vàroo	Wàrroo	Vàroo	bo-wàhoo	pānim-ghèn	Me-kāhār
	9	a-Hèevā	Hèevā	Hèevā	Hèevā	bo-hèevā	pānim-bāi	Me-kāfā
	10	a-Hòoroo	Ongofòoroo	Angāhòroo	Anāhòoroo	bo-hāhoo	pāroonèek	karirrom-k
The arm or hand		Rèemā	Nèemā	Ringā	Rèemā	Heimā		
Anum esjculcutum, or eddoch		Tàrro	Tāllo	Tāllo	Tarro		Oùbà	Nārèy
Bananas, sweet-plantanes		Māā Fèh-hee	} Foogee	(have none)	{ Māiga Fòotee	Māi	Munghee	Nā-cèk
A Beard		Oòmee	Oòmeemèeā	Goòmee	Oòmee	Oòmee	Poon-wāng	Nā-ghoòn
The Belly		òb.o	Fāttoo	K-òpoo	òboo	òpoo	Ghung	D-oòboom
The Bread-fruit		Oòroo	Māee	(have none)	(have none)	Oòroo, Māee		Gh-òoroo
A Canoe		a-Wāhā	Wāggā	te-wāggā	wagga	Wāā	Te-wāggā	Andītā
A Chief		A-Rèch	Hàrèekee		Hàrèekee	A-lā-āi	Alcèghee	Arèekee
Coco-nuts		Nèeā	Nèeoo	(have none)	(have none)	Nèeoo	Noo	Nèeoo
Dead, to die, kill		māttè	māttè	māttè			hāllèek	maròokee
A Dog		Oòree	Gh-òoree	gh-òoree	(have none)	(have none)	(have none)	(have
To drink		Aìnoo	aìnoo	aìnoo	hỳnoo	aìnoo	hỳndoo	Noòee
The Ears		Tàrrèhā	Tāringā	Tārèngā	Tārrèeān	Poneenohòe	Galinga	Ferdèang
To eat		āi	e-kāi	ekāi	māgho	māi, (viêtuals)	hoot	ānnee
The Eye		Māttā	Māttā	Māttā	Māttā	Māttā	Teewanya	Nāmee, n
A Fish		Eiya	Eèka	Eèkā	Eèkā	Eiyā	Tā-èekā	Tā-èekā
A Foot		āwāi	āwāi	wāī-wāi	āwāi	āwāi	hāā	Nāfoo
A Friend		Hòā, Tāo	Whòā	Hòā	Hèeò		ùlee, māilee	
Great		a-rāhāi, nòoee	Arāhāi	ārāhāi, nòoee	nòoee			fārāhòree
A Hatchet		Tòee	Tòghee	Tòghee		Tòee	Bābbānèw	Pāhā
Hair		arùuroo, hòoroo-hòoroo	Lo-òoroo	hòoroo		oòkho	Poon	Gvonèom
The Head		a-oòpo	òopo	òopo	A òpo	oòpo		kārāh
A Hog		Bòoā	Bòoàeeā	(have none)	(have none)	Boòāhā	(have none)	Boògā
A House		te-whàrre	Efàrre	te-fàrre	te-hàrre	te-whàrre	Oòmā	Nèemā
Land		Whennòoā	Fannòoā	Whennòoā	Hennòoā	Whennòoā	hāāp	Fennòoā
Little		èetee	eèdgee	èetee	èetee	èetèe		
A Man		Tāhāā		Tāngātā	Pāpā	Tèetee	āīt	Arromān
The Moon		Māràmā	Māràmā	Māràmā	Māràmàrā		Mālòk, Mathèenā	Māgòoā
The Mouth		Oòtoo	Mòtoo	Oòtoo	Oòdoo	Mètoo	Noo-ānya	Tarooèe
The Nose		Eỳhoo	Eèhoo	Ehèeoo	Eèyoo	Eiyoo	Mānīn-ya	Basfee-ang
Potatoes (sweet)		Goomàrro		Goomàlla	Goomàrrā			
The Sea		Tāi	Tāi	Mòdinnā			Dāllāi	Tāsfee
The Sun		Erā	Elòoā	herā	Erā		āt	Merỳ
Water		Evāi	Evāi	Evāi	Evāi	Evāi	T-evāi, oòè	T-avāi
A Woman		Wàheine	Fefèine	Wàhèine		Wàhèine	Tàmā	Bran
Yams		Oòwhee	Oòfee	(have none)	Oòhee		Oòfee	Noo-òok

"A Comparative Table of the Various Languages in the Isles of the South-Sea," as published in Forster's *Observations*, 1778.

Malay.	Tagalas.	Pampangos.	New-Holland.	Mexican.	Peruvian.	Chileese.
- - - - - -	yta - - - -	Ifa, Metong - -	- - - - - -	ce - - - -	- - - -	Quyn
- - - - - -	dalava, dolova - -	Ad-dua - - -	- - - - - -	ome - - - -	- - - -	Eppo
ega - - - -	tatl, ytlo - - -	at-lo - - - -	- - - - - -	Jei - - -	- - - -	Quila
pat - - -	apat - - - -	apat - - - -	- - - - - -	Nahuy - -	- - - -	Meli
ma - - -	Lima - - - -	Lima - - - -	- - - - - -	- - - -	- - - -	Quechu
n, a-nam - -	anim - - - -	anam - - - -	- - - - - -	- - - -	- - - -	Cuyn
oo - - - -	pito - - - -	pitu - - - -	- - - - - -	- - - -	- - - -	Relgi
span - - -	valo - - - -	valo - - - -	- - - - - -	- - - -	- - - -	Pura
belan - - -	Siyam - - - -	Siam - - - -	- - - - - -	- - - -	- - - -	Ailla
oloo - - - -	Polo, pobo - -	Apalo - - -	- - - - - -	- - - -	Chunca	Aılla
agan, Lingan - -	camas - - -	camavo - - -	- - - - - -	- - - -	Maqui -	{ Puilpa (brachium) / Cue (manus) }
ady } Rumph. { Tallas / a } { Javanice	Tarac, (camote grande)	Tugui - - -	- - - - - -	- - - -	- - - -	
ang (Rumph.)						
goot - - - -	gumi, Baba - -	Gumi (barbade) Baba -	- - Waller -	- - - -	- - - -	Pajun
ot, Pooroot - -	Tiyan - - - -	Attian, Butad - -	- - - - - -	- - - -	- - - -	Pue
cun, (Rumpf.)						
v - - - -	Berai (navio pequeño) -	Pangga, Lunday - -	- - Maragan -	- - - -	- - - -	{ Butawampa (navis) / Pichampo (navicula) / Dolio, (lembus, canoa) }
a - - - -	Hari - - - -	Ari - - - -	- - - - - -	- - - -	Apu (dominus)	{ Apò / Curaca (dominus) }
cor - - - -	Niog, Niyog - -	Uagot - - -	- - - - - -	- - - -	- - - -	
a-matayan - -	{ ca-matayan, hallimolan / patay (to kill) }	} matai - - -	- - - - - -	- - - -	- - - -	{ Lay (mori) / Langawyn (necare) }
atay, mattee - -						
ing - - - -	Darapova - -	Dapur - - -	- - Rotta -	- - - -	- - - -	Tewa
num - - -	Ynom - - - -	Inum - - - -	- - chuchala -	- - - -	- - - -	butun
nga - - - -	Taynga - - -	Balug-bug, Talinga, (bored ears) Melea -	- - - -	- - - -	- - - -	Pilum
can - - -	cain - - - -	can, afan, putat -	- - bootina -	- - - -	- - - -	Jen
a - - - -	Mata - - - -	Mata - - - -	- - Meul -	- - - -	- - - -	Ne
an - - -	Yfila - - - -	afan - - - -	- - - - - -	- - - -	- - - -	Challua
-kee - - - -	calis (foot of an animal)	Bitis - - - -	- - Edamal -	- - - -	- - - -	Namon
at, Toolan - -	{ Tiap,Lagoyo,Lagoma, / Catoto, Calagoma, Ca- / lagoya, Calli }	{ Lugud, Paffrag / Curang, Dugo }	- - }	- - - -	- - - -	
r - - - -	Daquila - - -	Dagul - - -	- - - - - -	- - - -	Hatun -	buta
ang, kapak campa	Daras, Pan-daras -	Daras - - -	- - - - - -	- - - -	- - - -	
boot - - - -	Bohoc - - -	Buac, Cavad -	- - Morye -	- - - -	- - - -	Lonco
la - - - -	Olo - - - -	Buntuc - - -	- - Waggheegee -	Tzontecortli	- - - -	{ Lonco / Towongen }
i, Bobbee - -	Babuy - - -	Babi - - - -	- - (have none)	- - - -	- - - -	Cuchy
ma - - - -	Bahay - - -	Balay - - -	- - - - - -	Calli - - -	- - - -	
t - - - -	Lupa - - - -	Labuad, Gabon -	- - - - - -	Lan - -	Lacta -	Tue
cheel } in quantity / dekit } in magnitude	onti, bali-balian -	intak, lati - -	- - - - - -	- - - -	- - - -	Pichi
ufia, Orang - -	Tavo - - - -	Tavo - - - -	- - Bàmmà -	- - - -	Runa -	Wento
an - - - -		Bulan - - -	- - - - - -	- - - -	Coilla -	
oot - - - -	bunga - - -	Bunganga, Afboc -	- - Yembe, Jembi -	Chal - -	- - - -	Oun
ng - - - -	Ylong - - -	Arung - - -	- - Bonjoo -	- - - -	- - - -	Ju
y kecheel - -						
t - - - -	{ Daggat / Laot, (mar alta) }	{ Dayat / Laut (mar alta) }	- - }	- - - -	- - - -	Louqien
a-harree - -	Arao - - - -	Aldao - - -	- - Galan -	- - - -	Inti -	Ante
- - - -	{ Tubig / Tambaang (freshwater) / Taffik (salt water) }	{ Sabug, Danum / Tabang (fresh water) / Alat (salt water) }	Poorli - -	Atl - -	Unuy -	ko
mpooang - -	Babaye - - -	Babai - - -	- - Mootjel -	- - - -	- - - -	Domo
y befarr - -	Obi - - - -	Ubi - - - -	- - - - - -	- - - -	- - - -	

should likewise imply, that the nations speaking the above mentioned languages, were the offspring of the Malays, which certainly would be proving too much.[16] I am therefore rather inclined to suppose, that all these dialects preserve several words of a more antient language, which was more universal, and was gradually divided into many languages, now remarkably different. The words therefore of the language of the South Sea isles, which are similar to others in the Malay tongue, prove clearly in my opinion, that the Eastern South Sea isles were originally peoples from the Indian, or Asiatic Northern isles; and that those lying more to the Westward, received their first inhabitants from the neighbourhood of New Guinea.

We have therefore, I apprehend, probable proofs that these islanders came originally from the Indian Asiatic isles, on which we have pointed out two races of inhabitants, such as we found them in the South Sea isles: it should seem therefore, that these two distinct races are descended from the two distinct Indian tribes. If we had good vocabularies of the various languages spoken in these isles, we should then be enabled to trace their original back to a particular tribe. But as we labour under a deficiency in this respect, I have endeavoured in the annexed table to give a general view of many languages, which of course, must confirm my former assertions. I flatter myself with having done as much as could be expected in my situation, and therefore leave the rest to better instructed, and more enlightened ages.

SECTION IV

Various Progress, which the Nations we saw, have made from the Savage State towards Civilization

Previous to other positions, mankind seem not originally to have lived in the extremities of what we commonly call the temperate zones; nor to have chosen these cold, inhospitable climates for their abode. The mild happy climate in, or near the tropics, the rapid growth of animals and vegetables in these places; the facility of procuring food, and shelter against the inclemencies of the weather; the variety and succession of fine and wholesome spontaneous roots and fruit, all lead us to suppose that man was originally settled there. We ought to be confirmed in this idea, by considering that the first nakedness of man in a savage state, is by no means calculated to bear the vicissitudes and inclemencies of the Northern and Southern extremities of the *temperate*, or the vigour of the two *frozen* zones; and that if ever men are found settled in these unhappy regions, it has been owing either to chance or cruel necessity.

The inhabitants of the islands in the South Sea, though unconnected with highly civilized nations, are more improved in every respect, as they live more and more distant from the poles. Their food is more varied, and abundant; their habitations more roomy, neat, and adapted to the exigencies of the climate; their garments more elegant, improved, and ingenious; their population is greater; their societies better regulated; their public security against foreign invaders more firmly established; their manners more courteous, elegant, and even refined; their principles of morality better understood, and generally practised; their minds capable of, and open to instruction; they have ideas of a supreme being, of a future state, of the origin of the world; and the whole contributes greatly to increase their happiness, in its natural, moral and social branches, both as individuals, and as a nation. On the contrary, the wretched mortals towards the frozen zone, are the most debased of all human beings, in every respect. Their food is scanty, loathsome, and precarious; their habitations the most miserable

huts that can be imagined; their garments rough, and by no means sufficient to
screen them against the rigours of the inhospitable climate; their societies thin,
and without any mutual ties or affection; exposed to the insults of all invaders,
they retreat to the most inhospitable rocks, and appear insensible to all that is
great and ingenious; a brutish stupidity is their general characteristic; and whenever they are the strongest, they are treacherous, and act in opposition to all the
principles of humanity and hospitality. May we not then infer from the above premises, that man unconnected with highly civilized nations, approaches in more
happy climates, nearer to that state of civilization, and happiness, which we
enjoy; that human nature is really debased in the savages, who inhabit the frozen
extremities of our globe, and that their present situation is as it were, a preternatural state.[2] I wish not to be misunderstood; the happiness which European nations
enjoy, and are capable of, becomes, on account of the degeneracy of a few profli-
gate individuals, very much debased, and mixed with the miseries, which are
entailed upon our civilized societies, by luxury and vice; if therefore the felicity of
several European or Asiatic nations, seem to be inferior to that of some of the
nations in the South Sea, it is owing to the above-mentioned causes, since it does
not seem to follow, that a high degree of civilization must necessarily lessen, or
destroy natural, moral, or social happiness.[3]

I believe the nations inhabiting the frozen extremities of our globe to be
degenerated and debased from that original happiness, which the tropical nations
more or less enjoy. I was first persuaded into this belief, from the state in which
we found the inhabitants of Tierra del Fuego and New Zeeland, and by comparing
their situation, with that of their neighbours.

The people on Tierra del Fuego, about Christmas Bay, were not numerous;
and if we are to judge from the general appearance of the country, and from the
numbers seen by other navigators, there cannot be a great population in these
inhospitable climates. These were the Southernmost lands, wherein we found
human creatures, who not only appeared to us to be wretched, but to be themselves conscious of their own misery, and forlorn situation; several boats, with
natives, came to our ship, and none of them had any other garment than a piece
of Sealskin, which did not reach so far as to cover half their buttocks, and came
barely over the shoulders; their head and feet, and whole body, were exposed to a
degree of cold in the midst of summer, which appeared to us sharp, though we
were well clad, having found the temperature of the air generally from 46° to 50°
of Fahrenheits thermometer; neither the men nor the women, had any thing to
cover their privities; their bodies smelled highly offensive from the rancid train
oil which they frequently use, and the rotten seals flesh which they eat; and I am
of opinion, their whole frame of body is thoroughly penetrated with this disagreeable smell. Their habitations consist of a few sticks, tied together, so as to form a

kind of shell, for a low, open, roundish hut; they join the neighbouring shrubs together, and cover the whole with some wisps of dry grass, and here and there a few pieces of seals-skin are tied over; one fifth or sixth of the whole circumference, is left open for a door, and the fire place; their utensils and furniture, which we had an opportunity of observing, consisted of a basket, a kind of mat-satchel, a bone-hook, fixed to a long stick of a light kind of wood, for disengaging the shell-fish from the rocks, a rude bow and some arrows.[4] Their canoes are made of bark, which is doubled round a pliant piece of wood, by way of gunwale, and a few sticks, of about the thickness of half an inch, are bent on the whole inside of the canoe, close to one another, so as to form a kind of strong deck, both for expanding the whole frame of the canoe, and preventing its bottom from being broken by walking on it; in one part of these poor embarkations, they lay up a little heap of soil, and on it they keep a constant fire, even in summer. Their food, beside the above-mentioned seals, are shell-fish, which they broil and devour; they were shivering, and appeared much affected with the cold: they looked at the ship and all its parts with a stupidity and indolence, which we had not hitherto observed in any of the nations in the South Seas, had all an empty stare in their countenances, and expressed hardly any desires or wishes to possess any thing which we offered, and thought it might become desirable to them; they were destitute of all convenience or ease, shewed no signs of joy or happiness, and seemed to be insensible to all natural, moral, or social feelings, and enjoyments, and occupied with nothing but their wants and wretchedness. This little tribe, observed by us, I suppose to be some outcasts of their brethren; for our officers, who landed in Success-Bay, reported, that the people there were much happier than those in Christmas-Harbour. If we again compare them with their neighbouring tribes on the continent, such as they are described by Mr. Thomas Falkner, who resided near 40 years among them, we must confess, that those are in every respect superior; they have horses, and a greater variety of food, supplying themselves by the chace; their garments are better calculated to defend them against the injuries of the climate; their arms both offensive and defensive, prove genius and an exertion of mind, of which the poor inhabitants of Tierra del Fuego seem utterly incapable; they have a kind of civil government, some regulations for the security of their societies; leaders and chiefs are at the head of their tribes in war, and in peace. Their behaviour is by no means inequitable, harsh, or inhumane; their minds shew vigour and courage, their language is copious, elegant, and has marks of a peculiar culture. In short they are infinitely less wretched than their neighbours on Tierra del Fuego, who, to all appearance, are only degenerated into that forlorn condition in which we found them sunk.

DUSKY BAY is the Southernmost place on New-Zeeland, we touched at; the latitude of the place where the astronomers observatory was fixed, being 45° 47′

PROGRESS OF
SAVAGES

South. We found this bay, which has several leagues of extent branching out into spacious inlets, stocked with many kinds of fowl, crowded with prodigious quantities of the best flavoured fish, and its rocks covered with numerous herds of seals; all which abundance would naturally invite people, who solely subsist upon fish and fowl, to settle here, and to become very numerous. But we found only three families in all this bay: their habitations consisted of a few sticks stuck into the ground, and meanly covered with flags and rushes: they had no idea of cultivating or planting; their garments were such as covered the upper part of the body, and left the legs and part of the thighs exposed, and they squatted down to shelter them under their clothes, which commonly were remarkably uncleanly; and the families settled here, seemed to be independent of each other. When we came to QUEEN CHARLOTTE's SOUND,[5] we found on the shores of that equally spacious water, four or five hundred people, and some of them paid deference to several old men, as *Tringoboohee, Goobaya*, and *Teiràtoo*, who were it seems their chiefs. Fish were in this place equally abundant, but of a sort inferior in taste and goodness; wild fowl, especially of the aquatic kind, were scarcer, and we saw but one seal, though our two ships resided here at different times. The people were clad in the same manner as in the former place; their habitations, especially on their hippas or strong holds, were better, cleanlier, and lined on the inside with reeds; they had no plantations, but they knew the names of *Tarro* and *Goomalla*, which the inhabitants of the tropical isles give to the *Arum esculentum* and the *Convolvulus Batatas*. This, in my opinion, evidently proves that they were descended from a tribe, who had cultivation, and who had lost or neglected this way of supporting themselves, either because they found greater plenty of fish, and animal food; or because they fled their country in so precipitate a manner, that they could not take any roots with them; or lastly, from mere supineness and indolence; for we saw them eat fern roots, a very insipid, coarse, and wretched food. Whatever may be the real cause, the climate would certainly allow of planting *eddoes* and *potatoes*, being in 41° 5′ South latitude; and it is evident that the natives were degenerated and debased from a more perfect and more happy state. The inhabitants of the Northern isle, who came off to us, had better boats, and were clad in finer garments; but we could not make many observations on their situation as we saw them only in a transitory manner; however, the published accounts of the preceding voyage, and those which I was favoured with by Capt. Cook, agree in this, that they had very extensive, regular, well-cultivated plantations, inclosed in very firm and neat fences, made of reeds; that they acknowledged the authority of a chief in a district of 80 leagues at least, where our people found justice administered by inferior chiefs; and that they seemed to live in that district in greater security and more comfortably than in any other part of the isle. *Hawksworth, vol. 3. p. 470.*

William Hodges, *View
in Pickersgill Harbour,
Dusky Bay, New Zealand*,
oil on canvas, April
1773. 654 x 731 mm.
National Maritime
Museum, London.

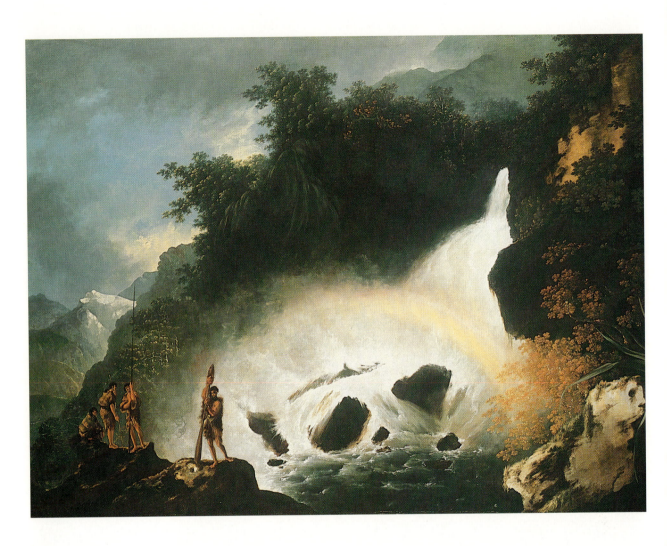

William Hodges,
[*Cascade Cove*] *Dusky Bay*, oil on canvas, 1775. 1346 x 1911 mm. National Maritime Museum, London.

William Hodges,
*A View Taken in the Bay
of Otaheite Peha*
[Vaitepiha], oil on can-
vas, 1776. 915 X 1371
mm. National Trust,
Anglesey Abbey,
Cambridgeshire.

George Forster, [*Ice
Islands with Ice Blink*],
gouache, 1772–1773.
350 X 545 mm. State
Library of New South
Wales.

Tahitian chief mourner's costume. Collected by Johann Reinhold Forster. Pitt Rivers Museum, Oxford (1886.1.1637b–1).

The natural inferences drawn from these data, seem to prove, that mankind being more numerous in or near the tropics, and very thinly scattered towards the cold extremities of our globe, the human species was originally settled in or near the tropics, and from thence spread towards the extremities. Secondly, the instances given here, evince likewise the truth of what we advanced before, *viz.* that the human species, when unconnected with the highly civilized nations, is always found more debased in its physical, mental, moral and social capacity, in proportion as it is removed from the tropical regions. It seems therefore probable that savage nations in cold climates, contract a harshness or rigidity in their fibres and frame of body, which causes sluggishness, indolence and stupidity of mind; their hearts grow insensible to the dictates of virtue, honor and conscience, and they become incapable of any attachment, affection or endearment.[6]

Let us now turn our eyes to O-TAHEITEE, the queen of tropical isles, and its happy inhabitants, and extend our view to all the Society and Friendly Isles. Though we found population to be very great in proportion to the extent of country, yet we were led to believe that a much greater number of inhabitants might be supported on these islands, and in ages to come might be found there, if no accidents should happen, or unless such manners and regulations should be introduced as tend to check or stop the progress of population. The fertility of the soil on those extensive plains, and numerous valleys, the rapid vegetation and constant succession of coco-nuts, bread-fruit, apples, bananas, plantanes, eddoes, potatoes, yams, and many other fine fruits and roots; the regular division of lands in private property, well and neatly fenced in; the particular care shewn by the inhabitants to the dogs, hogs, and fowls, which are their only domestic animals; the convenience and neatness of their houses and boats, their ingenious contrivances for fishing; the taste and elegance shewn in many of their utensils and houshold furniture; their dresses so well adapted to the climate, so curiously varied both in their texture and dyes; their delicacy of manners, true courtesy and politeness; their chearful and open behaviour; their goodness of heart, and hospitality; their knowledge of plants, birds, fishes, shells, insects, vermes, and all the branches of animated nature; their acquaintance with the stars, and their motion, with the seasons and winds; their poetry, songs, dances, and dramatic performances; their theogony and cosmogony, the various ranks and regulations of civil society; their establishments for defence, and for repelling and retaliating injuries offered to their state; all these conspire to prove that they are infinitely superior to the before mentioned tribes; and even point out the true causes of their greater happiness. The climate certainly contributes a great deal to their felicity, and might be justly deemed the main source of it. However, as we found farther to the West, new isles in the same happy climate, and in the same latitude, the inhabitants of which, were nevertheless, infinitely inferior in point of civilization, and more defective in the enjoyments of real happiness; it seems to follow, that there must be, besides the above-mentioned, some other cause of this remarkable circumstance.

All the ideas, all the improvements of mankind relative to sciences, arts, manufactures, social life, and even morality, ought to be considered as *the sum total of the efforts of mankind ever since its existence.* The first original tribes no doubt kept up connexions with one another, and thus they propagated and hoarded up useful knowledge, established principles, regulations, and mechanical trades for the benefit of their posterity. The sciences, the arts, manufactures, regulations, and principles of Egypt, and of the Eastern nations, were known, and partly adopted by the Greeks, from whom the Romans received their improvements; and we have recovered many, which were in use among the ancients, after they had been long neglected. From Chaldea and from Egypt two remarkable systems branched out, the one over India, China, and the extremities of the East, and the second over the West and North. Here and there we are still able to discover some remains; but in the interior Southern parts of Africa, and over the whole continent of America, few, if any, traces of those ancient systems, have been discovered. The more a tribe or nation preserved of the ancient systems, and modified and adapted them to their particular situation, climate and other circumstances, or raised new ideas and principles upon the first base or foundation, the more improved, civilized and happy must that tribe or nation be. The more a nation or tribe has forgotten or lost of the ancient systems; their situation, climate, and other circumstances, having obliged them to neglect or to depart from them without making up the defect by new principles and ideas, founded on the same plan, the more that nation or tribe is found to be degenerated, debased, and wretched. Various circumstances may have caused the loss and neglect of the ideas and improvements of the system, which their progenitors or mother-tribe still preserved; a number of men are obliged for instance, on account of intestine feuds in a nation, to abandon their native-country, and the climate wherein they were born and educated, in order to place themselves beyond the reach either of the power or outrage of their enemies; they wander over a great space of unoccupied ground, which is situated in a colder climate, than that which they formerly inhabited; the tropical fruits which grew in their native country spontaneously, are no longer to be met with; the roots, which there, by slight cultivation, gave them abundance of food, require here a very laborious and toilsome husbandry, before they yield the bare necessaries of life; because vegetation is not so luxuriant, so rapid, and powerful in climates, remote from the sun. Let us now suppose this clan, grown by length of time into a nation; new divisions supervening, force another portion, still further from the benevolent influence of the sun, where they find none of the spontaneous tropical fruits, where even the roots, their

former support, will not thrive, on account of the rigours of their winters, they
lose therefore, at once, their subsistence; and though they were obliged, in their
former country, to toil during a stated time, they had, however, the satisfaction of
collecting a certain food; but now, unacquainted as they are, with the spontaneous productions of this new climate, which might, perhaps, supply them with
eatables, they must roam over their new country in quest of precarious food; they
try to kill by force or address, some animals or birds or to catch some fish in the
rivers or seas, to procure a subsistence; this entirely alters their mode of living;
their habits, their language, and I might almost say their nature; their ideas are
quite changed, the improvements, which they had in their former situation, are
neglected and lost; the tree, from which they formerly made their garments,
grows not in this new climate; their retreat was so precipitate, that they had not
time to take some plants or shoots with them, nor any of the domesticated
animals, whose skins afforded them garments in their former country: they however, find themselves under the necessity of procuring some covering to screen
their bodies against the rigours of the climate, and the inclemencies of wind and
rain, to which they must now be more exposed than in their former situation,
their mode of living being quite altered. They find some grass, or the filaments of
some other plant, or the skins of birds and seals, to answer this purpose, and they
use them accordingly; their rambling way of life, in quest of food, obtained by the
chase or fishing, obliges them to change their abode as often as the game becomes
scarce, or the fish less numerous; they think it therefore not worth their while to
build neat, large, and convenient houses; a temporary hut, just sufficient to screen
them from the keen winds and the frequent showers of rain, snow, and hail, is
erected by them, in every new place to which they remove. The fathers retain
perhaps the names and ideas of things, which they enjoyed in their former situation; their children lose the idea, and the third or fourth generation, forget even
the names by which they are called; the new objects, which they find and begin
to use, oblige them to invent new names for them, and for the manner in which
they are employed; and thus even the language becomes altered; nay, their way of
subsisting, by the chace or fishing, obliges them to live in small tribes, distant
from others, in order to facilitate their subsistence. Formerly, when moderate husbandry and the spontaneous growth of fine fruits in a happy climate, enabled
numerous tribes to live close together, they then enjoyed more leisure for social
life, they had the advantage of being mutually and powerfully assisted, and they
communicated their improvements to each other: now they are deprived of the
charms and choice of society, which is confined to the few individuals of a family,
or a small tribe; they are destitute of any assistance or protection from their
friends; exposed to the fierceness of rapacious animals, perhaps to the barbarity of
some other tribe of savages; incapable of undertaking any work which requires

the united efforts of a multitude; they make no other improvements, but those which their narrow understanding comprehends, and is capable of; there being less chance of meeting with a man of genius, in a small, than in a greater number of human beings. Constantly intent upon the means of procuring the necessaries of life, especially food, every other pursuit, every other knowledge is neglected, and the ideas therefore, which are not connected with the chace or fishery, are absolutely lost to this race of men. They must therefore of course, by degrees, degenerate into a debased forlorn condition, and all the notions of improvements, the work of ages, and the result of the reason and the wits of thousands be forgotten; their reason, for want of being exercised, is at last brought so low, that nothing but the mere ideas of animal life, the instincts of brute creation remain; strangers to social feelings, and still more so to social virtues, they herd together by custom; sensuality,[7] and the enjoyment of the few wants of nature, make the whole field of their brutish desires; and of that bright image of divinity, of expanded and sublime knowledge, of the consciousness of good and virtuous actions, of the noble and generous struggle in the cause of virtue and social happiness, hardly a few sparks remain.

If we were to sum up the arguments, and evidence which we ought to collect from the above facts, it is certain, that on one side the mildness of the climate contributes greatly to soften the manners of mankind; and the rigours of the extremities of our globe, renders the fibres and whole frame of our bodies more harsh, rigid, and insensible, which undoubtedly operates upon the mind, and the heart, and almost totally destroys all social feelings; on the other side we find, that the influence of the climate far from being the only cause of the degeneracy of mankind on the extremities of our globe, evidently points us out the second great cause of degeneracy of the human race, the want of education, by which means the most useful notions, tending to improve our physical, mental, moral, and social faculties, are propagated, perpetuated, and lastly increased by new additional ideas.

Before I conclude this chapter, I beg leave to add a few reflections.

We have represented the savages living on the frozen extremities of our globe, as most debased, degenerated, and wretched: and it is nevertheless certain, that though their condition appear to us forlorn, and they themselves be in our eyes the outcast of the human species; they do not think so meanly of their own situation; nay, so far from supposing themselves unhappy; they rather glory in the advantages of their way of living, and none of them would exchange his cold climate for one that is more temperate, his wretched hut for a comfortable European house, nay, not even for the most magnificent palace; he thinks his piece of seals-skin a more becoming dress than the best silks and brocades; nor would he prefer a well-seasoned ragout to a piece of stinking seals flesh.[8] To be controuled

by wise laws and regulations, is what the spirit of some of these rambling barbarians could never brook; and independence, licentiousness, and revenge their
favourite passions, render them absolutely unfit for any well-regulated society,
and cause in them a general contempt for our way of living, where order and subordination take place. They think themselves happy, nay, happier than the best
regulated nation, and every individual of them is so perfectly contented with his
condition, that not even a wish is left in his breast for the least alteration.*

But a mind accustomed to meditation, and able to affix to every thing its
true value, must certainly perceive, that this situation of the savage or barbarian,
is nothing more than a state of intoxication; his happiness and contentment
founded on mere sensuality is transitory and delusive; the sum of all his enjoyments is so small, so defective in its particulars, and of so little value, that a man
in his senses cannot but think himself happy that he was born in a civilized
nation, educated in a country where society is as much improved as is possible;
that he belongs to a people who are governed by the mildest laws, and have the
happiest constitution of government, being under the influence of civil and religious liberty.

If therefore the happiness of the savage is not so eligible, as some philosophers will make us believe, who never viewed mankind in this debased situation;
it is certainly the wish of humanity, and of real goodness, to see all these nations
brought nearer to a more improved, more civilized, and more happy state, without the addition of these evils, which abuses, luxury and vice have introduced
among our societies. Human nature is capable of great improvements, if men only
knew how to proceed in order to effectuate this great and noble purpose. The
greater part of them are too unreasonable in their wishes, too rapid and violent in
their proceedings, and too sanguine in their expectations. They wish this change
should take place immediately, their methods for bringing it about are contrary to
human nature, and sometimes they overlook the progress of improvement,
because it is slow. If we consider the progress of man as an individual, from birth
to manhood, we find it very slow and gradual, though ever so much care be taken
to improve the body, as well as the intellectual and the moral faculties, and to
instill early into the mind the seeds of social virtue. We can never pass over the
years of childhood, and youth, and make infants men; not even by the most
accomplished education. Thus likewise, the approach towards civilization, must

---

* This is applicable to the savages of Tierra del Fuego, and the barbarians of New Zeeland: but the
inhabitants of O-Taheitee and the Society Isles, are beyond this state. None of the first two races of
men, upon the offer being made to them, shewed any desire to go with us to our own country; and
there are already seven or eight instances, to my knowledge, of persons from the latter isles, who
willingly offered to go with us to Europe.[9]

be left to time; it is a work of ages to bring the mind of a whole nation to maturity. Nor can it be forced or accelerated by the best instructions. From *animality* nations ripen into *savages*, from this state they enter into that of *barbarism*, before they are capable of *civilization*, and how many degrees of refinement does not even this situation admit?

Infancy is in individuals, merely animal life. In the same manner the lowest degree of degeneration in collective bodies is ANIMALITY. *Childhood* is undesigning, harmless, and innocent; private property and personal security of others, are ideas which the boy is to be taught when he emerges from infancy, for he knows of no other law than that of the strongest. The SAVAGE has likewise no idea of the personal security of any other besides himself, nor thinks better in regard to private property: he kills where he is the strongest, and he robs where he cannot otherwise obtain the possession of what he covets. *Adolescence* is the age of violent passions, breaking out in outrages against all the principles of morality; carrying away like an impetuous flood whatever opposes its desires: the youth has the dawning of understanding and reason, and if the mental faculties are not improved in this stage, and the passions made subservient to reason, he degenerates into profligacy, and brings on his own ruin. The BARBARIAN is likewise fiery and violent, without controul and principles, nay, capable of the most detestable outrages; nations in this state want education and improvement more than in any other. *Manhood* and a *mature age*, are similar to the CIVILIZED STATE, and have therefore several degrees.[10]

These remarks will give a general outline of the real condition of these nations, of the improvements which philosophers can with propriety wish for them, and of the progress they may be expected to have made from the little intercourse with Europeans. I have been frequently asked, what improvements and progress in civilization the inhabitants of the islands in the South Sea appeared to me to have made since Europeans came among them. A few years in regard to a nation, are a few moments in a man's life, a man may learn very useful things materially affecting his situation in life in a few hours; but it would be next to impossible to point out in his character, his mode of living, his conversation, and his actions a few hours after this acquisition, the advantages he can or will derive from thence; this holds likewise in regard to nations; a few years cannot bring on a material change among them. We carried hogs and fowls to New Zeeland; and dogs and pigs to New Caledonia, dogs to Tanna, Mallicollo, and the Friendly Isles, and goats to O-Taheitee; these animals will no doubt in time cause a material change in the way of living of these nations; but as we could give no more than one couple of goats and a few of the other species of animals, it will require a succession of years before they can multiply, and become so numerous, that every inhabitant may have several of them, and thus be enabled to employ them in food. The use of iron tools is another article, which would, in time, become a great improvement to their mechanical employments; but as those tools which we procured for them were by no means in sufficient number, that every man might be provided with a compleat set, the changes which they have produced, are, as yet, very inconsiderable; nay, as these isles have no productions, which might tempt any European nation to set on foot a regular and constant navigation to them; it is probable, that in a few years they will be entirely neglected; if therefore the iron tools imported, had been so numerous, that every man could have had his share, the natives would have entirely laid aside their own stone hatchets, stone chissels, and other implements, and would, perhaps, by length of time, have forgotten the manner of making them. This circumstance, must of course, have become very distressing to them; used to our tools, without possessing the art of making them, or the still greater art of procuring iron, from whence they might be manufactured, and having laid aside and forgotten the method of forming their substitutes of stone, they would, instead of being improved, have been thrown back several ages in their own improvements. We did not communicate intellectual, moral, or social improvements to the natives of the isles; nor could these be expected from the crew of a man of war; those who might be deemed capable of enlarging their minds with new ideas relative to science, arts and manufactures, of instilling the principles of true morality and virtue into their breasts, or of communicating to them notions of a well regulated government, and diffusing throughout a numerous nation, that spirit of charity, attachment, and disinterested love of the community, which ought to glow in the breast of every reasonable member of society, had neither time nor leisure for such an undertaking in the few days of our abode among them, especially as none had a thorough knowledge of the several languages, and as each had a different pursuit to attend, which had been delegated to him by his superiors, when this expedition was set on foot.

SECTION V

Food, and the Method of Procuring it, by Fishing,
Fowling, Hunting, and the wild spontaneous
Fruits. — Savage or barbarous State of a small
Number of Men. — Origin of Cannibalism. —
Means employed by Providence of improving
Human Societies

SED PRIMUM POSITUM SIT, NOSMET IPSOS COMMENDATOS ESSE
NOBIS, PRIMAMQUE EX NATURA HANC HABERE APPETITIONEM,
UT CONSERVEMUS NOSMET IPSOS.
  M. Tullius Cicero *de Fin. Bon & Mal.* 4[1]

ORIGIN OF
SOCIETIES

Having traced the general outline of the real condition of the nations we saw in
the course of our voyage, and endeavoured to assign the true causes of the
remarkable difference in their improvements; it now becomes proper to enter
into a more detailed description of the particulars relative to their food and population, and the various principles, manners, regulations, habits, and biass of mind
peculiar to each of the several tribes with which we became acquainted.

We observed in general, that the chief occupation of all the nations, which
live towards the extremities of our globe, consists in procuring their subsistence;
all their endeavours, contrivances and ingenuity, center in this great and necessary object: cloathing, habitation, security, liberty, property, and every other concern must give way to the first.

If we compare the situation of the inhabitants of *Tierra del Fuego*, and of the
Eskimaux, or *Greenlanders*, every circumstance proves the latter superior to the
inhabitants of the South extremity of America, though these have, in many
respects, the advantage of them in regard to the gifts which nature has bestowed
on their country.

The *Greenlanders* and *Eskimaux* can procure a variety of food, chiefly of the animal kind, from land and sea animals. They hunt equally rein dears and whales; kill seals and sea fowl, and likewise catch fish, especially salmon: but the wretched *Pesserai* is obliged to subsist chiefly on muscles and other shell fish, which he collects by means of a bone hook fixed on a long octangular pole, from the bottom of the sea, and from the rocks under water. We saw the Pesserais eat rotten seal's flesh, and they presented it to us as a great rarity; but though we examined the whole extent of Christmas-Bay in more than one boat, we never saw any seals. It is therefore probable, that they are either very scarce in this part, or that they occasionally migrate to other places, and return to the sound at certain seasons. One man among them had a piece of a guanacoes-skin for his clothing,[2] but amongst thirty or forty, whom we saw, he was the only one. Christmas-Harbour seems to have none of these animals, as its lands consist of small barren isles, without any woods or grassy places, which might afford food and shelter for these animals, and the summits of the hills were at the end of December entirely covered with immense masses of snow. It is therefore highly probable, that those *Pesserais* whom we saw there, remove to other places, where the guanacoes are found. Farther to the East, on *Tierra del Fuego* which consists of a large mass of land, without being divided into so many small islands; we and other navigators observed large woods of fine timber, and extensive plains covered with grass, and if any guanacoes are to be met with on *Tierra del Fuego*, it must be there;* but perhaps those animals are only to be found on the American continent. Our *Pesserais* therefore, in one or the other case, go to the continent, or to the Eastern regions of this great cluster of numerous isles. This however, proves that they change their abode, and transport themselves to very distant places, in order to procure their food, and likewise implies that they are much distressed for the means of procuring it; for they would certainly not remove, if they could provide at all times and seasons a sufficiency at the place of their abode. We did not observe that the *Pesserais* ever used the berries of a kind of ARBUTUS, which, in some places, is found in great abundance; nor can we recollect that they made use of any other vegetables by way of food, though it is probable that they do not entirely neglect them. On the contrary, the inhabitants of *Greenland* gather several kinds of berries to live upon, and likewise eat a kind of sea-weed.

The *Pesserais* whom we saw, were without any other covering than that of a small piece of seal-skin, or a part of a guanacoe-skin, hung over their backs, and seemed not the least concerned upon exposing their genitals; the women had only a piece of white birds skin about six inches square, hardly sufficient to be

---

* The Dutch navigators in the Nassau fleet, found some animals on *Tierra del Fuego*, which they called a kind of deer; but they are probably the guanacoes, common on the neighbouring continent. See *Recueil des Voyages faits pour l'Etablissement de la Comp. des Indes Orientales*, vol. iv.

called a badge of modesty; nor was this custom universal, for some of them were seen without it. The Greenlanders on the contrary, are all well provided with seal-skins, rein-deer-furrs and skins of water-birds; and these skins are further improved into a kind of convenient dress, well suited to the rigours of their winters; nay, they use the guts of certain fish and animals for under garments, or as we would call it instead of shirts and shifts; they formerly employed bones of fish and birds instead of needles, and they split the sinews of the rein-deer and whale, in order to use them instead of thread, which they handle with so much dexterity and neatness, that even our European furriers admire their skill. They are not contented with one set of cloaths, but on solemn occasions are provided with new suits.

Their habitations are adapted to each season; in winter they occupy warm and convenient houses, built of stone, and covered with beams, and a roof, though wood be very scarce among them, as they have no other than what is drifted to their shores, and thrown up by sea; they have windows for admitting day-light, made very curiously of seals guts, and maws of fish; the whole inside is hung with skins, and their elevated bed-places are covered with the finest furrs; and the entrance is contrived in a convenient and ingenious manner. Their method of dressing victuals, over a lamp of train-oil, in a kettle of pot-stone; and in a word, all their contrivances are proofs of their skill and ingenuity; their greater happiness, and their enjoyment of the lowest degree of conveniences. The summer they pass in neat and convenient tents, regularly built of poles, and covered with skins, with a transparent skin hung before the entrance, which admits light, and excludes the wind, rain, and cold. The poor *Pesserais,* on the contrary, wherever they are driven by necessity and hunger, have no other shelter than a few poles stuck in the ground, or small trees, which they find on the spot, tied together by leather straps or bast, and a few bundles of brush-wood fixed over them, by way of covering, all of which is encompassed by some old seals-skins; this kind of hut is open at least one fifth or sixth part of the whole circumference, and in this opening the fire is made, so that they remain exposed to the inclemencies of the weather, and to the rigors of the climate, which was far from being mild in the height of their summer. Notwithstanding all this, it appeared to me to be very singular, that a people, having a great quantity of the finest wood, should be so much at a loss, to make their situation a little more comfortable, by employing this timber, in building with it more convenient houses, and stronger boats. It cannot be said that they have no contrivance for cutting and shaping the wood to various purposes, because the poles, to which they fix their bone shell-hooks, are ten or twelve feet long, perfectly strait, smooth and octangular, which, in my opinion, evidently proves their skill in shaping wood; the same observation may be applied in regard to their cloathing; they have seal-skins, fox and guanacoe furrs; I saw that they had sewed parts of their seal-skins or guanacoe-skin cloaks, with sinews or small leather thongs, and yet they were not ingenious enough to carry this invention of sewing one step farther, by shaping their skins in such a manner, that they might shelter them against the inclemencies of their rigourous climate; these particulars strongly indicate the wretchedness and debased condition of these people. This miserable and forlorn condition of the poor *Pesserais*, appeared dreadful to us, who were accustomed to the conveniences of a civilized life: but habit, together with indolence and stupidity, render these hardships supportable; and they have hardly an idea that their situation can be improved; unless we believe that their indolence alone is so great, as to check even the least progress towards the enjoyment of greater and more desirable conveniencies; they seem to be the victims of the revenge or insolence of a more powerful tribe, who drove them to this inhospitable Southern extremity of the great American continent. All the nations found by the first European discovery, on the immense continent of America, were savages, just removed one degree from animality, rambling in the vast connected forests of this land, in small tribes: they all had very little clothing, and lived chiefly upon the produce of fishing, or the chace. Only two nations had a kind of civilization, and they lived within the tropics, and their improvements and progress towards a civilized state, were, according to their own historical monuments, of a modern date, and probably imported by a few families, whom chance, or cruel necessity, had thrown on these wild and inhospitable shores.

These considerations lead us to some natural inferences, viz. that as the number of inhabitants on the great American continent, was, in general very inconsiderable, their state far remote from civilization, and bordering upon animality; the rigors of the climate, on its extremities severe; the food for human beings very precarious; those men who are found on these extremities, certainly came from more happy and more civilized regions, and that only necessity could make the hardships supportable, which they of course must undergo: that the more wretched and forlorn their situation is, the stronger it proves, that the nation or tribe, of which they are descended, had already, in part, lost the principles of education, common to all happy nations, whom we generally find within the tropics; they must likewise be few in number, because they are descended from a straggling tribe, and are themselves not very prolific, owing perhaps to the want of natural heat, the harshness of their fibres, the poverty of their juices, and other causes, which are the consequences of their mode of living, and of the constitution of their climate. The great Mr. de Montesquieu* was of opinion, that

---

* Montesquieu *Esprit de Loix*, book 23, chap. xiii.

ORIGIN OF
SOCIETIES

the nations feeding chiefly on fish, were the most prolific, because the greasy, oily, particles of fish, seem to supply more of that substance which nature secretes for the purposes of generation, than any other kind of food.[3] This singular opinion, though retailed by many sensible copiers,* is not founded in nature, or confirmed by experience. In Greenland,† and among the Eskimaux,‡ where the natives live chiefly on fish, seals, and oily animal substances, the women seldom bear children oftener than three or four times; five or six births are reckoned a very extra-ordinary instance. The *Pesserais*, whom we saw, had not above two or three children belonging to each family, though their common food consisted of muscles, fish, and seals-flesh. The *New-Zeelanders* absolutely feed on fish, and yet no more than three or four children were found in the most prolific families; which seems strongly to indicate, that feeding on fish by no means contributes to the increase of numbers in a nation, but that there are other causes concurring, which promote population.

From the preceding arguments, it appears that the Pesserais are wretched on account of the inhospitality of their climate, and because they are descended from a degenerated race, and become the remote offspring of such happy tribes as are still possessed of the remains of the original system of education, of which little or nothing passed over with them into Tierra del Fuego.

Wherever we find nations or tribes in nearer or more immediate connexion, with those who had still the system of useful ideas, perpetuated by education, we likewise find the human species, as it were, in more vigour, and better civilization. The ancient Mexicans and Peruvians seem to be descended from those nations, whom *Kublaikhan* sent to conquer Japan, and who were dispersed by a dreadful storm, and it is probable that some of them were thrown on the coast of America, and there formed these two great empires. The Greenlanders and Eskimaux, in the very North of America, came later into that continent than any of the other American nations (the Mexicans and Peruvians excepted), for they are reckoned to be a foreign tribe, and they appear to be of a different race of men, by the language, the dress, the features, size, form and habit of body, and manners: probably they came from some of the numerous isles, which form the connexion between America and Asia. All these nations had better regulations and principles than their neighbours, and human nature seems with them to have been in more vigour, than with the rest of the American savage tribes; their later connexions with, and descent from Asiatic nations, accounts for the remaining ideas of arts and principles of social life, and of civilization; and likewise for the laws, regula-

* De Saintfoix *Essais Historiques sur Paris*, tom. ii. p. 181.
† Crantz's *History of Greenland*, vol. i. p. 161.
‡ Lieut. Curtis, in the *Philos. Trans.* vol. lxiv. part ii. p. 385.

tions and form of government introduced among them; but the *Pesserais* are in a quite different condition: for being descended from the straggling American tribes who themselves were much degenerated, they could not derive from them any idea of education, or any principles of social life, nor any regulations approaching to those which are usually to be met with, in civilized nations.

We may add to this, that their numbers are few, and that though their country be very little inferior in size to one moiety of Ireland, hardly 2000 inhabitants are found on this great extent of land.

In these small wild tribes, it is almost certain, that the still smaller societies, whom navigators have occasionally found, were nearly related to one another; which makes it probable, that they only keep together because they still find some benefit from their union and mutual assistance; and this makes the Europeans, who are used to civil society, believe, that the ties of friendship and blood still unite them; but it is quite otherwise, for it is not the interest of savages to form great bodies, in countries that are not rich in food and animal productions; as soon as they think themselves strong enough to set up a new family, they separate and remove to parts unoccupied by other families, where they have a prospect of supporting their wives and children, and perhaps a few younger brethren or sisters. This evidently points out the true cause of the debasement and degeneracy in savages; they can neither profit by the assistance, nor by the inventions and improvements of others, and the smallness of their numbers affords but a bad chance for a multiplicity of inventions or improvements. The instructions and good advice of long experience are lost to them, and the constant necessity of procuring a precarious food for the family, robs them of that leisure, which is necessary for instruction, and a more finished education. As soon as their numbers increase, that the country can no more feed the inhabitants, they must of course either oppress and expel, or kill others, in order to occupy their fishing and hunting places; or they are obliged to migrate to an unoccupied country; or they must devise new methods of procuring food with ease for their increased numbers. Seldom is their indolence conquered to that degree, that they migrate or become industrious, and find out a new kind of food, and a new way of living. Oppression is commonly represented to their minds as the easiest and surest method, they therefore dislodge their neighbours, or put them to death, and take their wives and children for their slaves and drudges. Thus grown elated with success, and powerful by extent of land, and enjoying those advantages, which supply them with the means of supporting themselves with greater ease, and making life somewhat more comfortable; they endeavour to extend their dominion, and every success enables them to emerge more and more from that state of debasement in which they were plunged; or if they should be opposed, checked, and even routed in the attempt, they will certainly be prompted to exert themselves again, that

ORIGIN OF
SOCIETIES

they may not lose that superiority which they had once attained; or they will study to make the misfortunes which their ambition had drawn upon them, less consequential, and to avert the miseries which otherwise would fall upon them. All this of course rouses their minds from that indolence and inactivity with which they were oppressed, and they in every respect conquer somewhat of that degeneracy to which they were reduced: for the human mind, left to itself in a continued course of uniformity either in happiness or wretchedness, has very little exertion; but add to it the springs of passions, which are most powerful in such tribes as are least improved in their mental faculties, and we shall find it amazing to what length they may carry a set of men, who lend no ear to any principles of morality, and who adjust their notions of rectitude by the extent of power only. Though naturally this principle cannot carry them very far, because they must sooner or later meet with a powerful opposition, from the united efforts of such tribes as will not lose their liberty; it has however, in general the benefit of communicating to all the tribes a willingness to exert themselves, to unite the interest of more families against the oppression of others, and to give them that dawning of civil society, which is alone the great improver and preserver of human happiness, in its physical, moral, and social sense.

If therefore the savages by an happy exertion of their physical and mental powers, rise one step higher in the class of rational beings, their situation no doubt, becomes upon the whole more improved; but at the same time this very state, though more vigorous and more active, often breaks out into such enormities, as make the heart ache, and are humiliating to human nature. New Zeeland offers us an instance of this assertion: whosoever casts an eye upon them with a view to compare their situation with that of the Pesserais, no doubt will allow that of the New-Zeelanders to be greatly preferable in every respect. They inhabit a milder climate both by situation and temperature, which has softened the fibres and organs, and taken off that rigour which certainly influences the mental and moral faculties of the Pesserais, by narrowing their minds, and brutalizing their feelings. From this somewhat less constricted and harsh state of their organization, their minds have acquired a larger and more liberal circle of ideas, improved by a greater population, and the advantages arising from thence by mutual assistance, improvements, instruction, advice, and education; their minds are bold and fearless. They are not without acuteness to comprehend sound reason, and not without docility in adopting such ideas and informations as are necessary and eligible in their situation. This has convinced them of the necessity and convenience of mutual attachments, and the propriety of forming larger societies, in order to preserve their liberty and independence; and as their actions are guided by violent passions, it is no wonder that we find among barbarous nations instances of fidelity and friendship, carried on with an enthusiasm, which would do honour to the most civilized nations, nay, which are hardly to be met with in a superior degree, in this age of refinement; unless we look for it into poems and romances, in the district of fiction and fable. Their principles of honesty, and public faith are noble, and romantic; but as they are jealous of their liberty and independence, the least thing is construed by them into offence, and they are too often ready to revenge an imaginary injury. Strangers especially are looked upon as persons to whom less forbearance is due than to their own friends. The wild notions of independence degenerated into licentiousness, arm their minds with an intrepedity, which would be meritorious, were it used only on real provoca-tion; but they work themselves up into a frantic madness, run into the most emi-nent dangers, and fight with a perseverance, which proves that death is no evil which they dread. In victory they are insolent, cruel, and vindictive, carrying it to the most unnatural and inhuman degree, viz. that of feasting upon the victims of their victorious prowess. They treat their women in the most oppressive manner, like the most abject drudges, or slaves, and the parents and relations frequently sold to the strangers the favours of the females, even against their will; which circumstances certainly proceed from the injurious and overbearing notions entertained in regard to their women, whom they do not think to be helpmates, but creatures intended for the satisfaction of brutish desires only, and destined to confirm them in ideleness and indolence. This idea prevailed so far, that we frequently saw the little boys strike their mothers, while the fathers stood by and would not permit the mothers to correct their children.[4] They have all a passion for ornaments, and dress; and they decorate the most common tools of husbandry or their arms, in a curious manner with volutes and scrolls, not altogether without taste. They are fond of romantic and fabulous tales, of music, songs and dances; even their fights are begun with a martial cadenced song and dance. They have some ideas of religion, and accounts of various invisible divinities, and a belief of the existence of the souls of their friends; but superstition seems not to have gained much ground among them, as far as we could observe. They have however, rites and customs peculiar to themselves, which they perform on certain occa-sions: for instance, in forming friendships and making peace, in announcing war and burying their dead, which last sometimes are sunk, it seems, in the sea. The natives of New-Zeeland, build some of their houses and cottages with an elegance and neatness, which makes them far superior to the wretched hovels of the inhabitants of Tierra del Fuego: for they are well covered on all sides with thatch, and the insides we found lined with reeds, so that they really had an appearance of neatness; and we sometimes saw several huts separated from the rest by inclo-sures of thatch, which I suppose was done with a view to screen them still more from the raging winds, and to shelter their fires, which are commonly made at the entrance of their huts. Their boats are stronger than those of Tierra del Fuego, and not without taste in their ornaments, nor without contrivance in their whole structure and shape, which, with the dexterous management of their paddles gives them an easy and swift motion. Their dress not only covers their nudities, but affords them shelter against the inclemencies of their climate, which is less vigorous in winter than that of Tierra del Fuego in summer: it is likewise woven with neatness, encompassed with borders, worked into various patterns of black, brown and white, ornamented on its corners with pieces of dogs-skin, and sometimes covered all over with patches of white and black dogs-skin, disposed in regular compartments. They wear over their garments a rug, made of the filaments of the flax-plant worked into a kind of mat, like thatch on its outside, which they call *Kegheea:* this is so very well calculated to keep off the wind, the rain, and the spray of the sea, that it is amazing that the poor inhabitants of Tierra del Fuego, who must depend solely on the sea for their food, in a climate remarkably colder, and more boisterous than that of New-Zeeland, have not hitherto devised a better and more convenient use of their seals and guanacoes skins.

The agriculture which is so well and so carefully carried on in many parts of the Northern island, incontestibly proves the superiority of the New-Zeelanders over the inhabitants of Tierra del Fuego. So that it might be superfluous in me to take up more time in multiplying the proofs of this so evident truth.

It seems likewise equally obvious, that the more improved state of the New-Zeelanders, is owing to several causes, viz. the mildness of the climate, the greater population, and also that they are more immediately descended from such tribes as had more remains of the general principles of education. In the extremities of the Southern isle of New-Zeeland, perhaps the numbers may be only equal to those of the Pesserais, but being more happy in regard to the mildness of their climate, and the preservation of such ideas and improvements as were handed down to them, by their more happy and less degenerated ancestors; even these straggling families are, in my opinion, to be ranked higher in the scale of human beings.

There is however one circumstance already alluded to, which seems to degrade them, viz. the odious and cruel custom of eating those, who are killed in their frequent feuds and petty wars. This has been represented by a late ingenious writer,* as originally introduced among the New-Zeelanders, by distress and hunger; but I cannot help dissenting from his opinion: for I did not find that these nations ever are so much distressed; they have prudence enough to provide in the proper season, stores of all kinds: when they catch more fish than they can eat, they carefully dry, and lay them up; their women go frequently up the hills, which

* Dr. Hawkesworth's *Compilation,* vol. iii. book ii. ch. 9.

are covered to an immense extent with fern, and dig up the roots, which they likewise dry, and preserve as a food to which they may have recourse, when neither fish nor any other kind of eatables are to be procured. We saw great quantities of these provisions in their huts, and frequently found them employed in preparing both fish and fern-roots, for the bad season. We were likewise told by Capt. Crozet, the friend and companion of the brave but unfortunate Capt. Marion; that when he got possession of the hippah or fortress of the New-Zeelanders, in the Bay of Islands, he found immense stores of dry fish, fern-roots, and other roots, in houses filled solely with these provisions.[5] It seems therefore, to me, by no means probable, that a nation perfectly convinced of the necessity of providing against the season of distress, and so very careful and active in collecting stores of eatables, should nevertheless have been induced by necessity and hunger, to eat the corses of those slain in battle. Nay, we heard from the natives, that they never eat those, who die a natural death, but either sink them in the sea, or bury them under ground: were necessity the true cause of this custom, why should they not feast upon the dead who formed the same community with them? But it will be objected, that hunger may be allowed so far to stifle all sentimental feelings of humanity, that they might suffer themselves to satisfy its cravings upon the corse of a slain foe, but that it will never carry them so far as to feed upon the flesh of those who lived in the same society with them. How specious soever this objection may be, it never can persuade me that hunger will make these nice distinctions, in a people, who have not those tender, humane feelings and emotions, of which we are capable, in so highly civilized a state, with a refined education, and principles infinitely superior to theirs.*

But I had reason to believe, that all the nations of the South Seas were formerly cannibals, even in the most happy and fertile climates, where they still live upon the almost spontaneous fruits, though their population be extremely great. The natives of Tanna gave us more than once to understand, that if we penetrated far into the country against their will, and without their permission, they would kill us, cut our bodies up, and eat them: when we purposely affected to misunderstand this last part of their story, and interpreted it, as if they were going to give us something good to eat, they convinced us by signs which could not be misinterpreted, that they would tear with their teeth the flesh from our arms and legs.[6]

---

* If the account given in the life of Pierre Viaud is to be credited; for the credibility of which, there are the greatest reasons, founded upon the joint testimonies of several respectable persons, and of such people who had no inducement to compliment the author with their testimonies; it may serve to prove still more the enormities, to which the rage of hunger may drive some wretches; and it likewise shews, how easily the more refined feelings of humanity are overcome, by the horrors of unconquerable want.

In Mallicollo, we had likewise some intimation that they were cannibals. The Taheiteans frequently enumerated to us isles inhabited by men-eaters: for instance, they said, that beyond Tabuamanoo is a high island called Manua, whose inhabitants "have but very few canoes, are ferocious, have wild and furious eyes, and eat men:" nay, we were at last told, that they themselves had formerly been *Tahéäi*, i.e. men-eaters. As the inhabitants of New-Zeeland certainly belong to the same race of people with the Taheiteans, it is evident that this custom has been common to the whole tribe. What is still more remarkable, it seems from thence to follow, that the want of a sufficiency of food in this isle, which is less fertile than the tropical countries, cannot have occasioned their cannibalism, since even the inhabitants of the happy and fertile tropical isles were men-eaters, without being forced to it by distress and hunger, and we must therefore certainly be convinced that there must be some other cause, which originally introduced this unnatural custom.

If we examine the whole oeconomy of their societies, we find that their education is the chief cause of all these enormities. The men train up the boys in a kind of liberty, which at last degenerates into licentiousness: they suffer not the mothers to strike their petulant, unruly, and wicked sons, for fear of breaking that

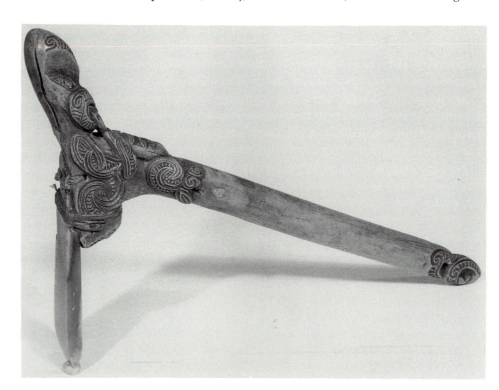

Toki pou tangata, Maori adze described by Forster as "a hatchet of green stone, the handle curiously carved" (see Gathercole, *"From the Islands of the South Seas, 1773–4"*). L. 460 mm. Collected by Johann Reinhold Forster. Pitt Rivers Museum, Oxford (1886.1.1159).

spirit of independency, which they seem to value above all things, and as the most necessary qualification for their societies; this naturally brings on an irascibility, which, in the men, cannot brook any controul, action or word, that can be construed according to their manners and principles into an affront, or injury; inflamed by passion, they are impatient to wreak their vengeance: wild fancy paints the injury so atrocious, that it must be washed in blood; they know not where to stop, and being more and more incensed by the power of imagination, they go to battle with a loud and barbarous song, each feature is distorted, each limb is set in a cadenced motion; they brandish their destructive weapons, and stamp upon the ground with their feet, while the whole band join in an awful, tremendous groan; the song begins a new, and at last the whole troop is lost in frenzy and rage; they fall to, and every one fights as if animated by furies; and destruction and carnage await the routed party: whosoever falls, is murdered without mercy, and the corses of the slain immediately serve to glut the inhuman appetites of the conquerors. When the bounds of humanity are once passed, and the reverence due to the bright image of divinity, is conquered by frenzy, the practice soon becomes habitual, especially as it is reckoned among the honours due to the conqueror, to feast upon the wretched victims of savage victory; add to this,

ORIGIN OF
SOCIETIES

Detail of the head of a *taiaha*, called "a battle-ax or halberd" by Forster (quoted in Gathercole, *"From the Islands of the South Seas, 1773–4"*). L. 1900 mm. Collected by Johann Reinhold Forster. Pitt Rivers Museum, Oxford (1886.1.1465).

that a nation which has no other animal food, than a few stupid dogs and fish, will soon reconcile themselves to human flesh, which, according to several known instances,* is reputed to be one of the most palatable dishes.

To us, indeed, who are used to live in better regulated societies, where for many years backwards, anthropophagy has been in disuse, it is always a horrid idea, that men should eat men. But I cannot help observing, that this barbarism is one of the steps, by which debased humanity, is gradually prepared for a better state of happiness; in the savage state, where man is just one remove from animality, wherein he has no other impulse for action, than want, he soon sinks into stupid indolence, which more and more debases all his powers and faculties: but scarce have the passions begun to act as the main springs of human actions, when man is carried from the first excentric action to a second, from one enormity to another, and from this or that shocking scene of cruelty, barbarism and unhumanity to others of a higher degree: these would grow to an outrageous height, were it not for certain circumstances, which at last naturally put a total stop to those inhuman practices. If therefore barbarians, who still preserve the shocking custom of eating men, meet with other tribes that have the same barbarous custom, and are strong or active enough, either by chance or bravery, to check their neighbours in their inhuman wrongs, they will soon be sensible, that their own numbers must decrease by these losses; they will therefore grow more cautious in provoking their anger or vengeance by new outrages, and will gradually become sober enough to be convinced, that it is more reasonable to lay aside the custom of eating men, and that a living man is more useful than one that is dead or roasted; they in consequence change their unnatural cruelty into a more humane behaviour; though it be not quite free from injustice and interest, it is however, less destructive to mankind, and prepares the way to a more humane and benevolent scene. Or let us on the other hand suppose, these barbarians meet with unmerited success, and always rout their neighbours, as often as they take the field; these humiliated foes, in order to avoid their utter ruin and destruction, will at last offer terms of accommodation; and though their condition should become as abject as possible, they will prefer it to a greater and unavoidable evil, involving the whole ruin of their tribe; the conquerors will soon discover, that by preserving the lives of their subjected foes, they may reap considerable advantages from their labour and united force, which will gradually improve their condition, and render them more and more happy.

---

* In the province of Matto-grosso, in Brazil, a woman told his Excellency Chevalier Pinto, who was then Governor, that human flesh was extremely palatable, especially if taken from a young person. And during the last dearth in Germany, a shepherd killed first a young person, to satisfy the cravings of hunger with his flesh, and afterwards several more, in order to please his luxurious palate.

This idea might be deemed imaginary; but upon examination, it will appear to be established in truth. In the Northern Isle of New-Zeeland, in a district of more than 90 miles, Captain Cook, found in his former voyage, the name of a great chief, called TEIRATOO, to be generally acknowledged;[7] and it should seem from thence, that the small tribes under his dominion, were either subdued by him and his adherents; or that they found it their interest, upon their own account, to acknowledge his authority, to become his subjects upon certain conditions, and thus to form one large political body, for greater security and defence; the better regulations, a security both of person and property, and a more impartial administration of justice, mentioned in the same account, prove beyond dispute, that from the violent state of cannibalism, the New-Zeelanders will soon arrive in their most populous districts, to a more settled and more happy state. For though the subjects for TEIRATOO still eat men, this custom is rather kept up on account of the vicinity of such tribes as still retain the same custom, otherwise their more improved situation would hardly admit of it.

"*Denique coetera animantia in suo genere probe degunt: congregari videmus & stare contra dissimilia: Leonum feritas inter se non dimicat: serpentum morsus non petit serpentes: ne maris quidem belluae ac pisces, nisi in diversa genera, soeviunt: at hercule! homini plurima ex homine sunt mala.*"
  Plin. *Hist. Nat.* lib. vii. Prooemii fine[8]

It is either the fault of some tribes, who are wanton, quarrelsome, and overbearing, when they are driven by more powerful nations, to such a desperate situation, that they become degenerate, and their offspring sinks to the lowest condition that can be intailed on mankind; or it is rather owing to cruel chance or accident, that they are brought into a forlorn state, wherein their progeny lingers for some time: in both cases Providence has wisely made a provision for preventing the perpetuity of misery and wretchedness in a nation, by infusing originally in the human soul, such faculties and powers, that when unfolded, or set in motion by unforeseen accidents, shall at last invigorate the minds of men, and supply them with the necessary means and strength for emerging from their debased condition, and enable them to resume gradually a higher rank in the scale of rational beings. The poor inhabitants of Tierra del Fuego, act only by instinct, by necessity and want, and in consequence of the accidental occurrences, which chance, or the natural changes of the elements and seasons throw in their way; but a more frequent intercourse with Europeans, or some other unforeseen accident, for instance, the fortuitous invention of iron, or some other useful metal; a discovery of the utility of some vegetable or tree in their climates;

ORIGIN OF
SOCIETIES

a new devise for catching fish, birds, and quadrupeds, in a more easy and expeditious manner than they have hitherto been accustomed to, must doubtless, sooner or later, bring on a revolution in their condition; new manners, new customs, a change of diet, of dress, weapons and utensils, must gradually produce a total change of their way of thinking and acting, introduce an alteration in their temper, facilitate the better regulation and security of their societies, and deliver them from that stupidity, torpor, and indolence with which they are now oppressed: for when once the mind is enlightened with new ideas, and new combinations, and a field opened to fancy and imagination in the recital of their actions, in their songs, dances, and various other representations; the passions, the great source of action in human life, will kindle in their breasts that Promethean fire, which will infuse strength and vigor into all the transactions of the community. Thus ought we to admire and adore that Providence, which, by the most simple means, always effects its intended purpose, and out of paternal care and tenderness, leaves the most degenerated race of men, not altogether destitute of faculties, powers, and means, by which they may emerge from their forlorn condition: nay, the very passions, which by their abuse and lawless condition, but too often become the causes of dangerous evils in human society, are employed by the wise Governor of the world, as subordinate causes, to forward the happiness of mankind, and to bring them gradually to a more mild, virtuous state, and to happiness of every kind. But at the same time that my most inward thoughts are prostrate in adoration before the great Maker and Father of the souls of all flesh; my heart is filled with the warmest wishes that it may please the alwise Providence soon to raise this brave and generous race of my fellow creatures from their unnatural state, to a condition, where humanity may characterise each action; that fellow-feeling, kindness, and universal charity may victoriously spread throughout all these barbarous nations, and restore that reverential awe due to man, the noblest work of God on Earth.

> . . . *Deus ille fuit* . . .
> *Qui princeps vitae rationem invenit eam, quae*
> *Nunc appellatur sapientia: quippe per artem*
> *Fluctibus e tantis vitam, tantisque tenebris,*
> *In tam tranquillo, & tam clarâ luce locavit.*
>   Lucretius, l. v[9]

SECTION VI

General Principles of National Happiness —
Increase of Population — Causes of Union —
Cultivation — Property — Society — Government

TUM GENUS HUMANUM PRIMUM MOLLESCERE COEPIT.
   Lucretius, lib. v[1]

The odious humiliating scenes of barbarism are so irksome and so tedious to the mind of the observer, that it gives pleasure to know that they are past. It is therefore not a common degree of selfdenial, fortitude, and heroism, required in a man, to resign his whole life to the education and improvement of barbarians; to have the scenes of cruelty and of debasement day after day before his eyes, to see his benevolent intentions opposed and defeated, and if any improvements take place, to observe their slow and tardy growth. On the other hand, it is next to impossible, to describe the pleasing satisfaction, and the agreeable feelings arising at the sight of happy scenes, in a nation abounding with benevolence, and shewing the first blossoms of social feelings. The passing through the gloomy scenes of the first, is a flight through utter and through middle darkness.

And now that I am returning to the bright regions of tropical countries, I feel the powerful influence of the great fountain of aetherial light, that gladdens every heart.

> *. . . Thee I revisit safe,*
> *And feel thy sov'reign vital lamp.*
>   Milton[2]

In order to treat the subject I have undertaken, with that order, clearness, and conviction, which its extensive utility, and interesting doctrines require, let us in a short excursion on the general principles of social life, and on the advantages and happiness, which reasonably may be expected in civilized societies, fix some ideas that may lead to the investigation of this great and interesting doctrine.

Man, such as he every where is, has a strong desire of being as happy as his circumstances will admit. The natural and most pressing wants, soon convince him that he cannot enjoy by himself even a moderate share of happiness; and that uniting with other human beings, is the most effectual means, not only of procuring the greatest degree of happiness possible in his situation; but also of insuring to him with certainty, an undisturbed enjoyment of it. He will soon be sensible that his own happiness procured by the assistance of the united efforts of other human beings, depend likewise upon their happiness; for no one who is doomed to be under continual pain, or overwhelmed with misery, will sincerely endeavour to contribute to the satisfaction of another, if he finds himself more wretched upon every effort to increase the happiness of his fellow creature. It must therefore be the interest of each individual who wishes to be happy, to promote the prosperity of the whole community to which he belongs; and from whom he expects acts of reciprocal kindness, that may tend to improve his own happiness. The happiness of every human being living in a society, depends upon the following principles.

First, Man has an organic body, requiring food, habitation, and dress, as means conducive to its support; and many other things necessary, in order to acquire these articles without great labour and peril, or in other words, to make life more agreeable and easy; these we would call the *principles of* PHYSICAL HAPPINESS.

Secondly, Man is likewise a rational, thinking, and freely acting being; his happiness therefore requires that he be able to procure the means of improving his intellectual faculties by instruction, and to preserve the rights and privileges of a free agency, which however, ought to be directed by charity and benevolence towards the promotion of his own happiness, and that of his fellow creatures. In a word, he ought to be enabled to live in a manner becoming the dignity of a rational and free being; and from thence we may collect the *principles of* MORAL HAPPINESS.

Lastly, As he is become together with others, a member of a community, with a view to the promotion of mutual happiness; he expects to derive from this union or society the means of enjoying with certainty, in a perfect and undisturbed manner his physical and moral happiness. Herein consist *the principles of* CIVIL OR SOCIAL FELICITY.

From hence it becomes evident, that whenever men are found to live in societies for the promotion of mutual happiness, they ought to enjoy *physical, moral* and *social felicity* in the highest degree possible, in their situation and circumstances.

But besides the abovementioned division of happiness we must allow, that it naturally must have many degrees, depending on the following circumstances.

First, The more *various* and *multiplied* the objects of *physical, moral,* and *social* enjoyment are, which a man or a whole society really can make their own, the greater must their happiness be; and on the other hand, the fewer and the less varied the enjoyments, and objects of enjoyment are, the more circumscribed and small is their happiness.

Secondly, The *longer the duration* of enjoyments of a man or society of men is, the happier they will find themselves: and the more fleeting and transitory their enjoyments are, in the same degree, must they experience unhappiness.

Thirdly, The more *extensive* and *general the influence* of all the enjoyment of a man or a society, is in regard to their physical, moral and social felicity, the more their happiness must be increased; and on the contrary, if their enjoyments have no effect or influence upon their own happiness, or that of others, then indeed it hardly deserves the name of happiness, or it is at least very inconsiderable.

By these few principles are we enabled to judge, with a tolerable degree of precision, of the happiness and civilization of the nations we met with in the course of our voyage; especially if we have a retrospect to the causes which promote felicity, and which hinder the same, or at least check its progress and more rapid increase.

For when men live in a genial climate, and enjoy the advantages of a happy organization, NATURE seems to do every thing vigorously, in promoting their happiness. Thus we see the early improvements, grandeur and happiness of the Assyrian and Egyptian empires; their climate is one of the mildest and most temperate; its inhabitants, even in their present degenerated, barbarous state, are endowed with a lively temper, and quick parts; nor are they destitute of good-nature and benevolence: no wonder, therefore, that ancient history is so copious on the state of their population, wealth, opulence, and happiness, which cannot be controverted, as the vast monuments and stupendous buildings of these nations are still subsisting, and witness the truth of their historians.

In climates nearly approaching the mild temperature of the former, the inhabitants are blessed with an organization proportioned to the softness of their climate, though probably descended from tribes that came from more rigid climates, and had been less happy in the preservation of the original systems of education; among these, national felicity could not be brought about with success, without the assistance of ART. Cecrops, Triptolemus, Theseus, Solon, Pisistratus, Miltiades and Aristides,[3] were the men, who, by art, assisted nature in Attica, and it required the efforts of the best and wisest men, during a space of 1130 years, before the Athenians could attain that pitch of happiness under Pericles, which made their empire the most respectable and happy in the contemporary civilized part of the world.

In climates still more unfavourable and rigid, not only the assistance of art, but that of CREATIVE physical POWER, as well as that of CREATIVE genius, is required to insure the happiness of the inhabitants, whose fibres had contracted a congenial roughness and rigidity, and who are continually subject to numberless checks and hindrances, to every improvement leading to national felicity. Such was the power and genius of Peter the Great; who, in half a century, raised his nation from indolence, barbarism, and stupidity, to that degree of happiness and grandeur, which it now enjoys under the mild and benevolent legislation of CATHARINE THE GREAT.

Such likewise are the various gradations of the happiness of the inhabitants of the South-Sea Islands; some have attained, in the course of nature, a degree of felicity, which is proportioned to their situation and condition; others are behind-hand in improvements and happiness, and can never attain it, unless nature be assisted by human art; in others, again, a whole new creation is required, to procure and to insure them that happiness which would set them upon a level with the first mentioned happy tribes. There are besides, so many concurring circumstances, that either promote or retard national felicity, that it is impossible, either to enumerate them all, or to describe the various hues of happiness arising from their different combinations. This, however, may be added to the former observations, that too great irritability, or too great rigidity of the human organization, equally oppose the progress of improvements and social felicity; the one causes a restless, passionate temper, in a fervent climate; the other creates stupidity, dullness and indolence, in the rigid and cold regions, found at the two polar extremities of our globe: and how difficult it is to conquer either the one or the other, may be easily proved from the hitherto fruitless attempts in civilizing the negroes of our plantations, or the Greenlanders and Laplanders of the North. I will not, however, deny, that perhaps the most proper means have not hitherto been employed, in bringing this difficult undertaking, even so far, that a rational probability of a very distant success, might be expected. The above-mentioned articles form the point of view, under which we now would wish every body to consider the more civilized state of the tropical nations in the South-Seas.

We found the isles in the South-Sea very populous; and from the accounts of former navigation, they were so, more than 180 years ago, and in the very condition, in regard to happiness, in which we ourselves observed them; so that we may be sure, that their civil or social establishment is of a long standing.

It is hardly credible, that the inhabitants were very numerous when they first occupied these isles; but the ease and facility with which they can support their lives, and satisfy the natural and most pressing wants, the early puberty in so mild and so happy a climate, the few diseases which are observed in nations used to a simple and salubrious food, are certainly reasons for supposing that they soon increased, and gradually filled the islands which they had occupied.

The first inhabitants had not the least difficulty in procuring their subsistence, as the sea and the fruits of various trees, sufficiently afforded them the necessary food: but in proportion as their numbers increased, their subsistence of course must become more precarious in an isle, which only yields, spontaneously, the necessaries for a certain determined number of inhabitants; they therefore soon found themselves under the necessity of devising some method of supplying the necessary food, principally by cultivating those plants, upon the wild produce of which they formerly lived. They began regularly to plant coco-nut-palms, bananas, South-Sea apples, yamboes, and bread-fruit trees, together with the yam, the sweet potatoe, the two kinds of eddoes, the tacca and the sugar-cane. These plantations being the work of the industry and foresight of some individuals, gave them a right to reap their productions; and as their example was soon followed by people equally solicitous for their preservation, this method of raising a sufficiency of food by industry and labour, became more universal; and when they found that the right of reaping the fruit of their own industry, was sometimes invaded by the indolent, the powerful, and the desperate, they began to form associations for the defence of their plantations, on which their very existence depended; they consequently stipulated, first among themselves, not to destroy one anothers plantations, to defend them jointly against the violence of others, and to give one another mutual assistance; in this manner the plantations were increased, extended, and in a manner surrounded by those of others; then every one began to look upon the land occupied by his trees or roots, as having a more immediate connexion with his person, or with the family or society to which he belonged; and hence arose the first ideas of property. Thus were gradually introduced certain regulations, agreed upon by mutual consent, and thus were soon formed those customary laws, which more or less take place among the nations that have property. The experience of several years soon taught them to distinguish the soil and season, most proper for each of the plants and roots; the most easy and useful method of preparing the soil for the reception and propagation of them, together with the means of averting danger from those vegetables, which are of so great consequence to them: the preservation of these eatables, by way of store, again required new efforts of genius and several experiments; and lastly, the preparation of them into various dishes, in order to avoid sameness and uniformity, still enriched their knowledge, and increased the stock of their useful ideas, and practical operations. Isles are, on account of their circumscribed size, more apt to promote and to accelerate civilization, than large continents; for in these, the inhabitants having too much room to roam over the country, and to disperse, in case of a disgust, or offence, they are prevented from entering into associations, and from making useful regulations relative to mutual assistance and mutual defence; and as they meet either with a sufficiency of spontaneous fruits, on a large tract of unoccupied land, or have opportunities to live by the chace, or by fishing, they constantly refuse to provide for their subsistence by a laborious, toilsome cultivation. However, in small islands, where the numbers of people are too inconsiderable for affording mutual security and assistance, or for forming a powerful society, and where there is no chance either for cultivation varied according to the difference of soil and exposures, or for extensive plantations, there likewise, it is in vain to expect so well regulated societies, as in isles of a tolerable size, and of various exposures and soils. It is therefore in my opinion evident, that the largest of the tropical isles, when all the other circumstances concur, must be the happiest and most civilized, as none of them is of too great extent.

Otaheitee and the neighbouring Society isles, are in this point nearer to happiness than any other nations we met with. They have a greater variety of food and in greater abundance, than any of the other nations. Their dress is like-wise more varied, a kind of refinement this, which most of the other nations either entirely want, or at least in a very imperfect manner possess. Their habita-tions are clean and roomy, and those of the better sort of people are even neat and elegant, as far as these advantages may be carried in its first rude beginning.

They have ideas of many things, which never occurred to other nations of the South Sea, their intellectual faculties, enlarged by instruction and exercise, are capable of comprehending, retaining, reproducing, and combining ideas, and though extremely quick of perception, and lively in their tempers, they are how-ever, equally jealous of their liberty and free agency; and what is still more happy, the simple but rational education, the happiest organization and the mildness of their climate concur in forming their minds for benevolence, and in filling their hearts with soft and tender feelings, and a charitable disposition. Any foreigner endeavouring to ingratiate himself with these generous friendly people, will soon succeed, though they can reap no benefit or advantage from a connection with him; and if he should happen to be sick, indisposed, distressed, or only tired, or wanting some refreshment; they will all vie one with another to assist, to nurse and to refresh him. Their hearts are capable of the warmest attachment, of the most generous friendship, and of the most tender connexions, of which, in our mixed and degenerating societies, we have very few instances; perhaps none at all, where such a disinterested, generous love, or such an enthusiasm of passion forms the basis of the tender connexion. Having myself felt all the tender emo-tions of a parent, during the soft moments of filial endearment, I flatter myself that I was in this case no incompetent judge; however I must confess that several of their children, and even of their more grown youths, had such winning and captivating means of ingratiating themselves with me; they shewed such confi-dence, openness, and grateful returns to the little trifling presents I used to make them; they became so attached to me, and were so studious of rendering me some small services, and of warning me against the thievish practices of some of their countrymen, that my heart could not resist their insinuating and innocently kind behaviour. I felt for many of them emotions, which were not so far distant from paternal affection and complacency, as might be expected, when we recollect the great difference of our manners and our way of thinking. But I found likewise on this occasion, what a great and venerable blessing benevolence is; when it is no longer the fashionable cant, borrowed from a favourite poet, or a moral romance, and dwelling only on mens lips; but when this best gift of heaven sits enthroned in the heart, fills the soul with gracious sensations, and prompts all our faculties to expressions of good-nature and kindness: then only does it connect all mankind as it were into one family; youths of distant nations become brethren, and the older people of one nation, find children in the offspring of the other. All those distinctions which ambition, wealth, and luxury, have introduced, are levelled, and the inhabitant of the polar region, finds a warm and generous friend in the torrid zone or in the opposite hemisphere. Still my heart was filled with tender affliction, and my eyes overflowed with tears of genuine sorrow, when I perceived that our own civilized countries, notwithstanding the numberless improvements they had received from the establishment of excellent laws, and the cultivation of arts and sciences; notwithstanding the frequent occasions of still greater improvement, and the glorious encouragement to virtue and morality, were far outdone in real goodness and benevolence by a set of innocent people, so much our inferiors in many other respects; and I could not help repeatedly wishing, that our civilized Europeans might add to their many advantages, that innocence of heart and genuine simplicity of manners, that spirit of benevolence, and real goodness, which these my new acquired friends so eminently possessed.

The Taheiteans as individuals, not only have the several good qualities above mentioned, of a domestic kind, but they are likewise sensible of the great advantages of a social or civil union: and as far as our imperfect knowledge of their language; our short stay amongst them, and the desultory instruction of *Maheine* and *O-Mai* would permit, I have reasons to think, that the beginning of their civil society is founded on paternal authority, and is of the patriarchal kind. The husband and the wife of his bosom, whom love unites by the silken ties of matrimony, form the first society. This union is, in these happy regions, first founded on the call of nature, in mutual assistance, and the sweet hopes of seeing themselves reproduced in a numerous offspring. In more degenerated nations, matrimonial union takes place from brutal appetite, is grounded upon the satisfaction of sensuality, the expectation of assistance from persons, whom oppression and custom has condemned to become drudges, and lastly the idea of gaining more strength and power from a numerous family of children. On the contrary, the mildness of the climate, the happiness of organization, and the kind and benevolent temper of this people, together with their more enlightened intellects, contribute very much to refine and to ennoble that soft passion which is the first beginning of this congenial harmony; and hence the brutish instincts, which were wants of the same low rank with hunger and thirst, are raised to a lasting, virtuous passion. This refinement of mutual love and matrimonial complacency, produces those tender regards with which this happy passion inspires its votaries for the beloved object; and it creates that mutual happiness, which is the result of all the more refined manners, and of their more polished behaviour towards one another. The offspring of such a happy couple early imbibe by the example of their parents, that kindness and benevolence, and those refined sentiments of love and happiness, which contribute so much to confirm the felicity of their parents, and wish to reduce them to practice, as soon as they feel the call of nature and find a partner whose sentiments are in unison with their own; so that these simple, but more exalted ideas of matrimonial union, are thus propagated and perpetuated in the progeny of a virtuous and tender couple. But before they attain that age of discretion and maturity, the fond parents take peculiar care of their education; they frequently check the wild flights of their unruly passions, and instill order, moderate industry, and the principles of benevolence and gratitude into their tender minds. I have seen mothers punishing obstinacy and disobedience, and though extremely fond of their children, they nevertheless are sensible enough thus far to do violence to their own feelings, that their children may not acquire a habit of ingratitude, obstinacy, and immorality; I have likewise heard them expostulating with their unruly little ones, and expressing their displeasure at their conduct; all which proves that they have ideas of moral rectitude, of order and filial subordination, and of the necessity of instilling these principles early into the minds of their children. Nor is this careful education without the good effects, which ought to be the consequence of it: for we saw many a family, where every individual belonging to it, gave strong marks of an attachment to the rest of the family, and evident proofs of those ties of benevolence which united them all. The younger part of them shewed reverence and respect to the older individuals, and at the least and most distant danger were alarmed and anxious for the welfare and safety of their parents. The injunctions of the parents were executed, with a readiness and truly exemplary affection. The father seemed to be the soul which animated the whole body of the family by his superior wisdom, benevolence and experience; in a word, they all assist one another and contribute their share of offices and labour towards the support, security and happiness of the whole family.

If several families find the wisdom, experience, valour, and benevolence of one head of a family to be superior to those of the rest, they all look upon him as their common father, they submit to his advice as to injunctions, and his councils become as sacred and inviolable as laws. This voluntary union into one great family, diffuses through them all that attachment, and benevolence, that spirit of order and regularity, which are the true promoters of morality, and universal happiness. If the son of this chief has skill, address and benevolence enough to tread in his fathers footsteps, he succeeds his father in authority, and thus a society gradually accustom themselves to look upon their chiefs with reverence, and accept the posterity of an equitable, benevolent leader, for their hereditary chief. As all the regulations for the weal of the society are chiefly issued by this ruler, as he is foremost in defending their liberty and property against any daring invader of their common right, as he decides between man and man in private disagreements, and punishes the wanton disturbers of public peace, all the authority of the whole community, centers in him; and as many advantages accrue to him on different occasions and opportunities offer of making acquisitions of property, either by the voluntary, general contributions, of all the inferior members of the community, or by the administration and distribution of the public property and wealth, it may be expected that he will become possessed of a greater share of wealth than any of the rest, which must gradually give him more influence and greater power: his family no doubt participate of this power, influence and wealth, and consequently form a class of people distinct from the commons.

If the society is attacked or injured by another society, and all unite to avert the injuries, to repel violence, and to retaliate upon the invaders and disturbers of the peace, the same wrongs which they intended to inflict; it is natural to suppose, that upon a very great provocation, and a consequently greater exertion of power, they may become victorious, which must, of course, make the condition of the vanquished tribe, inferior to that of the lowest of the victorious community, and create a new rank of people in their society. These seem to be the consequences of matrimonial union, of paternal authority, and the more general authority of a chief of a society, and the origin of ranks in O-Taheitee, the Society, and Friendly Isles.

The great chief is called *Aree-rahai:* the rest of his family are all Arees, and have some landed property, and among them we observed men of still greater rank and authority, who were chiefs of the differents districts, or Whennuas in the isle, and were called after the district, which was entrusted to their care and government; thus Hapaí O-Tu's father was *Aree n'O-parre,* chief of Oparre; O-Retti was chief of *O-Hiddea;* O-Amo was chief of *Papara;* T-Owha and Potatou were joint-chiefs of *Atahooroo;* Toppere had the direction of *Matavai* and Toomataroa that of *Tittahaw.* Besides these, is a class of people called *Manahounes,* who have landed property; and lastly, those belonging to the lowest rank of people are called *Toutous.*

As several words of the Malay language, are found in the O-Taheitee tongue, and its various dialects, they may be considered as proofs of the origin of these islanders. I am not willing to affirm that they are absolutely the immediate off-spring of the Malays; but it appeared to me very obvious from many concurring circumstances, that they were descended from some tribes, that are related to the Malays. The Tagalas and Pampangas are no doubt the offspring of the Malays; for Dr. Gemelli Carreri affirms, that they came from the continent of Malacca, and they themselves allow, that they came from Borneo.* The inhabitants of the Ladrones speak a language related to that of the Tagalas.† The vicinity of some of the New-Caroline islands, and the similarity of their customs and manners, make it highly probable, that the same nation is spread all over that great cluster of islands, extending for more than 30 degrees of longitude; and from thence to Byrons Island, and some of those islands where the Taheitean dialect is spoken, is not so great a distance. By this line I presume to trace the first migration of the tribes, who first peopled the Eastern South-Sea isles. If we add to this the great similarity between the manners and customs of the inhabitants of the Caroline islands, and those of the Friendly isles, this line of migration must appear to be something more than mere conjecture.

The most authentic accounts of a modern philosophic traveller‡ inform us, that a kind of feudal system is received by the Malays, which, as far as we know, admits of several ranks of men, very much in the same manner as we observed in the Society isles; and they possess likewise their lands by a kind of feudal tenure. The great chief or king, grants to the inferior chiefs, a district or province: under them, the rest of the Arees or chiefs have portions of land allotted to them; and the Manahounes, though not of the royal family, have likewise grants of land. The chiefs of the provinces, as well as the inferior Arees, have their demesnes cultivated by Toutous, who are obliged to raise fruits and roots, for the necessary food of their Aree; to fish, to build houses and canoes, to make cloth, to work their boats in war and peace, and to do every thing they bid them: and for this service they have the overplus of fruit and fish; which latter, the chief commonly distributes among all his vassals, very impartially, if they catch a considerable quantity at once. The Manahoune, his brethren, and offspring, cultivate the ground, which is granted to them; and I cannot say, that I ever observed Toutous attached to them. In war time, the great chief, with the advice of his relations, and of the chiefs of the provinces, who seem to have great influence in public

---

* *Voyage autour du monde* par Gemelli Carreri, tom. v. p. 64.
† See *Histoire des Isles Marianes* par le P. Gobien, Paris, 1700, 12mo. & the Abstract of the second book of Gobien, in des Brosses *Histoire des Navigations, aux Terres Australes*, vol. ii. p. 495.
‡ Mr. le Poivre.

affairs, orders an armament to be prepared; and as the shores only are inhabited, the attack commonly is made by sea: for that reason they have numbers of war-canoes, built and laid up under large sheds, which are immediately fitted out upon any such requisition, from the Lord Paramount; each inferior chief and Mana-houne is again either master of such a war-canoe, or he does service on board of one of them, as a warrior, and the Toutous are employed in paddling and working them. The chiefs of provinces regulate every thing in their districts, and adminis-ter justice, their authority being as great as that of the king. On extraordinary occasions, however, the king interposes his authority: thus I heard Oree, king of Huaheine, order his *Hoa** to go into a district of another chief, and bid him tell such were the words of the Aree-rahei; to apprehend the thieves, and seize the stolen goods, which he enumerated; the goods were in part restored the same day, and the next day he was ready to punish the thieves in our presence, had we not already been too far out at sea, and had we at first well understood his meaning. At O-Taheitee we saw the review of the naval armaments of two districts, which were destined to subdue a great revolted vassal, or feudal lord, on the isle of *Imeo*, in the district of *Morea*; and we were told, that every chief of a district must send his quota towards this expedition: and even the great chief of O-Taheitee-eetee, or Tiarraboo, would join in it as his duty required. O-Too, perhaps, not being well enough skilled in the noble art of war, was not intended to command the fleet, and therefore gave the dignity of high-admiral to T-Owha, chief of Atahooroo; though he told us at the same time, that he would likewise be in the fleet, in the quality of a warrior, or as we might call it, of a *knight*. These circumstances suffi-ciently prove, that their government is a kind of feudal system; but it has much of that original patriarchal form, blended with it, which rectifies the many defects of the feudal government, and for that very reason is infinitely superior to it, being founded on principles of kindness and benevolence, and on that primitive sim-plicity, which bears always the stamp of perfect undegenerated nature.

However, upon comparing every circumstance more minutely, as the Tahei-teans allow themselves to have formerly been cannibals, and likewise as their chiefs, Manahounes and warriors, are all of a fairer colour than the Toutous; it might not perhaps be inconsistent to suppose, that the first and aboriginal inhab-itants of the South-Sea isles, were of the tribe of the Papuas and people from New-Guinea, and its neighbourhood, and such as we found at Mallicollo, Tanna, and the New-Hebrides, and therefore were like them men-eaters.[4] It is probable, that either by accident, or on purpose, the ancient Malays of the Peninsula, of Malacca, gradually spread among the isles of the Indian seas; first over Borneo,

---

* *Hoa* signifies a friend, or chief-attendant on the king; we should call him a *lord in waiting*, of which the king of Taheitee has a good number, doing duty in their turns.

then to the Philippines; from whence they extended over the Ladrone islands, the New-Carolines, and Pescadores; and lastly, they removed to the Friendly-islands, the Society-islands, the Marquesas and Easter-island, to the Eastward; and to New-Zeeland to the Southward. This migration seems to have been successive, and perhaps several centuries elapsed, from the first removal of the Malays to Borneo, to the arrival of these tribes at New-Zeeland, and Easter-island. In each station they acquired a new tincture of manners and customs varied by climate, and the particular situation of each land which they gradually occupied; and being no doubt, opposed by the first aboriginal inhabitants, it cost a great deal of bloodshed, labour, and time, before they could entirely subdue them. In the larger islands, Borneo, Luçon, Maghindanao,[5] and some of the Moluccas, they were not conquered, but retired into the interior mountainous parts; and are still existing and known under the names of Byajos, Negrillos, Zambales, Allfoories, &c. &c. In the Friendly and Society-islands, the aboriginal inhabitants were subdued, and became Toutous. Their more polished and more civilized conquerors, established a mild and humane kind of government, wherein they introduced the oriental or Malay-feudal system, and endeavoured to wean their new subjects from that cruel cannibalism, which generally prevailed among all the aboriginal black tribes of the South-Sea. In this benevolent and humane undertaking they at last so far succeeded, that the name only, and a faint tradition of the existence of such a custom in O-Taheitee, are preserved. This hypothesis likewise accounts for the various traditions of the Taheiteans, who know, for instance, in their neighbourhood, an isle called *Mannua*, occupied by men-eaters, which, according to this conjecture, is a proof of its being inhabited by the aboriginal black race of people, who are, as far as we know, all cannibals. In New-Zeeland, I am of opinion, that the more civilized Malay tribes, mixed with the aboriginals, and the harshness of the climate, the roughness of the wild woody country, together with its great extent, contributed to preserve cannibalism, and to form a coalition of customs, wherein many points of civilization were totally lost, though the language was taken from the new-comers, and preserved blended with some words of the aboriginal tribe. *Savage-island*, whose inhabitants we found very tawny and ferocious, might perhaps be another island, which the Malay tribes have not hitherto been able to subdue; nay, as the inhabitants of TANNA, were likewise acquainted with a language totally different from theirs, called the FOOTOONA language, or that of IRRONAN, which we found to correspond with the dialect spoken at the Friendly-islands, it seems from thence to follow, that the Malay tribes still endeavour to spread, and to subdue the aboriginal tribes in the various South-Sea isles. These hints, it is to be hoped, may induce some future navigators more carefully to examine the languages, manners, customs, temper, habit and colour of body of the inhabitants of the various

South-Sea isles, in order still better to trace the origin and migrations of these nations; and to throw a still greater light on this interesting part of the History of Man.

It is however remarkable, that the nearer we approach to the Western or Friendly-islands, the greater is the respect, and the more numerous are external marks of subjection shewn by the common people to their chiefs and kings. In Easter-island, and the Marquesas, we observed hardly any difference between the subject and chief, if we except a more conspicuous dress, some attendants and the name of *Areckee* or *A-ka-hai*. In O-Taheitee, and the Society-isles, the lower ranks of people, by way of respect, strip off their upper garment, in the presence of their *Aree-rahai*. But at Tonga Tabu and Horn-Island,* the common people shew their great chief or Latoo the greatest respect imaginable, by prostrating themselves before him, and by putting his foot on their necks. In the Ladrone islands, the Tamolas or nobles are likewise highly revered, and none of the common people dare come near them, for fear of defiling them.† These circumstances in my opinion, prove, that the natives of the South-Sea isles changed some of their manners, and laid aside part of that stiffness, formality and humiliating respect paid to their chiefs in proportion, as they removed from the country, which gave birth to their first ancestors; and it is by this mixture of manners that the inhabitants of Taheitee have arrived at that happy mean which assigns the just bounds of prerogative to each rank of people, and thus places the true principles of happiness on a firm and solid basis. The king has a certain respect shewn him, which is decent and necessary, and he is invested with a degree of authority and power, sufficient to enable him to become beneficial to his subjects, without permitting him to oppress them; and he can acquire the title of father of his people, without ever becoming their tyrant. The chiefs of districts are both a support and check to the royal dignity: they form the great council of the nation, assembled on important affairs, especially war and peace: without their consent, the king cannot undertake any thing which might influence the public peace or safety, or punish any great Lord: without them the king is unable to execute great achievements, for if they should find him disposed to abuse his power, they would either refuse to assist him with the force of their district, or they would, perhaps, associate with those whom the king might be willing to oppress, and therefore prevent his progress towards despotism, by balancing his power, or by opposing his increase of prerogative. The war against the chief of Morea, on the island of Imeo, which the Taheiteans proposed to carry on, after our departure, and for which we saw such great preparations confirms the truth of this assertion. The

---

* See Mr. Dalrymples *Collection of Voyages to the South-Sea*, vol. ii. p. 41, 55.
† Des Brosses *Historie des Navigations aux Terres australes*, tom. ii. p. 484, 499.

chiefs of each district being subject to the king, dare not oppress their own sub-jects, who, in that case would either bring their complaints before his paramount, or they might form associations, in order to defend themselves against his rapines, oppression and despotism. The facility of procuring the necessaries of life, and even those articles which are here reckoned to be luxuries; together with the humane and benevolent temper of these nations have hitherto happily prevented the oppression of the Toutous; and if the morals of these people are not influ-enced and corrupted by the commerce and intercourse with European profligates, and by the introduction of new luxuries, which can be procured only by hard labour and drudgery, the happiness of the lowest class of people, will, probably be of long continuance; and forbid it humanity and benevolence, that any one of us should be wicked enough to form a wish or a plan to entail misery and wretched-ness, on a happy and harmless race of men!

They have undoubtedly customary laws and regulations relative to the good order of their societies, for the security both of their property and of the lives of individuals, and punishments which are inflicted on those who transgress these laws, and disturb the public peace. At the time when one of the natives had stolen a musket from a centry at the tents on Point Venus in O-Taheitee, the centry was carried on board under confinement, and previous to the punishment inflicted on him for the neglect of his duty, the articles of war were read before the whole ship's company assembled on deck; during this ceremony, it is custom-ary for every body to be uncovered. The natives, among whom were some of the king's relations, observing that something extraordinary was going forward, were particularly curious to know what the long *para-parou*, or speech signified; I told them it was *the word of the great king of our nation*; upon which they all agreed among themselves that it was MEERA; which I suppose from the above circum-stances to signify *law*, or *regulation*. They frequently told us that they killed thieves, by hanging a large stone to their necks and drowning them in the sea: however, in a nation which has so much innocence and benevolence, and so few wants, the greater part of which, may very easily be satisfied, this crime must be rare. Murder seems to be a crime unknown among them; though we frequently saw some of them disagree, and fight, yet the bystanders were always ready to part them, in order to prevent further mischief, and their hearts are not yet degraded to that degree of degeneracy and baseness, as to permit them to postpone ven-geance to another time, and to lay a plan in cool blood, and in a deliberate manner, to execute it with more certainty and security to themselves. Like true children of nature, their passions, the great principles of self-preservation and defence, prompt them to punish and repel their real or imaginary wrongs, and as soon as they have shewed that they are not destitute of a noble resentment, they yield to the endeavours of their brethren to establish peace and harmony, and are as easily reconciled to their antagonists.

Among the chiefs, instances of matrimonial infidelity are to be met with, which seem therefore, as in Europe, to be the vicious prerogative attached to rank and dignity. The natives told us, that adultery is punished with death among them, but we saw no instances of it, and those on the part of the husband which came to my knowledge, were no further punished, than that the justly exasperated wife, Juno like, treated her husband, with all the flow of bad language she was mistress of, and that she in great haste and wrath imparted some boxes on the ear to the fair one, whom she found desirous of encroaching upon her prerogative rights.

These happy isles have almost every article necessary for the supply of their wants; nevertheless their manners are already so far polished, that they like to be possessed of some articles chiefly of ornaments and luxury, which they cannot meet with in their own isle, or at least, not in such plenty as in others situated in the neighbourhood. Bora-bora, and O-Tahaw, are both well provided with coco-nut-palms, from which they manufacture an oil, well known in the East Indies; the inhabitants of Taheitee and its neighbourhood, use this oil perfumed, by means of various odoriferous plants, and aromatic woods, as an article of luxury to stain and to perfume their cloth, and even their hair, and sometimes their bodies. As the coco-nut-trees are not so plentiful in O-Taheitee as to enable the inhabitants to prepare a quantity of oil, to satisfy the great demand for it, and as on the contrary, the natives of Bora-bora, and O-Tahaw, cannot manufacture such a profusion and variety of cloth as they do at O-Taheitee, where the paper-mulberry-tree is much cultivated; there are persons who every year undertake a voyage from Taheitee to Tahaw and Bora-bora, in order to barter great quantities of cloth, for joints of thick bamboo-reeds filled with coco-nut oil. The Low-Islands have a race of dogs with long white hair, which the natives employ in fringing their breast-plates or war gorgets; and these low islanders cannot cultivate the mulberry-tree on their sandy, barren ledges of lands, which includes their salt lagoons; therefore these reciprocal wants, form a kind of commerce between the inhabitants of the high and low islands, and a mutual exchange of superfluities. The red feathers of parrots are employed in ornaments for their warriors, being fixed at the end of the tassels, which they wear like queues, and likewise in small bundles tied together with coco-nut-core, which they make use of in order to fix their attention during their prayers. The O-Taheitee parrot has but few and very dirty red feathers, but more to the West are islands, which have fine parroquets remarkable for beautiful red feathers. One of these isles is low, and destitute of inhabitants, at about ten days sail from O-Taheitee and is called Whennua-oora

PRINCIPLES OF
SOCIETIES

the *Land of red feathers*, to which the people from the Society Isles sometimes resort, in order to procure some of these red feathers, for they are the most valuable article of commerce, and there is nothing which a Taheitean would not give or grant in order to acquire some of these precious feathers. We brought some bright red feathers from England, but they soon found out they were only cocks feathers, and died red, and for that reason did not esteem them; they took them indeed, but refused to give any thing in return. Whereas, when we came the second time, in 1774, to O-Taheitee after we had been to Tonga Tabu, where the natives make various ornaments of red feathers, we procured for them not only numbers of hogs, the most valuable article of trade, but likewise mourning dresses, which the natives refused to part with before, when Mr. Banks was there, and during our first stay in their happy isle.[6] The rage after these trifling ornaments was so great, that Potatou a chief, whose magnanimity and noble way of thinking, we never questioned before, wanted even to prostitute his own wife, for a parcel of these baubles. All kinds of iron tools are likewise become great articles of commerce, since their connexions with Europeans. The Spaniards first made the inhabitants of all these islands acquainted with iron; and I am of opinion that even its O-Taheitean name is of Spanish origin; for when *Oliver van Noort* came in the year 1600 to *Guaham* one of the Ladrone Islands,[7] he saw more than 200 canoes full of natives coming off with coco-nuts, bananas, sugar-canes, fish, &c. and all wanted to exchange these refreshments for iron, crying aloud *hierro! hierro!* which is the Spanish name for iron, and in its pronunciation not very different from *yuree*, the Taheitean word for the same; and as the Ladrones as well as Taheitee, or at least some neighbouring isles, were first seen by Spaniards, there is very little doubt but the name of *yuree* is originally meant for *hierro*. The loss of one of Roggewyn's ships in 1772, on the low island of O-Anna, gave these islanders again a fresh supply of iron.[8] The anchors lost by Mr. de Bougainville at *O-Hidea* were afterwards taken up by the natives, and the king of Taheitee sent one as a rare present to Opunee king of Bora-bora. Lastly the English imported such quantities of iron-tools, especially hatchets, chissels, plains, saws, gimlets, and spikes and nails of all dimensions, that this commodity will not easily come into disuse among them, and is still less likely to be entirely forgotten. Especially as all these nations are very remarkable for preserving the smallest pieces of iron for many years: thus for instance, when we landed at *Tonga-tabu* one of the natives sold a very small nail carefully fastened in a handle of hard wood, and tied to it by strings of coco-nut-core. This nail was undoubtedly left by Taesman, who was there in 1643, and consequently had been preserved 130 years, and is now lodged amongst other curiosities in the British Museum. Beads of glass, since our several expeditions to the South Sea, are very common; as incredible quantities have been exchanged in these Seas for coco-nuts, yams, and bread-fruit. It is however, remarkable, that in O-Taheitee, those which were white and trans-parent were preferred, in the Friendly Islands, the black beads were in high esteem; and green ear-rings, and green or red glass buttons were most eagerly sought after in New-Zeeland. Each of these nations therefore had a peculiar taste. At *Tanna* the casuarina-wood for clubs was brought from *Irromanga*, hatchets made of black solid lava came from *Anattom*, and those of white shell from *Immer*. So that each country gives up its superfluities in exchange for other arti-cles, which are less common, and deemed either really necessary, or an improve-ment, or an article of luxury.

The acquisition of the various articles of commerce form the wealth and the opulence of individuals in these islands. Our stay at O-Taheitee has raised many persons from a low rank, and from poverty to affluence and a higher class; for when a man at Taheitee had acquired some wealth, he could keep it for his own use, or was permitted to dispose of it in such a manner as he pleased. This likewise was observed at Easter-island, the Marquesas, New-Zeeland, the New-Hebrides and New-Caledonia: but at the Friendly-islands the case was otherwise; *Attaha*, one of the inferior chiefs, was obliged to deliver all the presents he had received to their Latoo-Nipooroo; this was likewise practised by all the other chiefs; the priest was not obliged to pay this kind of homage or acknowledgment of his sub-jection to the great chief. Whenever the lower ranks of people at Taheitee stole any valuable articles, the chiefs either seized the whole booty, or at least shared the spoils with their Toutous, though they never deprived them by force of the effects, which they received in exchange for their eatables, cloth, furniture, and implements of war. However we found, that after some time, all this acquired wealth flowed as presents, or voluntary acknowledgments into the treasure of the various chiefs; who it seems were the only possessors of all the hatchets and broad axes; the use of which, they granted to their subjects, on certain occasions, prob-ably for some acknowledgment. What makes me more inclined to believe this circumstance, is the account of the very same custom observed at the *Caroline Islands*, where the inhabitants appropriate all the iron which they find on wrecked ships, to their *Tamoles* or chiefs, who have such tools made from them, as the size of the iron will admit, which they let for a high price to their subjects.* But the real wealth of the natives at Taheitee, the Society-islands, the Marquesas, the Friendly-islands, and even Easter-island, consists in the possession of their lands, which the manahounes cultivate with the assistance of their families; whereas, the possessions of their chiefs, as well as the royal demesnes, are under the inspection and cultivation of their own toutous: they feed the hogs and dogs of their masters, which constitute their greatest riches; they cultivate the banana-

---

* Des Brosses *Historie des Navigations aux Terres australes*, vol. ii. p. 485.

trees, take care of the bread-fruit and apple-trees, sugar-canes, yams, eddoes, tac-
cas, potatoes, and other useful vegetables; they plant the mulberry-trees, and
manufacture their bark; lay up stores of mahei or sower-paste, and provide the
indolent chiefs with food and raiment. It appears from hence, that the real wealth
and opulence of their chiefs depends upon the number of toutous, as well as upon
the extent of demesne they are possessed of. And that the toutou seems to be a
kind of property of the tribe of chiefs, alienable according to the pleasure of the
master, I collected from the following circumstance; as soon as our friend
Maheine had found his relations on O-Taheitee, he was presented by them with a
boy about 13 or 14 years old, called *Poë-tea-tea*, who became to all intents and
purposes his toutou, and was immediately remarkably attached to his new master
and his friends on board the ship.

We have already enumerated hogs and dogs among the riches of the natives
of Taheitee, to which we added goats in 1773, that had already produced a couple
of kids, at our return to Taheitee in the following year; but it is remarkable, that
these few domestic animals, were not even common over all the South Sea isles.
In all the low islands they have dogs, but no hogs; at the Friendly Islands
and Tanna, they had hogs, but no dogs, at New-Zeeland they had no hogs, and
at New-Caledonia they had neither hogs nor dogs. We gave at Amsterdam
and Tanna the first dogs; at New-Zeeland the first hogs and fowls, and at New-
Caledonia we left a couple of dogs, and another of pigs. They must formerly have
had dogs at Amsterdam, because they knew the animal, and were acquainted
with its name, *ghooree*, but have lost the species, as it should seem, by some accident. Though both the sorts of quadrupeds which are found in the South Seas, are
very prolific; thrive in the fine climate amazingly well, and soon come to maturity, they were however, not in such abundance, that every family could use them
for common food; but the bulk of the nation was obliged to subsist chiefly on
vegetables, the produce of their industry and moderate labour. In this circumstance I find a vestige of the infinite wisdom pursued in the works of nature, and
her general constitution, and trace therein a part of the grand plan, which has no
other aim than the greatest perfection of the whole.

The animal creation is not so much in the power of man, that he can by his
industry enlarge its prolific quality; for each animal is confined by invariable laws
of nature to certain limits in the propagation of its species; if therefore the whole
human race should subsist merely on animal food, and all mankind lead a pastoral
life; man would gradually sink into a situation, which is entirely inconsistent with
his physical, moral, and social happiness. Cultivation, or the art of raising by his
industry, care, and labour, a sufficiency of roots, herbs, and fruits for the subsistence and other purposes of human life, is the only foundation of all the felicity
which man ever can attain in this life. All vegetables, especially those which are

now become in various countries and climates, the chief food of mankind, naturally thrive with great ease, and are moreover, capable of being multiplied in a
stupendous proportion, by human industry. The nourishment which they afford is
salubrious, and well adapted to the structure of the organs, and the whole system
of animal functions in men. The infinite variety they afford, the excellent flavour
and rich taste of some vegetable productions, would soon cause them to become
the food of men, without ever cloying them. But there is something still more
advantageous in the universal and improved culture of vegetable food; the more
vegetables are cultivated, the more they become improved; which we may easily
confirm by the infinite variety of well tasted apples and pears, cherries and
plumbs, peaches and apricots, cabbages and turnips, potatoes and yams, and so
many other fruits, herbs and roots, which are meliorated by continued cultivation, and have afforded us new varieties and sorts of the same kind of vegetable.
The more and the better all vegetables are cultivated, the more they enable mankind to associate together, and to communicate to each other their assistance,
their experience, their ideas and improvements. Invention is more and more at
work, life acquires new ease and comfort, the ties of society become indissoluble,
all social feelings are rendered polished and refined; every one shares, in a higher
degree, the happiness, and is better enabled to alleviate the adversities of his
fellow-creatures; universal peace and order become more and more a check upon
the passions, and their wild flights; these regulations are gradually turned into
laws, and cause a more general equality of temper, and manners; this is the next
step to convince them of the great influence of vice and virtue, on their personal
and social happiness; and at last conscience and moral sentiments begin to awake
in every feeling breast, and prepare every one for that degree of happiness and
enjoyment, which humanity can attain in this transitory life. This therefore
shews evidently, that mankind, in a pastoral state, could never attain to that
degree of improvement and happiness, to which agriculture, and the cultivation
of vegetables, will easily and soon lead them. I do not, however, intend so far to
extol agriculture, and vegetable food, as to insist that mankind should entirely
neglect the culture, and domestication of animals; I am rather of opinion, that a
moderate share of animal food, mixed with vegetables, is very well adapted to our
organization, and that it is the joint care of animals and agriculture, which leads
mankind to the highest degree of content, and paves the way to perfect happiness. I congratulate, therefore, the Taheiteans, who are possessed of such a variety
and profusion of well-tasted and salubrious vegetable food, cultivated on their
happy isle, together with two domestic quadrupeds; and who made in our last
voyage, a new acquisition of the goat, a domestic animal; and to whose use Captain Cook, in his present voyage, carried rams and ewes, as well as bulls and cows;
because so valuable a present will enable that brave people to make many im-

provements in their domestic life. If rice, especially that kind which grows on hilly grounds, without requiring to be watered, as the common rice does, mayz, some pine-apples, chesnuts, dates, oranges, and lemons, together with the sago-palm, were added to their vegetables; they would form the most rational present, which ever was offered to a nation, and the most grateful returns we could make, to a kind, humane and hospitable people, who generously gave us all the refreshments we stood in need of, and enabled us to finish a navigation, which will for ever, stand unparallelled in the annals of all nations. The man who shall carry these vegetable productions to Taheitee, and the South-Sea isles, and at the same time teach the inhabitants their cultivation and use, will become a benefactor to mankind; he will deserve to be ranked with Triptolemus, Orpheus, and other heroes, and merit the thanks and reverence of grateful posterity.

The happiness resulting from the fertile climate, and from a profusion of fine vegetable productions, raised by the industry of the Manahounes and Toutous in Taheitee, and its neighbourhood; the very moderate and mild servitude of their Toutous, the order and regulation in their domestic societies, the benevolent and paternal affection of their chiefs, their association for the security of property and liberty, their commerce, wealth, and enjoyments, give us the best idea of the more refined and exalted situation of the inhabitants of Taheitee, and the Society-islands, above all the rest of the nations we visited in the course of our voyage. Convinced of the rectitude of order, and justice, as far as they relate to human societies; sensible of the pleasure arising from each common act of benevolence, and fired with the generous spirit of communicating happiness to as many as are willing to form with them the same society; they are likewise capable of that noble and disinterested desire to work for the common weal as much as lies in their power, which we call *public spirit* or *true patriotism*, and what is still better, they actually shew it on many occasions. I have seen a man eating a small proportion of bread-fruit, or other food, and nevertheless sharing this trifle out amongst several of his brethren, whilst it would admit of division. The solicitude of their chiefs, to strike a good bargain for their subjects, when they brought fruit, fish, or hogs to market, is likewise another proof of this assertion; nor can I omit the assistance they generally gave to one another; the detestation in which the better sort of people held all the thieves and robbers; the striking increase of happiness we observed in O-Taheitee, were, at our second arrival, after an absence of eight months, owing to the encouragement and minute inspection of the situation of every individual family under *O-Tu,* the resignation of the command of the fleet to T-Owha, made by O-Tu, and the readiness of T-Owha to undertake that expedition, though ill of the gout; the wisdom and public spirit with which they politely declined the assistance offered them by Capt. Cook for conquering the revolted island of Imeo. All these particulars give me the highest opinion of their *true patriotism*, and noble attachment to the weal of their country. This great maxim is the first germ of all noble social feelings and sentiments: it assigns to the various relations of man their true valour, and bids him act in consequence of each of them; it prescribes the simplicity and unity of principles, and the harmony of means for acting upon those principles. It teaches individuals to scorn to enjoy advantages which cannot become universal, or must be purchased at the expence of the happiness of the community, and makes of every individual a hero; who, if he lived in countries, where poets, orators, and authors, for gold lavish their incense, would have such monuments of eloquence raised to his memory, as are but too common in our adulatory age; and had he been born with those noble sentiments at Athens or Rome, he would have deserved to rank with Aristides, Agesilaus, Leonidas, Fabius, Africanus, Cato, and the sacred bands, who fill the temples of Grecian and Roman patriotism.[9]

The whole that has been said of the happiness of the Taheiteans, and inhabitants of the Society-islands, is not applicable to the rest of the nations in the tropical isles. In the Friendly-islands, cultivation is carried to a higher degree, which is likewise evident from the fences and partitions, so ingeniously contrived, and artfully executed between the various possessions of each individual family: but at the same time their government has still much oriental despotism and slavish subjection to chiefs and their Latoo, derogatory to that dignity and liberty, to which nature destined all her sons and daughters: the first is owing to the great population of these isles; the latter proves them to be nearer to that country, from whence they came, and where abject humiliations for chiefs and princes are common, and originally were introduced by preposterous obsequiousness and abject flattery, and afterwards established and propagated by tyranny and oppression. We were witness to their prostrations before their chief, but our stay was too short to be able to judge of their laws, and form of government. We found *Attaha* to have great authority at the place where we landed; there were, however, other chiefs, who had certainly more authority than he, which went so far, that he was afraid of sitting at dinner with us in their presence. One of these superior chiefs had great influence and weight with all the people in the boats, to whom some of our friends gave the title of lord high admiral; their priest was likewise a man of considerable authority, even to such a degree, that when all the other chiefs constantly gave the presents they had received from us to the Latoo, the priest kept to himself every thing that was presented to him; which seemed to intimate the subjection of their chiefs to Latoo, and the great authority this chief had assumed to himself. Several other chiefs were ready enough to order their people to do something, and we found their orders always respected; but I never saw them take any goods or fruits, from the inferior people, in order to give to us; nor did they rob their people of the things they had exchanged for various articles; this behaviour, should perhaps, teach us to think that they have made regulations for securing to individuals, personal property in these isles. In the Marquesas and Easter-island, there was hardly a distinction observable between the magistrate and the subject; they had the name of the dignity, they had some attendance, and were, on the arrival of strangers, better dressed; but their authority, if we may judge, from the few instances, we could observe during our short interviews with these people, seemed to be more familiar to the advice of a benevolent parent, than to the imperious dictates of a king. In the more Western isles of Mallicollo, Tanna, and New-Caledonia, we observed likewise chiefs, under the denominations *Aleeghee* or *Areekee*, but they were, upon the whole, not distinguished from their subjects, by rank or authority, and seem to enjoy only an hereditary title; and as to the laws of these people, we are not presumptuous enough to talk of things, which we had neither opportunities, nor time, nor sufficient knowledge of the language to observe. They had plantations in these isles, and we saw that several small families cleared spots of ground for that purpose, and it is very natural to suppose that they likewise reap the fruits of their labours. In general it appeared to us, that O-Taheitee and the cluster of high isles in its neighbourhood, were the only spots where civilization had made some progress, and where these advantages were not again over-balanced by defects in the constitution or government. I cannot dismiss this subject without observing, that though the tropical isles of the South-Sea, never may, perhaps, be so unhappy, if left to themselves, as to be again degraded to a more debased condition; they will on the other hand, never be able to make, unassisted, any great or rapid progress towards a higher civilization, or more improved condition, because the small size of their isles will not admit of these improvements: and in case they should attempt to make conquests and unite several small islands into one political body; many centuries must elapse before the little jealousies between the vanquished people and the conquerors will wear off, and by a happy coalition one powerful nation can be established; which, however, is absolutely required, if they are to make large strides towards improvement in science, morality, arts, manufactures, or husbandry: and thus together form one great scene of happiness.

SECTION VII

On the Principles, Moral Ideas, Manners, Refinement, Luxury, and the Condition of Women, among the Nations in the South-Sea-Isles

PRIMAE DEDERUNT SOLATIA DULCIA VITAE.
  Lucretius[1]

The happy inhabitants of the tropical islands in the South-Sea, occupy a rank in the class of human beings, which is by no means so despicable, as might, at first sight, be imagined; and the Taheiteans and their neighbours in the Society-islands, may claim the highest rank among these nations. They are certainly, for many reasons, superior to the cannibals in New-Zeeland, and still higher above the rambling, poor inhabitants, of New-Holland, and the most unhappy wretches of Tierra del Fuego.[2] In the same proportion the people at Tanna, and Mallicollo, exceed those at New-Caledonia;[3] the inhabitants of the Marquesas, stand higher than the people of the Friendly-islands, and these must yield to the Taheiteans, as every circumstance concurs to confirm their high rank. The organization of their bodies seems to me to be the most happy and susceptible of enjoyment and improvement, of all the other nations before-mentioned; the climate they live in, the vicinity of so many islands, peopled by the same nation, speaking in the same language, enjoying the same kind of government, accustomed to the same laws and regulations, instructed in the same principles, having the same ideas in regard to morality and religion, the same food, dress, habitations, and general manners; in a word, every thing contributes to connect and to form them for a higher degree of enjoyment.

   Men, of different inclinations, who are endued with rational souls, and capable of forming various ideas, are found to make advances to perfection only, when they strive to acquire a competent knowledge of a variety of objects, and take care to admit no other ideas among those who may serve them in life, than such as are perfectly conformable to truth, and which express to the mind the real qualities and properties of things; and when their thoughts and actions are directed by the strict rule of right. In this case they will soon discover that though there be a strong instinct in their breasts, prompting them to appropriate as much good to themselves as possible, yet the enjoyment of it will soon become more and more imperfect, and unhappiness, in some measure, the consequence; but by transferring acts of benevolence to other men, they soon open to themselves an inexhaustible source of enjoyment, because benefactions of an incredible variety may be bestowed upon an almost infinite number of fellow creatures, and thus we see the great *principles* of all rational human beings, ought to be CANDOUR and HUMANITY; which alone are capable of giving to all their ideas, desires, and actions, the true direction towards real, lasting happiness, and raise their nature to that exalted dignity, for which they were originally intended.

The tropical nations of the South-Seas considered in this point of view, seem to be deficient neither in *candour*, nor in *humanity*. For it is impossible to describe the inquisitive curiosity of these people relative to our country, government, religion, and the various arts by which our curious manufactures were carried on, I mean such as fell under their eyes, and could be understood by them. I was obliged to explain to them the difference between our stuffs made of wool, silk, cotton, and linen; by telling them the first was made of the hair of a *hog with teeth on the forehead,* (for thus they called our sheep when they first saw them)[4] the second, I explained to be the thread of a caterpillar; the third, I shewed to be a species of their cotton called *E-Vavài* or *Gossypium religiosum,* Linn. which is found in their isles, and the last I observed to be a kind of thread of a plant or grass; and they were all very attentive when I used to draw and twist some threads of their cotton in order the shew them the possibility of using it for that purpose. They were likewise very attentive while our armourer was forming hatchets on the anvil, or the carpenters grinding their tools; for which reason, Captain Cook gave them some grinding stones, and took care that they should be instructed in the proper use of these instruments. We were often obliged to explain to them our belief in the divinity; they used to ask how we called him in the British language, and endeavoured to pronounce the name of God; they were all attention, when according to their desire God was explained to be *without a maker,* invisible, almighty, and infinitely good; they required whether we addressed him in prayer, and whether we had priests and *marais,* i.e. places of worship, serving at the same time for burying places. All which, proves their inquisitive mind, and that they endeavour to acquire as many ideas as lye in their power. Nor were they destitute of knowledge and a system of useful ideas, preserved among the wise men of the nation; I include in this stock of ideas, their skill in cultivating certain plants for food and dress, and the choice of a proper soil for each of them, the various operations in preparing them for the various purposes required; the curious, and often very neat dresses, utensils, arms, and ornaments manufactured by them, with the simplest tools; their knowledge of the birds, fishes, and plants in their islands and their neighbourhood; their acquaintance with the winds and seasons, the names of the stars, and their rising and setting, and a knowledge of the situation of a considerable number of islands in those tropical seas; the art of navigating by the sun in the day time, and by the moon and stars in the night: the number and names of days in a lunation, and of lunations in a year. This exercise of their memories in retaining the various names expressing these ideas, and of other mental faculties confirming by their own experience the truth of the phaenomena, communicated to them by their parents and teachers, gives them a turn and as it were a predilection for the examination of truth; which, when applied to the purposes of common social life, gives a strong tincture of honesty and candour, which is most particularly necessary in all human transactions. But if we should require proofs of their humanity, we need only to quote the navigators in the Resolution, Adventure, Endeavour, Dolphin, and Mr. de Bougainville, at Taheitee, as so many monuments of their humanity and friendly disposition: they provided us with refreshments and vast quantities of hogs; they assisted us when we were often unattended a great way up in their country; they vied with each other in shewing us marks of their kindness and hospitality, invited us to sit down in the cooling shade of their houses, rubbed and chafed our wearied limbs, offered us a delicate dinner, prepared from the best of their fruits, undertook to become the bearers of our victuals and acquisitions of plants, shells, and fishes, in our excursions, carried us over all waters and rivulets on their backs, and fetched the ducks and other birds which we had shot; they entertained us with songs and dances, made us presents of cloth and provisions; and some of them were polite in every acceptation of the word, and treated us in a manner, which cannot but leave in our minds the most lasting impressions of their courtesy and benevolence.

These great principles of *candour* and *humanity*, which are so well understood, and so generally practised by these nations, have no doubt, a great influence on their MORALS and MANNERS. The first dawnings of the *law of nature*, taught them to be cautious, and abstain from doing harm to their fellow creatures; but *morality* gives the great practical lesson to make as many fellow creatures happy as possible. I will not however, maintain that those feelings of *moral sense* are absolutely the same at all times, in all climates, and among all nations: for I am well aware, that often the same nation approves of an action at one period of time, and at another condemns it. I am likewise not so ignorant as to deny that the same action is condemned by one people, and approved by another, or at least not reckoned to be criminal, because nations are in this respect likewise, similar to individuals: they gradually ripen to an age of maturity, and acquire in every age a more steady, and more refined moral taste; and if ever the bulk of the nation, or part of it, or even only individuals can dispel the prejudices surrounding their minds, and conquer the passions which influence their wills; they are sure to act

MANNERS

according to the dictates of their conscience, which is in that case *common sense relative to morals*, and the voice of the divinity strongly admonishing them of their duty; they then become sensible, that the actions of men living in a society, are by no means indifferent to the community, but that every individual is accountable for them to his fellow creatures. Upon the whole, though the actions of these happy people generally have a tendency to humanity and benevolence, they are actuated in some measure by a spirit of selfishness, the great root of corruption, and are therefore similar in that respect to the rest of mankind, whose actions are a compound of selfish and humane, benevolent behaviour; which is made use of according as prejudices, national character, and other circumstances prompt them to follow either the one or the other impulse: and even when selfishness carried away their desires, to covet for instance, the iron-ware, which we had, and induced one or more of them to purloin a nail or knife or some such trifle, they were however, not so absolutely lost to all moral sense, as not to shew by their immediate flight, that they had wronged us: nay, often some of the natives, who were either attached to us from principles of gratitude, or had a more generous and liberal way of thinking, and entertained stricter notions of morality, warned us against some persons whom they saw in the croud pressing officiously upon us, or whom they had seen once frustrated in their attempts upon our pockets; which at least proves so much, that though some were now and then tempted to act contrary to the impulse of conscience on account of an irresistible temptation, suggesting for a moment the principles of selfishness, there were however others, who acted strictly conformable to the dictates of morality; and even the criminals themselves were not without remorse, or insensible that their action was punishable, being wrong, and that we were able to call them to a strict account for it, and retaliate the wrongs they had been committing against us. I cannot leave this subject without mentioning that I found immorality and selfishness, far more prevailing among the great and the very lowest, than among the middle ranks of people. King O-Too, with his sister Tourai, being once on a visit to Captain Cook, were introduced into his state-room, where constantly a quantity of iron-ware lay exposed, in order to have as much of it ready, as was required for the trade which was constantly carried on. The Captain and I were the only persons who were with them. Captain Cook was called out by the officer on deck upon some business that admitted no delay, he therefore desired me to stay with the royal family. The absence of the Captain, and the great heaps of iron, suggested to Tourai the idea of profiting by this opportunity, and prompted her to purloin some of the fine iron goods; she desired her brother to divert my attention; he called me to the window and wanted to shew me something in the canoes surrounding our ship; I suspected their design, and went where he called me, but kept an eye on O-Too's sister, who immediately seized two large ten inch spikes and concealed them carefully under her garment. I acquainted Captain Cook at his return with the transaction, but we agreed to dissemble, and not to alarm their fears, that the briskness of the trade might not be interrupted. However, I made the following observations, that the sight of such treasures of iron, must have been very great temptations; because Tourai and O-Too might have had two or more spikes, upon barely asking for them, and that therefore the idea of acquiring them by stealth, should seem to be a sudden irresistibe impulse, capable of overcoming the turpitude of the action, the danger and shame of being exposed and regarded as thieves, and the king becoming himself accessary to the meanest transaction; however, the complaisance of the king for his sister, was, equally evident, and in some measure makes his condescension in my opinion, less culpable, nor would I wish by this observation to brand Tourai or O-Too, as people of abandoned morals, and capable of committing any immoral action; for I am persuaded from other reasons, that O-Too, was a well meaning man, inclined to fear that we might abuse the superiority of our power against him and his people; but at the same time benevolent, good-natured, and studiously promoting the wealth, power, and happiness of his people: though I believe him incapable of acting in so noble, distinterested, and generous a manner as Towha, who would have shone as a great character, in whatever nation he might have happened to live. The character of the sister, is in my opinion, less amiable than that of O-Too, especially if it be true, what a great many used to tell us, that she was a kind of a *Messalina,* demeaning herself so low as to admit Toutous to her embraces.[5] Besides this instance of the immorality and selfishness of the great, I can add another; *Waineeòu* and *Potatou* her husband, were so greedy after the possession of red parrots feathers, that having sold all the hogs, which they possibly could spare, together with a fine helmet, several breast-plates, and a mourning dress, they agreed to prostitute *Wainee-òu,* and she in consequence offered herself to Captain Cook, and appeared as a ready victim.

>   *. . . Tunica velàta recincta.*[6]

I must confess, having received a favourable and great idea of Potatou's character, this transaction made me ashamed of him; and being before elated with the thought of having found a nation, where one might at least find to the honour of humanity, less degeneracy joined to an amiable innocence and primitive simplicity, my spirits were damped by this unexpected scene of immorality and selfishness, in a family where I least expected to hear of it.

The principles of chastity we found however, in many families, exceedingly well understood and practised, to the great satisfaction of all those Europeans in whose hearts lewdness had not yet effaced every notion of purity and morality.

I have with transport seen many fine women, who with a modesty mixed with politeness, which would have graced the most exalted characters of our polite nations, refuse the greatest and most tempting offers made them by our forward youths; often they excused themselves with a simple *tirra-tane*, "I am married," and at other times they smiled and declined it with *eipa*, "no." But it is necessary to observe that a nation still enjoying that just and noble simplicity of manners, living in large houses with several families together, in the midst of their children, cannot conceal certain actions, which none of our Europeans, who have feelings and breeding, wished to commit in so great companies; this naturally makes all their children acquainted with transactions of which some European matrons perhaps may have no ideas, nor has love, and all its concomitant, and most mysterious endearments, enjoyments, and consequences, ever been stamped in these happy isles with a notion of turpitude. Virtuous women hear a joke without emotion, which amongst us might perhaps put some men to the blush. Neither austerity and anger, nor joy and ecstasy is the consequence, but sometimes a modest, dignified, serene smile spreads itself over their faces, and seems gently to rebuke the uncouth jester, for not being better acquainted with the purer enjoyments of modest and virtuous love, and with the practice of that respect which is due to those who are its religious votaries.

Thus the constant and excellent principles of *candour* and *humanity* teach the better individuals of this happy nation, the distinction between right and wrong, and spread, and confirm the notions of virtue and morality among them. But the actions of a people may be likewise considered, as far as they become expressive of a character peculiar to them, by which they give us an idea of their MANNERS. There are nations that have such strong outlines in their characters, forming so essential a contrast between them and other nations, that it is very easy to catch them, and to describe a picture perfectly resembling the original; the warlike institutions and laws of Lycurgus gave such a strong character to the Spartans, that nothing was more easy than to give a picture of Spartan manners: but to distinguish the inhabitant of Orchomenus from that of Megalopolis or of Mantinea and Tegea, by these characteristics was a more difficult task, because the features were so small, that the distinction was, as it were entirely lost. The characteristics of the South-Sea nations, are, upon the whole, very different from ours, and may therefore easily be traced; however, the difference between them and all the nations, which are just emerging from barbarism, is not so very considerable, nor is it possible to point out such features as would at once distinguish the inhabitants of each particular island, from those of the others in its neighbourhood, especially as our stay among them was so short, and their language so little understood by us: we shall nevertheless endeavour to give some faint outlines of their manners.

Man of the Island of Mallicollo [Malakula], engraving by J. Caldwall after William Hodges, early state. State Library of New South Wales.

The *general external appearance* of these nations, is, no doubt, very strongly contrasted to ours, and we have already mentioned something upon that subject in the section, treating of the colour, size, habit of body, &c. &c. of these nations, which renders it unnecessary to repeat the same argument again.

DRESS characterizes people most remarkably, nor is this uniform in the South-Sea-Islands. The inhabitants of Tierra del Fuego, we found destitute of such parts of dress, which modesty would employ, and necessity enjoin; in the Western islands of the Pacific Ocean, where the climate makes dress not abso-lutely necessary, the nations covered only those parts of their body,* which, by an almost general agreement, every nation on earth wishes to screen; but though their males, were, to all appearance, equally anxious in this respect with their females, this part of their dress served only to make that more conspicuous, which it intended to hide; and this device seems to be invented with as little delicacy and judgment as the famous *cod-piece*, which a few centuries ago made part of a man's dress in Europe; whether the care of preventing these parts from being wounded or hurt by branches of trees, briars, and insects, or real principles of pro-priety and modesty had first induced them to use so strange a method for covering their genitals, I cannot decide; however, among these same nations we observed, that only the age of maturity inspired them with these ideas of decency and mod-esty; for their little boys were stark naked, and little girls, below the age of eight years, had no other cover than a wisp of straw before, and another behind, fixed to a string tied round the waist. But though all these nations had no other parts of dress, to satisfy necessity in a cold climate, or modesty in a warmer; they found it nevertheless necessary to use various ornaments: in Tierra del Fuego, they painted their faces red, with a kind of ochre; in Tanna they somethimes laid on their faces black and white paint, in oblique alternating bands; the hair was sometimes divided into a great number of strings, not thicker than a crows-quill, and wrapt in strings of the bark of a bindweed, *(convolvulus)* which gave their heads a very odd appearance; the ears were generally pierced, and ornamented with rings of Tortoise-shell; nay, in New-Caledonia and Easter-Island, we found the hole enlarged to such a size, that four or five fingers might easily pass through, and the under part hung down almost to the shoulders. These preternatural apertures were commonly distended by scrolls of the elastic sugar-cane-leaves, or loaded with huge earrings, sometimes amounting to eighteen in number. The inhab-itants of the Friendly-islands had the ear perforated by two holes, through which they thrust, horizontally, a piece of bamboo reed, or a cylinder of tortoise-shell, or

---

* It is therefore remarkable, that in the engraved figure of a Mallicolese, which is found in Capt. Cook's Narrative of the voyage, a drapery has been spread over the body of the figure, in direct opposition to the universal custom of that country.[7]

"Man of the Island of
Mallicollo" [Malakula],
engraving by J. Caldwall
after William Hodges,
from Cook, *A Voyage
towards the South Pole*,
1777, Plate 47.

other shell. In Mallicollo and Tanna, several men had the *septum narium* perfo-rated, and the hole filled with a cylindrical stone; the heads of most of the men were bare; that of women often covered with a leaf of the *arum esculentum*, or the *dracontium pertusum*, or only surrounded by a fillet, or string. In New-Caledonia, many men had high cylindrical black caps, made of split bamboos, and coco-nut-core, which gave them a martial appearance; nor had several of these nations for-gotten to ornament their bodies, by puncturing them in various figures, and fill-ing the punctures with pounded coals or soot.[8] But the more civilized inhabitants of Taheitee and the Society-isles, living in the same mild tropical climate, have adopted a convenient, elegant dress: the lower part of the body is generally wrapt in pieces of this cloth to the middle of the calf of their legs, and the upper part is covered with another piece, having a longitudinal hole cut in the middle of it, through which they thrust their heads, and thus they cover their shoulders, half of their arms, their backs and breasts: sometimes these parts hang loose, and at other times they are tied fast to the body by the lower wrapper. This lower wrap-per is likewise adopted by the inhabitants of the Friendly-islands, with the entire omission of the upper-garment, which has the hole in the middle, and is called by the Taheiteans, *tèepoota*. In the Marquesas and Easter-Island, the same kind of cloth is used by the natives, though the full dress seemed to be only a garment of ceremony, when their chiefs and women appeared in state; the rest of the nation being but indifferently covered with short wrappers about the loins. Thus may we see the progress in the dress which originated from a necessary shelter against the inclemencies of the climate, and from a sense of modesty was improved to a coveting equally fitted for convenience and elegance.

The inhabitants of the Society-isles, are among all the nations of the South-Seas, the most cleanly; and the better sort of them carry cleanliness to a very great length; they bathe every morning and evening, in a rivulet, or the sea-water, and after they come out of the sea, they constantly undergo an immersion of their bodies in fresh water, for the ablution of the briny particles; before and after their meals they wash their hands; and were glad to obtain from us combs of all sizes and kinds, in order to adjust their hair, and likewise to free them from vermin, which, before the introduction of European combs, they frequently searched for, rendering this service to one another: they likewise anoint their hair, with per-fumed coco-nut oil, both to cause a fine smell, and to hinder the increase of vermin, which are instantly killed, as soon as their spiracula are stopt up with the oil. The want of scarcity of fresh water, in all the Low and Friendly-Islands, makes the natives less careful of ablution, and causes among them, I believe, these cuta-neous and leperous disorders, which we found so common among them. But the inhabitants of the New-Hebrides and New-Caledonia, we observed to be more cleanly, because fresh water is more common, and they were likewise careful in destroying the vermin.

The inhabitants of the Friendly-Islands constantly clip the hair of their beards, by means of two sharp bivalve shells; and I do not remember to have seen, in all these isles, one single man, with a long beard.* The hair of the head is commonly black, and flowing in beautiful natural ringlets; the natives, however, generally cut it short; and in a few individuals only, from Bolabola, we observed long hair.

Besides these articles belonging to the external appearance of the nations in the South-Seas, there are many others, which are equally characteristic, and the *language* is none of the least striking, curious and interesting. We acquired only a very imperfect knowledge of the many languages spoken in the various isles of the South-Sea; we shall therefore not pretend to be very full upon this subject, nor can it be expected; we shall only offer on that head a few general remarks.

The LANGUAGE of the Society-isles was better understood by us than any other, because we had made so considerable a stay among them, and had an opportunity of making use of the vocabularies collected in former voyages, and of conversing with the natives whom we had on board; the other dialects were only imperfectly understood. We found, however, that the language spoken at Easter island, the Marquesas, the Low, the Society, and Friendly-islands, and in New-Zeeland, is the same, and that the differences are hardly sufficient to constitute dialects. The languages spoken at the New-Hebrides, New-Caledonia, and New-Holland, are absolutely distinct from the above general language, and likewise differ among themselves. From a comparison of the vocabularies, in Schouten and le Maire's voyage, with one collected at the Friendly-islands, it appears, that they speak entirely the same dialect, in the Friendly-islands, and in those of *Hope, Coco's,* and *Traitor's,* to the North of the above islands. If we may be allowed to make an inference from one single word, I should think that at *Chica-yana,*† a low island, four days sail from *Taumaco,* the same dialect is spoken, since *ti-curi* or *tee-ghooree* is, in both places the name for a dog; nay, even at the NEW-CAROLINE-ISLANDS, they call the plaintive songs of their women *tonguer ifaifil;*‡ and in New-Zeeland, and the Friendly-islands, the same would be expressed by *tanghee fefeine,* which is not so very different, as to discourage our guessing at the

---

* We are therefore sorry, that we cannot, in this instance, say of the young artist's picture, representing the landing at the Friendly-isles, which is engraved for Capt. Cook's voyage, *omne tulit punctum qui miscuit utile dulci,*[9] as he made it a fine composition at the expence of truth, by giving all the men large bushy beards, contrary to the *costume* of the country, and by cloathing many figures from head to foot, with fine flowing draperies, in the finest Greek style, though the natives are constantly naked from the girdle upwards; the elegant form of their naked bodies would have produced as fine an effect, as the drapery: and in representations of this kind intended to accompany an history of a voyage, the chief requisite and merit is *truth;* which ought not to be sacrificed to whim and caprice.

† Dalrymple's *Collection,* vol. i. p. 159.

‡ Des Brosses *Hist. des Navigat. aux Terres Austral.* vol. ii. p. 486.

similarity of both languages. The language of *Chicayana*, is likewise, in my opinion, nearly related to that of the Tagalas, on the island of Luçon, because, in this tongue, *great* signifies DAQUILA, or TAQUILA,* and this is the name by which the natives of *Chicayana* distinguished the *great cardia*, or *cockles* from those which are smaller and more common.† The language of the Tagalas having an undoubted relation to that of the Malays, as may be easily collected from the comparison of the words of both languages; it can be no wonder that Malayan words were found in the Taheitean language, and its various dialects. These general observations on the language are so far curious and interesting, as they afford a farther confirmation of the origin and migration of these islanders.

But there are other observations, occurring on a more minute consideration of the language itself. The *first* is that at Taheitee, and the Society-isles, the natives have no sibilant in their language; and therefore having no use of their organs of speech in forming these sounds, they become at last utterly incapable of pronouncing any sibilant sound whatsoever. Their words, or even syllables, are never terminated by a consonant, for which reason the natives, in imitating the names of Europeans, always added a vowel at the end of such names as ended in a consonant; and this likewise has made their language soft and agreeable on account of the number of vowels; and wherever they met a sibilant, or consonant, which to their ear was not sufficiently euphonic, they immediately substituted another of more easy pronunciation: *Cook* was changed into *Toote*, and *George* into *Teoree*. The numerous vowels require a variation of dipthongs and accents, to produce a multiplicity of sounds, and a nicety of ear to observe all these little distinctions, which often occasioned a material alteration of the sense; as *ai*, to eat; *eài*, to copulate; *eìya*, fish; *aìya*, to steal or rob; *oìyo*, a noddy; *e-wài*, water; and *àvai*, the foot; *a hòw*, a dress or cloth; *à hoo*, a wind from behind; and *eoo*, the breasts; a dog is called *ooree*; a nail or iron *yuree*; and the male genitals *e-oure*.

The language is harmonious, and by no means harsh, when spoken in a manly manner, at Taheitee; at Huaheine, several people had the habit of pronouncing whatever they spoke, in a singing manner; and at the Friendly-isles, the singing tone of voice, in common conversation, was still more frequent, especially amongst women. The language of the Taheiteans, seems not destitute of some kind of culture, and shews a degree of civilization; for they have not only names for constellations, and single stars, for every plant or grass, but even for every insect, for every worm, every shell, fish, and bird, haunting their isle, and frequenting their shores; they have names also for all the parts of their body, and not only such as may be seen, but likewise for such as cannot be known but from

* P. Juan de Noceda y el P. Pedro de San Lucar *Vocabulario de la Lingua Tagala*, Manila, 1754, fol.
† Dalrymple's *Collection of Voyages*, vol. i. p. 149.

dissection. Like the old Britons, and Northern nations, they reckon not by days, but number the nights, if they want to express the interval of several days. As their minds are most used to things that strike the senses, they have no proper words for expressing abstract ideas; thus for instance they call the thoughts *the words of the belly, "parou no-te-oboo;"* a covetous man is called *tahata pirree-pirre*, or *piperriee*; and it should seem they had in their minds the idea of narrowness, or glueing and sticking together, when they formed the word, for *e-pirre* has the above significations; a generous man is called *tàhata-oowhoroa*, or literally, *the man of gifts or presents*; the HEAD of a human creature they call *oòpo*; that of a quadruped or fish, *òmee*; and that of a bird *pòa-arahòu*; the TAIL of a dog is called *àiro*; of a bird, *hòbe*; of a fish *eetèrre*; this last name is very remarkable, because it is expressive of the use the fishes make of their tail; for *ehoe-whateerra*, signifies a paddle for steering a canoe, or great boat; and the *eeterre* of fish, serves likewise for the direction of its course in the water. The males of the human species, they express by the word *tàne*; and the females, by that of *veheìne*; but the males of fishes, birds, or any animal, are called *ònee*; and the females, *òwha*: so that from these few instances, we may form some idea of the characteristic points in their language.

The COMMON OCCUPATIONS of the people of Taheitee, and the Society-islands, as well as those in all the islands of the Pacific Ocean are so very little varied, that Europeans, used both to a variety of occupations, and a round of amusements, would think their way of living highly insipid and uniform; they commonly rise with the sun, and as they have not a variety of garments to put on, they wrap themselves in the same clothes which served them for a cover during night, then go to the river or sea, and bathe; after which ablution each follows some occupation, either to fish at low water on the reef surrounding the island, or to dig up some ground intended for the plantation of the cloth-tree, which is commonly manured with broken shells; or to collect some bread-fruit, for making a sour paste, to be laid up for the season when none is to be had on the trees; or he climbs up to the elevated vallies between the mountains, and fetches from thence some loads of the large horse-plantanes; or he is occupied in felling large trees for making canoes or building houses; or his time is taken up in excavating a canoe, or sewing the several pieces together with cords made of coco-nut core: at other times he plants a young plantane-shoot, and surrounds it with pegs and sticks, that dogs, swine, and children, may not hurt or destroy it: the making of fish-hooks and of lines, from the filaments of a grass, or of cordage of various size and use, from coco-nut core, is another employment, or the manufacturing of a lance, a war-club, a breast-plate, a scoop for the canoe, a paddle, or some other such instrument, used in war or peace, is either his occupation or amusement. About noon, having washed his hands, he begins his meal of bread-fruit or sour-paste baked by hot stones under ground, and has perhaps, his brother and son for companions, whilst his wife and the females of the family, retire with their portion to another part of the house, or wait till the males have finished their meal. Clear water is their common drink, and frequently even sea-water. Another ablution of the hands concludes the dinner, and if the occupations in which he is engaged are not pressing, he rests on the ground in his hut, or if he be weary from constant hard labour, whether from a long walk, or from hard paddling, he refuses not to refresh his exhausted spirits by a seasonable sleep during the heat of the day, and in the cool of the evening returns to his former occupations with renewed vigour, till the declining sun bids him rest from the toils of the day; when after another slight repast, and another ablution, he lays down on the ground on a mat, and covers himself with his garment, by the side of his wife; unless he finds it more necessary to go on the reef with lighted links, in quest of a provision of fish.

The more barbarous, the less polished the manners of the nation are, the more MARKS OF CRUELTY towards strangers are generally observed; and in this respect, I should think, the natives of the tropical islands shewed the most favourable symptoms of friendship and philanthropy; for as soon as our ships arrived, they were received in the most friendly, generous, and cordial manner: even the attack made upon Captain Wallis,[10] I cannot suppose to have been concerted, unless some previous insult or offence, had been given, perhaps unknowingly, by our people, which roused their revenge, and as they were unacquainted with the effects of our fire-arms, they thought perhaps, they might venture an attack upon a set of men, who had offended or insulted them; and as the British people did not then understand their language, they possibly might have demanded redress and satisfaction for it, which, not being complied with, on account of the difference and ignorance of the language, they thought themselves in the right to retaliate the injury upon them; though this unlucky attempt, proved fatal to many of their brethren. Wherever we came, though the inhabitants had not the least idea of the execution our fire arms were capable of making, they behaved very friendly towards us: nay, after we had killed a man at the Marquesas, grievously wounded one at Easter-island, hooked a third with a boat-hook at Tonga-tabu, wounded one at Namocka, another at Mallicollo, and killed another at Tanna; the several inhabitants behaved in a civil and harmless manner to us, though they might have taken ample revenge, by cutting off our stragling parties; all which, in my opinion, sufficiently establish the friendly disposition of these several nations.[11]

We had no opportunities of seeing their method of punishing criminals, but we were told that thieves were either hanged or drowned with a weight tied to their necks; in either kind of punishment are no vestiges of cruely. In their wars all is over after the first onset, and it does not appear that they take any prisoners of war, or if they do, that they treat them in an inhuman or barbarous manner. We found not even the vestiges of making slaves of them in the sense that Eastern nations do, or still less by employing them to hard and toilsome labour, as we were used to do with those whom we send by thousands to our colonies. All that can be said against their friendly dispositions, is contained in some relations we heard of the devastations the people of Tearraboo or the little Peninsula made on O-Parre, after the battle of the Isthmus: it was reported that they burnt houses and canoes, and carried off all their hogs: but even this is in my opinion, not suf-ficient to represent them more cruel than the civilized nations of Europe, who plunder, waste, and burn with so much eagerness, and so little concern, that if we judge from thence, the actions above mentioned, seem by no means to brand the inhabitants of the South Seas with cruelty and barbarism. The natives of Bora-bora had conquered O-Raiedea and O-Taha, and some of their chiefs and warriors had occupied the lands of such people as had fled the country, but except in this instance, the conquerors had left every thing in the old situation; even the kings or chiefs of these islands, were alive and free, had a district to govern, had honours shewn them, and if we except the supreme power, they had not much changed their situation for the worse. There is hardly an instance of such moder-ation to be found in Europe. They had however, it seems, some notions, that strangers might be treated with less friendship and honesty, than their country-men, because no one of them hesitated a moment to steal or pilfer any thing, wherever he could lay his hands upon it, though they allowed it to be wrong, and though theft was punished in their country with hanging or drowning. They were, I believe, likewise in some measure excusable: for why came a set of strang-ers there, who had nothing to do on their shores? As they have no shipping or trade, or connexion with foreign nations, or any intercourse, or any wants making such an intercourse necessary,[12] they could not foresee that they should ever want the protection or favour of any European, and might therefore think it superflu-ous to gain their favour by honesty: but the generality behaved in so friendly a manner, as must endear their tempers and manners to all true lovers and promot-ers of universal philanthropy. However, though we find the islanders in the South Sea not without hospitality, they nevertheless think the strangers not quite entitled to all the friendship and benevolence which they bestow upon their own brethren, and in this respect they perfectly resemble all islanders in a less civilized situation, who commonly have a shy, reserved, and inhospitable character. Nor are the inhabitants of the islands in the South Sea quite free from a coarseness of manners, even to indelicacy in many respects, especially among the lower class of people; which appears from the disputes of many of them, wherein they fall to beating one another with the fist, and pulling one another's hair: and the numer-ous opprobrious names of *toùna, veheine wha-atùree, àiya, tahata-tàiva, dooe-dooaï, tahàta-peepèe ree* and others, corroborate this assertion.

MANNERS   The more fertile the isle of Taheitee is, and the more richly it affords all the
necessaries of life, and even those things which contribute to make life easy and
comfortable, the more does it contribute to the OPULENCE of the greater part of
the inhabitants; and really but very few are in such a situation, as to be called
POOR. Whenever we came to this happy island, we could evidently perceive the
opulence and happiness of its inhabitants; and those people of other South
Sea islands, who accidentally came to O-Taheitee always allowed it to be the
richest land, which they had seen. Opulence never fails to excite the appetite for
sensual pleasure, and if no restraint is laid on its gratification, it grows stronger
and stronger, so as at last to extinguish all the notions of propriety or decency.
This has been the case in all nations from all times. As long as the chiefs of these
islanders were few, the rest of the nation, preserved a kind of respect for these
leaders, who then it seems, were the heroes and best warriors of the nation. But
opulence, the fertility of soil and climate, and idleness at last increased the race of
chiefs to such a degree, that the wise men of the nation, the great chiefs of the
provinces and the whole nation itself, could not but be alarmed at their too great
number, and the disturbances which were doubtless too often made by an idle,
athletic, and numerous set of men. The respect which the rest of the nation still
had for their chiefs, and the great bodily strength of these drones, whose force was
unimpaired by labour, and daily inflamed by a preternatural indulgence in the
choicest fruit, and the fat of the land, made it more and more difficult to quell the
riots of these turbulent men. The married women have in all these isles a great
respect shewn to them, and their influence is great in all public and private
affairs; and as soon as the heir of a family is born, the father in a certain manner
loses his importance. These two circumstances made young men of rank and
property averse to marriage; and as they felt the strong calls of nature under the
influence of a powerful sun, they endeavoured to gratify their sensuality in such a
manner as was easy and most obvious; and as the other sex was excited by the
same causes to indulge themselves in sensual pleasure, the consequence was natural, that every kind of debauchery was introduced. These scenes of lewdness
nevertheless, could not be at first very common; but the children who were born
in consequence of this practice, became the object of serious public consideration: they had not been born in regular marriage, nor was it always possible to
point out the true father; they were therefore deprived of the right of inheritance,
on account of the uncertainty of their offspring; but continued to be stiled *Arees*,
and were allowed to belong to the family of chiefs, already grown too numerous,
turbulent, and powerful. As these chiefs, according to a former observation, were
the best warriors of the nations, the great chiefs and sage men thought it prudent
to institute an order of men, who should have great prerogatives, and great
honours paid to them, and who were to be the chief warriors; and that they might

not be too much attached to their wives and children, they were forbid marriage; and in the beginning of the institution, they were directed to abstain from all kinds of venery, as a practice that checked the boldness of spirit, and deprived men of that bodily strength so much required in their warriors. This society is called *Arreeoy,* and is still subsisting; though somewhat altered from its primitive institution.[13] There is no prerogative which a man likes more to boast of at the Society-islands, than that of an *Arreeoy;** they all belong to the class of warriors: as soon as an *Arreeoy* from another country appears, he is kindly received by the first *Arreeoy,* whom he meets; they exchange presents in cloth and garments, and he is entertained by his new host, with all the demonstration of friendship, and with the most unbounded hospitality. At certain stated times of the year the *Arreeoys* of one island remove to another, and there the days are spent in great feasts, wherein a profusion of the dainties of the country are consumed, and the nights are spent in music and dances, which are said to be remarkably lascivious, and likewise in the embraces of some girls, who officiate on these occasions like the priestesses and nymphs of the Paphian and Amathusian Goddess among the Greeks. We saw above seventy canoes sailing in one day from Huaheine to Raietea, with more than seven hundred people of both sexes on board, in order to assist at one of these feasts; when we arrived at Raietea, we found these *Arreeoys* removed from the Eastern side of the island, where they first had landed to its Western shore, and there we saw every house and shed crowded with people, and in every large house we observed heaps of provisions piled up, which were preparing by their women; and fishes, fowls, hogs, and dogs, were likewise dressed on this solemn occasion. During the night we could see these houses illuminated, and frequently heard the sound of their drums, which are used at their dramatic dances. And in a few days afterwards they removed to *O-Tahà,* and we were told, that they would even go as far as *Bora-bora,* before they would think of returning. So that several weeks must be spent in these feasts of *Arreeoys.* It is impossible that the frequent cohabitation with women, should not now and then be productive of an offspring; nay some of the modern *Arreeoys,* are so far degenerated, that they regularly keep a mistress, which, to all intents and purposes, is similar to a temporary wife, such as Muhammedans are used to marry for a certain time only.[†] But as this custom was contrary to the spirit of the original institution of Arreeoys, the Sages of the nation made another law, according to which, all infants, the offspring of the connexion of the Arreeoys with women, should be instantly killed after their birth; because, the increase of the Arees was thought to be detrimental to the state, and the original engagements of the *Arreeoys,* never

---

* See George Forster's *Voyage round the World,* vol. ii. p. 130.
† Chardin *Voyage,* vol. ii. p. 261, 263, de l'edit. in 12 mo. de 1711. Amster.

MANNERS

to cohabit with women, would else have been entirely defeated. *Boba,* the chief of O-Taha, was an Arreeoy, and nevertheless kept *Teinamai,* as a mistress, who was with child by him, at our second return to the Society-islands, and told us the child would be stifled the moment it was brought forth. Regulation and custom have established this inhuman practice; and nations which are not yet acquainted with those refined and sublime principles of virtue, which are established by the introduction of christianity into Europe, have frequently sacrificed the observation of a moral or social virtue to the greater security of the state, and even to a device for preventing imaginary evils; nay, which is worse, to a method of promoting either a martial spirit, or for teaching the stratagems of war. Thus for instance, the Spartans now and then sent their youths out upon the business of killing their Helotes; or ordered them to steal. However, we found these inhuman practices to be the effects of OPULENCE, LUXURY and SENSUALITY in a nation, which upon the whole, is not destitute of humanity, but rather inclined to practice kindness and goodnature, in a manner which would do honour to a more enlightened and civilized race of men.

The great profusion, and variety of choice fruit, delicious fish, and fine pork and dogs flesh, has likewise occasioned in the idle men belonging to the race of arees, a propensity to indulge themselves in the pleasures of the table beyond

Drum covered with shark skin, collected by Johann Reinhold Forster, probably from Raiatea in September 1773. H. 330 mm. Pitt Rivers Museum, Oxford (1886.1.1518).

what is usual. To excite their gluttony and voraciousness, they have invented the art of dressing these simple gifts of providence in a variety of dishes, nay, some sauces have been found out for stimulating appetite, and making some of the insipid victuals more palatable, and the quantities of the various kinds of fruit and meat which these drones can habitually swallow are hardly credible. Nor have they omitted to devise a method for procuring intoxication by the juice and infusion, of a kind of pepper-root. This same opulence has likewise been productive of distinctions in dress and ornaments. Their better people wear a variety of cloth distinct in colour and quality, and use it perhaps during a few days only, when they immediately change it. The fine white, and very soft cloth is the dress of their chiefs, and their women have a kind of wrapper or petticoat of a thin dark brown cloth, which is perfumed with their odoriferous coco-nut-oil. Red and yellow cloth of a very soft texture, is likewise part of the dress of the people of quality. Besides the distinction in dress, the chiefs are always served and attended by some of the lowest class of people, who dress and prepare their victuals, fetch water, and even cram them like animals that are to be fattened, and do all kind of service for them; while they indulge themselves in sloth and idleness, bathe twice a day, repose on a matt, with a wooden small chair under the head instead of a pillow; and do no kind of work unless they walk to see a friend or relation, nor are they unlike our grandees, who, from mere opulence, plunge into luxury and sensuality, and pursue the gratification of their brutish appetites, with the greatest eagerness, making it a kind of occupation necessary for their existence; they like them roam over the fertile plains of their isle, in quest of youth and beauty, and employ all the arts and guiles known in civilized countries, in order to debauch the unwary young females. When we sailed from O-Taheitee to Huaheine and Raietea in the year 1774, a female of the last mentioned island embarked with us at Taheitee in order to return to her native island. When we approached Raietea, she became very apprehensive, and told me she expected to be beaten by her father and mother, having been very naughty, and run away from them about a year and a half before, with a young *Arreeoy* of the family of the chiefs, who afterwards neglected her:* she was at Taheitee in the family of Tootaha's mother, and got her livelihood by working at the manufactory of the Taheitean cloth, and at the same time served for the gratification of the young men; in which profession she likewise attended our ship; and having on her return made her peace with her

---

* Capt. Cook seems to have expressed himself in such a manner, that his readers must understand that this girl was a native of O-Taheitee, and had run away from her parents in our ship; which could not be the case, since both her parents lived at Raietea; and though the circumstance happened as I related, it is equally probable, that her countrymen aimed a stroke of satire at her for running away with an arreeoy. See Cook's *Voyage*, p. 356.

parents, she took a trip to O-Taha, when the Arreoys removed to that island; but returned again in a few days to Raietea: which instance, in my opinion, clearly proves that *luxury* and *sensuality* naturally lead men to the most irregular and violent desires of gratifying their sensual appetites, ruining innocent young women, and of destroying the peace and happiness of families.

Among the innocent and harmless indulgences may be reckoned, the common practice of these islanders to rub and chase the wearied limbs of persons who have walked much, or used some violent exercise. This gentle chasing and pressing hinders the heated limbs from growing suddenly cold, and becoming stiff from a too sudden transition from one extreme to the other; and, as in these exertions, commonly a few muscles have been too much employed, and others less, it cannot but happen, that the equilibrium must be lost between the parts too much strained, and those which are so very little employed, which might cause dangerous effects, by cramps, convulsions, and other symptoms. The operation likewise invigorates the whole frame, and refreshes so much, that in the beginning I could not persuade myself, that this gentle squeezing of the tired limbs should produce so salutary an effect, had I not frequently had the experience.* When we had walked a great deal in our excursions, and sat down in order to take some refreshments, the natives of Taheitee and the Society Islands never omitted to rub our feet and arms, and to add this to the many little acts of kindness and hospitality, which they bestowed upon us with the greatest readiness and chearfulness; as they themselves never failed to perform this service to one another, on similar occasions.

The rank assigned to WOMEN in domestic society, among the various nations, has so great an influence upon their civilization and morality, that I cannot leave this subject, without adding a few remarks. The more debased the situation of a nation is, and of course the more remote from civilization, the more harshly we found the women treated.[14] In TIERRA DEL FUEGO women pick the muscles from the rocks, which constitute their chief food. In NEW-ZEELAND, they collect the eatable fern-roots (*Pteris esculenta, Polypodium medullare*), they dress the victuals, prepare the flax-plant, and manufacture it into garments, knit the nets for their fishing, and are never without labour and employment; whilst the surly men pass the greater part of their time in sloth and indolence: however, these are the least hardships of these unhappy females; for they are not only the drudges of the men, but are not even permitted to punish their unruly and wanton boys, who often

---

* The Chinese are equally fond of the same operation. See Osbeck's *Voyage*, vol. I. p. 231. Nor is it unknown, that the oriental nations use this rubbing or chafing in their public baths; which is said sometimes to cause so exquisitely agreeable a sensation, that the operated person is very nearly intranced. Mr. Lockyer, purser of the Ceres East-Indiaman, communicated this circumstance to me.

throw stones at their mothers, or beat them with impunity, under the eyes and sanction of their fathers; and they are looked upon as beings calculated for the mere satisfaction of brutal appetites, nor treated better than beasts of burden, without being allowed to have the least will of their own: which incontestibly proves, how much men, in a degenerated and savage state, are inclined to oppress the weaker party.

Et Venus in sylvis jungebat corpora amantum,
Conciliabat enim vel mutua quemque cupido,
Vel violenta viri vis, atque impensa libido.
    Lucret. lib. v[15]

The females at TANNA, MALLICOLLO, and NEW-CALEDONIA, were not in a much happier condition; for, though we never knew them to be beaten and abused by their own offspring, they were however obliged to carry burdens, and to take upon themselves every laborious and toilsome part of domestic business. This unhappy situation of the females among the savage and barbarous tribes of the South-Sea, has nevertheless been productive of an advantage, which, in our opinion, should rate them above their surly lords or oppressors; for, though the constant acts of indelicacy, oppression, and inhumanity, are so far from contributing towards the real contentment of the females, that they on the contrary reduce them to the most wretched beings; yet this very oppression, and the more delicate frame of their bodies, together with the finer and more irritable texture of their nerves, have contributed more towards the improvement and perfection of their intellectual faculties, than of those of the males. The various objects surrounding them make quicker and more vivid impressions on the senses of the females, because their nerves are finer and more irritable; this makes them more inclined to imitation, and more quick in observing the properties and relations of things; their memory is more faithful in retaining them; and their faculties thereby become more capable of comparing them, and of abstracting general ideas from their perceptions. This facilitates to them the various operations of their toilsome, laborious life, and often leads them towards new improvements. Used implicitly to submit to the will of their males, they have been early taught to suppress the flights of passion; cooler reflexion, gentleness, and every method for obtaining the approbation, and for winning the good-will of others have taken their place, and must in time naturally contribute to soften that harshness of manners, which is become habitual in the barbarous races of men; and all this may perhaps prepare them for the first dawnings of civilization. The males in barbarous nations look upon the women as their property, and this went so far, that in New-Zeeland the fathers and nearest relations were used to sell the favours of their females to those of our ship's company, who were irresistibly attracted by their charms; and often were these victims of brutality dragged by the fathers into the dark recesses of the ship, and there left to the beastly appetite of their paramours, who did not disdain them, though the poor victim stood trembling before them, and was dissolved in a flood of tears.[16] The barbarian knows hardly any law; the superiority of power decides every thing; it is therefore no wonder that he should extend his tyrannical sway over the weaker sex, and being himself a stranger to the more *tender feelings of love,* he is of course equally ignorant of the ideas of *modesty, bashfulness,* or *delicacy;* and if he forbids to his wife the connexions with others, and punishes the transgression of his commands on that head with great severity; it is not from the above principles, but in order to assert his right of property and dominion over her; for he would freely admit any stranger to his wife's embraces, if the equivalent for it were to his liking, or if prompted by some other consideration, which could satisfy his caprice or whim.

In O-Taheitee, the Society, the Friendly Isles, and the Marquesas, the fair sex is already raised to a greater equality with the men; and if, from no other reason, from this alone we might be allowed to pronounce, that these islanders have emerged from the state of savages, and ought to be ranked one remove above barbarians. For the more the women are esteemed in a nation, and enjoy an equality of rights with the men, the more it appears that the original harshness of manners is softened, the more the people are capable of tender feelings, mutual attachment, and social virtues, which naturally lead them towards the blessings of civilization. In O-Taheitee, and its neighbourhood, the women are possessed of a delicate organization, a sprightly turn of mind, a lively, fanciful imagination, a wonderful quickness of parts and sensibility, a sweetness of temper, and a desire to please; all which, when found connected with primitive simplicity of manners, when accompanied with a charming frankness, a beautifully proportioned shape, an irresistible smile, and eyes full of sweetness and sparkling with fire, contribute to captivate the hearts of their men, and to secure to them a just and moderate influence in domestic and even public affairs. We find the women esteemed at O-Taheitee, and its neighbourhood; they mix in all societies, and are allowed to converse freely with every body without restriction, which enables them to cultivate their minds, and to acquire that polish, which afterwards contributes to improve the manners of their young men; for, as it is one of the chief points of female education, in these happy isles, to learn the great art to please, they are instructed in all the means of gaining the affection of the males, of studying every winning art, and of habituating themselves to that sweetness of temper which never fails to merit the return of attachment, of friendship and love. Their frequent songs, their dances, their innocent laughter, and humorous mirth, all conspire to make the most lasting impressions upon the youths of the other sex, and to cement an union which is dissolved only by death.

> . . . *Fuit haec sapientia quondam*
> . . . .
> *Concubitu prohibere vago: dare jura maritis.*
> Horat. Art. Poet.[17]

But it is remarkable, that though the female sex has already so much softened the manners of their countrymen, there still remain some strokes in their customs, which seem to prove, that the fair sex did not always enjoy that esteem and equality, which is now allotted to them. Wherever women in a nation are considered as the drudges of the family, there they must be contented to take their victuals separately from their surly lords and husbands.* This inequitable custom, however, is universally received at Taheitee and its neighbourhood, and I was utterly unable to learn from them the true origin or cause of it; and in my opinion it is no more than a remainder of that subjection in which women formerly were held in the Society-Isles, before they came to their present improved condition.[18]

The state of MARRIAGE ought likewise to engage our attention, as we are here treating of women. As far as we could observe, *monogamy* was most universally introduced among the various nations of the South-Sea. There were, I believe, instances, especially among the people of quality, that a man endeavoured to have a love-affair with some of the many females, who were always ready to gratify such votaries on the first application; but I never heard, that a married woman ever yielded to the embraces of any lover.

As polygamy is so very common in all hot climates, and likewise among all barbarous nations, where women are looked upon as private property; it might appear very remarkable, that in the isles of the South-Sea, lying in a hot climate, where luxury had made a considerable progress,[19] and where the inhabitants were remarkably addicted to venery;[20] or at New-Zeeland, and in the more Western isles, where women were less esteemed, polygamy should not have been introduced. The reasons of this extraordinary phaenomenon are in my opinion to be looked for, first, in the more gentle and sweet manners of their females; secondly,

---

* *Labat* observed, that a negro-slave did not eat with his wife and children; but after he was satisfied, he gave them leave to eat likewise; and *Valentyn* found the women in Amboyna serving their husbands at table, and eating afterwards in private. The Guiana-men exclude their women from their meals, and in the Caribbee Islands women are not even permitted to eat in presence of their husbands. Labat *Voyage en Amerique.*

MANNERS

in the equal proportion of females to males existing in these isles; and lastly, in the great facility of parting with a wife, and taking another in her stead, of which we had several examples. *O-Amo*, the husband of *O-Poorea*, had another wife when we came to O-Taheitee; nor was she without a person who acted the part of a husband. *Potatou* had taken *Waineeòu*, and parted with his wife *Polatehera*, who lived with *Maheine* a young Oraiedea Chief. But I find myself obliged here to confess, that I am not as yet persuaded of the great and universal argument for monogamy, viz. the equal proportion of women to men; as, in my opinion, it is not clearly proved, that this just proportion takes place in all countries and climates. On the contrary, I am of opinion, that in Africa the constitution of food and climate, and the prevailing custom of marrying many wives, have, by length of time, produced a considerable disparity between the numbers of men and women, so that now to one man several women are born. In all kinds of animals, it has been observed, that in the two sexes when coupled, the most vigorous and hottest constitution always prevails; so that if, for instance, the stallion be more hot and vigorous than the mares, and not impaired by age and too often repeated covering,[21] the male foals in general will be more numerous; but if, on the contrary, the mares are more vigorous, the stallion old and exhausted by many copulations, their offspring will chiefly consist of females. If this be applied to the inhabitants of Africa, it is evident, that the men there, accustomed to polygamy, are enervated by the use of so many women, and therefore less vigorous; the women, on the contrary, are of a hotter constitution, not only on account of their more irritable nerves, more sensible organization, and more lively fancy; but likewise because they are deprived in their matrimony of that share of physical love, which in a monogamous condition would all be theirs; and thus, for the above reasons, the generality of children are born females. This observation is really confirmed by fact; for all the voyagers unanimously agree, that among all the African nations *polygyny* is customary*; nor has anyone observed, that there are many men among these nations without wives†, for every one is matched to one or more females. When a polygamous nation lives in the neighbourhood of monogamous nations, there is always a probability, that

---

* Oldendorp, (in his *History of the Mission of the Moravian Brethren in the Caribbee Isles, St. Thomas, St. Croix, and St. John*. Barby, 1777. 8vo.) says, vol. I. p. 293, "Polygamy is introduced among all the tribes of African negroes; those of Congo only, who are acquainted with the Christian doctrines and are baptized, are monogamous." But Lord Kaime, in his *Sketches of the History of Man*, vol. I. p. 197, says, "Among the Christians of Congo, polygamy is in use as formerly when they were pagans. To be confined to one wife during life, is held by the most zealous Christians there, to be altogether irrational: rather than be so confined, they would renounce Christianity."
† Bosman's *Description of the Coast of Guinea*, p. 180; who likewise p. 181, expressly declares, that "the number of women much exceeds that of the men."

the women necessary for so many men, who have more than one wife, are obtained by stealth, by force, or by commerce from the neighbouring nations: but in Africa all the nations are polygamous, every man is married, and has more than one wife; he cannot procure these numerous wives from the neighbouring tribes, where the same custom prevails; it is therefore, in my opinion, a clear and settled point, that the women born among these nations must be more numerous than the males.

Though the colonists settled at the Cape of Good Hope are monogamous, I observed in the various families of the town and country the number of females to prevail. The climate and food might influence them in some measure; but the chief reason which may be assigned for this appearance, is the licentious conduct of the young people there. The numerous female slaves imported from Madagascar, Bengal, Java, the Moluccas, and the coast of Papuas, give their young men many opportunities, and so great a facility of forming early and irregular connexions with these lascivious females, by which the vigour, and strength of constitution is exhausted in their males before marriage; that it is no wonder that the young women of the colony, born under a genial sun, never stinted for food, nor spent by labour, are more hale, vigorous, and blessed with a warm constitution; and that they during marriage, bring forth more females than males. It has been observed that in Sweden more females than males have been born during the latter part of this century. And it is reported that in the kingdom of Bantam* even ten women are born for one man. I wish therefore, that what I have here observed, may not be considered as a decided fact, but rather as reasons for doubting and continuing the enquiry with greater accuracy; as such a hint may lead to more authenticated facts, and serve to illustrate this curious part of the history of mankind. In the greater part of Europe it has been proved by the most accurate lists of mortality, that the proportion of men to women is nearly equal, or if any difference takes place the males born are more numerous, in the proportion of 105 to 100; here no doubt, providence has enforced the necessity of monogamy: how far the argument holds in hot countries, in Asia and Africa, is still uncertain. Perhaps the vicious habit of polygamy, has in a long succession of time inverted or viciated the general rule of nature, by the gradual enervation and encreasing weakness of males. Thus we find *polygyny* in one part of the globe, *monogamy* in another, and we have reason to suspect that *polyandry* is actually established at Easter-Island. In remote ages the Median women are said to have had several husbands at a time, and those were though ill provided, who were wedded to no more than five.† Nay, among the antient Britons ten or a dozen men kept but one

---

* Lord Kaime's *Sketches of the History of Man*, vol. i. p. 176.
† Strabo *Geogr.* lib. xi. p. m. 362.[22]

MANNERS

woman.* The women of quality on the coast of Malabar are allowed to marry as many men as they please.† And lately it has been confirmed that in the kingdom of Tibet, several men, especially if they happen to be brethren or relations, join together in maintaining one woman, and they used to excuse themselves that they had not women enough. Strange and unnatural as this custom may appear, it is however, not less true, and owes its origin undoubtedly to peculiar causes. In the vicinity of China, Bukaria, and India, where men are used to marry more than one wife, women must naturally grow scarce, being taken by main force or address, or by commerce: it is no wonder therefore that several men are obliged to maintain but one wife. Easter-island, when it was discovered in 1722, by *Rogge-wein* contained many thousands of inhabitants.‡ The Spaniards found in 1770 about 3000 people on it,* and we in 1774, scarcely 900.✦ This gradual diminution of inhabitants is a singular appearance; but what is still more remarkable, is, that among these 900 there were but about 50 women in all: so that the number of men to that of women was as 17 to one in this isle.[24] This strange proportion of men to women, could not have taken place long before our arrival there; for in a few years the number of men would by death come to a par, or nearly so, with that of the women. I suppose therefore, that as this isle has the strongest marks of hav-ing been once subject to a violent change from a subterraneous fire and earth-quake, it is highly probably that in a great revolution of this kind, the numerous inhabitants of the isle were destroyed. Nor is this circumstance very improbable, for Capt. *Davis* in the year 1687, felt a violent shock of an earthquake in this ocean, and not very far from this island.[25] In Otaheitee earthquakes are known and are thought to be under the regulation and conduct of *Maoowe* a peculiar divinity: but this is rendered more probable from the practice of the inhabitants of Easter-island, who to this very day, frequently form their habitations under ground, and support the whole fabric by walls of lose stones. Now if the disaster befel the nation in the day time, it is probable that a great many men being out of doors upon some business, might be preserved, whereas the women keeping more

---

* Caesar *de bello Gallico*, lib. v.[23]

† Dillon's *Voyage*, part i. chap. xxxii.

‡ Mr. Dalrymple's *Collection of Voyages*, vol. ii. p. 91, and 112.

* See Mr. Dalrymple's Letter to Dr. Hawkesworth, London, 4tº, 1773, page 34.

✦ Captain Cook's *Voyage towards the South Pole, and round the World*, vol. i, 289. It is said, "The inhabitants of this island do not seem to exceed six or seven hundred souls, and above two thirds of those we saw, were males." The disproportion between men and women is undoubtedly greater. Capt. Cook was sickly, and did not join the expedition over the island, being too weak. I am certain their houses contained no women concealed: and am equally sure that all the women I saw, did not exceed fifty; nor is it probable that they had restrained their females from appearing during our stay, as they were by no means of a jealous disposition.

at home, were involved in instantaneous ruin, by the tumbling of the wretched habitations, and no more than a few only that happened to be out of doors were spared, to become the mothers of a future and unhappy generation. These women we found still living in these huts, and they were most probably enjoyed by many husbands, nor were they afraid of encountering the embraces of a multitude from our ship, being accustomed to these rites on account of the reduced numbers of their sex, who were scarcely able to satisfy the desires of so many. If the above mentioned theory were admissible, and could be confirmed by facts and experience, the far greater proportion of boys, should be born in this isle: but the too numerous embraces of many might perhaps serve to frustrate the procreation of children, as is commonly the case with those unhappy females, who prostitute themselves to a multitude.

These few remarks are offered in hopes of conveying some ideas of the different manners and customs adopted among the various nations of the South Sea, in regard to their women in general, and during marriage in particular. They lead the thinking mind towards the investigation of truth, and the wise dispensations of providence relative to the generation of man; we observe, that though in a higher refined, more civilized, and more moral nation, *monogamy* seems to be the true and best means for perpetuating and encreasing mankind; yet when man is degenerated and debased by vicious habits, or involved in great misfortunes, we find *polygyny* and *polyandry* likewise employed, though I humbly presume they may be allowed, as matters now stand. But in case wise legislators had any authority, they could not better employ it, than by persuading these nations to return to MONOGAMY the primitive method ordained by providence for the propagation of mankind; and every encouragement ought to be given to so laudable a purpose.

The nations of the South Sea living all in monogamy, though descended from the nations on the Indian continent, who almost all are polygamous, prove indisputably, that perhaps neither wisdom nor virtue prompted them to adopt this measure, but that in all probability the first settlers in these isles brought an equal proportion of men and women with them, and that accident made it necessary to continue the measure, and to lay aside polygamy, the practice of which they had been accustomed to in the mother country.[26] The moderate size of these isles made it likewise necessary to continue this method; because if in a small isle, one man should encroach upon the rights of several men, by taking those females to himself, which originally were designed to be the wives of several, he could not remain unnoticed, and the injury done could not but be felt very grievously, and at length be in some measure repaired by restoring to every individual, what should have been his allotted share.

The young females of O-Taheitee and its neighbourhood, are not over scrupulous in admitting some lovers to their embraces before marriage. In other countries this would be a sufficient reason for excluding them for ever from the married state; but these nations think of such favours in a different light. If the birth of a child should happen to be the consequence, the youth is reputed the father, and the parents are entitled to all the privileges of regular marriages; if they have no issue, the female is not stamped with ignominy for such a trespass, but is always reputed capable of joining in matrimony with the best men of the nation.

> . . . *Jam proterva*
> *Fronte petet Lalage maritum*
> *Dilecta*
>   Horat. lib. ii. ode 5[27]

After marriage these very persons keep their compact with a chastity and fidelity which are highly meritorious.

When we were the second time at *O-Raiedea*, the chief of *O-Tahà*, called *Bobà*, came frequently to visit us; one day being on board, he saw his sisters coming towards the ship in a canoe, and pointing to his younger sister, desired me as soon as she came on deck, to say to her, *Veheina-poowa;* I did so, not knowing what would be the consequence, and her elder sister immediately lifted up the garments of the younger, shewing that she had the marks of puberty.[28] When she had done this two or three times, she refused to go through the same ceremony

Sydney Parkinson,
[*Tahitian Tattoo Designs*],
pen, wash, and pencil,
1769. 190 × 162 mm.
British Library.

again. I then enquired more carefully into the meaning of this transaction, and learnt, that in these isles, it is a kind of reproach, or want of dignity not to be of age, and to be destitute of the marks of puberty. As soon as they appear, the young women are obliged to undergo a very painful operation, viz. to have large arched stripes punctured on their buttocks: these curious marks are reputed honourable, and it is thought a mark of pre-eminence to be capable of bearing children. If therefore a man should reproach the person with the deficiency of these marks, she cannot in honour avoid refuting it by ocular demonstration.* The origin of these strange customs, it was not in my power to investigate. I contented myself therefore with collecting and recording the fact.

---

* Among the Thracians it was customary not to watch the chastity of their virgins, who were at liberty to admit any man they chose to their embraces; but they kept a strict watch over the conduct of their wives, whom they bought at a great price from their parents. To be punctured they thought a mark of nobility, to have no punctures, that of being basely born. Herodotus, *lib. v. c. 6.*[29]

SECTION VIII

Instruction, Private and Public. Origin and Progress of Manufactures, Arts and Sciences

Usus, & impigrae simul experientia mentis
Paulatim docuit pedetentim progredientis.
Lucretius, lib. v. p. 14, 51, 52[1]

ARTS AND
SCIENCES

Having endeavoured to display the principles of morality adopted among the nations of the South Sea, together with the characteristic lines, forming their manners, and the progress they had made in refinement and luxury; I lastly annexed some cursory remarks on their women. These several particulars, together with the observations on the population, the physical constitution of the tribes found by us in the South Sea, the causes of their diversity, the origin of their races, the first state of rude societies and their various progress, their laws of government, would be sufficient to enable us to form a competent idea of the real state of humanity in these countries. It remains only to complete the whole, by suggesting those arts, those ideas and principles, which these nations think most worthy of perpetuating among their progeny, and which therefore become the objects both of common and more exalted education.

Our trades and mechanical arts, as well as our sciences and historical knowledge, are the results of the inventions and observations of many thousands, who have lived at many different periods of time, and in countries very remote from one another. They may be just considered as the joint-stock of knowledge of all mankind, and a treasure, to which, all inquisitive individuals, and the more polished nations of Europe have free access. This immense store of knowledge can at present no longer be viewed and examined by one person: it is too vast to be comprehended by one individual, be he ever so great a genius. It is enough in the present condition of highly civilized European societies, to perpetuate the bulk, by dividing it into various branches, open for the exercise and investigation of a multitude, and their various circumstances and choice. Thus we have contrived not only to preserve each small branch in that perfection in which it is found, but likewise to make new improvements, and to add to it new discoveries. Our art of writing and printing, is the most efficacious means of preventing the entire oblivion of many useful observations, experiments, and discoveries, in each branch of human knowledge. But had mankind lived dispersed in the woods like savages or hunters, or had they continually rambled over great spaces with their herds, it would have been equally impossible to lay up so valuable and so immense a transfer, to increase it so constantly, and to make the advantages arising from their use so easy, and so common to every individual. The cultivation of such vegetables as serve for food to mankind, enables us in an especial manner, to form numerous societies. Many trades and mechanical arts, want the joint efforts of many arms, to give them that perfection, of which they are capable; and the more each art and trade is subdivided into smaller branches, the greater is the probability of bringing it to perfection and maturity. It is therefore evident that no other than numerous societies, in countries rich in such productions as are necessary for food and raiment, are best calculated for the greatest improvements, and most likely to promote the progress of acts and sciences, and their various branches. Egypt, on account of its happy constitution, caused by the *Nile's* overflowing every year the flat country, became very early the seat of agriculture, and cultivation of all kinds of vegetables, and for that reason pastoral life was laid aside, and even abhorred; population increased prodigiously, and the mechanical arts, the various branches of trade, and science began to be cultivated, received daily improvements, and the whole circle of human knowledge was more and more enlarged. The countries situated near the mouth of the rivers *Tigris* and *Euphrates*, were much of the same nature with Egypt; and it was there likewise, that agriculture, and the cultivation of trades, arts and sciences were known at a time when the rest of the world was still buried in barbarism. We find the same climate, the same constitution of the country, the same early use of agriculture, and the same progress in trade, arts and sciences, on the banks of the *Sind* and *Ganges* in India, and of the *Hoan-ho* and *Yan-tse-kian* in China. After these instances, the fact may be supposed so well established, that no doubt can remain about the truth of it. And in a certain degree may we likewise account for the progress which the arts had made in the Friendly and the Society-isles: these have a considerable population, which I suppose, at first obliged the inhabitants to increase the native productions of their lands, by a careful cultivation; the mildness of the climate, the great fertility of their soil, the progress they made in agriculture, enabled them to enjoy the advantages of mutual assistance, and to relish the charms of society; all these concurring circumstances gave rise to the first notion of perpetuating among their progeny, those arts, ideas, and principles, which form their system of education.

Though the more Western isles have the same advantage of a happy climate, are far from being barren, and the numbers of the people by no means inconsiderable; yet are they less improved, have fewer arts and improvements, and very imperfect ideas of science and useful knowledge; which remarkable difference seems strongly to prove, that there is still another great cause of the advancement of human knowledge in the Friendly and Society isles, but particularly in the latter; we have already pointed out the source of this difference, (chap. iv. page 196–198) viz. that the tribes from whom the two races of men in the South Seas descend, had unequally preserved by education and instruction, the systems of knowledge, which they had obtained from their more remote progenitors: it is therefore only necessary to give a more detailed idea of the education of these nations.

The first notions necessary for the way of life now in use in these islands, are instilled into the tender minds of the children by their parents: these notions may be divided into various branches, as varied as the objects are to which they relate; the more universally necessary objects of all nations, are food, raiment, and shelter against the inclemencies of the weather; the operations therefore relative to food, dress, and habitation are the first, which are taught the children by their parents. As these nations have not yet a multiplicity of artificial wants, and as their time is not yet taken up with any business more material than the three enumerated articles, their manufactures are in consequence very simple, and undivided in many branches; nay, they are all thought necessary for every individual in these isles, and for that reason every child is instructed in the best methods of cultivating the bread-fruit tree, the plantane-stalks, the roots of yams, and other eatable roots; the most expeditious ways for catching fish, the proper season and bait for each kind, and the places which they haunt and resort to, are told to their children; nay, all the fishes, shells, and blubbers, which in any ways may with safety be eaten, are named and shewed to them, together with their nature, food, haunts, and qualities; the devices for catching birds, for rearing dogs, swine, and fowls, and all the names of spontaneous eatable plants are communicated to their youths, together with their seasons and qualities; so that there is hardly a boy of 10 or 12 years old, who is not perfectly well acquainted with these articles. But as the bark of the mulberry tree, requisite for raiment, must be cultivated with a great deal of care and application, their youths are well instructed in the methods necessary for that purpose: and every young woman is early instructed in all the operations requisite for manufacturing and dying their cloth, and likewise in those of making mats, and other parts of their dress. The wood which is best calculated for building a house, a canoe, or other utensils, together with every operation for erecting a habitation, for making the various parts of a boat, and for navigating it by paddles or sails, are understood by every person, from the last toutou to the first chief of the land. In short, there is not one mechanical operation, which they do not teach to every youth, and which, after some time, he is not capable of executing with as much adroitness and skill as the best and oldest man in the nation.

It might seem that after all, these are but trifles in a system of education; but the very existence of these islanders depends upon the knowledge they have of the various vegetables, their cultivation and preparation into food, &c. &c. and also of the birds, fishes, shells, &c. which make part of their food. I had occasion to write down the names of 48 fishes, which they all reckoned eatable; and Captain Cook declared, those he had seen in his first voyage, and of which they heard the names from the natives were about 150. The very bread-fruit (*artocarpus communis*) called by the natives *ooroo*, has three varieties distinguished by peculiar

"A Branch of the Bread-fruit Tree with the Fruit," engraving by I. Miller, from Hawkesworth, *Account of the Voyages Undertaken . . . for Making Discoveries in the Southern Hemisphere*, 1773, Vol. 2, Plate 11.

names: thus for instance, the variety with more narrow pinnatifid leaves and oblong fruit, is called *maira*; another variety with oblong fruit, but a more rough, and as it were, scaly outside, they name *epatèa*; and still another oblong variety, whose rind has small mammillary prickles or warts, bears the denomination of *tat-tàra*. Of the banana (*musa paradisiaca*) they enumerate at least 13 different sorts, distinguished by different names, besides the large horse-plantanes: they cultivate at least two sorts of *arum*, viz. the common eddoes, with a blueish velvet leaf, (*arum esculentum*) called *tarro*, and the large kind, with green glossy leaves, which they name *àpe*, (*arum macrorhizum*). Besides these varieties of plants, they have also a kind of excellent apples, called *evèe*, nearly related to the Brasilian plumb (*spondias*). A large tree bears a kind of fruit involved in a stringy shell, in taste not greatly different from the chestnut, which they name *ràtta*, and we gave it the name of *inocarpus edulis*. Another large tree likewise growing in the East Indies, and known by the botanical name of *eugenia malaccensis*, is not uncommon in these isles; its juicy refreshing fruit is eaten in great quantities, and bears the name of *e-hàya*: there is another large plant, which these isles have in common with the East-Indies, known in the Molucca islands by the name of *pandang*, in Taheitee, by that of *e-whára*, and to which we gave the botanical name of *athro-dactylis spinosa*. (See *Forster's Characteres Gen. Plant. p.* 149, tab. 75.) Its fruit grows in large clusters, and when ripe, it has an agreeable smell, but the taste was to me very disagreeable and astringent; the natives find it more palatable: the same plant yields to them its large leaves, which dried, are employed for covering, with a good thatch, the roofs of their houses: the male-flowers of this plant are strewed on the head in the same manner as powder is used by us, and its agreeable smell is reckoned a fine perfume for the better sort of people, and called *heenànno*: the Banians have imported this plant into Arabia or *Yemen,* on account of its odoriferous male-flowers. Forskal believes they have only the male plant in Yemen, where it is called *keura*; one single spike of its flowers is sold for about eight-pence.* The *morinda citrifolia,* has, in Taheitee, the name of *e-nòno,* and its fruit is sometimes eaten by the lower class of people, when they can procure nothing better: the roots of the *tacca pinnatifida,* or, as the natives call it, *peea*; those of the *dracontium polyphyllum,* or *tevèh,* and of the *pteris grandifolia?* or *e-narè,* are frequently eaten; the second and last only in cases of necessity; when the leaves, of a kind of purslane (*portulaca lutea*) called *e-atoòree*; those of a *solanum* or *poorahèitee,* together with the stalks of the *boerhavia procumbens,* or *enoona-noona* are also eaten, after having been baked: the roots of the sweet potatoe, (*convolvulus batatas*) or *e-oomàrro,* and of the true yam (*dioscorea alata & oppositifolia*) or *e-oòwhe,* are regularly planted, and used as the best eatable during

---

* Forskal *Flora Aegyptiaco-Arabica.* Havniae, 1775, 4to. page 172.

the season, when the bread-fruit is not to be had: the kernel covering the inside of coco-nuts, is likewise frequently eaten by the natives. The knowledge only of vegetables fit for food, forms a considerable list of names, and of ideas connected with them; nor have we enumerated all those which are occasionally eaten. In the Friendly-isles, the *shaddock (citrus decumanus)* is common, and called *mòreea,* or *mòleea:* in Mallicollo they have *oranges:* in the isle of Tanna, the *eugenia iambos,* and an other *eugenia* are used for food: the natives likewise eat several sorts of figs, and of one species the leaves are dressed in a kind of pie, made of yams and plantanes; the kernels of the *(terminalia catappa)* and of the *sterculia balanghas,* are likewise eaten: at New-Caledonia, the bark of the *hibiscus tiliaceus,* which they cultivate, is used for food, but is, in my opinion, a wretched kind of aliment.

The next necessary care, after food, is RAIMENT; and in this respect the natives of Taheitee, and the neighbouring isles, are certainly well provided; it is therefore no small trouble to teach the young people all the various branches of manufactures relative to clothing. Their dress consists chiefly of three different sorts; the one is a kind of cloth manufactured from the bark of trees, the second consists of various species of matting, serving for various purposes; and the last article comprehends all the different ornaments and dresses appropriated for certain ranks, or used only on certain occasions, or for performing certain ceremonies or religious rites.

The art of making their CLOTH is comprehended under many branches.[2]

The *materials* of which they are manufactured are different: in general the cloths are made from the bark of trees; the best sort of cloth is from the bark of the *aoùta,* or *morus papyrifera.* This plant is very carefully cultivated, in a good and rich soil, which the natives take care to manure and prepare for the better growth of these plants, by mixing with it all kinds of shells; the ground which they destine for the nursery of *aoùta,* is commonly enclosed by deep trenches, in order to prevent men and animals from hurting the young trees; in this soil they plant the young shoots of the *aoùta,* in regular rows, at the distance of about 18 inches, or two feet; they lop off the leaves and branches that are sprouting out, which operation increases the main shoot, and invigorates its strait growth; as soon as the saplings have attained the size of an inch diameter, and the heighth of about six or eight feet, they are drawn up; the roots and tops are then cut off, and such parts of the root as have young shoots, are carefully preserved and planted again: of the strait main shoot, the bark is slit up longitudinally, and put into a running stream, under a board loaded with stones; when the water has rendered the filamentous part of the bark more flexible, dissolved the gummous substance which joins them, and softened the pulpy intermediate substance, then the women scrape the bark, in or near the water, on a smooth board, set in a oblique

ARTS AND
SCIENCES

direction. A thin bivalve shell (*tellina gargadia*) is the instrument they make use of
for this purpose, and they frequently dip the bark in the water during the operation; the small narrow slips thus prepared are carefully spread on plantane-leaves,
to the breadth and length which the piece of cloth is intended to have, or which
the quantity of bark will admit; and in this condition they remain a whole night,
and from the residuous gummosity of the bark, the fine filaments are so closely
joined, that the whole makes next day but one piece, after the water is drained or
evaporated. Great judgment is to be observed in spreading the slips of bark, for as
they are not of equal thickness, they are often obliged to mend those places where
the bark was too thin. These large pieces are carried to sheds, somewhat remote
from their habitations, where the women join in working: one or more sit at a
long, smooth, square piece of timber, on which they beat the cloth with a square
instrument of heavy wood, called *toa;* each of the sides of this instrument is fur-
rowed longitudinally by close grooves, of different dimensions, and the side which
has the coarsest grooves is applied first in beating, and gradually the finer ones are
used, till at the last operation the cloth is reckoned fit for use. This beating joins
the fibres so close together, that the whole being dry, is really of a good consistence, though the least moisture seems to dissolve the whole texture; some pieces
of the best sort of bark are beaten more than the common, which makes the cloth
fine and extremely soft, not much unlike our muslin. During the beating they

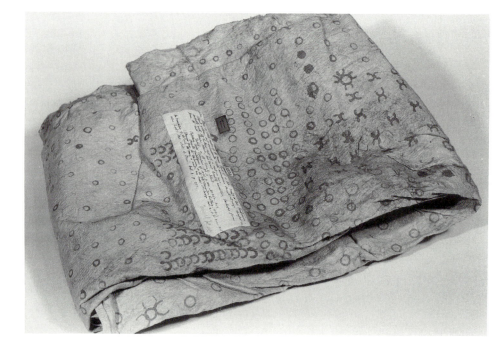

Piece of bark-cloth
from the Society Islands,
of the *apà* type referred
to by Forster; yellow
(presumably stained
with turmeric) and dec-
orated with red circles
produced by a bamboo
stamp. 2530 × 1600 mm.
Collected by Johann
Reinhold Forster. Pitt
Rivers Museum, Oxford
(1886.1.1234).

constantly sprinkle the stuff with water, which stands near them in cups of coco-nut-shells; after this operation the cloth is bleached, and washed, to make it whiter and softer; sometimes they make of such soft and fine cloth, (called in Taheitee *hoboo*) several large layers, which they join by a kind of glue, prepared from the root of the *tacca pinnatifida;* these layers are again consolidated by beat-ing, again rubbed, washed and softened, which operation makes it downy, smooth, and warm. The bread-fruit tree yields likewise a material for cloth; the natives plant the young shoots as the mulberry tree, the bark is stripped off, soaked, scraped, laid out, and beaten in the same manner, and the cloth it affords is somewhat coarser, and called *too-erroo.* A fig tree, called *eaoùwa,* nearly related to the *ficus indica,* and another kind, called by us *ficus aspera,* is likewise em-ployed, for making a species of cloth from its bark, which is always of brown or cinnamon colour; this cloth they call *òra,* and the way of manufacturing it is not different from the method described before; as this cloth resists the water more than any of the other two sorts, it is in high request, and chiefly worn by the people of quality, after being previously perfumed.

Not only the different of materials, but also the *destination* and *colour* causes various differences in the cloth: in general, every kind of cloth is called *ahoù;* but a garment, chiefly of the sort called *hoboo,* intended for the women, is named *paroovài:* if in the middle of a piece of about six feet in length, a longitudinal hole

Piece of bark-cloth from Tonga (detail). 2180 × 1400 mm. Collected by Johann Reinhold Forster. Pitt Rivers Museum, Oxford (1886.1.1226).

is cut, the natives call this dress *teèpoota*; it is a very common garment for both sexes, who put the head through the hole, and suffer it either to hang lose on both sides below the knees, or they inclose it by another piece of cloth, coming up almost to the breast, and serving instead of a wrapper. Pieces of cloth are used by both sexes as a sash, which covers their nudities; that which is worn by men, they call *màro*; that by women *parèoo*: red cloth is called *ewha-àïo*; the yellow kind is named *heapà*: there is a yellow cloth on which they make red figures, by dipping a bamboo reed in the red die, and stamping it on the cloth, this is known by the name *apà*; the sort which is not only brown, but covered with a kind of varnish or gummosity, they call *poowhìrree*. Their dies are very fine and bright, and would deserve more attention if they were lasting: the red die requires a good deal of labour and care in preparing it; the fruit of a small fig called *mattèe (ficus tinctoria)* affords a drop or two of a milky juice, when it is broken off from the tree; this juice is carefully gathered in a clean cup of coco-nut shell, and after having a sufficiency of it, they soak it in the leaves of the *etoù*, or *cordia sebestena*, which imbibe the milky juice, and soon tinge it of the finest crimson imaginable; the whole is gently squeezed out, and strained through the filaments of coco-nuts, and used to die cloth with: instead of the *e-toù*, sometimes the leaves of the *tahìnnoo*, or *tournefortia sericea*, are employed; or those of the *pohoòa* or *convolvulus brasiliensis*, or even those of the *e-poòa* or *solanum repandum*: the sole juice of the *mattèe*, affords a yellow colour; but the best yellow die is made of the juice dripping from the peduncles of the *hibiscus punctatus s. populneus*, or *e-mèero*: the watery infusion of the root of the *e-nòno*, or *morinda citrifolia*, dies a fine yellow; another kind is extracted from the *tamànnoo*, or the *calophyllum inophyllum*: one of the spurges called *epìrree-pìrree*, affords a hay brown colour; and the soaked bark of the *tootoòe*, or *aleurites triloba*, yields a gum or refinous substance, used by these people for varnishing their brown cloth (*poowhirree*).

MATS are employed for various purposes, and are either articles of dress, or are used for carpeting and bedding, or form their sails; those for dress are chiefly worn when they go a fishing, and in rainy weather. The bark of the *pooroù*, or *hibiscus tiliaceus*, is manufactured into mats, named *e-poorhòa*, which are very strong, and look as if they were made of a coarse flax or hemp; some of them are very fine, but have always a kind of harshness: the mat called *e-wharòu* is made from the leaves of a species of *athrodactylis*: the finest glossy white and shining mats, called *e-vanne*, are made of the membranaceous and best prepared part of the same leaves of *ewhàra* or *athrodactylis*, and sometimes of a kind of grass: another and very strong sort, manufactured of rush, is used to sleep on, which even the name of *Moèya* seems to imply: very nearly related to it is the sort, which is often striped or checked with black, and used occasionally for carpeting, or to dance on, in their dramatic pieces; these last mats are 20 or 30 yards in length; the bark of a tree, which I could never discover, forms their largest and very strong mats, called *hohòra,* one of which, when expanded upon a semi-oval frame, is an *eïya* or sail for their canoes.

The Taheiteans have various ORNAMENTAL and CEREMONIOUS dresses, which they manufacture in a most ingenious manner. After the death of a person of some note, one of the next relations puts on a kind of masquerade dress, called by them *Hèva,* which is very remarkable, as well on account of its curious workman-ship, as the strange assemblage of its parts and extraordinary appearance.[3] The enumeration of all the pieces belonging to it, with a short description of them, will not perhaps be thought superfluous, as it may set the arts of this people and their curious contrivances in no improper light. The first part of this dress they call *Ta-oòpo* or head-piece; it is formed of a piece of mat tied together into the form of a cone or a cap, to which they paste a piece of cloth reaching to the neck and shoulders, and covering the ears; they paste alternately red, brown and white transversal slips, in order to make this cap, and on its top they place a thick gar-land of glossy dark green pigeon feathers, to which sometimes red or yellow feathers are joined in small bunches, made of coco-nut filaments, the whole is encompassed by a kind of rope, formed of two kinds of Taheitee cloth, and other

ARTS AND
SCIENCES

"A Toupapow with a Corpse on it Attended by the Chief Mourner in his Habit of Ceremony," engraving by W. Woollett after William Hodges, from Cook, *A Voyage towards the South Pole,* 1777, Plate 44.

strings, tied together by the bark of various kinds of convulvuli, died black and red; this is called *Moyhò*. The next piece consists of several parts, the first of which is named *pa-tèea* to which they fasten the *pa-raè*, or frontlet; the *pa-oòto*, or mask before the mouth; and lastly, the *hoopà*, or stomacher, which form the most curious part of the whole dress. The *pa-teèa* is a large shell, of the oyster kind; they polish away its rough outside, and leave only a brown coating, which gives it much the appearance of turtle-shell; this shell is perforated on its margin by many small holes, which serve to fasten to it a border of shining dark green pigeons feathers, fixed on a plaited list of coco-nut filaments, and into this margin they fix a great quantity of tail-feathers from the tropic bird in a diverging manner; so as to appear like the rays of a luminous body: the *pa-ràe* is commonly joined to the *pa-teèa* by strings; this is again a shell of the same kind as the former, and has a very narrow hole, through which the person looks who wears the mask: below this is the *pa-ootoo*, or a thin black board, of the form of a segment of a circle, about a yard across, and about six or seven inches wide, to which they fix five mother of pearl shells, polished on both sides; on the extremities the two shells are again fringed, with pigeons feathers, as in the *pa-teèa*, and from them they suspend two tassels, of about 18 inches long, made of pigeons feathers, called *òrro-òrro*: the *hoopa* is made of small pieces of mother of pearl, of about an inch and a half, or two inches long, and one or two tenths of an inch wide, with a hole on each end, by which these small pieces are fixed in rows, so as to form a kind of apron or stomacher, there are sometimes 15 or 20 rows of these small pieces, in one *hoopa*. If we consider, that these holes are all bored by other sharp shells or bones, that the pieces must be ground of equal length and width, and then fastened in such a manner as to lie flat, it must be obvious, that the making of more than 2000 small pieces of mother of pearl, and the joining them together, is a work of immense labour, requiring much time and an unwearied patience, and what is still more, a nicety and accuracy in executing them, all of equal length and width: the *paràe* therefore, or the compound of these four pieces, is reckoned among the natives one of their most curious ornamental dresses; and which they seldom part with, unless for a very valuable consideration. Next to this follow the *ahou-aiboo*, which is a strong *teèpoota*, covered on its foreside with circular pieces of coco-nut shell, of about an inch and a half diameter, and disposed in rows; the *ahou-aiboo* is put over two other *teèpootas*, the lowermost of which is white or red in the widest, the next is brown and narrower, and the *ahou-aiboo* is the narrowest of all: these ahous they gather by a belt of two kinds of cloth, twisted together into a rope, and called *naoù-naoù*: over all this they spread on the back of the chief mourner a kind of mantle, made of netting of strings, and covered on the outside with glossy pigeons feathers; this cloak they call *ahou-roòpe*; in one hand the masked man, performing the ceremony, wears two strong mother of pearl oyster-shells, which he knocks against one another, and causes a loud noise, announcing his approach; these clappers are called *tettè*; the *pàyho* is held in the other hand, and consists of a stick, into which a row of sharp shark's teeth is fastened, with which they cut the people, who may happen to be dilatory in retiring at the approach of the solemn procession.* All the parts of this one dress are the most ingenious and most compound work they have on their isles, and must of consequence require a peculiar handiness and skill in executing with so much neatness and elegance.

The chief warriors who fight on the stages of their war-canoes, have likewise a dress peculiar to themselves, whose fabric requires some labour and ingenuity. The *awhoù* is a helmet of more than five or six feet high, formed of wicker work into the shape of a long cylinder; to this they add a frontlet, which is between three and four feet in length, it covers the front of the helmet or the half of the cylinder; towards the top however it does not lie close to the cylindric basket, but projects somewhat forward in a hollow shape; all this frontlet is covered with green glossy pigeons-feathers; sometimes they form of white feathers one or more borders round the whole frontlet, and to its outer edge they fix a great number of tail-feathers of the tropic-bird in a diverging manner, which gives the warrior a very grand appearance. These machines can by no means be worn, because they are so unwieldy, and at the same time so light, that the least breath of wind must almost overset the man, who should presume to wear one of them; so that I am of opinion these helmets are more for shew than real use, in defending the head against stones, or blows of clubs, and lances; it may possibly serve as a standard, to rally the troops about their leaders, which is not quite improbable, as we saw only single helmets in one or two war canoes, in a fleet of 169.[†] The warriors on the fighting-stage wear almost universally the gorget or breast-plate, called *ta-òmee*, likewise made of wicker-work, covered with semi-circular lifts of coco-nut fibres, which again are bedecked with shining glossy pigeons feathers, set off with two or three semi-circular rows of sharks-teeth, all which are bored and fastened to the breast-plate by strings; the whole gorget is fringed with long white dogs hair, imported from the Low-isles to O-Taheitee, and the Society-isles; on the top there are likewise mother of pearl shells, fringed with pigeons feathers; this breast-plate is hung on the neck by a string, and defends the breast against the thrust of one of their lances, headed with spines of the sting-ray.[‡] The making

---

* In Hawkesworth's Compilation, vol. ii. p. 234, plate No. 5, and in Captain Cook's *Voyage*, vol. i. p. 185, plate 44, is a representation of a man dressed in the *hèva* or mourning dress: but it must be observed, that the tropic bird's feathers go not beyond the *ta-oopo*, and are never fixed to the *pa-teea*, as has been improperly represented in the plate, drawn by Mr. W. Hodges.

† In Sydney Parkinson's *Journal, of a Voyage to the South-Seas*, plate xi. page 71; and in Capt. Cook's *Voyage*, vol. l. plate No. 61, p. 342: representation of this helmet may be seen; that in Parkinson gives by far the best idea of it.

‡ A good and faithful representation of one of these breast-plates may be seen in Hawkesworth's Compilation, vol. ii. p. 184, plate No. 8, drawn and engraved by Mr. James Roberts.

these war-dresses requires very curious and dextrous workmanship, and likewise a
good deal of time and patience.

The manufacturing various baskets, stools, cloth-beaters, and other utensils,
tools, and instruments, in use among these nations, is so multifarious, that a
minute description of them would require too much time; we must not therefore
enter upon the detail, but will confine ourselves to a brief description of the third
great branch of mechanical arts, exercised by these people, and relating to the
building of their houses. The materials, size, and destination of their houses and
buildings, constitute their difference. The wood of the *a-hoòdoo*, or *barringtonia
speciosa*, of the *inocarpus edulis*, or *ràtta*, of the *evee*, or *spondias pomifera*, of the
tamànoo or *calophyllum inophyllum*, and of the *oòroo* or *artocarpus communis*, are
the various materials used in building their houses. The natives call in general a
house *te-whàrre*; some are small and round, and are called *te-whàrre-potto*; those
which are very large and long, are named *tewhàrre tàrra*; and besides these, they
have houses or sheds to shelter their large double war-canoes. The common
houses are from 15 to 20 feet long, and 10 or 15 wide, the roof eight or nine feet
high in the middle, and about five or six feet on the sides, though the eves project
a good way beyond the sides, or posts.

The houses are all built with three rows of posts, supporting the roof
(*erà-woro*): the middle row of posts, (*epò-oo*) is about 16 or 20 feet high in the
large houses, and from eight to ten in the common or smaller ones; they support a
beam, forming the ridge of the roof, (*tocore-yore*) on which they fix the timbers,
or spars of the roof, (*ahèo*) which are again borne by a long beam, called *epài*,
under which a row of side-posts (*tooto-òroo*) is placed, standing on another beam
(*too-àrroo*) that rests on the ground: some times they fill these spaces between the
beams and posts on the sides of the house with bamboos, and this method of
building they call *parooroo*, but commonly all the underside is open. The roof
itself is formed of the leaves of the *athrodactylis indica*. Now and then I observed
the house open, but furnished below at the height of about one foot, with a fence
of bamboos. Some small houses are likewise included in a kind of partition made
of small sticks in the manner of hurdles. The natives commonly keep their hogs
during the night, in the house, and have in one corner of it contrived an inclosure (*pa boòa*) covered on the top with boards, on which they sleep.

The large war-canoes cost the natives infinite labour, and afford the best
specimens of their genius, industry, and mechanical arts; it is therefore no wonder
that they should be very careful in the preservation of these large boats, which are
the very means of their preservation and liberty, against the invasion of their
enemies. Huaheine has in its neighbourhood the isles of O-Raietea, Taha,
Borabora, and Mourooa, all under the dominion of *O-Poònee* a powerful chief,
who conquered Raietea and O-Taha, and would likewise have extended his

dominion over Huaheine; but the inhabitants of this island, with their chief *Oree*, were attentive to their true interest, and for that purpose kept constantly a large fleet in readiness under the above mentioned sheds. It was here likewise that I observed a double war-canoe, which required 144 paddles, and eight or ten steersmen to move it forward; the stage for fighting was roomy, and could contain about 30 men. These boat-houses are sometimes 40 or 50 or more yards long, about ten yards wide, and the eves of the roof are brought down within two or three feet of the ground. Sometimes the sides of the roof are in the shape of segments of a circle meeting at the top.

As I have here mentioned the large war-canoes of these nations, I will give a few hints relative to the structure of their boats. The inhabitants of the Society-isles distinguish their smaller canoes (*E-wàha*)* from the larger ones, (*pahèe*) and these are again different as their uses, for fishing, for long voyages from isle to isle, and for war. The latter have high sterns, and two of these boats being always tied together, towards the head of them stands a stage or platform (*Etoòtee*) raised on six or eight pillars about four or five feet high, and proportioned to the size of the boat. The warriors stand on these stages and fight the enemies who defend the shore. The boats are commonly built of the timber of the *E-avèe* or *Spondias pomifera* or the *E-màrra* or *Nauclea orientalis*. The keel is one piece of timber hollowed out, in the shape of a trough; in very large boats they employ more than one piece for the keel, but never exceed three. The next board is set on the keel in a diverging direction; the third board has a convex shape on its outside, but on the inside is concave, and the last board is set on this bilging board: these four boards are fitted amazingly tight and close, and afterwards fastened by cordage† made of the filaments surrounding the coco-nuts; and drawn together, that these

---

* The name *E-wáha* is certainly pronounced by the natives of the Friendly-isles and in New-Zeeland with a stronger founding of the aspirate *h*, by saying *Te-wagga*. In like manner the word *Teèhee* is changed into *Teéghee*, the word *Tahata* into *Tangata*, *E-hoe* or *Ehohe* is in New-Zeeland *Hogghee*, *Tohee* is *Togghee*, *Tareha* is *Taringa*, *Toohana* is *Tooghana*, &c. &c.

† The most antient and most simple manner of constructing embarkations, before the use of nails and iron to fix the planks to the knees and timbers, seems to have been that of sewing them together with strings. Plin. *Hist. Nat.* lib. xxiv. v. 40. *Cum sutiles fierent naves, lino tamen, non sparto unquam sutas.*⁴ In the ninth and tenth century of the Christian Aera, when all the vessels in the Mediterranean Sea were nailed together, a vessel was stranded on some part of the Syrian Coast, whose planks were all sewed together: this the author of the voyages to China of some Mahammedan travellers, published by Renaudot, p. 53, declared to be *an Arabian vessel from Shiras, whose construction is such that the planks are not nailed, but joined together in a peculiar manner, as if they had been sewed,* &c. &c. When the more civilized nations had better contrivances for the construction of their ships, by means of iron nails and bolts, the custom of sewing the planks of vessels together, was left to those that were less acquainted with the arts. The whole East has now the use of iron, and the custom of sewing the planks of embarkations is only found in the isles of the South Sea.

vessels are sufficiently water-tight, without any caulking; and though in the larger boats one person is constantly employed in baleing out the water, it never gains upon them. The head and stern are carved and commonly represent a rude figure of a man, called by them *E-teèhee;* which might be compared with the *tutelar genius* of the antient Romans and Greeks. Boats used for long voyages have on their foreparts small huts covered with thatch, and defended on one or two sides either with boards, or a partition of bamboos, and lined besides with mats, here the chief people sit by days, and sleep at night. The rest of these boats are nearly of the same structure with the war-boats; they have a mast, *(E-teèra)* a sail of mats in a frame *(Eìya)*; at the top of the mast they carry a bush of young branches of a tree, this bunch of rods is named *E-whatevà,* and from the top of the mast, or the uppermost part of the frame of the sail, one or two long garlands of feathers are hanging down called *Matìttee.* When they do not join two boats together, but have only one, across the middle of it a long beam is fixed, *(Patòa)* to which they fasten on one side small pieces of wood pointing downwards and joined to a piece of spar, shaped like a keel, i.e. triquetrous, which is nearly of the same length with the boat. This out-rigger they call *E-oà,* and it is fastened besides to the canoe by one or more cross beams. Such an apparatus must hinder the boat from overset-ting, and hardly retards the motion of the boat. The swift proas at the Ladrone-islands described in Lord Anson's voyage round the world, give the best idea of the utility of this apparatus.[5] To the projecting cross beams about the mast, the shrouds are fastened, and on the side opposite to the out-rigger, they fasten some-times a large stone in order to trim the boat by it.

The fishing boats are not unlike those intended for voyages, only the whole appartus is meaner, and the hut is less elegant, if any should happen to be fixed on the boat. This account will convince us that the natives of these isles are not defi-cient in the knowledge and practice of mechanical arts, and that they carefully preserve this knowledge, by early instructing their young people in all that belongs to their food, raiment, and habitations. If we consider that a stone adze, a chissel of the same materials, or of bone, and a piece of rough coral rock, together with a saw made from a part of the sting-ray's skin fastened round a piece of wood, are all the instruments to assist them in the structure of their houses and boats, we must certainly give ample testimony to their ingenuity. Their mechanical genius I particularly admired, having an opportunity of seeing one day a man busy in sew-ing a large canoe together: he employed a stick with a forked branch for the pur-pose of drawing the string more powerfully together; one of these branches he fixed against the lowermost plank; and to the other he had fastened the string or rope, which gave him an amazing purchase, and as soon as the string or rope was stretched to its utmost, an assistant struck a peg into the hole through which the string passed, to prevent its giving way again. Their methods of fishing and the several implements used for that purpose, afford many instances of their genius and spirit of observation. They make harpoons of reed (*E-tào-werro-eiya*) pointed with a hard wood shaped in the manner of the bearded head of an arrow. Their large seines (*oopèa*) are employed in shoal water only, and are of great extent and made of a kind of phaseolus and of a convolvulus. Their hooks (*Mattoù*) are formed of pieces of shells; those for catching of small fish are very neat, small, and of one piece; those for fish of a middle size, are made of mother of pearl-shell, and composed of two pieces, the shank is formed of the most bright and glossy part of the shell, and the hook is fastened to it by strings passing through some holes bored through both pieces, and for the better decoying the fish, they add some hair, feathers, or tufts of thread to represent the fins of small fish; this kind of hook they call *vìttee-vìttee*: the largest of all have a shank made of wood or bone covered with a brown mother of pearl-shell, and have a hook of tortoise-shell, which often is made of two pieces tied together. The strings for these hooks are made of a kind of nettle (*urtica argentea*) *Eroòa* which holds the strongest fish, (*viz.*) the Bonito or *Peeràra (Scomber pelamys)*, the Albecore or *Eàhai (Scomber Thynnus)*, and the Dolphin or *E-oòma (Coryphaena Hippurus)*: for all other purposes they use strings and ropes made of the *Emòhoo* or Cyperus alatus, the bark of *Pooròu* or Hibiscus tiliaceus, the bark of *Màttee* or ficus tinctoria and the *Epeèpee* or phaseolus amoenus. They make use of several plants and fruits, which when bruised and mixed with some minced meat of shell or cray-fish, and thrown into the sea inebriate fish to such a degree, that they may be caught by the hands, the chief fruit thus employed is that of the Barringtonia speciosa or *E-Hoòdoo*, and the leaves are those of the Daphne foetida or *Oào*, the Galega piscidia or *Ehòra*, and Lepidium Piscidium or *Enòu*. When they discover out at sea a quantity of birds hovering over a certain spot, they are sure that a number of fish is assembled there, and they hasten there with their sailing canoes and several *vittee-vittees* hung out on each side by a bamboo projecting from the canoe at a good distance, and they never fail to catch a great number of these fish. Thus we find that the attention which they bestowed on the various kinds of fish and their nature, gave them opportunities of making proper use of these observations for better and easier catching these animals, which make so material a part of their animal food.*

The most necessary ideas relative to food, garment, and habitation, form the first part of the education thought to be necessary among these islanders. The fertility of these isles, the mildness of their climate, together with the happy and joyful temper of their inhabitants, give them a general turn for sensual pleasures:

---

*The inhabitants of the Maledives are likewise very expert in catching all kinds of fish, with which their sea swarms; and as animal food of quadrupeds is not very common with them, fish are their most material food. See François Pyrard's *Voyage*, 4to. Paris, 1679, Part i. p. 88, 136, and 166.

ARTS AND
SCIENCES

the least happy occurrence in life is sufficient to inspire them with a high degree of glee, which sets their whole body in motion: they begin to frisk and DANCE, this makes a cadenced or measured breathing necessary; if in this situation man wishes to communicate his ideas to the by-standers, he will naturally give his words that kind of measure or cadence, which he has adopted with his breathing, this, together with the voice of exultation may be considered as the first origin of singing and MUSIC: if the ideas he wants to express by words, are the true feelings of the man, they will of course be more animated; the images rush forth with uncommon rapidity, he has not time to express the idea itself, he substitutes therefore any thing nearly related or similar to it, he pursues every lively quality of the thing or person he speaks of, and thus gives rise to POETRY, its imagery, metaphors, similes, and the frequency of epithets. When these arts have subsisted in a country for some time, the inhabitants find likewise a pleasure in representing by mimic actions and words certain well known scenes of life, interspersed with some coarse jokes, and some strokes of unpolished wit. The better they are able to imitate the true characters, the stronger they express the disharmony or disproportion of these actions or characters, and the greater is the pleasure they procure to their audience; and thus do they give life and existence to the DRAMA, a new kind of diversion. After these arts have once been applauded and become fashionable in a nation, it is very natural that either parents or some other persons, who have attained to some degree of perfection in these arts, should communicate to the rising generation the principles upon which they acted in order to obtain some eminence in their profession: and thus the second part of education is carried on among the more polished nations of the South Sea. Their dances, poetry, music, and dramas, are however by no means to be considered as performances which have any degree of perfection or excellence; they are the first rude beginnings of arts, and for that very reason they are in more general use, than the same arts are among us: females commonly dance at Taheitee and the Society-isles and men but seldom; however they are all acquainted with the steps and motions usual in this diversion. Every individual can compose verses *extempore*, and sing them at the same time; and their dramatic performances are commonly extemporaneous pieces, and a mixture of music, poetry, and dancing, so that the *Improvisadores* might here find in the opposite hemisphere people possessed of this admired qualification.[6]

The measured steps of their women, keep excellent time with their drums, which are beaten by fingers briskly and loud, and commonly accompanied by songs. The dress of the women in the greater dramatic dances has already been described,* and is not peculiarly connected with that art; however so much

---

* See Hawkesworth, vol. ii. p. 264, and George Forster's *Voyage*, vol. i. p. 399, and following.

appears from their clothes collected into long petticoats, that they by no means think the excellence of the performance to consist in the graceful motion of the feet, as they carefully cover them; but in the motion of their hands and fingers, they shew in my opinion, the greatest dexterity and elegance. They have generally long well shaped fingers, which are wonderfully pliant, so that they can with ease bend them so far back as to form with the rest of the hand a segment of a circle, and in this attitude they move them with a astonishing agility. This dance is called *Heèva-he-oòra*, and the motion of the fingers *Eòree*. But besides this, they shake their hips in a rotatory motion, both when they are standing and when they are leaning prostrate on their knees and elbows, with a velocity which excited our astonishment, and this is named *òne-òne*. There are other dances wherein they use measured steps, hold another by the hands and clap with them; which is called *pa-àta*. During the various kinds of dances, they never fail to make wry mouths, which, in our opinion, were the most extravagant and disgracing distortions, instead of being capable of giving the spectator ideas of gracefulness and harmony: habit has taught them to screw the mouth into an obliquely slanting direction by a kind of sudden convulsive motion of the lips, and custom only has made the sight of so unnatural and offensive a grimace a performance which pleases and merits applause. This distortion is called *ootoo-ròa* (large lips). There are other dances usual in their nocturnal festivals with the *Arreeoys*, which, none of our ships company had an opportunity of seeing, and are according to the accounts of the natives extremely indecent and lascivious; these are called *t'eài-morodèe*, and the women exhibiting them, *Too-àha*. The exercise of the common dramatic dances is very violent, the motion of the hands elegant, that of the feet not to be seen, that of the hips somewhat strange, and according to our notions indelicate; and lastly, that of the mouth horrid and disagreeable. The women when performing were always attended by a man, who accompanied the drums with a kind of song; and by some loud spoken words or the clapping of hands, directed their motions; which, in my opinion seems to intimate that they have a kind of plan in their dances, and that the transitions from the oblique steps, to the motion of the fingers and agitation of the hips, is in some measure connected with the words spoken by the master of the ballet.

Their MUSIC is by no means so perfect or harmonious as their dances or poetry: this branch of the polite arts having made but an indifferent progress among them. The flute in the hands of a Taheitean has no more than three holes, and is therefore incapable of a variety of notes, and the music they execute upon this instrument is but a poor humming: even their vocal music has no greater compass than three or four notes, however some of their songs were not quite disagreeable. The inhabitants of the Friendly Islands are better versed in music than the Taheiteans, and the tunes of their women had something pleasing to our ears when we first heard them at *E-Aoowhe* or Middleburgh. The inhabitants of Tanna* and New-Zeeland have in their songs greater variation and extent, which certainly intimate better and more improved talents for this branch of the polite arts.

The VERSES of the Taheiteans are always delivered by singing, in the true antient Greek style, and what is still more remarkable, we found that many of these verses were the productions of the moment, for we observed that their poetry had some relation to the persons on board our ship, or to some trans-actions which happened during our stay: but they had likewise many couplets or songs which had no reference to the persons or transactions occasioned by the presence of our ship. Their verses seem to be regularly divided into feet, and they observe the quantity and express it in singing. As to the beauties of their poetic style, we were not able to judge of them; because we were not sufficiently acquainted with their language; thus much however we observed that many words occurred in their poems which were not used in common conversation. The women on board our ship, seeing in the night the moon shine, frequently sung the following couplet or *pehai*.

Tĕ ōō | wă nō | tĕ Mālămă
Tĕ ōō | wă tĕ hēē | nārō
The cloud within the moon
That cloud I love!

We will transcribe one couplet from Hawkesworth which the natives com-posed when the Endeavour was at O-Taheitee.†

Epăhā | tāyŏ | Mālămă | tāiyĕ
Nŏ Tăbā | nĕ tō nŏtā | wă whănnō | māiyĕ
Perhaps with friendly light, this moon we view,
Has guided Banks, while to his friends he flew.

From the purport of this couplet it appears, that it was made when the moon was shining; and it may likewise be observed, that the syllables at the end of each

---

* When we were at Tanna, we heard every morning at day-break a solemn song, issuing as it were from the point lying to the East of the harbour, and this circumstance seems to prove that the natives of this island employ even their *Music* as part of their solemn worship of their Deity. We were still more confirmed in our suspicion, when we two or three times attempted to visit this East-ern point, and always found the natives ready to defend the sacred place by arms. See likewise George Forster's *Voyage*, vol. ii. p. 300, and 362.
† Hawkesworth, vol. ii. p. 205.

verse form rhymes, which cannot be thought to be the effect of accident, though all the other couplets in Hawkesworth, together with these two now before us, are without rhyme. From whence it seems to follow, that their poetry admits both of rhymes and of blank verse.

Another such couplet was frequently sung on board the Resolution, in 1774.

Awă | hēē tĕ păhēē | nŏ Tōōtē
Tĕ nēē | ā tŏ Tĕō | rĕe hŏrō ă - ē.

We can by no means vouch that this division of the metres and the quantities are perfectly true, but hearing the words, or reading those in Hawkesworth, we supposed that the quantities were such as we have marked over the words. In their prayers, and likewise in their dramas and on other solemn occasions,* the language is different from what we used to hear in their common conversation, and might justly be stiled a cadenced metrical performance or a *carmen* in the acceptation of the word as it is used in the formule delivered by the Roman *Feciales*, Livii. Hist. lib. i. cap. 24.

To the last branch of the liberal and polite arts exercised by the natives at Taheitee and its neighbourhood, belong their DRAMATIC PERFORMANCES. These are blended with dances and songs, with this restriction, that men only are the acting persons, in the same manner as at Rome, where no females were permitted to act. The drama is a simple representation of the common occurrences of life. A man entrusts his servants with the care of his goods, they fall asleep, and though they are lying on their masters property, the thieves are subtle enough to steal them away from under the persons who were appointed to watch them; sometimes the thieves are detected and severely beaten, and sometimes they return

---

* When we were in New Zeeland and the man in Dusky Bay was willing to come on board our ship, he pronounced a *carmen* or speech in a very cadenced and solemn manner, which lasted about two minutes, holding at the same time a green branch in his hand, as soon as he had finished this ceremonious formule, he struck the ship with the branch just as he had done before he began the ceremony, and then threw the branch into the ship. In Queen Charlotte's Sound, a party of Indians came on board our ship, whom we had not seen before, and one of them held a green flag in his hand, while another person delivered a long, solemn, and cadenced speech. The ceremony and solemn prayer of *Tupaya* on the first landing at *Huaheine* seems to have been of the same nature, and it was repeated by him on the first landing at *O-Raiedea*. See Hawkesworth, vol. ii. p. 251, and 256.

At our first landing in New-Caledonia, the Chief *Te-abooma*, and another Chief pronounced some cadenced, solemn speeches, intermixed with some short responses from certain old men. See George Forster's *Voyage*, vol. ii. p. 382. All which not only proves that the first interview and making of peace is a solemn act observed by nations of very different origin, and living at a considerable distance from one another, but also that their solemn speeches on these occasions are a kind of poem or cadenced metrical performance.

"Woman at Easter
Island," engraving by
J. Caldwall after William
Hodges, from Cook, *A
Voyage towards the South
Pole*, 1777, Plate 25.

the blows. In another farce, a man has a daughter, who has a lover; the father dis-likes him and refuses his daughter, and being afraid of being deceived he watches her closely, but in the dead of the night, the lover meets the fair one and per-suades her to run away with him; the consequence of this affair is the birth of a fine boy; the lady is in labour on the theatre and at last a large boy is exhibited, who immediately runs about the stage with the *placenta* and long *funis umbilicalis;* which is here not considered as indelicate, because every body is acquainted with the incident, the children of four or five years not excepted; and the oddity that the new-born child runs about and escapes the midwife, whose business it is to catch him, causes an universal and loud peal of laughter. The girls father upon seeing the cleverness of his grandson, is at last reconciled to his son-in-law.

Of this turn (though not in every particular) was the little extempore farce seen by some of our friends at Huaheine, and which seemed to be levelled at a girl, a native of *O-Raiedea,* who came with us from Taheitee in order to return to her parents, from whom she had eloped some months before with a young *Arreoy.* Though the piece was but rudely performed, it however put the girl to shame, and drew tears from her eyes, which naturally must have a good tendency, especially with such persons of her sex as might be tempted to follow her example. Upon the whole, this circumstance gives us a very good idea of the nation in every respect: If we consider the poor girl, who was thus exposed, her bashful behaviour and her tears are certainly irrefragable proofs of her modesty and repentance. In a genial climate, with a warm consitution, a feeling heart, and an education which made her acquainted with all the mysterious parts of love, even though she should not chuse to put them in practice, it was no wonder she yielded to the tender solicitations of a youthful and vigorous lover, when her own age and the natural levity of the whole nation, contributed to lessen the crime of her incon-siderate step, and still more so, the possibility of obtaining a husband without hurting her character. On the other hand, there is something so generous in her behaviour that I cannot help taking notice of it. She became the object of indeli-cate, but sharp and salutary satire, and gave by her tears ample testimony of the immorality of her behaviour, and that she felt herself aggrieved under self-condemnation, and was not unwilling to become a fair warning to a whole croud of young persons of her own sex. If again we consider the actors who took the opportunity of exposing immorality for the instruction of the rising generation; they must be thought highly commendable for having dared to lay aside for so salutary a purpose, the respect due to a lady and a stranger. She was under the protection of a set of foreigners, whose fire-arms indeed commanded respect; but these censors were not to be brow-beaten by power, or awed to silence by wealth, as is too often the case in Europe; they failed not to point the shafts of their satire at an object deserving censure, without regarding the consequences which might

accrue to themselves from thence, being fully convinced of the rectitude of their
action, and the salutary effects that might be derived for the benefit of the rising
generation. Lastly the whole audience deserved in my opinion, likewise to be
commended; for when the witty sarcasms were falling from the lips of their theatrical heroes, they laughed at their jokes; but when they observed that these shafts
of satire were not discharged at random, but made the person smart who was the
object of their instructive irony, when they saw the marks of returning modesty of
repentance and self-condemnation, in the attempts to hide her shame, and in the
copious tears of the poor girl; many an eye was moistened, and many a heart sym-
pathized with her; lastly, when the dramatic performance was over, every one was
eager to give her the most unfeigned and unsolicited marks of his esteem and
friendship, to comfort her in her distress and affliction, to countenance her modesty and return to her duty; and in a manner to thank her for having contributed
to the innocent mirth,* as well as to the instruction and the warning of her country women. If we reflect upon the want of feeling in the frequenters of our the-
atres, their indolence and inattention, and I may add their shameless effrontery,
we must give the palm to the O-Taheiteans, who, like the true children of nature,
have a sympathizing tear, and unrestrained feelings, the tribute and glory of
humanity, in readiness on all proper occasions.

> . . . *Mollissima corda*
> *Humano generi dare se natura fatetur,*
> *Quae lacrymas dedit: haec nostri pars optima sensus.*
>   Juvenalis[7]

Dances, music and poetry, are used at O-Taheitee to diffuse chearfulness and
mirth, the blessings of a social life, into the minds of the whole nation,† and the
stage is there, the instructor of virtue, and censor of immorality and vice; in a
sense by far more true than it is at present with the refined inhabitants of Europe.
When the polite arts become the promoters of so great and so universally beneficial advantages, even the most morose and gloomy philosophers must allow them
a place among the objects which ought to be communicated in a system of useful
and moral education. In this light therefore, these nations consider these arts;
every individual delights in the exercise of them, and endeavours to acquire
excellence in them. The professors of these arts are so far from being degraded by

---

* Thanks were returned to Lucius by the magistrates of a town in Thessalia, for having contributed
to their mirth in his sham-tryal. Apuleius *de Asino Aureo*.[8]

† Αιει δ' ημιν δαις τε φιλη κιθαρις τε, χοροι τε,
  Ειματα τ' εξημοιβα, λοετρα τε θερμα, και ευναι. Homeri Odyss. Θ 247, 248.[9]

them, that even the Princesses of the blood Royal think it not derogatory to their rank to exhibit their skill in dancing before a crouded audience of their father's or brother's subjects; and the actors were some of the *Hoas* or attendants upon the King. We hardly met with a single person, who was not able to sing a tune; and on all occasions the women subservient to the pleasures of our sailors, were singing their own extempore compositions. We had no opportunity of forming a judgment of the dances or drama of the other islands in the South Sea; as our stay among them was too short, and the knowledge of their respective languages too imperfect.

I cannot leave this subject without mentioning that the New-Zeelanders used likewise to exhibit to us their war-song, which was begun by one of them, and accompanied with vilent stampings, motions, and gestures, and the brandishing of their battle-axes; at the end of every stanza of the song, was a kind of burden,[10] which was sung by the whole band of warriors in chorus, with the loudest and most dreadful vociferations; which gradually worked them up to a kind of phrenzy, the only state of mind in which they fight. In O-Tahà I saw a funeral ceremony performed, wherein dancing was exhibited by three small girls, with occasional interludes by three men. Between the acts the friends and relations (*Hea-bìddee*) appeared dressed, in pairs at the entrance of the house, but came not in; and afterwards the whole place, about thirty feet long and eight feet wide was spread with cloth, which, was afterwards given to the drummers. I could not learn any other particulars relative to the meaning or tendency of this ceremony, except that it is not uncommon to celebrate the funerals of people of some rank by the rounds* of the chief-mourner, dressed in the *Hèva*, (described before p. 277, &c. &c.) and likewise by a dramatic performance, accompanied as customary, by dances and songs.

The knowledge of SCIENCES, as far as they are cultivated at Taheitee and its neighbourhood, lies no doubt, in a very small compass, if compared with ours; but it is sufficient to give them a great pre-eminence above the inhabitants of the other isles, and contributes in some measure to their greater happiness, whether in procuring more enjoyment, or in averting those evils which are the consequences of ignorance and stupidity. *Medicine, History, Geography, Astronomy, Navigation,* and *Divinity,* are almost the only sciences of which the Taheiteans have some ideas.

The nations of the South-Sea-Isles generally enjoy a perfect state of health, and we saw many of them, who had attained to old age, for we observed grey and even white hairs on their heads; and all the symptoms and attendants of old age; though I must confess, they could by no means determine with any degree of cer-

---

* Hawkesworth, vol. ii. p. 146.

tainty, how many years they had lived: for they think it satisfaction enough to live long, without minutely keeping an account of their age, by months or years. When Capt. Cook came to O-Taheitee in the year 1769, he saw TOOTAHA and calls him a middle aged man;* he was no doubt the younger brother of O-AMO and HAPPAI, who both were grey headed in 1774, when we came to Taheitee; their mother was still alive, and in my opinion between 60 and 70, she had white hair, and was very corpulent, and seemed still to retain so much vigour and strength, as to render it probable that she might live several years.

They have no doubt, in these isles diseases, but as far as I am able to judge, from what I saw, diseases are less numerous, and less common, than in our climates and societies. And many reasons may be assigned, which may induce us to believe the inhabitants more happy, and less subject to that croud of diseases, infesting our communities, and causing generally such a havock among our Europeans, as must shock even the feelings of the most-intrepid philosopher, or the most indolent beholder; for they are nothing less than scenes of death varied in many hundred shapes.

They all live in a climate which must be esteemed excellent; for if you do not use immoderate exercise, and purposely expose yourself to the powerful rays of a vertical sun, you always find it sufficiently temperate. The mitigating alternate sea and land breezes assuage the heat of the climate; and in all parts of the South-Sea which we visited, we found the inhabitants careful to keep under shelter during night, in order to avoid the cool and moist nocturnal air; and we observed in general, that in all other islands beyond Taheitee and the Society-isles, the natives had houses better calculated to exclude cold and moisture than those open sheds: nay, as the rains often came on in squalls, attended with cold winds from the cloudy summits of their hills, they are equally solicitous to take shelter at the first appearance of them. Their garments made of the bark of the paper-mulberry (*Morus papyrifera*) are at the same time a warm and a cool dress; sufficient to screen them against the rays of the sun, and likewise to keep off the noxious effects of cooling winds.

The fine tropical fruits, which afford a salubrious palatable and nourishing food, contribute likewise to preserve that healthy habit of body which the natives generally enjoy, for they are as yet strangers to the curse entailed on European societies, that a man comes into the world with a body, whose solids are infirm and relaxed, whose nerves are tortured by acute pains, whose fluids are poisoned with a *virus* which saps his vital from the very day of his birth, and who has this wretchedness settled on him, as it were by inheritance. Their gluttonous Chiefs and Arees it is true, stuff themselves with immoderate quantities of food, but it

* Hawkesworth, vol. ii. p. 84.

causes no other inconveniences than to make them fat and unwieldy. The finest fishes, and other marine productions, as cray-fish, shells, sea-eggs, cuttle-fish, and one kind of blubber, serve them instead of food; and though many of the latter are not eaten by us, they seem not however, to cause any diseases; especially as the common sort of people cannot have them in great abundance. As to animal food from hogs, dogs, and fowls, I am certain that their meat is but sparingly eaten; however, whenever they kill one of the two first animals, the chiefs indulge themselves in devouring the blood, the fat, the entrails, and so much of the meat, as few Europeans would be capable of eating at one meal; but as these indulgencies are not very frequent, and their stomachs prove strong and powerful digesters, they are seldom, if ever sick of a surfeit. Their common drink is fresh water, and in some few cases even sea-water, neither of which will prove hurtful. But the chiefs and principle people in these isles, use themselves to drink a liquor prepared by chewing the root of a kind of cultivated pepper, *(Piper methysticum)* which they put into a wooden bowl and infuse with common or coco-nut-water, and afterwards strain through coco-nut-core; which is then whitish, insipid, or partaking somewhat of the taste of a weak infusion of pepper.[11] This potion when taken in quantities, makes them drowsy, stupid, and intoxicated,* and causes bad consequences, which I will enumerate hereafter. In Taheitee this root is scarce and little used; in Huaheine and the other Society-isles they have great plantations of it; in the Friendly-isles it is still more liked and cultivated, and every where is presented as a sign of friendship. However upon the whole, but few persons use it; it cannot therefore influence the health of the nation at large.

The frequent use of moderate exercise, in walking from one place to another in their shady cool groves, in felling trees, and slowly excavating, rasping, and piercing their embarkations, or making other utensils, together with the gentle exercise of leisurely paddling their canoes, when they go a fishing, contribute

---

* It is the general character of all uncivilized nations to be addicted to drunkenness and inebriation caused by various vegetables. The antient Scythians procured intoxication by imbibing the fumes of hemp-seed thrown on hot stones. Herodot. *lib.* iv. 69, 70, 71. Maximus Tyrius *Orat.* xiii. § 6.[12] All the tribes of the Celtic and Teutonic nations brewed beer, ale, and mead; and so did some nations bordering upon the former, though greatly different from them. Pelloutier *Hist. des Celtes*, lib. ii. ch. 18. Tacitus *do morib. Germ.* c. 22, 23. King Alfred's *Orosius in Anglo-Saxon*, p. 26, 27. The Tchuktchi and Yukaghiri on the North-East extremity of Asia, infuse mushrooms, affording an inebriating liquor. All the Mungalic nations, and among others, the Khalmyks ferment mares-milk till it becomes inebriating, or distill a kind of spirituous liquor from it, which they call *Kumyss*. The Mohammedans use opium and smoak tobacco, which last custom among the Khalmyks is practised by women and children. The African Negroes are fond of brandy to excess, Romer's *Description of the Coast of Guinea;* and the same is observed of the Hottentots by Kolbe. Nor is any one ignorant how fond the American Savages, both in the North and in the South, are become of brandy. La Hontan, book xi.

greatly to their salubrious habit of body. However, as the heat of a vertical sun might cause too violent, and too general a relaxation of the solids, they prevent this by frequently bathing in sea-water, after which, they commonly perform an ablution in fresh water. They generally bathe every evening and morning, or at either time according as they have used themselves to it. But as an insensible and strong perspiration generally weakens our bodies very much in hot climates, and by carrying off too many liquids, renders them more obnoxious to putrid diseases, the natives of these isles would be equally subject to this inconvenience, if they had not a custom, which really seems to be intended to obviate the too copious perspiration, for at certain times they anoint their hair and head and the whole body, with the oil extracted from coco-nuts, and made odoriferous by adding the wood, the fruit, the flowers, and the leaves of several scented plants.* Upon the whole, their chearful temper, the absence of cares, their simplicity of manners, with the above enumerated causes, co-operate strongly to prevent the attacks of many varied diseases; and as the greater and more sensible part of these nations, adhere to an exemplary sobriety in every respect, this evidently contributes much to keep them in health, and in the enjoyment of real happiness.

We found in the isles but few people who were disfigured or maimed, or had any bodily imperfections: however they were by no means entirely free from them. For I saw some that squinted, others that had a film over one eye, and several blind of one eye. In the isle of Tanna I observed many who had a kind of weakness in the eye-lids, so that they could not lift them up beyond a limited extent, but were obliged to raise the head in order to see things that were upon a level with their eye. I have reason to believe that it is not merely an accidental ailment; for I saw a man and his little son of about five or six years, both labouring under the same imperfection, so that it might perhaps be owing to the manner of living in that family, or be caused by the insalubrious spot their hut stood on, or perhaps it is peculiar to this, and some other families, and is propagated.† I observed a few hump-backed, and also here and there a crooked person, some had distorted legs, and one man had a leg that was entirely withered and dried

* François Pyrard *Voyage*, b. i. p. 126, says the same of the people in the Maledive Islands.
† There are instances that dumbness and deafness have been propagated from parents upon children; likewise blindness has been entailed upon children; and people who have either four or six fingers on their hands, have procreated children with the same imperfection: in the same manner it is possible, that this defect might be propagated; though I am rather induced to suppose that this paralysis of the eye-lids was caused by the marshy situation of the huts in which the families lived, and from the constant smoak with which their huts are filled during night, in order to free the inhabitants of the numerous mosquitoes swarming in these marshy woods; there are likewise some kinds of wood, whose smoak makes people either entirely blind, or at least nearly deprives them of their eye-sight. See Osbeck's *Voyage*, vol. i. p. 320.

up. Among the robust New-Zeelanders, I saw a man of a fine figure with a lame hand. But as we were, especially in the beginning, very little acquainted with their language, and had a great deal of other business upon our hands, we could not minutely enquire into all the causes and particulars of these imperfections. I saw one man at Huaheine, who had a very great *Hernia umbilicalis,* and another in the same place with an immense expansion and schirrosity of the right testicle, which was grown to the size of a child's head, so that all the scrotum, and even the membrane over the penis was entirely filled up with it; and the aperture for making water, was driven to one side, and this man was nevertheless active, strong, and mounted the sides of our ship, with as great agility and unconcern, as if he were not in the least affected by this dreadful accident.

Among the diseases which we had an opportunity of observing in these nations, I must first reckon the *cough:* several laboured under it, especially towards night and in the morning; owing, as is probable, to their being too long exposed to cold rains or the cool of the night on the reef, when they are fishing, or perhaps being too slightly covered during night in their own houses.

Another disease was more common among the natives of these isles, which has various degrees and stadia, but in its utmost height and inveteracy seems to be a real kind of *Leprosy:* its slightest degree, is a kind of scaly exfoliation of the skin, of a whitish, or often a white colour.[13] Sometimes the whole body was covered with it, sometimes only one leg, sometimes both or the back only were affected with it; or perhaps only a few detached blotches on the body had this appearance. However we must distinguish from this symptom, two other appearances; the one, when we saw the bodies of the natives white and covered with a disagreeable roughness; and this being new to us, we imagined it might be some disease, but they soon undeceived us, by saying it was only sea salt, for the moment before they had been swimming in the sea, which we did not know. The second phenomenon is caused by the too frequent use of the before mentioned inebriating liquor prepared from the pepper-root: in this case the skin looks as if it had been parched and dried by heat and winds, it has a blackish appearance, and scales are even now and then separated from it. The eyes of people who use this liquor too freely are commonly red, inflamed, and sore, the body grows gradually emaciated, and the inhabitants become stupid, infirm, and dwindle away. All these symptoms, as we were told, were the consequences of the too immoderate use of the infusion of the pepper-root. But the scales of the morbous exfoliation, are not so harsh to the touch as those caused by sea-water, and there is generally a kind of tumour or swelling under it. In a higher degree of the disease I observed some ulcers in the white blotches, which appeared as if they were extending under the skin, honey-combed, and were running with red orifices surrounded by a red fungous flesh, sometimes between the white spots a livid or reddish hue of the part affected might be observed.

In the second kind or species of this terrible disorder, I saw several roundish or oblong people elevations on the skin, of the size of a crown piece. Some of them looked as if a part had been rotten, and fallen out and had turned into an ulcer filled with red fungosities. At *E-Aoowe*, or Middleburgh, in the Friendly-isles, a woman was afflicted with this kind, whose face swelled to an extreme degree, was one red, livid, and running sore, the nose was entirely rotten and had dropped off, the cheeks were of a red spungy substance. The eyes sunk deep in the head, red and sore: in a word, she was a most pitiable and miserable object.

I saw still another kind of the same disease, in the same isles of *E-Aoowe*. The back and left shoulder of a man as far as his upper arm was covered with a kind of ulcer, which was a quarter of an inch higher than the rest of the body. The whole was of a deep livid red, and the elevated margins towards the extremities were of a nasty yellow colour: it was not a running sore, though it had much the appearance of it. The natives have no peculiar name for this or any other disorders that cause ulcers, pimples, or eruptions, all are promiscuously called *e-pàe* or sores. I observed at *Tahà, O-Raiedea, Tonga-Tabbu,* and at *New-Caledonia* men with one or both legs enlarged to a monstrous size; the limb was entirely livid and felt hard, and the tumour was confined chiefly to the interval between the knee and instep, though it extended somewhat up the thigh, and even to the toes; however the leg was more swelled in proportion than any other part. Notwithstanding this, I observed the men could walk stoutly, and did not hesitate to wade through the sea-water almost up to their waist, and felt no other inconvenience as far as we could observe, than that they had a difficulty of breathing. This seems to be a kind of elephantiasis, such as some people have in the East Indies on the coast of Malabar.* At New-Caledonia, I saw two men each having an arm enlarged in the same manner.

When we arrived at O-Taheitee in 1773, we learnt that a Spanish ship had been there a few months before us, which the natives called *Paheè no Pèpe* or Pèppe's ship. To whose commander they gave the name of *t'Errire*; and by this ship's crew a disease had been introduced among them, which they called *e-pae-no-pèppe*, Pèppe's disease or sore. At the Cape of Good Hope, we heard from Mr. Crozet, Captain of a French East-India ship, and from the officers on board the Frigate Juno, in the Spanish service, under the command of Don Juan Arraos,

---

* On sait qu'il y a la maladie appelleé *pedes strumosi* parmi les Indiens qui se disont Chretiens de St. Thomas. *Miscell. Medic. Physic. Decur.* iii. tom. iii. *Observat.* 13. Sanchez *Dissertation sur la maladie Venerienne.*

that in the year 1773, Capt. Don Juan de Langara y Huarte had been with two Spanish ships upon discoveries in the South Seas, and had touched at Taheitee. The natives represented to us, that the disease of *o-Pèppe* caused ulcers, difficulty of breathing, a falling off of the hair, and lastly death; and that it had been communicated by co-habitation with women. We suspected this at first to be a venereal disease, but upon a further consideration, I am apt to believe, that as this Spanish ship came from Lima and Callao, where a great number of negro slaves are kept, who are frequently and chiefly subject to the various kinds of leprosis and elephantiasis, it might perhaps have happened that one or more of the crew might be infected with that kind of elephantiasis, which they communicated to the natives of these isles: for it is well known, that some species of leprosy may be communicated by cohabitation, that many lepers are very immoderate in venery, even a few moments before they expire, and that especially the elephantiasis described by Aretaeus and Paulus Aegineta, had some symptoms that are perfectly corresponding with those pointed out by the natives. We could see no person at the time of our arrival infected with that distemper, otherwise we should have inquired more accurately into its particular symptoms. And I do not intend to be positive that the disease was communicated to the natives by the people in the Spanish ship; for if an uncommon distemper should happen to break out at the time of the arrival, or stay of some strangers in a country, the strangers have often been accused of having given the infection, though they very little deserved such a charge.

When Captain Cook came in the year 1769, in the Endeavour to O-Taheitee, he found that half his crew when he left the Society-isles, were infected with the venereal disease,* and it was then suspected that Mr. Bougainville's ship's crew had communicated this disease. Mr. de Bougainville in his turn suspects the English in the Dolphin to have first introduced it:† and the gentlemen in the Dolphin assert they never had one man infected with the least venereal symptoms whilst they were at Taheitee or immediately afterwards.‡ When we came to Queen Charlotte's Sound, in New-Zeeland, in 1773, we had been out at sea for at least five months; none of our sailors had any symptom of this disease, which could hardly lie dormant for such a length of time; since from our leaving the Cape of Good Hope, they had been eating salt-meat and salt-pork plentifully, had no greens all that time, had indulged freely in the use of spirituous liquors, and were during the whole of the intermediate time, exposed to wet and cold, and all the rigours of the climate: circumstances that would soon have

---

* See Hawkesworth, vol. ii. p. 233.
† See Bougainville's *Voyage*. English translation, p. 274, and 286.
‡ See Hawkesworth, vol. i. p. 489, 490.

accelerated the breaking out of the distemper, and rendered it so virulent, that they must have had recourse to the assistance of the surgeon: yet, when we went out of Queen Charlotte's Sound, six months after leaving the Cape, a midshipman on board the Adventure discovered that he had been infected by one of the New-Zeeland females. In O-Taheitee, and the Society-isles, we found in 1773, the females communicated this disease to several of our people. From the Friendly-isles no infection was either received or communicated, because the people who laboured under it were not allowed to have any commerce with the females of those isles. The crew left the Marquesas and Easter-island without catching, or communicating the evil, because not a single person was infected with it, either before we visited those parts, or for some time after we had left them. At Taheitee and the Society-isles, the infection came in 1774 again into our ship; and as we staid only a few days at Namocka, I believe none either received or communicated it there. In the more Western Isles of Mallicollo, Tanna, and New-Caledonia our sailors had no connection with the females; but in New-Zeeland the disorder was again communicated to our crew. So that there is great reason to believe that the venereal disease has not been lately introduced into these isles, but was known there for a long time; especially as Ohedeeddee or Mahaine, the young man of Borabora, who went with us in 1773 from O-Raiedea, told us that this evil was very common in Bora-bora, where however, no European ship had ever touched; nay, he informed us that his own mother died of this disease before the arrival of Europeans in these isles.[14]

It seems to me therefore highly probable, that this infectious evil is of such a nature, that by a very libidinous life, and promiscuous cohabitation of males with females, it may very easily be caught; and we are now certain, that there is hardly a country to be found, where the young unmarried females are allowed such a lat-itude as at O-Taheitee and its neighbourhood in admitting a variety of young males, and abandoning themselves to various embraces without derogating from their character. Women of all ranks follow these practices from the earliest time, and after having passed through the embraces of hundreds, are married to the first people of the isle. It is therefore no wonder, that in a hot climate, in a libidinous nation, inclined to the leprosy and its various branches, a disease should pullu-late, which may become contagious only by cohabitation. We had opportunities of observing the most miserable objects in the last stage of this horrid evil. At Huaheine especially, we saw in 1774, a youth with a cadaverous look and com-plexion, covered with ulcers, especially under the arms, on the groin, and about the genitals, and wherever a congeries of glands is found in the human body. His eyes were almost extinct, his whole frame greatly reduced and emaciated, he dragged after him his languid excruciated limbs, the sad victim of brutal appetite and libidinous desire.*

---

* That the venereal disease is by no means to be considered as an evil imported into Europe from America, has been sufficiently proved by Mr. SANCHEZ, a very able and learned physician, (who has been for some time in Russia) in two little Treatises intitled: *Dissertation sur l'origine de la maladie Venerienne, Paris,* 1752, 12mo. *Examen Historique sur l'apparition de la maladie Venerienne en Europe, Lisbonne,* (Paris) 1774. It appears from his inquiries that the venereal disease appeared so early as in March, 1493, in Italy, and in Auvergne in France; at the very time when Christopher Columbus returned to Spain from America; for he landed at Seville, on the 15th of March, 1493, and in the middle of April in the same year he arrived at court, which then resided at Barcelona. From a book of *Peter Pintor,* a Spanish physician it appears, that the venereal disease raged at Rome, in March, 1493; and it is likewise to be collected from other writers, that about that time this evil spread all over Italy in the form of an epidemical distemper. *Pacificus Maximus,* a poet, whose book was printed at Florence, 1489, describes lib. iii. ad priapum, the venereal disease in such a manner, that no doubt can be entertained of its being known at that period of time. In the church of St. Maria del Popolo, at Rome, is a sepulcral monument, erected to the memory of Mario Alberti, *qui annum agens* xxx. *peste inguinaria interiit,* Anno. 1485, about eight years before Christopher Columbus returned from his first voyage. (See *Viaggiana, or detached Remarks on the Buildings, Pictures, Statues, Inscriptions, &c. &c. of antient and modern Rome,* London, 1776.) The Jews who were expelled from Spain, brought the disease into Africa, according to *Leo Africanus. Descriptio Africae,* lib. i. p. 86. edit. Elzevir. Lugd. Bat. 1632. 16° and it was there for that reason called *malum Hispanicum,* the Spanish evil. But Mariana, lib. xxxiv. cap. I. ad annum. 1492. says expressly, that the order for the expulsion of the Jews from Spain, was given in March, 1492, and only four months were allowed them, so that they were probably gone in June 1492, before Christopher Columbus sailed for the discovery of America. Nor are there testimonies wanting that in times still more remote, symptoms of the venereal disease were well known: Alfonsus I. King of Naples, died 1458, of the gonorrhoea, or as Tristano Carracciolo *de Varietate fortunae,* expresses it: *morbo insuper immundo & pertinaci, involuntario scilicet insensibilique, spermatis fluxu.*[15] Ladislas King of Naples, likewise died 1414, of an infection in his genitals; communicated to him by a girl, whom he kept, *l'Art de verifier les dates,* page 903; and in *Cardami Chronicle* from 1410-1494. More instances that the venereal disease had been known among the antients, are to be found in Joh. Zach. *Platneri Opusculis Tomo* ii. *Prolusione,* ii. *de morbo Campano,* p. 21. Lipsiae, 1748, 4to *Petrus Martyr de Angleria* mentions lib. i. epist. 67. dated April the 5th, 1489, that Ario Barbosa, professor at Salamanca, was severely afflicted with the *bubas* or *French disease.* Lastly from Muratori's *Collectio Scriptorum Historie Italicae,* tom. xvi. p. 554, 555. it appears from the *Chronicon Placentinum,* that in the year 555, after Christ, there was an epidemical pestilential distemper in Italy, which among other symptoms had these peculiar ones, that the glands began to swell to the size of a nut, particularly at the parts which modesty bids to conceal, which swelling was followed by an intolerable heat, and that those afflicted with that dreadful evil died in a day or two. All these arguments encourage me to suppose, that the venereal disease was not uncommon in antient times; that it however, broke out with new rage about the year 1493, and that fixing and attaching itself upon many other epidemical distempers, it became virulent, by being communicated by cohabiting with women. We need not wonder therefore that the disease should have made its appearance at Taheitee and its neighbourhood, long before the arrival of Europeans at their isle.[16]

Besides the above-mentioned diseases, *Towha,* then commander of the fleet, and one of the chiefs of Atahooroo, had symptoms which every body took for the gout; he was of a strong constitution, a corpulent habit of body, and owed this disease no doubt to intemperance, which is common amongst the great and wealthy of all nations. I observed likewise that the natives had frequently a sty in the eye, and some symptoms that usually attend the dropsy; and there may be some more diseases known among them, which our short stay made it impossible for us to discover. This however is certain, that though these nations are not without disease, they are upon the whole less subject to them than the Europeans, and we must therefore acknowledge, that they are in that respect physically happier than more civilized nations, who are generally more subject to various diseases.

Though there are among the islanders, especially those in the Society-Isles, men whom they call *Tahouva-mai,** who are a kind of physician, yet I could never learn that their knowledge was so considerable, that they could cure the above-mentioned diseases; for generally the natives ingenuously confess, that there is no *irrepòu,* or remedy against them. They have, however, some method of curing the venereal disease; because there is an instance of it mentioned in Hawkesworth's, vol. ii. p. 233, and we were likewise told, that they used some *irrepòu,* or remedy: but either the people to whom we spoke, did not know this remedy, and could not therefore inform us of it, or they concealed it from us, as a great and important secret, not to be trusted with a set of inquisitive strangers. They certainly used a kind of *Stachys, (Enèea-rohittee)*; a *Cotula (E-Vàinoo)* with another plant called *Etoòhoo* bruised as cataplasms upon their wounds, though I cannot determine how far those plants may be endued with healing qualities. The general sobriety of the natives, a sound constitution, and their happy and uniform climate, greatly contribute no doubt towards healing their wounds; so that the efficacy of their remedies cannot as yet be fairly decided, as a set of experiments must be tried in order to ascertain their virtue. I am however inclined to believe that they have among themselves some traditional knowledge of treating wounds by applying cataplasms of bruised plants; this knowledge is perhaps considerably inferior to that of the sons of Aesculapius, who, in the Trojan war, assisted the wounded Grecian horses with their remedies, and whose science was confined, it seems, to a few plaisters and chirurgical operations. The scars of wounds which we saw, were not all proofs of an equal success in their art. Some were really well healed,

---

* The Taheiteans call their priests *Tahouva*; pain, a wound, soreness, or disease, is called by them *mai* or *mamai,* from these two words, the word signifying a physician or surgeon, *Tahouva-mai* is compounded; as if the people meant to intimate that their physicians are in their opinion a kind of priests. And I am inclined to believe that their physicians employ in some instances charms or incantations, prayers or ceremonies against the disease. See Hawkesworth, vol. ii. p. 231, 232.

and others had large elevated seams. However, there were unquestionable in-stances of their skill and success in healing wounds. *O-Rettee* the chief, of *O-Hiddea*, and the friend of Mr. de Bougainville, had on the side of his forehead, an impression on the skull made by a large stone, of such a size, that a man's hand might be laid in it; and yet there were no visible scars of so dangerous a wound.

In the Friendly Isles we observed, that the greater part of the nation, had on each cheek-bone a spot, which in some only appeared to be of a different colour of the skin, in others we saw these round spots covered with a fresh scurf, and again in others they were quite red and wounded, as if they had been caused by some exulcerating plants, or by burning on it some substance similar to the *Moxa* of the Japanese,* and the natives intimated to us that it was done on account of a cold or pain in the eyes; however we had neither time nor opportunity to learn from them in what manner these round spots were produced.

The *Tahouva-mai*, or physician, is not only versed in the science of remedies against the diseases common among these islanders, but he has really a knowl-edge of nature, as far as is compatible with the confined ideas of the whole nation. I cannot but imagine that they must have some ideas of ANATOMY, as they are well acquainted with all the internal parts of the human body, which they could not have learnt but by examining some human corpse; and they have likewise pecu-liar names for all the internal parts of the body: thus for instance, they name *Roro* the brains; *o-hoòttoo* the heart; *paràïa* the liver; *hoòa-hoùa* the kidneys; *opoo-orahài* the stomach; *aòu* the bowels; *oboòboo* the bladder; *pow-ohoòre* the blind gut; *àwa* the womb or matrix; and *toa-hoùwa* the cawl or omentum. Besides they know all the plants and animals that are to be found in their isles, or in the seas surround-ing them, and have peculiar names for distinguishing them: nay, they seem to have examined the nature of each plant, and animal, since the name often expresses a peculiar quality of the plant or animal. Thus for instance, there is at

---

* All the Oriental physicians use some cauteries against diseases. The Arabs burn a cylinder of blue cotton cloth on the part affected by pain. The Indians and Malays, use various substances for cau-teries applied on diseased parts of the body, the most common of which is the pith of rushes, dipt in Sesam-oil. The Chinese and Japanese use the downy part collected from the young leaves of the common mugwort (*Artemisia vulgaris*) form a little cone of it, put it on the body and burn it. This remedy has been recommended and used by some Dutch physicians against the gout and rheuma-tisms, but has hitherto gained but an indifferent reputation. The Laplanders use the common punk or *boletus igniarius* for the same purpose: Kund Liem's *Description of the Laplanders*. The Bedwin-Arabs substitute common cotton. D'Arvieux *Voyage dans la Palestine;* which is likewise found by experiment to be as good as the *moxa* by Leeuwenhock. See Rob. Hook's *Philosophical Experiments and Observations*, p. 73. The rest of the authors who have written on the *moxa* are Valentinus Epis-tola ad Cleycrum, in the *Acta. Nat. Cur.* Kaempfer in his *Amoenitates Exoticae* p. 589. seq. and in the *History of Japan*, vol. ii. appendix p. 37. Lastly, Petrus Jonas Bergius *Materia Medica e regno Vege-tabili*, p. 673.

Taheitee a kind of *Loranthus*, which, like all the plants of this genus, grows on the branches and stems of other trees, like the *misletoes* and which probably is disseminated and propagated in the same manner, the seeds being first eaten by birds, and then voided on the branch of a tree, whereon they germinate and grow: this plant the natives call *toote-oopa*, dove's dung, from a kind of dove, *(oo-oòpa)* which is particularly fond of the seeds of this loranthus. There is a new species of *phyllanthus*, whose leaves shut up during night, which might not improperly be called the *sleeping* of the plant, and the natives have been shrewd enough to catch this little circumstance, and to call the plant from thence, *moë-moë*, sleepy: Linnaeus has observed this property in many plants, and calls it their *sleep*. The *Casuarina equisetifolia* affords a very hard and ponderous wood, of which the natives make the clubs used in war, and as war is called in their language *tòa*, they have adopted the name of *e-tòa*, for the tree. The seeds of the *urena lobata* have the same quality as the burdock buttons in our country, sticking to peoples cloaths; and as the word *pìrree* has the signification of glueing or joining fast together, they call the plant *pìrree-pìrree*. All these circumstances, seem to prove the sagacity and the spirit of observation of this people, who have investigated very carefully all the plants of their country, and attended to their various qualities, which they have preserved in the very name of the plant. Nor has their spirit of observation been wanting in distinguishing the various parts of plants: thus for instance the roots are called *èä*; *toòmoo* is the part of the stem within the ground, *(caudex intra terram)* and *e-ra-où* is the name for the stem above ground; the branches are called *àma*, the leaves *eloù*, the middle shoot *amòu*, the flower *teàrre*, the fruit *hoòerro*. What made me most attentive to these trifles are the names *oròe* for the spatha of the flowers of the coco-nut, and that of *te-pevaye*, signifying the bracteal leaves of a plant; which nice distinctions certainly prove a particular attention in discriminating these parts from the rest in a plant, and that they had in a manner, made botany their particular study; in which opinion we often were confirmed, when they pointed out to us, the differences in the species of plants; by the variety of flowers, the shape of the leaves, &c. &c.*

From the above observations we learn, that on account of wounds and diseases, mankind was first led to seek after remedies, by the examination of plants; and by attending more accurately to the parts affected by pain, to enquire into the interior structure of the human body. The want of happiness and enjoyment, prompted man to exert his industry and talents, in order to find out the means of restoring the loss of health and strength. The consciousness of his own weakness, rouzed him from his original indolence, and spurred him on to the exertion of industry, to the examination and study of himself, and the objects sur-

---

* They are likewise acquainted with the sexual system, especially in the coco-palm.

rounding him, and to seek for assistance in that very nature, of which he himself constitutes so considerable a part.

The preservation of the memory of transactions and men is not quite neglected in Taheitee; for they are able to give a good account of the things which happened in their isle; but this can only be said of the most recent transactions; for as they take no care to number their own years, they likewise are unable to say how long it is since an accident happened; all that they can do is to say that such a thing happened in my grand-father's, or great grand-father's time. The remarkable events, and the names of persons whose memory is deemed worth preserving, are recorded in verses of their own making, and occasionally sung, which form the rude annals of their HISTORY. In this respect, the Taheiteans are similar to all other nations, who have not the art of writing, or of perpetuating their ideas, the deeds of their great men, and the remarkable events which happen among them.

The next branches of science, of which the inhabitants of Taheitee and its neighbourhood have some knowledge, are ASTRONOMY, GEOGRAPHY, and NAVIGATION. I mention these three sciences purposely together, as they are closely connected, and as the knowledge of the two first has been made subservient to the last; and I believe likewise, that by their navigation they learnt so much of geography as they are acquainted with, and perhaps would not have attempted to observe the heavens, had it not been for the single purpose of directing them in their navigations to remote parts. So that necessity, not mere curiosity only, led them to the observation of the heavens. For as they are obliged to go now and then to the neighbouring isles, it often happens that a storm surprizes them at sea, and drives them far from their intended course, and separates them from their home, which they never would see again, had they not acquired some knowledge of the motion of the heavenly bodies. Those men among these islanders, who had acquired some ideas of the heavens, by necessity and a long experience, communicated them to the rising generation, in order to enable them to profit by their toils, and the study of many a night passed without sleep. Finding by cruel necessity that in an open sea nothing could guide them, but those luminaries which we see in the day, or which give their light to us in the night; they attended to the immense number of stars spread all over the firmament, some of which they soon discovered to have a motion peculiar to themselves, to describe again the same rounds which they had compleated before, and to perform their revolutions in different and stated periods of time, while the rest preserved invariably the same distance from one another.

The sky in this country is commonly clear and serene, and on a few days only in the whole year, is covered with clouds; so that the natives of the tropical isles have frequent opportunities of contemplating the heavens, and admiring during

A CHART

representing the

ISLES of the SOUTH-SEA,

according to

the NOTIONS of the INHABITANTS

o-TAHEITEE

and the Neighbouring Isles, chiefly

collected from the accounts of

TUPAYA.

I. of Danger or S. Bernardo

o-Ahourou 55   o-Rai-havai 53

o-Rima-tarra 52

o-Toomoo-papa 56   o-Karo-toa 54   o-Adeeha 49

Ururutu 48

Touteepa 57   o-Ahoua-hou 50

Navigators I.   o-Weeha 51   Woureeo 47

o-Reeva-vai 58   Mopeeha 44

Whennua-oora 45

o-Papatea 46   Moucoos

Tainuna 59   o-Rotooma 61   Scilly I.   Hows I.

Teresti (West)   o-Poppoa 62
Tootera

Palmerstones I.
o-Rimatema 60
o-Hittepotto 65   *Herveys I.*
o Savage I.   64 Te-Toopa-tupa-eahou   Moeno-tayo 63

Oheavai 78
o-Hitte-toutou-atu 66

o-Hittetoutou-nee 67
Te-Errepoo-opo-matte-hea 77

Ooporroo 76
o-Hitte-toutou-rera 68

Te-Orooro-Mativatea 74   Wouwou 75

o-Hitte-taiterre 69   o-Tootoo-erre 73

Te-Amaroo-hitte 70   Ouowhea 72

Te-Atou-hitte 71

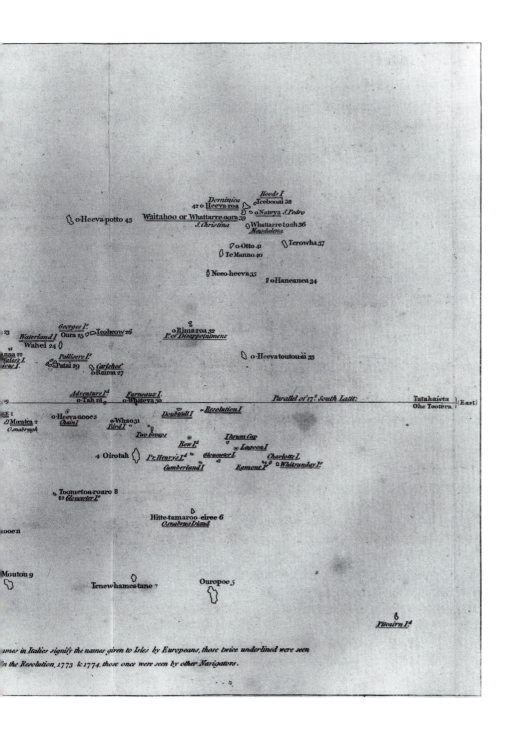

Hoods I
Dominica   Iceboooi 38
42 o Heeva-roa 39   o Nateva S.Pedro
o-Heeva-potto 43 Waitahoo or Whattarre-oora 39
                    S.Christina   Whattarre-toah 36
                                     Magdalena
                              o Otto 41   Terowha 37
                              Te Manno 40
                    Neeo-heeva 35
                              o Haneanea 34

Georges I.
23   Oura 25 Teoheow 26   o Rima-roa 32
Waterland I.   I. of Disappointment
Wahei 24
anna 22   Pallisere I.
atea I.   Patai 29   Carlshoff   o-Heeva toutou-ai 33
ieu I.   Oirairoa 27

         Adventure I.d   Furneaux I.   Parallel of 17° South Latit: Tatahaieta
9   o-Tah 28   o-Whaleva 30   Ohe Tootera   (East)
E 1   Resolution I.
o Moeatea 2   o-Heeva-nooe 3   o Whao 31   Doubtull I.
Ocnabrugh   Chain I.   Bird I.
                         Two Groups
                              Bow I.   Thrum Cap
                                        Lagoon I.
4 Oirotah   Pr.Henry's I.d   Gloucester I.   Charlotte I.
                 Cumberland I.   Egmont I.d   Whitsunday I.d

         Toometou-roaro 8
         Gloucester I.d

                    Hitte-tamaroo-eiree 6
                    Osnabrug Island

ooe 11

Moutou 9
              Tenewhamea-tane 7   Ouropoe 5

                                                      Pitcairn I.d

ames in Italics signify the names given to Isles by Europeans, those twice underlined were seen
  n the Resolution, 1773 & 1774, those once were seen by other Navigators.

Tupaia's Map (as
published in Forster's
Observations, 1778)

night the brilliancy of the stars. After the darkness of the night is over, they do not enjoy so long a twilight as we do; but the sun darts out at once as it were in full splendor from under the horizon, and shines with uncommon brightness and power, till he again sets on the opposite part of the horizon, when in a few minutes night spreads her sable hues over all the objects surrounding the happy natives of these isles. It must have been obvious to each beholder, that the sun rises and sets at certain times in points of the horizon diametrically opposite to one another, and at others, in points not much deviating from those situated either on one or the other side of them, for the whole difference cannot exceed fifty degrees. These regions of the horizon, are equally remarkable for the rising and setting of the moon nearly within the same space, and soon after they must likewise have found that five stars, (the greater part of which equalled or surpassed even the largest stars in apparent magnitude) rose and set within the same space of the horizon. This was sufficient to induce them to call that part of the heavens by a peculiar name. The place where the sun rises they called *Tataheìta,* and the place where he sets *Topa-t-erà.* They likewise found, that the sun from the time of rising came nearer and nearer to the zenith, that he removed farther and farther from that point till his setting, and that at certain times he was perpendicular over their heads; the line whereon the sun comes nearest to their zenith and upon it or the meridian, they call *T-erà-whattèa.* The Northern point of this imaginary line on the horizon, they name *Too-eroù,* and the opposite point *Toà.* They have likewise names for several points between these cardinal ones, which I heard mentioned, but I was not able exactly to determine either the number or the direction of them. If I am not mistaken, the whole horizon is divided into twelve points, so that two points would fall between two cardinals.

The natives of these isles could not help observing, that the bread fruit, their chief subsistence, grows but once during twelve months or revolutions of the moon; for during the space of seven months this fruit is gathered in abundance on the trees that bear it, but during five months they find none. This circumstance very naturally must lead them to investigate the true cause of it, the revolution of the sun. At the solstice in December, the sun is in its meridian altitude beyond the isle, towards the South of it, and in the solstice in June, he is in the Northern Hemisphere, and therefore passes twice a year through the zenith. About two months before and after the time of the suns reaching the Southern tropic, bread-fruit is very scarce, and during the season from August to March, this fruit is very plentiful, being ripe in March or the beginning of April, and this last season they call *Pa-oòroo,* from the name of bread-fruit. The mildness of the climate however is such, that there is always a tree here and there, which from its peculiar situation in a valley more elevated than the plain surrounding the isle, or from its exposure on the Southern side of a high hill, bears fruit at a time when the generality of trees of this kind have none; and it is from these trees that their chiefs and better sort of people have a constant succession of fresh bread-fruit, at a time when the rest of the people are obliged to live upon horse-plantanes, the fruit of the Ratta-tree, (*Inocarpus edulis*) the roots of eddoes, or the *Arum esculentum* and *macrorhizon*, and those of yams or *Dioscorea alata* and *oppositifolia*; or they then chiefly use the *Mahèe* or sour-paste prepared from fermented ripe bread-fruit.*

The whole of the bread-fruit season, including the time when they have none, is called *Tàoo*, and is therefore answerable to a year. They count the revolutions of the moon, and call them by the same name as the moon *Marama* or *Malama*. They enumerated to me thirteen names of moons or lunations, and then said *Hàre-te-tàoo*, the year is gone; and added still *Oomànnoo*, often, often, many times; which seemed to imply, that the cycle of the lunations is to be repeated every year. They begin the year about March, when they likewise begin to make their bread-fruit sour-paste or *Mahèe*, for which purpose immense quantities of the fruit are plucked off, which naturally creates some scarcity of this their chief aliment and must increase the same in proportion as the season advances. I cannot, from the mere enumeration of the thirteen names of months, prevail on myself to think that their year has thirteen lunations, but rather suppose that they have but twelve lunations, and now and then intercalate a thirteenth month, in order to keep the solar and lunar year in harmony; how often they do this, I pretend not to say. The names of the months are subjoined for the satisfaction of my readers.

1.	O-porore-o-moòa[†]	March
2.	O-porore-o-moòree	April
3.	Moorehà	May
4.	Oohee-eìya	June
5.	Hooree-àma (owhirree-àma).	July

---

* The description of the operations necessary for this purpose, is given in Hawkesworth, vol. ii. p. 198, 199.

† Some of the months have names, whose signification is known; of the rest I can give no account. 1 *Opororo-o-moòa*, signifies the *first hunger* or *want*; 2 *Oporore-o-moòree* has the signification of the *last hunger*; the foregoing observation on the scarcity of the bread-fruit about the time of its maturity, when it is plucked in quantities for making the *mahèe* or sour-paste, may in some measure account for the names of these two months. The fourth month *Oohee-eìya* has certainly a reference to *angling for fish*. The eighth month *O-Te-àree*, is thus called from the *young coco-nuts*, which probably are then most plentiful. The ninth month *O-Te-taì*, alludes to the *sea*. The eleventh *Wae-àhou*, to their *cloth*, and the twelfth *Pipìrree*, to some *covetousness* or *scantiness*, perhaps in food. The words included in *parenthesises* are the various readings of the name, having heard it pronounced by another person in a different manner.

6.	Tàowa	August
7.	Hooree-erre-èrre (owhirree-erre-èrre).	September
8.	O-Te-àree	October
9.	O-Te-taì	November
10.	Warehoo (Owarahew. Hawkesworth, v.ii. p.168)	December
11.	Wae-ahou	January
12.	Pipìrree	February
13.	A-oo-noonoo	

Each month contains according to the account given to me, twenty nine days, which approaches nearly to the real length of a lunation. If their year has but twelve months, it contains only 348 days; but if the thirteenth be added, it consists of 377 days; in the first case, the year is 17 days too short, and in the second, it exceeds the solar year by twelve days. This circumstance leads me to suspect, that they have some method of harmonizing the solar and lunar year unknown to us. What is more remarkable, I found that every one of the 29 days of the month has a peculiar name, which they have in common with the Persians, who appropriate to each day of the month a particular name. Their month begins from the first appearance of the new moon, and after the 28th and 29th day of the month, they added that the moon was dead, *màrama-màtte*, which proves that their months by no means consist exactly of 29 days; but that they contain sometimes 30, and sometimes 29 days only, according as the new moon makes her appearance sooner or later: for if they reckon exactly 29 days for a month, they would soon fall short of the new-moon, and then it could not be with propriety said of the two last days of the month, *màrama-màtte*, the moon is dead; by which expression they intend to say, that during these two days, the moon cannot be seen. Though I could not learn the meaning of any of the names of the days of the month, I will however give them here for the gratification of my readers.

1.	Tirrèo	10.	Oràboo
2.	Tirrohìddee (*Hoee-rohiddee*)*	11.	Mahàrroo
3.	O-hàtta (*Ha-òtta*)	12.	Ohoòa
4.	Ammee-àmma	13.	Mahìddoo
5.	Ammee-àmma hòy (*whaòttee*)	14.	Ohòddoo (*owhòddoo*)
6.	Orre-òrre	15.	Marài
7.	Orre-òrre-hòy (*ròtto*)	16.	Otoòroo
8.	Tamatèa	17.	Ra-òu
9.	Hoòna	18.	Ra-òu-hòy (*rotto*)

* The names included in parentheses are the various readings of the preceding name.

19. Ra-òu-hàddee (*whàddee*)
20. Ororo-tài (*tahài*)
21. Ororo-ròtto
22. Ororo-hàddee (*whaddee*)
23. Tarròa-tahài
24. Tarròa-ròtto

25. Tarròa-hàddie (*whàddee*)
26. Tàne
27. Oro-mòoa
28. Oro-mòoree ⎫
29. Omoòddoo ⎭ (màtte màrama)

Each day is divided into six hours, and the night into the same number; which they can guess at very nearly during the day, by the height of the sun: but few can guess at these divisions by the heighth of the stars during night. These hours, which answer to two of ours, have peculiar names, and are in length similar to the hours of the Chinese. Some of them only I could learn: they call midnight *Otoo-rahai-pò*; from midnight towards day-break is *Oetai yàow*; day-break is named *Ootaatahèita*; and sun rise *Erà-ooào*; when the sun grows hot, the time is called *Erà-t-oowèrra*; when he is in the meridian, they say *Erà-t-ooawatèa*; the part of the evening before sunsetting they name *ooaheihei*; and after sunset, *Erà-oo-opò*.

These divisions of time enable these islanders to observe the heavenly bodies with greater accuracy for their several purposes. They know that the fixed stars do not change their position in regard to one another, and have by long experience discovered which stars rise and set at certain seasons of the year; and by their help they determine the progressive motion of the planets, and the points of the compass during night. *Tupaia* was so well skilled in this, that wherever they came with the ship during the navigation of nearly a year, previous to the arrival of the Endeavour at Batavia, he could always point out the direction in which Taheitee was situated.

This attention to the great luminaries and the stars, rendered it necessary to distinguish each of them by a peculiar name. The sun has the name of *Erà*, and the moon that of *Màrama*, the planet Venus is called *Touroòa*, Jupiter *Matàree*, and Saturn *Na-ta-heèa*. The seven stars have the name of *E-whetto-owhàa*,* Sirius or the Dog-star *Ta-whettoo-ròa*; the stars forming the belt of Orion are named *E-whettoo-mahóo*, the milky way is known by the denomination of *T-èiya*, and a comet or blazing star by that of *E-whettoo-wèrra*; the natives have also a name for

---

* To give the literal signification of the names of all the stars, is a task too difficult for the imperfect knowledge of the Taheitean language I am master of, however I'll give here the interpretation of such names as are obvious to me. The seven stars are called *E-whettoo-owhaà*, or the *stars of the nest*; probably the natives abstracted from the position of the stars, the figure of a bird's nest. The Dog-star *Ta-whettoo roà* is the *great star*, and this name is very properly given. The milky way or *T'èiya* seems to signify a *sail*. A comet or *E-whettoo-wèrra* signifies the *burning star*.

a shooting star and call it *Epào*, and think that it is an evil genius passing rapidly through the heavens. They are doubtless acquainted with other stars, than those here enumerated, and by their rising or setting are enabled to judge of the time of the night, and likewise of the points of the heavens though they have no compass. It is very well known that their imperfect astronomical knowledge is only applicable to the parts of the world which are near to O-Taheitee, as the appearances would be greatly altered at a moderate distance from their isle, and be of no further use to them. We found however upon examination, that this moderate share of astronomy and the slightness of their embarkations did not hinder them from acquiring a very extensive knowledge of the islands in the neighbourhood. TUPAYA the most intelligent man that ever was met with by any European navigator in these isles, had himself been ten or twelve days sail to the Westward of O-*Raiedea;* which according to Capt. Cook's computation,* would make 400 leagues, or about twenty degrees of longitude. This man when on board the Endeavour, gave an account of his navigations and mentioned the names of more than eighty isles which he knew, together with their size and situation, the greater part of which he had visited, and having soon perceived the meaning and use of charts, he gave directions for making one according to his account, and always pointed to the part of the heavens, where each isle was situated, mentioning at the same time that it was either larger or smaller than Taheitee, and likewise whether it was high or low, whether it was peopled or not, adding now and then some curious accounts relative to some of them.[17] Of this chart a copy was obligingly communicated to me by Mr. Pickersgill, Lieutenant on board the Resolution, and who had been before twice at Taheitee, in the Endeavour, and in the Dolphin. Captain Cook was pleased also to communicate to me, two catalogues of such isles as he had heard named in his first voyage at Taheitee, and from Tupaya; I met with another copy of the chart, drawn after Tupaya's direction, in the possession of Joseph Banks, Esq. who, with great politeness and well known readiness to promote whatever has a tendency to become subservient to science, permitted me to take a copy of it. I remarked that the charts both agreed in general, and that the catalogues contained all the names which were found on the charts, and some few more, not inserted in them. I collected likewise many names and accounts of islands, when we were at Taheitee and the Society Isles. Some of the names were strangely spelt, as there never were two persons, in the last and former voyages, who spelt the same name in the same manner; it must therefore happen, that some of the names seemed to be different; though upon a more critical examination, I found them to agree better than might at first sight have been expected: this chart I have caused to be engraved as a monument of the ingenuity

---

* Hawkesworth, vol. ii. p. 278.

and geographical knowledge of the people in the Society Isles, and of Tupaya in particular: the isles are all numbered, that I might have an opportunity of referring to these numbers, and to add a few remarks, which may be thought necessary for illustration. The names themselves are spelt as I found them either in one of the catalogues, or the charts, or in my own register of observations, a preference being given to the best authority, and to the analogy of the language spoken in these isles. The chart includes about 20 degrees of longitude on either side of the meridian of 150 degrees West from Greenwich, or 40 degrees in all, and about 20 degrees of South latitude from about 7 degrees to 27 degrees; the parallel of 17 degrees running in the middle. It cannot be expected that this chart should be of such accuracy as to enable future navigators to make use of it: it is chiefly intended to give some idea of the geography of the inhabitants of the isles in the South Sea, and it will likewise serve to make every navigator cautious when he arrives at that part of the ocean comprehended in this chart; and probably may be the means of ascertaining the situation of these numerous and partly undiscovered isles.

1. O-Tahèitee, called by Capt. Wallis *King George's Island,* and by Mr. de Bougainville *Taïti.* Tupaya mentioned that in the life time of his great grandfather (*Medoòa no the Tooboòna*) a hostile ship (*Pahee-tòa*) had been there. And it is very probable, that Pedro Fernandez de Quiros was in the year 1606, its first discoverer,[18] who called it *Sagittaria,* according to the ingenious conjecture of Mr. Dalrymple in his *letter to Dr. Hawkesworth,* p. 17, and though this opinion has very lately been attacked; I am still of opinion, that Mr. Dalrymple's conjecture has not been invalidated by the shew of arguments opposed to it. It is about thirty leagues in circumference, and both Peninsulas are high land, which, especially in the Easternmost is extremely spiry, and has the strongest marks of being the work of a violent earthquake and subterraneous fire.

2. Maeatèa, was called *Osnabruck Island* by Captain Wallis, and *Pic de la Boudeuse* or *Boudoir* by Mr. de Bougainville. If the conjecture of Taheitee being Sagittaria is right, *Maeatea* must be *Dezena,* seen by Quiros February the 9th, 1606. It is about four or five miles in circuit, is high land, and the summit of the hill has the appearance of being excavated, as if formerly there had been a volcano, whose crater is now filled up.

3. O-Heeva-noòe, an isle to the Eastward of O-Taheitee, seems to be the same which Captain Cook called *Chain Island* in 1769, being a chain of low islands connected by reefs into an oval shape, about five leagues in length.

4. Oiròtah, is an island larger than Taheitee, inhabited.

5. Ouropòë, likewise inhabited, and larger than Taheitee.

6. O-HITTE-TAMARO-EÏREE, seems to be *Osnabruck Island*, seen by Captain Carteret in the year 1767, is low land, and probably not inhabited.

7. TE-NEWHAMMÈA-TÀNE, a low island.

8. TOÒMETO-ROÀRO, seems to be the cluster of low islands, seen likewise by Captain Carteret, and called by him the *Duke of Gloucester's Islands*.

9. MOUTOÙ, is larger than Taheitee and the Southernmost island, which Tupaya had seen; though his father had told him there were islands to the Southward of it.

10. MANNÙA is a high island, peopled by ferocious inhabitants, with wild and furious looks, and eating men, but having very little shipping: its situation is to the North East of *O-Hitte-roa*.

11. EÏTO-NOÒE.

12. O-HITTE-RÒA a high island, seen by Captain Cook in 1769.

13. TABBU-A-MÀNNOO, a small high island to the West of O-Taheitee, seen by Captain Wallis, and called *Sir Charles Saunders's Island*. Mr. de Bougainville heard of it, and calls it *Tapoua massou*. It is about six miles long. The Chief of this island in 1774, was called OÒPA.

14. EÏMÈO is high land, and was called *York Island* by Captain Wallis in 1767. Mr. de Bougainville named it *Aimeo*: It belongs to Taheitee.

15. HUAHÈINE is a high island, seen first by Captain Cook, its Chief in 1774 was OREE.

16. EA-WATTÈA, in the middle of the chart, is the name of the Meridian-Line.

17. O-RAIETÈA is a high island, seen first by Captain Cook; Mr. de Bougainville had heard of it, and calls it *Aiatea*. It was conquered by OPÙNEE chief or king of *Borabòra,* and the conquered chief is called Oo-oòroo: Tupaya said that in his grandfather's time a friendly ship had been there, of which we have no account in Europe, unless one of the ships of Roggewein came near this island.

18. O-TAHÀ is a high island, seen first by Captain Cook, and likewise conquered by OPÙNEE, the joint chiefs of it were OTÀ and BÒBA, Mr. de Bougainville seems to have heard of it, and called it *Otaa*.

19. BORABÒRA or BOLABÒLA is a high island, governed by OPÙNEE. Captain Cook saw it first, and it seems Mr. de Bougainville had heard something of it and called it *Papara*.

20. TOOPÀI is a low island, uninhabited, resorted to by the inhabitants of Borabòra for the purposes of fishing and fowling: sometimes the inhabitants of an island called *Papàä* frequent it.

21. MOUROÒA is a high island, under the dominion of OPÙNEE, first seen by Captain Cook. Mr. de Bougainville probably heard of it, and names it *Toomaraa*.

REMARKS ON THE HUMAN SPECIES IN THE SOUTH-SEA ISLES

22. O-ànna is a low island, on which a ship was wrecked, and some men perished, according to Tupaya's account: it seems to be the same which Admiral Byron called *Prince of Wales's Island*; for though some iron and brass, with the head of a rudder of a Dutch longboat, were found at *King George's Island*, it could not be the island on which the ship was lost; for the description and situation prove King George's Island to be (26) *Teokèa*; and the parts of the ship found there, might have been carried from *O-ànna*. The ship lost here, may, with great possibility, be supposed to be the *African Galley*, one of Roggewein's squadron, which was wrecked upon an island, called, for that reason, *Pernicious Island*.

23. O-Matèiva, or O-Matèa is a low island to the North East of *Raietèa*, and to the North West of Taheitee: a boat with three men and a woman, arrived from thence, some months before us, at Huaheine, where I saw the boat, similar to those at *Teokèa*, and the men were tattowed all over their faces and arms.

24. O-Wahèi seems to answer to *Waterland*, first seen by Schouten and Le Maire, in 1616. It is low land.

25. Oura, and

26. Teoheow or Teokèa, two low islands, at a few miles distance from one another, were seen by Admiral Byron, in 1765, and called *George's Islands*; we landed, in 1774, on the latter island, and learnt the true name of this island from the natives, who called it *Teoukea* or *Teokea*. On this island Mr. Byron found the carved head of a rudder, probably belonging to a Dutch long-boat, a piece of hammered iron, a piece of brass, and some small iron tools. He seems to indicate, "that in case the ship to which the long-boat belonged, sailed from this place in safety, it would not be easy to account for her leaving the rudder of her long-boat behind; and if she was cut off by the natives, there must be much more considerable remains of her in the island, especially of her iron work, upon which all Indian nations, who have no metal, set the highest value." These arguments seem to be very just, for the ship was lost on (22) *O-ànna*, the island before mentioned, and these trifles of iron and brass, were obtained by the inhabitants of *Teokèa*, either by trading with those at *O-ànna*, or as presents to the chiefs: for this is very customary in all these islands; thus for instance *Opùnee* chief of Borabòra, obtained one of Mr. de Bougainville's lost anchors, as a present from *Tootaha*, the chief of Taheitee.

27. O-Rai-ròa seems to be the island of *Carlshof* discovered in 1722 by Roggewein.

28. O-tàh corresponds in some measure with the situation of *Adventure's* Island seen by us in 1773.

29. O-PATÀI or OO-PATI, answers to the situation of the group of islands called by Captain Cook *Palliser's Islands*, in 1774.

30. O-WHARÈVA is probably the *Isle of Furneaux*, called thus by us in 1773.

31. O-WHÀO, must in all probability be the *Island of Birds*, discovered by Captain Cook in 1769.

32. O-RIMA-RÒA coincides nearly with the situation of the *Isles of Disappointment*, seen by Admiral Byron in 1765.

33. O-HÈEVA-TOUTOU-ÀI, to this island *Tupaya* added the following remark, "that the inhabitants are men-eaters, that their ships are large, and that the ship from Britain (the Endeavour) was but little in comparison."

34. HANEANÈA is a small island.

35. NEEO-HÈEVA is likewise small.[19]

36. WHATTÈRRE-TOÀ, seems to be *la Magdalena* discovered by *Mendaña*, 1595.

37. TEROWHÀ.

38. TEEBOOAI is from its situation very probably *Hood's Island* one of the *Marquesas*.

39. WHATÀRRE-OÒRA. In Mr. Bank's chart I find the name written *Whattèrre-ero*, and in two other lists the last word was spelt *oora* for *ero*, so that I think it is plain from the nature of the language that *Whatàrre-oòra* is the true writing of the name. The name *Waitàhoo* given to the isle of Christina by the natives themselves, confirms this still more, for we found that the inhabitants of the Marquesas never or at least very seldom pronounced the *r*; this was evident to me from a vocabulary of about eighty words not containing a single word with an *r*, and from the circumstance that all the words in the Taheitee language corresponded with the words of the language of *Waitàhoo*, with this difference only that the canine letter was either omitted or softened. In O-Taheitee the phrase *come hither* is expressed by *harre-mài*, in Waitàhoo by *hanna-mài*; the hand is called *reèma*, and in the Marquesas *heèma*; two is expressed *aroòa* at Taheitee, and *bo-hoòa* at Waitàhoo; three is *atòroo*, and *bo-dò-oo* at the latter place; five is called *reèma*, but at Waitàhoo *heèma*; great is *ròa*, and at the Marquesas *òa*. The island of *Dominica* was called *Oheeva-òa* instead of *Oheeva-róa*; and *Waitàhoo* in all probability is used in lieu of *Wattàrre-oòra*; for by dropping the *r*'s there remain *Wateae-oòa* or *Wattà-ooa*, in which an *h* has been inserted to compensate the elision of so many *r*'s, and pronounced *Wattà-hooa* or *Waità-hoo*. This is certainly the island of *St. Christina*, one of the Marquesas, discovered by Mendaña, 1595, and is high land.

40. TE-MÀNNO.

41. O-ÒTTO.

42. O-Hèeva-ròa, is high land, called by the natives *O-Heeva-òa,* and is the same which Mendaña called *Dominica;* seems to be populous, fertile, and the largest of the Marquesas.

43. O-Hèeva-pòtto.

44. Mopeèha or Motu-hèa, is a low island, but large, not inhabited, abounding however with fish, coconuts, turtle and pearls.

45. Whennua-oòra is a low island, has inhabitants, and has the same productions with the former.

46. O-Papatèa.

47. Woureèo is a large island, and inhabited.

48. Ururutù, inhabited.

49. O-Adeèha is an island to which men resort occasionally for fishing, but do not live continually on it.

50. O-Ahoua-hòu, large, and peopled.

51. O-Weèha.

52. O-Rima-tàrra, high land and inhabited.

53. O-Rai-havài.

54. O-Raro-tòa has inhabitants.

55. O-Ahouròu larger than Taheitee.

56. O-Toomoo-pàpa.

57. Toutèepa, a low island of no great extent, but is however inhabited.

58. O-reeva-vài; Tupaya added this remark, "fine hatchets come from thence to *Raiedea;*" whether these are iron or good stone hatchets cannot be determined from this account. If they had iron hatchets, they must have been there ever since the time of Abel Jansen Tasman, who was in this neighbourhood in 1643, or since the times of Schouten and le Maire, 1616. I obtained at *E-Aoowe* a small nail sticking in a kind of handle, which at least proves, how carefully the smallest pieces of iron are preserved by these people.

59. Tainùna.

60. O-Rima-tèma, from its position it seems to be the low island seen by us in the year 1774, and called *Palmerston's Island.*

61. O-Rotoòma is said to be larger than Taheitee.

62. O-Poppòa.

63. Moë-no-tàyo is a low island, and from its situation seems to be that which we called *Hervey's Island* in 1773.

64. Te-toòpa-tùpa-eahoù.

65. O-Hitte-pòtto corresponds with the situation of *Savage Island* seen by us in 1774.

66. O-Hitte-toutou-atù.

67. O-HITTE-TOUTOU-NÈE.

68. O-HITTE-TOUTOU-RÈRA.

69. O-HITTE-TAITÈRRE.

70. TE-AMAROO-HÌTTE.

71. TE-ATOU-HÌTTE.

72. OUOWHÈA.

73. O-TOOTOO-ÈRRE.

74. TE-OROOROO-MATIVATÈA.

75. WOUWÒU a small low island, but inhabited.

76. OOPÒRROO, a large island and well peopled.

77. TE-ERREPOO-OPO-MATTE-HÈA.

78. O-HEAVÀI is larger than Taheitee; *Tupaya* added "it is the father of all the islands."[20]

79. TEDHU-RÒA, a small island, a few leagues to the North of O-Taheitee, has no other inhabitants than those who occasionally resort to it from Taheitee.

80. O-WÀNNA, one of the low islands, East of Taheitee.

81. TATA-HAPÀI, 82. TAPY-ARÝ, 83. HAEDEDE, are three other names of islands, which I found mentioned in one of the lists, without any thing relative to their situation.

84. PAPPÄÄ is a low island, somewhat to the East of *Toopài* (20), whose inhabitants frequently go to this last mentioned island in order to fish and to catch turtle, but their language is not understood by the people of Borabora, who resort there for the same purpose.

As I have no account of the particular situation of the five last isles, I omitted the names on the chart. However the number of more than eighty isles, is abundantly sufficient to prove that the inhabitants of the Society-isles have a competent and extensive knowledge of the geography of their neighbourhood, considering the small size and slight structure of their embarkations, and the want of a compass; and that they cannot like the antient Phoenicians and the Greeks, follow the shores of an extensive continent, in order to make discoveries, but are obliged to cross large tracts of the ocean before they arrive at another island; and what is more remarkable, having no other provisions for these long navigations, than their sour paste, and some fruit, which cannot be kept above a few days in an eatable state; nor have they any vessels large enough to keep fresh water in for a long time; and yet with all these inconveniences, they have discovered lands at more than 400 leagues distance round their islands.

The Friendly-isles are a group where of *Tonga-Tabbu*, *E-Aoowe*, and *Namocka* are the largest; but we saw afterwards many small ones, and heard a still greater number named. The small islands off the North East point of *Tonga-*

Tabbu, were called WEWEGHEE. When we were sailing to *Namocka*, in 1774, we saw to the East of it some islands, whereof one was called O-MÀNGO-NOÒE and the other O-MÀNGO-EÈTEE, i.e. *great and little Mango*; they lay both to the North of our track; to the South of it we observed the isles of TONOO-MÈA and TEREFETCHÈA. South of *Namocka-nòoe* was NAMÒCKA EÈTEE, which last, Tasman called *Namocaki*, on his drawing. To the North West of *Namocka*, are two high isles, the Westernmost is called TOFOÒA, contains a Volcano, and is designed by Tasman, under the name *Amattafoa*, which spelling Captain Cook has adopted in his chart; the Easternmost of these isles is called by the natives OGHÀO, but by Tasman *Kaybay*. The Westernmost of the cluster of low isles, situated to the North and North East of Namocka, is called MOTTO-WÀ. The other little keys of this archipelago, were called O-TOOGHOÒA, O-OÒA, LOOGHELÀ-EI, FONNOO-ÀCKA, LAGHOLLÀ, OOFÀNGA, and WOFOÒGEE: these were all situated to the North of *Namocka*, but farther to the North East, the natives told us were the islands of OOVÈEA, WO-ALEE-ÀVA, OLEEFÀNGA, KO-FÒO, KO-E-E-ÒNNA, KO-NAGHOONÀMOO, O-FOOLÀNGO, MOU-E-E-ÒNNE, TOGHOÒROO, KOË-NOÒGOO, KO-ÒGEE, KO-NEÈ-MOO, and TONOO-NOO-OFOÒA.

Another account of some islands, lying still further to the West, is given by QUIROS, as it was communicated to him by a native of the isle of *Chicayana*,* and as deduced from his own observation and discoveries.

1. TAUMÀCO. Quiros saw in 10°. South latitude, 1250 leagues from Mexico, an island, eight or nine leagues in circumference, which was high and black, like a volcano, and its name he found to be *Taumàco*.
2. CHICAYÀNA. Four days sail from thence, is a low island, larger than TAUMÀCO, and in the language of the country, dogs are named *Te-cùri*, or *Te-ghoòree*, in the same manner as they call them at Tonga-Tabbu, and New-Zeeland, which may be construed into an argument for the identity of the language.
3. GUAYTÒPO, is another island larger than the two before-mentioned, at three days sail from Taumaco and two from Chicayana; the inhabitants of these three isles are friendly people.
4. MECAYRÀYLA is in all probability a low island, and inhabited, to which the natives of Guaytopo sail, in search of tortoise-shell, of which they make their ear-rings.
5. TUCÒPIA is a high island in twelve Degrees South Latitude, five days sail South West from Taumaco.

---

* See Dalrymple's *Collection of Voyages*, vol. I. page 151.

6. FONOFÒNO is the name of a cluster of small flat isles, three days sail from Tau-maco, though the voyage may be performed in two days with a fresh wind; the inhabitants are said to be very tall. The language differs from that spoken at Taumaco.

7. PÌLEN and NÙPAN are isles near the Fonofono isles.[21]

9. POURO is a large country very populous; its inhabitants are of a dun colour, at war among themselves, and have silver-headed arrows.

There are accounts in Herrera, Galvano, Argensola, and De Couto of some islands discovered by ALVARADO and GRIJALVA, which seem to be connected with the new Caroline Islands to the South in about 205 degrees West longitude from Greenwich, near the line: the names of these isles are given in Mr. Dalrymple's Collection of Voyages, vol. i. p. 35, 36, 37, 38, and 39; but as they were not men-tioned by the natives, I have forborn to speak of them as proofs of the Geograph-ical knowledge of the natives of these parts.

The foregoing account of the many islands mentioned by Tupaya is sufficient to prove that the inhabitants of the islands in the South Sea have made very con-siderable navigations in their slight and weak canoes; navigations which many Europeans would think impossible to be performed, upon a careful view of the vessels themselves, their rigging, sails, &c. &c. also the provisions of the climate.

The arts of dancing, music, and poetry, are generally understood by almost every individual from the highest to the lowest rank, but the sciences of physic and its various branches, those of geography, navigation, and astronomy, are known only to few. This ignorance extends so far that the greater part of the nation cannot count beyond ten: but those who have been instructed by their teachers can reckon as far as 200. I could not learn whether they can count beyond that number, but am rather inclined to believe they cannot. Their way of reckoning is by enumerating first the digits, 1 *a-tahài*, 2 *a-roòa*, 3 *a-tòroo*, 4 *a-hèa*, 5 *a-rèema*, 6 *a-hòno*, 7 *ahìddoo*, 8 *a-wàrroo*, 9 *a-hèeva*, 10 *a-hòoroo*; then they add a second ten as far as twenty, in the following manner: 11 *ma-tahài*, 12 *ma-ròoa*, 13 *ma-tòroo*, 14 *ma-hèa*, 15 *ma-reèma*, 16 *ma-hòno*, 17 *ma-hìddoo*, 18 *ma-wàrroo*, 19 *ma-heèva*, 20 *a-tahài-tàoo*. From thence they count by scores to 200; viz. they say for 21 *a-tahài-tàoo-màra-tahai*, literally one twenty with one; 30 is called *tàhai-tàoo-màra-hoòroo*, 40 *a-roòa-tàoo*, 50 *a-roòa-tàoo-màra-hoòroo*, &c. &c. The teachers are men, who have either from their fathers or other teachers acquired a knowledge, which, they again impart to others. These people are called *Tàhata-orrèro*, are very much respected, and commonly belong to the tribe of chiefs; which circumstance induces me to believe, that from their easy and independent circumstances, they are not under the necessity of communicating their knowl-edge to their pupils for any retribution; as there is little probability that a chief

should accept of a reward, or even honorary compensation, having himself a com-
petency, viz. land, a house, fruits, and trees that bear them; hogs, dogs, and fowls,
and lastly toutous to serve him.

The bulk of their science is the work of memory only, and by no means the
result of meditation, reflection, or reasoning. For I met with some of their chiefs
who had attempted to learn the names of the months and days, but knew them
only imperfectly, having taken no pains to preserve their knowledge; but those
professed teachers, *(Tahata-orrero)* were more perfect. However there must have
been a time when this knowledge was first introduced among them, and that man
who was its author must have had patience to attend with unwearied application
to the study of the heavens, and the motion of the heavenly bodies, and been
endued with sagacity to discover the true length of the solar or bread-fruit year,
and the duration of lunations, together with the beginning of the new moon. The
direction in which the remote islands are situated, which they know is a business
of the greatest difficulty, and required a remarkable skill, reflection, and combination of several incidental points; which evidently shews that this man had very
strong natural parts, and had used himself to apply them to the various occurrences of his life, and the objects surrounding him. It might perhaps be urged,
that this knowledge had been most probably carried along with them from Asia
and the more civilized nations of that continent. Though this perhaps might be
allowed in regard to other sciences, yet their knowledge of astronomy and geography, or their skill in determining with nicety the true situation of isles at the distance of 400 leagues from their own country, and directing the course of their
boats by the sun and stars,* proves evidently that this science must have had its
rise and progress among themselves; as many points could by no means agree, had
the Asiatic astronomy discovered in the Northern Hemisphere been carried to
Taheitee. The points where the sun rises and sets at different seasons, in countries
situated in the Southern hemisphere, differs from those in the Northern, so that
the Asiatic knowledge must have been in a great measure useless. The farther the
Asiatic country, in which we will suppose the Taheitean astronomy to have origi-

---

* The Endeavour, in which ship Tupaya sailed to Batavia, sailed first from Taheitee into forty
Degrees South Latitude, then she came by a North West course into twenty-eight Degrees, after this
she came by a South West course to about thirty-eight Degrees, and by a Western run to New
Zeeland, which islands were circumnavigated in runs of various directions to forty-eight Degrees
South Latitude, till by another Westerly course the coasts of New Holland were reached, along
which she sailed North and North West, up to about four Degrees North Latitude, and then West to
Savu, and lastly by the Streights of Sunda to Batavia. However, Tupaya was never at a loss to point
to Taheitee, at whatever place he came, even at Batavia at more than 2000 Leagues distance: which
evidently proves that he was perfectly well acquainted with astronomy and geography, as far as they
are necessary for these purposes.[22]

nated, is removed from the equinoctial line Northwards, the more sensible does this difference become, and renders it more probable that the inhabitants of these isles were the inventors of their own astronomy and geography: and if they had strength of mind sufficient to enable them to invent sciences which require accurate observations, and a remarkably strong sagacity; why may we not think them equally capable of being the inventors of the whole cyclus of their knowledge.

Macti ingenio este caeli interpretes, rerumque naturae capaces, argumenti repertores, quo deos hominesque vicistis.
Plin. lib. ii. c. 12[23]

SECTION IX

Religion, Mythology, Cosmogony, Worship, Origin of Mankind, Future State, Rites genethliac,[1] Nuptial, Sepulchral

FRAGILIS & LABORIOSA MORTALITAS IN PARTES ISTA (NUMINA) DIGES-
SIT, INFIRMITATIS SUAE IMMEMOR, UT PORTIONIBUS QUISQUE COLERET,
QUO MAXIME INDIGERET. ITAQUE NOMINA ALIA ALIIS GENTIBUS, &
NUMINA IN IISDEM INNUMERABILIA REPERIMUS.
Plin. *Hist. Nat.* lib. ii. c. vii[2]

The Contemplation of the infinite power and wisdom of the creator and governor of the world, the fountain of all good, the witness to, and judge of all our actions; and on the other hand the sense of our own weakness and wants, together with the impossibility of obviating or avoiding many great and remarkable incidents of our lives, impress our minds with awe and respect, with a confidence in, and love towards this friendly distributor of mercies. If again we examine our faculties both of body and mind, the enjoyments of which we are capable, especially of a rational sort, and the thirst after everlasting life and happiness which every individual feels strongly in his breast, notwithstanding the prejudices of education, and the wiles of vice and predominant luxury; it becomes more and more evident that the Supreme Being deserves our humble adoration, our warmest attachment, and our unfeigned love: that we ought to exert our faculties in examining and studying the immense and infinite powers and perfections of this being; that it should be our chief thought and earnest endeavour to imitate, and to approximate the bright virtues of this great prototype of perfection and goodness; to behave in a manner becoming the many ties and relations by which the creator has been pleased to connect us with him and other subordinate beings. The above ideas or others to the same purpose, form the ground work of true religion, of all natural obligations, moral virtues and religious worship. The ideas of the inhabitants of the South Sea islands on this head, are we may suppose, less clear, perfect and refined: however they acknowledge an almighty invisible lord and creator of the universe, who executed the various parts of his creation by various subordinate powerful beings. They are of opinion that he is good and omniscient; that he sees and hears all human actions, and is the giver of all good gifts. They feel their own wants, and therefore apply for redress to the Supreme Being, and offer to him, with a grateful heart, the best gifts of their lands. They acknowledge to have a being within their bodies, which sees, hears, smells, tastes, and feels, which they call *E-teèhee;* and they believe, that after the dissolution of the body, it hovers about the corpse; and lastly, retires into the wooden representations of human bodies, erected near their burying places. They are convinced of the certainty of a happy life in the sun, where they shall feast on breadfruit, and meat which requires no dressing; and they think it their duty to direct their prayers to this Supreme Divinity, or *Eatoòa-rahài.* Those who have more leisure among these people, are very desirous of learning what is known relative to this and all other inferior divinities, and to practise such virtues, as by the general consent of mankind constitute good actions; these are briefly the general outlines of their religion and worship.

Though these principles are generally adopted among the greater part of mankind, provided they are not so much degraded and debased as to have lost even these universally acknowledged notions of the Deity, and of the duties we owe him; there is, however, no impropriety in believing that these very notions are the venerable remains of a tradition, which may have been brought over from the Asiatic continent. We do not, however, mean to insinuate, as if their notions of the Deity and his worship were of such a complexion that they could not have been learnt but by tradition; there are, however, many reasons which confirm me in this opinion; *first,* as their language, their manners, customs, and many other circumstances, prove the Asiatic origin of the nation, why should we not also suspect their religious principles to have been derived from the same source: *secondly,* the indolence and supineness of mankind is so great in most matters, which require reasoning, attention, and judgment, or which, suppose a great many abstract ideas, that we rather choose to follow a beaten track, than to strike out a new one, by dint of argumentation, and by a constant exertion of attention and judgment. It seems therefore more natural, that these nations should have adopted the notions of their ancestors or forefathers, than to imagine that they formed the whole system of their religion, by the mere strength of their understandings. *Lastly,* there is, beyond all doubt, so great an agreement between the religious principles of Taheitee, and its neighbourhood, and these of the rest of the East, that we cannot hesitate a moment in pronouncing them to have been imported from Asia; nay, if we go one step further in our enquiry, we must soon find, that there is not a country, nor a nation existing, which has not preserved some ideas in their religion, which, when attended to, prove that they were handed down to them by tradition: now, by going backward into remote ages, there must be at last a place where we must stop; and this, though ever so remote in antiquity, seems to have obtained these notions from the very source. Mankind, collectively in its infant state, is exactly as the individual in the first years of his existence: the ideas of a Supreme Being, and the obligation of worshipping him, are by no means of such a clearness and evidence, that they should be easily discovered by a child; those who have the care of his education are therefore solicitous, at this early period, when the faculties of apprehending, judging, and reasoning, are not yet developed or strong enough in the child, to treat the great truth of the existence of God, and the obligation of worshipping him as a precept, or as an universally acknowledged, indisputable axiom; and inculcate it as such into the minds of their children. Afterwards, when they find the faculties, by exercise and education, to be more enlarged, and to have acquired more strength, they lead their pupils back, and teach them to investigate the existence of God and his attributes, together with the nature and obligation of worshipping him, by arguments and by the force of reasoning. Divine Providence seems then in this respect, to have treated mankind like children; and to have given the first notions of himself and his existence, as an axiom, and inforced its worship by precept, conforming these great and salutary truths to the infant state of mankind; as long therefore as the use of reason and of the intellectual faculties is not yet practised in a nation, these religious notions must be communicated by precept and tradition: but as soon as men feel themselves strong enough, they will no longer trust to tradition, the instructor of their childhood, in this great and interesting truth, and soon find that it is impossible to be mistaken in this important argument, as the existence of this Infinite Being is written with so legible characters in every object surrounding them: they soon go back to themselves, and investigate their own mental and sensual faculties, and from thence are gradually led to acknowledge the duties they owe to God, themselves, and all the rational, animated, organic, and inanimated creation, which they either find co-operating with, or subordinate to themselves. The people at Taheitee preserve their notions relative to the Deity and his worship by tradition, and are as yet unable to investigate the necessity of the existence of God, the nature of his attributes, and the duties they owe him by reason; they are therefore still in the infant state of humanity, not yet ripened to the use of argument and reason in religious matters: and, according to the present situation of affairs, a long time must pass, before they will be able to bear the evidence of these doctrines, and the radiancy of this truth; we have only therefore to wish that we may be permitted to see the minds of these excellent people irradiated by the bright religion taught by nature and reason; which may prepare them for a due reception of the doctrines of the Christian dispensation.

Their present system of religion is a polytheism, which may be called one of the best and least exceptionable as yet known. The name EATOÒA, admits a very great latitude in its interpretation; for though it properly signifies a *Divinity*, it may likewise be interpreted a *Genius*. However they admit a Being whom they call *Eatoòa-rahài*, which is the supreme *Deity* above all. Each of the isles surrounding Taheitee, has its peculiar god, or as we may justly call it, its *tutelar Divinity*. Taheitee is under the peculiar guidance and government of ORÙA-HÀTTOO; over Huaheine presides TÀNE; over O-Raiedea ORÒO: over O-Tahà ORRA; Borabora has its TAÒOTOO; Mauroa its OTÒO; and in Tabua-mànoo TARÒA is the chief god. This is always the Divinity whom the high priest of each isle addresses in his prayers at the grand Marai of the prince of that island. The great Deity they think to be the prime cause of all divined and human beings and as this nation has introduced every where the idea of generation, it has applied the system of generation to the origin of their inferior Divinities, and for that purpose the natives though it likewise necessary to attribute to the EATOOA-RAHAI, a being of the female sex, from whose conjunction all the inferior Eatoòas, and even mankind are descended; and in this respect they call the great Deity TA-ROA-T'EAY-ETOÒ-MOO the great procreating stem: but his wife is not of the same nature with him; their gross ideas imagined a coexisting material hard substance necessary, which they call O-TE-PÀPA a rock. These procreated O-HEÈNA the goddess who created the moon, and presides in the black cloud which appears in this luminary; TE-WHETTOO-MA-TARÀI the creator of the stars; OOMARRÈE the God and creator of the Seas; and ORRE-ÒRRE* who is the God of the Winds. But the sea is under the direction of 13 Divinities, who all have some peculiar employment, as their name often seems to imply: their names are the following: 1. OOROO-HÀDDOO, 2. TAMAOÒEE, 3. TA-ÀPEE, 4. ATOO-AREEÒNO, 5. TANÈEA, 6. TAHOU-ME-ÒNNA, 7. OTA-MA-ÒU-WE,† 8. OWHÀI,‡ 9. O-WHÀTTA, 10. TA-HOÒA, 11. TEOO-T-EÌYA,* 12. OMA-HÒOROO, 13. O-WHÀDDOO. The great God TAROA-T'EAI-ETOÒMOO lives in the sun, and is represented as a man, who has fine hair, reaching down to the very ground; he is thought to be the cause of the earthquakes, in which case the natives call him O-MAOÙWE, and he is likewise the creator of the sun; a rude representation of this deity, under the attribute of *O-Maoùwe*, was observed by Captain Cook, in 1769, when he made the tour of Taheitee in a boat: it was formed of basket-work, and covered with black and white feathers. This is the only instance of a figure or representation of their divinities which I ever heard of; and Capt.

---

* *Orree* signifies wind.

† *Ma-òu* signifies a shark.

‡ *Owhài* is called a stone or pebble.

* *T'eiya* is a fish or a sail of a canoe.

Cook does not mention that any respect or reverence was paid to this rude figure of *Maoùwe*. The natives have a tradition that the great Deity procreated the inferior divinities, each of whom created the part of the world allotted to his peculiar care: one the seas, another the moon, the stars, the birds, fishes, &c. &c. *O-Maoùwe* created the sun, and then took the immense rock *O-Te-pàpa*, his wife, and dragged her from West to East through the seas: when the isles, which the natives now inhabit, were broken off; after which he left his great land to the East, where it still exists. The care and government of each island was committed to the inferior divinities, enumerated before. The god *Tàne*, is not more particularly addressed than the rest of his brother divinities, nor is he supposed to take a greater part in the affairs of mankind,* except at Huaheine, which place is under his peculiar inspection, and where he is worshipped as the tutelar divinity of that country. Besides these divinities of the second class, there are others of a still inferior rank, and though called *Eatooas*, are no more than what the Greek or Roman Mythologists would have called *Genii*, or *Dii Minorum Gentium:*[3] one of them, called Orometoòa, is of a malignant disposition, resides chiefly near the *Marais* and *Toopapous* (places of burial) and in or near the boxes, or little chests, including the heads of their deceased friends, each of which, on that account, is called *Te-wharre no te Orometoòa*, the house of the evil genius *Orometoòa*. The people at Taheitee are of opinion, that if their priests invoke this evil genius, he will kill, by a sudden death, the person on whom they intend to bring down the vengeance of this divinity. Their priests are, I suppose, not the most conscientious persons, and, if bribed, will not scruple to poison the man who is devoted to destruction, and afterwards ascribe the sudden death of such a person to the malignity of *Orometoòa*; and this seems to be the more probable, as I was told with the strongest asseveration, that it was not uncommon to see the prayers of the priests to their *Orometoòa* fulfilled. I heard likewise of another genius, or inferior divinity, called Oromehouhoùwe, who had the same power of killing men, with this difference only, that he was not addressed by prayer, but is only worshipped by hissing.† The last kind of genius is called Tèehee; the natives told us, that was the thing which

---

* Hawkesworth, vol. ii. p. 239.

† It is remarkable that this mode of worshipping the deity or a genius by hissing was likewise adopted by the Egyptian Priests according to the testimony of Nicomachus Gerasenus Harmon. Manual. i. ii. (*in Meibomii auctoribus Antiquae Musicae, vol.* i. *p.* 37) Αρμονια αποτελει δραστικας δυναμεις και τελεστικας των θειων. διο οτ'αν μαλιστα οι θερινοι (λεγε θεοριμοι) το τοιουτον (λεγε το θειον) σεβαζονται σιγμοις τε και εναρθροις και ασυμφωνοις ηχοις συμβολικως επικαλουνται *Harmonia perficit potestates operatrices & divinorum effectivas. Quare Theurgici, cum sanctissimo colunt numen aliquod, invocant illud sibilis & poppysmis, sonisque qui articulationes & consonas non habent.*[4]

sees, hears, smells, tastes, and feels within us, which forms the thoughts,* and, after death, exists separately from the body, but lives near the burying places, and hovers about the corpse or bones, deposited there, is likewise an object of their reverence, though addressed only by hissing: they informed us farther, that these *Tèehees* inhabit chiefly the wooden figures, which are erected near the marais; and are, according to the sex of the person deceased, either males or females: they are likewise dreaded; for according to their belief, they creep, during night, into the houses, and eat the heart and entrails of the people sleeping therein, and thus cause their death.

The inhabitants of Taheitee shew their reverence to their divinities in various manners, *first* by the appropriation of certain places for religious worship, which they call MARÀI. These places are commonly on points projecting into the sea, or near it, and consist of a very large pile of stones, generally in the shape of an Egyptian pyramid, with large steps; sometimes this pyramid makes one of the sides of an area, walled in with square stones and paved with flat stones: the pyramid is not solid, but the inside is filled with smaller fragments of coral stones. Sometimes there are one or more sheds standing at a little distance from the marai, for the reception of such people as attend the marai on account of praying or performing the funeral rites of their relations. Sometimes there are spars fixed in the ground and joined by cross beams in a firm frame at a small distance from the marai, and likewise small stages raised on pillars of various heights and dimensions. The stages are called *Whattas*, and are intended for the reception of the hogs, dogs, fowls and fruits, which the natives offer to their gods. The large frame is sometimes thirty feet high, and about twenty or more wide, and often entirely covered with bananas hung up for the gods with many garlands of flowers, and ornamented with green branches.† Lastly, near the marais are twenty or thirty single pieces of wood fixed into the ground, carved all over on one side with figures about eighteen inches long, rudely representing a man and a woman alternately, so that often more than fifteen or twenty figures may be counted on one piece of wood, called by them *Teèhee*. To ornament the marais and to honour by it the gods and the decayed buried there, the inhabitants plant several sorts of trees, near them; above all the *Casuarina equisetifolia* or *Toa-tree* is the most common, not only in Taheitee and its neighbourhood, but even in the Friendly islands; where exceeding large trees were observed by us, near their *Assayetoòcas*

---

* The Taheiteans have no expressions for abstract ideas. *Thoughts* certainly do not convey a corporeal idea, and required therefore a peculiar turn in order to be expressed by words: the Taheiteans have called them *parou no te oboo* words of the belly.
† The plants employed for that purpose are chiefly the *Pooràoo* or *Epòoa-taròoroo* or Crataeva, the *E-mòtoo* Melastoma malabathrica, and the *Awa-waidai* or Piper latifolium.

or places of burial and worship. The *Tamànoo* or Calophyllum inophyllum, is likewise planted near the *Marais*, as is the *E-meero* or Hibiscus populneus; with the *Ewharra* or Athrodactylis; and lastly the *Etèe* or Dracaena terminalis, of which there is one variety with red flowers, and red veins in the leaves, with many others.

The second mark of reverence paid to their divinities, consists in the appointment of certain days appropriated for their worship. Though I cannot with any precision point out any day which they peculiarly celebrated as an anniversary feast or holiday; it is nevertheless certain from the accounts I repeatedly heard, that they did observe some days as feasts.

Another way of declaring their respect for their divinities is the appointment of certain persons for the peculiar performance of prayers, rites, and ceremonies. Each great chief or king of an island chooses from among the inferior chiefs an intelligent person, who is to be his *Tahòuwa* or priest; whose business it is to pray and offer up sacrifices, and to perform the rites which are deemed requisite on each occasion. This dignity is hereditary and descends to the son. Each chief of a province has likewise a priest, and the inferior ranks of people have in the same manner peculiar priests, who cannot perform rites and offer up prayers for men of a higher class: it is observed by Hawkesworth, vol. ii. p. 239. that even the priests for the males cannot perform the same office for the females; and that each sex has marais, to which the other sex is never admitted, though they have marais common to both. These circumstances indeed we never heard, but it is not improbable that they have these singularities in their mode of worshipping.

The acts of devotion, which these nations pay to their divinities are likewise of various kinds: the first is the invocation or prayer addressed to one of their deities. The prayers themselves are either spoken loud or offered tacitly by the priest: for each peculiar ceremony they have short sentences, which they deliver on that occasion; the language seems to be more formal, sententious, and almost totally different from that used in common life: for none of us were able to understand the least sentence of their prayers, though we were possessed of large vocabularies, and had acquired a tolerable share of knowledge of their language. Besides the prayers which the priests of each class deliver upon certain occasions, the laymen themselves are not excluded from saying their own prayers, and performing many ceremonies of their worship: for when a young man at Taheitee, in 1773, chose to sail with us to Huaheine, before he eat his supper, he repeated a kind of prayer, and took a very small piece of the fish, which was intended for his supper, and laid it near him on the table, as an offering for the Eatoòa. The natives told me when I enquired about their mode of worship, that the priest sometimes delivered his prayer so low that nobody could hear any thing, yet he was heard by the Eatoòa, who is then near the marai, and speaks to the priest again, and though there were ever so many people present they could not hear a single word spoken by the Eatooas, whereas the priest (*Tahouwa*) understood it all. The inferior divinities according to our former observation are revered only by a hissing sound.

A native of the Society-isles no sooner comes within sight of a marai, than he strips his garment from his shoulders, and pays it the same respect which he shews his prince, by uncovering his shoulders: which most undoubtedly proves that a very peculiar reverence is shewn to the place, and which they would not do, unless they were persuaded, that a being of a superior rank lived there, and well deserved such a mark of reverence.

Not contented with prayers and mere professions, delivered by words, the natives of these islands endeavour likewise to add to them some sacrifices of the animals and fruit of their country. I have frequently seen hogs, dogs, or fowls roasted, covered with a fine piece of cloth, and exposed on a kind of altar, built near the marai for that purpose: I likewise saw great scaffoldings in the neighbourhood of the marai, wholly covered with bananas, and plantanes, as sacrifices or offerings to their gods; but I never saw any thing else offered to their divinities, nor did I ever hear that they sacrifice men. However, as Captain Cook seems to have investigated the subject very carefully,[*] it is not improbable[†] that they think it expedient to punish their criminals in this manner, by devoting them as sacrifices to their God: nay, as we have already mentioned,[‡] that in more remote times canibalism was introduced among the Taheiteans, and the inhabitants of the Society Isles, it is highly probable that these human sacrifices, are the remains of the canibalism of these islanders; with this difference, that they now stay and offer the criminals to the Gods, without eating them; whereas they formerly added that inhumanity and barbarism. Though the restriction of killing only *bad men*, for the reconciliation of the favour of their Gods, seems very much to mitigate this cruel custom, and by all appearances sanctifies the impious rite into a legal necessary action; it is, however, again debased in the most detestable manner, by leaving the choice of the person, who is to be devoted to the gods to

---

[*] See Cook's *Voyage*, vol. i. p. 185.

[†] Almost all the antient nations sacrificed men; the Egyptians excepted; who never were addicted to this cruel and barbarous custom; and wherever it is mentioned in old writers that the Egyptians practised this method in order to appease the anger of their gods, it is to be understood of the Arabian shepherds, who undoubtedly were used to reconcile their divinities by human sacrifices, and who once had over-run and conquered all Egypt. On the subject of averting the anger of the gods, by the effusion of human blood, among all nations none has written with greater learning, than the ingenious Mr. BRYANT, in his *Observations and Inquiries relating to various Parts of ancient History*, p. 267–285.

[‡] See Cook's *Voyage*, p. 327, and likewise p. 358, 359, and 360.

the caprice of the High Priest; who, on this occasion, has an opportunity, not only of indulging his private revenge against any man, by whom he may think himself injured, but also of practising at the same time one of the most abominable scenes of priest-craft that ever took place; for it is said, that on certain occasions, when the nation is solemnly assembled, the High Priest alone enters the house of God, or the marai, and after staying there for some time, he returns and informs the congregation, that having conversed with their great God, he was ordered to ask for a human sacrifice, and then mentions the person whom the deity desired to have offered; this man is immediately seized and killed, being beaten till he be dead. The circumstance, that such criminals only as had nothing wherewithal to redeem themselves, are devoted to death, proves besides, that the priest has an opportunity of satisfying his avarice. What has been hitherto said on this peculiar part of the religious worship practised in the Society isles, confirms us more and more in that general truth, that the greater part of mankind, when left to themselves, in their religious principles, and modes of worship, have always more or less deviated from that noble simplicity, which the true adoration in the spirit and truth requires, and which is so fully held forth in the Christian dispensation; wherein the ideas of the Deity are pure, and capable of filling the mind with humility, confidence, and adoration, and prompting every professor of that religion, to the practice of all moral and social virtues, and lastly, excluding all priest-craft from its true and genuine votaries.

The human sacrifices being left to the choice of the priest, who pretends to converse with the Deity, intimate, that these nations have some idea of a communication of the will and pleasure of the Deity, by means of their priests. I was told, that in dubious cases of great consequence, the priest did actually consult the divinity, and pretended to bring back the answer to the people; which seems to imply that their marais are looked upon as ORACLES, where the Deity may be consulted, and his answer is plainly heard by the priest, and communicated to those who desire to be instructed, and guided by it. This idea has likewise pervaded all mankind, for there is hardly a nation to be found, either antient or modern, which had it not inserted amongst its religious tenets, that the Deity had reserved to himself the prerogative of instructing mankind on the most important occasions, especially such as greatly influence their happiness.

The Taheiteans relate, that the great god TARÒA-T'EAY-E-TOÒMOO, having by his wife O-TE-PÀPA, begotten many divinities of both sexes, who created the various parts of this world, and who now preside over them; having likewise produced the various isles, by dragging *O-Te-pàpa* through the seas, he at last begot by her a son called O-TÈA, who was the first man: and according to their tradition, his limbs were all rolled up in a figure like a ball, but his mother carefully expanded them to the shape in which men now appear. A daughter was likewise begotten by the same parents, whose name is O-TE-TÒRRO, who became the wife of O-TÈA, and from this couple they believe all mankind to have been descended. This traditional history of the origin of mankind, accounts at once for many points of their religion and philosophy: *first*, as they think man to have been born of their great gods it is plain that they must think their deities similar to mankind, in their external appearance, and this is confirmed by the figure of *Maouwe*, which Capt. Cook met with in his first voyage. *Secondly*, though they always protested that God could not be seen, they had, however, made a human figure to represent *Maouwe*, which seems to intimate that this representation of a god, was rather reckoned to be a symbolical figure, than a real representation. *Thirdly*, since they believe that the being which is possessed of sensation and of thinking, or as they call it, of forming the speech in the belly (*paroù-no-te-òboo*) exists after death in a separate state, and is then even unseen capable of actions similar to those it performed when combined with the body, viz. of seeing, hearing, receiving pleasure from the actions of their friends, and of shewing its displeasure by killing people; it is evident that they think of an invisible being, very distinct from the body, and endowed with a free agency. This they call TEÈHEE and represent it frequently under the rude figure of a man or woman, seldom exceeding eighteen inches in heighth; which again seems to indicate that this figure is not intended to be the real figure of the invisible soul, but only its emblem. *Fourthly*, as they think man to have descended from their supreme deity, it is evident they must likewise imagine man to be in some inferior degree homogeneous to their divinities, or *vice versa* their divinities are according to their opinion analogous to man, and as they often told me the great *Eatoòa* could not be seen, or in other words was invisible, this analogy cannot lie in the body the only visible part of man, and must therefore consist in the part capable of thinking and reasoning, which in some measure is analogous to the scriptural phrase of the *image of God*, after which man was first made. *Lastly*, as they attribute to O-TÈA the first man but one wife, this circumstance seems to imply that they think monogamy to be the lawful or most reasonable method for propagating mankind.

The inhabitants of the South Sea have certainly some notions of a future state; but I must confess, I am at a loss how to conciliate their ideas on that head. They told us that the being, which had sensations and thoughts, did not decay with the body but was well (*woùra*) and existing near its old habitation the body and the remains exposed on an elevated stage, or even near the bones when buried, or the head preserved in a little chest: it is for this being that they expose various fruits and meat near the burying place; and the little wooden images or *Teèhees* are, as we were told, the receptacles of the invisible *Teèhees*, or what we would call souls, according to our way of thinking. And notwithstanding this most positive assertion, they told us almost in the same breath, that after their death the departed met in the sun, and attended *Maòuwe*, and feasted there with this deity upon bread-fruit, and the meat of hogs or dogs, which needs no dressing; and some even ventured to say that they were to have a constant succession of liquor prepared from *àwa* (*Piper methysticum*). This state they call the meeting or assembly of the heavens or sky (*Touroòa-t'erài*).* However the people of rank only, have hopes of being received in this assembly of the heavens after their demise; and perhaps this idea is formed from the *Touroòa* or meeting of the states of the nation, where only the higher ranks of the nation have a right to sit. The *toutous* or lower sort of people meet after death at the *taya-hòboo*, which I am unable to explain. We never heard that any of these places was to be considered as a state of punishment. The *Touroòa-t'erài* seems to be a place of enjoyment and happiness, in some measure similar to the *Valhalla* of the Northern nations, where the heroes killed in battle met at ODIN's palace, feasted upon the meat of the boar *Serimner*,† and drank ale or mead out of the skulls of their enemies. The actions of men do not seem to influence in the least their future state according to their doctrine: but I am fully persuaded, that the people of these islands were frequently awed from committing bad immoral actions by the fear of meriting the displeasure and the anger of the Gods; for when I discoursed with them upon various subjects, and in order to try their way of thinking and principles, asked them why they did not kill their children or any other persons, they always replied the Gods would be angry: when I continued to ask whether this anger or displeasure would cause punishments to be inflicted, they constantly answered in the affirmative; when I asked whether this anger would take place after death, they still affirmed it; but I never could obtain any information concerning the method, place and duration of the anger of their Gods for such crimes. Nay, having one day attempted to dissuade TEINAMAI from killing the child that she was shortly to bring forth, and seeing her obstinate in her design, I represented upon this very ground to her, that the *Eatoòa* would be very angry (*wòriddee*) on that account against her; but she very coolly replied, that this might perhaps be the case of the *Eatoòa no Pretànee* i.e. the British God, but the *Eatoòa* of *O-Raiedèa* knew her to be with child by an *Arreeoy*, whose children must not live, and would therefore not be angry. From the above account however I think we have reason to conclude that they are not quite without some notions of a future state attended with rewards and punishments. Their religion therefore is not altogether disinterested,

---

* The word *Tooroòa* signifies the meeting or assembly of the states in Taheitee, wherein the king, the chiefs of provinces, priests, inferior chiefs, and manahounes have a right to sit, but the *hoas*, or king's attendants, though present, must stand.

† See the EDDA, in various places, and likewise Jo. George Keysler's *Antiquitates Selectas Septentrionales*, p. 149. seq.

but greatly influences their morals; and in my opinion seems well adapted to the weak and infant state of their reason; and though they go through all the acts of reverence and adoration both by words and actions, they certainly perform them with a childish simplicity and humility, from the little knowledge they have early imbibed of the greatness, goodness, and excellence of the Supreme Being, and likewise because they have been taught to dread the anger and displeasure of a being whose power is infinitely superior to that of any other they have an idea of.

After the *birth of a child,* they do not observe any ceremonies whatever, excepting that of depressing in some degree its nose, and giving it a name from some object or other which is nearest at hand, or which from some circumstance becomes remarkable. The king of Taheitee was called *O-Too,* which is the name of a grey heron: the chief of the isle of St. Christina, one of the Marquesa-islands, was called *Ahònoo,* which signifies a turtle; one of the chiefs at Taheitee related to *O-Too* was called *Teèhee* the soul or a carved figure, which is the symbol or emblem of the soul. The chief of the province of Tittahàw had the name of *Toumàta-ròa* a great hat, and many more of that nature, much too tedious to mention. However in this early period of life, the male children undergo a ceremony or operation on their genitals, for a piece of bamboo reed is thrust into the prepuce, and the membrane slit by means of another bamboo-reed, (to which a very sharp edge is given by tearing it) in order to prevent its contracting over and covering the glans. This operation is performed merely from principles of cleanliness, by the priest, though there is not any religion or religious ceremony mixed with the custom; for which reason it is not performed on a certain day after the birth of the child, nor at any certain age; but when the child is capable of attending to it, that the prepuce may not again join over the glans, then the operation is made, which, from its nature cannot properly be called a circumcision. Both sexes have many marks on their skin, made by puncturing the part with a toothed instrument of bone, dipt into lamp black and water, and by this method they imprint marks which are indelible for life. The men have sometimes not only a black part on their buttocks, but sometimes on the arms and even their sides, and various other parts of the body marked in this manner. The toothed instrument is called *Eoòwee-tatattaòu,* a spatula of wood, with which they constantly stir the black colour, and on one end of which they have contrived a kind of small club of the thickness of a finger, is the second instrument employed on this occasion; with the small club they give repeated gentle strokes on the toothed instrument, in order to make it pierce the skin. This spatula is called *Tatàë,* and the black colour *arahoà-tattàou.* The arches which they design on the buttocks obtain the name of *avàree;* the parts which are one mass of black on the buttocks are named *toumàrro,* and the arches which are thus designed on the buttocks of their females, and are honourable marks of their puberty, are called *toto-hoòwa:* the priests are the only persons entitled to perform these operations, and are paid for their trouble in cloth, fowls, fish, and after the natives had obtained European commodities, in nails and beads.

In their *marriages* some ceremonies are observed, but the authorities we have for talking of them are of no great weight, because the only people who were present, did not understand enough of the language, to obtain information relative to the signification of several transactions and ceremonies they saw performed in their presence. The young Borabora man *Maheine* was married to the daughter of *Topèrre* chief of the district of *Matavai*, during our second stay at Taheitee. We were told that he had been sitting on the ground by the side of his bride, holding her hand in his, being surrounded by ten or twelve persons, chiefly women, who repeated some words in a recitative or singing tone, to which Maheine and his bride gave some short responses: some food was presented to them, and Maheine gave a part of it to his bride and she to him, which action was likewise accompanied by certain words, and lastly they bathed in the river. This is the whole account of the ceremony, which has been observed and recounted. Persons of little curiosity with a very slender knowledge of the language, were certainly not the best qualified for enquiring into the reason and signification of any transaction or ceremony, and we did not hear of those circumstances till we had quitted the isle, otherwise we should have endeavoured to obtain some information on that head.

The ceremonies usually performed on the demise of persons of rank in Taheitee are more curious than any other seen or described, and contain briefly the following circumstances. As soon as the person is known to be dead, the relations and friends resort to the house he occupied when alive, and there join in lamentations and other signs of grief over the loss of their friend, which continues all that day and night, till the next morning; when the body is wrapped in some of their white cloth, and carried to the neighbourhood of the marai, where the remains of the deceased in future are to be deposited; if that place be distant, the corpse is carried in a boat and conveyed thither on a bier covered by a little thatch in the form of a small house. The corpse is then carried near the shore, attended during the whole time by the priest, who repeats some prayers before the corpse is taken, and continues to repeat them till he reaches the marai. He then renews his prayers and sentences, and sprinkles sea-water towards the body, but not upon it; which is repeated several times, the body having been taken away and carried back each time; till at last a small inclosure being made near the marai, and a kind of open shed called TUPAPÒU,* raised on posts six or seven feet

---

* One of the *Tupapous* is represented in Cook's *Voyage*, vol. i. p. 185. pl. xliv. and another in Hawkesworth, vol. ii. p. 234, pl. Nᵒ. v.

from the ground, being finished, the corpse or bier is deposited under the shed either on posts or on a stage made on purpose, and left there till the flesh putrifies and separates from the bones. Meat, fruit, and water are often brought to the *Tupapòu* and left at a small distance from it; nor do the relations forget to ornament the *Tupapòu* with cloth and garlands of the ewharra-fruit (*Athrodactylis*) and coconut-leaves. And near it are generally to be seen one or more trees of the kind called *Casuarina equisetifolia*. The female relations testify their grief by tears and by cutting the crown of the head with a shark's tooth: the blood flowing from the wound as well as the tears shed on this solemn occasion are received on pieces of their cloth and then thrown under the bier, as well as the hair cut off by some young people on this occasion. Some days after these ceremonies have been performed, one of the nearest relations takes up the *hèva*-dress described before p. 277 and holding in one hand a clapper made of two large mother of pearl shells; and in the other a flat cudgel set with shark's teeth along its edge, he begins a solemn procession from the house of the deceased by a long circuit to the *Tupapòu*, preceded by two or more people almost naked and blackened by a mixture of charcoal and water, who are called NINÈVA i.e. *insane* or *mad*, supposing them to be transported by the phrenzy of grief, for if the chief mourner performing the *hèva*, should happen to meet any person during his circuit, he would run at them and strike them with the shark's teeth fixed on his stick. For which reason, no sooner is the noise of the two shells heard, than every one leaves his habitation and endeavours to obtain shelter at a distance, and out of the reach of the shark's teeth: near the corpse, and the places where men live, a kind of sentence or prayer is pronounced. This procession is performed for about five moons at certain intervals; which become less frequent at the end of the interval than at the beginning; each relation takes this procession in his turn, and now and then the priests in company, and at the desire of the relations repeat their prayers near the corpse and offer to their deities some offerings of fruit or meat. After the flesh is decayed, the bones are scraped, washed, and buried in the marai, if the person deceased was a chief, but without if he belonged not to that class. The skull of a chief is not buried with the bones, but wrapped in cloth and put in a long box*

---

* The method of disposing of the corpse of the dead at Taheitee, seems to be at first sight very strange, but upon more mature examination, the same practice is found to obtain among many other nations, both antient and modern. When I was in Russia in the summer of the year 1765, I observed in the great desert to the East of the Volga, several Khalmyks exposed in the same manner for putrefaction. I saw one lying dead in a hut in his cloth; I found round the hut several callico and silk vanes on long sticks fixed in the ground, on which several lines in Tibetan characters were printed. I met with another corpse in a little house of wood six feet long and two feet wide, and when I came near a fox escaped out of it, who had been preying on the dead body: besides the vanes above mentioned, the khalmyks had fixed about this sepulchre pieces of wood pierced in the middle

which the natives call *Te-whàrre-no-te-orometùa,* of which mention has been made before p. 325. After this burial of the bones the relations now and then renew some funeral ceremonies with the priest, who takes a bunch of the red feathers of a parroquet called *oòra,* and twisted together with coco-nut filaments, and fixes them on a small pointed stick in the ground; (these feathers are in high estimation with these people and become the emblem of the divinity, and serve

---

by a hole, through which the sticks were thrust on which the wooden vanes almost constantly moved by the least breath of wind; these pieces of wood were on the two opposite sides hollowed out like spoons of about seven or eight inches long and five wide, and covered on the hollow part with Tibetan characters. The lamas or priests of the khalmyks say that as often as the vane or this wooden instrument moves round, the substance of the prayers for the repose of the deceased, is as it were offered up to God. In the *Archaeologia* of the Society of Antiquaries of London, vol. ii. p. 233. is inserted a Memoir, written in 1767; wherein I have described the six modes of burial usual among those who follow the religion of the Dalai-lama. According to the first mode they burn the corpse of their Lamas, Khans, Noions, and other people of rank, and preserve their ashes mixed with frankincense, and send the whole to the Dalai-lama in Tibet. 2. They keep the bodies in a coffin and afterwards cover them with stones. 3. Some are carried to the tops of mountains and left there a prey to birds and beasts. 4. Some are carried to an inclosure full of dogs, and there the burier feeds the dogs with the flesh severed from the bones, and casts the bones into the water, and gives the skull to the relations of the deceased, who carry it respectfully home. 5. Some corpses are thrown into the water. 6. Others are buried under ground. The mode of burial is fixed and determined upon by the priest according to the hour in which a person dies, as each time requires a different way of burying. These circumstances are confirmed by Dr. P. S. Pallas, F.R.S. in his *Travels through several Provinces of the Russian Empire,* vol. i. p. 362, 363 and partly by John Stewart, Esq. F.R.S. *in his account of the Kingdom of Tibet, in the Philos. Trans.* vol. lxvii. pl. ii. p. 478. In the island of Formosa or Tayovan the inhabitants keep the corpses of their deceased in their houses on an elevated stage, and put fire under them in order to dry them, after the ninth day they wrap the body in mats and cloth, and expose them on a still higher stage; after the body has been thus kept during three years the bones are buryed. *Relation of the Island of Formosa* by Candidius. The people in Corea do not bury the remains of their deceased friends till after three years are elapsed. Du Halde's *Hist. of China.* The indians upon the river Oronoko suffer the corpses of their chiefs to putrefy and when the flesh is decayed they dress the skeleton with jewels of gold and ornaments of feathers, and suspend it in a hut. See the *Voyage of Sir Walter Raleigh in Hakluyt's Voyages,* vol. iii. p. 644. edit. 1598. *Appollonius Rhodius Argonautic.* lib. iii. p. 207. and likewise *Aelian. var. Historiae,* lib. iv. ch. i. mention that the Colchi sew the corpse of their deceased relations in raw hides of oxen, and hang them up by a chain in the air.[5] The inhabitants of Chili put their deceased in the attitude of a child in the mother's womb, and then they expose them on a stage six feet high. *Supplement to Anson's Voyage.* All these accounts evidently prove, that many nations observe the same custom with regard to the corpses of their deceased friends as at O-Taheitee, in exposing them to putrefaction and afterwards burying the bones only. And though some of them differ somewhat in their method of treating the remains of their relations, there are however others who do not bury them under ground, but sever the flesh from the bones, and preserve the skeleton dressed out and finely ornamented in caves under ground, (such for instance are the customs of the Moluches, Taluhets, and Divihets) or in small huts near the sea coast, sometimes at 300 leagues from their habitations (which is done by the Tehuelhets). See Falkner's *Description of Patagonia,* p. 118, 120.

to fix their attention during the ceremony) opposite to this bunch of feathers a young plantane is placed, which is the emblem of friendship, peace, and expiation; the priest stands with the relations over against the bunch of red feathers and repeats his prayers, after which he deposits on the grave some coconut-leaves twisted into various shapes and knots during his prayer, and the relations likewise leave a few provisions.

Instead of a man, I saw at *O-Taha* a woman wear the heva-dress; a ceremonious dance was performed at the same place, and the nearest relations appeared well dressed with presents of cloth for the drummers and musicians. From all the ceremonies of the burial it appears, that the people at Taheitee and its neighbourhood, have an idea of a separate state, in which the *Teèhee* or soul lives though not united with the body. I was not able to discover when they supposed the soul removed or left the neighbourhood of the corpse and the bones. For it has been already observed, that they imagine that the chiefs and better sort of people go to *Màouwe* into the sun and feast on bread-fruit, and meat of dogs and hogs, which requires no dressing, in the assembly of heavens or *Te-roòa te-rai*. The time when the deceased are thought to go to this assembly remains therefore unsettled.* The Egyptian doctrine of the transmigration of the soul has been, I believe often mentioned, but seldom understood. The Egyptians were of opinion, that the soul of man was obliged after the DECAY of the body to animate the bodies of animals, birds, and fish, till after a revolution of three thousand years the same soul again resumed the direction of a human body.† They embalmed the body of the deceased, in order to hinder its decay and putrefaction, and to prevent the tedious transmigration of the soul through so many bodies of animals, and to facilitate its transition from one human body (after the interval of 3000 years) into another.‡

---

* We shall in the next chapter give an account of the doctrine of the soul as it is received among the inhabitants of the Caroline islands, which can be employed for the illustration of the doctrine of the Taheiteans.

† Herodot. lib. ii. Nº 123.[6]

‡ During all that time in which the body was not decayed the Egyptians imagined the soul to remain near it. At Memphis especially was a lake between the burying place and the city, and close to it a fine green meadow, which was the ELYSIUM: for so Servius remarks ad Aeneid. vi.[7] *Vireta prope Memphin amoena sunt, in quibus Aegyptiorum sepulcra sunt, haec Elysios campos vocant. Palus prope est, loto & calamis plena, & graviter olet. Per hanc paludem vectantur cadavera; hinc dixit Orpheus, vehi per Acherontem.*[8] Hom. l. 4. Odysseae, ubi loquitur Proteus: *sed te Elysium campum, & ultimas terras Dii immortales mittent,* &c. &c. Homer in the Odyssey, Ω 13. calls it:

——————— ασφοδελον λειμωνα
Ενθα δε ναιουσι ψυχαι.————.[9]

A meadow full of herbage, where the soul lives. The words Αχερουσια and *Elysium*, have their origin from words in the Egyptian language, which have a reference to *fertility, grass,* and *rushes.* Near it were the ηελιοιο πυλαι the ports or gates of tl   n, i.e. of a temple of serapis or the sun,

This doctrine has furnished a hint for fixing with some probability, the time of the departure of the souls of the Taheiteans for the *Te-roòa-te-rai;* it seems to me to take place when all the flesh is entirely decayed, and nothing but bones are left. The difference between the doctrine of Egypt and that of Taheitee is evident and needs no comment, but it appears that they agreed in thinking the soul to remain about the body as long as any flesh continued undecayed. I am far from thinking that the people in the South Sea derived their sepulchral rites, and their opinions relative to the soul from Egypt, for I have frequently observed that the same customs are observed at very distant places. It is therefore possible that mankind may have accidentally employed upon certain occasions the same customs without having an opportunity of borrowing them from places so very remote.

In the Friendly isles, (though we twice visited them) we made a very short stay, so that we could not make many observations on their religion and the rites and ceremonies that are in any ways related to religion; however we find they used the word *Eatoòca,* we saw one of their priests perform some rites, and heard him repeat a long prayer, opposite to one of their burying places, called by them Affayetoòca.* I was told that they buried the remains of their deceased friends within the house or *Affayetoòca,* which was filled with pieces of coral stone. I found in the house two rude figures of a man similar to the *Teèhee* at Taheitee. I inquired whether they called it an *Eatoòca,* they said no; I again asked how they called it, and I was told *Teèghee;* I inquired whether they prayed to it, this they denied, and kicked the figures with their feet, to shew that they did not pay the least respect to them.

In New-Zeeland, the people were very ignorant in regard to religion, however they had the names of *Eatoòca* and *Teèghee,* which latter they represented by a small ill shapen figure of a man, cut in the green nephritic stone, and this they commonly wore on a string round their necks: for as they have no fixed place of abode, but are constantly removing, they cannot erect a figure of a *Teèghee* on a certain place, lest it should be destroyed by some hostile party: another reason for doing so is, because they never bury the corpses of their deceased relations, but sink them with stones in the sea; it is therefore impossible to rise any other monuments to the memory of their friends, than such as they can wear and carry along with them. They likewise wear in commemoration of their deceased rela-

---

and λευχας πετρα or that part of the city of Memphis called *Leucotiche* by Thucydides, lib. i. c. 104.[10] The marais of the Taheiteans are constantly near the sea, in a pleasant spot, surrounded by verdure and fine shady trees.

* The name *Affayetooca* seems to signify *the house of God:* for *farre* is a house in the Friendly-isles and *E-atooca* is in the name of God, which would form the word *E-farre-tooca* or *E-ffaye-tooca.*

tions some of their teeth about their neck; I have seen some men and women wearing whole strings or necklaces of teeth about their necks.

In Easter-island they bury their dead near the ranges of gigantic stone figures, which serve in lieu of the wooden Taheitean *Teèhees*, (because wood is extremely scarce on their island) for I was told that these figures represented their deceased chiefs or *hareekees;* I observed many human bones scattered on the surface of the stone parapet wherein the stone pillars were erected. I measured a thigh bone by my own and found them nearly of the same length.

At the Marquesas we discovered no signs of their burying places, as none of us penetrated to the top of the hills, where we discovered from on board the ships some long stakes standing upright, nearly in the same manner as the *Teèhees* at Taheitee, and which by several were considered as fortifications. Mendaña saw in the year 1595, in the same island, not far from the town, somelthing which he calls "an oracle, surrounded with palisades, with the entrance to the West, and a house almost in the middle with the door to the North, in which were some figures of wood ill wrought, and there were offered some eatables, among which was a hog; this the Spanish soldiers took down, and wanting to take away other things, the Indians hindered them, saying by signs, that they should not touch them, intimating that they respected that house and figures."* From this account it appears to me evident, that the place they saw was a place of worship and burying, or in a word a marai. It likewise seems to intimate, that they had the same manner of worshipping, the same offerings of hogs and other eatables, together with the wooden Teèhees as at Taheitee, and that the whole of their religion and notions of divinity are nearly the same as in the Society-isles.

On Mallicollo we made no observations either on the religion or worship of its inhabitants, as we staid only one day on the island. I have not the least doubt that the hymns which some of the inhabitants at Tanna sung every morning at day break, were part of the worship they paid to the divinity, as the solemn tone, and stated regularity with which it was heard, seem to confirm this opinion. Of their manner of burying we saw not the least vestiges. At New Caledonia on the summit of a barren hill we observed stakes stuck in the ground, with branches on the top, and a whisp of dry grass, and we were told that this was one of their burying places: close to the sea-shore we saw likewise an inclosure made of sticks, round a tumulus of about four feet high, on which were placed several sticks, on the tops of which several large *turbines* were sticking: and we were informed by the natives that this was the burying place of the chief of the district. On the island of *Ballabeea* lying to the N.W. of New Caledonia, our people, who were sent there by Captain Cook, found a large sepulcral tumulus of one of their chiefs,

---

* Dalrymple's *Collection of Voyages*, vol. i. p. 68.

who was killed in battle by the inhabitants of *Mìngha* or *Mínda*, a great island sit‑
uated Northward or North Westward of their own isle, and whose natives were
warlike and at war with them. Lastly I found some miles from the place where our
ship was at anchor at the foot of the large ridge of hills running along the whole
island, a house of one of their chiefs, and behind it a range of wooden pillars,
about ten or twelve inches square, and eight or nine feet high, with a carved
human head on the top. The old man who lived in the above house, intimated to
me by signs, that it was his burying place, but as we were then in quest of *Heebài*
the Captain's friend, in order to present him with a boar and a little sow, I had not
time to inquire more particularly, especially as it was the last day before our depar‑
ture, and I was desirous of collecting some birds and plants which I had seen, and
which were not easily to be obtained. These sepulcres with the carved figure of a
human head, seem to intimate that the natives of this island had almost the same
manner of burying the dead, and of fixing a human figure or a *Teèhee* near it, as
the inhabitants of Taheitee.

The whole account of the religion, worship, and various rites in use among
the inhabitants of the islands in the South Sea, shew that it is the least excep‑
tionable system of polytheism. It has the stamp of all the inventions and works of
mankind in its imperfection and error; but it is in my opinion less cruel, and not
so much clogged with superstition as many others, which were or still are in use
among nations who are reputed to be more civilized and more improved. Their
religion requires of its votaries a kind of worship, it teaches them to look upon the
deity as the giver of all good gifts, as the being who hears their prayers, and is will‑
ing to assist mankind when invoked, and to reward the good: and these doctrines
afford the only origin of all honesty, faith, and justice; or in a word of all social
ties and social virtues, without which there would be no comfort, and still less
real happiness in human societies.

Atque haud scio, an pietate adversus Deos sublata, fides etiam, & societas humani generis,
& una excellentissima virtus, justitia tollatur.
  M. Tullus Cicero, *de Nat. Deor.* lib. i. p. 7. Elzev[11]

SECTION X

Recapitulation. General View of the Happiness of the Islanders in the South Sea. Short comparative view of various Manners and Customs usual in the South Sea Isles, with those of other nations

NEC SOLUM IN RECTIS, SED ETIAM IN PARVIS ACTIBUS INSIGNIS EST HUMANI GENERIS SIMILITUDO.
    M. Tullus Cicero, *De legibus*, lib. i. p. 305. ed. Elzevir[1]

MANNERS
COMPARED

Having finished our observations on the inhabitants of the isles in the South Sea, we have only to bring into one point of view what has been the result of nine long dissertations, in order the better to form a just idea of their real happiness.

The inhabitants of the isles in the South Sea which we visited, are upon the whole very numerous. We found that the farther the nations live from the equinoctial line, the less numerous they are, and of those within the tropics, they are the most numerous who are more civilized than the rest. Though it be highly difficult to ascertain the population of Taheitee, it is however possible to form an idea, which comes very near to its real numbers. We took an opportunity of making some inferences from the number of war canoes, which we saw reviewed, and confirmed our conclusions by a view of the size and extent of the fertile plain surrounding the isle, by calculating the number of bread-fruit trees growing on this plain, and the quantity of breadfruit-trees necessary for the support of one man, shewing that many more men might receive subsistence than we had allowed. This standard afforded us a rule wherewith to compare or to measure the population of all other isles; and lastly we supposed more than one million of inhabitants to live on the isles which we had seen and visited. We observed, that the inhabitants of the islands in the South Seas are remarkably different in colour, form, habit, and natural turn of mind; and that the people at Taheitee and the Society-isles, with those at the Marquesas, the Friendly-isles, New-Zeeland and Easter-island seem to constitute a race of men entirely different from those as New-Caledonia, Tanna and Mallicollo, and all the rest living in the New

Hebrides. We added a small account of the Pesserais, prefixing to it a dissertation proving the existence of a nation taller and more athletic than the rest of the American tribes; though not so tall as the fabulous accounts of a gigantic race would make them. The causes of the difference observed in the races of men are the subject of another section. Some suppose men to be divided into species materially and essentially different from one another. Others on the contrary are of opinion that some races of men as well as the Ouran Outangs are different from us, which however is inadmissible if we take into consideration the exercise of reason and common sense, the formation of ideas, the language of the heart, the refinement of moral sentiment, with the gifts of speech founded on the variety, power and extent of voice and articulation, and even on the whole structure and mechanism of our bodies. The other proposition, according to which men are of different species, is equally groundless, because the most different species can procreate children, and if the different marriages with persons of one kind be continued for a few generations, the difference at last entirely vanishes. The objection that this difference is so great, that it remains incomprehensible how it was originally produced is examined, and it is proved that it intirely depends upon physical causes; it is likewise shewn that the transition from a fair to a dark complexion is very soon brought about, but the contrary requires a longer time, and the interval of more generations, and even then is scarcely observable: so that if the same race of people should pass through a long and gradual circuit, the one through hot countries, and the other immediately by a sudden transition to the same climate; those who have passed through the fervid climate would preserve a darker hue, than those who at once should pass to the same without making any stay in the intermediate climates; and both would afterwards in the new climate preserve in some measure the hue and complexion they brought from the country which they left last: upon these premises we ventured to suppose that the two races of men in the South Sea arrived there by different routs, and were descended from two different sets of men. This surmise might be rendered more probable and ripened as it were into fact, if any record or historical proof could be alledged in favour of this opinion: but how can we expect to find such historical proofs, where no records are kept? However the five nations of the first enumerated race seem to come from the Northward and by the Caroline-islands, the Ladrones, the Manilla and the island of Borneo, to have descended from the Malays: whereas on the contrary, the black race of men seems to have sprung from the people that originally inhabited the Moluccas, and on the approach of the Malay tribes withdrew into the interior parts of their isles and countries. The language of these two races in some measure proves the assertion, especially as it is evident that the five first branches speak only dialects of one *general language* preserving several words of the Malay-language; whereas the three tribes of the latter race, have not even a similarity of speech among themselves; and that none of these languages has the least or most distant reference to any American language spoken on the Western coasts of America. When we consider the difference in the happiness and enjoyments of the various tribes who were visited by us in the course of our circumnavigation; it is evident that the nations become less happy in proportion as they are removed from the tropics and the benign influence of the sun. The warm tropical climates seem to have been originally the seat of the human race, which removed to the two colder extremities of the globe, when forced either by chance or cruel necessity; the wretched and uncomfortable situation of the Pesserais and New-Zeelanders, when compared with the real state and enjoyment of the Taheiteans, clearly prove that these tribes are really debased and degenerated from their original happiness, and that the rigours of the climate first influence the body and afterwards the mind and the heart. But if we compare the inhabitants of the more Western isles in the South Sea with the Taheiteans, we find that the latter far surpass the former in every respect; which intimates that though the climate greatly influences the happiness of a nation, it is however not the only cause of its real felicity; that education contributes as much, if not more, towards the good state of a people; and that the removal from the tropics towards the colder extremities of the globe, together with the gradual loss of the principles of education greatly contribute to the degeneracy and debasement of a nation into a low and forlorn condition. Mankind is therefore to be considered in various situations, comparable with the various ages of men from infancy to manhood; with this difference only, that men in their collective capacity ripen but slowly from animality, through the states of savages and barbarians into a civilized society, which has again an infinite variety of situations and degrees of perfection. It is therefore not to be expected, that from a short and slight intercourse with Europeans these nations should make a rapid progress in civilization and happiness, especially as other concurrent circumstances on our side were against it. We then returned to a comparative view of the Pesserais and the Eskimaux, and found the former to be in the lowest state of degeneracy and debasement. The New-Zeelanders we observed to be infinitely superior to them: we then took a view of the most probable means by which the poor Pesserais may one day or other emerge into a state one degree, at least more remote from their forlorn condition, and that the increase of population and want of food may prompt some tribes to oppress others; who either will unite in order to resist their oppressive brethren, or reduce them to subjection; in both cases they must become less unhappy. The barbarian is capable of strong exertions of physical and mental powers, and though outrageous and violent, is forced by the resistance of others to be guarded and cautious, and to unite with others into societies, which sooner or later introduce a mildness of manners, so that even the very unbounded and irresistible eruptions of their passions in the end serve to soften their fierceness and ferocity. Canibalism, one of the most inhumane and atrocious customs, is not introduced into large societies by want and hunger, but by the most unnatural and violent spirit of revenge, and must after some time be laid aside as a custom which is inconsistent with itself. In order to judge of the happiness of mankind, it is necessary to define the various kinds of happiness they are capable of, in regard to their different faculties and state. The most pressing wants which are to be satisfied first, are food, habitation, and raiment; and an easy method of procuring them, together with the advantage of being free from bodily pain, is the first principle of *physical happiness*. The means of improving the intellectual faculties, and of preserving the rights and privileges of a free agency in man, without interfering with the happiness of others, form the principles of *moral happiness*. The advantages arising from the union of men in society, and a certain undisturbed enjoyment of physical and moral happiness, in conjunction with others, form the principles of *civil or social felicity*. Each state requires certain duties without the fulfilling of which, no happiness can be obtained. And the various kinds of happiness have likewise various degrees, in the number and variety of enjoyments, in their long and undisturbed duration, and in the influence they have upon the happiness of others. Nature alone promotes in some climates these various kinds and degrees of happiness; in some nature assisted by art, can produce these effects; and lastly, in others creative physical power and creative genius can only bring about such desirable ends. These general principles convince us of the various kinds and degrees of happiness in the various tribes visited by us in the South-Seas. The great increase of population in an isle of some size, made it necessary to unite into societies for mutual defence and assistance, and gave rise to the formation of property, and exerted cultivation. This required laws and regulations, and persons who should superintend their execution; anarchy reigns among the barbarous tribes, and despotism takes place among those which are more civilized and nearer related to Eastern despotic countries. Cultivation enables mankind best to enjoy the highest degree of happiness, and it is therefore preferable to the rambling state of shepherd nations, or what is still worse, the wild tribes that live by fishing and hunting. Men in society advance towards perfection by a strict regard to truth or *candour*, by *humanity*, and by perfecting their *moral ideas and moral sense*, of which various examples are produced among the inhabitants of the South Sea. The characteristic actions of people, form their *manners*, which accordingly are described in the nations we saw, together with the refinements in their manners, and even their luxury, with some account of the probable origin and progress of their *Arreeoys*. The situation of the fair sex in the various tribes we saw, is represented; they are slaves and drudges among the savages and barbarians, but upon a greater equality with the males in Taheitee, and the isles occupied by the fair race of men in the South-Sea. Marriage is kept sacred among all those nations whom we found to be monogamous. At the same time that we mentioned various instances of *Polygyny,* of which the consequence seems to be a greater proportion of women born, we endeavoured to point out the most probable cause of *Polyandry* now perhaps existing at Easter-island. The young women at Taheitee, before marriage, are under no restriction; but chastity after puberty and marriage, is highly honourable. The advantages of education consist chiefly in perpetuating the joint stock of knowledge of our fore-fathers, and making occasional additions. In Europe, this knowledge is sub-divided into various branches, and cannot now be lost, because the art of printing, so happily discovered, is so universally practised. But the islanders are constrained to teach their mechanical arts, especially such as are necessary for procuring food, and constructing their habitations, to every individual from the Prince to the slave. Historical records they have none, if we except a few verses made occasionally to perpetuate the names and actions of some individuals. They are acquainted with the polite arts of music, dancing, and poetry, of which a few outlines are given, particularly of their extemporaneous verses and drama. In describing the progress they have made in the art of medicine, we took occasion to mention the diseases of the country, especially the leprosy and the venereal disease, and made some observations on the latter. Geography, astronomy, and navigation, are in some measure understood among them, in confirmation of which the isles are described, and our readers referred to a map, drawn according to the informations given by Tupaya; their hours, days of the moon, and the number and names of the moon in their year, are enumerated together with those of the cardinal points, and of some stars. To their education likewise belong the ideas relative to the Deity and religion. Their system of polytheism is explained, and the names and functions of their gods and geniuses enumerated, their mode of worshipping described, their ideas on the subject of the origin of the world and its isles, as well as of mankind in general, and on their state after death, together with the various rites and ceremonies at birth, marriage and death, are particularly laid open and described. This general view of the history of these islanders, enables us to form a judgment on their real happiness; which is by no means equal among all the nations we visited in the course of our voyage, but it progressively varied from the wretched existence of the poor Pesserais to that of the unsettled life of the people in the Southern island of New-Zeeland; to the more comfortable situation of the tribes in the Northern isle, where the cultivation of ground has taken place with many regulations for securing their societies against the power and oppression of their neighbours; to the still more happy state of the natives of New-Caledonia and the New-Hebrides, where they depend still more on cultivation, and seem to be less ferocious; to that of the inhabitants of the Friendly-isles, where cultivation flourishes in the most perfect manner, but under the disadvantage of despotism, from their chiefs and their kind, or *Latoo-nipoòroo*; to the more increased felicity in the Marquesa-islands, where cultivation is well understood, but not in so high a degree as at the Friendly-isles, though their government is upon a more liberal plan; and at last to the degree of happiness which undoubtedly is highest among all the isles of the South-Sea, at Taheitee, where the mildness of the climate, and of government, concur with the greater extent and fertility of the island, the gentle temper of the inhabitants, and their courteous manners and improved minds, to increase their happiness, and make it most conspicuous and lasting.

The first view will convince the unprejudiced observer, of the great happiness which reigns at O-Taheitee and the Society-isles. All the inhabitants are of an agreeable temper, and lovers of mirth and joy; I never saw any one, of a morose, peevish, discontented disposition in the whole nation; they all join to their chearful temper, a politeness and elegance which is happily blended with the most innocent simplicity of manners. Their youth shews indeed a great deal of levity, which with a maturer age, ripens into a more placid countenance and behaviour; and experience, together with their good natural parts endow them with true prudence and solidity for their conduct in life.

They are possessed either of land as their own property, or enjoy a sufficient share of fruits and roots in lieu of the cultivation of the lands belonging to their chiefs, to whom they give likewise a share of these productions. The great fertility and mildness of the climate, reduce the number of their wants, and at the same time afford them after a very moderate labour, a great affluence of food and raiment, and very neat habitations, well adapted to the climate. The pampered epicure in Europe knows hardly the multifarious ingredients of his disguised ragouts, and his palled appetite remains indifferent to the almost infinite variety carried to his table from every quarter of the globe; nor has he the satisfaction to know how or where these things are produced, or manufactured, while the more happy inhabitant of Taheitee plants his own breadfruit tree, and plucks the fruit for his own use; the banana tree raises by his industry and care, its elegant stem, its picturesque leaves, and the delicious fruit all in one year; the yam, the eddo, the tacca and many other roots are the produce of the soil cultivated by his own hands: he catches the fish for his dinner, his wife rears and feeds the dog, the hog, and the fowl, which on great occasions serve for his meal; in short, there is not a single article of his food, which owes not its existence to his or his fathers industry or care; who planted the trees, which furnish cocoas, apples, and other nuts and fruits. In regard to clothes, the Taheitean is most certainly happier than the European, whose dress requires more time, labour, and devices; and to whom folly and fashion have made many articles seem to be necessary, which are really frivolous and absolutely useless; the Taheitean dress is easier obtained and made;

elegant, simple, and answering every purpose in their situation. Their houses are neat and well suited to the climate, and the manners of the nation; I pretend not here to say that these three great articles, food, raiment, and habitation, are in every respect at Taheitee, superior to our food, our dresses, our materials, and houses; it must be allowed these articles are among us, more ingeniously contrived and varied, and better adapted to all seasons, climates, and ranks; but it cannot be denied that these people enjoy a happiness which is more attainable by every individual, for there cannot be an instance among them, that ever a person died for want of shelter, cloth, or food; even the meanest obtain their share with great ease and in affluence; none is doomed by a hard master to perpetual toils and unremitted labour, which requires a continual exertion of all his strength: for the natives work gently, and more for the sake of exercise, than to obtain their livelihood by it. The fertility of the country enables them to satisfy their little wants, and to form societies, where they can mutually assist one another, both by their labour and by the instruction and knowledge, which willingly flows from the lips of their wise men and fathers; they hear the noble actions of their ancestors celebrated by songs, and consecrated by the gratitude of posterity; their minds therefore are early devoted to candour and humanity, to truth and to virtue; their societies are well regulated; their chiefs have a great love and paternal predilection for the happiness and welfare of their subjects, who, in their turn, are attached to their superiors by love and a truly filial duty. The vices which are usual among them, are yet so few in number, and of so harmless a tendency that few societies can boast such innocence, and simplicity of manners. Every individual is convinced that the chiefs can have nothing in view in the administration of affairs, but the happiness of the whole community, and the satisfaction and contentment of every individual, and this they prove in return by that exemplary love, attachment, respect and obedience, which they chearfully shew to their chiefs. While the youth of both sexes was singing and dancing, and those of a maturer age, active as well in their duties as enjoyments, we have often seen the venerable hoary senior looking upon the more busy scenes of life with a complacent smile and a serenity, which bore witness to the happiness enjoyed by all ranks and ages: in a word we are perfectly convinced that these islanders really enjoy a degree of felicity, which is seldom observed in the more civilized countries, and which is here still more enhanced by the generality with which it is diffused over whole nations, by the facility with which it is attainable, and by the just proportion it bears to the present state of these islanders, to whose condition this happiness is perfectly adequate, and which if enlarged would become incompatible with their capacities.

We have now and then illustrated in notes the CUSTOMS of the natives in these islands, and represented some of them to be SIMILAR to customs which formerly did, or at present still prevail among other nations very distant from those we had seen; but we have also collected more of these parallel customs; not always with a view to prove that nations, which chance to have the same custom, owe their origin to one another; but rather to convince ourselves that this similarity does not always give sufficient foundation for such a belief. At the same time we may suspect, that some of these customs were really common to two nations, on account of their common origin.

The custom of cutting or puncturing the body with instruments dipped in a mixture of water and lamp-black, and forming thereby various figures on the various parts of the body, we found established all over the islands of the South Sea, with this difference only, that some marked chiefly the face, as the people at New-Zeeland; others imprinted indelible figures all over the body, as at the Marquesas; some produced only large blotches on the buttocks, which is chiefly customary at the Society-isles and Taheitee; others again have only a few black or blue spots on their lips, which is the custom of the women at New-Zeeland. Strange as this custom seems to be, it has been however received among many nations; the Tunguses,* and the Greenlanders[†] sow into the flesh of the faces of their children, various figures, by a thread dipped into a black substance. The ancient *Huns* formerly were used to make incisions into their cheeks, in order to prevent the growth of the beard.[‡] Though this seems not to be the reason which prompted the New-Zeelanders to cut various deep figures and scrolls into their faces, but rather that of the very obvious ones to making their aspect more terrible to their enemies, and inuring the young men to endure pain; it has however, in the course of nature, produced the same effect, and almost eradicated the hair of the beard. In all America the savages are used to puncture some part of the body with black figures. *Pietro della Valle* observed the Arabians had likewise adopted this custom. The women of the Bedouins of the desarts about Tunis and Tremesen punctured their lips according to the testimony of Boullaye le Gouz. The Arabian women in Palestine used the same custom as D'Arvieux and de la Roque have observed. Besides these black carved scrolls on the faces of the New-Zeelanders, we frequently observed perpendicular deep furrows marked on their foreheads; these however were cut in the phrenzy of their grief, with a sharp shell, for the loss of a friend or near relation. The O-Taheitean women wound the crown of the head under the hair with a shark's tooth, to prove the sincerity of their grief: and the antient Huns wounded their cheeks on all

---

* Gmelin's *Voyage to Sibiria*, vol. i. p. 77, and vol. ii. p. 648, &c. &c.
[†] Crantz *History of Greenland*, vol. i. p. 138.
[‡] Ammianus Marcellinus, lib. xxxi. c. 2. and Jordanes *Hist. Get.*[2]

occasions, where they wanted to testify their grief for the loss of a great man or a relation.*

The inhabitants of Tanna have on their arms and bellies elevated scars, representing plants, flowers, stars and various other figures. They are made by first cutting the skin with a sharp bamboo reed, and then applying a certain plant to the wound which raises the scar above the rest of the skin. The inhabitants of Tayovan or Formosa† by a very painful operation express on their naked skins various figures of trees, flowers and animals. The great men in Guinea have their skin flowered like damask.‡ And in Decan the women likewise have flowers cut into their flesh on the forehead, the arms and the breast, and the elevated scars are painted in colours, and exhibit the appearance of flowered damask.*

The inhabitants of Mallicollo and Tanna, wore a cylindrical stone in the *Septum narium;* and the same part was found perforated in the natives of New Holland, by Mr. Banks and Capt. Cook,✦ but instead of a small stone, a bone of a bird five or six inches long, and nearly as thick as a man's finger, was thrust into the hole, and Dampier observed likewise in the men of New Britain such long sticks thrust into the hole of the gristle between the nostrils.♥ In the Friendly isles the natives had two holes made into the lap of their ears, and they wore a small stick stuck in these two holes; the same with a long stick were likewise found in the ears of the inhabitants of the Isle of Garret Dennis, near the coast of New Guinea.★ The people of Tanna, Irromanga, and Mallicollo wore large ear-rings of turtle shell of more than an inch in diameter, and three quarters of an inch broad. On their arms we observed bracelets of coco-nut-shell and small plaited shell-work, and we saw the hair of the natives of Namocka and the Friendly-isles, powdered white, blue or orange; the white is no doubt made of shell-lime, the orange extracted from turmeric, which affords a very strong and deep colour, but the blue we could never obtain; nor learn how it was manufactured. The Papooas wore rings in the ears, in both nostrils, and the perforated gristle between the nostrils. They used bracelets on their arms above the elbow and wrist, and their hair was powdered with shell-lime.§ Capt. Carteret observed that the inhabitants of the isles called by him New Ireland and the Admiralty Islands, powdered both their

---

* Agathias lib. v. Menander Protector, l. viii. And Sidonius in *Panegyrico ad Avitum.*[3]

† *Relation of Candidius.*

‡ Prevo[s]t *Histoire des Voyages,* tom. i.

* Tavernier's *Voyage.*

✦ Hawkesworth, vol. iii. p. 575.

♥ Dampier's *Voyage,* vol. iii. p. 203, and 205.

★ Dampier ibidem.

§ Jaques le Maire *dans la Collection des Voyages qui ont servi pour l'Etablissement de la Compagnie des Indes,* vol. iv. p. 648.

hair and their beards.* And others have observed the natives of Garret Dennis Isle to dye their hair of divers colours, viz. red, white, and yellow.† The Tripolitan ladies in Barbary strew the hair of their children with vermillion.‡ The antient Gauls employed the assistance of art to heighten the red colour of their hair, and the chiefs strewed them with the dust of gold,* which luxury was likewise adopted by the Jewish ladies,⁺ and Saint Jerome in one of his Epistles piously exhorts a Roman lady not to indulge her daughter in these fashionable vanities of the times; *ne irrufet crines, et sibi anticipet ignes gehennae.*⁵

Some nations daub their faces with various colours, either to appear more terrible to their foes, or to compliment their friends with a more pleasing aspect. The most indolent and miserable wretches on Tierra del Fuego, use ruddle or ochre, and some train-oil, to improve their unmeaning physiognomy with a brighter glare of dulness and stupidity. The New-Zeeland ladies never failed to put on the same kind of *rouge* mixed with grease, before they came on board to offer the uncouth favours to our sailors. Mr. Hodges being employed to draw the face of one of these coquetting ladies, and seeing how highly they valued their own bad red colour, immediately mixed some vermillion with linseed oil and daubed her whole face. She was in raptures at this refinement, and all her people of both sexes admired her charms, which had been thus heightened, but her rouge betrayed all the persons who had sacrificed at the shrine of the Paphian goddess with this fair priestess. Nor is the use of the red confined to the ladies only, because the males were if possible still more fond of it. But the inhabitants of the island of Tanna, were by no means contented with the red colour; they improved upon it, by adding the shining black, of a kind of black lead, or black wadd (*Molybdaenum plumbago.* Linn.) and a white prepared of shell lime, and then laying each on alternately, in oblique broad stripes a-cross their faces. In the Admiralty-isles, Captain Carteret saw likewise people, who had marked their faces with white streaks.♥

The ear-laps of the people at Easter-island, and the New-Hebrides, were distended to an enormous size, so as to hang down to their shoulders: they used for that purpose some scrolls of the elastic leaf of sugar-cane, and this is much affected by several nations in America, and likewise at Siam, where they use the same scrolls of leaves, in order to aggrandise the hole; nor is this custom unknown

---

* Hawkesworth, vol. i. p. 599, and 604.
† Dampier's *Voyage*, vol. iii. p. 202.
‡ *Etat des Royaumes de Barbarie.*
* Diod, Sic. lib. v. p. 305. edit, Wechel.⁴
⁺ Josephus.
♥ Hawkesworth, vol. i. p. 605.

in Africa, where several negro women use large solid ear-rings, of six inches diameter;* and in the North of Asia the Mungalic tribes wear ear-rings of about a foot long. On the coast of Malabar the holes in the ears are so large, that a man's hand may pass through with ease; nor is this a wonder, as their ear-rings weigh sometimes above two ounces each.†

The nails of the people of quality at Taheitee, and the neighbourhood, are of a great length, so that sometimes the part standing beyond the finger, is equal to one of the joints: the dancing girls, (who are always persons of quality) have also very long nails: and this custom is likewise common among the women of the Gold-coast in Africa‡: the Mandarines in China, carefully preserve their long nails as a proof or mark of their nobility and rank; and keep on purpose small cases of bamboo over them during the night, to prevent accidents✸: in Siam, the dancing girls make use of false nails, made of brass, in order to come up to this fashion✦: at Maghindanao, (commonly called *Mindanao*) the nails of the thumb on their left hand are never cut; and the people in Java are said to wear long hair and long nails.♥

The figure of the nose seems to have been an object worthy the attention of the midwives at Taheitee; and since, they are of opinion that a broad, somewhat flat nose, is ornamental, they depress the nose immediately after the birth of the child, and repeat this action upon the child, whilst it is still tender, which we have already observed, page 332. Though this custom might appear very singular, it has been however useful in other nations. The women of the Hottentots squeeze the noses of their children flat with the thumb:★ and in Macassar they flatten the noses of the children, and repeat the operation several times every day, softening at the same time the nose with oil or warm water.§

It is a kind of luxury introduced at Taheitee, to anoint the hair with an odoriferous oil; and the same custom has been observed among the inhabitants of the Maldive-islands.‡ The natives of Tanna are remarkable for the growth of hair on their body; we observed several individuals who were very hairy, hardly one part

---

* *Voyage de Brue.*[6]
† Dillon's *Voyage to the East-Indies:* English translation. London 8vo. 1698. p. 107.
‡ Prevot *Hist. des Voyages*, tom. iv.
✸ Osbeck's *Voyage to China*, vol. i. p. 270.
✦ De la Loubere *Voyage*.
♥ *Voyages faits pour l'Etablissement de la Compagnie des Indes Orientales* (Amsterdam 1702.) vol. i. p. 392.
★ Kolben's *Description of the Cape of Good Hope*, English translation, vol. i. p. 52.
§ Gomara *Historia general de las Indias*.
‡ Pyrard *Voyages*, vol. i. p. 80.

of their body being exempted from this extraordinary growth of hair; for I saw one, who was even on his back covered all over with hair. Nor is this uncommon in other places, for the inhabitants of the Maldives were observed to be more hairy over the whole body, than the Europeans.*

As to defects and diseases, we found some in the isles, which by other navigators had been observed in other places. In Tanna we saw men and children who could not lift up their eyelids, and were therefore obliged to raise their heads in order to bring the object parallel with the axis of the vision; and Dampier found this defect among the people of New-Holland.† In the same manner the thick elephants leg, which was observed at the Society-isles, and at New-Caledonia, was not uncommon among the Naïrs of Calicut and in Ceylon.‡

Nor must we forget several strange customs which are common to places at very considerable distances from the South Sea. In Mallicollo the inhabitants were shy on first approaching our ship in their canoes; however, when they saw that they were permitted to approach unmolested, and with safety, they took sea-water in the hollow of their hands, and threw it on their heads; and when we landed, they desired us to go through the same ceremony, which they interpreted as an act of friendship. The inhabitants of Pulo Sabuda, near New Guinea, used the same ceremony, as a sign of friendship:* nor is it quite improbable that the Mallicolese are the offspring of some of the tribes on or near New Guinea; but on the coast of Guinea in Africa, the natives will not come into a ship, unless the Captain first come down over the side, dip his hand into the sea, and sprinkle his own head with it; which they look upon as a sign of friendship, and as an oath or superstitious ceremony, without which they will not venture to come on board an European ship;✦ however, it is by no means probable, that the people of Guinea had any intercourse with the natives of New Guinea or Mallicollo.

Captain Cook and Mr. Banks found on O-Taheitee, and in the other Society-isles, sometimes the under jaws of their vanquished enemies, hung up as trophies; and the underjaws of the slain foes, are likewise hung up before the houses of the conquerors on the coast of Guinea, as marks of honour, and the first step gained towards obtaining nobility.♥

Having before, (Chap. vi. Sect. iii. p. 186) hinted at the great probability, that the nations of the first race (inhabiting Easter-island, the Marquesas, the

---

* Idem, vol. i. p. 81.
† Dampier's *Voyage*, vol. i. p. 464.
‡ Francois Pyrard's *Voyages*, vol. i. p. 280.
✱ Dampier's *Voyages*, vol. iii. p. 186.
✦ Villauld de Bellefond *Relation des cotes d'Afrique appellèe Guinée* (Paris 1669, 8vo.)
♥ Atkin's *Voyage to Guinea*, 8vo, 1737, p. 80, and Villauld de Bellefond.

Society and Friendly-islands, and New-Zeeland) are descended from some of the isles situated to the East of the Philippines, commonly called the Caroline-islands; it might not, perhaps, be improper to give here a sketch of the manners and customs of the people living in the Caroline-islands, since this will carry this probability to the highest degree possible, as their manners are so similar and so nearly related to those of the people in the islands of the South Seas just mentioned.*

The inhabitants of the island of ULEE (one of the Caroline-islands) and its district, are of various colours, some are fairer than the rest, like Mestisos, who have a Spanish father and an Indian mother; others are similar in colour to the Indians at the Philippines; and others again are like mulattoes sprung from a negro and an Indian woman. The most tawny people are of the lowest class, and serve instead of domestics. They all live chiefly upon fish, which they catch in great abundance, upon cocos and seven sorts of roots, similar to those used in the Marian-islands. They have fowls, and catch all kinds of birds especially of the aquatic sort, which they use for food; but they are without any quadruped. The houses of the common people are small cottages covered with thatch of a kind of palm leaves (probably the *Athrodactylis*) but those of their chiefs or TAMOLES are large, painted, and ornamented on the inside. Their boats are high both before and behind, and the planks are sewed together; to one side of the boat out-riggers are fixed, which are also fastened to a long spar placed parallel to the boat to prevent its oversetting: at the prow and poop, and likewise at each end of an out-rigger, projecting from each side of the mast, are small apartments; the sails are manufactured of a mat of palm leaves.

The common occupation of men consists in preparing the soil for the cultivation of various roots for their subsistence; for which purpose they clear the ground of the woods with their stone-hatchets, in a very troublesome manner, and then set fire to the wood when perfectly dry; the smoak and fire of which is often seen at a great distance out at sea. Fishing takes up a great deal of their time, and they use for that purpose among other contrivances, a basket. The building houses and boats together with the making their arms, are likewise allotted to the men. The women assist the men in sewing and planting their roots, and are besides occupied in dressing their victuals, and preparing cloth from the bark of a *plane-tree*.† The tree called by them *balibago* is likewise employed in the manufacture of cloth by their women.

---

* This account of the manners of the people in the new Caroline islands has been abstracted from des Brosses *Historie des navigations aux terres Australes*, vol. ii. p. 445–511. In order to prevent repetitions, we shall only refer the reader to the passages of this work, to Capt. Cook's *Voyages* and those of George Forster.

† The plane-tree here mentioned is most probably the *Morus papyrifera*, since its jagged leaves might be mistaken for those of a plane-tree.

In their domestic life they are very sober and uniform; they rise with the sun, and go to sleep when it sets. For their meals they keep no regular time, but eat whenever appetite prompts them, and whenever opportunity offers: However they eat but little at a time, and repeat it often. They bathe three times a day, and are always very neat and cleanly. Their king or great chief resides in the isle of ULEE, and another lives in that of LAMUREC, and all the chiefs or *Tamoles* of the neighbouring isles are subjects or vassals of these two kings. Each island contains a great many noblemen or *Tamoles* of the royal family and one of them governs the isle. A kind of gentry inferior in rank are next to the *Tamoles*, and the low people are still more subjected; each of these ranks of men shew great respect to their chiefs.

Those who are willing to pay a visit to their chiefs, shew their respect amongst others by painting their bodies with a kind of an aromatic yellow paste;* this is likewise observed on their festivals; but the chiefs are almost constantly painted in this manner. The raiment of the common people consists of a piece of cloth wrapped round their loins and thighs, part of which passes between their legs. The women are dressed in the same manner, with this difference only, that the cloth reaches down to the middle of their legs, whereas that of the men hardly covers the knees. The upper part of the body is naked; however sometimes a kind of cloak with a hood to it is worn by them over their shoulders. The chief wears a piece of cloth with a hole cut in the middle of it, through which he puts the head, and has one part hanging down the breast and to the knees, and the other reaching as far down behind. The women wear bracelets of tortoise-shell above their elbows, and in their ears, rings made of the same substance, in which they sometimes put odoriferous flowers, or small beads of coco-nut-shells. The men use a kind of cap or fillet, made of plaited filaments, stuck round with birds feathers standing upright. Their body is marked with various lines dispersed in various compartments, but the women and children are without them. They are a set of people having well-proportioned limbs, but their chiefs are remarkably tall and lusty, their hair is black, long, and falling in curls; their beards are strong and bushy, their noses broad, their eyes large, lively and piercing. In their temper is a mixture of the greatest good-nature and benevolence; therefore if ever they quarrel, they are never carried away so far by their passion or hatred as to kill their adversary: the highest pitch of their vengeance is to fight their foes at fisty cuffs, and as soon as some of the by-standers interfere and separate the combatants, their anger is over and they are easily reconciled, especially by a few presents made to the person offended. If ever any one commits a heinous crime, his pun-

---

* In the Friendly isles, Easter Island, and all the New Hebrides, they stain their bodies and cloth sometimes with a yellow aromatic powder, extracted from turmeric.

ishment never extends further than banishment to one of the neighbouring islands. Though the breach of conjugal fidelity is reckoned a great crime, it is however deemed venial, and the injured husband easily forgets the offence for a handsome acknowledgement: but he is still at liberty to divorce the wife upon such occasions. The wife is likewise permitted to separate herself from her husband upon any slight offence, displeasure or disgust. One curious custom however prevails among them, according to which a man marries the wife of his deceased brother, in case he has left no children to inherit; this custom, as far as we know, is no where practised among the inhabitants of the islands which we had occasion to visit. The common people are contented with one wife, though it be not unlawful to marry more than one, and with the chiefs and nobles it is looked upon as a mark of rank to have more than one wife; nay, the King of the district of CITTAC residing at the isle of HUOGOLEU or TORRES, has nine wives. Among themselves they keep strictly honest, and pilfer only from strangers; they covet iron above all things, and every one who obtains some, either by purchase from Europeans, from shipwrecks, or by stealth, is obliged to bring it to the chief, who orders such tools to be made of it, as the size and form of the iron will best admit, and then his subjects hire them for their own use at a certain price.

Their benevolent and friendly disposition gives unity and friendship to their societies; their lively and joyful temper prompts them to mirth and all kinds of sports, and the enjoyment of pleasure; they are amazingly addicted to laughing, and are fond of little witty agreeable stories of a jovial turn; they shew true politeness and good breeding in all their manners and behaviour, and speak very pertinently and wisely on all kinds of subjects; their hearts are capable of being melted at the recital or sight of distress or wretchedness, and a generous tear never fails to steal down their cheeks, the tribute of benevolence and humanity. In their social and festal meetings, they have much singing and dancing. Their females often sit down in small companies, and sing languishing songs, accompanied by motions of the head and hands expressive of the same sentiment, these they call *Tanger ifai-fil,** or the *complaint of women*. Their songs are not without a regular measure and harmony, and they beat time by striking their thighs. In their dances the men stand in two lines opposite to one another; their heads are stuck with feathers and flowers, odoriferous herbs hang from their noses, and from the ears hang down ornaments made of plaited coco-nut filaments. The dances consist chiefly in cadenced, harmonic, and uniform motions of the head, arms, hands, and feet.

---

* We have already made use of this word, to render our opinion more probable; according to which the nations of the first race of people in the South Seas are descended from the inhabitants of the Caroline Islands. See p. 249.

The chief sometimes holds up a piece of cloth, which is given to him who first can seize it, all the competitors starting at the same time for it.

In case they should be injured by neighbouring societies or tribes, they avenge their wrongs by war. They chiefly use lances and darts for arms, which are barbed with points of human bones, and constantly exercise themselves in throwing lances and stones at a mark. They march up regularly in three lines, the first consisting of young men, the second those of a middle age, and lastly the old men stand behind, and no sooner is one of the first rank killed, than the man behind occupies the empty place. They have no defensive weapons, but endeavour to avoid the missile arms of the enemy by agility: their wars are by no means bloody and cruel; the death of two or three men commonly decides the victory, and the conquerors announce their conquest by a loud triumphant shout, and insulting words against the routed party.

They have an idea of the immortality of the soul, and of a state wherein the good are rewarded and the wicked punished. When common people die, their corpses are thrown into the sea. But the bodies of their deceased chiefs are painted yellow; the assembled people cut locks of their hair and beards, and throw them on the corpse in testimony of their grief, to which they add in loud vociferation the praises of the dead, and lastly abstain all that day from eating. After this ceremony the corpse of the deceased is inclosed in a small stone apartment in their own houses, or buried at some distance from their habitations and the sepulcre inclosed in a stone-wall. From time to time they expose near the grave fruits and other eatables, that according to their opinion the deceased may suck them: for they suppose the souls of those who are gone to heaven, return on the fourth day and live invisibly among their friends and relations. These souls are looked upon as good genii, and in every undertaking they are addressed for assistance and success, the priests being supposed to have an intercourse with them.

These and many other traditional doctrines are communicated by certain teachers to the youth of both sexes, in houses appropriated for that purpose. The boys especially learn the names and directions of the 12 winds of their compass, the names and motion of the brightest stars; the situation and names of the various neighbouring isles, and by what course they must steer for each of them. The teachers likewise communicate to them their traditional doctrines of religion. It is observed that though they have no knowledge of a maker of Heaven and Earth, they however acknowledge a good and great spirit, who is the great Lord of Heaven, to whom many spirits both good and evil are subordinate: these spirits are celestial beings different from those who inhabit the Earth, they have a body, and marry in the style of their chiefs, more than one wife. The oldest spirit known among them is called *Sabucoor*, and his wife's name is *Halmelul*. Their son was *Eliulep*, (i.e. the great spirit) and their daughter *Ligobuud*. *Eliulep* married

Leteuhieul, a woman born in the island of *Ulee,* and had by her a son called *Lugueiling,* (i.e. middle of heaven) whom these nations worship as the great lord of heaven, of which he is presumptive heir: *Leteuhieul* died in the prime of her youth and her spirit flew to heaven. *Eliulep* adopted a young man, born in the island of *Lamurec,* called *Reschahuileng,* who, being tired with living on earth, ascended to heaven, in order to enjoy the delights of his father: his mother being still alive at *Lamurec,* he came to her into the middle region of the air and communicated to her the mysteries of heaven. The sister of *Eliulep,* called *Ligobuud,* finding herself with child in the middle region of the air, came down to earth, and brought forth three children. She was astonished to find the earth to be barren and dry; by her powerful word the earth was covered with herbs, flowers, and fruit-trees; she covered the earth with verdure, and peopled it with reasonable men. No death then took place on earth, for in lieu of it a short sleep befel the men the last day of the moon, who revived at her re-apparition on the horizon, as if awaking from an agreeable slumber. But *Erigerigers,* an evil spirit, who was displeased with the happiness of mankind, brought about a kind of death, against which there is no remedy, and since that time, he who dies once is certainly dead: this evil genius is called *Elus melabut,* (i.e. malevolent spirit): the rest are called *Elus melafirs* (benevolent spirits). *Morogrog,* an evil spirit, expelled from heaven, brought fire first upon earth. *Lugueiling,* the son of *Eliulep,* married two wives, one of celestial origin, who brought him two children, *Carrer* and *Meliliau;* the other of terrestrial origin, born at *Falalu,* in the province of *Huogoleu,* by whom he had a son, called *Oclefat;* this young man, upon hearing that his father was a celestial spirit, attempted to mount to heaven, but fell down and wept: hereupon he kindled a great fire, and went up in the smoke to his celestial father, whom he embraced. In the isle of *Falalu* is a pond of fresh water, which the natives fear to approach, because they suppose the Gods bathe in it. The sun, the moon, and the stars, have, according to the opinion of these people, rational souls, and are inhabited by numerous celestial nations. These islanders have neither temples, nor carved or any other images; and they never think it necessary to make any offerings or sacrifices, except a few of them, who seem to worship their deceased friends. At the island of *Yap* or *Panlog,* the inhabitants worship a crocodile; observe incantations making knots of palm-leaves. And to the East of the five clusters of isles, called Carolines, there are many more islands, especially that of *Falupet,* the inhabitants of which worship the shark, *(Tiburon).*

These isles are very numerous, and have inhabitants of a brown colour, like those of the coast of Philippines; but the inhabitants of *Panleu* or the *Palaos,* are like negroes, savage and barbarous; they go naked, and are canibals; and are for that reason, detested by the inhabitants of the Caroline-islands, who look upon them as dangerous to deal with, and the fiends of mankind.

The chiefs at the Caroline-islands are much respected; they wear long beards, and sit on a high seat, like a table, and give audience; those who want to talk to a chief, bow very low, then sit down, hear his commands, and go away after another bow, or they sometimes kiss his hands and feet; or they take the foot of the chief gently with the hand, and rub their face with it. They think it likewise a mark of respect to lull the Tamaoles asleep by songs.

These few remarks on the manners, customs, opinions, and religion of the natives in the Caroline-islands, if compared with those of the inhabitants of the South Sea isles, of the first race, prove that they bear a strong resemblance; and as this similarity of almost every circumstance can hardly be accidental, especially if we consider the vicinity of both clusters of isles, and the correspondence in the stature, colour, habit of body, and turn of mind of the inhabitants, and the probable successive migration of these tribes from isle to isle; it is almost beyond a doubt, that they are very nearly related to one another; and that from these Caroline-islanders, the inhabitants of the Eastern South Sea islands were descended at some distant period. This consideration leads us to another, *viz.* that these islanders having no other than vague traditional reports in lieu of historical records, it is impossible to know any thing of their origin or migrations; and that no distant guess or conjecture could ever have been formed unless by paying a particular attention to their peculiar customs and manners, and likewise to their language; of the first we have given as good an account as our historical proofs would admit; the latter some future navigators must investigate more carefully. A stronger proof of the advantages of civilization, cannot be given, than results from this total uncertainty, respecting the origin of these nations: if we have been able to produce any arguments that lay claim to probability, it is because our minds are improved by civilization, and our talents, natural and acquired, have enabled us to form a judgment as nearly approaching to truth as these subjects will allow. Our minds therefore should be impressed with the most unfeigned feelings and acts of gratitude to Providence for the blessings of a more exalted civilization and education, which give us in every respect so great a superiority over these nations, and assign to us so high a rank in the scale of rational beings; and how much ought not this to encourage us to act up to this greater knowledge, and to maintain by humanity and virtue the exalted station we occupy.

Quum natura hominis imbecillior sit, quam coeterorum animalium, quae vel ad perferendam vim temporum, vel ad incursiones a suis corporibus arcendas, naturalibus munimentis providentia coelestis armavit; homini autem quia nihil istorum datum est, accepit pro istis omnibus miserationis affectum, qui plane vocatur HUMANITAS, *qua nosmet invicem tueamur.*
LACTANTIUS, lib. iii. c. 17[7]

SECTION XI

On the Preservation of Health in long Voyages— Account of our Diseases, and the Remedies and Preventatives used on our Voyage[1]

IDEO UTILE EST SCIRE UNUMQUEMQUE, QUID, & QUANDO MAXIME CAVEAT.
Corn. Celsus *de Medicina*, lib. ii. praef.[2]

PRESERVATION OF MARINERS

After the discovery of America and the East Indies, by the way round the Cape of Good Hope, the history of the first long navigations, abounds with the most melancholy accounts of a dreadful and alarming mortality raging on board the vessels. Death, in its multifarious and terrible approaching symptoms, without remedy, though none of the least sources of human misery, is, however, exceeded by the loss of thousands of young, hale, and very useful sea-faring men, who, in a great commercial state are an irreparable loss, and must become alarming to the state, either during the time of or on the eve of a war. The mortality was felt again on certain occasions in later times; and the principles both of sound policy as well as of humanity, should prompt every man of knowledge, and who has an opportunity of making observations on this great and interesting subject, to communicate his observations to the public, together with his proposals for the preservation of so useful a set of men as mariners are; that those who are intrusted with the conduct of naval affairs, may have an opportunity of trying these proposed remedies and prophylactics, and upon finding that some answer and others do not, the public may be enabled to profit by their experience, and thus preserve the lives of many thousands of useful members to society. It has been frequently the practice of the great officers for naval affairs in the various commercial nations, not only to recommend many of these things by way of experiment, but likewise to encourage those by rewards, who had the good fortune or skill to discover some new method of preventing in any manner the premature loss of mariners by diseases, especially those of the putrid kind. But none of the maritime powers can boast so many essays, and so many successful attempts for saving the lives of mariners as Great Britain.

The legislative and executive branches of government, together with all the public learned bodies, as well as individuals, concurred in this noble and benevolent career. The last voyages undertaken under the royal patronage, planned by wisdom, supported by national munificence, and executed with the most indefatigable labour, and a noble exertion of knowledge, experience, and perseverance, are the most undeniable proofs of this spirit of emulation, in this important business to mankind. In consequence of it, that great and able navigator, Captain Cook, has communicated to the world the method he employed for the preservation of the healths and lives of his ship's company, and its success. The Royal Society has crowned his paper with the presentation of Sir Godfrey Copley's golden medal, to testify her approbation of the excellent method proposed by him. The learned president of the Society, has, upon this occasion, illustrated the method used by the navigator, with that perspicuity, learning, experience, and both medical and natural knowledge, which are peculiar to him, and have procured him the merited applause of the learned world. After these publications it might seem superfluous, to say any thing more on a subject so ably set forth: however, as I have had frequent opportunities of investigating this subject with care and attention, and can give some necessary details on the preparation and use of the antiseptics; and lastly, as I flatter myself not only to be able to propose some material improvements on many parts of this method, but also to suggest some important hints, which may lead to still greater discoveries; I thought it on the present occasion by no means superfluous to publish my observations and remarks on ths same subject, hoping that they may in course of time become useful and interesting. I am besides so well persuaded of the candour, humanity and zeal for encouraging every attempt which tends to improve science, and to promote the benefit of mankind both in my friend Capt. Cook and in the learned president of the Royal Society, that I have not the least doubt of being not only absolved by them, of the charge of envy or a desire of rivalship in the same career, but likewise of being commended for being emulous of becoming useful to mankind and perhaps the occasion of saving the lives of many useful and necessary members of society.

The most common and at the same time most dreadful evil infesting the crews of ships sent out on long voyages, is the Sea-Scurvy; which according to the last observations of Dr. Macbride, and those of Sir John Pringle is of the putrid kind. Some authors have assigned the sea-air to be one of its causes, but it is impossible to make good this assertion, since people living near the sea, or in small islands surrounded by the sea and its air, enjoy their health as well as those who have inland habitations. Salt provisions contribute no doubt a great deal towards spreading this disease in a ship, especially if they have been lying for a long space of time in salt and are become putrid; as this must accelerate its symptoms and bring on a general putrescence of the whole habit of the human body.

But the chief causes, originally depositing the fomes[3] of putrescence into our body, have in my opinion, hitherto not been attended to, and still less have they been placed in that point of view, in which I flatter myself to represent it to the public; and which I trust may lead us to find out the remedies against this dreadful scourge to sea-faring people.

We find that the blood of animals imbibes through the lungs a considerable portion of phlogistic matter; for when a quantity of inflammable air made by pouring some weakened oil of vitriol on steel filings, contained in a bladder or vessel, is breathed into the lungs and exhaled again into the same vessel, it not only after 20 or 30 reciprocal breathings ceases to be inflammable, but on the contrary will extinguish a burning candle put into it; which circumstance incontestibly proves, that the inflammable air, when in the lungs had been deprived of its phlogiston, and consequently that the latter had been absorbed into the blood. That ingenious and accurate philosopher, Dr. Priestley, inferred from the experiment wherein common air becomes, by being inhaled into the lungs unfit for the purposes of respiration or giving nourishment to the flame of a candle, "that the use of the lungs is to carry off a putrid *effluvium,* or to *discharge that phlogiston,*[4] which had been taken into the system with the aliment, and was become, as it were, *effete;* the air that is respired serving as a *menstruum* for that purpose."* And adds, that what he had before "concluded to be the use of respiration in general, he had now, he thinks proved to be effected by means of the blood, in consequence of its coming so nearly into contact with the air in the lungs: the blood appearing to be a fluid wonderfully formed to imbibe and part with that principle, which the chemists call phlogiston." It appears however from the experiment just mentioned, and which may easily be repeated, that the blood instead of discharging any phlogiston, imbibes it only from the air, and at each inhalation decompounds the common air,† which is a compound of *empyreal air,*‡ (i.e. dephlogis-

---

* Experiments and Observations on different kinds of air, by Joseph Priestley, L.L.D. vol. iii. p. 56. In the *Philos. Trans.* vol. lxi. P. i. p. 226.

† Dr. Priestley had no doubt left in his mind, that *atmospherical air* consists of the nitrous acid and earth: Priestley, vol. ii. p. 35. Mr. Sage in his *Elements de Mineralogie docimastique,* thinks common air to consist of phosphoric acid, Phlogiston and Water, vol. ii. p. 377, 378.

‡ The words *empyreal air,* are used in an acceptation, which is not yet adopted as to the composition with air: but as this integrant part of air is very pure, *gives life and aliment in flame,* and admits more exhalations from the lungs, before it comes unfit for respiration than common air, it may not improperly be called *empyreal air:* and being a compound of a subtle acid and phlogiston, it is analogous to a *dulcified acid,* which may by a higher rectification become *Ether.* The word ETHER has been adopted in chemistry from the notions of antient Philosophers, who called the substance they supposed to exist beyond our atmosphere by that name: and in the same manner the more refined and purer regions beyond the atmosphere were called by the antients the EMPYREAL HEAVENS. It will therefore be no impropriety to call this integrant part of common air, EMPYREAL AIR.

ticated air of Dr. Priestley) and of such air as will not support the flame of a candle. This *empyreal air* Mr. SCHEELE,* has proved to be compounded of a very subtle acid and a phlogiston. Consequently in every inhalation, the common air yields to the blood its empyreal part, which contains a good deal of phlogiston, and leaves the rest unfit for respiration. The empyreal air acts as an other, or dulcified acid upon the lungs and the heart, and consequently as a gentle stimulus. Were the acid too prevalent in its composition, it would cause convulsions, and too much phlogiston would likewise be hurtful, as we shall shew in the sequel. The dulcified acid or ethereal air is therefore found the most convenient. All the operations of our body are produced either by chemical processes or by mechanical powers, or both. The empyreal air, on account of its dulcified acid, stimulates the heart, and causes its continual motion, and on account of its phlogiston entertains and diffuses that natural heat, which is absolutely necessary for the functions of life.

All organic bodies both animal and vegetable consist of an acid, some phlogiston and absorbent earth. The proportions of the integrant parts vary, and are sometimes modified by additions of some other substances. The addition of food and the attraction of juices by the roots, are the means of increasing the growth and supporting the life both of vegetables and animals. All animal bodies require a continual supply of food, from whence both by a chemical and mechanical operation juices are extracted; which are assimilated as much as possible to those contained in the body, and rendered nearly homogeneous to its constituent parts; these juices circulate in the form of blood through the body, and gradually form a secretion of various parts, constantly depositing insensible atoms of matter, replacing continually those atoms which are incessantly wasted by perspiration, and friction, by labour, walking, &c. These atoms deposited by the blood and other juices are analogous to the mixtures contained in the various substances employed as food; if therefore the acid particles prevail in the nourishment, it is an *acidulated diet*; if the phlogiston is most copious, it yields a *phlogistic diet,* and if the absorbents and alkalies preponderate it becomes an *alkaline diet*. Health depends partly on the just medium or mixture between the various diets: for according as the quality of the diet prevails in the food, so must the juices be changed which are circulating in the body, and which afterwards constitute the solids. If the acids prevail, the fibres of the body become too crisp and much inclined to *convulsive symptoms*; if the phlogiston becomes too copious, *inflammatory and eruptive* diseases may be apprehended, and if the alkaline parts are the chief ingredients of our food, *putrid diseases* must be the natural consequences.

---

* *Chemical Treatise on Air and Fire,* by Charles William Scheele, Upsala, octavo, 1777 (written in German).

I wish to be understood, without misconstruction; I pretend not to say that an acidulated diet is the only cause of convulsive and spasmodic symptoms, or the phlogistic of inflammatory diseases, or the alkaline of putrid: for there are no doubt many other causes productive of the same effects, under various circumstances; nay, there are external causes which throw the whole habit into the same morbific state that may originate from a certain kind of food.

Fresh food, both of the animal and vegetable kind, contains a proportionate salubrious mixture of acids, phlogiston and alkalies; especially if it be dressed without any disguise of rich sauces, full of spice and other ingredients, not properly assimilated to our habits; it is therefore no wonder, that *caeteribus paribus*, fresh food is not so pernicious as salted. But if we examine the water, the flesh, and all the aliments eaten by the people in ships during long voyages; we find that they have left that equal mixture of parts, which alone entitled them to the rank of salubrious food. The *water*, if ever so good when fresh, commonly in a few weeks stinks intolerably, especially in hot climates, and is often full of aquatic insects, and in case those insects perish in the water, they putrefy, that is, their organic parts are again restored to a mixture of their integrant elementary parts; and they form commonly a real liver of sulphur,* whose noxiousness and septic quality is well known. The *flesh* is salted in order to preserve it the longer; but common salt is by no means an antiseptic, when mixed with animal substances. The latter when dead, by an intestine motion of their elementary integrant parts are gradually dissolved; the volatile parts of phlogiston, and acids volatilized by phlogiston fly off; then the volatile alkaline parts leave the mass; and the remainder is a magma, nearly related to a hepar sulphuris; which after a still longer period of time becomes an alkali, or an absorbent earth. The addition of the large quantity of salt cannot prevent the flesh from real putrefaction, but only retards its progress. We found, that our meat, which had been really the best of its kind, was become in fact very little better than putrid; all its fat had been corroded by the salt, and its smell, both in a raw and boiled state, was extremely offensive, though it had been towed in a net of ropes for twenty-four hours at the stern of the ship; by which operation a great proportion of the saltness, together with part of the stench had been carried off, and the bare tough muscular fibre strongly impregnated with salt alone remained. The gelatinous part, which is the chief nutriment in flesh, was all lost, and nothing was left but a strongly alkaline part, which is known to be a great promoter of putrefaction. The *bread* is made for the English navy of wheat, and is baked into flat cakes, without the addition of yeast or other leaven. The flatness of the bread is the means of excluding moisture, which would otherwise be expelled by fire. It is impossible to preserve the bread

---

* Mr. Sage *Analyse des blés*, Paris, 1776, 8vo. p. 106, seq.

against the attacks of weavils, which exist by thousands in it. In their larva or grub state they pierce bread very much, and in their perfect insect state they deposit their eggs in it. If unfortunately the casks containing the bread have not been well seasoned before, or are still green, the bread grows mouldy, contracts a musty taste and smell, and becomes really rotten. If the casks be good, they are still subject to the alkaline and septic effluvia of the putrid water, in the casks and flesh, or those from the bilge-water, and the bad air caused by the breathing and perspiration of many hundred persons, which penetrates to the best secured and most secret places, and infects every thing with its septic quality. I need not mention that in some few cases the sea-water may reach the bread-casks, which naturally must spoil them, and woe to the poor mortals who are under the cruel necessity of living upon bread affected by such an accident. It is true, all possible care is taken to secure this most necessary article against such accidents, but I have been told that sometimes they happen in spight of all providential care. White *pease* are an article of food daily served at dinner in the form of soup, which is, in my opinion, one of the best aliments that can be given in long voyages, as they are full of fixed air, and contain likewise a considerable portion of phlogiston; they are liable, by the intestinal digestive fermentation, to part with their fixed air, which is on sea voyages one of the most necessary articles that can be found in aliment. We had the misfortune to have on board the Resolution, pease for our provision, that had been, I suppose, kiln-dried; for though they were boiled over so long, they remained whole; the husk parted, and left the two halves of the pease, as hard as if they had only been parched. The pease on board the Adventure had not this bad quality, which effectually prevented the easy digestion of this excellent food: it is, however, of great consequence to take aliments, which are easily digested on long sea voyages, because many circumstances concur to weaken the digestive power of the stomach and intestines in these circumstances. Government was used to allow *oil* to the ship's company for making their puddings, and for dressing their victuals in such manner as the sailors like best. Captain Cook says, *oil (such as the navy is usually supplied with) has the contrary effect*; i.e. is not antiscorbutic, but septic. From the hint thrown out by this able navigator, it should seem that the navy is usually supplied with an oil of inferior sort, and bad quality, either actually rancid, or such as is on the point of becoming so. How ill suited oil is in such a state to health, I leave to those to judge who know what effects acids have upon our frame. *Wheat* or *oatmeal* are provided for the navy for breakfast, and are both most excellent aliments for men, who are deprived of fresh vegetable diet, during a long space of time.

We have hitherto examined the food on board of such ships as are performing long voyages: we are next to examine the other parts of the oeconomy of a sailor. The great numbers of people perspiring and breathing in a ship, must natu-

PRESERVATION OF
MARINERS

rally render the air between decks at last unfit for breathing; or at least so much charged with alkaline and septic effluvia, that it must be very difficult to preserve the health of the seamen in the midst of such a cloud of infecting steams; this will become more evident, by considering that the bilge-water in the pump-well, is more than sufficient to fill the whole ship with noxious effluvia. After we left Plymouth, in the year 1772, and gradually came into warmer climates, a most intolerable stench began to spread throughout the ship; the bilge-water having become highly putrid, and diffusing its noxious effluvia from the motion, continually forming and presenting new surfaces for the evaporation of the offensive particles. No parts were more infected by this smell, than my own and my son's cabins, because they were nearest to the main mast, and consequently close to the opening of the pumps from whence this horrid stench was communicated to the upper parts of the ship. I was then little acquainted with naval affairs, and communicated accidentally my sentiments to the Captain; he immediately supposed the bilge-water to be the cause, and explained to me the situation of the pump-well, and that all the moisture of the ship must be collected in that place; he added the ship had been detained for such a long space of time at Sheerness and Plymouth, that it was no wonder if the water should have become putrid: its depth was measured, and found to be a few inches high only, which is never thought sufficient to make it worth while to pump it out; the water therefore remained, and the stench continued for some time, till it gradually became less offensive: however I then recommended the use of fire and fumigations between decks as the best remedies against this dreadful stench and the noxious effluvia of this sink. I find by my journal, that my advice was followed during our passage from Madeira to the Cape Verd Islands, anterior to the 8th of August, and that the air was rarefied by charcoal fires, and sometimes by setting fire to brimstone or pitch, or even to a mixture of gun-powder and vinegar.* When this was done, all hands were called on deck, all the skuttles and hatchways were shut, and the smoak confined, so that it had time likewise to destroy the vermin. When this operation was done during winter, I generally found the thermometer in my cabin to rise, and to remain higher during the first twenty-four hours; the difference

---

* The friend of Capt. Cook mentioned by Sir John Pringle in his *Discourse,* who observed that the old twenty gun ships, had their *galley* or kitchen in the fore-part of the *orlop,*[5] and suspected this circumstance to contribute much towards their being remarkably less sickly, than those ships of the same size of a modern construction, is certainly very right in his suspicion. When I was at Plymouth in the year 1772, expecting the arrival of the Resolution, Dr. Irving visited with me a Dutch man of war, then lying there: we found the kitchen in the middle part of the *orlop,* somewhat before the main mast, and enquiring how they found the ship in regard to healthiness, when out at sea for some time, we were told, that it was remarkably healthy. The smoak was very great and the heat in the middle of a very warm day, was to us, almost intolerable between decks.

however seldom exceeded two or three degrees: for the fire was made between decks, and the smoak only penetrated into my cabin by the chinks and crevices of the deck.

The next object falling under examination, are the *persons* themselves sailing in the ship, and their dress. In general we find mankind of the same turn of mind; among all ranks of men are such as love neatness of their persons and cleanliness both in regard to their bodies and their cloths; and likewise there are others, who from an invincible connate indolence or sluggishness are always dirty, and though they have a sufficient change they become however so uncleanly, that it seems almost an inherent quality to them; no wonder therefore, that persons of both these qualifications should be found in a ship's company. The same cloth constantly put on without any change, must very naturally imbibe a great part of the effluvia carried off by perspiration, and being constantly worn, the pores must again imbibe the impure vapours; and as the filthiness in their external behaviour causes them to postpone their washing, many pores must by this neglect be stopt up, and the insensible perspiration prevented. All which circumstances contribute greatly toward accelerating the effects of the scurvy.

Let us now consider how far the aliments on board a ship can be made antiseptic in long voyages; for it can be no remedy against the scurvy to give the patients a small dose of physic; since the greater part of the food of a sailor is either putrid or at least in such a state, that it must highly promote and accelerate the putresence of the whole habit: it becomes therefore absolutely necessary to provide a substance by way of aliment, which will keep a long while at sea without decaying, and which will yield in quantity those particles, which are generally wanting in the putrid food. The *flesh* must be salted, and of course is liable to lose by lying long in salt those particles, which when boiled down, first yield a gelatinous substance, and lastly a kind of glue, the only nutritive parts contained in all meat; this aliment is therefore one of those which cannot be preserved in a good condition, be it ever so good in its kind, and which of course must become more and more noxious in proportion to the space of time it has been lying in salt.

The *bread* is the second article of food, which likewise cannot be kept perfectly good for a long space of time; especially the wheaten ship's biscuit is more liable to become mouldy and musty and worm eaten, than any other of the same kind. I have likewise found from my own experience, and that of a great many persons on board our ship, that the wheaten biscuit causes obstructions, and as seafaring men are generally inclined to constipation, this aliment tends greatly to increase the evil. I am therefore of opinion that bread would be infinitely more wholesome if it be made of rye, or of equal parts of rye and of wheat mixed together, or even of wheat alone, provided the flour be not quite ground fine, and separated only from the coarsest bran; and lastly the bread ought to be made with

leaven or sour-paste. What convinced me chiefly that these precautions would
make the bread more salubrious, was the experience we had of such bread from
the Cape of Good Hope. When we left this last mentioned place in November,
1772, we had taken in there as much of their bread as our ships could stow away
with convenience, in lieu of the bread which had been eaten during the passage
from Plymouth to the Cape. The biscuit we obtained at the Cape, was made of
wheat, which had not been ground into the finest flour, nor had the bran been
bolted, and it was prepared with four leaven. This bread, according to my own
experience, and that of many of our ship-mates, stimulated the viscera so gently
that it procured stools more regularly than the wheaten biscuit. The example of
the Russian soldiers and sailors, who have no other than rye-biscuit, prepared
with sour-paste and of a flour from which hardly any bran has been separated, and
who with this bread alone and hardly any other aliment, are healthy, and seldom
or ever plagued with the scurvy, confirmed me still more in my opinion. The only
precautions which ought to be taken with this bread are to eat it always after it
has been soaked, and never when it is quite dry, and secondly to bake large loaves
of this bread and then to cut them into small cubes of about an inch and an half,
and bake them over again. This bread is certainly less subject to become mouldy
or musty, or worm-eaten; its acidity and hardness making it less likely to become
food for the worms: its coarser particles stimulate the intestines and procure easy
stools, and its acidity not only acts as an antiseptic, but causes a greater fermentation with all the other aliments, and consequently discharges more fixed air,
which sweetens and meliorates the putridity of the salt flesh, and with the copious inflammable parts of the pease mixes into a food more analogous to our juices
and whole animal system. The only difficulty I foresee, will arise from its being a
novelty, and every body versed in naval affairs will find that no set of men are
brought with greater reluctance into an innovation than sailors. But the example
of the officers, together with a gentle treatment will no doubt in a little time get
the better of this difficulty, and introduce an aliment on board the English navy,
which will greatly contribute to the more healthy state of the ships company, and
thus preserve the lives of many an useful member to society.

The *sowerkrout,* lately become of more universal use, is of such an excellence
as an antiseptic as needs no further comment. Its preparation is well understood
in Germany, Denmark, Sweden, and Russia; and has lately been so well prepared
for the King's ships in England, that it would be needless to dwell on this subject:
however, as there may be persons desirous of using this salutary food, and at the
same time ignorant of the method of preparing it, I will here annex the following
account: solid heads of cabbages are taken and cut asunder, and then put into a
kind of box, running in groves over a machine, similar to those of a less size used
for cutting cucumbers into slices for salad, which of course must be supposed to

be greater and proportioned to the business, which is to be performed by the machine. The iron planes for cutting the cabbages into slices, are made from 12 to 18 inches in length. While the box is drawn backwards and forwards over this machine; the heads of the cabbages must be gently pressed during the operation, and new ones gradually laid in; by which means the cabbages are cut into thin slices, and fall into a large tub, whereon the machine is laid. These slices of cabbages are, by some persons, mixed up with salt and caraway-seeds (*Carum Carvi*, Linn.) or by others with salt and juniper-berries, and then beaten into a cask, or vat, (whereof the head has been taken out) till it yields some juice. The instrument serving for that purpose, is either a large club of about five or six inches in diameter, or a large and strong butter-staff. Caraway seeds are to be preferred to juniper berries; since the first are very nourishing, and serve, when reduced into flower, to whole Tartar nations for food, when boiled with mares milk; and because they yield by fermentation, a great quantity of fixed air; and are known to increase the milk of wetnurses; qualities, which alone would be sufficient to recommend the seeds preferably to juniper berries. If the casks wherein the *sowerkrout* is to be prepared, has been a wine, or brandy, or vinegar cask, the fermentation succeeds upon the whole better, and imparts to the sowerkrout a more vinous taste. Some rub the inside of the cask with sower-leaven, in order to accelerate the fermentation, which latter circumstance may be omitted, if there is time enough for letting the cabbage go through a regular and gradual fermentation. The stamping a new quantity of sowerkrout on the first layer of it is always continued, till the whole cask be full. Then it is necessary to bring the cask, containing the sliced and stamped cabbage, into a place which has a moderate temperatur, and, if possible, above 50 or 60 degrees of Fahrenheits thermometer: because the warmth greatly promotes, and accelerates its vinous fermentation. As soon as it becomes acidulated, which will happen in 10, 12, or 14 days, according to the degree of warmth, in which the cask is kept, the vat may be removed to a cellar, and there preserved. In the beginning a quantity of juice is found standing on the top of the fermenting cabbage, and with a stick a hole is made in the middle of the cask for the better circulation of the fermenting liquor. If this cabbage be destined for a long sea voyage, the cabbage is taken out of its juice, and in this dry state closely packed in empty casks: but if it be intended to be consumed at home, a clean board fitting the cask, and loaded with weights for depressing the fermented cabbage, is put on the top of it. Of such fermented cabbage or *sowerkrout*, about a pint was served to every individual of our ship's company, twice or three times in a week; and it is to this most excellent antiseptic, that we chiefly ascribe the little progress which the scurvy made on board our ship. Our ship's company grew at last very fond of it, especially when they observed its salutary effects in preventing the scurvy. We had 60 casks of it on board, and about a month before

PRESERVATION OF
MARINERS

we reached the Cape of Good Hope, in March 1775, the whole quantity was apprehended to have been consumed; and the loss of it was severely felt by our ship-mates. However, when we arrived at the Cape, and all the hold was cleared, we still found two casks, of one of which a part was left, when we arrived at *Fayal*, in the Western islands, in July 1775, and was given away by Captain Cook, to the British Consul, who relished it very much, and it was then found to be as good as when first made in October, 1771.

Another salutary food is *wheat* and *oatmeal*, for breakfast; the wheat being more nourishing, is certainly preferable to the *oatmeal*; but as the *sooins* (a kind of acidulous jelly, and found by experiment to be very antiseptic) is prepared from the last article: it will always be ranked amongst the salutary food of a ship's company.

Pease the common food of sailors is no doubt while fresh and uncorrupted very salutary; however as they abound in phlogiston, and are not sufficiently mixed and rendered analogous to our alimentary vessels, it would not be amiss to allow some vinegar to the sailors for their pease-soup, which by its acidity will correct this excellent food, and by intestine fermentation disengage its fixed air, and render it by this means more antiseptic and salubrious.

Instead of *oil* it is undoubtedly preferable to allow some *sugar* to people in-tended to go on long voyages, according to the opinion of Capt. Cook.* Sugar is one of those vegetable substances, which contain an acid of phosphorus, and an oily inflammable principle; and which on account of the just and proper propor-tion of the acid and phlogiston in its mixture, ferments in general more easily, yields more freely a vinous fermentation, and when mixed with other substances which are not in actual fermentation, it sooner communicates a fermentation to them, than any other known vegetable substance. This quality no doubt makes sugar one of the best antiseptics, and its use will greatly contribute to rectify the putrescence of the salt food eaten on board a ship, and prevent the scurvy from breaking out.

The use of *sweet-wort,* or the infusion of malt, ground in a coarse manner into *groats* or *grits,* is at present so generally known to be the best prophylactic against the scurvy, that it would be superfluous to recommend its utility; since Dr. Macbride, Sir John Pringle and Captain Cook have put this matter entirely out of doubt. The wort was prepared by infusing two or three pints of boiling water on one pint of good malt, ground in a coarse manner: the infusion was kept in a warm place near the fire of the galley, and closely covered to prevent its growing cold: of this liquor the persons threatened by the scurvy drank every day one or

---

* Capt. Cook's *Voyages towards the South Pole, and round the world,* vol. ii. p. 290.

two pints warm, two or three hours before and after their meals; those who had already some slight symptoms of the scurvy, drank a quart of this wort, twice a day; and lastly, those who were very much attacked by that dreadful evil, were allowed three quarts and more. I observed wonderful effects of this remedy on board our ship. Amongst other scorbutic patients, we had two who were scarcely a few days out at sea, when the first symptoms of the scurvy constantly appeared, and rapidly increased to a very violent and dangerous degree; their gums were bleeding and ulcerated, their teeth loose, their feet oedematous,[6] with large, livid, and purple blotches; the swelling, when pressed by a finger, would leave a pit for a good while; the urine smelt offensively putrid, and contained long filaments: and one of the men lost entirely the use of his limbs, which became contracted: these two patients were not only quite restored by the copious use of the *sweet-wort*, but one of them acquired a quite new set of gums, the old ones being much impaired, and having fallen gradually away by ulceration; and the other was, in his contraction, much relieved, by constantly applying the warm *grains* of malt, (after the infusion of sweet-wort had been drawn off) to his crippled limbs; I saw another man, whose swelling and purple blotches on the feet disappeared, by frequent fomentations with these hot *grains*. The quantity of malt we had on board, amounted to 11 large casks; and during the two first years, kept remarkably well; but in the third year, some lumps were found mouldered in the casks, though some other parts still remained very good; the wort procured from this malt was inferior in quality, but by increasing the quantity of malt and lessening that of water, the infusion was still found a powerful and excellent antiseptic. It has been objected against the infusion of malt, *that it will not cure the scurvy at sea;** since this *antiscorbutic sea-medicine will only prevent the scurvy from making any great progress for a considerable while.*† But if we consider the two or three cases before mentioned, we shall be obliged to allow that they cannot be considered otherwise than perfect cures. For we must likewise remark on the other hand, that as long as the patient, (who is restored to health by the use of the sweet-wort) remains on board, the causes which produced the scurvy are not removed; the putrid water continues to be his drink, the putrid salt-flesh his diet, and the putrid air is at all times inhaled by him, at least during night, between the decks, all which circumstances keep up and increase the *fomes* of putrescence in the body. A person therefore with a bad habit of body, may be said to have been perfectly cured of the scurvy, without daring to leave off the use of the sweet-wort all the time he remains on board, for fear of being again attacked by the same evil, whose fomes he is continually taking in by way of food, and even by his breath. Malt, as every

---

* Capt. Cook's *Voyage*, vol. ii. p. 289.

† Idem, ibid.

body knows, is made of barley, and of all the kinds of grains used for food, which have some analogy with the tribe of grasses, it contains more of a sugar-like extract than all the rest. When the malt is manufactured, the grains of barley are macerated, and then left to ferment in a moderate degree of warmth. This fermentation promotes the growth of the blade, and of the first roots; but it likewise sets free the sweet particles, which were lying as it were dormant, and enveloped in the glutinous and starchy substance.* The sweet substance analogous to sugar, is more capable of promoting fermentation than any other; the malt being dried just at the moment when this sweet substance is freed from the others by fermentation, preserves this precious sweet juice; and when it is extracted from the malt by the infusion of boiling water, the liquor is richly charged with the saccharine particles promoting fermentation, sweetening the putrescent parts of the salt flesh, and discharging copiously fixed air, which is the only substance capable of resisting powerfully the dreadful effects of putridity.

We come now to the *water*, which is one of the most simple and most necessary elements; and which, if become putrid and offensive, greatly increases the scene of misery, which opens upon so brave and so useful a set of men as the sailors, who devote their health and their lives for the defence of their country. We observed, that though ventilation takes off a great deal of the offensive smell of the water, it remains however ill tasted, putrid and very unwholesome. I have, by several experiments, found that putrid water contains a liver of sulphur, and as nothing quenches more effectually and more suddenly the spreading effluvia of the liver of sulphur, and takes off its loathsome taste than quicklime, I would propose that quicklime dissolved in water, should be poured in such quantities into the putrid water, as may be sufficient to suppress both its bad taste and smell. The proportion cannot be ascertained, as the degree of putridity of the water is various, and must of course require either a greater or less quantity. The quicklime in an instant makes the water potable, and in some measure impregnates it with fixed air, which by the putrid fermentation is entirely gone off. If the water thus prepared be decanted from the precipitate, it will not only be palatable, but likewise limpid and clear.†

The same limewater poured into the putrid bilge-water of the pump-well, will in an instant, precipitate its putrid particles, and render the water inoffensive; to which operation I would always add the rarefaction of the air in the

---

* Sage *Analyse des blés*. Paris, 8vo. 1776.
† Since the above was written, I have been informed, that the addition of limewater to the fresh water, intended for the use of the people on board of French ships, has entirely prevented its becoming putrid; when the same water, without the addition of limewater, grew very putrid and intolerably offensive.

pump-well by fire; and am sure that both remedies joined together, will not only effectually hinder the effluvia from becoming noxious by their effects, but also prevent the water from recovering its prutrescency so soon.

We had on board our ship the *rob of lemon and oranges;*[7] which has by no means been found to succeed in obviating the effects of the scurvy; and though used on purpose by one or two men by itself without the addition of any other remedy, our excellent surgeon, Mr. PATTON, was of opinion that it did not even stop the progress of the scurvy.

Besides this preventative, we had the *marmalade of carrots*, which consisted of the inspissated[8] juice of carrots, extracted by boiling and afterwards evaporated by fire to the consistence of a syrup, Mr. MUZEL-STOSCH of Berlin, had recommended this marmalade to the Society for promoting Arts, Manufactures and Commerce; who referred the same to the Board of Admiralty, by whose orders some of it was prepared, and given to the surgeons of our ships, in order that they might make proper trials of it: they found after some experiments, that it had nearly the same effect as the rob of lemons, and perhaps had moreover the good quality of keeping the belly open, and preventing that constipation which is so general in sea-faring men; but it did not cure any scorbutic symptoms, nor even prevent the increase of the evil. The inspissation of the juice of lemons and of carrots by fire, has perhaps deprived these two antiscorbutic substances of those properties, which might be expected from them, if less exposed to the fire; I am therefore of opinion that the *expressed juice of lemons* by itself is a more powerful antiseptic, than either the rob or the marmalade of carrots; but as it has been very justly apprehended, that the expressed juice of lemons will not keep in a good condition for a long space of time; I only beg leave to mention, that the Captain with me obtained about thirty gallons of lemon-juice at the Cape of Good Hope, to which quantity we added about a fifth or a sixth part of brandy or rum which preserved the lemon-juice during the space of thirty-two months in so good a condition, that it really appeared to us to be as good, as if it had been fresh expressed. This acid mixed up with sugar and given to scorbutic patients, will undoubtedly with the other remedies greatly promote their recovery. These few remarks and hints will I hope disclose such a method of preventing the deleterious effects of the scurvy on board the Royal Navy, by effectually sweetening of the food and water, and meliorating the noxious effluvia of the confined air between decks; especially if they be added to the various methods proposed and tried by Capt. Cook, in regard to the cleanliness of the persons, the airing of the bedding, changing of clothes, the airing of the ship by fire and fumigation, and the regulation of keeping the crew at three watches, instead of putting them as is commonly termed, at watch and watch.

By the help of the regulations just now exhibited, and some of the before mentioned prophylactics, our whole ship's crew enjoyed in general a very good state of health: and though we often passed in a few weeks from extreme cold, (where we were surrounded by hundreds of ice-islands, and had snow and sleet pouring down on our decks;) to the most intense degree of heat, i.e. from 27° to 80° or 90° of Fahrenheits Thermometer, we were not deprived of the inestimable blessing of health.

The diseases which prevailed in the ship, when we were in the cold antarctic regions, where we often had hard blowing weather with snow, sleet, and cold penetrating rain and fogs that were continued for several days, consisted chiefly in slight *colds,* rheumatisms, sore throats, and swellings of the glands: which latter circumstance was, according to my opinion, caused by the ice-water; for when we filled thirty or forty casks with small pieces of ice, on which some dissolved ice-water was poured, and then struck them down into the hold, the temperature of the air was commonly very suddenly altered, so that from 50° of Fahrenheits Thermometer, the mercury at once fell down to 35°; and besides this it is well known that ice expels all fixed air from water, nor is the melting of the ice by fire, an operation which can properly restore its natural quantity of fixed air to it. The want of which may very probably cause obstructions in the glandular system of our body.

Besides the above, the chief diseases were *fevers.* However our ship's company was more free from them, than might be expected on a voyage, where we underwent so many changes of climate. In the year 1774, in February, March, and April, after we left the cold climates, and were advancing towards the milder regions, the Captain, my son, my servant, and two or three persons more in the ship were attacked by the *bilious colic;* among its symptoms were acute pains, and the disease rose to a dangerous height; the Captain especially grew by neglecting the disease in the beginning, very weak, and had for about twenty-four hours a continued hiccough, however, by the indefatigable assiduity and skill of Mr. PAT-TON, our excellent surgeon, the patients were restored to health; and though they recovered but slowly whilst we were at sea, for want of fresh and nourishing food, restoratives and greens; yet as soon as we came to Taheitee they durst not venture to eat any of the common fruits of the country, as bread-fruit, coco-nuts, and bananas, because they renewed their pains; but having at last ventured to eat the fine apples of this country, *(Spondias)* which have a peculiar kind of tartness joined to an agreeable sweetness much approaching to the taste of pine-apples; they soon felt the salutary effects of this most excellent fruit, and were in a few days perfectly restored.

The *sea-scurvy* did not make such ravages on board our ship as might have been expected, on account of the regulations enumerated before and the use of the excellent prophylactics and remedies, which were freely administered, and of which we have spoken very fully.

The *venereal disease* was very frequent among our ships-company, so that sometimes thirty or forty persons were at once infected; but the vigilance and skill of Mr. Patton always prevented this disease from rising to any great height, and from leaving any dangerous effects. I cannot conclude this article without mentioning, that I have lately learnt from a letter written by Dr. HENSLER, Physican to the King of Denmark, to a friend of mine, who kindly communicated its contents to me, that he has collected many very old historical facts from Chronicles and Records, by which it appears beyond a possibility of doubt, that this evil was known in various parts of Europe several centuries before the discovery of America by Christopher Columbus in 1493, and it is particularly to be remarked that in the North of Germany the friars and monks were observed to disseminate the evil more than any other set of people. As this learned and ingenious gentleman intends to communicate to the public the result of his enquiries, which I have here the happiness to announce, we shall be farther convinced by irrefragable proofs, of the facts already asserted in the *Philosophical Transactions*, vol. xxvii and xxxi. N⁰· 365, II.

I cannot omit here a circumstance which befel us, and might perhaps have proved fatal to many of us, if proper care had not been taken to prevent the ill consequences of it.[9] When we were at anchor at Port Sandwich in Mallicollo, on the 23d of July, 1774, our people caught in the night two or three large reddish fish, which they immediately cleared of the garbage and scales, and cut the belly and gills open, with some of the fins, so that when I got up in the morning I suspected them to be a new kind of fish, as we were not able to describe or examine them in this mangled state: but as we hoped to stay many nights more in that place, I expected to obtain other specimens for examination; however we removed from that port the day after, without catching another fish of the same kind. When we were at New Caledonia, a sailor caught another fish of the same species during the night, and had unfortunately thrown away the garbage, scraped the scales, and cut away the gills and fins. The scarcity of fresh food made this last fish a desirable object, notwithstanding the eating of the former had caused very alarming symptoms. The sailor therefore salted the fish, and let it hang three or four days, and then eat it in company with his mess-mates, without feeling the least bad effects from this imprudent step. The fish had in its mangled state a similarity to the red gilthead (*Sparus Pagrus*, Linn.) which is the more probable, since Quiros observed that his whole ship's crews were poisoned at the same place by a fish, which he called *Pargo*.* The same night that the reddish fishes were caught at Mallicollo, several rock-fish, (*Labri*) an Indian sucking-fish, (*Echeneis Neucrates*) and a shark nine feet long were likewise caught and eaten that day,

---

* Dalrymple's *Collection of Voyages*, vol. i. p. 140, 141.

without causing any alarming symptoms. When we came to New-Caledonia, a native killed at the mouth of a fresh-water river on the reef, a new cartilaginous fish of the genus called by Linnaeus *Tetradon*. The Captain's Clerk bought it for the Captain, and after we had made a description and sketch of it, it was ordered the next day for dinner. My son as well as myself told Capt. Cook that we were of opinion the fish was not proper for food, as it belonged to a suspicious class; but the Captain was of opinion, that he had eaten the same kind of fish in the last voyage on the coast of New Holland, and this was sufficient to quiet our apprehensions. Whilst we were at supper, the servant shewed us the liver, which looked very tempting, for people who had been for some time deprived of fresh food; we had it therefore fried, but as it came after supper, I ate of it about the size of two half-crown pieces, and the Captain with my son only tasted it, each to the size of about half a crown piece. It had no bad taste and we expected to have a good dinner of the fish next day. In the morning about three o'clock I awoke from an uneasiness similar to that when the stomach is out of order on account of a surfeit. I sat upright in the bed and found my head giddy and swimming, I wanted to remove a chair from before the bed, which in my hands was as light as a feather, and I found I could not distinguish heavy things from light ones. When I began to walk, I reeled from one side of the cabin to the other. I felt in the stomach a heaviness and a burning, which extended all the length of the gullet, as if it had been excoriated, and my extremities were benumbed. I had a stool and in order to alleviate the stomach, endeavoured to void by vomiting its contents, but this caused such a burning all along from the mouth to the stomach, that I thought the whole to be wounded. I waked Dr. Sparrman and spoke to him about my situation; as he was separated only by a deal partition from the Captain's state room, Capt. Cook overheard our discourse, and tried to get up, when he found that he had the same symptoms which I experienced. I then waked my son, who was in the same situation. The Captain sent for our surgeon Mr. PATTON, who prescribed us plenty of warm water, in order to free the stomach of any remains of this dangerous diet, and then gave us some diaphoretics, and salts, which in a few days restored us to our former health; though the giddiness of the head, the numbness of our hands and feet, a constant chillness, and some few pains were not quite removed till after almost eight or ten days. A dog which had eaten the remainder of the fried liver, and a hog given me by an old man at Tanna, which had devoured the garbage of the fish, fell likewise very sick, and the latter died the next day. Several natives coming on board, saw the fish hanging, and gave us to understand by signs, that it was unwholsome food, for they pointed to their stomach, and showed that it caused pains there, and afterwards laid their hand to the cheek and ear, and made a motion of the head as if they were going to sleep. I feigned not to comprehend the meaning of these signs, and as if I believed they wanted the fish to eat, I ordered it to be given to them; but they shewed the most unequivocal signs of abhorrence, when it was offered to them.

The fishes eaten at Mallicollo, caused in the evening violent reachings, gripes and looseness, preceded by an uneasiness similar to that which I had felt; a violent head-ach and pain in the face, with a burning heat, followed immediately after this; and extended to the hands and legs. The pulse was by no means feverish or strong, as might have been expected from the great heat which every one felt, but was rather low and weak. About sixteen or eighteen persons who had eaten of the fish were all ill of this poison, and had more or less the same symptoms, to which we must add the same torpor in the extremities. The pains continued for several days in the stomach and in all the limbs, with the heat and also a giddiness, which would not suffer them to walk or hardly to stand. All along the throat they felt a pain equal to that of an excoriation in that part. In some few patients the salival glands were swelled, and discharged an extraordinary quantity of saliva, so that it run out of their mouths involuntarily. In a few a painful erection of the penis was observed: and some even found that their teeth were grown loose. When they recovered it was but slowly, and as often as they were exposed to cold, the pain and stiffness of the limbs returned, and upon the whole every evening the symptoms of restlessness, pain and heaviness were renewed, nay, after the expiration of a fortnight when they were quite free from pains and other symptoms, they found themselves chilly. The surgeon prescribed the same remedies, which we had taken by his direction. A tame Taheitean parroquet, which had eaten a very small morsel of the fish died in great agonies. All the dogs, which had been fed with the bones, fins and entrails of the fish, fell violently sick and continued so for a long while: one that had retired into a boat and was lying in some water became quite paralytic, and was ordered to be cast over-board to shorten his agonies: another dog equally sick, received from his master an infusion of tobacco by way of emetic, but he fell a sacrifice to the remedy. A hog which had eaten of the entrails, likewise died within 24 hours.

The circumstances here related seem to intimate, that the *Sparus Pagrus* or *Pargos* is not a poisonous fish, but only become noxious, when it has taken some dangerous food. The fish which were caught at Port Sandwich, together with the *Pagrus*, proved wholesome, which proves that their food differs from that of the *Pargos*. The *Tetrodon Sceleratus* alone seems to be poisonous of itself, since the natives of New Caledonia were acquainted with its noxious and deleterious quality; but if we again consider, that the *Tetrodon* caused the same symptoms as the *Pargos*, (only in an inferior degree, because we ate so very little of it) it is obvious, that the *Tetrodon* likewise must have received this deleterious quality from the nature of its food. I wish to have had it in my power to examine the entrails of all these fish, because I do not in the least doubt, but the examination of them would have immediately shewed the true cause of these symptoms; and as nothing occurs, which might have caused these effect, I suspect that these fish live chiefly upon blubbers, *(Medusae)* some of which we know to be of a very burning quality, when brought into contact with our skin, and probably would be capable of producing all the abovementioned symptoms if taken internally. It might be here objected, that if the blubbers are so noxious, how happens it that the fish eat them without being affected in the same manner as we were: but if we consider, that fish eat, without injury, even manchenil-apples *(Hippomane Mancinella)* which would kill a man; it becomes so much the more probable that fishes may live on a food, which to men is highly noxious. The natives, however, seem to be well acquainted with the poisonous quality of the fish: it would be adviseable therefore to enquire of them whether it may be eaten with safety, and they are every where good-natured enough to give fair warning when there is the least danger. This circumstance leads us to make the following remarks: the first is, that mankind ought to be considered as the members of one great family; therefore let us not despise any of them, though they be our inferiors in regard to many improvements and points of civilization; none of them is so despicable that he should not, in some one point or other, know more than the wisest man of the most polished nation. This knowledge may be easily obtained from them by friendliness, kindness, and gentleness; and if so bought it is cheaply obtained. The second observation points out the necessity of sending out men versed in science, and the knowledge of nature on all occasions to remote parts of the world, in order to investigate the powers and qualities of natural objects; and it is not enough to send them out, but they ought likewise to be encouraged in their laborious task, liberally supported and generously enabled to make such enquiries as may prevent their fellow creatures in future times from becoming sacrifices to their own ignorance.

Quibusdam & iis quidem non admodum indoctis, totum hoc displicet, philosophari.
Quidam autem id non tam reprehendunt, si remissius agatur: sed tantum studium, tamque
multam operam ponendam in eo non arbitrantur.
　M. Tullius Cicero. *De finibus bon. & malor.* lib. i. initio[10]

FINIS.

List of Subscribers

Rev. Dr. Adams, Master of Pembroke
    College, Oxford.
Wellbore Ellis Agar, Esq.
Agriculture Society, at Manchester.
Mr. William Allin, of Newark, Bookseller.
All Souls College Library, Oxford.
Mr. Alstroemer.
Mr. Thomas Armiger, Surgeon.
Alexander Aubert, Esq; F.R.S.
Rev. Dr. Bagot, Dean of C.C. Oxford.
Joseph Banks, Esq; F.R.S.
Rev. Dr. Barton, Warden of Merton
    College, Oxford.
T. Butterworth Bayley, Esq; F.R.S.
T. Beauclerck, Esq.
Count de Belgioioso.
Rich. Henry Alex. Bennet, Esq.
Rev. Mr. Beuzeville.
Mr. Birt, Hertford College, Oxford.
John Blanket, Esq.
R. Wilbraham Booth, Esq; F.R.S. 2 Copies.
Rev. Dr. Brown, Canon of C.C. and Prof.
    of Hebrew, Oxford.
Count de Bruhl.
Paul Jacob Bruns, M.A. Oxford.
Anthony Champion, Esq.
Rev. Mr. Eusebius Cleaver.
William Constable, Esq; F.R.S.
Thomas Cornewall, Esq.
Alexander Dalrymple, Esq; F.R.S.
Edward Delaval, Esq.
Sir Francis Drake, Bart.
Matthew Duane, Esq; F.R.S.

Rev. Mr. Ereleigh, M.A. Fell. of Oriel
    College, Oxford.
Exeter College Library, Oxford.
Thomas Falconer, Esq; Chester.
Signor Paolo Greppy, of Milano.
Dr. Heberden.
Rev. Mr. Hornsby, F.R.S. Prof. of
    Astronomy, Oxford.
Mr. William Hudson, F.R.S.
Rev. Mr. Hughes, Fel. of Jesus Col.
    Oxford.
John Hussey, Esq; Hertford College,
    Oxford, F.S.A.
Benjamin Hyatt. Esq.
Rev. Mr. Cyril Jackson, B.D.C.C.C.
    Oxford.
William Jackson, Esq; C.C.C. Oxford.
Rev. Dr. Jeffreys, Canon of C.C. Oxford.
Rev. Dr. Benjamin Kennicott, Canon of
    C.C. Oxford, F.R.S.
Edward Leeds, Esq.
Right Rev. Shute, Lord Bishop of Llandaff.
John Lloyd, Esq; F.R.S.
Right Rev. Robert, Lord Bishop of
    London, F.R.S.
Rev. Dr. Long, All Souls Coll. Oxford.
Rev. Mr. Lucas, M.A. Winchester Coll.
    Oxford.
Mr. Mainstone.
Samuel Martin, Esq.
Rev. Dr. Jeremiah Milles, Dean of Exeter.
Mrs. De Missy.
Dr. John Monro.

Paul Panton, Esq.

General Pascal Paoli, F.R.S.

John Peachey, Esq.

W. P. Perrin, Esq; F.R.S.

Joseph Plymley, Esq; Pembroke Coll. Oxford.

Mr. Daniel Prince, Bookseller, at Oxford, 7 Copies.

Sir John Pringle, Bart. Pres. R.S.

Rev. Mr. Proster, M.A. Fell. of Baliol Coll. Oxford.

Rev. Mr. Putman, F.R.S.

Rev. Mr. Richards, M.A. Fell. of Exeter Coll. Oxford

Mr. Riollay, M.A. Fell. of Hertford Coll. Oxford.

Mr. Roide, C.C.C. Oxford.

Right Hon. Earl of Shelburne.

Henry Allured Shore, Esq; Hertford Coll. Ox.

——— Shuttleworth, Esq; F.R.S.

Rev. Dr. Smallwell, Canon of C.C. Oxford.

Philip Stephens, Esq; Sec. of the Admiralty.

Rev. Mr. Stinton, M.A. Fell. of Exeter. Coll. Oxford.

Rev. Dr. Stonehouse, Hadley, in Berks.

Rev. Mr. Tilson.

Thomas Tyrwhitt, Esq.

Benjamin Vaughan, Esq.

William Vaughan, Esq.

Warrington Academy, Library.

Rev. Dr. Wheeler, Regius Prof. of Divinity, and Canon of C.C. Oxford.

Rev. Mr. White, Laudian Prof. of Arabic, Oxford.

Thomas White, Esq; F.R.S.

Rev. Mr. Williams.

Rev. Mr. Winstanley, M.A. Fell. of Hertford C. Oxford.

Edward Wynne, Esq.

APPENDIXES

Appendix I: Forster's Pacific Placenames

Forster	Modern/Indigenous
SOCIETY ISLANDS	
Taheitee, Otaheite[1]	Tahiti
Taha	Tahaa
Bolabola, Borabora	Bora Bora
Tiarraboo, Tearraboo	Tiarapu
Raietea, Ulietea	Raiatea
Wharre Harbour	Fare (Huahine)
TONGAN ISLANDS	
Eaoowhe, Middleburgh	Eua
Tonga-Tabboo, Amsterdam	Tongatapu
Namocka, Rotterdam	Nomuka
O Ghao	Kao
Tofooa	Tofua
VANUATU (NEW HEBRIDES)	
Ambrrym	Ambrym
Annatom	Aneityum
Apee	Epi
Aurora	Maewo
Espiritu Santo	Espiritu Santo
Immer	Aniwa
Irromanga, Erromango	Erromanga
Irronan	West Futuna
Isle of Lepers	Ambae (formerly Aoba)
Mallicollo	Malekula, Malakula
Pa-oom	Paama
Sandwich Island	Efate
Tanna	Tanna

---

[1] Cook voyage participants among other early visitors frequently prefixed the article O to names; hence *Omai* is properly *Mai*, *Otaheite* properly *Tahiti*, and so on.

Three-Hills Isle	Mai
Whitsuntide	Pentecost

MARQUESAS

Heevaroa, Dominica	Hiva Oa
Onateyo, Saint Pedro	Motane
Waitahu, Saint Christina	Vaitahu[2] (Tahuata)

OTHERS

New Caledonia	New Caledonia, Kanaky
New Holland	Australia
Savage Island	Niue
Turtle Island	Vatoa
Waihu[3]	Easter Island, Rapanui

[2] Vaitahu is the name of a bay and valley, not the whole island.
[3] Waihu is the name of a cove, not the whole island.

Appendix II: Forster's Polynesian Linguistics

When the British Admiralty appointed Reinhold Forster to replace Joseph Banks as naturalist on Cook's second voyage to the Pacific, they got more than they had bargained for. Reinhold Forster, the "tactless philosopher" as Michael Hoare called him, was an all-around scholar, the eighteenth-century German "Universalgelehrte," equally as well versed in philosophy, theology, and ethnography as in geography, botany, and zoology. Furthermore, he knew foreign languages, modern and classical ones, altogether seventeen, among them Coptic, which he had studied in depth. Of all the early scientists who had accompanied exploring expeditions to the Pacific, Reinhold Forster had the best academic qualifications to quickly acquire communication skills in the various native tongues and to collect linguistic data that were more reliable than the impressionistic and naive descriptions that untrained amateurs had provided so far.

While Forster's contributions to the natural sciences have been the focus of attention, either critical or laudatory, from the day the expedition returned to England, his linguistic research remained practically unknown. George Forster's account of the second voyage, published in 1777, included not a single word list of a Pacific language. This is surprising, as it was an established practice to add to the accounts of voyages word lists of the exotic languages one had encountered. Bougainville had done so, and so had Hawkesworth, who edited the journal of Cook's first voyage. *Observations* does include a table of South Sea and Pacific Rim languages, basically for comparative purposes. It contains the numbers 1 through 10 and thirty-six basic vocabulary items, such as body parts.

Forster carried out linguistic fieldwork in New Zealand, Easter Island, Vanuatu, the Marquesas, and Tonga, but the most extensive research was done in the Society Islands. The linguistic data and his comments on the Pacific languages were never published, but Forster frequently made use of his language studies in his numerous publications on the Pacific by quoting from the vocabularies the native names of plants, trees, animals, fishes, and so on. When he died in 1798, the Royal Prussian Library in Berlin purchased Forster's private book collection of about seven thousand volumes. Among them were three manuscripts containing linguistic material collected on Cook's second voyage.

Forster's task to learn the Tahitian language had been greatly facilitated by information available from the first voyage. For the Society Island language Cook had given him a word list compiled by Monkhouse, surgeon on the *Endeavour*. During the long months at sea en route to Tahiti, Forster had the chance to study this vocabulary thoroughly. It seems that he appreciated Monkhouse's efforts very highly, not only because the data were based on knowledgeable informants, "good authorities," as he put it, but also because the author took "pains to express the sounds of the Otaheitee Language as accurately, as can be done with English letters."[1]

Apart from Monkhouse's vocabulary, Forster had other sources at his disposal. There was Bougainville's Tahitian word list, which contained about six hundred words. Forster did not have a high opinion of Bougainville's linguistic achievements, and pointed out that the French navigator had spent only a very short time in Tahiti (eleven days). Furthermore, the Polynesian words had been transcribed in French orthography and elicited from an informant, Aotooroo, who in Forster's opinion could not be relied on, as he had a "vicious pronunciation."

Forster was equally suspicious of a word list that had appeared in the first printed account of Cook's voyage published by an anonymous author[2] in 1771 (not in 1772 as stated by Forster). He considered it "excessively ill spelt" with "many r's inserted where none were wanted." Another vocabulary of the Tahitian language had been given to him by Isaac Smith, Captain Cook's cousin, who was a midshipman on the first voyage and served as a master's mate on the *Resolution*. According to Forster, this vocabulary was not very different from the one published in the anonymous account of the first voyage.

Some linguistic information Forster gleaned viva voce aboard ship from Samuel Gibson, a corporal of the marines. Gibson had the reputation of having acquired a better knowledge of Tahitian than any other European.[3] It appears that he had learned the language from his Tahitian girlfriend when the *Endeavour* first visited Tahiti.[4] Captain Cook used to take him along on excursions as an interpreter.[5] Forster was doubtful about Gibson's language proficiency, saying that he had "forgotten many words, others he mistook, & several he pronounced wrong." Gibson was probably competent enough to communicate about simple matters, but on one occasion when, in his presence, Cook asked a Tahitian informant questions about human sacrifices, a topic that required a wider knowledge of language, Gibson failed to understand what was being said.[6]

Forster's main informant in language matters was a young man from Bora Bora by the name of Mahaine or Oe-diddee. Forster met him in Raiatea. Mahaine, a relative of Opunee, the great chief of Bora Bora, had expressed the intention to go to England on the *Resolution*. Cook decided to take him along, thinking that Mahaine might be useful as an interpreter when making landfalls on other islands in the Pacific. Mahaine, then seventeen or eighteen years old, joined the *Resolution* on 17 September 1773. He accompanied Cook on his visits to Tonga, New Zealand, Easter Island, and the Marquesas. His ability to communicate with the native population of these islands greatly facilitated the task of the explorers. However, when the *Resolution* returned to Raiatea on 4 June 1774, Mahaine, much to the regret of the Forsters, had second thoughts about visiting England and decided to stay behind.

During the nine months' cruise through the South Pacific, Forster revised with Maheine the word lists he had obtained from the first voyage and his own collection of Tahitian words, to which he added new words elicited from Maheine. It should be mentioned that the language of Bora Bora, although very similar to Tahitian in its phonology, morphology, and syntactic structure, cannot be assumed to have had exactly the same word inventory, although today the lexical differences have been leveled out. Occasionally Forster comments on a lexical variation—for example, in the case of taio[7] 'friend': Mahaine says the word taio is not known in Bora Bora.

The manuscript containing the various vocabularies of the South Sea languages is preceded by some general observations about the internal relationship of the Pacific languages and their affinity with Malay. Forster also deals with the problems of transcribing hitherto unknown languages, using Tahitian as an example. He was well aware that English orthography was not ideally suited for transcription, especially as far as the vowel sounds are concerned, as one letter can stand for more than one sound (e.g., a in master [a], in care [e], and in late [ei]). The use of the English spelling system was definitely not Forster's preferred option as we will see in the following; but as he was in the service of the British crown, it was of course expected that his linguistic data should make sense to someone who was used to "sounding letters" the English way. Also, as Forster was using Monkhouse's data as the groundwork of his collection, it would have made little sense to abandon the established model of transcription altogether. So rather than devising a new transcription system or defining the letters of the alphabet in terms of the sound values they have in French or German, languages whose orthographies are more regular and consistent, Forster, nolens volens adopted the English notation. However, he introduced a number of diacritic signs to disambiguate some letters and to refine the transcription. He drew up rules that uniquely define the phonetic value of each letter or combination of letters. To illustrate the sound values he gave examples of English words in which the particular letter is used (e.g., "a without any addition is to be pronounced as in the English words came, able, disable").

Tahitian has a five-vowel system consisting of the high vowels i and u, the mid vowels e and o, and the low vowel a. Vowel length is phonemic—that is, the difference between long and short vowels is used to distinguish words. In modern Tahitian orthography, the phonemic difference between short and long vowels is marked by a macron: parau 'to speak' vs. pārau [pa:rau] 'mother-of-pearl'; tumu 'origin' vs. tūmū [tu:mu:] 'blunt,' etc.

The long vowels are so-called pure vowels without an offglide. They are realized very much like the respective Italian vowels. Polynesian languages have a relatively small sound inventory, and the kinds of sounds that occur were not too difficult to identify and mimic for someone like Forster, who was familiar with more than a dozen languages. The phonotactic structure is also simple. Tahitian does not have any consonant clusters, and the only syllables allowed are open ones, which means that only two basic syllable types occur: CV, and V (C = consonant, V = vowel [monophthong or diphthong]).

Because of the small number of consonants and the limited phonotactic possibilities, many words contain sequences of two or more vowels or consist entirely of vowels. This fact was observed and commented on by many of the early explorers. Forster continues the tradition when he states that Tahitian is a difficult language for Europeans to learn, "because the transposition of a few Vowels, the change of the Accent, & the addition of another Vowel, entirely alter the signification of Words."[8]

The Tahitian consonant system is composed of a relatively small number of phonemes. It is characterized by the absence of a voiced-voiceless distinction in the stop series, the absence of sibilants, and the absence of sounds made at the velar point of articulation.

stops	p	t	ʔ
fricatives	f,v		h
nasals	m	n	
liquids		r	

/p/ and /t/ are realized as nonaspirated stops. The English visitors had difficulties recognizing the nature of the bilabial and alveolar stops. /p/ is rendered sometimes by *p*, sometimes by *b*, and /t/ likewise by *t* and *d*. Forster had the same problem. On the other hand, Bougainville and the Spanish missionaries consistently transcribe *p* and *t*. Being native speakers of a Romance language, they had no difficulty in identifying the nonaspirated Tahitian stops. Decades later the London Missionary Society missionaries realized that the p/b, t/d distinctions were linguistically irrelevant in Tahitian and introduced the standardized spellings *p* (for *p* and *b*) and *t* (for *t* and *d*). The Polynesian glottal stop ʔ proved to be a major problem for all European visitors.[9] Although this sound occurs in English and German, it has no contrastive function, and linguistically untrained native speakers are normally not aware of its existence.

Forster did not identify the glottal stop as a distinctive sound unit in its own right either, but he noticed some unusual auditory qualities, which he associated with the realization of certain vowels. Unfortunately, the description he provides is somewhat vague and only allows us to speculate whether he is trying to describe a glottal stop. He writes: "*a* with a circumflex below, is to be pronounced long & and with a guttural sound [this could refer to a glottal stop], something through the Nose or with a Rhinismus" (this does not apply to a glottal stop at all). His occasional use of a hyphen to separate syllables includes cases where the following syllable starts with a glottal stop: for example, pa-atta *pa'ata* 'dance'; mara-ai *mara'ai* 'east'. This notation gives the impression that he recognized the glottal break; however, the overwhelming number of words in which he represents two identical vowels separated by a glottal stop by a simple vowel proves that he had no clear understanding of the articulatory characteristics of this sound at all (e.g., tata *ta'ata* 'man'; papa *papa'a* 'crab'; mora *mo'ora* 'duck'; tee *ti'i* 'image'; and so on).

/ f /

The Tahitian /f/ is realized as [f] or [ɸ]. The bilabial fricative is commonly encountered after *o* and *u*. At the time of European contact, the bilabial pronunciation must have been predominant in all phonetic environments as we can gather from the *wh* transcription used by the English explorers and also by Forster (e.g., whattoo *fatu* 'owner'; owha *ofe* 'fish'; atoowha *tufa* 'to distribute'; and so on). English *wh* was pronounced as a fortis voiceless labio-velar fricative [hw], for example in *whine* [hwain] as opposed to *wine* [wain], a distinction still made in careful conservative speech, is a fairly good approximation of a bilabial voiceless fricative.

In some Tahitian words, /f/ has changed to /h/; given the articulatory parameters of /f/ realizations, this change is not difficult to explain. The sound change never gathered enough momentum to affect all lexical items. It was, however, well under way at the time of European contact as evidenced by occasional *h*-transcriptions from Forster's word list: honnoo *fonu* 'turtle'; hawarre *ha'avare* (from an earlier fa'avare) 'lie, deception'.

/v/

Like its voiceless counterpart, the phoneme /v/ can be realized as a labiodental fricative [v] and as a bilabial fricative [β]. A third variant with secondary velar articulation [w] also exists in Tahitian. Forster generally transcribes Tahitian *v* as *w* and occasionally as *v*. As no special mention regarding the pronunciation of *w* or *v* is made in his list of transcriptions, we can assume that he assigned to them the phonetic value they have in English (i.e., that he used *v* for voiced labiodental and *w* for voiced bilabial fricatives). No distribution pattern based on the segmental environment or phonotactic position can be established for *v* and *w* from Forster's data (e.g., weevo *vivo* 'flute'; owawa *vava* 'dumb'; ta-eeva *taiva* 'to cheat'; waha *vaha* 'to carry').

/r/

Tahitian /r/ is phonetically an apical trill similar to the rolled *r* in Scottish or in Italian, but much shorter (i.e. consisting of fewer taps of the apex). Forster makes no reference to this very important feature of Tahitian /r/; on the contrary, he lists it as one of the sounds that "are in general to be pronounced as in English." A variant of the trilled *r* is the *r* pronounced with a single tap. It sounds very much like the allegro realization of an intervocalic -d- in American English. There are quite a few cases where Forster transcribes *d* where the alveolar stop represents an underlying /r/ (e.g., porodi *porori* 'hungry'; dahy *rahai* [popular pronunciation of *rahi* 'big']; etoro-eida *toroire* 'Mimosa peregrina'; aeda *ira* 'fleshmark').

/h/

Tahitian /h/ is pronounced like *h* in English. If preceded by a back vowel, *u* or *o*, it retains the vowel's lip rounding and becomes labialized. Between a preceding *i* and a following *o* it is realized as a voiceless palatal fricative. Forster distinguishes a simple *h* and an *h* "strongly pronounced like a double *hh* or like in the Hebrew". This *h* he marks with a stroke at the top. The distribution of his ordinary and "strongly pronounced" *h* doesn't follow any pattern that would allow us to link them to phonological conditioning; it's very likely a case of over-differentiation.

In spoken Tahitian, *h* can trigger a very interesting phonological process if it is preceded by a short stressed vowel. This process, which is best described as translaryngeal vowel copying, consists of moving the vowel preceding *h* to a position immediately following *h* while retaining a copy of it in the original position. The shifted vowel retains the stress—that is, the word stress changes from the penultimate to the ultimate syllable—and forms a new vowel sequence or a diphthong with the vowel in word final position (e.g., *ráhi* > *rahái* 'big'; *réhu* > *rehéu* 'ashes'). If the final vowel has the same quality as the shifted one, vowel copying results in a long vowel (e.g., *páha* > *pahā* 'perhaps').

Here are some examples from Forster's word list showing that this phonological process was already operative at the time of European contact and included cases where the vowel preceding *h* was unstressed: awahy [vaháí] < *váhi* 'to open'; awahai [auaháí] < *auáhi* 'fire'; atahai [taháí] < *táhi* 'one'; eahai [aháí] < *áhi* 'sandalwood'; pahou [paháu] < *páhu* 'drum'.

Forster had difficulties with the auditory identification of *h*; he sometimes did not hear it all, or he transcribed *h* where none was called for. These errors would not be worth mentioning if not for the fact that Forster thought he was better than Bougainville, whom he had criticized for his inability to identify *h*. Examples from Forster's word list include madooa-owy for *metua hoovai* 'parent-in-law'; toee for *tohi* 'cut with an axe'; e-mohoo for *mo'u* 'Cyperus alatus'; oomaraha *ume re'a* 'yellow fish'; tooha for *tua* 'loin'; hopea for *'ope'a* 'swallow'; and so forth.

Both Forsters were quite confident that they were highly qualified and capable of carrying out research on the languages in the Pacific. In fact, from their criticism of English and French linguists, one must conclude that they considered themselves superior to their colleagues because of their German language background. Criticizing the English spelling of "Tupia" as found in Hawkesworth, George Forster argues in *Reise um die Welt* that his spelling ("Tupaya") is far more correct because it has been devised by him, a native speaker of German. He goes on to say that Germans not only have a greater disposition for learning foreign languages, but are also incomparably more accurate in pronouncing and spelling foreign words.

The older Forster shared his son's opinion. According to him the English write foreign names in an arbitrary way, leaving people in doubt regarding what the true pronunciation of the word should be.[10] The French were unsuitable as field workers because of their problems with the *h* sound. "The French seldom pronounce the h, though it be sometimes written in their language. Mr Bougainville therefore entirely omitted the h in his Vocabulary, & never took notice of any Gutturals."

In his German publications, such as his translation of Dixon's *Voyage*, Forster modified the transcription of Polynesian words by spelling them according to the rules of German orthography, and for instance replaced the English spelling of the names of the Hawaiian islands by what he considered a less ambiguous German version ("Owaihie" instead of "Owhyhee").[11]

Oceanic Words in Observations

Forster's transcription is followed by the corresponding entry of John Davies' dictionary of 1851, which standardized the Tahitian orthography. In some instances no corresponding word can be found in Davies, possibly because of a lacuna in his collection or because he deliberately omitted items in cases where a term had become obsolete or was considered improper and offensive. The omitted words are also missing from Jaussen's dictionary of 1861. The Tahitian lexicon has undergone rapid changes. About two-thirds of the words recorded in nineteenth-century dictionaries are no longer known to the present language community. For words still in use today we have adopted the modern orthography based on Y. Lemaître's dictionary, which marks vowel length by a macron and represents the glottal stop by an apostrophe.

Forster	Standard orthography	English
CAROLINES		
balibago	?	tree (probably *Ficus* sp.)
tamoles	?	chief
tangeurifaifil	?	complaint of women
EASTER ISLAND		
areckee	ariki	principal chief
hareekeè	ariki	principal chief
MALEKULA		
aleeghee	ariki	principal chief
areekee	ariki	principal chief
MARQUESAS		
a-ka-hai	haka'iki	chief
TAHITI		
a-hèa	fa	four
a-hèeva	iva	nine
a-hìddoo	hitu	seven
a-hòno	ono	six
à hoo	hū	fart
a-hoòdoo	hutu	*Barringtonia speciosa*
a-hòoroo	ahuru	ten
a-oo-noonoo	a unu unu	name of a month
a-rèema	rima	five
a-roòa	rua	two
a-tahài-tàoo	tahi ta'au	twenty
a-tahài	tahi	one
a-tòroo	toru	three
a-wàrroo	varu	eight
ahèo	'ā'eho	reed
ahoù	'ahu	garment
ahou-aiboo	'ahu ipu	type of garment
ahou-roòpe	'ahu rupe	type of garment
a hòw	'ahu	garment

Forster	Standard orthography	English
ai	'ai	to eat
àiro	'aero	tail of quadrupeds, birds, and rays
aìya	'eiā	to steal
àiya	'eiā	thief, to steal
àma	ama'a	branch
ammee-àmma-hoy	hamiama ho'i	day of the moon cycle
ammee-àmma	hamiama	day of the moon cycle
amòu	mō'ū	generic term for *Cyperaceae*
aòu	'ā'au	bowels
aoùta	'aute	*Morus papyrifera*
apà	apa'a	thick cloth
àpe	'ape	kape (*Arum costatum*)
arahoà-tattàou	'ārahu tatau	tatoo color
aree n'O-parre	ari'i no Pare	principal chief of Pare
aree-rahai	ari'i rahi	paramount chief
aree	ari'i	chief
arees	ari'i	chief
aroòa	rua	two
arreeoy	arioi	Arioi
atòroo	toru	three
àvai	'āvae	foot
avàree	?	tatoo on buttocks
àwa	eve	the secundines of a beast
àwa	'ava	kawa (*Piper methysticum*)
awhoù	fau	sort of headdress
dooe-dooaï	?	insult (not attested elsewhere)
eä	a'a	root
e-atoòree	aturi	kind of purslane (*Portulaca lutea*)
e-avèe	vi	*Spondias pomifera*
e-hàya	'ahi'a	*Eugenia malaccensis* (the native red apple)
e-hoòdoo	hutu	*Barringtonia speciosa*

Forster	Standard orthography	English
e-màrra	mara	*Nauclea orientalis*
e-mèero, e-meero	miro	*Hibiscus punctatus, H. populneus*
e-narè	nahe	*Pteris grandifolia*
e-nòno	nono	*Morinda citrifolia*
e-oà	o'a	ribs of a timber boat
e-oomàrro	'umara	sweet potato
E-oòma	ume	surgeonfish (*Acanthuridae* sp.)
e-oòwhe	ufi	yam
e-oure	ure	penis
e-pàe, e-pae	pae	rough skin
e-pae-no-pèpe	pae no Pepe	Pepe's disease
e-pirre	pi(piri)	covetous, niggardly
e-poòa	pua	*Solanum repandum*
e-poorhòa	pura	mat made of *Hibiscus tiliaceus*
e-ra-où	rā'au	stem, tree, wood
E-tào-werro-eiya	tao vero i'a	fish-spearing harpoon
E-teèhee	ti'i	Tiki
e-teèra	tira	mast
e-tòa	toa	*Casuarina equisetifolia*
e-toù	tou	*Cordia sebestena*
e-vàinoo	vaianu	*Adenostemma viscosum*
e-vanne	vane	fine mat
e-vavài	vavai	cotton (*Gossypium religiosum*)
e-wàha	va'a	canoe
e-wài	vai	water
e-whára	fara	pandanus
e-wharòu	fara	mat made of pandanus
e-whatevà	fatea	female of roa plant (*Pipturus argenteus*)
e-whetoo-mahóo	fetu mahu	stars forming
e-whettoo-owhàa	fetu ōfa'a	belt of Orion (not attested elsewhere)
e-whettoo-wèrra	fetu verovero	twinkling star
Eàhai	a'ahi	albacore (*Thunnus* sp.)
eài	ai	to copulate
eaoùwa	aua	fig tree species
eatoòa no pretànee	atua no Peretani	God of Britain

Forster	Standard orthography	English
eatoòa-rahài	atua rahi	Principal God
eeterre	tere	to slide, move along, swim (fish)
ehoe-whateerra	hoe fa'atere	steering oar
ehòra	hora	*Galega piscidia* (poisonous plant used for fishing)
eipa	eipa	no, not
eìya, eiyà	i'a	fish
eìya	'ie	sail
eloù	rau	leaf
Emòhoo	mō'ū	*Cyperus* (generic term for *Cyperus* sp.)
eneèa-rohitee	niuroahiti	*Leucas decemdentata*
enoona-noona	nuna nuna	*Boerhavia procumbens*
enòu	nau	*Lepidium piscidium*
eoo	u	breast
eoòwee-tatattaòu	'ohe tatau	tattooing instrument
eòree	'ori	to dance, to shake
epài	pa'e	anything to put under to support the joists under a floor, sill, threshold, etc.
epào	pao	shooting star
epatèa	patea	breadfruit species
epeèpee	pipi	bean (*Phaseolus amoenus*)
epìree-pìrree	piripiri	spurge
epò-oo	pou	post
erà-oo-opò	rā 'ua hopo	time after sunset
erà-t-oo awatèa	rā 'ua avatea	time when the sun is in the meridian
erà-t-oo wèrra	rā 'ua vera	time when the sun gets hot
erà-woro	rauoro	pandanus leaf
erà	rā	sun
eràooào	rā 'ua ao	sunrise
Eroòa	roa	a small tree, the bark of which is used like hemp for cordage, nets
etèe	ti	*Dracaena terminalis*

Forster	Standard orthography	English
etoòboo	tupu	name of a plant
etoòtee	tuti'i	sort of scaffold on which the warriors stood in a seafight
etoù	tou	*Cordia sebestena*
evee, evèe	vī	*Spondias pomifera*
ewha-àïo	faaio	red and white cloth
ewhàra, ewharra	fara	pandanus
goomalla	'umara	sweet potato
ha-òtta	hoata	day of the moon cycle
hanna-mài	hanna mai	come here
harre-mài	haere mai	come here
hea-bìddee	apiti	a couple
heapà	hapaa	yellow cloth
heèva he-oòra	hiva hura	dance (hula)
hèva	heva	mourning garment
hoa	hoa	friend, attendant of a chief
hoboo	hopuu	fine native cloth, very white
hoee-rohiddee	hirohiti	day of the moon cycle
hohòra	hohora	mat
hoòa-hoùa	huahua	kidney; modern meaning is vulva, testicles
hoòerro	huero	seeds of trees and plants
hoòna	huna	day of the moon cycle
hoopà, hoopa	hupi	part of a mourner's headdress
hooree-àma	?	name of a month (not attested elsewhere)
hooree-erre-èrre	?	name of a month (not attested elsewhere)
irrepòu	rapa'au	medicine
ma-hèa	ma fa	fourteen
ma-hèeva	ma iva	nineteen
ma-hìddoo	ma hitu	seventeen
ma-hòno	ma ono	sixteen
ma-reèma	ma rima	fifteen
ma-ròoa	ma rua	twelve

Forster	Standard orthography	English
ma-tahài	ma tahi	eleven
ma-tòroo	ma toru	thirteen
ma-wàroo	ma varu	eighteen
mahàrroo	maharu	day of the moon cycle
mahèe	mahi	breadfruit paste
mahìdoo	maitu	day of the moon cycle
maira	maire	breadfruit species
malama	marama	month
manahoune	manahune	commoner
maraì	mara'i	day of the moon cycle
marai	marae	marae, place for worship
màrama-màtte	marama mate	the moon is dead
marama	marama	month
màrama	marama	moon
màro	maro	piece of cloth worn by men instead of breeches
matàree	matari'i	the Pleiades
matìttee	matiti	pendant
màtte-màrama	mate marama	day of the moon cycle
màttee, mattèe, matteè	mati	*Ficus tinctoria*
mattoù	matau	fishing hook
meera	?	law, regulation
moë-moë	moe moe	*Phyllanthus* sp.
moèya	moe'a	strong mat to sleep on
moorehà	muri 'aha	name of a month
moyhò	moiho	piece of twisted cloth oiled for a torch
na-ta-heèa	natauihe	name of a star
naoù-naoù	?	kind of belt
neenànno	nīnano	flower of the *Pandanus odoratissimus*
ninèva	neneva	insane
oboòboo	opupu	bladder
o-hàtta	hoata	day of the moon cycle
o-hoòtoo	hutu	heart
o-porore-o-moòa	paroro mua	name of a month
o-porore-o-moòree	paroro muri	name of a month
o-te-àree	te'eri	name of a month

Forster	Standard orthography	English
o-te-taì	te taʻi	name of a month
oào	oʻoao	*Daphne foetida*
oetai yàow	ʻua tae ao	time between midnight and daybreak
oohee-eìya	hiaʻia	name of a month
ohòdoo	hotu	day of the moon cycle
ohoòa	huʻa	day of the moon cycle
oìyo	ʻoio	seabird (*Anous stolidus*)
òmee	ʻōmiʻi	head of animals, especially fish
omoòddoo	mutu	day of the moon cycle
òne-òne	?	shake hips in a rotary motion
ònee	oni	the male of beasts, birds, insects, fish
ooaheihei	ua hihi	time before sunset
oomànnoo	ʻua mano	often
oopèa	ʻupeʻa	seine
oòpo	upoʻo	head
oòra	ʻura	red feathers
ooree	ʻurī	dog
ooroo, oòroo	ʻuru	breadfruit
ootataheìta	ʻua tatahiata	daybreak
ootoo-ròa	ʻutu roa	wry mouth
opoo-orahài	ʻopu rahi	stomach
òra	oraʻa	brown native cloth
oràboo	ōrapu	day of the moon cycle
oro-mòoa	roʻō mua	day of the moon cycle
oro-mòoree	roʻō muri	day of the moon cycle
oròe	ʻōroe	sheath of coconut
ororo-hàddee	ʻoreʻore fati	day of the moon cycle
ororo-ròtto	ʻoreʻore roto	day of the moon cycle
ororo-tài	ʻoreʻore tahi	day of the moon cycle
orre-òrre-hòy	ʻoreʻore hoʻi	day of the moon cycle
orre-òrre	ʻoreʻore	day of the moon cycle
òrro-òrro	ʻoroʻoro	ornament of feathers
otoo-rahai-pò	tuʻi raʻa pō	midnight
otoòroo	turu	day of the moon cycle
òwha	ufa	female of beasts, birds, insects, fish
owhòddoo	hotu	day of the moon cycle

Forster	Standard orthography	English
pa boòa	pā pua'a	pig enclosure
pa-àta	paata	to excite merriment or laughter
Pa-oòroo	pa uru	season of the year (when breadfruit is plentiful)
pa-oòto	pautu	part of mourner's dress
pa-ootoo	pautu	part of mourner's dress
pa-ràe, paràe	parae	headpiece of mourning dress
pa-teèa	pātia	fence of upright sticks; fork
paheè	pahī	ship
paheè-no-pèpe	pahī no Pepe	Pepe's ship
para-parou	paraparau	to converse
paràïa	para'ia	liver of a beast
parèoo	pāreu	loincloth worn by women
parooroo	pāruru	side panel of a native house
paroovài	paruai	calico, cloth
paroù-no-te-òboo	parau no te 'opu	words from the belly
pateèa	patia	fence of upright sticks; fork
patòa	pātoa	*Oxalis corniculata*
pàyho	paeho	a sword set with shark's teeth
peea	pia	*Tacca pinnatifida*
peeràra	pirara	bonito (*Scomber pelamys*)
pehai	pehe	couplet, song
piperriee	pipiri	niggardly
pipìrree	pipiri	name of a month
pìrree	piri	to adhere, to stick to a thing
pìree-pìree	piripiri	*Urena lobata*
pòa-arahoù	porahu	head of a beast
pohoòa	pōhue	generic term for *Convolvulaceae*
pooroù, pooròu	purau	*Hibiscus tiliaceus*

Forster	Standard orthography	English
poowhìree, poowhirree	puhiri	brown native cloth
pow-ohoòre	pou'ōhure	rectum
ra-òu-hàddee	ara'au fati	day of the moon cycle
ra-òu-hòy	ara'au ho'i	day of the moon cycle
ra-òu	ara'au	day of the moon cycle
ràtta	rata	*Inocarpus edulis*
reèma	rima	five
ròa	roa	great
roro	roro	brains
ròtto	roto	day of the moon cycle
t-èiya	te 'ie	sail; in *Observations*, Milky Way
t-erà-whatteà	ra avatea	meridian
ta-òmee	taumi	breastplate
ta-oòpo	tāupo'o	headdress
tahài	tahi	day of the moon cycle
tahata pirree-pirre	ta'ata piripiri	niggardly man
tahata tàïva	ta'ata tāiva	cheat
tàhata-oowhoroa	ta'ata fa'ahōro'a	generous man
tàhata-orrèro	ta'ata orero	orator
tahata-peepèeree	ta'ata pipiri	niggardly man
tahéäi	taehae	savage man
tahìnnoo	tahinu	*Tournefortia sericea*
Tahouva-mai	tahu'a mai	native doctor, healer
tahoùwa	tahu'a	priest (pre-contact religion)
tamànnoouu, tamànoo, tamànnoo	tāmanu	*Calophyllum inophyllum*
tamatèa	tamatea	day of the moon cycle
tàne	tane	husband, man
tàne	tane	day of the moon cycle
tàoo	tau	season
tàowa	ta'a'oa	name of a month
tarro	taro	taro
tarròa-hàddie	ta'āroa-fati	day of the moon cycle
tarròa-ròtto	ta'āroa-roto	day of the moon cycle
tarròa-tàhai	ta'āroa-tahi	day of the moon cycle
tatàe	compound of tā	tattooing instrument
tataheìta	tatahiata	place where the sun rises

Forster	Standard orthography	English
tattàra	tatara	breadfruit species
ta-whettoo-ròa	te fetu roa	big star
taya-hòboo	?	place for dead tautaus (heaven)
te-pevaye	piavai	case covering banana blossom
te-roòa-te-rai	ta'urua te ra'i	heaven (pre-contact religion)
te-whàrre	fare	house
te-whàrre-potto	fare poto	round house
tewhàrre tàrra	fare tara	long house
te-wharre no te orometoòa	fare no te 'orometua	house of malevolent ghosts
t'eài-morodèe	te ai moro iti	native dance (obscene; ai = intercourse)
teàrre	tiare	flower
teèhee	ti'i	image of a spirit, Tiki
teèpoota	tīputa	name of a garment
tettè	'atete	tinkle, rattle
tevèh	teve	*Dracontium polyphyllum*
tirra-tane	taratane	married woman
tirrèo	tireo	day of the moon cycle
tirrohìddee	tireohiti	day of the moon cycle
toa	toa	*Casuarina equisetifolia*
toà	to'a	South
toa-hoùwa	to'ahua	fat lining the ribs of animals
too-àha	tua'a	lewd, shameless, profane
too-àrroo	tuaru	ridgebeam
too-eroù	to'erau	North
too-erroo	tuoro	native cloth
toòmoo	tumu	trunk of a tree
toopapou	tūpāpa'u	spirit of the dead
toote-oopa	tūtae 'u'upa	*Loranthus* sp.
tooto-òroo	tuturu	post, prop for support
tootoòe	tutu'i	*Aleurites triloba*
topa-t-erà	topa te rā	place where the sun sets
toto-hoòwa	tatau hua	tattoo pattern
toumàrro	?	black tattoo (not documented elsewhere)

Forster	Standard orthography	English
toùna	taona	malediction
touroòa	ta'urua	Venus (star)
touroòa	ta'urua	name of a public feast
touroòa-t'erài	ta'urua te ra'i	heaven (pre-contact religion)
toutou, towtow	tautau teu	attendant on a chief
tupapòu	tūpāpa'u	spirit of the dead
vae-ahou	fa'ahu	name of a month
veheina-poowa	?	young female showing the marks of puberty (not attested elsewhere)
veheìne	vahine	woman
veheine wha-atùree	vahine fa'aturi	prostitute
vìttee-vìttee	vitiviti	fishing hook
warehoo	varehu	name of a month
whaddee, whàddee	fati	day of the moon cycle
whaòtee	?	day of the moon cycle
whatta	fata	scaffold for any purpose
whennua	fenua	land
whenua-oora	fenua 'ura	land of the red feathers
wòrriddee	'ua riri	angry
woùra	'ua ora	alive
yuree	'āuri	iron
TANNESE		
doogoos	tukwus	hot spring
pahà-bìttaf	pahapitov	black axe
pahà-bushan	paha kusan (or "pusan")	shell axe
TONGA		
affayetoòca	fa'itoka	burying place
ataha	taha	one
eatoòca	'atua	god
ghooree	kulī	dog

Forster	Standard orthography	English
latoo	latu	paramount chief
mòleea	moli	orange
tee-ghooree	kulī	dog
teèghee	tiki	statue
ti-curi	kulī	dog

Notes

Abbreviations

Beaglehole	*The Journals of Captain James Cook on his Voyages of Discovery*, ed. J. C. Beaglehole. Cambridge, 1955–1967 (vol. 2: *The Voyage of the* Resolution *and* Adventure, *1772–1775*, unless otherwise indicated).
DSB	*Dictionary of Scientific Biography*
Hakluyt	works issued by the Hakluyt Society; o.s. = old series, 1847–1899; n.s. = new series, 1899–present.
Hoare	Michael E. Hoare, *The Tactless Philosopher: Johann Reinhold Forster (1729–1798)*. Melbourne, 1976.
Joppien and Smith	Rüdiger Joppien and Bernard Smith, *The Art of Captain Cook's Voyages*. New Haven, 1985–1987.
Journal	*The* Resolution *Journal of Johann Reinhold Forster, 1772–1775*, ed. Michael E. Hoare. London, 1982 [Hakluyt, n.s., 152–155].

Introduction

Johann Reinhold Forster and His *Observations*

1. This account is a brief one in part because there are good biographies and readily available, albeit generally unsympathetic, accounts of the post-voyage controversies (see n. 4 below). The most exhaustive biography is Michael Hoare's *The Tactless Philosopher: Johann Reinhold Forster (1729–1798)* (Melbourne, 1976), but for the period most relevant to the *Observations*, Joseph S. Gordon's detailed dissertation, "Reinhold and Georg Forster in England, 1766–1780" (Duke University, 1975), is also very useful. Other sources include Hoare's summary biography of Forster up to the time of the voyage, in the introduction to his edition of Forster's *Resolution Journal* (*Journal*, 1–54). On Forster's work in Russia before his move to England, see G. Steiner, "Johann Reinhold Forsters und Georg Forsters Beziehungen zu Rußland," in *Studien zur Geschichte der russichen Literatur des 18. Jahrhunderts*, ed. H. Grasshoff and U. Lehmann (Berlin, 1968), 2:245–311; and Roger Paul Bartlett, "J. R. Forster's Stay in Russia, 1765–1766: Diplomatic and Official Accounts," *Jahrbücher für Geschichte Osteuropas* 23 (1975): 489–495. The literature on George Forster is much more considerable and includes valuable editorial material in *Georg Forsters Werke*, gen. ed. Gerhard Steiner (Berlin, 1968–); of particular relevance here is Ruth Dawson, "Georg Forster's *Reise um die Welt*: A Travelogue in Its Eighteenth-Century Context" (Ph.D. diss., University of Michigan, 1973).

2. Properly Johann George Adam Forster. His work in German generally appeared under the name Georg Forster, and this is how he has been referred to by German and most other scholars. He was christened George, but this is less important than the fact that he was speaking and writing almost exclusively in English in the period relevant here, and this makes it seem more appropriate

to use the English form of his name. On the other hand, though the *Observations* and some of Forster senior's other English publications gave his name as John Reinold (as it was Jean Renaud in French), he is so generally referred to as Johann Reinhold that it would have seemed perverse to reinstitute the anglicized name. Though his use of this form may be interpreted as an effort to emphasize his family's British origins and diminish his foreignness within the London milieux, it should be recalled that in the period names were frequently translated on title pages (Bougainville, for instance, became Lewis de Bougainville for Forster's 1772 translation).

3. Detailed accounts of the voyage are numerous; that most salient here, for its discussion of Forster's findings in the various places visited, is Hoare's in his "Introduction" to Forster's *Journal*. O. H. K. Spate's *Paradise Found and Lost* (vol. 1 of *The Pacific since Magellan* [Rushcutters Bay, NSW, 1988]) provides a fresh appraisal and situates the voyages effectively in the longer history of mercantile expansion.

4. On the post-voyage disputes, the editor of Cook's journals and author of his biography, J. C. Beaglehole, took an extraordinarily opinionated and hostile attitude toward Forster; his discussion in *The Life of Captain James Cook* (London, 1974), 461–470, together with other anti-Forster remarks scattered through annotations and the introduction to the second voyage (*Journals*, 2: xlii–xlviii), has evidently molded the views of a number of other writers, who generally have nothing to say about Forster beyond remarking on his notoriously fractious personality. If there is a reality behind the plethora of allusions of this kind, it has been blown out of all proportion and has obscured a whole range of conceptual and political questions concerning not only the dispute itself, but the character and status of science on the voyage and in the period. The accounts of Hoare, 151–184, and of Gordon, 206–256, though they understand the history in the same terms of personal character and motivation, are considerably more sympathetic to Forster. Bernard Smith appears to have been the first modern commentator to draw attention to the wider importance of Forster's *Observations* (see his *European Vision and the South Pacific*, 2d ed. [New Haven, 1985], 86–87).

5. The only surreptitious account from the second voyage was John Marra's *Journal of the Resolution's Voyage* (London, 1775). George Forster was exempted by his youth from the Admiralty's prohibition.

6. Gordon, 214. An extract from a draft fragment is printed here; see 413 below.

7. Gordon, 214–215. The agreement was published as an appendix to George's *Letter to the Right Honourable the Earl of Sandwich* (London, 1778).

8. Beaglehole, 2: clxviii.

9. Ibid., 2: cliii.

10. Hoare, chaps. 9–12.

"On the Varieties of the Human Species"

1. Quoted in Ian Simpson Ross, *Lord Kames and the Scotland of His Day* (Oxford, 1972), 333–334.

2. Henry Home, Lord Kames, *Sketches of the History of Man* (Edinburgh, 1774), bk. 1, 271 (here cited in the 1807 edition).

3. "The Legal Needs of a Commercial Society: The Jurisprudence of Lord Kames," in *Wealth and Virtue*, ed. Istvan Hont and Michael Ignatieff (Cambridge, 1983).

4. For stylistic reasons I use "Society Islands" in the modern sense to refer to the whole archipelago of Tahiti, Moorea, Huahine, Raiatea, Tahaa, Bora Bora, and some smaller islands; in its original application it referred only to the last four, which constitute a distinct cluster, but Forster often uses it more inclusively and does not, in any case, ever systematically develop contrasts or discriminations between the Tahitians and the inhabitants of other islands within the Society group.

5. George Louis le Clerc, Count of Buffon, *Natural History, General and Particular*, trans. William Smellie (London, 1866), 1:331, 406.

6. J. S. C. Dumont d'Urville, "Sur les îles du grand Océan," *Bulletin de la Société de Géographie* 17 (1832): 1–21.

7. This analogy between fecundity or barrenness in one sphere of life and another is not an isolated comparison but something that structures the whole of Forster's exposition: vegetable and animal kingdoms are evoked through the same aesthetic progression from most pleasing to least, from Tahiti through other tropical islands to New Zealand and Tierra del Fuego, that is pivotal to the account of human variety: "We have observed how much the least attractive of these tropical countries, surpasses the ruder scenery of New Zeeland; how much more discouraging than this, are the extremities of America; and lastly, how dreadful the southern coasts [i.e., Antarctica] appear, which we discovered. In the same manner, the plants that inhabit these lands, will be found to differ in number, stature, beauty, and use" (113); "We have seen by what degrees nature descended from the gay enamel of the plains of the Society Isles, to the horrible barrenness of the Southern SANDWICH LAND. In the same manner, the animal world, from being beautiful, rich, enchanting, between the tropics; falls into deformity, poverty, and disgustfulness in the Southern coasts" (128).

8. Buffon, *Natural History*, 1:252.

9. For speculation about why the responses of some Pacific islanders to early European visits were very different to those of others, see Nicholas Thomas, *Entangled Objects: Exchange, Material Culture, and Colonialism in the Pacific* (Cambridge, Mass., 1991), 83–110.

10. Forster makes a good deal more of this contrast than Cook, who recognizes no one from his previous visit to Queen Charlotte's Sound and infers that these people too change their place of residence frequently (*A Voyage toward the South Pole and round the World*, London, 1777, 1:127–128).

11. George Forster, *A Voyage Round the World* (London, 1777), 1: 216.

12. I'm grateful to Jonathan Lamb, who suggested the salience of this passage in these terms to me.

13. Adam Smith, *The Theory of Moral Sentiments* (London, 1767), 4:1, 1–10.

14. See Margaret Jolly, " 'Ill-natured Comparisons': Racism and Relativism in European Representations of Ni-Vanuatu from Cook's Second Voyage," in *Colonialism and Culture*, ed. Nicholas Thomas, special issue of *History and Anthropology* 5 (3/4) (1992): 331–363.

Looking at Women

1. *History of the Voyages and Discoveries made in the North* (London, 1786), xiv.

2. For the French ambassador's anecdote, and a fuller discussion of its implications, see Spate, *Paradise Found and Lost*, 81. On curiosity, see my "The Great Distinction: Figures of the Exotic in the Work of William Hodges," in *New Feminist Discourses: Critical Essays on Theories and Texts*, ed. Isobel Armstrong (London, 1992), 320–322.

3. Forster and Cook both observe with relief the success of Cook's temporary prohibition on trade between the islanders and crew at Tongatabu. Cook adds that "the different tradeing parties were so successfull to day as to procure for both Sloops a tollerable supply of refreshments in concequence of which I gave the next morning every one leave to purchase what curiosities and other things they pleased, after this it was astonishing to see with what eagerness every one catched at every thing they saw, it even went so far as to become the ridicule of the Natives by offering pieces of sticks stones and what not to exchange, one waggish Boy took a piece of human excrement on the end of a stick and hild it out to every one of our people he met with" (Beaglehole, 255). See also

Journal, 2:531–532, and 3:488. Forster himself seems to have viewed his collection of exotic curiosities as a resource that could be sold for personal profit in times of hardship; see Hoare, 177.

4. On exoticism, see my "Curiously Marked: Tattooing, Masculinity, and Nationality in Eighteenth-Century British Perceptions of the South Pacific," *Painting and the Politics of Culture*, ed. John Barrell (Oxford, 1992), 102–104.

5. William Wales, *Remarks on Mr. Forster's Account of Captain Cook's last Voyage Round the World, in the Years 1772, 1773, 1774, and 1775* (London, 1778), 34–35; also 3. See also 54–55. The grounds of the argument between Wales and the Forsters have been extensively discussed. See, for example, Hoare, 173–179. For Forster's comments on "unofficial" collecting, see, for example, *Journal*, 2: xlv–xlvi.

6. *Journal*, 3:390.

7. Ibid., 391.

8. *Journal*, 2:356–357.

9. See, for example, ibid., 302–303. Several of these incidents are also reported in *Observations*.

10. *Journal*, 2:308–309.

11. Ibid., 307.

12. John Millar, *The Origin of the Distinction of Ranks: or, an Inquiry into the Circumstances Which Give Rise to Influence and Authority, in the Different Members of Society* (this 4th ed., Edinburgh, 1806), 100, 102, 90–91.

13. Ibid., 98. *Journal*, 2:309. Millar's argument is for a remoralization of the principles of commerce, achieved at least in part through representing the vices associated with women as a kind of inoculation for the healthy body of society.

14. Millar, *Origin*, 424. Millar sees the "liberty of divorce" in the late days of the Roman empire as a sign of luxury and debauchery—clearly not the basis for virtuous monogamy. It is interesting to note that it is from this discussion of monogamy and polygamy that Mary Wollstonecraft quotes in her *Vindication of the Rights of Woman: With Strictures on Political and Moral Subjects* (1792), chap. 4.

15. Forster, however, does not specify the character of the difficulties he sees as attendant on marriages in Europe. He sometimes seems to have in mind difficulties that might be resolved through reform of the marriage and divorce laws—in his comments on the rarity of "tender connexions" comparable to those of the islanders, for example—rather than the financial and social difficulties of getting married in the first place.

16. The appropriation of these terms to the Arioi may imply a covert allusion to same-sex desire, which Kames and other theorists represented as characteristic of late commercial societies.

17. Despite the absence of the "notion of turpitude," Forster claims that the women of the Society Islands exhibit what appears to be a natural modesty. See *Observations*, 289–290 and 243–244. Mary Wollstonecraft comments: "Nothing can be more absurd than the ridicule of the critic, that the heroine of his mock-tragedy was in love with the very man whom she ought least to have loved; he could not have given a better reason. How can passion gain strength any other way? In Otaheite, love cannot be known, where the obstacles to irritate an indiscriminate appetite, and sublimate the simple sensations of desire till they mount to passion, are never known. There a man or woman cannot love the very person they ought not to have loved—nor does jealousy ever fan the flame." "Hints: Chiefly designed to have been incorporated in the Second Part of the Vindication of the Rights of Woman," in Janet Todd and Marilyn Butler, eds., *The Works of Mary Wollstonecraft* (London: Pickering, 1989), 5:271.

18. The differences I have discussed between the representation of women in the *Journal* and

the *Observations* might be accounted for, in rather a weak sense, by the notions of class division in Tahiti that Forster constructs in the published text.

19. Henry Home, Lord Kames, represents variety of food and drink as the primary form of luxurious appetite; see *Sketches*, bk. 1, sketch 8, "Progress and Effects of Luxury."

20. On women and the division of labor, see John Barrell, "The Birth of Pandora and the Origin of Painting," in his *The Birth of Pandora and the Division of Knowledge* (London, 1992), esp. sections 2 and 3. On the construction of women as morally superior, see my "The Wanton Muse: Politics and Gender in Gothic Theory after 1760," in *Beyond Romanticism: New Approaches to Texts and Contexts 1780–1832*, ed. Stephen Copley and John Whale (London, 1992), sect. 4.

21. A further and significant problem for Forster's argument is indicated by his acknowledgment that the men and women of Tahiti take their food separately.

"A Kind of Linnaean Being"

Many thanks to Nicholas Thomas for supplying photocopies of the manuscripts of Forster's Warrington lectures from Berlin, the two Bartlett articles on Forster's Russian travels, and much patient, constructive advice. Thanks also to Victoria Luker and Holly Rothermel for their helpful criticisms and suggestions on several versions of this essay. I have drawn extensively on Michael Hoare's biography *The Tactless Philosopher* (Melbourne, 1977) and his introduction to *The Resolution Journal of Johann Reinhold Forster* (4 vols.; London, 1982).

1. March 15, 1774. *Journal*, 233–234.

2. December 21, 1774. *Journal*, 438–439.

3. See the *Oxford English Dictionary*, 2d ed., 5:60.

4. Michel Foucault's discussion of the discontinuities between "Renaissance" and "Classical" natural history in *The Order of Things* (New York, 1970) still has much to recommend it, in part because he focuses on the changes in the ways the *materials* of natural history were disposed, displayed, and controlled, rather than doing a history of ideas of classification and order. He describes the advent of "Classical" natural history in the mid-1600s as the opening of a gap between thing and sign, "a new way of connecting things both to the eye and to discourse" (131) that disintegrated the element of "resemblance" in which the objects of "Renaissance" natural history moved.

5. Still most useful and subtle for describing "mercantilism" as the economic construction of a "nation" out of "territories," not as a failed experiment in the theoretical analysis of wealth and economic policy, is Gustav Schmoller, *The Mercantile System and Its Historical Significance* (New York, 1897). For a more detailed discussion of mercantilism as practiced in particular areas of administration in Germany and Russia, see Marc Raeff, *The Well-Ordered Police State: Social and Institutional Change Through Law in the Germanies and Russia, 1600–1800* (New Haven and London, 1983); Albion Small, *The Cameralists* (Chicago, 1909).

6. Tore Frangsmayr, "Linnaeus in his Swedish Context," in *Contemporary Perspectives on Linnaeus*, ed. John Weinstock (Lanham, Md., 1985), 183–193. Frangsmayr points out that royally patronized scholarship at the Swedish court was a heavily ideological activity. Furthermore, in the 1740s and 1750s Sweden was, even more than Britain, the obligatory stop on any young German administrator's education. Among others, Friedrich Anton von Heinitz, founder of the Royal Mining Academy at Freiberg and director of mining in Saxony and Prussia, and Johann Beckmann, who as professor of economy at Göttingen introduced the term "Technologie" into German, formed extensive, sometimes illicit connections in Sweden. The memoirs of the Royal Swedish Academy, which Linnaeus helped found in 1749, were a prized source of economic information—for those who could read Swedish. See Wolfhard Weber, *Friedrich Anton von Heynitz: Innovationen im frühin-*

dustriellen deutschen Bergbau (Göttingen, 1976); and Ulrich Troitzsch, *Ansätze technologischen Denkens bei den Kameralisten des 17. und 18. Jahrhunderts* (Berlin, 1966).

7. Lisbet Koerner, "Nature and Nation in Linnaean Travel," paper given to conference "Visions of Empire: Voyages, Botany, and Representations of Nature," William Andrews Clark Library, Los Angeles, 17–20 January 1991. Koerner shows that this notion of "oeconomy" was itself probably drawn from seventeenth-century British physicotheologians like Robert Boyle, William Derham, and above all John Ray, long the reference point for Swedish naturalists visiting Britain. I thank Dr. Koerner for providing me with a typescript of her talk.

8. Franz A. Stafleu, *Linnaeus and the Linnaeans: The Spreading of Their Ideas in Systematic Botany, 1735–1789* (Utrecht, 1971), is an excellent account of Linnaeus' writings and the way in which Linnaean apostles colonized gardens and cabinets around the world. A map of the apostles' travels is reprinted in Wilfred Blunt, *The Compleat Naturalist* (New York, 1971), 186. For further reading on Linnaeus' system and method, see James Larson, *Reason and Experience: The Representation of Natural Order in the Work of Carl von Linné* (Berkeley, 1971).

9. See Linnaeus to Forster, July, 1772, in *Journal*, 136n1. For Solander, see R. A. Rauschenberg, "Daniel Carl Solander, Naturalist on the *Endeavour*," *Transactions of the American Philosophical Society*, n.s., 58 (1968): 1–66.

10. Forster to Thomas Pennant, October 1768, quoted in Hoare, 37.

11. The doctrine of "cameralism," the German version of mercantilism, was made the center of higher education in Prussia when Friedrich Wilhelm I founded the chair of Kameralwissenschaft at Halle in 1727. This was a crucial episode in the dissolution of the Renaissance university and the bureaucratization of higher learning in Germany. Halle served as the model for Sweden's first chair in economics, endowed by Gustav III at Uppsala in 1741 along with Linnaeus' appointment there. See Anthony La Vopa, *Grace, Talent and Merit: Poor Students, Clerical Careers, and Professional Ideology in Eighteenth-Century Germany* (Cambridge, 1988), 49–53; William Clark, "From the Medieval Universitas Scholarium to the German Research University: A Sociogenesis of the Germanic Academic" (Ph.D. diss., University of California, Los Angeles, 1986); and Charles McClelland, *State, Society, and University in Germany, 1700–1914* (Cambridge, 1980).

12. For "improving pastors" and the identification of moral and agricultural health in German reformed religion, see Henry Lowood, "Patriotism, Profit, and the Promotion of Science in the German Enlightenment: The Economic and Scientific Societies, 1760–1815" (Ph.D. diss., University of California, Berkeley, 1987), 136–138. Forster was an active participant in the patriotic societies upon returning to Prussia in 1780, publishing essays on tanning and agricultural pests among other topics in the *Halle Weekly*; in England, he offered the Society for the Encouragement of Arts, Manufactures, and Commerce a paper on "the best and profitablest Manner of breeding bees," that most characteristic topic of improving rural economists. See Lowood, "Patriotism, Profit and Promotion of Science," 160–173.

13. Unable to afford membership in the Danzig Gesellschaft Naturforschender Freunde, Forster corresponded with and supplied plants to a major figure within the society, Gottfried Reyger, between 1760 and 1766. Reyger wrote the first flora of Danzig and was the first in Germany to record flowering seasons of local plants. Hoare, 22–23.

14. Ibid., 25.

15. Roger Paul Bartlett, "Foreign Settlement in Russia under Catherine II," *New Zealand Slavonic Journal*, n.s., 1 (1974): 1–22.

16. Forster gave his version of events in a much later biographical notice on his son. J. R. Forster, "Ueber Georg Forster," *Annalen der Philosophie und des philosophischen Geistes. Philosophischer Anzeiger*, 14 January 1795, cols. 9–16; 15 April 1795, cols. 121–128.

17. These diplomatic memoranda are quoted in Roger Paul Bartlett, "J. R. Forster's Stay in Russia, 1765–1766: Diplomatic and Official Accounts", *Jahrbücher für die Geschichte Osteuropas* 23 (1975): 489–495. The Russian account further relates that despite Forster's demands for the humane treatment of subjects, "he did not limit himself to frequently beating the Cossacks who escorted him in the desert; once, he had the temerity to fire on them with his rifle and wounded his interpreter."

18. Pallas to Pennant, 1778, reviewing Forster's summary of the natural history of the steppes, "Specimen Historiae Naturalis Volgensis," which Forster read to the Royal Society in June 1767; quoted in Hoare, 46. Pallas described Forster's assignment as "pointing out proper places for establishing Colonies" and judged him "a very unskilful project-maker."

19. Koerner, "Nature and Nation in Linnaean Travel," 37n34.

20. Forster's career in England has been too well documented by Joseph Gordon, "Reinhold and Georg Forster in England, 1766–1780" (Ph.D. diss., Duke University, 1975), to need repeating here. I am interested in how Forster's self-consciousness as a confirmed Linnaean natural historian developed.

21. See "A Letter from Mr. John Reinhold Forster, F.A.S. to the Hon. Daines Barrington, Vice-Pres. R.S. on the Management of Carp in Polish Prussia," *Philosophical Transactions*, 61 (1771): 310–325; "Specimen Historiae Naturalis Volgensis," *Philosophical Transactions*, 57 (1767): 312–357; "A Letter from Mr. J. R. Forster, F.A.S. to M. Maty, M.D. Sec. R.S. containing some Account of a new Map of the River Volga," *Philosophical Transactions*, 58 (1768): 214–216. These were probably the "Charts" that had so interested the British envoy in St. Petersburg.

22. Hoare, 58. Forster announced the "system" in the "advertisement" to his *Introduction to Mineralogy* (1768), a short classification of mineral bodies that served as the basis of his lectures.

23. Quoted in Hoare, 55. All following quotations of Forster's Warrington lectures are taken from J. R. Forster, "Lectures on Natural History, & especially on Mineralogy. Part the 1st containing the Introductory lectures on the Earths & Stones, with the Petrefactions, or all the true Fossils. Begun to be read & composed 1767 & 1768" (MS germ. oct. 22a, Deutsche Staatsbibliothek—Preussischer Kulturbesitz, Berlin). Page numbers are cited in parentheses in the text. I thank the Deutsche Staatsbibliothek for permission to cite this manuscript.

24. Hoare, 57ff. Pennant, a gentleman naturalist with an estate in northern Wales, gained renown for his British birds and mammals, and with many colony-minded fellows of the Royal Society like Barrington and Dalrymple had an avid interest in the natural history of the Arctic. His *Arctic Zoology* (1782–1785) served for decades on expeditions searching for the Northwest Passage.

25. See the useful Forster bibliography at the end of Hoare, 337–372.

26. Forster described the natural history treasures being unloaded from the *Endeavour* at Greenwich to Pennant, 13 August 1771 (*Journal*, 45). The dedication of the insect catalogue to Banks declared Forster's readiness "not only to pray for every good fortune and a happy safe return, adorned by new spoils of the sea and the antipodes, but also, if it pleases God, to endure the same perils with you, to share with you the same pleasure the study of nature gives, under a new sky." Trans. and quoted in *Journal*, 1:46. Hoare also detects a certain British chauvinism in Forster's notes to Bougainville and Bossu; *Journal*, 1:42.

27. Quoted in Hoare, 68–69. Hoare suggests the reviewer may have been Forster himself, who reviewed several voyages for the *Review*.

28. *Journal*, 48–50.

29. Forster to Pennant, June 1772, quoted in Hoare, 77.

30. *Journal*, 127, 130–133.

31. *Journal*, 309–310.

32. Forster's *Enchiridion Historiae Naturali Inserviens* (Halle, 1788), a handbook of Linnaean classification for traveling natural historians that Forster composed on board the *Resolution* during 1773 and 1774, was one response to such difficulties. The natural historian, Forster warned prospective travelers, had to have the Linnaean method and language drilled into him or at least carried with him in a convenient book well before setting foot in unfamiliar country; the natural historian's conscious wits had to be saved for constant and exhausting vigilance: "In effect, we were continually beset by an immense crowd of inhabitants, of a very inquisitive people, who were above all interested in our weapons and all our iron instruments. Very agile, crafty men, always moving, surrounded us everywhere." Once back in the relative safety of the ship, the big battle was to stay awake long enough to describe and draw everything that had been seen and collected, before memories faded and specimens decayed or dessicated. J. R. Forster, *Manuel pour servir à l'histoire naturelle des oiseaux, des poissons, des insectes et des plantes,* trans. J. B. F. Léveillé (Paris, An VII [1799]), xviii–xxii.

33. Forster agonized over whether or not he was seeing the Marquesas Islands and blamed previous navigators for the uncertainty, which could long ago have been resolved had they "taken the prudents Step to inquire the Natives, for the Names of the Islands they saw. . . . Then all the future Navigators can enquire for the Name of what they see, & then they will easily make out, whether it is new or not." *Journal,* 480.

34. As it happened, the chronometers failed during the voyage, and the scramble to assign blame back in England embroiled not only Wales and Arnold, but the Forsters as well. More than Forster's philosophical competence was questioned; in the war of pamphlets that followed, Georg complained that Wales had portrayed his father as "a piratical pretender of knowledge, biased by system, guilty of continual misrepresentations, inconsistent, unworthy of credit, contemptible, ignorant and illiterate, unmannerly, uncivil, indelicate, unskilful, inattentive, rash, timorous, absurd, silly, blabbing, unsociable, ill-tempered, lying, bribing, knavish, artful, deceitful, abusive, indignant, spiteful, revengeful, arrogant, slanderous, proud, covetous, cruel, execrable and finally mad." Imputations of philosophical skill and gentility run together in such debates, especially in disputes over one's "credit-worthiness," and especially in affairs of colonial speculation.

35. Forster to Pennant, 19 November 1772, quoted in *Journal,* 1:100.

36. 4 July 1774. *Journal,* 3:551–552.

37. *Journal,* 647.

38. Hoare, 128. One springbok and a dozen birds survived the journey home. Right until landing at the Cape, Forster fretted about the loss of family, friendship, and patronage that might await him after two and a half years incommunicado. "Those therefore who send people out upon such a long Expedition do not think, that we lose so many valuable connexions in Life. I am no more young, if I should have been unfortunate enough to have lost in my Absence, my best Friends & Patrons, I must begin life as it were again, which must cast a damp upon my Spirits, which are after such a cruize none of the highest" (*Journal,* 4:97–98).

39. Hoare, 151–152.

40. As commonly occurred, one diary escaped the Admiralty, that of an *Adventure* seaman, James Burney. Howard T. Fry, *Alexander Dalrymple (1737–1808) and the Expansion of British Trade* (London, 1970), 129.

41. *Journal,* 443, 447.

42. George Forster, "Letter to Sandwich," in *Werke,* 4:15–16. See Hoare, 160, for an account of the debate.

43. George Forster, *A Voyage round the World, in His Brittanic Majesty's sloop,* Resolution (London, 1777), 1:7–8.

44. Hoare, 183, 185–186.

45. Pliny the Elder, *Natural History*, Book II, trans. H. H. Rackham (Cambridge, 1938), 1:291. Forster's reliance on heathen Classical authority to evoke this natural historical theodicy is not just a display of learning, but a conscious heterodoxy born of the reformation in theology and philology in which Forster was embroiled, not least by his Göttingen correspondent Johann David Michaelis. Natural history had to defend itself against charges of "barbarism" from the universities because of its constant need to neologize and depart from the rules of Latin rhetoric. Part of the Linnaean exercise of classification, as Forster outlined it in his *Enchiridion*, was a derivation of the generic and species names from valid Classical sources and its attribution to a modern natural historian. The frequent use of Classical sources is thus an appropriation of university erudition for a "barbaric" enterprise that often descended into the vulgar vernaculars. See Forster's defense of Latin usage in his *Manuel pour servir. . . .*

46. *Journal*, 480.

47. *Journal*, 605–607.

48. Recruiting native cultures was a major tool in the Linnaean's armory. In his own travels through Lapland, part of his campaign to make the great northern wilderness Sweden's "East Indies," Linnaeus made much of his acceptance by the Lapps as one of their own. He would often appear for lectures or sit for portraits in full Lapp dress (much as Forster donned the Polynesian *ahu*). It is also worth recalling that when Forster returned to St. Petersburg to propose his constitution for the Volga colonies, he brought two colonists with him to testify. See Blunt, *Compleat Naturalist*, 118, for a picture of Linnaeus in his costume, and Koerner, "Nature and Nation in Linnaean Travel," 22, 45n69.

Advertisement for the Observations

1. This was evidently circulated with copies of George Forster's *Voyage round the World;* the only copy we have sighted is bound with one of the copies of that book in the National Library of Australia (at call number NK5009).

Forster's Observations

Preface

1. Forster refers here to Georges Louis Leclerc, Comte de Buffon, *Histoire Naturelle* (Paris, 1752–1768); Isaac Iselin, *Über die Geschichte der Menschheit* (1768); and Torbern Bergman, *Physical Description of the Earth* (in Swedish) (Uppsala, 1766). It will be seen that the *Histoire Naturelle* is one of the most frequently quoted and cited works here, but though Forster broadly shares Buffon's environmentalism, he took exception to many of Buffon's particular claims and arguments, in part as a means to privilege direct observations of the kind he had made himself, over Buffon's largely secondhand, synthetic knowledge (he had already written a fairly critical assessment of the ornithological section of the *Histoire Naturelle*, in the *Critical Review* 32 [1771]: 209–224). From Iselin's philosophical history of the human species (also briefly noticed in the *Critical Review* 33 [1772]: 340), Forster draws upon the emphases on the role of education in progress and the status of women as a crucial index of it; in this regard, his reading of Kames' *Sketches of the History of Man* (Edinburgh, 1774) was also evidently important (and Kames' influence is also manifest in later editions of Iselin's book). Forster's citation of Bergman must be seen in the context of his efforts to secure Swedish patronage after the debacle with the British Admiralty, but it also reflects a perception of

how a philosophical historian ought to relate to his public. Forster was no doubt impressed by Berg-man's aestheticized cosmography, which put the natural historian in the position of moral philoso-pher and political economist, and gave his writings equivalent salience and scope.

2. The references here are to Johann Blumenbach's *De generis humani varietate nativa* (Göttin-gen, 1776) and John Hunter's *Disputation inauguralis, quaedem de hominum varietatibus* (London, 1775). What Forster draws from Blumenbach is, first, the basic thesis of the unity of the human species (affirmed also by Hunter) and, second, a qualified environmentalism (advocated also by Buffon)—though the notion that climate would provide sufficient determinations of human variety is rejected: "There are, however, two ways, in which men may gather experience of a change of climate. . . . They may emigrate and so change the climate, and it may also happen that the climate of their native country may sensibly become more mild or more severe, and so the inhabitants may degenerate" (*The Anthropological Treatises of Johann Friedrich Blumenbach*, ed. Thomas Bendyshe, London, 1865, 71). What is retrospectively taken to be more important by historians of physical anthropology—Blumenbach's classification of races into Caucasian, Mongolian, etc.—was incorpo-rated only into the third (1795) edition of his treatise and in its preliminary expressions was less salient to *Observations*. Blumenbach's types were originally defined strictly on physiological grounds, but, drawing on Forster, he incorporated a brief reference to manners and temperaments into later editions of his essay (*Anthropological Treatises*, 100). Forster followed Hunter in under-standing the effect of climate more in the inclusive modern sense of environment than in that of latitudinal zone. Heat, air, topography, clothing, and behavior (notably kinds of labor) that related to the degree of exposure of the body to the sun all affected skin color (*Anthropological Treatises*, 369–370).

Journal

1. The original is mispaginated here; the "Journal," which begins at page 9, finishes at page 16, and the text of chapter 1 begins again at page 9. This could suggest that the "Journal" was added at a late stage, but there is a disjunction in any case between the preface (i–iii) and contents (i–iv) and the beginning of the text: there are no pages numbered 1–8.

2. Apparent discrepancies between this "Journal" and the voyage journals of Forster and Cook result from Forster's having changed dates from naval to civil time; under the former the day is from noon to noon, so for example the anchorage off Madeira takes place on 29 July, the evening of 28 July in civil time.

Chapter I, Section I

1. "I would reckon this too among the crimes of our ingratitude, that we are ignorant of her [the earth's] nature" (Pliny 2.159).

2. The most obvious example of despotism would have been the French ancien régime; but Forster, having been associated with Warrington radicals and embittered by what he saw as the tyrannical behavior of powerful figures in the Admiralty such as Lord Sandwich, may also have had Britain in mind (see J. S. Gordon, "Reinhold and Georg Forster in England, 1766–1780," Ph.D. diss., Duke University, 1975, 291–292). In *Observations* Forster avoided overt discussion of the con-troversy concerning the publication of the results of the voyages—that for him at least marked the Admiralty's inadequate recognition of natural history—but there are implicit references that cannot have been missed by informed readers at the time.

Chapter I, Section II

1. ". . . where no tree revives under a summer breeze, a region of the world over which brood mists and a gloomy sky" (Horace, *Odes*, 1.22.17–20).

Chapter I, Section III

1. Trade relations in southern Vanuatu are discussed by Matthew Spriggs in "Landscape, Land Use, and Political Transformation in Southern Melanesia," in *Island Societies: Archaeological Approaches to Evolution and Transformation*, ed. Patrick Vinton Kirch (Cambridge, 1986), 6–19. For ethnohistoric background on the region, see Spriggs' "Vegetable Kingdoms: Taro Irrigation and Pacific Prehistory" (Ph.D. thesis, Australian National University, 1983); and Ron Adams, *In the Land of Strangers: A Century of European Contact with Tanna, 1774–1874* (Canberra, 1983).

2. Ignivomous: fire-vomiting, i.e., actively volcanic.

Chapter I, Section IV

1. Marc-Joseph Marion du Fresne's exploratory and trading expedition of 1771–1775 met with disaster when Marion and some thirty men were killed by Maori in the Bay of Islands; participants in Cook's voyage learned of these events from Julien Marie Crozet at the Cape in March 1775 (Beaglehole, 656). The main publication is A.-M. de Rochon, *Nouveau voyage à la mer du sud* (Paris, 1783); see also Spate, *Paradise Found and Lost*, 120–122; and, for an account attempting to recover Maori perspectives, Anne Salmond, *Two Worlds* (Auckland, 1991).

2. In fact the "discoveries" of Yves Joseph de Kerguelen-Tremarec were largely fraudulent; his book, *Relation de deux voyages dans les mers Australes & des Indes* (Paris, 1782) was suppressed by the French government. See John Dunmore, *French Explorers in the Pacific* (Oxford, 1965–1969), i, 196–249.

3. William Heberden (1710–1801), physician.

4. "The lower regions [of air] are also warm, first because of the exhalation of the earth, which carries with it a great deal of warmth; second, because the rays of the sun are reflected back and make the air more genially warm with reflected heat as far as they are able to reach" (Seneca, *Natural Questions*, 2.10.3).

Chapter I, Section V

1. This is the first passage in which Forster introduces a rhetorical continuum that structures and animates his exposition throughout the book: the progression from the dead barrenness of the far south through gloomy, stunted, and indolent temperate life forms to the happy luxuriance of the tropics. In some contexts, as in his account of the varieties of the human species, the order is reversed, and the most aesthetically appealing and improved example is presented first, and then those that are successively more debased. It will be noted that much of his language is similar, whether he is speaking of plants, animals, or humans: here, for instance, the suggestion that seals and penguins are slow, unwieldly, and torpid parallels the response to Tierra del Fuegians, who are found to be ugly and indolent. The tropics are understood to be naturally improved, in almost the same sense as human improvements produce a happier and more benevolent civility, in Tahiti than in New Zealand (although Forster's usage on these points is hardly consistent: the Tahitian character is said elsewhere to be as "amiable as that of any nation, that ever came unimproved out of the hands of nature" (155), which sits awkwardly with the statement that Tahiti is "a country improved by art" (114), even though it should be noted that the improvement of land is seen to be causally associated with the refinement of a people, rather than identical or coincident with it.

It should also be noted that Forster's emphasis on the harsh and sterile character of the southern lands, which is also graphically expressed in some of Hodges' pen and watercolor sketches, implicitly contradicts the notion that the postulated Great Southern Land was fertile and luxuriant (see n. 6, 412–414).

2. "... pars mundi damnata a rerum natura et densa mersa caligine" (Pliny, *Natural History*,

[hereafter, Pliny], 4.88): "a part of the world that lies under the condemnation of nature and is plunged in dense darkness."

3. This account of cyclical and seemingly chaotic decay recalls a memorable passage in George Forster's *Voyage Round the World* (London, 1777), 1:177–180, which is in turn based on a briefer section in Forster senior's *Journal* (265–266). In those texts the emphasis is on the limited capacities of the Maori to transform the environment, upon which point they were unfavorably compared with the Tahitians.

4. Forster's quotation corresponds essentially with the standard text. "[Earth] receives us at birth, and gives us nurture after birth, and when once brought forth she maintains us always, and at the last when we have been disinherited by the rest of nature she embraces us in her bosom and at that very time gives us her maternal shelter . . . kind and gentle and indulgent, ever a handmaid in the service of mortals, producing under our compulsion, or lavishing of her own accord, what scents and savors, what juices, what surfaces for the touch, what colors! how honestly she repays the interest lent her! what produce she fosters for our benefit!" (Pliny 2.154, 155).

Chapter II, Section I

1. "Hoc elementum [aqua] ceteris omnibus imperat": "This element [water] is lord over all the others" (Pliny 31.1).

2. "O spring of Bandusia, brighter than crystal, worthy of sweet wine and flowers" (Horace, *Odes*, 3.13).

3. Jesse Ramsden (1735–1800) was a renowned manufacturer of scientific instruments.

4. See George Forster, *Voyage*, II:308, for the uneasiness of the Tannese.

Chapter II, Section II

1. Eddoes: taro (*Colocasia esculenta*) was one of the most important Oceanic cultivated plants, often grown intensively in irrigated terraces. See Spriggs, "Vegetable Kingdoms."

Chapter II, Section III

1. What Forster refers to as the duodecimo edition of the *Histoire Naturelle* corresponds in pagination to the fifth edition (Paris, 1752–1768). His quotations here and elsewhere will be found to be fairly literal and close translations.

2. Forster had visited Buffon in Paris in the summer of 1776 (Hoare, 165).

3. James Lind (1716–1794) was the author of the important *Treatise on Scurvy* (Edinburgh, 1753) and *An Essay on the Most Effectual Means of Preserving the Health of Seamen in the Royal Navy* (London, 1757); the advantage of his method of distilling seawater was that it required no chemical additives (*DSB*, viii, 361–363).

4. "It is their nature to shine in darkness with a bright light when other light is removed" (Pliny 9.84). The preceding sentence, "The class shellfish includes the finger-mussel, named from its resemblance to a human fingernail," is omitted.

5. This citation, which Forster copied from Buffon, has not been traced, but must be to one of the numerous works of the physicist and chemist Robert Boyle.

6. For a survey of the interest in a southern continent, see Spate, *Paradise Found and Lost,* chap. 4. Anglo-French exploratory rivalry followed particularly from the observations of de Lozier Bouvet in 1739; those enthusiastic about the possibility of a large southern landmass, and the attendant scope for colonization, included Maupertuis and Buffon as well as Charles de Brosses (1709–1777; writer on antiquities, languages, and fetishism as well as exploration) and Alexander Dalrymple (1737–1808; author of numerous hydrographic and geographic works). The definitive rejection

of the hypothesis is generally regarded as the major navigational accomplishment of Cook's second voyage; see, for example, Beaglehole's *Life of Captain James Cook* (London, 1974), 475.

Forster referred to the debate more directly in one of the draft essay fragments that reviewed the history of the exploration of the Pacific. The beginning of this text is missing but clearly refers to discoveries made as by-products of commercial expeditions and proceeds as follows:

The Geographical Knowledge of a fourth part of the globe was still to be acquired, & though of no immediate use, might however turn out beneficial in time. A profitable peace succeeded to a War [the Seven Years' War, 1756–1763] which had been glorious to *Great Britain,* and gave a liberal and enlightened Prince an opportunity of displaying his Patronage of Learning and Science to an eminent degree. Four successive voyages to the South Seas were made under his auspices with no other aim, than that noble one of extending our Knowledge, wholly free from the interested motives which had been the cause of every former Voyage. Two of these Enterprises had already gone forward, when a Spirit of Emulation in a Rival power produced a similar disinterested Voyage of Discovery under M. de *Bougainville!* The two English ones which followed under Capt. *Cook,* compleated the Investigation of the South-seas, determined what was uncertain before, found out all that was still unseen from the Line to the Antarctick, and lastly exploded the deep rooted Notions of a Southern Continent!

Almost as soon as the Southseas came to be known in Europe, the opinion that it contained a huge tract of Land became familiar to the Learned, and this supposed new Continent claimed a place in all the Charts & Plates that were published. The infatuation went so far, that tho' not an atom of this land had been seen, yet it was laid down quite across the whole ocean from the Coast of *New Guinea* to opposite the Straits of *Magelhaens,* and as it had been easy to the Geographers to create the land, they found not the least difficulty in singling out a Discoverer: *Hernando Gallego* who discovered a few islands under the line a little from the Coasts of America, was pitched upon as the happy Inventor of this blessed Country, which was said to surpass all others in fertility, beauty, excellence of climate, and to abound in those things for which alone the Spaniards could turn Discoverers, I mean Gold Pearls & Gems. It was indeed owing to this way of thinking of the Spanish government, that every Navigator in their service endeavoured to represent his Discoveries as overflowing with riches, well knowing how little they could be valued at home, if looked upon as destitute of this qualification. From hence the *Solomon Islands* so much talked of, and as often removed further West from Peru, as the Roman *Ultima Thule* to the Northward of their Empire, were cried up as another *El Dorado,* and every man whose Genius led him to Discoveries in the South Seas, was obliged to use the search of these isles as the pretext to his going out; though their existence was founded on no better grounds than that of the Southern Continent.

The opinion that there was a Continent in the Southsea was so firmly adopted by *Quiros,* that when he found those large lands which he called *Terra del Espiritù Santo,* he never once doubted that they were a part of it, though in order to carry on his search of it, he was obliged to have recourse to the old method of gilding his former Discoveries in the Eyes of government, and inferring the vast abundance of Silver and Pearls in a Country where the metal is probably a total Stranger, and the pearls a great rarity.

The subsequent Voyage of Tasman convinced the World that Quiros's Land was an Island; but the discovery of New Zeland gave new support to the Continental Doctrine, and though it was allowed that no part of the *Terra australis* reached the Tropick, yet it was believed and asserted to extend all the Temperate Zone; nor could the later Voyages, though they always cut off some part of the supposed land by their tracks which extended always to a greater distance from the American shores, destroy the infatuation. Philosophers not content with quoting authorities & Discoverers of the Continent, and asserting that it was impossible to *discover* it hereafter, because it had not been seen before, tortured the imagination to invent mechanical & mathematical reasons to demonstrate the absolute necessity of Land in the Southern Hemisphere, and declared the World could not perform its revolutions without that due proportion of Earth to counterbalance the Solid Weight of the Northern half. Nor were there wanting idle hands to delineate & determine beforehand the magnitude, and the very figure of this lump. A mountain of Ice seen in the meridian of the Cape of Good Hope, and taken for a Promontery, came very opportunely to the assistance of these presuming Geographers, who now extended their Continent all along the Skirts of the Southern *Atlantick* Ocean.

But Cook's two Voyages at last triumphed over the Continent. The first by cutting off *New Zeeland* and running into 40° South in the midst of the South Sea gave it a sensible shock; the last intirely distroyed it by crossing this sea in four different latitudes & examining it from the Torrid to the Frigid Zone, besides probing the Nonexistence of the famous Cape *Circumcision,* and abolishing all the little refuges that the favourers of this ill founded opinion might still have left.

A further draft fragment on the "Geography of the South sea" appears to follow on this; it locates the sea between America and New Guinea and points out that while its warmer parts justify the name "Pacific," the storms encountered in the far south make that name "highly improper." These drafts are certainly from an earlier stage of composition than those on population and disease.

The longer passage quoted reflects positions familiar from Forster's other writing: the disparagement of speculative and cabinet-based philosophy, the advocacy of the special authority of the learned empirical traveler, the privileging of a quest for knowledge from which commercial motives had been purged, and the celebration of British ventures against those of Spain and France (marked also in some of his annotations to his translation of Bougainville's *Voyage Round the World*). If this text and this kind of writing were deliberately omitted and underemphasized respectively in the *Observations,* this may be so for generic reasons: the overtly patriotic history may have been appropriate in collections of voyages, which were frequently restricted to the discoveries of the author-compiler's nation, but perhaps seemed less fitting in a natural history treatise, which associated its author with a non-national Linnaean brotherhood (including Kalm, Osbeck, Forsskål, and others) rather than a peculiarly British exploratory venture. In this register, Forster was inclined to emphasize the limited and tentative character of many observations, rather than the exhaustiveness of the voyage's discoveries.

Chapter II, Section IV

1. The theory of the formation of ice was crucial not only for the debate about the southern continent (because de Brosses and Buffon took ice as evidence for the presence of land; see Forster's quotations from Buffon, and Spate, *Paradise Found and Lost,* 71–73), but also for the equally important geographical and mercantile problem of whether or not there was a navigable northwest passage between the Atlantic and Pacific that would provide access to lucrative Asian trade. Daines Barrington (1727–1800) was concerned with this question and supported Forster before the voyage and through much of the controversy concerning post-voyage publication arrangements; but he so strongly adhered to the view that Forster rejected, that seawater could not freeze, that he later withdrew his patronage (Hoare, 160, 180; Gordon, "Reinhold and Georg Forster in England," 219–220).

2. No paper of Robert Boyle's in the *Philosophical Transactions* seems to correspond with this

reference, but the work referred to is evidently his *New Observations and Experiments in Order to an Experimental History of Cold* (London, 1665), which was discussed in several articles in the first volume of that journal (1664–1665), for example at 8–9, 46–52.

3. On Bouvet, see O. H. K. Spate, "Between Tasman and Cook: Bouvet's Place in the History of Exploration," in *Frontiers and Men*, ed. J. Andrews (Melbourne, 1966).

4. Strabo, *Geography* (hereafter, Strabo), 7.3.18.

5. Edward Nairne (1726–1806), author of essays on seawater, astronomy, electricity, etc.; Bryan Higgins (1737?–1820), chemist.

6. The passages quoted in this note are as follows: (1) " . . . [the northern sea] they call the frozen sea or the sea of Cronos. Others also call it the dead sea because of the weak sun" (Dionysius Periegetes, *Orbis Descriptio*, 32f.); (2) "[the Argo] burst out into the Ocean. The articulate Hyperboreans call it the sea of Cronos, and the dead sea" (Orphica, *Argonautica*, 1081f.); (3) Strabo (2.4.1. iv): "Trans Suionas aliud mare, pigrum ac prope immotum, quo cingi claudique terrarum orbem hinc fides, quod extremus cadentis iam solis fulgor in ortum edurat adeo clarus, ut sidera hebetet"; (4) (Tacitus, *Germania*, 45.1): "Beyond the Suiones is another sea, sluggish and almost motionless, with which the earth is girdled and bounded; evidence for this is furnished in the brilliance of the last rays of the sun, which remain bright enough from his setting to his rising again to dim the stars"; (5) "To the north is the ocean; beyond the river Parapanisus where it washes the coast of Scythia, Hecataeus calls it the Amalchian Sea, a name that in the language of the natives means 'frozen'; Philemon says that the Cimbrian name for it is Morimarusa (that is 'Dead Sea') from the Parapanisus to Cape Rusbeae, and from that point onward the Cronian Sea" (Pliny 4.95); (6) "One day's sail from Thule is the frozen ocean, called by some the Cronian Sea" (Pliny 4.104).

7. Forster's source for Amerigo Vespucci was no doubt Ramusio's collection of *Viaggia*; for Gonzalo García de Nodal, see O. H. K. Spate, *Monopolists and Freebooters*, vol. 2 in *The Pacific since Magellan* (Canberra, 1983), 25–26; their findings were first published in Madrid in 1621.

8. The French and British navigators are all discussed at least in passing by Spate in *Monopolists and Freebooters* and *Paradise Found and Lost*; his annotations contain useful references to original sources and the modern literature.

9. "All that region is covered with rime and hail that never thaws, and imprisons the ice of ages; the steep face of the lofty mountain rises stiffly up, and, though it faces the rising sun, can never melt its hardened crust in his rays" (Silius Italicus, *Punica*, 3.479–482).

10. Some of these statistics were published in Cook, *A Voyage towards the South Pole*, ii, 294–316; see also William Wales and William Bayly, *The Original Astronomical Observations, made in the course of a Voyage towards the South Pole* (London, 1777).

Chapter III, Section I

1. "Atmosphere is, indeed, an essential part of the universe" (Seneca, *Natural Questions*, 2.4.1).

2. "Apples" refers to the "Malay Apple" or *'ahi'a*; see Douglas Oliver, *Ancient Tahitian Society* (Honolulu, 1974), 245, for this and general background on indigenous subsistence.

3. Compare Beaglehole, 140; *Journal*, 280–282.

4. Jean de Thevenot (1633–1667), traveler in the Middle East.

5. Peter Shaw (1694–1763), physician and chemist.

6. "Vocatur et columna, cum spissatus umor rigensque ipse se sustinet; ex eodem genere et aulon, cum veluti fistula nubes aquam trahit" (Pliny 2.134): "There is also what is called a column, when densified and stiffened moisture raises itself aloft; in the same class also is a waterspout, when a cloud draws up water like a pipe."

Chapter III, Section II

1. This refers to Frézier's *Voyage de la mer du sud*.

Chapter III, Section III

1. The astronomer William Wales also had a particular interest in the *aurora australis*, which may well have been sighted by earlier voyagers but appears indeed to have been "discovered" by those on the *Resolution* in the sense that they were the first to publish an account of it. This was one of many characterizations of light, ice, and atmospheric phenomena in Forster's text that appear to have entered into Coleridge's "Rime of the Ancient Mariner," according to Bernard Smith's persuasive discussion (*Imagining the Pacific* [New Haven, 1992], 166–167).

Chapter IV, Section I

1. "My mind is bent to tell of bodies changed into new forms" (Ovid, *Metamorphoses*, 1.1f.).

2. The polarity between torpor and agility, between indolence and vigor, which here corresponds with the character of life in frigid and tropical climates respectively, directly recalls the vocabulary of Scottish Enlightenment works such as Kames' *Sketches of the History of Man*, which Forster cites. A primitive or socially degraded condition is generally equated with slumber; a people undergoing one form or another of advancement are "roused." Forster's usage differs from Kames' in that the conditions that produce indolence in humans are understood to apply similarly to animal and plant life, as is evident in this passage.

Chapter IV, Section II

1. This recalls the passage in George Forster's *Voyage* above (see n. 3, chap. I, sect. v, 412).

2. The thesis that the practice of agriculture was fundamental to a more advanced state of civility turned on the point that it required some system of property and was therefore conducive to regulation and government. See Adam Ferguson, *An Essay on the History of Civil Society* (Edinburgh, 1767), 123–124, and for an illuminating discussion, J. G. A. Pocock, "Tangata Whenua and Enlightenment Anthropology," *New Zealand Journal of History* 26 (1992): 28–53.

3. Cf. *Journal*, 542.

4. Cf. *Journal*, 615–617.

5. Cf. *Journal*, 583–584.

6. "It was not at that distance discernible from what mountain the cloud issued, but it was found afterwards to Vesuvius. I cannot give you a more exact description of its shape, than by comparing it to that of a pine-tree, for it shot up a great height in the form of a trunk, which extended itself at the top into several branches; because I imagine, a momentary gust of air blew it aloft, and failing, left it there; thus causing the cloud to expand laterally as it dissolved, or possibly the downward pressure of its own weight produced this effect. It was at one moment white, at another dark and spotted, as if it had carried up earth or cinders" (Pliny the Younger, *Epistles*, 6.16).

Chapter IV, Section III

1. Forster was correct in proposing that coral had been raised in certain places; islands formed in this way include parts of the Tongan archipelago and Niue, as well as Vatoa (Turtle Island).

Chapter IV, Section IV

1. The distinction between low and high islands has been crucial to subsequent geographical observation in the Pacific; the differences between the natural resources on atolls and mountainous islands were of course of great consequence for indigenous subsistence production systems.

2. "... nothing remains therein to be recovered; merely ashes and earth with not a seed [of flame]" (*Aetna*, 429f.). Forster attributes these verses to Cornelius Severus but they are not his. *Aetna* dates from the first century A.D. and appears in the Loeb *Minor Latin Poets*.

3. For the voyage of Jacob Roggeveen, notable for first contact at Easter Island and several Tuamotuan atolls, see O. H. K. Spate's discussion in *Monopolists and Freebooters*, 220–228. The standard modern edition is *The Journal of Jacob Roggeveen* (Oxford, 1974); Forster's source would have been Alexander Dalrymple's *Historical Collection of the Several Voyages and Discoveries in the South Pacific Ocean* (London, 1770–1771), 2:85–120. While Easter Island is certainly of volcanic origin, the destruction Forster noted was the result of recent warfare, not late eruptions.

4. In a number of Polynesian cosmologies the god Maui is credited with having pulled islands up from beneath the sea while fishing from his canoe. Forster's gloss on this, that he "dragged a land" through the ocean, seems something of a distortion.

Chapter V, Section I

1. "Omnis natura vult esse conservatrix sui, ut ... in genere conserveter suo": "Every natural organism aims at being its own preserver, so as to secure ... its preservation true to its specific type" (Cicero, *De Finibus*, 4.16).

2. Here again we find the aesthetic continuum that organizes Forster's description and evaluation of variety: tropical plants are more beautiful, luxuriant, and useful than those of temperate or frigid zones, which come later and last respectively in both the exposition and the implied history of gradual migratory degeneration. The integration, within a description of this kind, of the question of the utility to humankind of different plants and animals, recalls Buffon's treatment of domesticated animals in the *Histoire naturelle*.

3. Poisoning was a relatively common fishing technique in the Pacific.

4. It will be noted here and at a number of other points that Forster ranks the Tahitians above the Tongans, which may surprise readers familiar with the social evolutionary typologies put forward by nineteenth- and twentieth-century ethnologists: in most of these schema, the Tongan and Hawaiian polities (the latter unknown to the British until Cook's third voyage), represent the apex of Polynesian development. While Forster would certainly have agreed that Tongan society was more socially stratified than Tahitian, he regarded this accentuated social differentiation as a regressive feature, understanding it as a variety of Asiatic despotism; this is essentially how John Webber depicted it in his sketch of "Poulaho, King of the Friendly Islands, drinking Kava," which was engraved for the official account of the third voyage (Rudiger Joppien and Bernard Smith, *The Art of Captain Cook's Voyages* [New Haven, 1985–1987], 3:318–319). It is notable that Forster's understanding of Oriental despotism turns more upon behavior and an unseemly subservience than on the elaborate courts and luxury that were perhaps more common in eighteenth-century evocations. This suggests that his interest was less in associating Tonga with the Orient than with extending the political critique of despotism, which had been advanced by the Scottish writers among others, to the Tongan case. For twentieth-century scholarly interpretations of the Tongan polity, see E. W. Gifford, *Tongan Society* (Honolulu, 1929); Noel Rutherford, ed., *Friendly Islands: A History of Tonga* (Melbourne, 1977); and Valerio Valeri, "Death in Heaven: Myths and Rites of Kinship in Tongan Kingship," *History and Anthropology* 4 (1990): 209–247.

5. Cultivation based on the use of the plough was seen to be crucial to the growth of civilization by a number of eighteenth-century writers, because its technical processes produced marks of appropriation and demarcation, which in turn entailed property, property rights, and government (see Pocock, "Tangata Whenua and Enlightenment Anthropology," 31–32). Some Pacific societies, however, were recognizably "civilized" in certain ways, in the absence of plough agriculture; in Tonga, in particular, an elaborate division of private property was identified. Forster's remarks here

upon the attractive and regular spacing of trees and his evocation of an idyllic and ordered pastoral scene suggest that he understood the civilizing effect of agriculture in less technologically determinist terms. Elsewhere (221) he argues that the labor required to tend fruit trees and root crops leads people to agree to refrain from trespassing on one another's plantations and jointly defend them against others; from this follows "certain regulations" and "customary laws." The martial emphasis upon the importance of an external enemy for defense and internal union recalls Ferguson, though the principle is not privileged to the same extent.

6. Forster was in fact misled by the testimonies of those sailors and officers who claimed that the plants of New Caledonia resembled those of Australia (New Holland); he might here have heeded more his own polemical caution concerning the unreliability of "unphilosophical travellers."

7. George Everard Rumphius was the author of *Herbarium Amboinense* (1750), a key botanical text that Banks took on the first voyage in the *Endeavour*.

8. Forster's source for the voyage of Quiros was Dalrymple's *Historical Collection of the Several Voyages and Discoveries in the South Pacific Ocean* (London, 1770–1771); the standard modern edition is *The Voyages of Pedro Fernandez de Quiros, 1595 to 1606*, ed. Clements Markham (London, 1904–1905; Hakluyt n.s., 14/15); the reference to nutmegs is at 443.

9. See Beaglehole, 433–437; *Journal*, 537–538. For an attempt to account for the singular hostility of the people of Niue to visiting mariners, see Thomas, *Entangled Objects*, 88–93.

10. In fact, there are good reasons for believing that polity and population on Easter Island did decline considerably over the period between the visit of Roggeveen and that of Cook; see n. ‡, 264.

11. Tacca: arrowroot was of minor importance in the Tahitian diet (Oliver, *Ancient Tahitian Society*, pp. 252–253).

12. Philip Brown (d. 1779) was a doctor and botanist; the travels of Per (Peter) Loefling (1729–1756) to Spain and South America had been translated by the Forsters; Nikolaus Josef Jacquin (1727–1817) and Joseph de Jussieu (1704–1779) had also engaged in botanical research in America, though Forster may also have had the more extensive publications of Antoine de Jussieu (1686–1758) in mind.

Chapter V, Section II

1. Gay enamel: a lustrous appearance comparable to an enamel painting.

2. In finding the animals of the far south impoverished and deformed, Forster recapitulates the continuum evoked elsewhere in the character of the topography, flora, and human life.

3. What Forster says here is basically correct. Archaeological investigations have shown that on some islands dogs and/or pigs were introduced by Polynesian settlers but died out before European contact. For overviews of Oceanic prehistory, dealing with the transportation of domesticated animals among other topics, see Peter Bellwood, *Man's Conquest of the Pacific* (Auckland, 1978); and Patrick Vinton Kirch, *The Evolution of the Polynesian Chiefdoms* (Cambridge, 1984).

4. Thomas Pennant (1726–1798) was an important naturalist, travel writer, and antiquarian who supported and worked with Forster from 1768 on; see Smith, *Imagining the Pacific*, 37–38; and Hoare, 57–66 passim.

5. See Richard Walter and Benjamin Robbins, *A Voyage Round the World in the Years MDCCXL, I, II, III, IV, by George Anson*, ed. Glyndwr Williams (Oxford, 1974), 122–124 (first published in 1748 and extensively reprinted).

6. Georg Wilhelm Steller (1709–1746) was a naturalist on Bering's expedition in the north Pacific of 1740–1741; see Spate, *Monopolists and Freebooters*, 231–244.

7. Pehr Forsskål (1732–1763) was a pupil of Linnaeus' who died of malaria while conducting

botanical research in southern Arabia; Forster refers to his posthumously published *Flora aegyptiaco-arabica* (Copenhagen, 1775).

8. Pierre Louis Moreau de Maupertuis (1698–1759) wrote on the distinctiveness of species and the nature of hybrids (see *DSB*, 9:186–189), as well as on physics and mathematics.

9. Giovanni Antonio Scopoli (1723–1788), Italian naturalist, author of *Entomologia carniolica* (Vienna, 1763) and *Introductio ad historiam naturalem* (Prague, 1777), among other works.

10. For twentieth-century studies of indigenous economies in New Zealand and the Society Islands, see Raymond Firth, *Primitive Economics of the New Zealand Maori* (London, 1929); and Oliver, *Ancient Tahitian Society*, esp. chap. 9 (though in neither of these is the ethnohistoric reconstruction entirely thorough or satisfying; Anne Salmond, *Two Worlds*, is more up-to-date for New Zealand).

11. Forster's differentiation of Tahitians, "western" islanders, and Tierra del Fuegians on the basis of their respective possession of luxuries, conveniences and necessaries, and bare necessities alone recalls Kames: men in "the hunter-state" were preoccupied with satisfying their bodily needs "and have no time nor zeal for studying conveniences. The ease of the shepherd-state affords both time and inclination for useful arts; which are greatly promoted by numbers who are relieved, by agriculture from bodily labour . . . the surplus hands are employed, first, in useful arts, and, next, in those of amusement. Arts accordingly make the quickest progress in a fertile soil" (*Sketches in the History of Man*, new ed., Edinburgh, 1807, 128); for similar discriminations, see Millar's *Distinction of Ranks* (4th ed., Edinburgh, 1806), 3–4. Had Forster encountered a pastoral population, his discourse would have been more directly articulated with the evolutionary narratives of the Scottish writers, but there is evidently much common ground in the approach to the basic question of the preconditions for civil and moral improvement.

12. Feathers were used by Tahitians in a variety of ornaments but were valuable specifically because they were associated with deities and formed essential components of wicker incarnations of deities *(to'o)* and feather girdles *(maro),* which were the emblems of high chiefly titles (see Oliver, *Ancient Tahitian Society*, 74–78). Potatou's enthusiasm to acquire red feathers from the British might be seen in the context of the fact that a flag left on the island by Wallis in 1767 was subsequently woven into one *maro*, presumably because the Tahitian aristocrats sought to incorporate the singular divine foreignness of the British. On this theme see Marshall Sahlins, *Islands of History* (Chicago, 1985), 74. On the process of barter, see *Journal*, 497, and Beaglehole, 382–383.

13. The fish-poisoning incident is described again in the book's conclusion, 373–376 for Quiros' account, see *The Voyages of Pedro Fernandez de Quiros*, ed. Markham, 390–391 and 447–448.

Chapter VI (preliminary matter)

1. "Some wonder at the heights of mountains, the huge waves of the sea, the deep courses of rivers, the vast compass of the Ocean, and the circular motions of the stars—and they pass themselves by, without wonder"; this is loosely based on Augustine, *Confessions*, 10.8.64–67.

2. *Essay on Man*, epistle 2, l. 2.

3. *Paradise Lost*, bk. 12, ll. 149–151.

4. Forster's assertion of the authority of the "philosophical" traveler, as opposed, on one side, to his "unphilosophical" counterpart, and on the other, to speculative writing uninformed by personal travel, is clearly political and self-serving. However, his claims that scientific travelers had neglected people, while writers on the human species were either unsophisticated or speculative, were warranted, to some degree; even the Linnaean travelers he admired offered little that could retrospectively be called anthropological description or inquiry. The cabinet writers he had in mind no doubt included Rousseau, Voltaire, Montesquieu, and Kames.

5. With respect to the degeneracy of highly civilized societies, Forster was enunciating a standard civic humanist position, which took commerce to be a source of vice (see n. 4, chap. vi, below).

Chapter VI, Section I

1. Cicero should here read "Non enim temere nec fortuito sati et creati sumus, sed profecto fuit quaedam vis quae generi consuleret humano": "For not to blind hazard or accident was our birth and our creation due, but assuredly there was some power which looked to the interests of mankind" (*Tusculan Disputations*, 1.118). Forster alters the tense to read "there is some power."

2. This section corresponds with the draft "On the human Species in the South Sea Isles. On its numbers and population" in Berlin (MS. germ. oct. 79). The prefatory paragraph in the manuscript does not appear in the published text and reads: "Having made a few Remarks on the Vegetable and animal System as far as we could observe something worthy [of] the attention of the learned world: we at last come to the human species, & intend to conclude with some observations on the Population, Colours, Habit, Form, Varieties, Migrations, & endemial Diseases of the inhabitants of the various Countries we have visited in the course of this expedition." The word "conclude" here suggests that Forster may not have anticipated devoting such a large proportion of the book to the human species, though the topics he mentions are more or less those that he in fact proceeds to address. Much of the wording in the remainder of this draft accords closely, though not quite word for word, with the text as published, which incorporates a good deal of elaboration and some reordering of paragraphs. For instance, the following sentences read "We shall begin with O-Taheite one of the largest most prosperous & richly-cultivated islands in the Pacific Ocean. The high Hills of this happy country are without inhabitants: & if we except a few fertile, well watered Vallies, which lie between the high mountains & contain a few Cottages, the whole interior country is unimproved & such as it came out of the hands of Nature"; it will be seen that this approximates the opening sentences of the chapter as published. Among other small differences is a mistake in the arithmetic in the manuscript, where 27,000 men, each with a wife and child, is said to add up to 82,500 rather than 81,000 as is correct here (148).

3. Cavallas: a kind of mackerel.

4. The notion of luxury was highly contested in eighteenth-century debate. In the aristocratic form of what has been defined by J. G. A. Pocock and others as the discourse of civic humanism, commerce, opulence, and luxury were taken as basic sources of effeminacy and political corruption; among the works Forster had certainly read that expressed these conceptions in an elaborate way was Kames' *Sketches of the History of Man*. This vocabulary remained salient in the second half of the eighteenth century, in forms increasingly adapted to a political economy in which commercial acquisitiveness was accorded a more neutral status; this shift can be detected for instance in Ferguson, who insists on the distinctness of luxury and vice (*Civil Society*, 382–383). Forster's view seems intermediate between that of Kames and Ferguson: while retaining the former's sense that opulence is almost inevitably conducive to sensuality and vice, he is less preoccupied with this as a cause of degeneracy, emphasizing instead the preservation or loss of accumulated learning. His view of Tahiti will be seen to be ambivalent, as while he here refers to the absence of luxury, he later refers to the limited commerce in ornaments and associated goods and clearly sees both the aristocracy and the adolescent libertine Arioi society as to some extent corrupted and corruptible on the basis of this sensuality, in conventional civic humanist terms (see, e.g., 231 and 256).

On the discourse of civic humanism, see J. G. A. Pocock, *The Machiavellian Moment: Florentine Political Thought and the Atlantic Republican Tradition* (Princeton, 1975), 430–431 and chaps. 13 and 14 passim; and, for more accessible summaries, John Barrell, *The Political Theory of Painting from Reynolds to Hazlitt* (New Haven, 1986), 3–10; and Stephen Copley, *Literature and the Social Order in*

Eighteenth-Century England (London, 1984), 3–18. Luxury specifically is also extensively discussed by John Sekora in *Luxury: The Concept in Western Thought, Eden to Smollett* (Baltimore, 1977).

5. Cook similarly estimated the Tahitian population on the basis of numbers of canoes (Beaglehole, 409). For more recent assessments, see Norma McArthur, *Island Populations of the Pacific* (Canberra, 1967); and Kirch, *Polynesian Chiefdoms*, 19. Like most early-contact figures, Forster's were considerably exaggerated, though less than the 204,000 proposed by Cook.

6. Aristocratic and political relationships in Tahiti and the Society Islands generally were not well understood by early visitors, and a good deal has remained obscure. Douglas Oliver's *Ancient Tahitian Society* provides an accessible, though not wholly satisfactory account; for a more detailed analysis, see H. A. H. Driessen, "From Ta'aroa to 'Oro: An Exploration of Themes in the Traditional Culture and History of the Leeward Society Islands" (Ph.D. thesis, Australian National University, 1991).

7. I.e., the Tuamotu archipelago, consisting of some 76 atolls, occupied by a total of perhaps 7,000 people in the early-contact period.

8. Here Forster foreshadows an argument concerning the progressive effect of cultivation that is developed at greater length at 221 and elsewhere; but here population growth is accorded a more definite causative role.

Chapter VI, Section II

1. ["And again, as regards the various arts and faculties and institutions of mankind, most of them . . . flourish in any latitude whatsoever] and in certain instances even in spite of latitude; so that some local characteristics of a people come by nature, others by training and habit" (Strabo, 2.3.7; the first part not included).

2. "Brisk" here probably means not "brusque" but "vigorous," the point thus being that while the first race are ranked higher than the second from the viewpoint of beauty, physique, and various criteria of civility, the latter tend to be more continually active than the former, among whom the chiefs particularly lapse into indolence. This reading would resonate with wider ambiguities in Forster's exposition and evaluation of the peoples concerned.

3. *Aree* transliterates *ari'i*, Tahitian for "chief" and cognate with Polynesian words with the same meaning, *ali'i, aliki, ariki,* and so on.

4. *Manahune:* commoners of intermediate rank in Tahitian society, possibly with some property rights, and often differentiated from servants or *teuteu* (Forster's "towtows").

5. Here and elsewhere Forster is informed by Montesquieu's physiology, and specifically the argument that "fibres" are hardened in cold climates and relaxed in the tropics, though his understanding of the consequences for temperament, vigor, and indolence inverts Montesquieu. (Note that, in this context, "climate" refers usually to a latitudinal zone—frigid, temperate, or torrid—rather than environment in a more particular sense.)

> Cold air contracts the extremities of the body's surface fibers; this increases their springs and favors the return of blood from the extremities of the heart. . . . Hot air, by contrast, relaxes these extremities of fibers and lengthens them; therefore it decreases their strength and spring. Therefore, men are more vigorous in cold climates. . . . As you move toward the countries of the south, you will believe you have moved away from morality itself: the liveliest passions will increase crime. . . . The heat of the climate can be so excessive that the body there will be absolutely without strength . . . laziness there will be happiness. (*The Spirit of the Laws,* trans. and ed. Anne Cohler, Basia Miller, and Harold Stone [Cambridge, 1989], 231, 234)

While these propositions influence Forster's understanding at a number of points—where he attributes a "natural levity" to the Tahitians, for example—he by no means follows Montesquieu closely, representing the peoples of the tropics as more vigorous and industrious than those of, say, Tierra del Fuego; but this difference is attributed more to the preservation of education (an emphasis he derives from Isaac Iselin) than to the direct effect of temperature upon the body. Forster also elsewhere rejects Montesquieu's claim that a diet of fish is conducive to a more fecund population.

6. This is wrong. Marquesans lived generally on valley floors, though occasionally they resorted to elevated fortifications.

7. Here and elsewhere "puncturing" refers to tattooing (the Tahitian *tatau* was anglicized through the Cook voyage publications).

8. Toys: artifacts or knicknacks rather than playthings.

9. In equating the nations of ancient Europe with the barbarians of the periphery, Forster was employing a rhetorical and comparative device that had, of course, a long history in European responses to the non-European world; John White's sixteenth-century drawings of Americans and ancient Britons are notable among early examples. However, this form of comparison became far more systematic after Lafitau's *Moeurs des sauvages amériquains comparées aux moeurs des premiers temps* (Paris, 1724), which equated the Iroquois with the Hellenes. Forster would have had at least secondhand familiarity with Lafitau's arguments, and Scottish Enlightenment writers such as Ferguson frequently temporalized difference in the same way. "In their present condition," he wrote of the Americans, "we are to behold, as in a mirrour, the features of our own progenitors" (*Civil Society*, 122).

10. The reference to Strabo is not clear, but at 4.4.3 he says of the Gallic peoples, "But as for their custom relating to the men and the women, (I mean the fact that their tasks have been exchanged, in a manner opposite to what obtains among us), it is one which they share in common with many other barbarian peoples." Tacitus says, "When they [the Germans] are not entering on war, they spend much time in hunting, but more in idleness—creatures who eat and sleep, the best and the bravest warriors doing nothing, having handed over the charge of their home, hearth, and estate to the women and the old men and the weakest members of the family: for themselves they lounge about" (*Germania*, 15.1).

11. The curvilinear forms of Maori carving and *moko* (facial incision, frequently referred to as tattooing but technically distinct) were clearly aesthetically challenging to the European observers: while observations on much Pacific material culture were various or indifferent, Banks, Cook, and Parkinson, on the first voyage, all found Maori carving striking, ingenious, and peculiar (see Bernard Smith, *European Vision and the South Pacific* [New Haven, 1985], 123–125; and Thomas, *Entangled Objects*, 130–138).

12. This note refers implicitly to the old polygenetic argument that negro hair was a form of wool, specifically different from the hair of whites, which had been reiterated by Edward Long in his pro-slavery *History of Jamaica* (London, 1774). Forster both differentiates the hair of the western Pacific islanders from this "wool" and suggests that a common, climatically determined process accounts for both varieties.

13. For the contrasts between voyage attitudes to the people of Vanuatu and eastern Polynesia, see Jolly, " 'Ill-natured Comparisons,' " 331–364.

14. Quiros in fact encountered the people of Espíritù Santo, not Malekula; for his attempt to settle on the island, see *The Voyages of Pedro Fernandez de Quiros*, 241–286.

15. Cf. *Journal*, 567.

16. This is somewhat modified. The original Latin reads "Medio vero terrae salubri utrimque mixtura, fertiles ad omnia tractus, modicos corporum habitus magna et in colore temperie, ritus molles, sensus liquidos, ingenia fecunda totiusque naturae capacia," which translates as "Whereas in

the middle of the earth [i.e., the part of the world between the Ethiopians and the frosty north], owing to a healthy blending of both elements [i.e., heat and damp], there are tracts that are fertile for all sorts of produce, men of medium stature with a marked blending even in their coloring, gentle customs, clear senses, intellects fertile and able to grasp the whole of nature" (Pliny, 2.190). Forster's Latin omits the reference to the "medium stature and marked blending" of the inhabitants.

17. Magalhaens: Magellan. Forster elsewhere maintained that it was "right to spell proper names as they are written in their original language" (translation of Bougainville's *Voyage*, 5 n.).

18. Omai, properly Mai, a Raiatean brought back to Britain with Furneaux in the *Adventure*, was an object of great curiosity in London; like Joseph Banks' natural history, curiosity itself connoted license, and this presumed literalization of its promiscuous character is thus consistent with other moral ambiguities. On Omai, see Smith, *European Vision*, 80–82; E. H. McCormick, *Omai: Pacific Envoy* (Auckland, 1977); and Guest, "Curiously Marked."

19. Compare Cook's perceptions: Beaglehole, 597–598.

20. This term is elsewhere used by Forster as an ethnic label for these people.

21. Train-oil: here meaning oil boiled down from seal fat, presumably used primarily to protect and insulate the skin.

Chapter VI, Section III

1. "Therefrom Venus unfolds forms with varying chance, and recalls the look, the voice, the hair of ancestors" (Lucretius, *De Rerum Natura* [hereafter, Lucretius], 4.1223f.).

2. ". . . idle fancies are shaped like a sick man's dreams" (Horace, *Ars Poetica*, 7f.).

3. Monboddo actually wrote "they are the Ouran Outangs, who, as I have said, are proved to be of our species by marks of humanity that I think are incontestable; they have one property more of the species than the quadruped savages above mentioned, which have been found in different parts of Europe, that they walk erect" (Of *the Origin and Progress of Language* [Edinburgh, 1773]), 1: 289.

4. Connate: inborn, innate.

5. *Paradise Lost*, bk. 8, ll. 471–477, 488–489. In the poem this is Adam's direct speech; hence Forster has altered "my heart" to "his heart."

6. "Specifically" is here used technically, "specifically different" meaning "of different species."

7. Forster uses "race" roughly as an equivalent to subspecies; in some cases, as here, "variety" is equivalent to this, but elsewhere it refers to a more exclusive kind. Hence, the eastern and western Pacific islanders are considered to be two distinct races, which are further divided into varieties such as the Society Islanders and Marquesans, the New Caledonians and Tannese, and so forth.

8. Herodotus, 3.101.

9. Towtows or properly *teuteu* were domestic dependants or "servants" in higher-status or chiefly families; see Oliver, *Ancient Tahitian Society*, 750–751, 859–860.

10. The ambivalence of Forster's view is evident here: the elaboration of private property in Tonga is a positive feature, because it produces greater sophistication in agriculture, but it also has negative ramifications in the development of despotism (cf. particularly 237).

11. Endemial: endemic.

12. In emphasizing the relation between habit and bodily form, Forster is indebted to John Hunter (see n. 2 to preface, 410).

13. The "immense" time scale for environmentally-induced change in the complexion and physique of humans forestalled the critique generally offered of the monogenist, climatic determination view: that blacks transposed to temperate latitudes did not become white as whites in the tropics did not become black. While Forster is nowhere explicit about the kind of chronology he

imagines for the development of variation in the human species, it is suggested at a number of points that individual human lives were but moments in the process.

14. Forster here proposes that if a particular people remain sedentary in one zone for a sufficiently long period, they attain a "certain standard character." This evidently approximates the "original type" that he perceives behind distinct groups of varieties such as the eastern or western Pacific islanders, and bridges what would otherwise appear to be a discrepancy in his exposition of human variety: on one side, races are presented that possess a singular physique, color, and turn of mind, while on the other, the interest is in a continuous series of locally-adapted varieties. The unifying term is migration: its absence—that is, long residence in one climate—results in the stable and distinctive races that elsewhere degenerate or shade into one another after a succession of displacements.

15. Diodorus Siculus, 2.43.6; "next come the two mouths of the river Don, where the inhabitants are the Sarmatae, said to be descended from the Medes" (Pliny, 6.19).

16. Forster correctly saw Polynesian languages and Malay as being related; all are part of the larger Austronesian family. The "Persian" and "Braminic" elements in Malay are not related, as he suggests, to a more ancient ancestral language, but to the more recent Indicization and Islamicization of southeast Asia.

Chapter VI, Section IV

1. "Whatever booty chance had offered to each, he bore it off; for each was taught at his own will to live and thrive for himself alone" (Lucretius, 5.960f.).

2. Preternatural: nonnatural or abnormal.

3. In emphasizing that a high degree of civilization does not necessarily lead to a failure of happiness, Forster differentiates his position from that, for instance, of Kames, who saw the history of civilization in almost cyclical and tragic terms: an improved sociality gives way inevitably to selfishness, opulence, degeneracy, and so on (see, e.g., *Sketches*, i, 275, 280–281, 324–326).

4. A field drawing by Alexander Buchan from the first voyage was consistent with Forster's perception of the wretchedness of the Tierra del Fuegians; but the image was romanticized and classicized by G. B. Cipriani and in an engraving by Bartolozzi after Cipriani that appeared in Hawkesworth's publication (see Joppien and Smith, 1:15–19).

5. The differences to which Forster was responding were very real. The Polynesian settlers of New Zealand had to contend with the fact that the principal tropical plants of their ancestral economies—coconuts, bananas, breadfruit, and the like—would not grow, but sweet potato could be cultivated in much of the North Island and the northeastern fringe of the South. While the northern half of the North Island perhaps contained about 80 percent of the population at the time of contact, the larger part of the South supported nomadic food gatherers who probably amounted to only 15 percent. These contrasts were most striking to those who had been on the first voyage and had therefore visited the most densely populated region, but Forster encountered both the cultivators of Queen Charlotte's Sound and the foragers of Dusky Bay and refers to the account of the first voyage. For the richest account of the Dusky Bay encounter, see George Forster, *Voyage*, 1:123–188; also *Journal*, 238–265; Beaglehole, 109–139; and Cook, *Voyage towards the South Pole*, 1:69–91.

6. Forster again draws on Montesquieu's understanding of the effects of climate upon human "fibres"; see n. 5 to chap. VI, sect. II, 421.

7. While sensuality is often attributed to luxury and opulence, it here characterizes a social condition dominated by wanton passion rather than educated reason.

8. There is an inconsistency between this statement and what is said on 192, where the people of Tierra del Fuego are said "to be themselves conscious of their own misery." In the latter part of the

paragraph, however, Forster is primarily referring to the New Zealanders' vital licentiousness, rather than the wretchedness of the Tierra del Fuegians.

9. The extent to which native peoples found their own mode of life satisfactory or were, to the contrary, interested in the ways of Europeans was frequently adduced as an index of progress, as was the related question of their treatment of strangers: those who were hostile were considered more backward than those who were friendly.

10. The homology developed here between the individual life cycle and social evolution was implied by much usage that infantilized various non-Western peoples and anticipated more explicitly by a number of other eighteenth-century writers (see, e.g., Ferguson, *Civil Society*, 122; and Kames, *Sketches*, iii, 203). However, Forster's specific identifications between the dispositions of savages and infants and those of adolescents and barbarians are more elaborate than most earlier formulations. Ferguson differentiated between savages and barbarians on the grounds of the former's lack and the latter's rudimentary possession of notions of property, but it is not surprising—given the centrality of the development of forms of property for his argument—that he was less concerned to contrast the manners or temperaments peculiar to each stage. Other writers made no clear discrimination between the two states. See Harriet Guest, "The Great Distinction: Figures of the Exotic in the Work of William Hodges," in *New Feminist Discourses*, ed. Isabel Armstrong (London, 1989).

Chapter VI, Section V

1. "But let it be granted to begin with, that we have an affection for ourselves, and that the earliest impulse bestowed upon us by nature is a desire for self-preservation" (Cicero, *De Finibus*, 4.25).

2. Guanacoes: a kind of wild llama, producing a wool used in garments.

3. See *The Spirit of the Laws*, 435.

4. For the coercive prostitution of Maori women, see George Forster, *Voyage*, 1:210–212, and for the boy attacking his mother, 1:510. It appears that this was the only such incident witnessed by either Forster but that members of the crew maintained that they had "frequently" observed violence, and in particular, sons striking their mothers.

5. Forster met Crozet at the Cape in March–April 1775 on the voyage home (*Journal*, 731n.). See also n. 1 to chap. I, sect. IV, 411 above.

6. *Journal*, 599, 628.

7. Beaglehole, 1: 203. Beaglehole is extremely sceptical concerning Cook's interpretation that "Teeratu" was some kind of paramount chief; see his introduction to that volume, cli–cliii.

8. "All other living creatures pass their time worthily among their own species: we see them herd together and stand firm against other kinds of animals: fierce lions do not fight among themselves, the serpent's bite does not attack serpents, even the monsters of the sea and the fishes are only cruel against different species; whereas to man, by Hercules, most of his evils come from his fellow man" (Pliny, 7.5).

9. "He was a god . . . who first found out that principle of life, which now is called wisdom, and who by his skill saved our life from the high seas and thick darkness, and enclosed it in such calm waters and a bright land" (Lucretius, 5.8–12). Forster intends this to be read as "God it was . . . who first found [etc.]," but Lucretius is in fact praising Epicurus.

Chapter VI, Section VI

1. "Then first the race of men began to soften" (Lucretius, 5.1014).

2. *Paradise Lost*, bk. 3, ll. 21–22.

3. Cecrops: mythical first king of Athens; Triptolemus: legendary figure who taught men agri-

culture; Theseus: Athenian hero and king, killer of the Cretan Minotaur; Solon (c. 640–c. 560 B.C.): Athenian lawmaker; Pisistratus or Peisistratus (c. 600–527 B.C.): Athenian warrior and ruler; the reference is probably to the younger Miltiades (c. 550–489 B.C.), warrior with Darius, subsequently influential in Athens; Aristides or Aristeides (d. c. 486 B.C.): Athenian general and key figure in the formation of the Delian League. Forster's point is that Athenian civility was the product of a long process of military and political accomplishment.

4. A "two strata" theory of Polynesian migration and social class differentiation, which took chiefs to be conquerors, and commoners to be the descendants of an indigenous inferior race, was widely entertained by later ethnologists, but retains no credibility today.

5. I.e., Luzon and Mindanao, in the Philippines.

6. See *The Endeavour Journal of Sir Joseph Banks*, ed. J. C. Beaglehole [Sydney, 1961], 1: 288–289.

7. For the voyage of Oliver van Noort, see Spate, *Monopolists and Freebooters*, 5–9; Forster's source was no doubt the account in Purchas' *Pilgrimes*.

8. For the ramifications in Polynesian history of Roggeveen's loss, see H. A. H. Driessen, "Outriggerless Canoes and Glorious Beings: Pre-Contact Prophesies in the Society Islands," *Journal of Pacific History* 17 (1982): 3–28.

9. Aristides: Athenian politician (c. 520–c. 468 B.C.); Agesilaus: Spartan king (444–360 B.C.); Leonidas, Spartan king at battle of Thermopylae (d. 480 B.C.); Fabius: probably either Maximus Rullianus, hero of wars against Etruscans, Gauls, and Samnites in the fourth century B.C., or Maximus Verrucosus, who defended Rome against Hannibal; Africanus: Scipio Africanus (236–184 B.C.); Cato (234–139 B.C.). All these figures exemplify a specifically martial patriotism.

Chapter VI, Section VII

1. "She [i.e., Athens] first gave sweet solace for life" (Lucretius, 6.4).

2. Here again a low rank in "the class of human beings" is equated specifically with nomadism.

3. There appears to be a slip of the pen or printer's error here, since Forster elsewhere (notably at 159–164) ranks the people of New Caledonia above those of Tanna and Malekula.

4. The Tahitians among other Pacific islanders did in fact respond initially to European animals in the way Forster suggests, regarding introduced quadrupeds such as goats, sheep, and later cattle as variations upon pigs.

5. Messalina: promiscuous wife of the emperor Claudius.

6. " . . . clad in her ungirt tunic" (Ovid, *Fasti*, 3.654).

7. In fact, Hodges' drawing, and a canceled proof plate here reproduced, were more ethnographically accurate; see Joppien and Smith, 2:87–92.

8. On British responses to Polynesian tattooing see Guest, "Curiously Marked." On the Polynesian art forms themselves, Alfred Gell's *Wrapping in Images: Tattooing in Polynesia* (Oxford, 1993), is the most stimulating discussion.

9. "He has won all applause who has blended profit with pleasure" (Horace, *Ars Poetica*, 343).

10. Wallis' narrative is in John Hawkesworth, *An account of the voyages undertaken by the order of His Present Majesty for making discoveries in the Southern Hemisphere, and successively performed by Commodore Byron, Captain Wallis, Captain Carteret and Captain Cook, in the Dolphin, the Swallow and the Endeavor.* (London, 1773), 1: 363–522.

11. For debate about these incidents of violence, see Wales' *Remarks* and George's *Reply*.

12. This point has already been qualified; see 231–233 and 234.

13. The Arioi society consisted of younger and notably aristocratic islanders dedicated to the

cult of the deity ʻOro, which was celebrated through feasting, theatrical performances, and so on. Though marked by promiscuity—and therefore frequently discussed to one end or another by mariners, missionaries, and travelers—Arioi were obliged to restrain from reproducing (presumably so that illegitimate offspring of high-ranking individuals could not makes claims upon titles or property) and therefore extensively practiced infanticide. See Oliver, *Ancient Tahitian Society*, 913–964; and, for more recent interpretation, Gell, *Wrapping in Images*, chap. 4.

14. The kind of identification between social advancement and the status of women developed here was a commonplace of Enlightenment social theory; see, for example, Millar's *Observations*, Kames, and Iselin (see Harriet Guest's essay).

15. "And Venus would unite lovers in the woods; for each woman was wooed either by mutual passion, or by the man's fierce force and reckless lust" (Lucretius, 5.962–964).

16. Though relatively little direct criticism of common sailors enters into the *Observations*, Forster clearly regarded them as depraved and brutal, particularly in this context of prostitution, in which, in contradistinction to relations at Tahiti, women were offered against their will by their male relatives; there is a more extensive and sharply critical passage in George's *Voyage* (1:210–216). For attempts to reconstruct indigenous perceptions of these relationships, see Marshall Sahlins, *Historical Metaphors and Mythical Realities* (Ann Arbor, 1981), 38–42; and Caroline Ralston, "Changes in the Lives of Ordinary Women in Early Post-Contact Hawaii," in *Family and Gender in the Pacific*, ed. Margaret Jolly and Martha Macintyre (Cambridge, 1989); both of these deal with Hawaii rather than Polynesia generally.

17. "In former days this was wisdom . . . to check vagrant union, to give rules for wedded life" (Horace, *Ars Poetica*, 396, 398).

18. The argument here that segregated eating is a vestige of a more barbaric order constructs the Society Islands as an advance upon other Pacific nations (and specifically New Zealand); this progressive evolutionary model inverts the temporality postulated elsewhere. In other sections of the book, Forster construes the tropical populations as exemplars of an original condition and the more debased inhabitants of colder regions as subsequent offshoots from them (see Nicholas Thomas' essay in this volume).

19. In several passages in the latter third of the book, particularly as here where Forster discusses promiscuity or other forms of vice, the presence and effects of luxury in Tahiti are noted, inverting the emphasis in certain earlier statements (for example, 253).

20. Venery: sexual indulgence.

21. Covering: copulation.

22. Strabo's text (11.13.11), which says that both Median men and women had at least five spouses, is thought to be corrupt (note to Loeb edition, 314).

23. This refers to Caesar's *Gallic War*, 5.15: "Groups of ten or twelve men have wives together in common, and particularly brothers along with brothers, and fathers with sons."

24. The invariably difficult exercise of estimating early-contact populations is complicated here by the fact that Easter Island underwent catastrophic ecological deterioration over the seventeenth and eighteenth centuries and moved into a self-destructive dynamic of endemic warfare (Kirch, *Polynesian Chiefdoms*, 264–278; Nicholas Thomas, *Out of Time: History and Evolution in Anthropological Discourse* [Cambridge, 1989], 59–64). Hence the population may have been as high as seven thousand at the time of Roggeveen's visit, but it was certainly considerably lower by 1774; nevertheless, the figure of nine hundred seems too small, as there are sound estimates of about fifteen hundred for the first half of the nineteenth century. Though there are various reasons why men may have considerably outnumbered women, Forster's observation of only fifty suggests that most were in hiding; this parallels the responses of some other Pacific populations who, by reason of their

cultural construction of political relationships, did not regard foreigners as chiefly beings to be welcomed (see Thomas, *Entangled Objects*, 91–93).

25. For the buccaneer Edward Davis, see Spate, *Monopolists and Freebooters*, 149–151. Forster's source was presumably [David Henry], *An Historical Account of all the Voyages round the world performed by English Navigators* (London, 1774).

26. The loss or abandonment of ancestral customs in the course of migration is again pivotal to Forster's discussion: while he mostly sees such changes as detrimental to systems of knowledge and civility, here, as in the case of the Tahitian amelioration of the kind of despotism that still prevailed in Tonga, the modification amounts to an improvement.

27. "...soon Lalage will seek a mate with bold forwardness, and will be more doted on than..." (Horace, *Odes*, 2.5).

28. For discussion of this passage in the context of eighteenth-century notions of ornament, see Guest, "Great Distinction." The arches tattooed on women's buttocks are depicted in Hodges' "View Taken in the Bay of Otaheite Peha" (see color plate S).

29. The note is a direct translation of Herodotus 5.6.

Chapter VI, Section VIII

1. "Practice and therewith the inventiveness of the eager mind taught them little by little, as they went forward step by step" (Lucretius, 5.1452f.).

2. For a useful survey of Polynesian bark-cloth, see Simon Koojiman, "*Tapa* Techniques and *Tapa* Patterns in Polynesia: A Regional Differentiation," in *Primitive Art and Society*, ed. Anthony Forge (New York, 1973); a small volume with printed accounts of the process of manufacture, incorporating this passage of Forster, with actual specimens cut from pieces collected on Cook's voyages, was published by Alexander Shaw in 1787 (*A Catalogue of Different Specimens of Cloth . . .*, London).

3. The chief mourner's dress was particularly an object of fascination for Banks, on the first voyage; see n. 6 to chap. VI, sect. VI, 426.

4. "Though ships were made with sewed seams, yet it was with flax that they were sewed and never with esparto [a Spanish or African grass]" (Pliny, 24.65).

5. See Walter and Robbins, *A Voyage Round the World in the Years MDCCXL, I, II, III, IV, by George Anson*, 305–308.

6. The improvisation of verse was at this time regarded as a peculiarly Italian capacity.

7. "... Nature, who gave tears to human kind, confessed that she had given a tender heart" (Juvenal, *Satires*, 15.131–133).

8. Apuleius, *Metamorphoses*, 3.11.

9. "We always take delight in feasts, in music and dancing, in fresh clothes, warm baths, and [comfortable] beds."

10. Burden: in the sense of a refrain or chorus.

11. The beverage referred to is the narcotic generally known as kava, still consumed widely in the western Pacific but now abandoned in Tahiti and the rest of eastern Polynesia.

12. The classical references are to Herodotus, 4.73–75; Tacitus, *Germania*, 22f.; and Maximus Tyrius, 21.6.

13. The term leprosy is used loosely here, probably in fact to relate to yaws.

14. See Howard M. Smith, "The Introduction of Venereal Disease into Tahiti: a Re-examination," *Journal of Pacific History* 10 (1975): 38–45. Forster is incorrect in arguing that venereal disease was already endemic in Tahiti; but yaws, which he is unlikely to have distinguished it from, was. There has long been Anglo-French argument about whether Bougainville's or Wallis' voyage was responsible for the introduction of syphilis, but Smith establishes that it was very likely to have been the latter, who visited in June 1767, eight months before Bougainville.

15. " . . . from, moreover, a filthy and pertinacious disease, and involuntary and imperceptible flux of semen"; Tristano Caracciola, *De Varietate Fortunae*, in *Rerum Italicarum Scriptores*, ed. L. A. Muratori et al., vol. 22.1, p. 75.

16. These references to medieval sources on the history of venereal disease have been among the most difficult of Forster's citations to trace. For example, with respect to Pintor, it is unlikely that he saw the original book of 1499, and unclear whether his source was Luisini's 1728 treatise (*Aphrodisiacus*, Leiden), the abridged translation of this work (J. Armstrong's *Synopsis . . . of venereal diseases*, London, 1737), or some other book altogether. Of the works listed, we have been unable to trace *L'art de verifier les dates*, the *Cardamic Chronicle*, and the work of "Joh. Zach."

17. Tupaia's chart, together with associated lists of island names, has fueled much debate concerning the nature of Polynesian geographical knowledge, the question of whether the settlement of Polynesia proceeded primarily through deliberate or accidental (drift) voyages, and some related issues concerning early European contact; see Andrew Sharp, *Ancient Voyagers in Polynesia* (London, 1957); Jack Golson, ed., *Polynesian Navigation*, 3d ed. (Wellington, 1972); G. R. Lewthwaite, "The Puzzle of Tupaia's Map," *New Zealand Geographer* 26 (1970): 1–19; Robert Langdon, "Of Time, Prophecy, and the European Ships of Tupaia's Chart," *Journal of Pacific History* 19 (1984): 239–247; and H. A. H. Driessen, "Outriggerless Canoes and Glorious Beings Revisited: A Reply to Robert Langdon," *Journal of Pacific History* 19 (1984): 248–257. While some of the islands listed by Forster were certainly often visited by Tahitians, problems concerning orthography and other factors make identification, in many cases, a speculative project outside the scope of these annotations. The following list incorporates reasonably clear identifications, mainly of larger islands in the Societies, the Tuamotus, the Marquesas, and the Austral islands. The fullest and generally most adequate effort to correlate the various lists obtained by participants in the Cook voyages and others with present geographical knowledge remains G. M. Dening's "The Geographical Knowledge of the Polynesians and the Nature of Inter-Island Contact," in *Polynesian Navigation*, 102–153.

1.	Tahiti	22.	Anaa
2.	Mehetia	25.	Kaukura
9.	Tubuai	27.	Rangiroa
12.	Rurutu	28.	Tahanea
13.	Tubuai Manu	30.	Fakarava
14.	Eimeo (Moorea)	31.	Hao
15.	Huaheine	42.	Hiva Oa
17.	Raiaetea	48.	Rurutu
18.	Tahaa	50.	Mangaia
19.	Bora Bora	52.	Rimatara
20.	Tupai	53.	Raivavae

18. Quiros did not in fact sight Tahiti; see O. H. K. Spate, *The Spanish Lake*, vol. 1 in *The Pacific since Magellan* (Canberra, 1979), 127–138, for his voyage of 1605–1606.

19. It typifies the difficulties of interpreting the list that, while number 35 is a convincing transcription of Nuku Hiva, in the Marquesas, this is hardly a small island in eastern Polynesian terms.

20. "O-Heavài" probably refers to the ancestral Polynesian homeland, known as Hawaiki, Hawai'i, and Savai'i in various languages, rather than the island of Savai'i in Samoa, as is proposed by Dening among other commentators.

21. There is no number 8.

22. On Tupaia, see Beaglehole, 1:111–156 passim; he died on 26 December 1770, at Batavia.

23. "All hail to your genius, you who interpret the heavens and grasp the facts of nature, discoverers of a theory by which you have vanquished gods and men!" (Pliny, 2.54).

Chapter VI, Section IX

1. Genethliac: relating to birth or birthdays.

2. "Frail, toiling mortality, remembering its own weakness, has divided those [deities] into groups, so that each may worship in portions what he is especially in need of. Consequently, different races have different names for the deities, and we find countless deities in the same races" (Pliny, 2.15).

3. "Guardian spirits" or "gods of inferior orders."

4. Forster's Latin here translates, in places loosely, the Greek of Nicomachus Gerasmus. The Latin may be translated: "Harmony brings to perfection the active powers and productive arts of the gods. For that reason, the cultic magicians, when they worship some god or other with especial piety, invoke him with hissing and an inarticulate buzzing without consonnants" (Nicomachus Gerasena, *Excerpta* 6). The main deviation from the Greek is that Forster quotes Nicomachus as writing εναρθροις (articulate) but translates him as intending αναρθροις (inarticulate).

5. Apollonius Rhodius, *Argonautica*, 3200–3209; Aelian, *Varia Historia*, 4.1.

6. Herodotus, 2.123.

7. "There are pleasant green meadows near Memphis in which are the tombs of the Egyptians—they call the meadows the Elysian fields. There is a marsh nearby, full of lotus plants and reeds, and it gives off a heavy odor. Across this marsh are carried the corpses. Thus Orpheus says, 'to be carried across Acheron.' " This does not in fact appear in Servius' commentary on the Aeneid (the passage Forster has in mind is 6.637–678, on Elysium), nor has the last phrase attributed to Orpheus been traced in Orphica's *Argonautica*.

8. " . . . where Proteus says: 'but the immortal Gods will send you to the Elysian field and the ends of the earth' " (Homer, *Odyssey*, 4.563f.).

9. I.e., belonging to Acheron, a river in Hades.

10. Forster's "A meadow full of herbage, where the soul lives" loosely translates his quotation from Homer, which might more fully be rendered "A meadow of asphodel, where dwell the spirits [of the dead]." Αχερουσια (Acherusia) is the name of a lake that in ancient times lay in a plain of the same name in Epirus in northwest Greece, near ηελιοιο πυλαι (Gates of the Sun) and λευχας πετρα (White Rock), a promontory on the coast of Epirus or on the nearby island of Leucas. The landscape of this region is referred to by Homer in *Odyssey* 24:11–14 and was reputed to contain the entrance to Hades. But Forster compares (or confuses) the features of this landscape—plain, lake, gates of the sun, white rock—with the landscape around Memphis in Egypt, where Servius situates the Elysian fields or plains alongside a rushy lake. Nearby, Forster adds, were the temple of Serapis (whom Forster identifies as a sun god) and Leucotiche (White Walls), which according to Thucydides was an area of the city of Memphis.

11. "And in all probability the disappearance of piety towards the gods will entail the disappearance of loyalty and social union among men as well, and of justice itself, the most excellent of the virtues" (Cicero, *De Natura Deorum*, 1.4).

Chapter VI, Section X

1. "The similarity of the human race is clearly marked not only in good deeds but also in small ones." This is something of a departure from Cicero, *De Legibus*, 1.31: "The similarity of the human race is clearly marked in its evil tendencies as well as in its goodness."

2. Ammianus Marcellinus, 31.2.2; Jordanes, *Getica*, 127f.

3. Agathias, *Historia*, 5.20.2; the reference to Menander Protector has not been traced; Sidonius Apollinarius, *Carmina*, 7.238–240.

4. Diodorus Siculus 5.28.1f. He says that the hair of the Gauls is blonde and is lightened with limewater. At 5.27 there is a reference to the abundance of gold, but none to the strewing of gold dust through the hair.

5. "Let her not dye her hair red, and let her not anticipate for herself the fires of hell" (Jerome, *Epistles*, 107.5, paraphrased).

6. Andre Brue's voyages to Africa of 1697–1715 were published in Thomas Astley's *New General Collection of Voyages and Travels* (London, 1745–1747), 2:27–138; Forster's source was probably Prevost d'Exiles' *Histoire générale des voyages*, of which the first ten volumes were a translation of Astley.

7. "For although the nature of man is weaker than that of other animals, which a heavenly providence has strengthened with natural protections, either for enduring the force of the seasons or for warding off attacks from their bodies—because none of these has been given to man, in their place he has received the affection of pity which is usually called humanity, by which we ourselves protect each other" (Lactantius, *Institutiones Divinae*, 3.23.9).

Chapter VI, Section XI

1. A draft among the Berlin manuscripts—"5. On the Diseases incident to Europeans in these Climates, & on the Preservation of their Health in long Voyages," of twelve manuscript pages—corresponds in subject matter with this section but is much more descriptive and less systematic than the text that was published. There is nothing in the draft corresponding to the general section on phlogiston and varieties of food and the association between certain deficiencies and certain illnesses. The section of the manuscript that is closest to the book is the last part, dealing with the fish-poisoning incident; see n. 9 following.

2. "So it is of use that everyone should recognize against what, and when, he should be most on his guard" (Celsus, *De Medicina*, praef.).

3. Fomes: substances containing contagious effluvia, sources of infection.

4. Phlogiston was believed to exist in combination with all combustible bodies.

5. Orlop: the deck covering the hold of a vessel.

6. Oedematous: characterized by retention of fluids and consequent swelling.

7. Rob: the juice.

8. Inspissated: thickened.

9. See *Journal*, 649–651; for the significance of this incident as a fitting conclusion to the book, see Michael Dettelbach's essay in this volume. Three and a half pages of the draft referred to above (n. 1) relate to this section and are clearly based on Forster's journal. The degree of similarity to the published text may be judged from the first few lines of the relevant section, which in the manuscript read "Before I conclude this Article, I cannot omit a Circumstance which befel us, & might perhaps have proved fatal to many of us, if proper care had not been taken to prevent the ill consequences of it. When we were at Mallicollo at Anchor, our People caught in the Night 2 or 3 large reddish Fish, which they immediately cleared of the Garbage & Scales, & cut the Belly & Gills open, so that when I got up in the morning I suspected them to be a new kind of Fish." This section concludes with a statement of the natives' willingness to provide advice concerning the risks or otherwise of consuming particular fish—"they are good-natured enough every where to give You a fair Warning in such Cases"—but lacks the rhetorical embellishment that Forster has added in the final version.

10. "Certain persons, and those not without some pretension to letters, disapprove of the study of philosophy altogether. Others do not so greatly object to it provided it is followed in dilet-

tante fashion; but they do not think it ought to engage so large an amount of one's interest and attention" (Cicero, *De Finibus*, 1.1).

Appendix II

Forster's Polynesian Linguistics

1. MS Forster, section I, part 2, in Stiftung Preussischer Kulturbesitz, Berlin.

2. *A Journal of a Voyage round the World, In his Majesty's Ship* Endeavour, *In the Years 1768, 1769, 1770, and 1771*. The author is thought to be James Magra.

3. "He it was among our people who possessed the best knowledge of the [Tahitian] language" (Beaglehole, 884).

4. While in Tahiti Gibson deserted together with Webb. They were caught and punished. "It appear'd that an acqueentence they had contracted with two Girls and to whom they had stron[g]ly attached themselves was the sole reason for their attempting to Stay behind" (Beaglehole, *Endeavour*, 116).

5. "I went one day to a marai in Matavai in company with Captain Furneaux, having along with us, as I had upon every other occasion a marin who was with me last voyage and who spoke the language tolerably well" (Beaglehole, 233).

6. Cook politely refrains from mentioning Gibson by name when he states "but we were not masters enough of their language to understand them" (ibid.).

7. *Taio* was thought to be a word universally understood by all Pacific islanders. When making contact with the native population of a newly discovered island the Europeans used to shout "tayo, tayo" to indicate that they were coming as friends.

8. MS Forster, section II, part 1, in Stiftung Preussischer Kulturbesitz, Berlin.

9. In the orthography of modern Polynesian languages the apostrophe ' is used to represent the glottal stop.

10. "Die Engländer schreiben fremde Namen äusserst willkürlich und man kann nicht genau bestimmen, welches nach unserer Art die wahre Ausprache sei." (*Reise*, 182n1).

11. "Ich habe deshalb die Namen der Inseln so geschrieben, wie sie ein Deutscher aussprechen sollte: folglich Owhyhee, Owaihie; Mowee, Mauï; Morety, oder Morotai, Morotay (wie es Cook schrieb); Ranai, Ranay; Whahoo (oder wie es Cook schrieb: Whoahoo) Wahuh; Attoói, Atuai, und Oneehow, Oniehau" (*Reise*, 182).

Bibliography

A. Works by George Forster and Johann Reinhold Forster

Forster, George. 1777. *A Voyage Round the World in His Brittanic Majesty's Sloop*, Resolution. London. [The only modern edition, ed. Robert L. Kahn, constitutes Band 1 of *Georg Forsters Werke*, Berlin, 1968].

———. 1778. *A Letter to the Right Honourable the Earl of Sandwich*. London.

———. 1778. *A Reply to Mr. Wales' Remarks*. London.

Forster, Johann Reinhold. 1767. "Specimen Historiae Naturalis Volgensis." *Philosophical Transactions* 57:312–357.

———. 1768. *Introduction to Mineralogy*. London.

———. 1768. "A Letter from Mr. J. R. Forster, F.A.S. to M. Maty, M.D. Sec. R.S. containing some Account of a new Map of the River Volga." *Philosophical Transactions* 58:214–216.

———. 1771. "A Letter from Mr. John Reinhold Forster, F.A.S. to the Hon. Daines Barrington, Vice-Pres. R.S. on the Management of Carp in Polish Prussia." *Philosophical Transactions* 61: 310–325.

———. 1773. "Observations on some Tartarian Antiquities, described in the Previous Article." *Archaeologia: or Miscellaneous Tracts Relating to Antiquity* 2:227–235.

———. 1776. *Characteres generum plantarum, quas in itinere ad insulas maris australis collegerunt, descripserunt, delinearunt annis MDCCLXXII–MDCCLXXV*. London. [See also Elizabeth Edgar, "Preface to *Characteres Generum Plantarum* by J.R. and G. Forster, a translation," *New Zealand Journal of Botany* (1969), 311–315].

———. 1786. *History of the Voyages and Discoveries Made in the North*. London.

———. 1788. *Enchiridion Historiae Naturali Inserviens*. Halle.

———. 1795. "Über Georg Forster." *Annalen der Philosophie und des philosophischen Geistes. Philosophischer Anzeiger*, 14 January, cols. 9–16; 15 April, cols. 121–128.

———. 1799. *Manuel pour servir à l'histoire naturelle des oiseaux, des poissons, des insectes et des plantes*, trans. J. B. F. Léveillé. Paris.

———. 1982. *The* Resolution *Journal* (see under Hoare).

Hoare, Michael E., ed. 1982. *The* Resolution *Journal of Johann Reinhold Forster*. London.

B. Works Referred to by Forster

*Works already listed in section A are not included here; * indicates a book known to have been in Forster's library on the voyage; see Smith, Imagining the Pacific, 242–243, and Hoare, Journal.*

Adanson, Michel. 1757. *Histoire naturelle du Senegal . . . avec la relation abrege d'un voyage fait en ce pays, pendant les annees 1749, 50, 51, 52, 53*. Paris. [English ed., London, 1759.]

Anglerius (Petrus Martyr). *Opus epistolarum*. Amsterdam.

Armstrong, J. 1737. *A Synopsis of the History and Cure of Venereal Diseases*. London. (This book is possibly one of Forster's sources for information from Petrus Pintor [qv] and other writers.)

Atkins, John. 1737. *A Voyage to Guinea, Brasil and the West Indies*. 2d ed. London. [Forster's source may have been the extract in Astley and Prevost d'Exiles.]

Barentz (see under Renneville).

Barrington, Daines. 1775. *The Probability of Reaching the North Pole Discussed*. London.

Baster, Jobus. 1759–1765. *Opusculas subseciva, observationes miscellaneas de animalculis et plantis guibusdam marinis, eurumque ovariis et seminibus continentia*. Haarlem.

Beckett, William. 1720. "A Letter Concerning the Antiquity of the Venereal Disease." *Philosophical Transactions* 31: 47–65.

———. 1720. "A Letter . . . In Answer to Some Objections Made to the History of the Antiquity of the Venereal Disease." *Philosophical Transactions* 31: 108–112.

Beeckman, Daniel. 1718. *A Voyage to and from the Island of Borneo*. London.

Bergano, Diego. 1732. *Vocabulario de la lengua pampango en romance*. Manila. [Later editions include Manila, 1860.]

Bergman, Torben. 1766. *Physisk beskrifning ofver jord-klotet*. Uppsala.

Blumenbach, Johann Friedrich. 1776. *De generis humani varietate nativa*. Göttingen. [Later editions include *The Anthropological Treatises of Johann Friedrich Blumenbach*, trans. and ed. Thomas Bendyshe, London, 1865, and New York, 1969.]

Boscovich, Ruggiero Giuseppe. 1772. *Journal d'un Voyage de Constantinople en Pologne en 1762*. Lausanne.

Bosman, Willem. 1705. *A New and Accurate Description of the Coast of Guinea*. London. [Ed. J. R. Willis and J. D. Fage, London, 1967.]

Bougainville, Louis Antoine de. 1772. *A Voyage Round the World . . . in the Frigate "La Boudeuse" and the Store Ship "L'Etoile,"* trans. J. R. Forster. London. [French text, ed. Jacques Proust, Paris, 1982; facsimile of English edition, Amsterdam, 1967.]

Bouguer, Pierre. 1729. *Essai d'Optique sur la gradation de la lumière*. Paris.

Bourzes, Father. 1730. *Lettres Edifiantes et Curieuses, Ecrites des Missions Etrangères*, t. ix. Paris. [The full work appeared in 34 volumes over 1702–1776.]

Bouvet (see under Dalrymple, 1775).

Brosses, Charles de. 1756. *Histoire des navigation aux terres australes*. Paris. [John Callender is basically a translation.]

Brue (see Prevost d'Exiles).

Bryant, Jacob. 1767. *Observations and inquiries relating to various parts of ancient history*. London.

*Buffon, Georges Louis Leclerc, Comte de. 1752–1768. *Histoire naturelle, générale et particulière, avec la description du cabinet du Roi*. Paris. [The pagination of what Forster refers to as the duodecimo edition corresponds with this fifth edition.]

Candidus, Georgius. 1725. "Relation de l'état de l'isle Formosa." In R. A. C. de Renneville, *Recueil des voyages qui ont servi à l'établissement et aux progrez de la compagnie des Indes Orientales*. Rouen. [Forster apparently used the edition of 1754.]

Canton, John. "Experiments to prove the luminousness of the sea arises from the putrefaction of its animal substances." *Philosophical Transactions* 59:446.

Carracciolus, Tristanus. 1934–1935. *Opusculi storici*, ed. G. Paladino. Bologna. (The work referred to by Forster appears to have been part of Muratori's *Rerum Italicarum Scriptores*, qv.)

Chardin, Jean. 1711. *Voyages de Monsieur le Chevalier Chardin, en Perse, et autres lieux de l'Orient*. Amsterdam. [This was the first full edition; modern editions include *Sir John Chardin's Travels in Persia*, London, 1927.]

Clayton, William. 1776. "An Account of the Falkland Islands." *Philosophical Transactions* 66: 99–108.

Cook, James. 1777. *A Voyage towards the South Pole and round the world, performed in His Majesty's Ships the* Resolution *and* Adventure. London. [Facsimile, Adelaide, 1968.]

Court de Gebelin, Antoine. 1773–1782. *Monde primitif, analysé et comparé avec le monde moderne.* Paris.

Crantz, David. 1767. *A History of Greenland: Containing a Description of the Country.* London.

Cronstedt, Axel Fredrik. 1772. *An Essay towards a System of Mineralogy.* London.

Curtis, Roger. 1774. "Particulars of the Country of Labradore, extracted from the Papers of Lieutenant Roger Curtis, of his Majesty's Sloop the *Otter*." *Philosophical Transactions* 64: 372–388.

Dalrymple, Alexander. 1769. *Memoir of a Chart of the Southern Ocean.* London.

———. 1770–1771. *A Historical Collection of the Several Voyages and Discoveries in the South Pacific Ocean.* London.

———. 1773. *Letter from Mr. Dalrymple to Dr. Hawkesworth.* London.

———. 1775. *A Collection of Voyages, Chiefly in the Southern Atlantic Ocean.* London.

*[Dampier, William]. 1729. *A Collection of Voyages in four volumes. . . .* I: *Captain William Dampier's voyage around the world.* London.

D'Arvieux, Laurent. 1717. *Voyage fait par ordre du Roy Louis XIV dans la Palestine.* Paris.

Dillon, ———. 1698. *Voyage to the East Indies* (Eng. ed.). London.

Discourse sur les vignes Dijon. 1756.

Du Halde, Jean Baptiste. 1736. *The General History of China.* London. [Translation of *Description géographique, historique, chronologique et physique de l'Empire et de la Tartarie Chinoise,* Paris, 1735.]

Falkner, Thomas. 1774. *A Description of Patagonia.* Hereford.

Ferber, Johann Jacob. 1776. *Travels through Italy in the years 1771 and 1772,* trans. R. E. Raspe. London.

Fernandez Navarrete, Domingo. 1676. *Tratados historicos, politicos, ethicos, y religiosos de la monarchia de China.* Madrid.

Forsskål, Pehr. 1775. *Flora Aegyptico-Arabica.* Havniae.

Franklin, Benjamin. 1774. *Experiments and observations on electricity.* 5th ed. London.

*Frézier, A.-F. 1717. *A Voyage to the South-Seas, and along the Coasts of Chili and Peru.* London.

*Gemelli Careri, G. F. 1699–1700. *Giro del mondo del dottor D. Gio Francesco Gemelli Careri.* Naples.

Gmelin, Johann Georg. 1751–1752. *Reise durch Sibirien.* Göttingen.

Gobien, Charles le (see under Bourzes).

Gomara, Francisco Lopez de. 1749. *Historia general de las Indes.* Madrid.

Goree, Father. 1710–1712. "A Relation of a New Island, which was Raised up from the Bottom of the Sea, on the 23rd of May, 1707, in the Bay of Santorini." *Philosophical Transactions* 27: 354–375.

Gumilla, Joseph. 1741. *El Orinoco ilustrado.* Madrid.

Halley (see under Dalrymple, 1775).

Hamilton, Sir William. 1772. *Observations on Mount Vesuvius, Mount Etna, and other Volcanos: in a Series of Letters, addressed to the Royal Society.* London.

Hawkesworth, John. 1773. *An account of the voyages undertaken by the order of His Present Majesty for making discoveries in the Southern Hemisphere, and successively performed by Commodore Byron, Captain Wallis, Captain Carteret and Captain Cook, in the* Dolphin, *the* Swallow *and the* Endeavor.

Hawkins, Richard. 1622. *The Observations of Sir Richard Hawkins Knight, in his Voyage into the South Sea.* London. [Republished as Hakluyt o.s., vol. 1.]

[Henry, David]. 1774. *An Historical Account of all the Voyages round the world performed by English Navigators*. London.

Higgins, B. 1776. *Observations on the Floating Ice which is Found in High Northern and Southern Latitudes. (A Second Supplement to [Barrington's] The Probability of Reaching the North Pole)*. London.

Hunter, Dr. John. 1775. *Disputation inauguralis, quaedem de hominum varietatibus*. Edinburgh. [Subsequently published in *The Anthropological Treatises of Johann Friedrich Blumenbach*, ed. and trans. Thomas Bendyshe, London, 1865.]

Hunter, William. 1776. *De codem argumento*. Edinburgh.

Iselin, Isaac. 1768. *Über die Geschichte der Menschheit*. Basel.

Jordanes (6th c.). *The Gothic History of Jordanes in English version*, ed. C. C. Mierow. Cambridge, 1915.

La Faye, Jean Baptiste de. 1703. *Etat des royaumes de Barbarie, Tripoly, Tunis, et Alger*. Rouen.

Kaempfer, Engelbert. 1727. *The History of Japan, together with a Description of the Kingdom of Siam*. London.

Kames, Lord (Henry Home). 1774. *Sketches of the History of Man*. 2 vols. Edinburgh. (Editors' citations are to the "new edition" of 1807, 3 vols., Edinburgh.)

Keeling (see Purchas).

Keysler, Johann George. 1720. *Antiquitates Selectae Septentrionales et Celticae*. Hanover.

Knivet, Anthony. 1625. *The admirable Adventures and Strange Fortunes of Master Antoine Knivet which went with Master Thomas Candish [Cavendish] on his Second Voyage to the South Sea*. In Samuel Purchas, *Pilgrimes*, vol. 4, book 6, 698–710. London.

Kolben [also Kolb, Kolbe], Peter. 1731. *Description of the Cape of Good Hope*. London.

Labat, Jean Baptiste. 1742. *Nouveau voyage aux iles de l'Amerique*. Paris.

*La Caille, Nicolas Louis de. 1763. *Journal historique du voyage fait au cap de Bonne-Esperance*. Paris.

La Giraudais, de (see under Pernety).

Lahontan, Louis-Armand de Lom d'Arce, Baron de. 1703. *Nouveaux voyages de M. le Baron Lahontan dans l'Amérique septentrionale*. The Hague.

La Loubere, Simon de. 1705. *An Historical Account of the Kingdom of Siam*. London.

Le Cat, Claude Nicolas. 1765. *Traité sur la couleur de la peau humaine en général, de celle des nègres en particulier*. Amsterdam.

Le Maire (see under Renneville).

Leem, Knud. 1808. "An Account of the Laplanders of Finmark." In *Voyages and Travels*, ed. J. Pinkerton, 1:376–490. London. (Forster would have used a Danish or Latin edition of about 1767.)

Leo Africanus. 1632. *The History and Description of Africa*. (Many editions in several European languages from 1550 on; we have not identified the edition in Latin, edited by "Elzevir," that Forster refers to. A translation by J. Pory, first published in London in 1600, is the basis for R. Brown's edition of 1896: HS n.s. 92–94.)

Lind, James. 1777. *An Essay of Diseases incidental to Europeans in hot climates*. London.

Linnaeus (Carl von Linné). 1766–1768. *System Naturae*. 12th ed. Holmiae.

Lomonosov, M. V. *Memoire on the ice mountains*. Swedish Memoirs of the Academy of Stockholm, vol. 25 (German ed.).

Luisini, Luigi. 1728. *Aphrodiasicus*. Leiden.

Macky. 1742–1743. "Part of a Letter . . . being an Extract from the Books of the Town Council of Edinburgh, Relating to the Disease There, Supposed to be Venereal, in the Year 1497." *Philosophical Transactions* 42: 420.

Mairan, Jean Jacques Dortous de. 1744. *Dissertation sur la glace*. Paris.

Mariana, Juan de. 1699. *The General History of Spain*. London.

[Martens, Frederick]. 1694. *An Account of Several Late Voyages and Discoveries to the South and the North . . . by John Narborough and others.* London. [Forster evidently used a French edition; republished in Hakluyt, o.s., 18.]

Modern Universal History (see under Sale).

Monboddo, Lord (James Burnet). 1773[–1792]. *Of the Origin and Progress of Language.* Edinburgh.

Montesquieu, Charles de Secondat, Baron de. 1748. *De l'esprit des loix.* Geneva. [Modern editions: *Oeuvres complètes de Montesquieu,* ed. André Masson, Paris, 1950–1955; *The Spirit of the Laws,* trans. and ed. Anne Cohler, Basia Miller, and Harold Stone, Cambridge, 1989.]

Muratori, L. A. 1723–1751. *Rerum Italicarum Scriptores.* Mediolani.

Nairne, Edward. 1776. "Experiments on Water obtained from the Melted Ice of Sea-Water, to ascertain whether it be Fresh or not; and to determine its Specific Gravity with Respect to Other Water." *Philosophical Transactions* 66: 249–256.

Navarette (see Fernandez Navarette).

Noceda, Juan de, and Pedro de San Lucan. 1754. *Vocabulario de la lengua Tagalo.* Manila.

Oldendorp, C. G. A. 1777. *Geschichte des Mission der evangelischen Brüder auf den caraibischen Inseln.* Leipzig.

Osbeck, Pehr. 1771. *A Voyage to China and the East Indies,* trans. J. R. Forster. London.

Pallas, Peter Simon. 1771–1776. *Reise durch verschiedene Provinzen des Russischen Reichs.* St. Petersburg.

Parkinson, Sydney. 1773. *A Journal of a Voyage to the South Seas, in His Majesty's Ship, the* Endeavour. London. [Later editions include a facsimile of the 1784 edition; London, 1984].

Pelloutier, Simone. 1750. *Histoire des Celtes.* The Hague.

Pennant, Thomas. 1766. *British Zoology.* Warrington.

*Pernety, A. J. 1771. *History of a Voyage to the Falkland Islands.* London. [Trans. of *Journal historique d'un voyage aux îles Malouines . . . et deux voyages au détroit de Magellan,* Paris, 1769.]

Petrus Martyr (see Anglerius).

Phipps, Constantine John. 1775. *A Voyage Towards the North Pole.* Dublin.

[Pigafetta, Antonio]. 1550–1559. *Viaggio di Antonio Pigafetta.* In Giovanni Battista Ramusion's *Navigazioni e Viaggi.* Venice. [Republished, Turin, 1978.]

Pinto, Chevalier. n.d. "Vocabulary of the Brazilian Language." Ms.

Pintor, Petrus. 1499. *Ad beatissimum.* Rome.

Poivre, Pierre. 1770. *Travels of a philosopher: or, Observations on the manners and arts of various nations in Africa and Asia.* Glasgow. [Trans. of *Voyage d'un philosophe, ou observations sur les moeurs et les arts des peuples de l'Afrique, de l'Asie, et de l'Amérique,* Yverdon, 1768.]

Prevost d'Exiles, Antoine François. 1746–1791. *Histoire générale des voyages.* Paris. [Precisely which edition Forster used is not clear; volumes 1–10 were a translation of Thomas Astley's *New General Collection of Voyages and Travels,* London, 1745–1747.]

Priestley, Joseph. 1772. "Observations on Different Kinds of Air." *Philosophical Transactions* 62: 147–264.

———. 1775. "An Account of Further Discoveries in Air." *Philosophical Transactions* 65: 384–394.

Pringle, Sir John. 1776. *A Discourse on Some Late Improvements of the Means of Preserving the Health of Mariners, Delivered at the Anniversary Meeting of the Royal Society.* London.

Purchas, Samuel. 1625. *Purchas his Pilgrimes.* London. [Numerous later editions; best modern reprint is Glasgow, 1905–1907.]

*Pyrard, François. 1679. *Voyage de François Pyrard de Laval, contenant sa navigation aux Indes Orientales, Maldives, Moluques, Brésil.* Paris. [Republished as Hakluyt, o.s., 76–80.]

Raleigh, Sir Walter. 1598. "The Voyage of Sir Walter Ralegh himself to the island of Trinidad." In Richard Hakluyt's *The Principal Navigations, Voyages, Traffiques and Discoveries of the English Nation*. London. [Vol. 7, pp. 280–349 in the 1907 ed., London].

Ray, Benjamin. 1751–1752. "An Account of a Water-Spout, rais'd off the Land, in Deeping-Fen, Lincolnshire." *Philosophical Transactions* 47: 477–478.

Reland, Adrian. 1706–1708. *Dissertationum Misscelanaearum*. Trajecti ad Rhinum.

Renaudet, Eusebius. 1733. *Ancient Accounts of India and China by two Mohammedan Travellers*. London.

*Renneville, R. A. C. de. 1754. *Recueil des voyages qui ont servi a l'établissement et aux progrez de la compagnie des Indes Orientales*. Paris.

Rios Coronel, Hernando de los. 1621. *Memorial y relacion para su Magestad . . . y en las islas del Maluco*. Madrid.

Roggewein, Jacob. 1702. In *Recueil des voyages qui ont servi a l'Etablissement de la compagnie des Indes Orientales*. Amsterdam. [The modern edition is *The Journal of Jacob Roggeveen*, ed. Andrew Sharp, Oxford 1974.]

Romer (see under Bosman).

Roy, William. 1777. "Experiments and Observations made in Britain, in order to obtain a Rule for measuring Heights with the Barometer." *Philosophical Transactions* 67: 653–788.

Rumphius, George Everard. 1741–1750. *Herbarium Ambioinense*. Amsterdam.

Sage. 1776. *Analyse des blés*. Paris.

———. 1777. *Elémens de minéralogie docimatique*. Paris.

de Saintfoix, _____. 1759. *Essais historiques sur Paris*. London.

Sale, George, et al. 1759. *The Modern Part of an Universal History from the Earliest Account of Time*. London. [Referred to as the *Modern Universal History*; there are a number of editions, this being the folio that Forster consulted.]

Sanchez. 1752. *Dissertation sur l'origine de la maladie venerienne*. Paris.

———. 1774. *Examen historique sur l'apparition de la maladie venerienne en Europe*. Paris.

Scheele, Charles William. 1777. *Chemical Treatise on Air and Fire* (in German). Uppsala. [Forster's English translation published as *Chemical Observations and Experiments on Air and Fire*, London, 1780.]

Sonnerat, Pierre. 1776. *Voyage à la Nouvelle Guinée*. Paris.

Stewart, John. 1777. "An Account of the Kingdom of Thibet." *Philosophical Transactions* 67: 465–492.

Tavernier, J.-B. 1684. *Collection of Travels through Turky into Persia*. London.

Toland, John. 1726. "History of the Druids." In *A Collection of Several Pieces*. London.

Valentyn [Valentijn], François. 1726. *Verhandeling deer zee-horenkens en zeegewassen in en omtrent Amboina en de naby gelegene eylanden*. Dordrecht.

[Valtravers]. 1776. *Summary Observations and Facts Collected from Late and Authentic Accounts of Russian and other Navigators*. London.

Venegas, Miguel. 1759. *A Natural and Civil History of California*. London.

Viaud, Pierre. 1771. *The shipwreck and adventures of Pierre Viaud*, trans. from French by Mrs. Griffiths. London.

Villauld de Bellefond. 1669. *Relation des côtes d'Afrique appellée Guinée*. Paris.

Voltaire. 1765. *La Philosophie d'histoire*. Amsterdam [Ed. J. H. Brumfitt in *The Complete Works of Voltaire*, vol. 59, Geneva, 1969.]

———. 1770–1772. *Questions sur l'encyclopédie*. Amsterdam? [Incorporated in *Dictionnaire philosophique*, t. 51–56 of *Oeuvres complètes de Voltaire*, Paris, 1875–1876.]

C. Works Referred to by the Editors

Works already listed in sections A and B are not included here.

Adams, Ron. 1983. *In the Land of Strangers: A Century of European Contact with Tanna, 1774–1784*. Canberra.

Barrell, John. 1986. *The Political Theory of Painting from Reynolds to Hazlitt*. New Haven.

———. 1992. *The Birth of Pandora and the Division of Knowledge*. London.

Bartlett, Roger Paul. 1974. "Foreign Settlement in Russia under Catherine II." *New Zealand Slavonic Journal*, n.s., 1: 1–22.

———. 1975. "J. R. Forster's Stay in Russia, 1765–1766: Diplomatic and Official Accounts." *Jahrbücher für die Geschichte Osteuropas* 23: 489–495.

Beaglehole, J. C. 1974. *The Life of Captain James Cook*. London.

Beaglehole, J. C., ed. 1955–1967. *The Journals of Captain James Cook on his Voyages of Discovery*. Cambridge.

———. 1961. *The Endeavour Journal of Sir Joseph Banks*. Sydney.

Bellwood, Peter. 1978. *Man's Conquest of the Pacific*. Auckland.

Bendyshe, Thomas, ed. 1865. *The Anthropological Treatises of Johann Friedrich Blumenbach [and John Hunter]*. London.

Blunt, Wilfred. 1971. *The Compleat Naturalist*. New York.

Boyle, Robert. 1665. *New Observations and Experiments in Order to an Experimental History of Cold*. London.

Clark, William. 1986. "From the Medieval Universitas Scholarium to the German Research University: A Sociogenesis of the Germanic Academic." Ph.D. diss., University of California, Los Angeles.

Copley, Stephen, ed. 1984. *Literature and the Social Order in Eighteenth-Century England*. London.

Davies, John. 1851. *A Tahitian and English dictionary*. Papeete.

Dening, G. M. 1972. "The Geographical Knowledge of the Polynesians and the Nature of Inter-Island Contact." In *Polynesian Navigation*, ed. Jack Golson. Wellington.

Driessen, H. A. H. 1982. "Outriggerless Canoes and Glorious Beings: Pre-Contact Prophesies in the Society Islands." *Journal of Pacific History* 17: 3–28.

Dixon, George, and Nathaniel Portlock. 1789. *Der Kapitaine Portlock's und Dixon's reise um die Welt*. Berlin.

———. 1984. "Outriggerless Canoes and Glorious Beings Revisited: A Reply to Robert Langdon." *Journal of Pacific History* 19: 248–257.

———. 1991. "From Ta'aroa to 'Oro: An Exploration of Themes in the Traditional Culture and History of the Leeward Society Islands." Ph.D. thesis, Australian National University.

Dumont d'Urville, J. S. C. 1832. "Sur les îles du grand Océan." *Bulletin de la Société de Géographie* 17: 1–21.

Dunmore, John. 1965–1969. *French Explorers in the Pacific*. Oxford.

Ferguson, Adam. 1767. *An Essay on the History of Civil Society*. Edinburgh.

Firth, Raymond. 1929. *Primitive Economics of the New Zealand Maori*. London.

Foucault, Michel. 1970. *The Order of Things*. New York.

Frangsmayr, Toer. 1985. "Linnaeus in his Swedish Context." In *Contemporary Perspectives on Linnaeus*, ed. John Weinstock. Lanham, Md.

Frezier, A.-F. 1716. *Voyage de la Mer du Sud*. Paris.

Fry, Howard T. 1970. *Alexander Dalrymple (1737–1808) and the Expansion of British Trade*. London.

[Gathercole, Peter] n.d. *"From the Islands of the South Seas, 1773–4"; an Exhibition of a Collection Made on Cap^n Cook's Second Voyage of Discovery by J. R. Forster*. Oxford.

Gell, Alfred. 1993. *Wrapping in Images: Tattooing in Polynesia*. Oxford.

Gifford, E. W. 1929. *Tongan Society*. Bernice P. Bishop Museum Bulletin 61. Honolulu.

Golson, Jack, ed. 1972. *Polynesian Navigation*. 3d ed. Wellington.

Gordon, Joseph S. 1975. "Reinhold and Georg Forster in England, 1766–1780." Ph.D. diss., Duke University.

Guest, Harriet. 1989. "The Great Distinction: Figures of the Exotic in the Work of William Hodges." In *New Feminist Discourses: Critical Essays on Theories and Texts*, ed. Isobel Armstrong. London.

———. 1992. "Curiously Marked: Tattooing, Masculinity, and Nationality in Eighteenth-Century British Perceptions of the South Pacific." In *Painting and the Politics of Culture: New Essays in British Art, 1700–1850*, ed. John Barrell. Oxford.

———. 1992. "The Wanton Muse: Politics and Gender in Gothic Theory after 1760." In *Beyond Romanticism: New Approaches to Texts and Contexts 1780–1832*, ed. Stephen Copley and John Whale. London.

Hoare, Michael E. 1976. *The Tactless Philosopher: Johann Reinhold Forster (1729–1798)*. Melbourne.

Hunter, John (see under Bendyshe).

Jaussen, Tepano. 1898. *Grammaire et dictionnaire de la langue tahitienne*. Paris.

Jolly, Margaret. 1992. " 'Ill-natured Comparisons': Racism and Relativism in European Representations of Ni-Vanuatu from Cook's Second Voyage." *History and Anthropology* 5: 331–363.

Joppien, Rudiger, and Bernard Smith. 1985–1987. *The Art of Captain Cook's Voyages*. New Haven.

Kalm, Peter. 1770–1771. *Travels into North America*. Trans. [George and] Johann Reinhold Forster. Warrington.

Kerguelen-Tremarec, Yves Joseph de. 1782. *Relation de deux voyages dans les mers Australes et des Indes*. Paris.

Kirch, Patrick Vinton. 1984. *The Evolution of the Polynesian Chiefdoms*. Cambridge.

Koerner, Lisbet. In press. "Nature and Nation in Linnean Travel." In *Visions of Empire: Voyages, Botany, and Representations of Nature*, ed. David Miller. Cambridge.

Kooijman, Simon. 1973. "*Tapa* Techniques and *Tapa* Patterns in Polynesia: A Regional Differentiation." In *Primitive Art and Society*, ed. Anthony Forge. New York.

Lafitau, J.-F. 1724. *Moeurs des sauvages amériquains comparées aux moeurs des premiers temps*. Paris.

Langdon, Robert. 1984. "Of Time, Prophecy, and the European Ships of Tupaia's Chart." *Journal of Pacific History* 19: 239–247.

Larson, James. 1971. *Reason and Experience: The Representation of Natural Order in the Work of Carl von Linné*. Berkeley.

La Vopa, Anthony. 1988. *Grace, Talent, and Merit: Poor Students, Clerical Careers, and Professional Ideology in Eighteenth-Century Germany*. Cambridge.

Lemaître, Yves. 1973. *Lexique du tahitien contemporain*. Paris.

Lewthwaite, G. R. 1970. "The Puzzle of Tupaia's Map." *New Zealand Geographer* 26: 1–19.

Lieberman, David. 1983. "The Legal Needs of a Commercial Society: the Jurisprudence of Lord Kames." In *Wealth and Virtue*, ed. I. Hont and M. Ignatieff. Cambridge.

Lind, James. 1753. *A Treatise on Scurvy*. London.

———. 1757. *An Essay on the Most Effectual Means of Preserving the Health of Seamen in the Royal Navy*. London.

Long, Edward. 1774. *The History of Jamaica*. London.

Lowood, Henry. 1987. "Patriotism, Profit, and the Promotion of Science in the German Enlightenment: The Economic and Scientific Societies, 1760–1815." Ph.D. diss., University of California, Berkeley.

[Magra, James]. 1771. *A Journal of a Voyage Round the World, In his Majesty's Ship* Endeavour, ... London.

Markham, Clements. 1904–1905. *The Voyages of Pedro Fernandez de Quiros, 1595 to 1606*. London (Hakluyt n.s. 14/15).

McArthur, Norma. 1967. *Island Populations of the Pacific*. Canberra.

McClelland, Charles. 1980. *State, Society, and University in Germany, 1700–1914*. Cambridge.

McCormick, E. H. 1977. *Omai: Pacific Envoy*. Auckland.

Meckel, Johann Friedrich, the Elder. 1748. *Tractatus anatomico-physiologicus*. Göttingen.

Millar, John. 1771. *Observations concerning the Distinction of Ranks in Society*. [Later eds. entitled *The Origin of the Distinction of Ranks*]. London.

Oliver, Douglas L. 1974. *Ancient Tahitian Society*. Honolulu.

Osbeck, Pehr. 1771. *A Voyage to China and the East Indies*. Trans. Johann Reinhold Forster. London.

Pocock, J. G. A. 1975. *The Machiavellian Moment: Florentine Political Thought and the Atlantic Republican Tradition*. Princeton.

———. 1992. "Tangata Whenua and Enlightenment Anthropology." *New Zealand Journal of History* 26: 28–53.

Raeff, Marc. 1983. *The Well-Ordered Police State: Social and Institutional Change Through Law in the Germanies and Russia, 1600–1800*. New Haven.

Ralston, Caroline. 1989. "Changes in the Lives of Ordinary Women in Early Post-Contact Hawaii." In *Family and Gender in the Pacific*, ed. Margaret Jolly and Martha Macintyre. Cambridge.

Rauschenberg, R. A. 1968. "Daniel Carl Solander, Naturalist on the *Endeavour*." *Transactions of the American Philosophical Society*, n.s., 58: 1–66.

Rochon, A.-M. de. 1783. *Nouveau voyage à la mer du sud*. Paris.

Ross, Ian Simpson. 1972. *Lord Kames and the Scotland of his Day*. Oxford.

Rousseau, Jean-Jacques. 1755. *Discourse on the Origin of Inequality*. London.

Rutherford, Noel, ed. 1977. *Friendly Islands: A History of Tonga*. Melbourne.

Sahlins, Marshall. 1981. *Historical Metaphors and Mythical Realities*. Ann Arbor.

———. 1985. *Islands of History*. Chicago.

Salmond, Anne. 1991. *Two Worlds: First Meetings between Maori and Europeans*. Auckland.

Schmoller, Gustav. 1897. *The Mercantile System and Its Historical Significance*. New York.

Scopoli, Giovanni Antonio. 1763. *Entomologia carniolica*. Vienna.

———. 1777. *Introductio ad historiam naturalem*. Prague.

Sekora, John. 1977. *Luxury: The Concept in Western Thought, Eden to Smollett*. Baltimore.

Sharp, Andrew. 1956. *Ancient Voyagers in the Pacific*. Wellington.

———. 1957. *Ancient Voyagers in Polynesia*. London.

———, ed. 1974. *The Journal of Jacob Roggeveen*. Oxford.

Shaw, Alexander. 1787. *A Catalogue of Different Specimens of Cloth*. . . . London.

Small, Albion. 1909. *The Cameralists*. Chicago.

Smith, Adam. 1767. *The Theory of Moral Sentiments*. London. (Cited from the "Glasgow" edition of Oxford, 1976.)

Smith, Bernard. 1985. *European Vision and the South Pacific*. 2d ed. New Haven.

———. 1992. *Imagining the Pacific: In the Wake of the Cook Voyages*. New Haven.

Smith, Howard M. 1975. "The Introduction of the Venereal Disease into Tahiti: A Re-examination." *Journal of Pacific History* 10: 38–45.

Spate, O. H. K. 1966. "Between Tasman and Cook: Bouvet's Place in the History of Exploration." In *Frontiers and Men*, ed. J. Andrews. Melbourne.

———. 1979. *The Spanish Lake*. Vol. 1 in *The Pacific since Magellan*. Canberra.

———. 1983. *Monopolists and Freebooters*. Vol. 2 in *The Pacific since Magellan*. Canberra.

————. 1988. *Paradise Found and Lost*. Vol. 3 in *The Pacific since Magellan*. Rushcutters Bay, New South Wales.

Spriggs, Matthew. 1983. "Vegetable Kingdoms: Taro Irrigation and Pacific Prehistory." Ph. D. thesis, Australian National University.

————. 1986. "Landscape, Land Use, and Political Transformation in Southern Melanesia." In *Island Societies: Archaeological Approaches to Evolution and Transformation,* ed. Patrick Vinton Kirch. Cambridge.

Stafleu, Franz A. 1971. *Linnaeus and the Linnaeans: The Spreading of Their Ideas in Systematic Botany, 1735–1789.* Utrecht.

Stagl, Justin. 1990. "The Methodising of Travel in the Sixteenth Century: A Tale of Three Cities." *History and Anthropology* 4: 303–338.

Thomas, Nicholas. 1989. *Out of Time: History and Evolution in Anthropological Discourse.* Cambridge.

————. 1991. *Entangled Objects: Exchange, Material Culture, and Colonialism in the Pacific.* Cambridge, Mass.

Troitzsch, Ulrich. 1966. *Ansätze technologisches Denkens bei den Kameralisten des 17. und 18. Jahrhunderts.* Berlin.

Valeri, Valerio. 1990. "Death in Heaven: Myths and Rites of Kinship in Tongan Kingship." *History and Anthropology* 4: 209–247.

Wales, William. 1778. *Remarks on Mr. Forster's Account of Captain Cook's last Voyage Round the World, in the Years 1772, 1773, 1774, and 1775.* London.

Wales, William, and William Bayly. 1777. *The Original Astronomical Observations, made in the course of a Voyage towards the South Pole.* London.

Weber, Wolfhard. 1976. *Friedrich Anton von Heynitz: Innovationen im frühindustriellen deutschen Bergbau.* Göttingen.

Walter, Richard, and Benjamin Robbins. 1974. *A Voyage Round the World in the Years MDCCXL, I, II, III, IV,* ed. Glyndwr Williams. Oxford. (First published in 1748.)

Wollstonecraft, Mary. 1792. *A Vindication of the Rights of Woman.* London.

Index

Place-names and other terms generally follow Forster's usage. References to illustrations are in **boldface.**